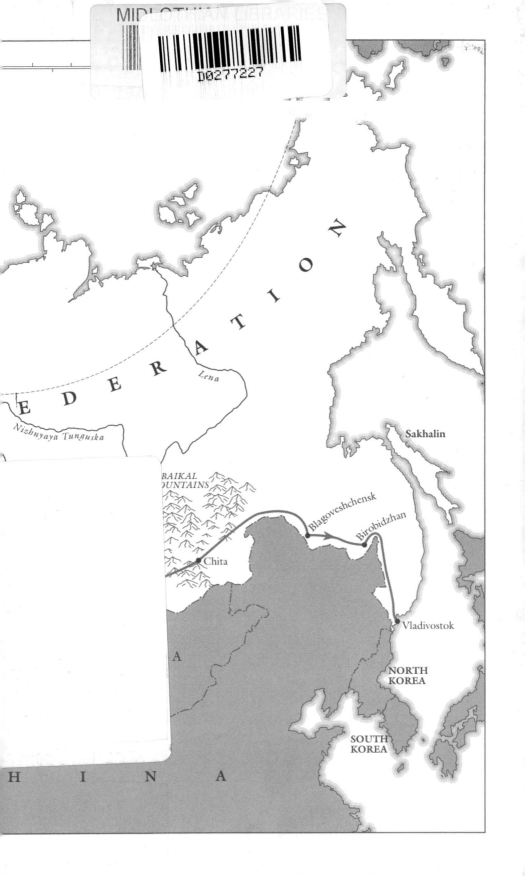

F E D E R A T I O N

*Lena*

*Nizhnyaya Tunguska*

Sakhalin

BAIKAL
MOUNTAINS

Blagoveshchensk

Birobidzhan

Chita

A

H I N A

Vladivostok

NORTH
KOREA

SOUTH
KOREA

# RUSSIA

By the same author
*Richard Dimbleby: A Biography*
*The Palestinians*
*The Prince of Wales: A Biography*
*The Last Governor: Chris Patten and the Handover of Hong Kong*

# JONATHAN DIMBLEBY

RUSSIA

## A JOURNEY TO THE HEART
## OF A LAND AND ITS PEOPLE

BBC
BOOKS

This book is published to accompany the television series entitled
*Russia: A Journey with Jonathan Dimbleby*, produced by Mentorn Media
and first broadcast on BBC2 in 2008.
Series producers: George Carey and Teresa Cherfas

1 3 5 7 9 10 8 6 4 2

Published in 2008 by BBC Books, an imprint of Ebury Publishing.
A Random House Group Company

The Random House Group Limited Reg. No. 954009
Addresses for companies within the Random House Group
can be found at www.randomhouse.co.uk

A CIP catalogue record for this book is available from the British Library.

Hardback ISBN 978 0 563 53912 4
Trade paperback ISBN 978 1 846 07540 7

The Random House Group Limited supports the Forest Stewardship Council (FSC), the leading international forest certification organization. All our titles that are printed on Greenpeace approved FSC certified paper carry the FSC logo. Our paper procurement policy can be found at www.rbooks.co.uk/environment

**Mixed Sources**
Product group from well-managed
forests and other controlled sources
www.fsc.org Cert no. TT-COC-2139
© 1996 Forest Stewardship Council

Commissioning editor: Martin Redfern
Project editor: Christopher Tinker
Copy-editor: Esther Jagger
Designer: Jonathan Baker at Seagull Design
Maps: Peter Wilkinson
Picture researcher: Sarah Hopper
Production: David Brimble

Printed and bound in Great Britain by Clays Ltd, St Ives plc

To buy books from your favourite authors and register for offers, visit www.rbooks.co.uk

For Jessica

# CONTENTS

# ACKNOWLEDGEMENTS

I am indebted to many individuals without whom it would have been impossible to write this book. George Carey was the originator of the BBC television series *Russia – A Journey with Jonathan Dimbleby*, which the book accompanies. Without his passionate commitment as executive producer, the television programmes (and therefore the book) would not have seen the light of day. Between them, he and Teresa Cherfas (as joint series producers) plotted and reconnoitred my route through Russia and did much of the preliminary research for all five films. In addition, Teresa Cherfas acted as my translator for almost the whole journey; her skill and sensitivity in this role were invaluable. Even when I took a different view from either of theirs, our discussions were invariably stimulating. I am much in their debt.

My three directors – Hugh Thompson (films 1 and 2), Jamie Muir (films 3 and 5), and David Wallace (film 4) – read and commented on those parts of the book covered by their films; their own research was also helpful. In addition, Jamie Muir not only undertook detailed research on my behalf, but read the entire manuscript; his scholarly comments clarified a wide range of issues and saved me from several egregious errors.

I owe a similar debt of gratitude to Dr Lyuba Vinogradova, who scoured the manuscript, bringing consistency to my spelling of Russian words and names, correcting dates and facts, and, on matters of judgement and interpretation, offering a consistently helpful and constructive critique of my attitudes and assumptions.

Maria Kolesnikova and Anastasia Serdyukova not only provided me with vital research, but – well beyond the call of duty – became my eyes and ears on the ground (especially when I was away from the camera), acting both as guides and interpreters. They were stimulating and refreshing companions who taught me more about Russia than I think they will ever realize. Many other individuals helped me along the way. I cannot name them all here, but Olga Fleshler, Katya Golitsine, Yulia Korneva, Anzor Kushkhabiev, Magomedkhan Magomedkhanov, Tatiana Tikhomirova and Andrei Toporkov were especially generous with their time and their insights. Similarly, our Russian production manager, Marina Erastova, not only navigated our team through Russia's administrative and organizational shoals, but made my own experience far more enjoyable than it might otherwise have been. But I am grateful above all to the scores of Russians who welcomed me into their lives with warmth and generosity. Without their readiness to talk to me about themselves and their Motherland, the book would have been stillborn.

The films have been blessed by the technical brilliance of my colleagues on camera and sound, but all of them also played a part in shaping my experience and my responses to it. My gratitude to cameramen Simon Ffrench (film 1), David Niblock (films 2 and 3), and Peter Harvey (films 4 and 5); and likewise to sound recordists James Pursey (films 1 and 2), Ivo Hanak (film 3), Neil Laycock (film 4), and Mick Duffield (film 5). In London my production managers Fiona Frankland, Fiona Herson, Sarah Mires and Carmelina Palumbo eased my professional aches and pains and were remarkably tolerant of my foibles.

I have been exceptionally fortunate in my editor at BBC Books, Martin Redfern, whose comments and suggestions have been unfailingly constructive and thoughtful. I am grateful to him and his colleagues (especially project editor Christopher Tinker and my meticulous copy editor Esther Jagger) for meeting a very tight schedule with such superb professionalism. My agent at David Higham Associates, Veronique Baxter, and her colleague Annabel Hardman have been a constant source of support and sound advice throughout the long process from commission to publication; and my PA, Stella Keeley, kept my life in order throughout.

I would not have been able to undertake this project, nor would I have completed it, without the sustained nurture of my wife Jessica. She has endured my frequent ups and downs with stoic patience. Her wise counsel was given unstintingly despite the fact that, a few months after Russia started to dominate my working life, she became pregnant with her first child, our daughter Daisy – who celebrated the end of my journey by reaching the grand old age of six months. For this and other blessings, *Russia – A Journey to the Heart of a Land and its People* is dedicated to Jessica.

All those named above have between them contributed greatly to this book. None of them is responsible for any of its errors, which – as ever – are mine alone.

# INTRODUCTION

It was an irresistible invitation: to make an epic journey across Russia from Murmansk in the far northwest of the country to Vladivostok in the far southeast. The route would be some 10,000 miles in length and would allow me to explore the past, the present and the future of the largest country in the world. Travelling principally by road, rail and boat, I would experience a land and its people from ground level. I would visit great cities and tiny villages, I would explore forests and mountains, huge lakes and long rivers, and – most importantly of all – I would have a chance to meet hundreds of Russians in all their rich diversity. The journey would take a total of eighteen weeks, enough time to delve beneath the surface and discover some of the realities of life in a resurgent nation that for me – in Churchill's aphorism – was still 'a riddle wrapped in a mystery inside an enigma'. Perhaps, I told myself, I would be able to reveal the enigma, unwrap the mystery and solve the riddle. It was a journalist's dream.

I would not quite be an innocent abroad. As a television reporter I had been to Russia before, but that was during the Cold War when it was impossible to have a free and open conversation with anyone. Attempting to interpret a pyramid of Soviet half-truths and evasions for the benefit of a Western audience for whom Russia meant the Gulag, nuclear weapons and vodka was, to put it mildly, a challenging frustration. My fleeting impressions of the Soviet Union in the late seventies and early eighties was of a society stricken by repression, viciousness and corruption; of a political and social environment corroded by bad faith and self-delusion. Although I was able to glimpse and record a little of the material and spiritual poverty of everyday life in Moscow, I felt myself to be deeply ignorant of the humanity that trudged to and fro in front of the camera's eye. So, like most observers, I gave a half cheer when President Mikhail Gorbachev ushered in the era of *perestroika* and *glasnost*; when I met him before the fall – an encounter that I describe in these pages – I very nearly gave a full cheer. But, aside from a long weekend in Moscow in the celebratory days following the final collapse of the Soviet Empire in 1991, I had not been back since. I was intrigued at the thought of discovering how Russia had altered and where the nation was heading.

In the decade following the demise of the Soviet Union, Russia came to be regarded internationally as something of political joke, a fallen giant that no longer threatened the victorious superpower and could therefore be safely consigned to the margins of history. But from the start of this century and the arrival of Vladimir Putin in the Kremlin that patronizing and blinkered assumption had been rudely exposed. The international community came belatedly to realize that the ownership of huge energy reserves in the form of oil and gas, in a world where demand is dramatically growing as resources sharply diminish, had given Putin's Russia a muscle-flexing source of international power and influence. Russia, we had all come to appreciate, would matter very much indeed and could be ignored only at our peril.

Against that background, I had a host of questions in my mind. What is the relationship of Russians to one another and to those who rule over them? How do Russians see themselves in the world today? What role do they want their nation to play? What are the sources and origins of these aspirations and attitudes? And after so many centuries of suffering what is it to love 'Mother Russia'? I knew that those and many other questions would take me not only on a long physical journey but on a political, cultural and psychological one as well. Intrigued by what it means for people to say, 'I am Russian', I wanted to understand better their sense of the past, their individual histories and beliefs and ambitions, and to illuminate, if possible, the elusive nature of the 'Russian soul'. The opportunities seemed limitless and exhilarating.

The invitation had come from one of television's grandees, George Carey, who had managed to sell the idea of a five-part documentary series called *Russia – A Journey with Jonathan Dimbleby* to the controller of BBC2. He then sold it to me. But as soon as he had done so, I got cold feet, feeling suddenly overwhelmed by the sheer scale of the task to which I had committed myself. Half in panic, I told myself I was taking a terrible risk with my life that was not so much physical as professional. To make the Russian programmes I would have to give up the security of a stimulating perch at the edge of the political arena as the presenter of ITV's weekly flagship political programme, *Jonathan Dimbleby*. And for what, I asked myself: the insecurity of an unknown venture in an alien land without a compass? Although I would be travelling with a producer, a director, a researcher and camera crew, and despite the fact that I would have a translator and interpreters at my side (I had no more than half a dozen words of Russian at my command and I could not read the Cyrillic alphabet), I felt that I would be very alone, if not entirely lost.

To ward off the demons of insecurity that now started to assail me, I told myself that I would become a twenty-first-century version of the Victorian traveller. Baedeker in one hand, journal in my knapsack, I would be open to every experience, shying away from nothing, however eccentric or bizarre it might seem. Russia has always invited contradictory epithets – romantic and brutal, harsh and generous, brooding and exuberant, raw and sophisticated, crude and subtle. In writing a book about my journey to accompany the TV series, I would have the space to attempt a resolution of these contradictions, or at least to make sense of them. I would be able to immerse myself in a country that straddles half the globe, and would investigate the complexities of a nation that embraces – or rather strives to contain – so much ethnic, cultural and religious diversity.

My route was to take me deep into rural Russia, travelling south from Murmansk through Karelia via St Petersburg and Moscow (hoping to peer beneath the carapace of these great cities to hear the beating heart of the new Russian metropolis) to the edge of the Black Sea. From there I would traverse the war-torn Caucasus until I reached the Caspian Sea and the mouth of the Volga. Following the course of that vital artery for hundreds of miles, I would pass through the cities of Volgograd, Samara and Kazan before heading eastward once again, to cross the Urals into the vastness of Siberia, with its massive deposits of oil, gas and precious metals, until eventually I reached the Pacific coast and my final destination, Vladivostok. *Russia – A Journey to the Heart of a Land and Its People* would be the story of that journey, a personal odyssey in which I would have the chance to describe anything and everything along the way.

In an attempt to bring perspective and shape to the journey, I decided that I would sketch in the principal historical events that have shaped the Russian drama – from the arrival of the Vikings and the later invasion of the Mongols through to Ivan the Terrible and Peter the Great, and in the twentieth century from the Bolshevik Revolution and murder of the last tsar through to Lenin, Stalin, Gorbachev, Yeltsin and Putin. (There is a timeline on page 543 for quick reference.) I would also draw on the glorious wealth of Russian literature, especially that of the nineteenth century, to distil some of the insights of Gogol, Dostoevsky, Lermontov, Tolstoy and others, both to illuminate their own tumultuous times and, through them, to explore the character of the Russian psyche. In short, I told myself as I imagined this huge canvas in front of me, I was entitled to be daunted but I should not let myself be intimidated: I was about to have a once-in-a-lifetime experience.

And that is just about how it has turned out, though not quite in the way I had expected. For example, I did not foresee in 2006 when I set out on the first leg of my journey that relations between Russia and the West would deteriorate so sharply and rapidly. When I started out, the international 'jury' had not even begun to form a coherent view of Putin's Russia. But since then, Putin's increasingly autocratic rule at home, combined with his international assertiveness, has started to disconcert more and more observers. I witnessed Putinism at close quarters, discovering and confronting the profoundly disquieting attitudes of most, though by no means all, Russians to the values and principles that a Western liberal holds dear. I have tried to understand and explain their deepening aversion to Western democracy, but I have not refrained from expressing my views about it. I have also come to believe that a quasi-ideological gulf between 'them' and 'us' makes it likely that Russian resurgence will find itself on a collision course with the West. This does not mean that a new Cold War is in the offing (an outcome that would be inimical to Russia's immediate and long-term interests as an energy superpower), but a reversion to a form of peaceful coexistence is more likely than the positive collaboration that optimists like me had expected a decade ago. To a child of the Cold War, who rejoiced unequivocally at the fall of the Berlin Wall, this is a dispiriting prospect.

I was shocked too by the accelerating corruption of the political process within Russia: notably the absence of free and fair elections, the supine torpor of the parliamentary body, the Duma, the muzzling of the media, the intimidation of the judiciary and a profound contempt for human rights. I did not set out to be an uncritical traveller, but the extent to which this retreat from the guiding principles of a free and open society has eaten into the soul of the nation shocked and dismayed me. Even though I had a huge number of gloriously challenging, stimulating, amusing and exhilarating encounters with Russians of all kinds – encounters that form the bedrock of this book – and found among them some of the most generous and warm-hearted people you could hope to find anywhere, I could not quite shake off the disquieting sense that I was travelling through a crypto-fascist state by any other name.

But all that formed part of my 'exterior' journey. In parallel, I gradually came to realize that I had also embarked on an 'interior' journey and that it would have been wrong to conceal this. Throughout the two years I have spent on this project my perspective on Russia has been affected, if not shaped, by an emotional volatility that troubled me especially when I was away from home. While I never set out to write an objective account of my journey across Russia, I found that, day after day, I was turning to my notebook to record my sharply fluctuating moods. After rereading those notes and recognizing the extent to which these emotions (which would swing rapidly from delight to despair) had coloured my outlook, I decided that – except in bad faith – I could not pretend that it had been otherwise. Some of these feelings therefore surface from time to time in my narrative. But I can only make sense of these passages for the reader by outlining the background to what has been a roller-coaster period in my personal life.

A little over three years before I embarked on my Russian venture, I met an opera singer called Susan Chilcott who was the leading lyric soprano of her generation. In May 2003 we started to have an affair. Some months earlier, after treatment for breast cancer, she had been given the all-clear. But very soon after our relationship began she discovered a secondary lump in her breast, and two days later her oncologist told her that the cancer had spread to her liver. No further treatment was possible; she had only a short time to live. Although Sue protested that I should not turn my life upside down for her, I felt that I had no choice but to be by her side for the final months of her life. In so doing, I had chosen to leave my wife Bel with whom I had shared thirty-five years of marriage and to whom I had always believed myself bound as a partner for life. I still do not adequately understand the intensity of passion and pity that animated my decision; only that I felt I had to follow my heart and what seemed to be my duty. For the next three months I lived with Sue and her four-year-old son Hugh. They were precious days of intense joy mingled with deep sorrow until, on 4 September 2003, Sue died in my arms.

It was a tragedy for those who loved music and had heard Sue sing or seen her on stage. I found myself broken by a grief that was more dreadful than I had ever imagined such pain could be. For day after day I could barely bring myself to get out of bed in the morning. Nor did I care whether I lived or died. I could not rest, I could not sleep, I could not think. With the benefit of hindsight, I feel now that only my wonderful family and a small handful of close friends saved me from going out of my mind. When I went back to work, colleagues at the BBC and ITV were astonishingly sensitive and forbearing.

I began to hope that I could return to our family home. But although my adult children, encouraged by Bel, were more loving and understanding than I could ever have hoped, I was in no condition to repair the damage I had inflicted on our marriage. Bel understandably decided that she could take no more, and, a few months after Sue's death, moved out of our farmhouse to start a new life with a close family friend. Now I felt doubly bereft and bewildered. The very foundations of my life seemed to have collapsed. I did not know who I was or where I was going, and I could see no way out of the long, dark tunnel in which I now found myself.

And then, in the spring of 2004, I met Jessica. Gradually and cautiously, over the following months we formed a relationship as she helped to nurture me back to a better state of health. But it took far longer than I had expected and I was still frequently stricken by waves of grief that welled up unexpectedly, drowning out every other sensation and not leaving me until I was utterly drained and exhausted. This lasted, gradually becoming less frequent but no less intense, for months, a year, and then two years. Even in January 2006, when I had to make the choice between Sunday politics and the Russian project, I was in such a state of inner turmoil that my doctor warned that I would descend into a serious depression unless I put myself on a course of drugs. As it happened, I resisted this advice and that wave passed.

If the Russian journey was, in professional terms, an irresistible challenge, it became, in personal terms, a very simple decision. Jessica was at work during the week; I was working at weekends. It was clear that if we were to have a life together, I would have to recover my weekends for both of us to share. For this reason alone, the Russian invitation arrived at just the right moment. But it took a long time for me to restore the mental equilibrium that I had once taken for granted. My journey through Russia played what, in retrospect, I believe to have been a crucial part of my recovery – a parallel journey – and that is why, in an effort to be true to my experience, I have not pretended otherwise.

Jonathan Dimbleby
*Moreleigh, Devon*
*February 2008*

Murmansk

*Arctic Circle*

FINLAND  KARELIA

*White Sea*
**Solovki**

Kem

*Lake Onega*

Petrozavodsk

*Lake Ladoga*

*River Neva*

St Petersburg

Staraya Ladoga

Novgorod

*Volkhov River*

R U S S I A

■ Moscow

N

| 0 | | | | 200 miles |
| 0 | | | | 300 kms |

➤ Route taken

# PART ONE
# FROM MURMANSK
# TO NOVGOROD

The Russlandia Hotel, the best in the Arctic city of Murmansk, calls itself 'your home on the top of the world'. Some home. I was sitting in the Ice-Breaker nightclub, where customers were welcomed by a sign instructing us that we were forbidden to enter with hand-guns about our persons. Otherwise, disappointingly, there was no echo of the Wild West. The Ice-Breaker, I gradually discerned through the gloom, was designed like the mess room of a ship, complete with portholes offering a submariner's glimpse into a simulated azure sea. There was canned laughter from a fuzzy TV screen that hung from the ceiling and, leaking from the walls in discordant rivalry, retread dance music on a loop. The bar was empty except for a scatter of businessmen and tourists from Finland, here for the salmon fishing. They engaged in desultory banter with a trio of hookers while consuming beer and vodka in gargantuan quantities. Although consuming lots of booze is supposed to break the ice, it was hard to think of any place on earth less likely to do so.

It could have been midday or midnight. The stygian Ice-Breaker concealed the fact that outside it was broad daylight, as it would remain for twenty-four hours a day during this brief midsummer break from the long Arctic winter that otherwise embraces this inhospitable territory in the far northwest of Russia. To fit myself for purpose, I was reading Nikolai Gogol's subversive little masterpiece, his 'Diary of a Madman', in which the father of the modern Russian novel chillingly reminds us that sanity and insanity are two sides of the same coin, or, rather, arbitrary points along the spectrum of 'normality'. In the sure-ality of the Ice-Breaker, sleepless with fatigue, I found it easy to imagine myself as Gogol's demented hero who has deluded himself that he has become the new king of Spain, and who therefore endures unspeak-able torture in the fond belief that it represents a rite of passage rather than the sadism of a prison warder beating him to a pulp for daring such *lèse-majesté*. But that way, of course, madness lies.

My grasp of Russian was confined to pleasantries – 'good morn-ing', 'please' and 'thank you' – and I had to summon up the resolve to order a cup of coffee. I gestured as best I could and finally a bored waitress alighted on my repeated use of the word 'cappuccino'. A while later she returned with a small cup of bitter black coffee. Gogol, I noted lugubriously in my diary, was absolutely right to instruct us that what we like to believe to be the gulf between the real and the surreal, the sane and the insane, is paper-thin.

I slumped into gloom, my constant companion since leaving England. A familiar question wormed its way out of my subconscious: 'What, in the name of God, am I doing here?' As a child I was sent to boarding school by loving parents who obeyed the middle-class conventions of the day. They thought they were sending me off for a good education; I cried myself to sleep every night for a week at the start of every term. Nothing much has changed except that – for the most part – I have disciplined myself to hold the tears at bay. But homesickness still grips me, and whenever I am away I still count the days until I get back, marking them off in my head, and sometimes in my diary, like a prisoner waiting for release. Yet I was supposed to be on what I had told myself to regard as the 'journey of a lifetime'. The cliché alone was enough to suggest bad faith – though at one level, of course, it was just that kind of venture. Who would not – in principle – donate what remained of their eye teeth in return for the chance to explore the largest country in the world and to write about the experience as well? Friends and colleagues had been encouragingly envious. So why, I wondered, was I whingeing to myself: 'Wish I wasn't here.'

## MURMANSK AND
## THE GREAT PATRIOTIC WAR

Murmansk is quite a challenge. It has no beauty or grace. Architecturally it is a museum to the worst of the Soviet age. There is not even one of those neo-imperial grotesqueries that self-glorified Stalin and still preside over the Moscow skyline. This outpost in the Arctic is drab and ugly, designed and constructed as if its purpose was not so much to celebrate the triumph of the proletariat as to oblige the human spirit to submit: 'Who? Whom?' writ large in dreary tiers on the slopes leading up from the harbour.

Ignorance is the polar opposite of bliss (what absurd aphorist suggested otherwise?) so I put aside Gogol and plunged into my briefcase in search of my notes about Murmansk. If you want to begin to understand the Russian people, wise counsellors had advised me, you really have to have a sense of Russia's past. So, I reminded myself, Murmansk was once a small fishing port in the Kola Peninsula whose surrounding waters, blessed by a quirk of the Gulf Stream, defy temperatures that can fall below minus 25 degrees centigrade and thus remain navigable throughout the severest winter. Down the centuries its inhabitants eked out a living by trading in fish and furs, and, if they had a lucky break, walrus tusks as well. The port barely registered on the map of Russia until well after the turn of the nineteenth century, when the last of the Romanovs, Tsar Nicholas II, decided that the empire needed an all-weather naval base for the new Arctic fleet that he had commissioned to defend the northern flank of the Imperial Motherland. With the hubris that so often characterizes the powerful – and the purblind – he named his new city Romanov-on-Murman, as though his dynasty would last for ever. But after his overthrow in 1917 and his gruesome murder at the hands of the Bolsheviks a year later, Romanov-on-Murman was renamed Murmansk.

Russia's new leader, Vladimir Ilich Lenin, was careful not to throw the military baby out with the water from that revolutionary blood-bath. The facilities at Murmansk were rapidly expanded so that by the outbreak of World War II, the little fishing port had become a major military headquarters, destined by 1941 to play a key role in the what the Russians call the Great Patriotic War against Nazi Germany. It was the landfall for Allied convoys bringing military supplies from America and Britain through the treacherous waters of the Arctic for the hard-pressed Soviet front line to the south and especially around Leningrad. Murmansk was therefore a critical link in that vital supply chain, and both its port and railhead were prime targets for the Luftwaffe, which in 1941 blitzed the city to such effect that only a handful of pre-war buildings survived.

After a day – or was it night? – of non-sleep I crawled out of bed and took myself off to get a better sense of the city. Driving through potholed streets lined by concrete housing blocks and shops so reticent that they seemed to be ashamed to proclaim their role in the new market economy, I saw nothing so garish as a colourful sign or window display, merely a half-open door here and there beckoning you without welcome. Murmansk seemed to be trapped in a Soviet time warp. But then, on one of the main streets, I found a sudden splurge of bright colour defying the drabness: flower shop after flower shop in fierce rivalry, with blooms of every hue skilfully but garishly arranged in bouquets without regard for those subtleties of shade and tone that Western sophisticates like to regard as 'tasteful' or 'stylish'. This unexpected exuberance of clashing reds, oranges and purples hinted at a *joie de vivre* in Murmansk that had hitherto seemed entirely absent. And since there was not a cemetery in sight, nor a Palace of Wedding Ceremonies (the Soviet equivalent of a Register Office), I gave the citizens of Murmansk the benefit of the doubt. Perhaps they just liked the colour to offset their dour surroundings.

As the elderly people carrier wheezed up the long climb to the tabletop of the city, I looked down to see a lake dotted with skiffs and pedalos and, on the grassy banks, children and dogs and family games. Suddenly Murmansk acquired humanity and I could, for a moment, imagine that it was the Serpentine in Hyde Park on an early summer day. Up on the peak, the harbour is overlooked by a soaring stone monument from the base of which there is a spectacular view over the bay and the peninsula beyond. It was absolutely quiet that day, but in the silence it was not hard to imagine the distant drone of Nazi bombers advancing low over the hills towards the docks and the marshalling yards: the roar of the Heinkels as they came overhead, the thunder from the Soviet anti-aircraft guns, the waterspout trails through the harbour, the sheets of flame, the ships ablaze, the loco-motives and goods wagons smashed into matchwood. The dead would have lain in their thousands in the surrounding streets or buried in the ruins of their bombed-out homes. As I looked down at the apparently comatose port, I could imagine the survivors – those who had not perished and were too weak to flee – cowering from a sustained bombardment that caused more damage (95 per cent of the city was razed) than in any other Russian city except Stalingrad.

Today the port, like the city, is in sharp decline. I watched a couple of cargo ships offloading lethargically in the only dock that seemed to be active. In the bay, merchantmen rode at anchor idly in the haze. Until the end of the Cold War this waterway was a high-security mili-tary zone, home to the Arctic fleet of nuclear submarines. It is still a nuclear base, both for naval submarines and for a fleet of polar ice-breakers. But nowadays, if you are well-heeled, you can take a weekend cruise on one of the latter (coloured crimson, with an emblematic white bear painted on the superstructure) to the North Pole itself. Although I had accreditation from the government in Moscow, I half expected to be stopped by a police officer or even an agent of the FSB (the Federal Security Service, the born-again equivalent of the KGB). Slightly to my disappointment, however, no official, uniformed or otherwise, betrayed the slightest curiosity in my presence on what had once been top-secret terrain.

As I got closer to the monument, it revealed itself as a vast figure cast in concrete, towering some 40 metres above me, a giant of a military man gazing out across the bay. My instinctive sneer at Soviet realism – so crassly assertive and crudely heroic – was swiftly rebuked by the gentleness and sorrow in the massive but delicately chiselled profile of this Unknown Soldier. It was the meaning within the form that mattered, the knowledge that he represented the millions who died to save the Soviet Union from the Nazi invasion. At his feet lay wreaths left by veterans and posies placed by newly-weds around an Eternal Flame that flickers in peaceful reverence over the 'Hero City', as it was belatedly designated by the Kremlin in 1985.

Before leaving Britain I had a smattering of knowledge about the Arctic convoys and the notorious 'Murmansk Runs', described in the official US naval history of World War II as involving the negotiation of 'more hazards' than any other form of naval duty in that conflict. The combination of treacherous waters, enemy attack from air and sea, and temperatures well below freezing meant that the convoys had only a very modest chance of returning unscathed. Between January 1942 and March 1943, one out of every three merchant ships (forty-five out of 143) that set out from America and Britain on the Murmansk Run did not return.

The calamity that struck Convoy PQ17 in July 1942 is especially poignant. In the grandiloquent words of Sir Winston Churchill, writing some years later, it was 'one of the most melancholy episodes of the whole of the war'. The most 'melancholy' truth is that it was an entirely avoidable episode. On 4 July, as they were nearing Murmansk and at the most dangerous point on the voyage, thirty-five Allied merchantmen laden with tanks, aircraft and other supplies for the Russian Front suddenly found themselves abandoned by all sixty-one of the Allied warships escorting them. Incomprehensibly, as it seemed to them at the time, the merchant fleet was ordered by the Admiralty in London to 'scatter'. Simultaneously, their naval escort was instructed to 'withdraw to the Westward at high speed' – in short, to flee. But from what? In the absence of any other compelling evidence, the Admiralty had heeded intelligence reports to the effect that an enemy task force led by the most dreaded of all battleships, the *Tirpitz*, was closing in fast on the convoy. In reality the German fleet was still at anchor 300 miles away in the Norwegian Altenfjord. In the absence of naval support, the Allied merchant ships became sitting targets for the Luftwaffe and the German E-boats, which did indeed close in fast. Altogether twenty-four of the thirty-five vessels in the convoy were lost; some three thousand of the 'bravest souls afloat', as Churchill described them, perished in the icy waters of the Arctic.

On the outskirts of Murmansk, in a mosquito-infested birch wood, there is an ill-kempt and lonely cemetery. In one forlorn little corner I came across an orderly row of graves honouring a small number of those Allied seamen who were lost at sea or killed in the port itself. All of them were young; some of them teenagers. One headstone, in remembrance of J.B. Anderson, Steward's Boy, aged sixteen, bears the inscription, 'His leaf perished in the green, blasted by Arctic gales'. I counted twenty similar headstones. Further into the cemetery, I walked the length of a simple stone wall inscribed with the names of the Soviet soldiers and sailors who died defending Murmansk. I lost count after reaching twenty thousand names, but of course that was only a tiny fraction of the estimated 11 million Russian military personnel who died in the Great Patriotic War. It seems oddly unpatriotic for an Englishman to note that this grand total is some thirty times greater than the equivalent figure for Britain (382,600); in any case, as George Bernard Shaw noted, it is the quality, not the quantity, of suffering that matters. But no wonder the vast statue of Alyosha, as it has been nicknamed locally, is a place of pilgrimage for every generation in Murmansk.

I was taken to meet a veteran of the Great Patriotic War. Yevgraf and his wife Nina live on the eighth floor of a high-rise block that towers over a square of littered waste ground. The stairwell smelt faintly of urine and the walls were covered with graffiti. Among the specimens of post-Soviet self-expressionism were the choicer sentiments of American rap artists punctuated by familiar expletives, more or less in English, like 'Motherfucer [sic]' and 'Kunt [sic]'. I indulged the grumpy old man's reflection: 'So this is what their grandfathers died for in this city.' And then, less mindlessly, I remembered that young people in the new Russia are said to be as alienated as their Western counterparts, a phenomenon, I reminded myself, that I hoped to explore later in the journey.

On the eighth floor, beyond the grime and protected by a heavily locked door, we entered another world – yesterday's world. Nina looked after her modest flat with exquisite care. We removed our shoes and entered the sitting room, where Yevgraf showed me a row of wartime medals of honour pinned on a neatly pressed blue suit that he brought from a wardrobe for inspection. On a sideboard a black and white photo of a pretty fourteen-year-old boy – who was about to join the Soviet navy – smiled innocently into the room. For his part in the Great Patriotic War, Yevgraf, now a rosy-cheeked seventy-eight-year-old, was revered by the Russian state. He had a kindly smile and a chirpy manner that reminded me of the Cheeryble Brothers in *Nicholas Nickleby* and, once I had been pampered into a comfortable chair, he was only too keen to regale me with his memories of the Arctic convoys. But Nina had prepared a feast for her foreign guests and she insisted that food came first. We were soon eating from a table laden with cold chicken, cod's liver pâté, potatoes, Russian salad, olives and vodka. Yevgraf filled my glass and then held his own aloft. 'I would like to propose the first toast. I am very glad that you have come to see us and that our friendship and cooperation has continued to this day. I was there when the very first convoy arrived in 1941. I wish you health. The most important thing is health and that our friendship should never end.' It was the first of many such toasts.

Unprompted, he described the German air raids. 'We had anti-aircraft guns, but the Germans started to fly in very low and our guns could not target them without hitting our own people. So they just bombed and bombed. Nothing was left of Lenin Street except broken chimneys. And when the boats docked they were simply blown up.' The citizens soon ran short of food. 'The children were given 200 grams of bread a day, the grown-ups had 300 grams,' he explained, taking two slices of bread from the table to demonstrate what that meant. 'It was not enough, of course, so parents would cheat – faking ration cards, doing anything to feed their children. We had cabbage as well. But it was not enough. And then, in December 1943, the bread ration was cut to 75 grams and sometimes we didn't have that. We ate berries, and people boiled their boots and removed the bark from the birch trees to eat the green sap beneath. Sometimes people took the needles from the pine trees and screwed them into balls to chew. By the spring, when the grass began to grow, nettles and other plants as well, it got easier.'

In 1943 the teenage Yevgraf began to take part in the Soviet naval patrols that went from Murmansk and (in the summer), once the sea ice had melted, from Archangel to meet the Allied convoys. 'One day I saw a ship sunk by a German submarine. The bows rose up into the air and the men on board just slipped off into the sea. I saw their arms and legs flailing in the water. They were screaming for help. But we were not allowed to stop to pick them up. It was a nightmare. You see people dying and there is nothing you can do about it. You can't do anything. It was just terrible. A nightmare.' His eyes filled with tears.

We proposed more toasts and drank much more vodka until I was soon as lachrymose as Yevgraf. His final toast was to those who had lost their life in the Great Patriotic War: 'To all those who died: the

English, the Americans, Canadians and Dutch. They all died. I would like to drink to them. They died so that this should never happen again.' I responded with what I hoped he would regard as a suitable sentiment: 'Sometimes in the West we forget what was done for us by the Russian men and women who fought and died in such terrible numbers. You not only saved Russia from Nazism, but you saved us as well. And I thank you from the bottom of my heart.' The virtue of a toast, I was beginning to discover, is that it allows you to circumnavigate the embarrassment that would otherwise deter the expression of sincere emotion between strangers. Of course, the vodka helps.

After a while, Yevgraf took a battered accordion from its place beside the wardrobe and started to play a medley of American and Russian wartime songs. His 'Roll out the Barrel' was especially touching; wrapped up in the past, his expression radiated a camaraderie with the British that surmounted the suspicion and disapproval of his own superior officers. He put his instrument aside, remembering that joyous conspiracy of illicit amity. 'I wish that I and my fellow Russian veterans who played our part in the Murmansk Runs could join the Remembrance Day Parade in London. We have asked, but apparently we are not eligible.' Then, after a pause: 'Governments cause wars. People don't want wars. People want peace. We want friendship.' We had come full circle. With one more toast, we hugged each other and clung on for a moment as though to convince ourselves that what he had said was true. I tottered off into the midday – or was it midnight? – and returned to my hotel.

Back in the isolation of the Ice-Breaker nightclub, I wondered what Yevgraf would have made of my surroundings. He reminded me of so many war veterans that I have seen or heard before: his modesty, his spirit, his unsought heroism. I was born in 1944, soon after D-Day, but the two world wars of the twentieth century did not form any part of my childhood education. At school the study of history ended at the outbreak of World War I – unhappily, the concept of 'contemporary' history had not yet been pioneered – and the little I learned about that charnel house came from reading Siegfried Sassoon and Wilfred Owen. Although my father had faced danger and witnessed horror as a BBC war correspondent in World War II, he rarely spoke of his experiences. My rudimentary knowledge of both conflicts therefore sprang only from what I had read as an adult and seen in documentaries. And even these did not really give me a real feeling for what it must be like to endure the full horror of the battlefield. That came with my own limited but first-hand experience of warfare as a jobbing reporter who has trotted quite a lot of the globe. I still catch my breath with remembered fear at being caught in crossfire during the Turkish invasion of Cyprus, or crossing the Green Line in Beirut past a bloodstained corpse hanging out of the driver's seat of a bullet-spattered car and knowing myself to be in the sights of a sniper's rifle. Seeing the wasted dead and meeting the mutilated survivors of wars in the Middle East, Africa and Latin America filled me with disgust and despair. War may indeed be 'the continuation of politics by other means', but it is no less unspeakably terrible for that.

In *The March of Folly*, the historian Barbara Tuchman, analysing the 'woodenheadedness' of war-like governments down the ages, cites an unnamed fellow historian who damned Philip II of Spain with the words 'no experience of the failure of his policy could shake his belief in its essential excellence'. As I sat alone in the submarine gloom, a news bulletin flickering on the television screen showed the latest carnage from Iraq, and I noted that the same phrase could equally well serve as the political epitaph for the architects of that conflict. The images provoked an onrush of isolated despair: despair at the folly of war, at the hubris of our political leaders and at their glib mastery of the shifting half-truths with which, trapped in the bunker of history, they have sought to deflect their critics. At least, I thought, Yevgraf and his comrades-in-arms had an unequivocally valid cause for which to fight and die. At which I returned to Gogol and the 'Diary of a Madman' and one last glass of vodka.

## SOUTH TO THE WHITE SEA

The journey south from Murmansk to Kem on the edge of the White Sea was a trundle by train. We had a fifteen-hour journey ahead of us. Our carriage was full when we got in, and it smelt of humanity and food. My fellow passengers had already taken up residence on their bunks, which were tiered in twos and ran laterally down the length of the compartment. They stood open to a corridor, a permanently busy thoroughfare that separated them from a row of longitudinal bunks, one of which was mine. Quite like boarding school, I reminded myself. The curtains, faded orange and grubby, were drawn even though it was still a White Night afternoon. My fellow passengers had brought food with them, as the only other source of sustenance was the samovar for hot water and tea at the end of each carriage. But the samovar, which promises Eastern romance and without which no Russian novel is complete, proved disappointing: no more than a huge and absurdly complicated kettle that even Heath Robinson would have been hard put to invent. True, it gushed hot water from a gas heater, but it had no other redeeming feature that I could detect. Yet the samovar is still spoken of in Russia with reverence, as though it were blessed with the same cultural resonance as a coffee ceremony in Ethiopia or a tea ceremony in China. Perhaps I am simply too ignorant or insensitive to get the point.

We passed through an unrelenting forest of birch trees and conifers, pressed up against the railway line and obscuring whatever they might have concealed: more forest, I presumed. I settled myself in for long hours of enforced inaction. The train was in no hurry, and I soon adjusted to the swaying amble. I watched a shabby little man shuffling down the carriage bearing a small bag bulging with what looked at first like maps, but which turned out to be recipes. His shoes were so old that they were worn through at the toe. He stopped mechanically by each bunk, holding out his wares for inspection. An overweight mother with a blotchy face and a baby on her lap examined the recipes with an air of indifference and in a manner that suggested she was unaccustomed to looking at words rather than pictures. After ten minutes of perusal, she finally glanced up. I thought she was going to return the recipes, but instead she held up two of them enquiringly. He nodded. She riffled through the detritus that surrounded her child and herself to extract a purse from a cavernous handbag, and gave him three or four coins. He nodded and shuffled on. The transaction had been completed without a word being exchanged between them.

At home I am one of those travellers who is immediately irritated when the 'train manager' comes on the tannoy to announce a delay. I raise my eyebrows and sigh as if to say, 'Late again', with the accomplished ennui of the seasoned traveller. On this train, though, I adapted to impotence without demur. I stared out of the window, allowing myself to become hypnotized by the trees, by the nothingness of this meandering journey. I fell asleep.

After a couple of hours I woke again, bleary-eyed. A little way down the carriage an attractive woman, who looked to be in her mid-forties, sat quietly opposite her daughter, their modest picnic neatly unfolded on the drop-down table between their bunks. Rather hesitantly, I went to interrupt them. They at once invited me to join them. They were on their way back home, heading south from Murmansk, a journey that would last forty-eight hours. Sayukin, the mother, elegant but careworn in a black dress that was clearly her Sunday best, introduced her daughter. Karin was a pretty girl with an elfin face and olive eyes, who was anxious to practise her English but was enchantingly modest about her prowess. She had just been interviewed for a place at Murmansk University, where she wanted to study English, French, Spanish and two other, yet to be determined, foreign languages. She had top grades from her school, and she told me that she loved Shakespeare, particularly *King Lear*. Her dream was to qualify as an interpreter because she wanted to travel and see the world.

The problem, her mother intervened to explain, was that the family had very little money – too little, at any rate, to buy her way into one of the better courses in Russia. In fact, they were not at all sure they would be able to afford a place at any university. Buy? I had assumed that universities were free and that a place was entirely dependent on merit. Not so, Karin explained, not in the new Russia. There were, of course, free places, but where there was strong demand, you had to buy your way to the front of the queue. Of course it was illegal, but that was how the marketplace in education worked. Suddenly Sayukin leant forward to say with unexpected ferocity, 'It is insulting if my child is a much better student, but someone who is not as good as her gets a place when she doesn't. There are some colleges that you can enter only by paying fees, and she can't begin to aspire to that. I find that really bad.' I commiserated, drank a toast to Karin's future and headed back to my perch at the window.

Across the corridor a large, coarse woman with a blotched, pock-marked face and an air of truculence was in altercation with another passenger who had arrived to claim the same seat. Neither yielded, despite the patient efforts of our *provodnitsa* – the superintendent assigned to every carriage on Russian trains – who was dressed in a neatly pressed blue uniform and carried real authority. It transpired that they were indeed both booked in the same seat, but for different days. In the end, using to her advantage the fact that she was already in occupation, truculence won the argument, even though it was her ticket that was wrongly dated. She looked exhausted, but glared across as if daring me to judge her.

I felt reproached for my aversion to this belligerence when I discovered that behind the sour exterior was a very unhappy woman. She had just come from the hospital in Murmansk, where she had been treated for an inoperable brain tumour, and was now on her way back to the orphanage where she worked for a pittance looking after abandoned children. She was sick and in pain. I had to remind myself – more often than I should need to – not to judge by appearances alone.

After another brief and fitful sleep, I woke up and began to stare once more at the passing landscape. We had been on the train for fourteen hours and the backdrop to the journey had changed perceptibly. The conifers were now interspersed with oak and ash, evidence of a marginally milder climate as we moved away from the tundra and into the steppe. On one side of the train a wide, shallow river tumbled and gurgled around smooth, white boulders; on the other a lake stretched into the distance, a flurry of whitecaps chasing towards the train. I noticed that the silver birches were swaying, not wildly but busily, in the wind and noted in my diary, with the anxiety of a fair-weather sailor, that the wind must be at force 5 gusting 6 on the Beaufort scale, perhaps 25 miles an hour.

This only mattered because Kem is on the edge of the White Sea, and we were due to go directly from the station there to catch a ferry. We were bound for a remote archipelago called Solovetskie Ostrava, renowned for its natural beauty, revered as a holy place, and notorious for the crimes of the Gulag that were perpetrated on its hallowed ground. The three-hour sea-passage to Solovki, as the islands are universally known in Russia, is known for sudden storms even in summer; in winter it is not navigable because it is covered in ice. I added a further note to my diary: 'Could be a rough crossing.'

By the time we reached the jetty, careering there from the station in a beaten-up taxi as if, in our driver's mind, death by dangerous driving were a guarantee of immortality, the wind was still rising – certainly force 6 and probably gusting 7 or 8. My trepidation grew when we joined the throng of people trying to board the dilapidated and rusting hulk of a ferry that was supposed to take us to our destination. We had been told that seats had been reserved for us and that there was safe storage for our equipment and cases. But what had been intended as an orderly process had become a free-for-all, with many more would-be passengers than places. The ferry, the only one of the day, was now perilously overloaded with tourists and pilgrims who had been transferred from three other smaller ferries deemed too frail to attempt the crossing in such weather.

Once outside the harbour, those passengers who could find no space in the cabin had to remain on the open deck, where most of them tried to find shelter on the leeward side away from the stinging spray whipped up by the wind and the sea. As a result, the ferry was listing heavily to starboard as the mounting seas rolled in on the port beam. The sun, which had provided a picture-post illusion that all was well, disappeared behind the dark clouds that now shouldered towards us. It started to rain in ice-cold horizontal slivers. I was in light summer clothes, having foolishly forgotten to bring an overcoat, let alone the oilskins that are really required in this kind of weather. Very soon I was shivering. I saw that others were in a similar state. The chill had silenced conversation, and the ferry became suffused with a mood of apprehension.

After forty-five minutes or so we were in open water, breasting short, steep, ugly seas. We pitched and rolled, sometimes to what seemed to be the very extreme of 45 degrees. The boat shuddered, stayed poised on that edge for an eternity, then rolled back to start the same process all over again, as if to torture us with the possibility that what we feared was inevitable. Some passengers clutched each other in alarm. Others were crossing themselves; yet others, more resolute, started to sing what sounded in the roar of the wind like a Russian version of 'Abide with Me'.

With the courage of real fear – I had images in my mind of those ferry disasters in Third World countries, where scores of people are drowned in avoidable tragedies – I decided to confront the skipper. I slid and slithered to the upper deck and staggered across to the wheelhouse. Pulling open the door, more drowned rat than ancient mariner, I yelled over the wind and engine, 'I am a sailor and this weather is getting worse. This boat is overloaded and you are putting our lives in danger.' In retrospect the words seem embarrassingly melodramatic but I believed then, as I do now, that I was telling the truth. At first – with that infuriating combination of indifference and contempt that I was starting to think was a genetic peculiarity of the Russian people – he affected not to hear me, but looked resolutely ahead at the confused and breaking seas. On my third exasperated attempt he simply said, 'I shall not turn back.' Beside him, leaning against the wheelhouse door, was his emaciated ship's mate, sodden with alcohol, clutching on to a rail for support, his bloodshot eyes staring with benign vacancy into the middle distance. I reckoned there were more than two hundred passengers on a boat designed for, at most, half that number. Two hundred souls and two crew, one of whom was a psychopath and the other roaring drunk. I eyed the life-rafts, securely fastened to the deck. If we were to capsize, none of us would have any hope.

I returned to the aft deck and, gesturing at those huddling on the leeward side, urged them to move across to windward to balance the boat. A few bold souls did as I asked – only to retreat again in the face of the wind, the rain and the sea. Not from heroism but from fear I chose to follow my own advice, and stood facing the elements in the forlorn hope that if the boat did capsize, I would at least be on the top side and not trapped underneath.

As it happened, the skipper was a skilled helmsman and managed to chart a course through the breaking seas that now raced towards us with white foaming crests that towered above us before sluicing water across the deck. Sometimes two waves would collide to become a single waterspout, a sudden and alarming ejaculation of energy. I stood shivering and soaking, wishing that I was as fatalistic as our malevolent skipper. Beside me a woman read from her prayer book, never turning the page, a look of concentrated terror on her face.

It seemed an endless journey, but in fact it lasted no more than three and a half hours. Gradually, as we entered the lee of the islands, the sea and the storm subsided. We tied up alongside the jetty and, numbed by fear and cold, I felt a surge of that anger that sometimes accompanies relief: anger at the elements, at the skipper, at the state's systemic indifference to health and safety, and at the Russians in general for being so intolerably fatalistic. I wanted to find someone in author-ity to whom I could complain, but there was nobody; I subsided, totally exhausted. The following day I was perversely reassured to hear that the lead item on the regional news was the 'freak storm in the White Sea, which had felled trees and in which some small boats had been lost'. The only lasting irritation was caused by a devout Orthodox Christian who told me, with the smugness of those who are blessed with certainty, that I should not have been afraid, that I had been shepherded by the Lord and that it was His will that we had survived; moreover, had we perished, it would have been God's will as well. Fine, I wanted to retort, so long as you have faith, so long as you think you have been 'chosen', and so long as you believe that your afterlife will be better than your life on earth: I don't.

## SOLOVKI: THE FIRST GULAG

The next day, with a gentle haze and a soft sea breeze and a few small boats bobbing in the harbour, I was reminded at once of the Isles of Scilly. But there the comparison stopped. Solovki is billed as one of the holiest places in Russia, but throughout the country's turbulent and cruel history it has been the site of unholy horrors that – for me – shrouded the entire archipelago in a sinister embrace. According to Orthodox legend, Solovki was first settled in 1429 by two monks, Savvaty and German, who made landfall on the island in a small sailing boat. It is said that the two would-be hermits had survived the perils of the White Sea courtesy of two Orthodox angels, who had already prepared the ground for them by beating up a poor woman who had been unwise enough to collect firewood on what had been ordained by the Almighty as a retreat reserved for the exclusive use of these God-fearing males.

Despite the desolation, the intense cold and a woeful lack of food, the two holy men managed to survive on Solovki for six years until the elements forced them to retreat to the mainland. Soon afterwards Savvaty died, but German, joined by another monk called Zosima, returned to Solovki where the latter had a dream in which he saw a church hovering in the sky above them. Obeying what they took to be a command, the two monks built a wooden church on what is now the site of one of the most famous monastic complexes in Russia. All three men – Savvaty, German and Zosima – were later sanctified as Solovki's founders, and their remains are buried there today for pilgrims to revere.

At first glance Solovki, which is dominated by high, buttressed white walls, from within which towers and onion domes sprout glitteringly into the evening sun, seems to be as much fortress as holy place, more kremlin (as it is properly called) than monastery. Its past explains why. Solovki has had to endure two major sieges. The first – in the latter half of the seventeenth century – followed the monks' refusal to obey an edict requiring them to bring their liturgical practices into line with changes imposed on the Orthodox Church by the Patriarch in Moscow. This defiance by the 'Old Believers' of Solovki, foreshadowing a schism that was to last well into the second half of the twentieth century, was regarded by the tsar as an act of insolent apostasy. Determined to break their resistance, he ordered a blockade of the island to force the rebels into submission. The siege lasted six fruitless years, and it took a further three before Imperial troops finally found a way into the kremlin, where they discovered fourteen emaciated survivors too weak to offer any resistance. But the tsar was implacable: the 'Old Believers' had committed a capital offence, and they were summarily executed.

Solovki again came under siege during the Crimean War in the mid-nineteenth century. On this occasion, bizarrely, the invasion took the form of two frigates of Her Britannic Majesty's navy, which headed down from the Baltic into the White Sea to harass Imperial Russia from the north, while Tsar Nicholas's navy was already some 1000 miles away to the south resisting the combined might of Britain, Turkey and France in the Black Sea. When the two British warships anchored just outside the harbour on 6 July 1854, the monks rang the monastery bells, and the inhabitants of Solovki gathered for safety inside the kremlin walls. Receiving no response to their demand that the island surrender, the British let fly with what the Russian annals – perhaps overstating the case – record as a nine-hour barrage of cannon-fire directed at the monastery. Inside, the monks processed around the gallery of the cathedral, carrying an icon of the Virgin Mary and chanting prayers to her for their salvation. Eventually the British gave up and sailed on, leaving behind a miracle: their very last cannonball hit the icon, but the legendary presence of the Virgin Mary ensured that none of the faithful was hurt. Solovki abounds in miracles.

By the end of the nineteenth century the island was virtually self-sufficient, and it prospered both spiritually and materially. A tannery, an iron foundry and a paper-mill added to the income derived from an intricate network of fish farms and kitchen gardens to meet the growing needs of a burgeoning settlement. By this time Solovki had become a destination for summer pilgrims, with up to fifteen thousand devotees a year from all over the Russian Empire making the trek to its holy places. Then, in 1917, the Bolshevik revolution intervened, resolving to liquidate all false gods. The real horror was about to unfold.

Apologists for the Soviet Union liked to believe that the Terror, of which the Gulag was the most ubiquitous example, sprang from a peculiarly demented excess of revolutionary zeal for which Josef Stalin himself – not the system – should take the blame. In fact, the atrocities perpetrated in the name of the Bolshevik revolution started very soon after his predecessor, Lenin, seized control of the state apparatus. As early as 1918, during the Civil War, Lenin oversaw the publication of a document called 'The Resolution on Red Terror', which decreed, *inter alia*, that the 'safeguarding of the Soviet Republic from class enemies' required 'isolating them in concentration camps'. The isolated monastery on Solovki promised to be an ideal location for this experiment.

In Lenin's perverted vision these concentration camps were to be progressive institutions, 're-education' centres for political and other criminals, which were to stand in sharp contrast to the capitalist prisons in the West, where offenders were customarily locked away without prospect of rehabilitation. Many Western liberals, let alone fellow-travellers, were content to accept this conceptual analysis and, perhaps from wishful thinking, displayed a marked lack of curiosity about how the system operated in practice. Solovki was the prototype for the Gulag empire developed by Stalin from Lenin's blueprint. It was a model of its kind: when the official files were opened after the collapse of the Soviet Union, they revealed that between 1923 and 1938, one hundred thousand prisoners were sent to the island, of whom forty thousand died either from disease and starvation or at the hands of the prison authorities.

There was little excuse for the purblindness of the West's liberals and leftists. The first glimmer of the truth about Solovki began to seep out in 1925 after a particularly intrepid prisoner managed to escape to Finland, smuggling out with him an account of what he had endured. S.A. Malsagov was a White Russian officer who surrendered to the Bolsheviks in 1922 and was sent to Solovki after being accused of 'monarchist, bourgeois, anti-socialist tendencies'. There he joined his fellow 'class enemies', who included landowners, engineers, lawyers, artists, writers, teachers, doctors and students, as well as priests and monks. These 'politicals' were outnumbered, however, by a gruesome collection of common criminals.

The camp commandant, whose real name was Nogtev but went by the nickname of Palach ('executioner'), was described by Malsagov as a deaf, 'semi-educated' drunkard. Nogtev coined a slogan to welcome new inmates: 'Here you are not subject to Soviet rules,' he warned, 'but Solovki rules.' To emphasize this point he required the newly arrived 'class enemies' to run back and forth along the quay until they were exhausted. Then he would select one of their number at random and summarily execute him with a pistol shot in the head.

Palach's administrative brainwave was to place the 'political' prisoners under the charge of the *shpana* – common criminals – whose number included convicted murderers, burglars and rapists. It was a terrifying ordeal. On his arrival, Malsagov was allocated to Hut

Number 6, which was already overflowing with *shpana*. 'The stench was so awful that I nearly collapsed,' he recorded, 'drunken yells and drunken weeping; the most disgusting abuse.' On his first night, the convicts – 'starving, half-naked gallows-birds, dying by the score daily from scurvy and syphilis' – prised open the suitcases and boxes belonging to the 'politicals', plundering them of all their provisions and possessions. When one of the looters stole 'too much' booty, he was punished by three fellow criminals, who 'were hitting him over the head with pieces of wood; he was dripping with blood, but still refused to give up the linen he held under his arm'. There was, Malsagov noted with no apparent irony, 'an unwritten internal discipline [that] binds the ordinary criminals together'.

The camp also held women prisoners, who were degraded beyond measure: 'dumb, dirty flesh, an object of barter at the disposal first and foremost of the camp personnel'. The younger women became their concubines. 'If they refused the improved rations that accompany this abasement, they knew that they would very soon die of under-nourishment or tuberculosis.' Today a notice at the edge of the harbour invites new arrivals to respect the ecology of the archipelago by resisting the temptation to pick flowers or hunt animals, and only to picnic in designated zones. With no sense of irony, the administrator of District 50 (as Solovki is now known) writes: 'Dear Visitors, We hope that a keeping of the rules will not be difficult for you...' As if.

Outside the gigantic walls of the kremlin, the settlement of Solovki irresistibly conjures up images of the American west in the nineteenth century: a dusty main street, clapboard houses on either side, a scatter of tumble-down barns half-filled with hay for the winter, a few scruffy goats and sheep picking at a rubbish heap, an emaciated cow grazing on the scrubby verge. The permanent inhabitants are readily distinguishable from the visitors. They have a hangdog, resentful manner, as if the outsiders, pilgrims and tourists who rent apartments or stay in lodgings and use the island for walking and biking in the brief summer reprieve from a near-Arctic winter are unwelcome intruders. The locals slouch as they wander about their business, their clothes threadbare and stained, their poverty in sharp contrast to the well-heeled visitors from Moscow and St Petersburg. Both sexes bear the scars of a severe climate in which for much of the year they endure extreme cold, darkness and storms – and in which, living on nugatory benefits, they do little but drink the long winters away with cheap vodka. A disproportionate number of them appear to be disfigured or disabled. Family feuds and violence are commonplace; a few months earlier, a young man was murdered outside the café where visitors to the holy island relax over lunch.

From the centre of the township a choice of quiet tracks leads you by various routes into the wooded interior of the island. In summer the landscape is deceptively benign; hills and valleys form a natural bowl for a series of artificial lakes intersected by the intricate chain of canals built by the monks in the sixteenth century to breed and harvest fish. On one summit, at the top of a hill called Sekirnaya, I was led into a glade that shelters a small white church with a long view over the White Sea. If it had been blessed with a different history, it would be the kind of haven where even an atheist might find sanctuary. But in the early days of the Gulag it was used as a punishment block, and the chanting of monks was replaced by the screams of tortured prisoners. There is no peace here.

My guide was one of Solovki's senior administrators. Marina had given up a career as a nuclear scientist to settle permanently on the island, where she had dedicated her life to the service of the Orthodox Church as the – unpaid – head of Pilgrim Services. She knew every detail of what had happened in this simple church, which was now under restoration, and where, as they peeled away at the fabric, the restoration team had uncovered an inscription written by one of the inmates: 'Comrades, remember Lenin's legacy. Solovki is a school that teaches thugs to kill again.' Among the more exquisite forms of punishment was a peculiarly cruel procedure by which prisoners were forced to sit on thin poles, suspended so that their feet could not touch the ground. As they became exhausted and benumbed, they lost their balance and fell – only to be beaten for insubordination and hoisted once more on to their agonizing perch. Alternatively, such 'social parasites', as the prisoners were officially designated, were tied up naked to a tree in the heat of the day and left for mosquitoes to torment. At the end of the day the victims would be cut down, their bodies devoured and bloodied. 'Very often,' Marina said, as I swatted away a cloud of mosquitoes, 'they died.'

Such tortures accounted for only a minority of the forty thousand recorded deaths at Solovki. Most of the victims died from starvation, disease and neglect. The prison hospital was always overcrowded. As Malsagov and others recorded, the doctors would from time to time order the 'wards' to be cleaned, sluiced down and disinfected. To facilitate this procedure the patients were carried outside, where the temperature was very often minus 20 degrees centigrade. During one winter so many prisoners perished from cold and hunger that the frozen bodies had to be stored upright in the makeshift morgue, for which one of the monastery's cellars had been commandeered. Perhaps all this is what the camp authorities had in mind when they greeted new prisoners with a revolutionary slogan that read: 'With an Iron Fist, We Will Lead Humanity to Happiness'.

Gradually the Gulag 'system' acquired a more sophisticated purpose. Under Stalin, the Bolsheviks decreed that the prison camps should be turned into self-sustaining and profit-making enterprises. The ever-growing number of 'class enemies' – according to Anne Applebaum's meticulously researched *Gulag: A History*, some fifty thousand prisoners had been incarcerated in eighty-four camps by the mid-twenties – were the means to that end. On Solovki the prisoners became, in effect, beasts of burden at the service of the camp commandant as he sought to turn the desolate island into a socialist 'profit centre'. Their daily food rations were distributed according to the number of tasks they were able to perform. The more work they did – digging ditches, carting bricks, laying roads – the more they ate. Thus a defining socialist slogan –

'From each according to his ability, to each according to his need' – was turned on its head. The strong were fed; the weak starved.

Any doubts about the Gulag were slow, very slow, to infiltrate the collective unconscious of that army of romantics and ideologues in the West who saw in the Soviet revolution a new dawn for all mankind. But by 1928 Malsagov's revelations and other clandestinely distributed 'subversive' (*samizdat*) reports about Solovki had finally raised a few European eyebrows. Determined to assuage this anxiety, the Soviet authorities summoned the authentic 'proletarian' author Maxim Gorky to the rescue. Although his international star was on the wane, Gorky was still lionized by a gullible intelligentsia in Europe and America, who not only believed him to be his country's greatest living writer, but saw in him proof that it was possible for Russian artists and intellectuals both to express themselves freely and to be loyal Soviet citizens.

His track record had indeed been impressive. Two weeks after the October Revolution of 1917 he had been free to write that 'Lenin and Trotsky don't have any idea about freedom or human rights. They are already corrupted by the dirty poison of power...' Later he compared Lenin unfavourably to the last tsar. In response the Russian leader wrote him a letter: 'My advice to you: change your surroundings, your views, your actions, otherwise life may turn away from you.' In 1921 he duly retreated to the southern Italian town of Sorrento, where he had lived in the years leading up to the outbreak of World War I, a refugee both from the despotism of Tsar Nicholas II and from the cruel Russian climate that had aggravated his poor health. But this time, once again in self-imposed exile, he chose the same healthy climate not only as a prisoner of the TB by which his body was racked, but, discreetly, as a political refugee from the revolution of which he had originally been the intellectual world's most eloquent champion. For this reason, even *in absentia* he was sedulously paraded by the Kremlin as an unvarnished hero of the revolution.

In 1928, after painstaking negotiations with the Soviet authorities, he returned to the Motherland to attend celebrations organized to mark his sixtieth birthday. When he arrived in Moscow he was given an ecstatic welcome from a great crowd at the Belorussky station. Overwhelmed by this popular embrace, which contrasted gratifyingly with the indifference with which he was treated by the people of Sorrento, and flattered by the blandishments of the Soviet leadership, he elected never to leave the country again. Who better to quash the rumours and silence the whispers about the Gulag system at Solovki?

Gorky arrived on Solovki in June 1929, accompanied by a phalanx of state officials, and was taken around the prison complex, which had been spruced up with fresh paint and flowers for the occasion. One of the inmates was Dmitry Likhachyov, a young graduate fresh out of Leningrad University. Likhachyov had been sentenced to five years' hard labour for the arcane crime of denouncing Bolshevik reforms to Russian orthography. Later to be revered as a great scholar, and a fearless defender of Alexander Solzhenitsyn and Andrei Sakharov, Likhachyov treated his incarceration on Solovki as an opportunity to study what he described wryly as 'criminal folklore'. To this end he kept a secret diary, complete with pen and ink drawings, which is now preserved in the Pushkin House in St Petersburg, and in which he noted, when news of Gorky's forthcoming visit reached Solovki, 'All we prisoners were delighted. Gorky will spot everything, find out everything. He's been around. You can't fool him…' But they did.

Although Gorky spent three days on Solovki, he managed to avoid almost all contact with the convicts. However, he did have one meeting with a young inmate who was no more than a boy. Their conversation lasted at least half an hour, during which the writer was apparently left in no doubt about the horror of life in this concentration camp. He was also taken to what passed as the 'library', where he was shown a group of men ostentatiously reading newspapers the wrong way up. As if to demonstrate that he had got the message – that 're-education' at Solovki was a great lie – Gorky walked over to the men and carefully turned one of their papers the right way up. The prisoners rejoiced that he had seen the light. They were mistaken.

After his visit to the punishment block in the church on the top of Sekirnaya, one of the Moscow bureaucrats accompanying Gorky made an official note in the prison log to the effect that conditions there were 'appropriate'. In his own hand Gorky added at the bottom, above his signature, 'He could have written "excellent".' He then departed to write of Solovki, 'There is no impression of life being over-regulated. There is no resemblance to a prison; instead it seems as if these rooms are inhabited by passengers rescued from a drowning ship.' For good measure he added, with leaden triumphalism, 'If any so-called cultured European Society dared to conduct an experiment such as this colony and if this experiment yielded fruits as ours had, that country would blow all its trumpets and boast about its accomplishments.' Two years later he accepted Stalin's invitation to settle permanently in Moscow, where he was provided with a grace-and-favour mansion, two dachas in the country and the staff to run all three.

After Gorky's departure from Solovki, the small boy to whom he had granted an audience was removed from his compound and not seen again. According to Likhachyov, the prison guards also embarked on a drunken killing spree. 'One bullet per person,' he noted. 'Many were buried alive, just a thin layer of earth over them. In the morning the earth on the pit was still moving.' Gorky's determination to avoid the truth, his cowardice in the face of the facts, leaves me to wonder, What if? What if he had revealed the truth about the first Gulag? Would it have made any difference? Perhaps not. But at least Stalin's apologists in Europe and America would have had even less excuse for their silence in the face of what Solzhenitsyn, citing Solovki in the opening chapter of *The Gulag Archipelago*, would describe as the 'cancer' that spread until, by the time of Stalin's death in 1953, 18 million Soviet citizens, most of them as slave labourers, had passed through the Gulag system.

Within the walls of the kremlin, I visited a little museum dedicated to the victims who died at Solovki. Their innocent faces stared out in rebuke from faded photographs: intelligent and sensitive young men looking thoughtfully towards the future, but with no idea of what was to befall them. There were scraps of letters as well. One of them was written by a teenage boy to his parents in 1921: 'There are 800 of us…it is hard to believe that anyone can come out of here alive. I am very sick. If you can, please help us… Your son.' Four months later, the caption records, he was drowned in the White Sea while trying to escape.

Echoing the Orthodox view, Marina told me with profound sincerity that the redemptive feature of Solovki was that it created, in her precise words, 'many more martyrs for our faith'. I was instantly reminded of Monty Python's *Life of Brian* – always look on the bright side of life. Only five years ago, she went on, a monk was walking through the woods below the church on Sekirnaya when he had a vision in which he was told that bodies lay under the ground where he was standing. The monks brought spades to the place that he identified and, sure enough, they came upon a pile of corpses in prison uniform. Marina took me to the same spot, where there are now four or five unmarked crosses. As we entered the little glade, she stopped, stood in silence for a few moments, and then began to chant with delicate musicality a prayer for their souls. Her voice lilted through the trees as I smacked at the mosquitoes on my face. It is generally supposed that there are many more 'martyrs' for the Orthodox cause yet to be disinterred on this 'holy' island. Unknown, unnamed.

On my last morning on Solovki I woke up early with a familiar feeling of dread. My room faced the Holy Lake beyond the eastern walls of the kremlin. A breeze ruffled the water, the light was soft, the sun still low in the sky, shadows shortening over the gleaming leaded spires and golden domes. I should have been elated by the simple beauty of the moment. Instead I found myself fighting a losing battle with despair. I noted in my diary, 'I wish I was away from here. I can't understand the language. I can't read the alphabet. I am like a blind man who is also deaf. I want to escape. I am lonely and homesick. I know I must school myself to discipline these feelings. I have to be a public person. I have to deliver. But it is draining me.' Then, uncontrollably, my eyes started to prick and I was soon sobbing with self-pity, the monastery a blur in the distance. I feared that I was heading back down towards a depression that would coil around me and suck me into its vortex.

## THE MAGIC OF KARELIA

I was in a reverie, sitting on the deck of a three-masted brig, a replica of an eighteenth-century square-rigged Baltic trader. We were making 4 knots in a balmy breeze, the spars were creaking gently and, for the first time in Russia, I felt content. The skipper wore a peaked cap, Cowes-style, and had a crew of two – one of whom, his wife, was preparing a stew for us below in the galley. I was half-reading a scholarly history of the Orthodox Church, but letting my mind wander, lulled by the slight motion of the boat. Memories of the TV series *The Onedin Line* floated into my semi-consciousness as I basked in the warmth of the late afternoon sun, imagining myself in a world away from where I was. But this feel-good sensation was for all the wrong reasons. Instead of being uplifted because I was travelling across Russia, I had allowed myself to become so mesmerized by the flow of water past the hull, eddying in our wake, that I had inadvertently transposed myself back to the coastal waters of the west of England and to one of those summer afternoons in Start Bay, where for the last forty years or so I have sailed back and forth a little way from the safety of Dartmouth harbour. In reality, we were crossing another measureless inland sea called Lake Onego, and the capital city of Russian Karelia, Petrozavodsk, had just faded into the haze behind us.

The skipper invited me to take the helm, indicating the compass course I should steer towards our destination some ten hours away to the south. One of the delights of sailing in fine weather is that you can both concentrate on steering in the right direction at the fastest comfortable speed *and* allow your mind to wander. In such circumstances it really is, for a while, the journey, not the arrival, that matters. I began to feel as if I could go on for ever in this never-never environment, wondering at the vast scale of the landlocked seas that form a necklace of silvery waterways stretching to the horizon in every direction that you could navigate for day after day without ever making a landfall. The very thought filled me with that sense of the numinous that even – or perhaps especially – non-God-fearing folk discover in the presence of the natural world.

Before we left Petrozavodsk, hoping to experience a little of what it must have been like for the early traders in these uncharted waters and heading for the remote hinterland of Karelia, my bemused driver, only half in jest, asked: 'Are you really going there – to the Far East? I wouldn't if I were you. They are savages there.' Romantics and anthropologists view Karelia through a somewhat different prism, and speak of its mysteries in hushed, awed, almost mystical terms. Its forests are said to guard ancient rites and rituals; there are fauns among the fauna; gods and devils in the birches; white witches (as well as black) in the villages, who brew up alchemical mixtures to rescue (or ruin) the lives of a pagan people who have more faith in their magic than in orthodox means, whether medicine or religion. After a more or less sleepless voyage through the day–night, in which I watched the sun fail to set before it began to rise again, I now felt half-inclined to believe it all.

Just before 4 a.m. we drifted into the mouth of a wide river that, in the early morning mist, reminded me of the Mekong delta. I could just pick out across the water a clutch of single-storey dwellings, silent hamlets set in the trees and among the fields. As we got closer to our landfall, there was the sound and then, in the pre-dawn obscurity, the sight of cranes groaning as they loaded a couple of brightly lit coasters, one with sawn timber and the other with gravel. In what many Russians describe nostalgically as the Soviet era, the sawmill and the gravel pit produced their annual quota regardless of the laws of supply and demand. But they also provided jobs for an otherwise unemployable workforce. Now the businesses are in private hands, the market rules, and hundreds of workers have been laid off with no hope of other work. Not surprisingly, many ordinary Russians neither welcomed the collapse of the Soviet Union nor relish its capitalist alternative. We docked at a worn-out jetty alongside two elderly tugs, in one of which a seaman slouched over his wheel, smoking a cigarette as he waited for instructions that he knew would never come. I caught his eye and he stared back blankly, as Russians so often do, but I detected no sign of the threatened savagery.

On the contrary, the forests of Karelia seemed both enchanting and enticing. It was at once apparent that 'Russian' Karelia (the region known historically as Karelia embraces large tracts of Sibelius's Finland as well) was indeed other-worldly. Small rural settlements clung to the edge of long, empty roads that passed through forests girdled and laced by streams, rivers and tributaries, all of which seemed to lead down into Lake Onega. There was a dreaminess in the atmosphere, a surreality that nurtured fantasy.

We were met by an anthropologist who had made the forests of Karelia his special subject. Andrey had agreed to guide me through the social and cultural complexities of a region to which he had devoted twenty years of his professional life. Like many Russian academics I had met, he liked a drink, but the impact of alcohol appeared to have no detectable effect on his academic precision as he explained the anthropological features of the various communities on his patch. He was mercifully free of the self-regarding jargon that so many anthropologists deploy to reassure themselves that their field of study is a genuine scientific discipline rather than a form of upmarket journalism. He was also quick to cut to the chase. 'Would you like to meet a white witch? I think it can be arranged,' he said.

The next day we drove deep into the forest, leaving the highway to follow a track that emerged on the edge of a silky-soft stream that meandered through reedbeds and over gravel towards a wider flow where a clutch of small boats drifted in the current, each with its fisherman huddled amidships. There we abandoned the car and crossed the stream by a narrow, rickety footbridge that led on to an island where we could make out the roofs of wooden houses among the trees. I glimpsed two statues side by side, almost hidden behind a jumble of shrubs in an ill-kempt miniature park. One was a Victorian tribute to an indistinct worthy of local renown, the other immediately familiar but incongruous: the stocky figure, the bald pate, the rounded bullet head – like David Lloyd George without the flowing locks – and the right arm outstretched, at once protective and threatening. It was Lenin in white mock marble, one of a job lot that must have been churned out by the truckload for distribution into every corner of what had once been his empire, but now half-covered in ivy.

We found our way to a dilapidated little house that seemed to fit Andrey's promised bill to perfection. It was painted blue, faded with age, and it tilted slightly from the vertical, which made it look as though it had been lifted from the pages of a children's book featuring the nursery rhyme about the old lady who lived in a shoe. There was a barking dog on a chain outside, which I circumnavigated with care. A baby slept in a pram. We were greeted formally by a middle-aged woman and a young girl (her daughter, I presumed), who stared at us with unblinking curiosity. Andrey explained our purpose. We were led through the kitchen past an old cooking range festooned with pots and pans, and up some stairs to a surprisingly spacious living room, where my white witch was waiting to receive us.

Babushka Valentina, known to everyone in the locality and beyond as Baba Valya, must have been at least eighty years old. A rotund and diminutive woman, she had a pale, doughy face that seemed to have been pressed directly on to her shoulders without thought of a neck. Her eyes were dark, like twin currants buried in deep folds of pastry, and her gaze was piercing. She welcomed us with a gesture of her hand but without a smile, her manner indicating that she was accustomed to due deference. We sat around her on rickety chairs as she held forth without need of invitation, speaking slowly and with assurance, pausing only when a yellow budgerigar flew across the room to settle on her shoulder. I was mildly relieved to see that my white witch had a white cat that knew it had no chance of catching the bird.

'I am a healer. I have this gift. I understand. I know things. When people come to see me I can tell what is wrong. If they have cut a finger, I can stop the bleeding; even if a vein is cut, I can staunch the flow. If small children are brought to me, I will say the words that will allow them to grow up healthy and strong. Mothers bring sick children to me when they are babies, when the hospital can't help, and I make them well.'

Communication with Baba Valya was a slow process. Not because of any infirmity on her part – she spoke with clarity and precision – but because she spoke in a Karelian dialect that Andrey, whose English was imperfect, had to translate into Russian for my translator, Teresa, to pass on to me in English. I am generally impatient at such inevitable but cumbersome procedures, but Baba Valya's certainties were so extraordinary that the delay did not matter at all. 'When people come to see me with an ailment I walk over,' she continued, gesturing to a curtain behind which was a stove, 'and I say some magic words and brew tea for them. And I say, "Dear one, I have a pure soul and I can help you." Often they have bought medicine from the doctor, but it is very expensive and the trouble only goes away for a few days – then they are ill again. But I don't make them pay, and they get better, so many people want to see me.'

Baba Valya explained that her healing powers had been passed down to her by her grandfather when she was a young child. 'There were no doctors here then, but I had a very good memory from the age of three, so I was able to retain everything he told me. He had these books, old Russian books, and I think that some of his knowledge was in those books. I never had the books, but remembered everything he said. My granddaughter also has a wonderful memory – she is very sharp. When I am old and close to death, but while my soul is still living, then I will pass my powers on to her.' The granddaughter was the little girl whose baleful stare had greeted me at the porch.

I asked tentatively whether she had the ability to cast evil spells as well. For a moment she looked affronted by my temerity – as if, as the writer Malcolm Muggeridge did once on the BBC's *Panorama*, I had asked a surgeon who had just triumphantly separated a pair of 'Siamese' twins, 'Could you join them together again?' But she replied calmly, 'Some people can, but I can't. I don't know how to do it – and, in any case, why should I want to harm people?' Then she softened and twinkled, saying, 'Anyway, if I could do witchcraft, I'd use it on my son. He's forty-three and he still isn't married. I would find him a bride.'

Andrey intervened to warn that I was entering delicate territory, but I pressed on to ask about the spirits of the Karelian forest. Did they really exist? Did she believe in them? Her answer was enchanting and very possibly enchanted – and to me at that moment it made as much sense as the competing certainties of monotheistic religions: there is One God and only One God, and you had better know that he is Ours and not Yours. 'I am a Christian,' she said, 'but I also know that there are demons and sprites in the forest.' She made contact with the latter (but never the former) through what she believed to be 'christianized' spells. This kind of contact was very important, she explained, otherwise the cattle belonging to the villagers would be at risk when they were driven out to the forest to forage. 'I used to protect the cattle with my spells, making sure the wood sprites would look after them. My cows would always come back safely of their own accord, even after five hours in the forest. But others, who didn't know about my spells and whose animals had not been protected, would have to go searching for them high and low because their animals would not come back. When they realized I had this special skill they asked me, "Come and help us. Please help us," and I did. In this way I found myself looking after seventy-five, maybe a hundred cattle.' I began to feel myself under her spell. Why not, I thought?

What difference is there between talking to sprites and praying to the Almighty?

All this had happened in the last century under the eyes of the secret police at a time when the Communist Party was making strenuous efforts to stamp out false gods of all kinds by harassing, threatening, bullying, arresting, sentencing, imprisoning, deporting and sometimes killing those who dared openly to defy the secular certainties of the Soviet Union. But the security services in Karelia evidently turned a blind eye to Baba Valya and to those who solicited her magic charms. 'On one occasion,' she said, 'I was told by the manager of our cooperative that the cattle were to be pastured near the village, so it would be unnecessary for me to make contact with the wood sprites, so I should not do so. I obeyed him. During that night the animals were attacked by bears and five animals died.'

Baba Valya's survival as a white witch may owe something to the fact that her heretical belief in the supernatural was widely shared in this tightly knit community. Nonetheless, she was careful to weave her spells with discretion, treating those members of the community who sought her out, but not daring to 'advertise' her wares beyond that close circle. Today she needs no advertisement. Word of mouth means that those who believe in the power of magic come in their scores from as far afield as Moscow and St Petersburg; among their number lawyers and politicians, not to mention doctors of medicine, for whom the occult evidently has a potency that science has yet to dispel. I found myself in awe of Baba Valya and, more generally, at the resilience of the human spirit – the indomitable, dogged refusal to surrender faith, however irrational or heretical it may appear to secular souls like me or, in his time, to Comrade Stalin.

Feeling rather guilty about the bad faith I was about to reveal, I was curious enough to ask if she could do anything to help my own ailment – an intermittent backache that, I explained, had a habit of degenerating into spasm without warning and at the most inconvenient times, invariably immobilizing me. She said nothing but stared at me intently for at least a minute. Then she muttered something as an aside to Andrey, which made him shift uncomfortably and which even Teresa seemed reluctant to pass on. 'What did she say?' I insisted, no longer sceptical. 'She says that she can try to help, but you are suffering in another way. It is your psychological state. Your nervous system is damaged.' 'How do you know?' I asked Baba Valya in dismay. 'I don't know how I know, but I can tell,' she replied enigmatically and unhelpfully. 'Can it be treated?' I demanded. Another flurry of dialogue among her, Andrey and Teresa elicited an unconvincing 'yes' of the 'keep the bad news from the patient' variety. Anyway, she consented to do what she could about the physical manifestation of my psychological distress.

Advised by Andrey, I had brought a packet of tea with me as an offering. I gave it to her and she disappeared behind a curtain, where I could glimpse her turning it round and round in her hands, all the while murmuring to herself almost inaudibly, as old people will. This lasted for what seemed an interminable time, but was probably no more than three minutes. Then she handed the tea back to me with the instruction that I should drink it and afterwards bath in salt water. Following this ablution, I should fill a glass with the bath water and drain its contents. Afterwards I should rinse my body in fresh water.

She beckoned me into an adjoining room where there was a small table by the window. Gesturing for me to roll down my trousers to expose the upper part of my buttocks and to roll my shirt up to the chest, she required me to lean forward over the table, resting my front on its surface. She asked me for my name, then took a knife and, pressing the point gently to the skin, worked her way up and down my spine, all the while muttering to herself an incantation in which I could occasionally distinguish the word 'Jonathan'. This procedure lasted about ten minutes and proved to be a surprisingly soothing experience. When it was over I thanked her profusely. She admonished me: 'You need more treatment, and you will only get better if you really believe.' Then she added, as though I had just taken Holy Communion, 'God be with you.'

As we said our farewells, a neighbour arrived in a state of some agitation. Her dog had gone missing. They had searched up and down the river bank without success. Could Baba Valya use her magic to help? The old lady smiled and promised to try. And this, I thought, was Russia in the twenty-first century; Karelia, I concluded, certainly was 'other'.

The following day the packet of tea split and the contents disappeared into the folds of my suitcase. I also failed to bath in salt water. My back, however, recovered. But then it always does – for a while.

A while later we set off for Devil's Nose, a place shrouded in mythology and academic disputation about the exquisite petroglyphs scored in the rocks there perhaps five thousand years ago by the first settlers in Karelia. We headed towards this prehistoric site down a long, slow-flowing river that meandered gently through the forest. It was quite extraordinarily beautiful; the water so still that it offered a precise mirror to the silver birches that flanked our route to the river's edge; so clear that the reflected tips of the trees seemed to reach down 30 metres or so below the surface, just as they reached up to the same height above. It was mesmerizing – or rather, to be precise, it would have been so had we been travelling silently by skiff or punt. But we had a 40-mile journey and limited time, so we had hired a speedboat. That may give a false impression. Ours was not one of those gleaming, little plastic wave-pounders that pollute every vulgar resort around the world, but a battered veteran made of tin, which had seen twenty-five years of service. It was designed, in Soviet style, to be robust and work-man-like and would not have been out of place on the Serpentine half a century ago; except that it had an equally ancient outboard engine that reeked of leaking fuel and poured black carbon into the atmosphere once our skipper, who was himself fuelled by vodka, managed to fire it up. Since the engine cover had long since been discarded, its innards were exposed to the air and, as the throttle appeared to be beyond our skipper's control, we progressed at only two speeds, dead slow or flat out, when the shriek of the engine was deafening.

It might have been exhilarating as we careered downstream at 25 knots had it not been for the fact that our way was strewn with tree trunks, partly submerged but upright, as if they had been pile-driven into the river bed; only a few centimetres of seal-like head showed above the surface. The skipper more or less knew his way, twisting through this lethal obstacle course with a panache that deserted him only when we struck one of the logs and the boat half-leapt from the water. After that I concentrated intently, pointing to left and right at each barely visible obstruction in the vague hope that we might avoid being fatally speared.

After two hours of this, we emerged from the secrecy of the river into the late evening sunlight and the skipping waves of the lake. In fits and starts – the fuel was dirty – we arrived at Devil's Nose. I had always been a philistine about cave and rock paintings, sensing their significance but not feeling it. The petroglyphs at Devil's Nose, however, turned out to be enchanting. Aside from a solitary fisherman who helped point us in the right direction, we were alone with this spectacular evidence of Russia's prehistory; alone as the sun slid towards the horizon, throwing a copper-golden light across the rock as though we were on stage waiting for Wotan, Fricke and Brunnhilde to appear before us. You could see at once why our ancestors had chosen this spot to record their existence.

The chiselled images of a fish, a spear, an otter, four delicate swans with two cygnets, and the Devil himself are so clearly etched on the rock that the artists might have downed tools only yesterday. The Devil's face is rectangular, his one good eye (the other is closed) glaring at the sky; his arms are outstretched, one hand holding a fish, the other with fingers apart as if in imprecation. A natural crack in the rock bisects his body from top to bottom and then runs to the water. Local folklore claims that animals (even humans) were sacrificed here and their blood poured into the crack and thence into the reddening water. On the rock above the Devil's head an Orthodox cross, presumed to have been carved into the rock by local monks in the fifteenth century, is in perpetual mortal combat with this evil force, neither ever victorious.

Had this site been in Europe or America, it would surely have been fenced off, access denied to all except headset-wearing ticket-holders enjoined not to step on these precious relics. As it was, I wandered freely but reverentially among these ancient wonders, tracing their outlines with my fingers and feeling a sense of wonder and delight. Ever since the discovery of these petroglyphs in 1845, scholars have speculated on their meaning and purpose. As one of their number has pointed out recently, the experts are in accord only in discerning that rock art is 'deceptively simple'. Are the animals and figures at Devil's Nose, and the many others scattered on the eastern shores of the Karelian seas and lakes, an artistic commentary on the significant realities of daily life? Are they holy sites where the gods may be appeased? Are they shrines at which to worship the Devil? Do they reveal a relationship with the cosmos that modern man can only guess at? I was about to leave Devil's Nose in awe of the unknown and unknowable when the modern age rudely intervened: a mobile phone rang with the news that Roger Federer had won yet another Wimbledon championship.

As if to confirm that magic, myth and folklore properly define a Karelian identity that has survived the totalitarian certainties of the Soviet age, we heard about a troupe of babushka singers who performed at weddings and other celebrations, and were anxious to display their art to the visiting foreigner. We were instructed to find our way to a hamlet and thence to an orchard adjoining a cottage that was available to them for rehearsals. There they would entertain us. The babushkas (literally 'grandmothers' or 'old ladies') were dressed in traditional peasant costumes: ample skirts woven in shades and patterns of red, black and green, white blouses and multi-coloured shawls. They smiled at us and then, without further ceremony, they were away, dancing and jigging and singing in piping unison. Their songs were of joy and sorrow, of love and loss. The words, steps and music passed down to them by parents and grandparents belonged to a folk culture that had hardly changed for centuries. It was a touchingly unaffected performance.

I applauded vigorously, my hands working overtime. At this I was arrested, almost literally, by one of the babushkas with a toothless smile – to be precise, she had only two visible teeth and they were filled with gold – and a face lined by age and hard labour, but that was more than redeemed by deep brown eyes that flashed, it could be fairly said, coquettishly. She told me, to the immense mirth of her fellow troupers, that I was 'a very handsome man'. Not exactly encouraged by this, and uncertain of protocol, I went towards her and was at once enfolded to her breast. After a while, during which I struggled to avoid suffocation, she released me, declaring that this was the first time she had been held by a man for many years. How sad it was, she lamented, that 'I am now so old that my breasts are dry'. Wretchedly searching for the appropriate gallantry, I replied, 'I am delighted to meet you, to see your wonderful clothes, your smiling face and your beautiful eyes.' But these words, which had been intended to bring an early end to our tryst, had the opposite effect, seeming merely to increase her mischievous ardour. While her friends fell about in laughter at her lack of inhibition, she exclaimed, 'Even when I was a girl no one ever told me I was beautiful – but now that I am old this charming man says the most wonderful things to me!'

I tried to change the subject, asking, with an effort at serious enquiry, about the challenges of life in post-Soviet Karelia. She shot back: 'It is terrible because we have no men, no love.' And then, as though this had nonetheless unleashed a genuine emotion among all of them, she and her friends competed with stories of their own losses and sorrows, the true tales that folkloric songs turn into poetry. Only one of the nine babushkas was not a widow. 'Our men die young,' they explained, 'from hard work and vodka.' I was reminded of a shocking statistic: life expectancy in modern Russia for a man who has reached the age of twenty has fallen to fifty-eight years, and even that calamitous figure is on a downward trajectory. The principal culprits are violence, road accidents, AIDS, chain-smoked tobacco and a toxic intake of cheap liquor. Russia is facing a catastrophic population implosion, with numbers predicted to plummet from 150 million today to perhaps no more than 120 million over the next forty years.

The babushkas did not speak of this, nor did I ask them, but they were forthright about their travails. Life, they insisted, was worse now than it had been in Soviet times. They spoke of poverty, insecurity and unemployment; of young people who either left for the city or wasted their days drinking or taking drugs; of a lack of respect and decency; of a world that, seen from their perspective, was going to hell in a handcart. I left the Karelian glade touched by their warmth and frankness, reminding myself yet again that such open conversations would have been impossible a generation ago.

## TSAR PETER'S CITY

I had never been to St Petersburg before. Of course I had seen photographs and – like most people – gasped at the massive scale of the city and at the wonders of the Hermitage. But, slightly disappointingly, my first sight of the city was from a taxi that brought me in through a sprawl of suburbs – which had somehow failed to find their way into the best of the guide books. However, I had to walk the last part of the way towards my lodgings and, losing my way, I found myself suddenly facing one of the city's most famous sights, the Anichkov Bridge that crosses the Fontanka Canal on Nevsky Prospect. Guide book in hand, I stared up at a neo-classical quartet of warriors, each astride a half-tamed stallion. It was portentous but magnificent. Later I wandered along the Fontanka in the evening light passing the palaces, peeling blue and fading pink, wondering both at the grandeur itself and why it left me so unmoved. I had expected to enthuse about

St Petersburg but the longer I stayed and the more I discovered about the city, the more challenging this became.

Of course, St Petersburg is an astonishing achievement, the product of visionary genius, but it is an artifice, a grand folly, a faintly absurd statement about Russia and about the genius in question, Peter the Great. Although St Petersburg was conceived partly in the image of great cities like Venice and Amsterdam, its canals thread their way through a stage set built for visual effect rather than playing the role of necessary thoroughfares for the purpose of communication and trade. Not that St Petersburg is boring. On the contrary, its delights are obvious: grand vistas, glorious palaces, fine bridges, the River Neva, the Hermitage where you can walk through a labyrinth of delight for days without ever finding your way (I made a beeline for the Rembrandts and the two adjoining rooms that are given over, respectively, to Picasso and Matisse), the Summer and Winter palaces, *The Bronze Horseman*, St Isaac's Cathedral and the street where you can stroll for an eternity, Nevsky Prospect. But for me that is not quite the point. I like cities that emerge from the past. St Petersburg was imposed on the future, an arrogant assertion of will, a confidence trick that leaves me bedazzled but cold.

By almost any reading Tsar Peter I's vision for Russia, which he sought to realize in St Petersburg, was every bit as obsessive and ruthless as that of the Soviet Union's first 'tsar', Lenin. Both men had relentless conviction and energy. Both were despotic. Both were so powerful and charismatic that their absolute authority was never seriously put to the test. Both conducted a gigantic social experiment with the Russian people as their guinea pigs. And both were revolutionaries. Sitting in a café on Nevsky Prospect, I felt that my comparison was smart but maybe too glib. So I was reassured to read in Laurence Kelly's marvellous *A Traveller's Companion to St Petersburg* that this 'insight' of mine was very far from being original.

Kelly cites an anecdote reported by the French ambassador just before World War I, in which the chamberlain to the Russian Imperial

Court, Nicholas Besak, explains for the benefit of his companion why Tsar Peter was indeed a revolutionary:

> All Peter Alexeievitch liked was destroying things. That is why he was so essentially Russian. In his savage despotism he undermined and overturned the whole fabric. For nearly thirty years he was in revolt against his people; he attacked all our traditions and customs; he turned everything upside down, even our holy Orthodox Church…. He destroyed for the sheer delight in destroying, and took cynical pleasure in breaking down the resistance of others…. When our present-day anarchists dream of blowing up the social edifice on the pretext of reconstructing it en bloc, they are unconsciously drawing their inspiration from Peter the Great. Like him they have a fanatical hatred of the past; like him they imagine they can change the whole soul of a nation….

The conversation between the diplomat and the courtier took place on a bitterly cold evening as they stood beneath Falconet's famous statue of *The Bronze Horseman*, which depicts the city's founder staring out across the Neva River towards the Peter and Paul Fortress, where, so legend has it, on 16 May 1703 Tsar Peter cut a swathe of turf in the swamp and declared, 'Here shall be a town'. In his glorious ballad 'The Bronze Horseman', which most Russian children are still required to learn by heart, Alexander Pushkin contemplates to perfection both the magnificence and the menace in the god-like founder of St Petersburg: 'Terrible was he in the surrounding gloom. What strength was in him…. Oh, mighty master of fate! Was it not thus, aloft on the very edge of the abyss, that you reined up Russia with your iron curb?'

To me the chubby figure of Peter astride his warhorse looks somehow both complacent and menacing – like a spoilt child who has more than he needs; his outstretched arm, like that of Lenin in his most famous revolutionary pose, both promises a new dawn and demands absolute obedience. In person, he was evidently less physically impressive than Falconet's sculpture and numerous other depictions suggest. Despite his imposing height – at nearly 2 metres tall, he dwarfed his contemporaries – he was, in the words of one of them, 'long, on weak, spindly little legs and with a head so small in relation to the rest of his body...he looked more like a sort of dummy with a badly stuck on head than a live person. He suffered from a constant tic and was always making faces: wrinkling, screwing up his mouth, twitching his nose, wagging his chin.' A young Italian visitor to the Imperial Court confirms this unflattering impression, albeit more graciously: 'Peter was tall and thin.... For his great height, his feet seemed very narrow. His head was sometimes tugged to the right by convulsions.'

From his youth, Peter had been driven by an imperial ambition of breathtaking audacity and imagination: to transform Russia into a great European and maritime power that would be a force for all the world to reckon with. In 1696 he challenged the might of the Ottoman Empire in the south for control of the Black Sea, ordering the construction of the first Russian naval fleet for that purpose. And then, in the north, he advanced to confront the formidable King Charles XII of Sweden for control of the Baltic Sea. Although he failed disastrously against the Turks and was obliged to sue for peace, the Great Northern War of 1700–21, in which he led a coalition of European powers against Sweden, proved far more successful. Despite early setbacks, he seized the Swedish army's stronghold on the Neva and, in 1709, established his imperial capital on the site. It would be called St Petersburg, not apparently in self-glorification, but after the Apostle who very conveniently shared his name.

Peter I's military adventures and diplomatic excursions – which did indeed secure Russia a junior place at the European Top Table – were not merely an exercise in imperial muscle-flexing. They formed the backdrop for an even bolder enterprise: a social and cultural transformation of his realm that he sought to accomplish by ripping up the traditional and essential fabric of Russian society, the customs and traditions that had evolved over more than five centuries. His intention was to uproot his subjects from their Asiatic past, which he regarded as barbaric, superstitious and brutish, and to force them to adopt a new – European – identity. This, he believed, would fit Russia for the brave new tomorrow of his implacable imagination.

He set about his task with resolution. Between 1697 and 1700 he travelled extensively throughout Europe, often going from capital to capital incognito in search of the latest, enlightened ideas. He visited Paris, Rome, Königsberg (modern Kaliningrad), Amsterdam (where he worked as a shipwright at the East India Company headquarters) and London (where he was taken round the Observatory, the Arsenal, the Royal Mint and the Royal Society, and where he even attended the review of His Britannic Majesty's Fleet at Deptford). As a result of these eclectic experiences, his new model navy was constructed on Dutch and English lines; his military academies on the Prussian and Swedish models; his legal system was imported from Germany; and his government borrowed its formal structure from the Danish court. He also indulged a voracious appetite for European arts and sciences. St Petersburg was to be the fulcrum, the beacon and the symbol of the new Russia.

The Peter and Paul Fortress, designed as a defensive outpost, is a forbidding monument to an astonishing but pitiless vision. Its foundations were dug out and laid by soldiers and half-starved labourers working in chain gangs in the swampy, pestilential waste-land of the Neva valley. Lacking even the most basic tools like picks, shovels and wheelbarrows, they were obliged to dig away with their bare hands and to carry soil and stones in the folds of their tattered clothing. Nonetheless, the Peter and Paul Fortress was completed on schedule within five months. Peter himself took up residence in a modest, austere log cabin (which is still preserved), where he drew up detailed plans in his own hand for the future of the city. Under his presiding genius it grew at a fantastic speed, so that by 1710 the court was able to decamp from Moscow to take up permanent residence in the new capital. But the price was exorbitant: it is estimated that the construction of St Petersburg cost the lives of a hundred thousand labourers – serfs and convicts – who perished from hunger and disease to make the tsar's dream come true.

More than a century later an emissary from France, the Marquis de Custine, wrote, 'In Russia, at that time, everything was sacrificed to the future; everyone was employed in building the palaces of their yet unborn masters.... There is a certain greatness of mind evidenced in this care that a chieftain and his people take for the power, and even the vanity, of the generations that are yet to come.' Although Peter and his successors – especially Catherine the Great – hired designers, architects, engineers and craftsmen from all over Europe to master-mind the construction of the palaces, the boulevards, the bridges and the canals according to the imperial template, yet his subjects, most of whom were bonded to their labouring masters as serfs, were merely slaves to this grandiose vision. A contemporary visitor – uncharacter-istically concerned about the fate of the tsar's subjects – noted that 'the common people talked of life as a burden from which they wanted to be freed. When sick, they lie on the floor hardly concerned whether they recover or die.... They won't even take medicine.'

Their masters did not escape either. The boyars, as they were known, had been accustomed to a life of companionable isolation among their families, their serfs and their animals, living on their far-flung estates in relative modesty. Now those who owned more than thirty serfs were ordered to attend upon Peter the Great in the new capital. The first hundred families arrived in 1716. Once they had constructed their St Petersburg town houses (a nobleman with five hundred serfs in his possession had to build a two-storey palace; smaller landowners clubbed together to find the money for a lesser dwelling), they were compelled to remain in St Petersburg as courtiers.

Humiliation was piled upon humiliation. The boyars were told not only how to build their houses, but how to converse with one another. Peter was also troubled by their table manners, ordering them to abjure from spitting food on to the floor and using their knives as toothpicks. To modernize their appearance he required them to copy him by shaving off their beards (it is said that Peter himself took shears to the beard of one recalcitrant nobleman) and to discard their traditional costumes in favour of European modes of dress. Nor did they have any choice in the matter. Thanks to a new imperial edict, they found themselves assigned to the service of the state as servants of the court, officially defined as 'slaves'. Detained in St Petersburg at the pleasure of the tsar, they had to surrender to him the title deeds both to their estates and to their serfs, which were then in effect leased back to them, but liable to forfeit if they failed to live up to his exacting standards.

Yet the journals written by contemporary travellers suggest that Peter's despotic approach had at best a limited effect. With patronizing, almost racist, disdain, one of them described the nation's nobility among whom he found himself as 'the barbarians'. Another, an English doctor, noted that 'they know not how to eat peas and carrots boiled but, like swine, eat them shells and all'. Indeed, in the privacy of their own palaces the boyars did not entirely surrender their Russian souls to Peter's European blueprint. The internal courtyards around which the self-consciously European apartments of the tsar's architectural Legoland were erected remained defiantly bucolic. Pigs, poultry and cattle, tended by serfs who lived among their livestock, had the run of what were supposed to be elegant outdoor vestibules on the French and Italian model. This obstinate subversion by the boyars was frequently made manifest when their cows and sheep escaped to wander the boulevards of the city, in open defiance of Peter's edict forbidding such desecration.

But they could not escape the Table of Ranks, the imperial game of snakes and ladders devised by Peter (and maintained by his successors) to facilitate the tsar's divine authority and by which they were kept in perpetual rivalry with each other. A passion for promotion and a terror of demotion became ruling obsessions. This Gilbertian corruption of the human psyche soon became entrenched – a suffocating culture that ate into the very marrow of the Russian soul. Under Peter and his successors, those members of the nobility who rose to the top of the Table of Ranks amassed great wealth. By the end of the eighteenth century the Sheremetev family, a case study in Orlando Figes's fine cultural history of Russia, *Natasha's Dance*, owned no fewer than 800,000 hectares of land and a million serfs. They were the largest landowners in the world, far richer than their 'grander' British counterparts, the Bedfords or the Devonshires. At their principal residence in St Petersburg, Fountain House on the Fontanka, they maintained a staff of 340 serfs; in the same period the Devonshires employed a mere eighteen live-in staff.

Balls and banquets were on the grand scale – *grandes bouffes* of gluttony in which precedence was all. Etiquette demanded that the young always stood in the presence of their elders. Food was served first to those of higher rank and only afterwards to those lower in the pecking order. As Figes notes, 'If the top end wanted second helpings, the bottom ends would not be served at all.' Prince Potemkin, famously cherished by Catherine the Great as statesman and lover, once asked one of the latter, a minor member of the nobility, whether he had enjoyed the feast at his table. The famished young officer replied – illustrating the universal truth that where there is precedence you will also find deference – 'Very much, Your Excellency, I saw everything.'

St Petersburg soon acquired all the trappings of a great European city. By the early nineteenth century, a fashion for Western art (in deference to the incontinent passion and bottomless purse of the eighteenth-century Empress Catherine), as well as for the theatre, opera and ballet, gave visitors from the West the impression that the city really was, in Pushkin's phrase, 'a window on Europe'. But if there was magnificence, it was on the surface. The eminent Russian polemicist Alexander Herzen likened Catherine the Great's Winter Palace to a ship 'floating on the surface of the ocean, [that] had no real connection with the inhabitants of the deep, beyond that of eating them…it imposed itself on the nation as a conqueror. In that monstrous barrack, in that enormous chancellery, there reigned the cold rigidity of a camp. One set gave or transmitted orders, the rest obeyed in silence.'

Seeing through the city's glittering façade, the Marquis de Custine detected a profoundly damaged society for which the canny French diplomat held Peter the Great directly responsible. In St Petersburg, he wrote, Peter had constructed

> a box, from which his chained boyars might contemplate, with envy, the stage on which is enacted the civilization of Europe; a civilization which, in forcing them to copy, he forbade them to emulate! Peter the Great, in all his works, acted without any regard to humanity, time or nature. All his ideas, with the faults of character of which they were the consequence, have spread and multiplied under the reigns that followed.

Similar sentiments were expressed by another in the words of the Russian polemicist Petr Jakovlevic Chaadaev, likewise writing more than a century after the birth pangs of Peter the Great's dream: 'To give a pledge of the Enlightenment he threw over us the mantle of civilization. We assumed the mantle but never arrived at enlighten-ment.' He continued despairingly in his First Philosophical Letter:

> The problem is that we never grew up with other peoples, that we do not belong to a single great family of the human race, either to the West or to the East, that we do not have the tradition of either the one or the other. We stand as it were outside time, and the world-wide upbringing of the human race has not reached us. The wonderful bond of human ideas in the succession of genera-tions and the history of the human spirit, which has brought this spirit throughout the rest of the world to its present status, has had no influence on us at all. Truly what has for long already formed the essence of life and society is still only theory and spec-ulation for us.

For me the story of the creation of St Petersburg is comedic tragedy: a parable of pride, arrogance and insecurity, which, along with courage and docility, are hallmark characteristics of the Russian people even today. It also offers a compelling political lesson: that no individual, however ruthless, can remould the essential character of a nation by force; that although the despot may for a time, even a long time, impose his will, he cannot uproot an inherited culture; and that, although subject peoples may find themselves obliged to submit for a time, their will can never be broken. The only way to make progress is by way of example, with reason and sensitivity, in what is a collaborative venture or nothing. The dismal failure of all Russia's rulers, from Peter the Great to Stalin, to appreciate this suggests a fatal flaw of character that has perverted the course of Russian history with tragic consequences for its long-suffering and brutalized people.

## MEETING THE INTELLIGENTSIA

That, at any rate, was how it seemed to me as I perched on a window seat of my palatial nineteenth-century guest-house looking down towards Nevsky Prospect. On the Fontanka, salesgirls competed with each other to megaphone the best deals for boat rides to the perpetual drift of tourists meandering along the capital's main thoroughfare clutching their guide books. Despite the warning of my solicitous housekeeper that I should not venture out at night, I joined the throng, hoping to stumble towards some measure of understanding as to why St Petersburg should make me feel morose. The local girls are pretty – often sensationally so in the prevailing uniform of mini-skirts and halter-tops baring a few inches of midriff – but, to my jaundiced eye, they seemed to lack animation. Heavily made up with powder-puff white faces and mauve lipstick, they reminded me of dolls or catwalk models as unreal as the city in which they strolled with carefully manicured ennui. Maybe it was merely the grumpy lust of late middle age – why should they all have such long legs and tiny waists

with chestnut hair cascading over their shoulders? – but they reinforced my feeling that there is a hollowness at the heart of the city, that
same unreality noted by early visitors to Peter the Great's imperium, a
stage that is today as artificial as that on which their forebears were
required to strut almost three centuries ago.

I was invited to a party to meet some of the city's glitterati. To be
precise, a delightful friend of a friend organized a party for me to meet
some of her friends, all of whom, it was immediately apparent, were
very chic, very elegant and very confident of their place in the new
Russia. As a small child – not only awkward but verging towards the
diminutive, I was gifted by my peers with the nickname 'Stumpy' – I
loathed parties. Aware of my prospective terror at the very thought of
balloons, jellies, parcel passing, blind-man buffing, clowns (who might
single me out to be their victim), magicians and eightsome reels, my
parents were wonderfully accommodating. So long as I agreed to
attend just one party a year, my mother would turn down all the rest
on my behalf. Thus each Christmas season I duly went to the house
next door to endure the requisite two hours of purgatory. I have never
lost that incipient dread, though more than fifty years on, I hope I
now manage it rather better. Nonetheless, as I looked around at this
elegant *galère* of St Petersburg musicians, artists, academics, designers
and writers, most of them dressed in designer fashions, which like their
owners, seemed to have dropped in lately from New York, Paris or
London, that familiar ancient dread knotted my stomach once again.

As it turned out, everyone was charming in the cool and detached
kind of way of such gatherings. They were clever and funny but determinedly supercilious, as if that were the style for this year. An interior
designer called Sergey told me that since the collapse of 'the dictatorship of the proletariat' the city had fallen under the malign sway of a
governor who imposed 'the dictatorship of bad taste.... We need a
dictator with good taste,' he said – and I think he meant it. So what
was his taste? 'I try to combine misery and luxury together,' he
replied, at which I murmured an appreciative, 'Really?' before moving

on, reminding myself of the party scene in Pushkin's *Eugene Onegin*: 'No lasting truths or dissertations – and no one's ears were shocked a bit by all the flow of lively wit.'

Feeling myself to be something of a spoilsport, I steeled my sinews to ask a serious question: what were the prospects for democracy in post-Soviet Russia? I tried first with a louche-looking composer of what he told me was 'industrial music'. 'Well, I don't want the past to return, but sometimes I am so angry with the people about me that I think we need some big stick, some dictator to beat us,' he replied, with no apparent irony, adding, after a pause, 'Well, perhaps not a dictator but a strong leader, one leader only.'

A painter, another Sergey, who was languidly dangling a small child from his shoulders, picked up the theme. 'Nothing has really changed in Russia, you know,' he counselled. 'Ten years, fifteen years ago, some people – good people – entered politics, but once they were there they changed completely. That's the impact of power. And it has frozen Russia from the fifteenth century until now. But, my friend, don't speak to me of democracy. I don't believe the word has any meaning in the modern world.'

I moved on to interrupt a conversation between two exquisitely tailored young women, who told me that I should visit St Petersburg in winter when it was especially beautiful. However, they added, they themselves would not be there as they would have departed for softer climes, probably India, 'Because, you know, St Petersburg is dark, cold, wet and depressing for so much of the time that you need one big break.' Emboldened by the not quite chilled and rather too sweet champagne, I enquired about modern Russia. They said they were very happy with how things were. 'And democracy?' I asked, venturing again into that terrain where no Russian I had yet met wanted to dawdle. Of course I knew that, for the many downtrodden, impoverished post-Soviet citizens in this brave new capitalist world, democracy signified on the one hand American imperialism and on the other anarchy, crime, insecurity, unemployment and inflation. But perhaps these fragrant, well-heeled and apparently so very Westernized citizens of the new Russia would have some sympathy with the concept.

'Why democracy?' they retorted in concert. 'Is Germany free? Or America?' I suggested that, broadly speaking, taking into account the right to vote in free elections and the supremacy, for most of the time, of the rule of law, that yes, on the whole, both states could fairly be called democracies. 'Well,' one of them countered, 'I don't like that type of democracy. Democracy for Russia would be death because people don't like democracy at all.' For good measure, her friend added, 'Nobody cares about anything here. That is part of our life and part of our freedom. We have freedom because everyone can choose.' Can you then be free in a dictatorship?' I asked in an effort at philosophical enquiry. 'We have dictatorship already, so we are free,' I was told.

And with that, one of the most beautiful and delicate daughters of Putin's Russia threw back her head, held her empty champagne glass high in the air and chortled mockingly at my leaden curiosity about such irrelevant notions. There was no meeting of minds. If ever I needed any reminder that Russia's political culture is different, deeply different from ours, this was it. They were as serious as I was and as genuinely baffled by my preoccupation as I was by their insouciance. I gave up and got quietly drunk instead.

The next day another of the party-goers, an architectural historian who held down a senior but evidently mind-numbing administrative role at the Hermitage, took me on a guided tour through one of the city's many semi-formal gardens. They reminded me of St James's Park in London – not surprisingly, as St Petersburg owes much to Catherine the Great's passion for eighteenth-century English land-scaping. Alexey Le Porc was both mordant and nostalgic, and, to an extent, shared my impression that St Petersburg was a city of illusions. 'There is no natural life here. It was created as a dream and it remains superficial. You become addicted to it, though, to these strange, very dark winters and your total depression. Then spring comes. It has a fantastic blue sky – sorry to be sentimental – your ideal blue. And there is the gold of the spires and then the citizens shine. It was cold, cold, cold and then it becomes suddenly extremely hot and people go about like idiots, doing nothing, just dreaming.'

I noticed that Alexey used the word 'Leningrad' interchangeably with 'St Petersburg', and wondered if he had a soft spot for the Soviet era. He answered obliquely – but far more seriously than his peers at the party: 'The city was an idealistic dream, and I was raised in an idealistic society. As a child I could recognize such an entity as "the Soviet people", and that is why for many Russians, and especially for my generation, the collapse was such a shock. We couldn't understand why there had been this kind of divorce... [Communism] ...was very repressive ideologically, but it had its dreamy side as well. It was, in many respects, a highly idealistic society. We had no opportunities, but we also had no desires. We were equal even at different levels. Now we have to become Americanized and it is happening to all of us. We have to become like everywhere else in the world. I don't like it. It doesn't make any sense. I now look at young people and see they have very different values. I thank God that personally I am not motivated by the market economy, that I am not twenty, and that I will not end my life like they will.'

I thought of all those artists, writers, intellectuals and musicians of the Soviet era who had had to dance to the Kremlin's tune or face denunciation or, worse, exile in Siberia – and I asked yet again about democracy. Was it an issue for him? 'We have no democracy – there is no democracy in Russia.' Would there ever be democracy? 'No. After fifteen years from the end of Communism, we have now a one-party system.' Was there anything more to be said? What about freedom? 'Yes, we have freedom to talk, but freedom has advantages and disad-vantages.' And what were the downsides? 'The true vulgarity of this society. It is incredibly vulgar. Look how people are dressed on the streets. Sometimes we think that the Soviet restrictions were good because shorts were not allowed in this city and the police would immediately stop you. It was aesthetically nicer.' I thought he was joking and replied flippantly, 'You're just a style fascist.' But he was not joking at all. 'I'm not a fascist,' he shot back with genuine resentment. Again I had fallen into that gulf of understanding and attitude that was disguised by the European grandeur of our surroundings and the sophistication of my interlocutor. But it was an important discovery for me: to find a leading member of St Petersburg's cosmopolitan elite expressing views that, from my perspective, seemed to verge on the Neanderthal.

After my first taste of life at the top with St Petersburg's intelligentsia – how could they be so carefree, frivolous and irresponsible about such crucial concepts? I wondered gloomily – I had to remind myself again that their Russia is very different from my Britain; that for them, the concept of democracy is so far from being the point as to be virtually irrelevant. But as I walked past the statue that was erected after the collapse of the Soviet Union to honour that great scientist and human-rights campaigner Andrey Sakharov, I allowed myself to wonder what he would have made of their apparent indifference to the values for which he had striven with such persistence.

It was refreshing to meet a fellow journalist who inhabited a rather different world. Diana was the editor of a small group of local newspapers that had a combined circulation of 360,000 in the St Petersburg region. Brisk, opinionated and blessed with a brittle-sharp intelligence, she was in her mid-forties with an editorial team who looked half her age. I sat in on the weekly editorial meeting, which was animated by a flow of suggestions and the competition for space. I felt myself to be in a world I understood. In a city where it was still a novelty to be free to move from one district to another, to choose where to live, to buy your own flat and to improve it according to your own taste, their focus was on local issues. But, according to Diana, the St Petersburgers who formed her readership (which excluded the cultural elite) were disillusioned. The heady days of *perestroika* – the sense that you could change your country, change the world – were long gone. Now everyone was more 'egotistical', she said. 'They think only about themselves and their immediate families.' But this had offered an opportunity that her proprietors had been swift to exploit.

'There are lots of problems with living conditions, especially in the heart of the city where the buildings are very old. But we don't only concentrate on rubbish dumps and broken pipes which would be...' she paused and drawled, 'rather boring.' Her readers wanted stories about schools and clinics and hospitals, and her approach was one that would find favour with the old school of regional editors in Britain. 'We try not simply to be negative but to find solutions. We want to improve the community. If we find one person who is fighting to solve a problem and others read about it, it helps them fight as well.' Her team also tried to find local angles to national issues. Of course, this is standard practice for any astute local paper, but their stories were of an unusually dramatic order: the two little girls who went to visit relatives in Beslan and were trapped in the siege but survived the massacre; more bizarrely, the anguished mother who got in touch to say she had lost contact with her son after he joined the army. It transpired that he had been 'bought' by a senior officer as a slave, but – thanks to the efforts of Diana and her team – he was released.

I commented that such a story would have been on the front page on any national newspaper in Britain. 'I am sure of that,' she replied, 'but unfortunately this kind of thing happens very often in Russia. But it is not very often reported.' Diana did not need to tell me what could happen to reporters who were too inquisitive: their bodies were prone to turn up in alleyways or basements; the authorities would deplore such criminality and promise that no stone would remain unturned until the culprits were found; and, of course, the crime would never solved. But, to use that cliché of my trade, Diana was genuinely intrepid. She had reported from what she called 'a lot of hotspots in the former Soviet Union' and was not at all naive about the risks that faced her colleagues. She explained her own freedom to print most of what she wanted. 'It is partly because the paper is owned by a Swedish company that encour-ages free speech, but largely because local newspapers in Russia offer no significant threat to the ruling establishment either in St Petersburg or Moscow.' Thus Diana felt free to take Putin to task in her editorial columns – not on matters of policy, which did not form part of her remit, but, for instance, his 'gross and vulgar' use of language in public. 'I wrote that he could speak like that, if he wished, at home, but not when he was addressing us on television.' She was deluged with readers' letters, not all sympathetic to her stand. One woman who worked in a government institute had collected 155 signatures to her letter of complaint to the newspaper for being offensive about the President. 'So we published her letter,' Diana said, 'and I added a sarcastic footnote saying, "Don't forget to send it to the KGB".'

She fears that the pressure on what remains of the free press in Russia is growing. 'My reporters are always asking, "Are we able to write about this?" and I am always having to reply, "Does it matter to our readers?" If it does, we print.' But even in her own young team she detects 'a censor sitting inside them, a self-censor. And self-censorship is getting tighter and tighter.' She looks back with nostalgia on the early years following the collapse of the Soviet Union, when she saw the clouds part to offer a glimpse of the promised land. 'I think journalists of my generation were the luckiest people in the world.... After being in a cage we were suddenly let free. It was like a tiger had been let go. Now I have this strange feeling that we are going back to the times I thought we had left behind.' An image of the St Petersburg party two nights earlier came into my mind, along with the thought that it only takes good men to do nothing...

Diana's greatest fear is a tide of nationalism that she sees rising inexorably across the country. Nationalism's bedfellows in Russia, as elsewhere, are xenophobia and racism. 'This is a very painful topic right now, especially in St Petersburg,' she said. 'Pushkin's window on the West,' I murmured as she continued: 'There have been many racist attacks in recent years here. We ran a story about a little child who was killed this way. And since then we have followed her family, seeing how her mother and father have managed. And we always write about those foreign students who are attacked. What is really painful is the reaction of the readers. I don't count exactly – maybe it is thirty to seventy against us – but they write saying, "Why are you writing about poor black people being attacked? Why do you not write about poor Russian people being attacked by blacks?"'

What dismays her even more is the way in which nationalism is used so openly as a political tool by the Kremlin and endorsed by the leadership of the Orthodox Church. 'The Church is growing more and more powerful, so that I can see us moving very fast to a position where "national" and "Orthodox" are entwined in a very dangerous way.' How so? I asked. 'The danger is very clear. The young kids who are making these racist attacks are listening to the Kremlin and to the Church. They watch the TV and they get the impression that their ideas are right.' She spoke with anger, and again I thought of the party where I had met smart, rich people with abundant talent who had surrendered their souls to the freedom of the market and, with a Panglossian flourish of a champagne glass, chosen to believe that, in Russia, all was for the best in the best of all possible worlds. But, I suggested to Diana, St Petersburg was widely supposed to be a great international city. 'It's a dream,' she responded. 'A fantasy?' I mooted. 'No, "dream" is better. With a dream you can have hope. Unfortunately, we are now heading in the opposite direction.'

## GOGOL AND DOSTOEVSKY:
## ECHOES OF THE FUTURE

Dreams, fantasies, illusions. In search of illumination, I hurried back to the nineteenth century and to Gogol. His satirical stories, many of which were inspired by his time in St Petersburg, are infused with a sense of the absurd and a taste for the phantasmagorical. In the 'Diary of a Madman' and, consummately, in *The Overcoat*, Gogol conjures up a terrifying world in which the principal protagonists find themselves apparently free but always in chains. They are ordinary individuals tormented by unseen powers and influences that eat them up and spit them out; little people who have dreams that become nightmares that they do not begin to comprehend. His work is anarchic and subversive, a mocking indictment of the social mores of his age, and, with withering detachment, it illuminates the Russian psyche in a way that no biography or history can ever quite emulate.

*Dead Souls*, Gogol's last masterpiece, is an epic satire that could serve as a commentary on Putin's Russia as easily as it did on that of the nineteenth-century Tsar Nicholas I. The novel's anti-hero is a conman called Chichikov, whose scam is to buy from gullible and greedy landowners the identity of those of their serfs who have died since the last population census and on whose 'dead souls' they would otherwise still have to pay tax until the next census. In the process of relieving his 'victims' of their financial burden, Chichikov manages to buy his way into high esteem as a 'property owner' of substance, with four hundred serfs to his name. Government officials fall over themselves to ingratiate themselves with him. Before long, as more and more of his fellow citizens became party to this bizarre enterprise, the rot has eaten into the soul of almost everyone of note in his community.

Eventually Chichikov is arrested, but so widespread is the web of corruption over which he presides that it is impossible to find him guilty without exposing the complicity of almost every official in the realm. In the final passage of the book, the haughty but ineffectual governor-general who had felt himself obliged to authorize Chichikov's release summons the town's entire bureaucracy, including 'those who did not take bribes and those who did, those who violated their conscience, those who half violated it, and those who did not violate it in the least'. Once they have gathered in his mansion, the governor-general pleads with them to mend their ways. 'I know that there are no means, no threats, no punishments sufficient to eradicate wrongdoing; it is already too deeply rooted. The dishonest business of taking bribes has become a necessity and a need even for those who were certainly not born to be dishonest. I know that by now it is almost impossible for many people to swim against the current,' he acknowledges, before urging them 'to remember the duty that awaits a person in whatever position he occupies. I invite you to make a closer examination of your duty and the obligations of your official position on this earth.' One may presume that these grandiloquent vapourings were treated by the governor-general's audience then as they would be today, in the unlikely event that one of Putin's satraps were to venture a similar rebuke to those who grease the wheels of capitalism in twenty-first-century Russia.

Fyodor Dostoevsky penetrated even further than Gogol behind the social façade of Russia. Dostoevsky arrived in St Petersburg from Moscow in 1837 at the age of sixteen to study at the Military Engineering Academy. Seven years later he took the momentous decision to resign his commission and devote himself exclusively to literature. The following year he published his first novel, *Poor People*. The critics fell over themselves to acclaim him as Gogol's heir, while Dostoevsky himself was to acknowledge his debt to the first master of the 'modern' Russian novel with the words, 'We have all emerged from under Gogol's Overcoat.'

One of his own masterly short stories, *White Nights*, opens with a description of St Petersburg in summer: 'It was a lovely night, one of those nights, dear reader, which can only happen when you are young. The sky was so bright and starry that when you looked at it the first question that came into your head was whether it was really possible that all sorts of bad-tempered and unstable people could live under such a glorious sky.' But there is a much grimmer world beneath the surface of the city, behind the façade. It is a subterranean, troglodyte world where 'there is quite a different sun...the light it sheds on everything is also different... [In these places] the people also seem to live quite a different life, unlike that which surges all around us.'

That passage rang in my ears as I left the boulevards that run from Nevsky Prospect and lost myself in the alleyways that are hidden away from the main thoroughfare. I found myself in a courtyard, surrounded by the faded, peeling walls of a once grand palace, now a tenement. Two ill-kempt, pasty-faced youths were sitting on a stone block, incuriously staring into the distance, their senses benumbed perhaps by the thud of heavy-metal music that came from a window somewhere above them or, more probably, by the drugs that are as easily available on the streets of St Petersburg as in any other large city. A narrow passage leading off the courtyard led to a stairwell where a faint smell of urine lurked in the damp, stale air. An elderly woman in a baggy sweater and grubby pastel skirt, her face lined and grey, shambled past me to disappear up the stairs. A cat sat with triumphant indifference in this wasteland, basking in the one half-ray of sunlight that just penetrated the gloom.

In *White Nights* Dostoevsky describes a cramped apartment where 'everything was dark and grimy, and the cobwebs were thicker than ever'; the view from the window was to a 'gloomy and dingy' building, 'the plaster on its columns peeling and crumbling, its cornices blackened and full of cracks.' It was as though he had seen precisely what I now saw more than 150 years later.

When the Bolsheviks came to power the owners of St Petersburg's grand palaces and apartments were required to open their doors to the workers and to live communally with them and their families. The elegant drawing rooms where members of high society, all aware of their very special place in the life of the city, had once delivered themselves of *bien pensées* in fashionable French, were partitioned to make cramped and overcrowded apartments for homeless proletarians. Today, some 15 per cent of the 5 million residents of St Petersburg – 750,000 people – still live in conditions that, had they been in Glasgow or Manchester or London, would have been condemned as unfit for human habitation long ago.

I was taken to see the inside of one of these Soviet hangovers by a social scientist who had spent much of the last decade studying the dynamics of communal living. Ilya Utekhin suggested we visit the flat in which he himself had been reared and from which he had only recently escaped. Leaving the gloom of a grubby, potholed courtyard, we entered through a rusting steel door and climbed up a broad, palatial stone staircase that, in his grandmother's day, had been thickly carpeted. The walls were now covered with graffiti, some of it in English and most of it obscene. Stepping carefully over a used condom, we arrived at Ilya's former residence. The door into the apartment was locked and bolted, but he still enjoyed squatter's rights there. Once inside, it took a while to adjust to the semi-darkness; the single light bulb that hung forlornly over what had once been a grand vestibule offered more shadows than light.

We walked tentatively down a long corridor towards the communal kitchen. On either side we passed the doors to about ten modest bedrooms in which the thirty residents (down from fifty in Ilya's youth) who still lived there were afforded a degree of privacy. There was one small, grubby bathroom that was shared among the lot of them. My instinct that it must have been impossible for eight, nine, ten families to share such a cramped space without coming to blows was reinforced when we entered the kitchen where each family had its own mini-kitchen with its own ancient gas cooker and blackened utensils. There was barely space to squeeze between them. The brown linoleum on the floor was torn, discoloured and encrusted with dirt. In places the plaster on the ceiling had fallen away; in one corner the flowered wallpaper, spotted with mildew, had come adrift and drooped disconsolately over a cracked enamel sink that had a single cold, dripping tap.

I have always thought that even the most primitive conditions in African villages are preferable to urban slum-living, and Ilya must have seen my dismay. 'Of course, today it is different from Soviet times. Then you could find intellectuals, professors, military officers living cheek by jowl with drunkards and prostitutes and drug addicts. There were strict rules and a great deal of litigation as neighbours informed on one another in the hope of getting more space or privileges.' There was even a Leningrad journal devoted to reporting communal issues, in which grievances could be aired and the idle or troublemakers exposed. But order more or less prevailed, even if ideological commitment to the communal principle was conspicuously absent.

It sounded to me as dreadful in those days as it appeared today. But Ilya, who now lived in a large apartment of his own with a young family, was disconcertingly upbeat about living conditions that he no longer had to endure. He conceded that 'communal kitchens cause communal scandals' in which 'people yell at one another as if they are in an Italian opera', but, he explained with scholarly precision, to minimize the risk of friction the families tended to eat in separate shifts, avoiding one another as much as possible. He showed me the rota for cleaning the communal spaces; a pervasively sour smell, however, suggested to both of us that this particular communal principle had ceased to operate in practice.

According to Ilya, the public spaces in and around the apartment were regarded as 'a kind of no man's land for which no one has any responsibility'. On one occasion when he was still living in this apartment he invited a friend, a French philosopher, to stay with him. 'He saw a piece of human excrement on the stairwell. When it was still there the next day he asked, "Why don't you remove it?" And I had to think: I am living here, so why haven't I removed it? Why don't I do as he says? It led me to start an entire research project in an effort to understand the ideas behind this notion of "territory"; what is mine and what is public, and where do my responsibilities start and finish.'

Ilya went on to surmise that even in the twenty-first century, many of those who still have to endure communal living are not resentful because their material surroundings are of very little concern to them. 'Soviet people,' he said, using the term interchangeably with the word 'Russian', 'separate their life here [pointing to his forehead] from their everyday life. Their life here [pointing to his head again] is concerned with self-realization or the spiritual life. Everyday life is sleeping, eating, washing dishes – things like that are not important.' I found this hard to believe, but merely said that I was glad that I did not face a similar predicament; that I had a choice. I was relieved when he murmured, with a self-deprecating chuckle, 'Me too.'

Yet again, in *White Nights*, Dostoevsky pre-echoed Ilya's insight into the Russian psyche. 'Oh what is there in our humdrum existence to interest him', his anti-hero soliloquizes, speaking in the third person the better to impress a young lover with his poetic other-worldliness.

> Look at those magical phantoms which so enchantingly, so capriciously, so vastly, and so boundlessly, are conjured up before his mind's eye in so magical and thrilling a picture, a picture in which, needless to say, he himself, our dreamer, occupies the most prominent place.... And how easily, how naturally, is this imaginary, fantastic world created! As though it were not a dream at all! Indeed, he is sometimes ready to believe that all this life is not a vision conjured up by his overwrought mind, not a mirage, not a figment of the imagination, but something real, something that actually exists.

St Petersburg is filled with other pre-echoes. Seventy years before the Reds and Whites fought each other in the streets here, Dostoevsky was sentenced to death for subversion. He had joined a group of like-minded spirits known as the Petrashevsky Group, which called for the emancipation of the serfs and fundamental reform of the judicial system. On 23 April 1849, along with other members of the group, he was arrested and imprisoned in the Peter and Paul Fortress, where he languished for eight months until sentence was pronounced. On 22 December he and his associates were taken from prison to Semyonovskaya Square, where the punishment – execution by firing squad – was read out for the crowd to hear. 'We were all made to kiss the cross, a sword was broken over our heads, and we were told to put on our execution shirts,' he wrote later to his brother. 'Then three of us were tied to the posts to be executed. I was the sixth, and therefore in the second group of those to be executed. I had only one more minute to live.' At that point, in a piece of nastily contrived political theatre, a soldier galloped into the square to announce that Tsar Nicholas I had decided that their lives should be spared. Dostoevsky was sentenced instead to eight years' penal servitude for 'taking part in criminal plots' and for circulating 'insolent attacks against the Orthodox Church and the government'.

In a long line of oppressive autocrats that had begun with Ivan the Terrible some three hundred years earlier, Nicholas I proved himself to be one of the most whimsically malevolent of all Russian tsars. In this instance, after subjecting one of the Empire's creative geniuses to exile in Siberia, he later arbitrarily halved the sentence to four years – which merely served to emphasize his boundless capriciousness. But the punishment was not without effect. When Dostoevsky was released in 1854 he emerged, in the words of his translator, the Russian scholar David Magarshack, as 'a passionate adherent of the most reactionary forces in Russia'. But even though the privations he endured may have turned the radical into a reactionary, they failed to tame his independence of spirit. In 1862 he returned to St Petersburg, intending to found a new periodical that he wanted to call *Pravda* (Truth). In the Soviet era, as a kind of sick joke, *Pravda* was the name given to the official daily mouthpiece of the Kremlin; but in Dostoevsky's case – in a move worthy of Gogol at his best – the authorities banned his prospective publication on the grounds that its title was too provocative.

The similarities between the treatment meted out to Dostoevsky by the tsarist state and that which would be endured less than a century later by his peers in the Soviet era again suggest a malign thread that runs through the history of the Russian political psyche, uniting tsars and Bolsheviks and, I am already tempted to think, the Putinists who rule the nation today. There is another thread too. In 1880, by now thoroughly rehabilitated by the state and revered throughout Russia, Dostoevsky made a speech to mark the unveiling of the Pushkin Monument in Moscow: in it he declared that the Russian character had a unique genius for universality and thereby a mission to become the unifying force of all Europe. This nineteenth-century vision, stirring that romantic fatalism by which Russia has long been stricken, could almost have been deployed as part of that twentieth-century political credo that, blending Bolshevism with nationalism, underpinned an ideology that sought to justify Soviet 'internationalism'. But there is also a gloriously redemptive quality in the Russian soul. As if to prove that Dostoevsky understood the deeper recesses of the national psyche better than any other novelist – something that Stalin also believed, and perhaps this is why he banned *Crime and Punishment* and *The Brothers Karamazov* – more than fifty thousand mourners attended the great man's funeral in 1881.

It was with this in mind that I crossed the city to pay my respects at the Finland Station, which turned out disappointingly to be the nondescript terminus of a suburban line that would have tested even John Betjeman's affection for the unexceptional. But it was to this spot that Lenin returned from more than a decade in exile in Germany to take up the leadership of the Bolshevik revolution. He is there still, high on a plinth in the square, cast in bronze, his right arm held out in exhortation, cast in the same heroic mould as the founder of the city. Although the citizens of St Petersburg could not have realized it – and some never would – his arrival was to scrape them out of the tsarist frying pan only to grill them over the Leninist fire.

As I walked around the statue, it was easy to picture the scene a little before midnight on 3 April 1917. Tsar Nicholas II had been overthrown, Alexander Kerensky's provisional government was in office but not in power, and the workers controlled the streets. The square was packed with an excited crowd and surrounded by armoured cars waiting for Lenin's arrival. A military band struck up 'La Marseillaise' as his train rumbled in to deposit him into the hands of an armed escort and a phalanx of loyal comrades. After a huddle with them in what had been the imperial waiting room, Comrade Lenin emerged to address the expectant crowd.

According to Gorky, writing before he had succumbed to Stalin's blandishments, Lenin was a professional revolutionary who knew nothing of human suffering, and for this reason he had 'a pitiless contempt, worthy of a nobleman, for the lives of ordinary people.' This lacuna must have been well disguised because he reportedly mesmerized his audience with heart-warming slogans that could just be heard above the hubbub. Such phrases as 'imperial slaughter', 'lies and frauds' and 'capitalist pirates' that fell easily from his lips were well-judged opiates for a people who had been exploited for centuries and saw in the Bolshevik revolution a glimmer of hope. Thus delivered of these inspirational sentiments, he was borne off through the ecstatic onlookers and taken away in an armoured car to the Winter Palace to prepare the Russian people for the dictatorship of the proletariat that, with the consent of most of them, he would soon impose upon them. In the late 1970s, in the bloodbath of revolutionary Ethiopia, I had watched aghast as young neo-Leninist ideologues 're-educated' rival revolutionary Marxists, who had been rounded up and imprisoned for this purpose, by requiring them to chant slogans like 'Revolutionary Motherland or Death' before executing them as 'counter-revolutionary' enemies of the people. In the case of Russia in 1917, I now think it was a case of 'Romantic fatalism or Death'. And, of course, there was to be death on a scale that revolutionary Ethiopia, even at its bloodiest, would never be able to emulate.

## THE SIEGE OF LENINGRAD

By the time of my pilgrimage to the Finland Station I had acquainted myself with some of the salient facts about the siege of Leningrad in World War II: that it had lasted for some nine hundred days; that 1.2 million civilians had died in the Nazi bombardment or from starvation and disease; and that this number was greater than the number of those who had perished either at Stalingrad or from the atomic bombs that destroyed Hiroshima and Nagasaki. I had also read about the astonishing lengths to which the besieged population had been driven in order to survive, but I had recoiled so sharply from the evidence that the dreadful detail of their agony had remained a blur in my mind. But now that I was in the city itself, where almost every physical trace of the siege has been obliterated, I felt obliged to understand better.

In the guest-house where I was staying I riffled through a sheaf of letters written by ordinary citizens during the bitter winter of 1941–2, by which time up to seven thousand people were dying of hunger every day. That this correspondence survives is due, ironically, to the institutional paranoia of the Kremlin, which, fearing defeatism among the populace, ordered their letters to be intercepted by the regional branch of the NKVD, one of the precursors of the KGB. But far from being defeatist, the private feelings stolen from their authors by the security services are merely heart-breaking:

With every day that passes, life in Leningrad gets worse. People are beginning to swell up because they are eating patties made from mustard. Flour dust, which used to be used for making wall-paper paste, cannot be bought for love nor money.

There is a terrible hunger in Leningrad. We go to the fields and the scrap heaps and gather all sorts of roots and dirty leaves from animal feed...and even that's a rare find.

I was witness to a scene when a cabbie's horse collapsed on the street from malnutrition. People ran over to it with axes and knives and began cutting it up into pieces and carting them home. It's awful. These people had the look of executioners about them.

Our beloved Leningrad has turned into a heap of dirt and corpses. Trams have long since ceased to run, there it no light, no fuel, the water is frozen, the rubbish isn't cleared. And, most important, we're tormented by hunger.

We've become a herd of hungry beasts. You walk along the streets and come across people swaying like drunks, collapsing and dying. We've become used to seeing such sights and pay no attention because today they are dying but tomorrow it will be me.

Leningrad has become a morgue, the streets have become avenues of the dead. In every house, the cellar is a dump for corpses. There are cavalcades of dead bodies lining the streets.

Dmitri Shostakovich was Leningrad's most eminent citizen. Already recognized, alongside Sergei Prokofiev and Igor Stravinsky, as one of his country's great contemporary composers, he had remained in the Soviet Union throughout the worst of Stalin's Terror. Subjected to lavish praise, interspersed with denunciation and intimidation, he survived by judiciously avoiding public criticism of Stalin. After the collapse of the Nazi–Soviet Non-Aggression Pact caused by Hitler's invasion of Russia in June 1941, Shostakovich applied to join the Red Army, but was twice turned down on account of his poor eyesight. He then applied successfully to join the People's Volunteer Brigades, writing that 'only by fighting can we save humanity from destruction'. Such was his international reputation that he appeared on the front cover of *Time* magazine in the uniform of a Soviet firefighter, waiting to defend Leningrad from the encircling Panzer divisions with which Hitler – who had likened the city to 'a viper' that had to be crushed – expected to accomplish his crazed urge to obliterate its very existence. But it was Shostakovich's extraordinary 7th Symphony, which he dedicated to 'my native city', that was his greatest contribution to the morale of the nation.

I had repeatedly listened to the Leningrad Symphony, as the 7th is generally known, hoping to conjure up the visual images that so readily float into the mind when I hear, for instance, Beethoven's Pastoral Symphony or Tchaikovsky's 1812 Overture. But with the monumental 7th, I could not do it. Although the slow movement is achingly mournful and dignified, it remained an elusive, abstract experience, eliciting powerful moods rather than potent images. Then I came across a piece of journalism by the *Observer* writer Ed Vulliamy in which he vividly described the extraordinary occasion, on 9 August 1942, when the Leningrad Symphony was performed by a scratch orchestra of starving musicians in the besieged city. The images flooded back to the music.

As Vulliamy relates the story, Shostakovitch wrote the Adagio by candlelight in what was clearly a frenzy of creative inspiration while Leningrad was under bombardment by the Luftwaffe – though he was forced to finish the manuscript in Moscow a little after Christmas 1941, by which time he had reluctantly obeyed the party's instruction to evacuate his native city. The 7th had its première the following March in the Soviet capital and then, after a microfilm score had been smuggled out to the West, it was performed in America to huge acclaim.

A première in Leningrad was harder to accomplish. In 2001 Vulliamy tracked down the last few surviving members of the Leningrad Radio Orchestra of those days. One of them, Viktor Koslov, a clarinettist, recalled for the reporter what it was like to endure the winter of 1941–2 and what he saw when the snows began to melt in the spring of 1942. It was terrible to read and I longed to disbelieve his testimony. But why should an aged musician lift a powerful taboo except in the name of the truth?

> Some were dead, some were half-dead, sometimes from injuries they had done to themselves. People were cutting off and eating their own buttocks. We only really saw what winter did when the snow began to melt.... Decomposing, dismembered corpses in the streets that had been hidden under the ice. Severed legs with meat chopped off them. Bits of bodies in the bins. Women's bodies with breasts cut off, which people had taken to eat.

It was at this time that a light plane from Moscow, flying over the encircling German army, dropped Shostakovich's score into the city. The symphony orchestra was re-formed and rehearsals started for what was to be the most important concert ever held in Leningrad. Another of Vulliamy's interviewees, Edith Katya Matus, recalled her arrival at the first rehearsal: 'I nearly fell over with shock. Of the orchestra of 100 people, there were only 15 left. I didn't recognize the musicians I knew from before, they were like skeletons.... It was evident we couldn't play anything, we could hardly stand on our feet!' The conductor, the now forgotten Karl Ilich Eliasburg, took to the rostrum and said, 'Dear friends, we are weak but we must force ourselves to start work.' He raised his arms to begin but, according to Matus, no one had the energy to move:

> The musicians were trembling. Finally those who were able to play a bit helped the weaker musicians, and thus our small group began to play the opening bars. And that was the beginning of the first rehearsal.... I remember the trumpeter didn't have the breath to play his solo and there was silence when his turn came around. He was on his knees, poor man.... Everybody did his best, but we played badly, it was hopeless.

Yet gradually, week by week, they found the strength to persevere, although many of the musicians collapsed from hunger and four died from starvation. As some fell out, others took their place, until, re-inforced by musicians from military bands serving at the front, the orchestra was finally ready to perform. Eliasburg took to the airwaves to announce the event, declaring: 'This performance is witness to our spirit, courage and readiness to fight. Listen, comrades!'

On that August evening, the entire population of the city was reportedly in the Philharmonic Hall, or sitting by their radios in ruined apartments, or listening in their trenches at the front line. An artillery-man called Savkov described sitting with his comrades, listening with closed eyes: 'It seemed that the cloudless sky had suddenly become a storm bursting with music as the city listened to the symphony of heroes and forgot about the war but not the meaning of war.' The German invaders too were able to hear the great work, either because their guns had been silenced by an unusually ferocious barrage on the previous night or because they could not resist listening to the message of musical defiance wafting across from loudspeakers directed at them from the Russian trenches.

As I stood in the auditorium of the Philharmonic Hall during a break in rehearsals it was not hard to conjure up that hour in that place on that August day in 1942. The empty scattered chairs, the abandoned music stands and the silence seemed to bear witness to an heroic and indomitable spirit. In the history of the siege it was the best and the worst of times. The surviving citizens were suffering as never before, but the German grip on the city was already slackening. The onset of another terrible winter and alarming setbacks to the south were haemorrhaging the invaders' ability to sustain the siege. It would last eighteen more months and see many more deaths, but Leningrad was not throttled and would not succumb.

## A NIGHT AT THE OPERA

The musical maestro of St Petersburg, lionized around the world, is the artistic director and conductor of the Mariinsky Theatre, Valery Gergiev. He is a striking figure and gloriously alive. He has a time-roughened face, hair that knows no order, but eyes that are kind and sad, that seem to know truths through music that the rest of us only guess at. I sat enthralled five rows from the orchestra pit as he joined forces with the famous American soprano Renée Fleming in a wide-ranging programme that entranced the locals and a host of foreign tourists who had managed to beg, steal or buy tickets to see the two stars in performance.

On the rostrum Gergiev reminded me, perversely, of Pete Sampras at Wimbledon as he stood half-crouched, swaying, in front of his orchestra. He does not use a baton and his right arm does all the work. As a result, he has an over-developed shoulder muscle on that side, like the hard-serving tennis star. He sweats profusely and, when you catch a glimpse of his face as he looks towards the first violins, he has a distant look of intense concentration. Although he is disdained by some critics for spreading himself too thinly across too many orchestras, Gergiev's force of character, energy and musical genius have turned the Mariinsky – opera, ballet and orchestra – into a world-class act. On this particular evening he had conjured a warm, rich – if occasionally rough-edged – sound from his orchestra. His presence on the platform was mesmeric, and Fleming sang as deliciously as the world of opera has come to expect of her. At the end of the performance they were summoned back for an extended encore.

Suddenly and unexpectedly I found myself in tears, burying my face to hide the sound. Fleming had chosen Natasha's aria from *The Queen of Spades*, which Sue had sung opposite Placido Domingo, with Gergiev conducting, at her Covent Garden début a few years earlier. I was not there, but I had heard the tape of a voice so beautiful, soaring, rich and anguished that I had at once understood what Placido meant when he had described Sue to me after her death as a glorious artist who sang from her soul. He had also told me that as a rule he retreated to his dressing room in the long gaps between his own scenes, but in Sue's case he had been unable to tear himself away. 'I stood in the wings. I had to watch Susan. That is how you distinguish great artists from the others. You can't take your eyes off them. Yes, she was a great artist.' His words, which I had treasured ever since, flooded into my mind and, as Fleming's voice soared over my head, I wept for the woman that Placido had described so touchingly as 'someone who lit up a room as soon as she entered'.

As Fleming – Sue's transatlantic peer – completed the famous aria to a roar of approval, I could think only of my own loss, of Sue's death. To compound this onrush of renewed grief, Fleming then chose the third of Richard Strauss's *Four Last Songs*, the most anguished of this most overwhelming orchestral song cycle. This was a coincidence too far. Only weeks before she died Sue had been hard at work on this very music, still hoping to honour a commitment to sing the entire cycle at the Sydney Opera House later that year. But each day when she returned from her lesson, the pain from her rapidly progressing cancer was worse. To ease her distress we increased the doses of morphine day by day, but as her liver swelled it pressed more and more on her diaphragm. She was finding it impossible to take the deep breaths needed for such a demanding role. One afternoon she came home to her cottage and said bleakly, 'I can't do it.' This was the final admission that there would be no Sydney Opera House, no more stages, no more of that lyrical voice that those who heard it thought came from heaven itself. I did my best to comfort her. Later I was sitting at the kitchen table when she came up behind me and said gently, 'I'm going to sing you your own last song.' Putting her arms around me, she placed her lips close to my ear and crooned – if that is the term to describe the quiet acceptance of the inevitable that her voice seemed to express – the third of the *Four Last Songs*. I heard it through a mist of sorrow but felt that, if there were a heaven, then we were both together there at that moment. In the Mariinsky, though, as Fleming did the very same music great justice, I felt broken once more, my eyes blurred and stinging, my chest heaving, my hands shaking with the terrible spasm of familiar pain that racks those who grieve and that made me once more want to rage and roar against the heavens for this most absolute, final, implacable, cruel fact: that Sue could not, would not, ever come back.

Afterwards there was a dinner and I found myself sitting between Fleming and Gergiev, still red-eyed but under control. Both spoke of Sue with affection and admiration. Gergiev, who had conducted her as Natasha in *The Queen of Spades*, echoed Placido. 'She was an extraordinary presence, a great artist, and a very lovely person.' Pathetically, I felt comforted by this informal, personal epitaph. At least he knew

*A toast with Yevgraf, a survivor of the Nazi attack on Murmansk: 'To all those who died ... They died that this should never happen again.'*

*With babushki singers in a remote part of Karelia: 'It is terrible we have no men, no love.'*

*Solovki is considered to be one of the holiest places in Russia, but has been the site of such unholy horrors that the entire archipelago is shrouded in a sinister embrace.*

*Baba Valya is a white witch who says she is a healer – 'Why should I want to harm people?'*

*The petroglyphs at Devil's Nose, Karelia, were carved some 5000 years ago. Human sacrifices are said to have been performed over the Devil's torso.*

*'Two exquisitely tailored young women' at a party for the St Petersburg glitterati, insisting that 'democracy for Russia would be death'.*

*St Petersburg is an astonishing achievement, a grand folly, an arrogant assertion of will, a bedazzling confidence trick.*

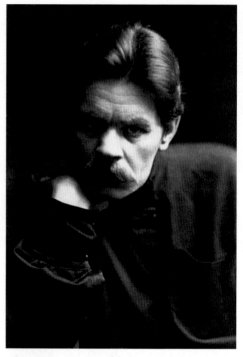

'What strength was in him … Oh mighty master of fate.' Russian schoolchildren still learn by heart Pushkin's ballad about Peter the Great, depicted here as The Bronze Horseman.

Maxim Gorky is celebrated as Russia's first 'social realist' but when he visited the notorious labour camp on Solovki he chose not to see the inmates' plight.

On the eve of the Russian revolution Lenin stood before a huge crowd outside Finland Station, St Petersburg, to denounce the 'lies and frauds' of imperialism's 'capitalist pirates'.

*Valentin is a diminutive, one-armed optimist. In Lake Ladoga the fish stocks have declined and his livelihood is now as precarious as the spin of a roulette wheel – 'a casino'.*

*St Sophia Cathedral in the ancient city of Novgorod where 'even the secular soul is soon mesmerized by the theatre of faith'.*

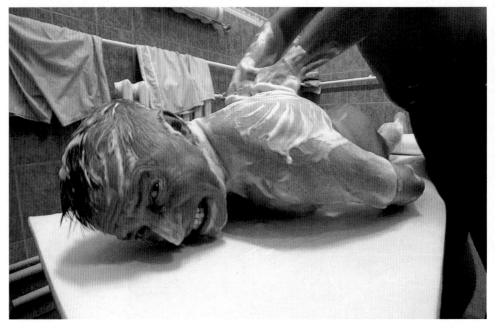

The Russian bath-house promised
'maximum pleasure ... the health and joy
of full life, harmony and self-confidence'.

In Red Square the famous department
store GUM has been transformed to a
degree that would have the embalmed
corpse of Lenin turning in its catafalque.

what those who loved her knew but what the rest of the world would never now know.

That night all this was in my mind and I could not sleep despite the red wine that I had imbibed at dinner to numb the senses. I looked out of my window at the canal that, in the half-light, reflected the old apartment blocks along its edge, and thought, 'I want to be out of this city – away from this netherworld that they call the "White Nights".' And I asked myself resentfully, 'Is there really any romance in the conjunction of these two contradictory words? Or is it just a piece of salesmanship, repeated endlessly by tourist brochures determined to transform natural gloom into unnatural beauty?' I wanted, with an overwhelming surge, to be back in England, in Devon, back home where I belong, where I could perhaps find some order in which to settle and grow again the roots that might give back meaning to my life – and where at least I would be among the people I love. I felt intensely alone and totally consumed by self-pity.

## FROM LAKE LADOGA TO NOVGOROD

On a calm summer day a fisherman called Valentin, a diminutive, one-armed optimist, took us out into Lake Ladoga, which borders St Petersburg to the east, in his rusting old trawler. He had silvered wispy hair, a walrus moustache, a face crinkled like a walnut, and the kind of laugh that forces you to laugh as well, even when you have no under-standing of the joke. He had acquired a smattering of misplaced American slang, and gesticulated so vividly that I hardly needed a translator to understand his story. He had been born in St Petersburg in 1941, a child of the siege. Most of his family had perished there, but his father had been serving in the navy and was thus able to purloin extra provisions for his wife and baby son – just enough to avoid star-vation. After school Valentin had himself joined the navy, and later became a fisherman working for a state-owned company. His child-hood dream had been to have a boat of his own, an ambition he realized soon after the collapse of the Soviet Union and in which he still proudly rejoiced.

Valentin regarded Lake Ladoga with that mixture of respect and fear that all wise seamen have for the deep. It is the largest lake in Europe (107,000 square miles in area), more than 125 miles in length and with a maximum depth of 230 metres. During the siege of Leningrad it was a lifeline to the city, a corridor for weapons and supplies brought south from where they had been landed by the Allied convoys in Murmansk. In summer, cargo ships plied the vital route; in winter, when the lake was frozen, the supplies were brought over the ice along the 'road of life' in handcarts and trucks. It was a hazardous run and there was no protection from the Luftwaffe – an astonishing, hardly imaginable, feat of endurance. On this tranquil summer day, meandering along the same route, it was hard to imagine that indomitable resolve to which Lake Ladoga had once borne silent witness. In those days, as others fought for their survival, I was a contented infant safely asleep in a pram in the English countryside.

Lake Ladoga is prone to severe storms that are whipped up unexpectedly and with deadly effect. I sat with Valentin in his little cabin, drinking vodka while we inched our way across what was on this occasion a glassy surface and he told me stories of storms in which he and his crew had almost lost their lives. They didn't sound like fishermen's tales, although, at that point in the story when they were 'almost' swept on to the rocks for a second time, I detected a repetitive flourish that suggested that the events he was describing had not exactly died in his imagination. There was no exaggeration, however, when he described the decline in his catch over the last few years. 'Casino,' he said in English, repeating the word as he gesticulated how he and his two shipmates laboured to cast their nets only to haul them in and, time and again, find them empty – at which point he put his one hand over his head in a theatrical gesture of despair. He explained that he went out three days a week in the summer season and barely caught enough to meet his overheads. He shrugged in resigned acceptance of his fate, explaining that before pollution and over-fishing took their toll this part of the lake used to deliver a rich harvest for the St Petersburg market.

We were not in the lake so much to fish as to sail into the mouth of the Volkhov River to get some sense of what it must have been like 1200 years earlier when Viking invaders sailed south via this route on their way from Sweden to the Black Sea. I stood in the bow trying to imagine the fear of the tribespeople in the settlements that lined the shore as the Viking warships, at first silent silhouettes in the distance, gradually emerged into full, terrifying view: forty or fifty oarsmen on each side, rowing in perfect harmony, and in the belly of each vessel the same number of men equipped with swords, shields and helmets, waiting to leap ashore to pillage and plunder. In mythology, if not in demonstrable fact – scholars strenuously contest the available evidence – the Varangians, as this branch of the Viking race is known, were the founders of what eventually became the modern Russian state. One of their leaders, Rurik, is described in the twelfth-century *Primary Chronicle*, a compilation of ancient records, as the first leader of what became known as Rus. Thus, via a myth that at least does no violence to known facts, it is possible to trace a dynastic history of Russia that runs from Rurik through to the first tsar six centuries later.

As I was indulging my imagination, but also trying to grasp this alien and convoluted history, Valentin, who was on the foredeck beside me, leapt up and turned around to face the wheelhouse, yelling at his helmsman and gesticulating skywards with his arm in evident panic: 'Turn around, turn around.' I looked up and saw that we were within 30 metres of a thick line of massive power cables strung from one bank of the river to the other. Unless we were able to stop in time, the top of the boat's mast looked certain to collide with the lowest electric cable, which would at once conduct thousands of volts through the boat. We would surely all be electrocuted. Transfixed, I could see the inevitable with absolute clarity in slow motion: the cables inching closer, the boat slowing, stopping and almost turning – but surely too late. I shouted at everyone to get their feet off the steel deck and stand on wood – anything but metal. We waited, watching, silent, impotent. I glanced across at Valentin. He was motionless, a look of horror on his face. The line of cables crept closer and closer, but more slowly. By now the top of the mast was no more than a metre from the cable. A metre between life and death – or so it seemed. But then, at last, the boat was arcing to port and we started to creep away from mortal danger. Wanting to break the mood, I essayed some feeble remark about the Vikings having had a much easier time on their journey south to Constantinople. No one laughed.

We headed back downriver towards Lake Ladoga. On our way, Valentin explained his moment of panic. In Soviet times he had been a dinghy sailor, good enough to race for his country. One day he had been testing a new Italian design in a fresh wind. He was wearing a harness, leaning out to keep the boat on an even keel, his arm around the high-tensile shroud that ran almost to the top of the mast. It was dusk and he did not see a power cable ahead that was drooping low over the water. He sailed straight towards it, the mast clipped the wire and eleven thousand volts shot through his body. Astonishingly, he survived, but at the point where he had been holding the shroud his arm was almost severed, incinerated by the electric current. He also lost most of his left foot, which, like his arm, had to be amputated. No wonder he had looked so terrified a few minutes earlier.

After this adventure we decided to desert the river and make our way south by road until we reached Staraya (Ancient) Ladoga, the first Viking settlement on the Volkhov. Today three Viking burial mounds, one of which is reputed to contain the remains of Rurik himself, stand in vigil at the water's edge, unexcavated and unprotected. Of the original Staraya Ladoga itself, nothing remains above the ground but a walled fortress of medieval origin, carefully restored in recent years, that now guards an archaeological site of international significance. While we were there, students on vacation from St Petersburg were at their painstaking task of digging, sifting, weighing, logging and poring over the ground like police officers at the scene of a murder, searching for any clues that might help piece together a fuller story of the Viking invasion.

The Vikings did not merely rape, pillage and lay waste the homes of those who were foolhardy enough to resist their progress. Nor were they merely sophisticated boat-builders and navigators. They were also skilful administrators with a system of laws and a power structure conceived to secure stability and prosperity. According to the ancient chronicles, the warring tribes who lived in the region realized that they could turn the Viking occupation to their own advantage. At some point – mythology is not precise about dates – they apparently said to themselves, 'Let us seek a prince who may rule over us and judge us according to the law.' Rurik, one of three brothers, emerged as the chosen one. Whatever the truth of this legend, it is beyond doubt that Staraya Ladoga began to flourish as an entrepôt, and the archaeological evidence – coins, necklaces, rings, bracelets, combs, knives, urns and utensils – is there to prove it.

The professor in charge of the excavation – as he had been for more than thirty years – was working alone in a small, grubby cabin a little way from the dig. He sat at a wooden desk, the floor round about him strewn with old cardboard boxes filled with fragments of iron and clay – his life's work. Anatoly Kirpichnikov was a shabby, dishevelled figure in a sweat-stained T-shirt. I presumed him to be about seventy years old; his face was lined and his eyes mournful behind a pair of thick spectacles that were as grimy as the precious relics at which he peered with loving intensity.

He did not welcome my arrival, but gruffly, to the point of hostility, demanded to know what I wanted from him. Although by now I had immunized myself against such first encounters, it was dispiriting – he had, after all, agreed to meet me. I had prepared myself for a conversation with one of the grand old men of Russian archaeology, a leading member of the Academy of Sciences, and I had deluded myself that he would be only too delighted to welcome a stranger from another land. Instead here was Mr Grumpy and, sweltering in the heat, I started to feel pretty much the same way. So I stalked off ostentatiously to the nearby museum, which was in a fierce race against the professor for state funds. By so doing, I hoped, I would add insult to his evident sense of injury; I imagined that he might now be a relic of the Soviet Union, perhaps bitter that he now lacked the status, salary and security that would have been guaranteed in the old days.

But to my surprise, a couple of hours later, when I next passed the professor's hut he emerged to beckon me inside. He had cleared his worktop to make space for a loaf of bread and a large cheese. There were glasses and a bottle of chilled vodka that he had pulled from the fridge. I was clearly forgiven. He filled the glasses and started to talk enthrallingly about his passion for archaeology. 'You never know what the earth will reveal,' he enthused. 'You are looking and looking and suddenly see something. It's such a thrill. It's like a card game, gambling for very high stakes. It's riveting. You forget about everything else. And then you hit the jackpot.' He filled our glasses again and, flushed with an excitement that made him seem young again, picked up a simple Orthodox cross in bronze. 'You see this?' he said, holding the crudely fashioned piece tenderly in his hand. 'It fills me with trepidation. It comes from the twelfth, maybe the fourteenth century. It had the power of the divine. People wore them to protect themselves, and today it causes me great trepidation to touch these things that people wore with such faith.'

After a further glass of vodka, Anatoly started to talk about himself. He was seventy-one years old and had been born in St Petersburg, so as a small child he had been through the siege. His mother had been obliged to sell all the family's possessions to buy food. 'One day my mother – she is an icon to me, like all mothers – was hit by shrapnel. When they told me that she was badly wounded I understood that I would be without her, that she would die.' Tears filled his eyes as he spoke quietly and without affectation about a loss felt so keenly so many years later. As an orphaned schoolboy at the end of the Great

Patriotic War, he remembered that his mother had once told him that the family had relatives in England, White Russians who had fled in 1917 after the Bolshevik revolution. He went on: 'She had a small photograph of them hidden away, but she had never dared to make contact with them because it was far too dangerous in Stalin's time. It was very, very dangerous to look for anyone abroad. It was forbidden.'

Nevertheless, at the age of ten Anatoly decided to write to the BBC in London because he knew that it symbolized everything that was good and honourable in England. 'I had the idea to ask them to help me. I wrote and said I had no mother and that as we were allies perhaps they could help me find my relatives in England.' He heard nothing. But that disappointment was as nothing compared to the effect he believed his letter had within the Soviet Union. 'I was a young boy,' he went on. 'I had no idea until much later that with that letter I had sentenced myself to a lifelong punishment. I became an archaeologist, and later an established specialist in my field, and, of course, I wanted to attend conferences abroad. But I was always forbidden to leave. I wasn't even allowed to go to Bulgaria. I was invited again and again to go to Denmark by one of my European colleagues who happened to be a Communist. Each time I applied for a visa – eight times in all – I was summoned by the authorities in Moscow. "Why do you want to go?" they would ask. I would explain that I was studying the Vikings, and they would say, "Very interesting, but are you aware that Denmark is a member of NATO?" And they always refused me a visa. No explanation.'

It was not until 1986, with the introduction of Gorbachev's *glasnost* and *perestroika*, that he finally achieved his ambition to travel to Europe. And it was not until the collapse of the Soviet Union that he discovered, through a friend, that his boyhood letter to the BBC had been intercepted by the KGB and held on file, where it had been used against him for the next four decades. By this time, after yet another vodka, I was feeling thoroughly ashamed of my premature irritation with this warm, sad man. We embraced as he described me as a 'soulmate' and, arms about each other, his disdain for the Soviet system tumbled forth in a cathartic flood of bitter memories. 'It was a time of total degradation. Until then Russia had been open to the rest of the world. But Communism destroyed people, annihilated them. It destroyed faith, it destroyed human values. All it offered were values for the herd. After 1917, Russia lost the twentieth century.'

Anatoly's Vikings, ever restless, pressed on along the Volkhov River on their way southwards in search of trade and conquest. Some 150 miles south of Staraya Ladoga, they established another settlement that later became known as Novgorod. According to the ancient chronicles, it was here in 859 that Rurik is said to have founded his suzerainty. As Staraya Ladoga slowly faded in significance Novgorod blossomed to become one of the finest cities in all Europe, the trading heart of northern Rus, with profitable links to Germany and Scandinavia. Rurik's successor, Oleg, driven further south by a restless impulse to reach Constantinople (now Istanbul), chose Kiev (now the capital of Ukraine) as his new stronghold; but Novgorod retained its commercial importance as a leading member of the family of competing principalities that formed the mini-power blocs of the new state of Kievan Rus.

Today the city is adorned by cathedrals, churches and monasteries that owe their origins both to the wealth created in the early Middle Ages and to a profoundly important decision made by Vladimir the Great, who emerged as the ruler of Kievan Rus in 980. In a move reminiscent of Peter the Great more than seven hundred years later, Vladimir determined to break with the past, to 'Europeanize' Rus, in this case by destroying its pagan, atavistic culture. Convinced that a monotheistic faith was more suited to an emerging nation that was entitled to be treated on equal terms with the other great powers of Europe, he sent emissaries to study Judaism, Islam, Roman Catholicism and – in Constantinople – the Greek Orthodox Church. Eventually, for reasons that are the subject of much speculation and dispute, he selected the latter branch of Christianity for all the subjects of Rus. Perhaps he was motivated by diplomatic factors – Constantinople was a fabulously wealthy commercial centre at the heart of the then known world; perhaps it was because he had been informed by his emissaries that the political relationship between Church and State in Constantinople placed the Patriarch entirely at the disposal of the Emperor; or perhaps, as some scholars suggest, it was because he was attracted by vivid descriptions of the exotic ritual and liturgical splendour by which an authoritarian Church held the faithful in thrall. Perhaps all these considerations, and even, as the mythology suggests, a genuine conversion of Pauline proportions, played their part in his choice. Whatever the explanation, Vladimir and the entire warrior class under his command were formally baptized into the Orthodox Church in 987 by senior members of the Greek clergy dispatched from Constantinople for the purpose. Obedient in every respect to the Greek Orthodox blueprint, Vladimir at once ordered that pagan idols be destroyed and thrown into rivers or lakes, and that heathen temples be replaced by churches.

His religious conversion was an astute political move of the moment, but would also become a very mixed blessing. Declaring, 'I believe in One God, the Father, who is unbegotten, and in the only Son, who is begotten and in one Holy Spirit,' Vladimir, the erstwhile tribal leader of a pagan people, found himself with an entry ticket into the magic circle of European monarchs. But the Church to which he had committed himself was very different from its Western rivals and counterparts. To an extent that is as hard to exaggerate as it is precisely to pinpoint, Vladimir's decision was truly fateful. Orthodoxy was a powerful opiate that taught that material concerns were to be abominated; that life on earth was merely a transition towards either heaven or hell; that renunciation on the one hand and spiritual ecstasy on the other were cardinal virtues; and that suffering and mortification were the defining characteristics of a heavenward soul.

As an agnostic who veers towards atheism, it is not hard for me to find myself sharing the view that the impact of the Russian Orthodox Church through the centuries has retarded social and cultural progress in a way that only obscurantists and mystics could possibly welcome. I had never thought to find myself in agreement with a right-wing American academic who had been – to my student eyes – an intransigent Cold War warrior, but in *Russia under the Old Regime* the historian Richard Pipes has written a masterly analysis of the trajectory of Russian Orthodoxy. 'No branch of Christianity has shown such callous indifference to social and political injustice,' he writes, adding, 'The ultimate result of the policies of the Russian Orthodox Church was not only to discredit it in the eyes of those who cared for social and political justice, but to create a spiritual vacuum. This vacuum was filled by secular ideologies which sought to realize on this earth the paradise that Christianity had promised to provide in the next.' No one could put it better.

None of this stopped me from succumbing to the ethereal grandeur of a city that has been carefully restored to something like its former glory. Against the blue sky of a summer Sunday morning, with solemn bells ringing out across the city from magnificent silver and gold domes, Novgorod is touched by a magical variety of tones, shades, textures and designs that cannot fail to impress. Summoned by bells to the cathedral of St Sophia, even the secular soul is soon mesmerized by the theatre of faith: the enveloping incense, the curl of white smoke rising to mingle with the shafts of sunlight that pierce the gloom from high above the nave, the icons in deep red and gold, the murals that glorify saints and martyrs, the guttering candles, the swish of priestly robes, the long beards and cowls that disguise holy faces, the chants and incantations from ancient manuscripts, the tinkling of tiny bells and, not least, the reverence of the faithful.

As I shuffled through the congregation crowded into the five naves to observe the outward forms of their devotion – making the sign of the cross, offering obeisance before the bones of long-dead saints, or simply responding to instructions from the altar – I had to remind myself that the freedom to worship openly without fear of discrimination is still a novelty for those communicants who endured the disapprobation of the state in the Soviet era. I looked again at the grannies, the mothers, the fathers (not so many of them), and at the children and toddlers, cosseted and cuddled by loving relatives – and the innocence and simplicity all around suddenly moved me to an imprecise compassion for their religious conviction that, from my perspective, has contributed balefully, if not ruinously, to the tortured history of the Russian people.

As obedient followers of the Orthodox Church, the peasants, most of whom were serfs, lived for centuries in a cultural prison run by the priesthood. While western Europe emerged from the Middle Ages to glory in the Renaissance and then the Age of Enlightenment, the Orthodox Church led its followers in the opposite direction, denying any expression of humanity's creative impulse except through religious symbols. Secular art was specifically forbidden; Russian landscape painting, even allegory, did not exist. There were no secular plays or secular poetry; no journals or magazines. The use of musical instruments was forbidden. Only the Orthodox chant, the heavenly plainsong of monks and priests, was permitted; a sound so insistently spiritual that the mind is swiftly numbed by the senses, themselves in servitude to ecstasy. It does not take much imagination to appreciate how, for century after century, the peasantry cowered under the stern spiritual protection of Orthodoxy's Almighty; nor to realize why Russia remained for so long a cultural desert.

Despite this, by reason of its location and its outward – westward – perspective, Novgorod was not entirely immune to European ideas of progress. When Kiev, 'the mother of all Russian cities', was sacked by the Mongols in 1240, Novgorod was spared. With the Rus now split into two separate and competing principalities, the city's pivotal position on the cultural and economic crossroads between East and West brought power and wealth to a huge region that ran from the Baltic to the Urals. Before long the city fathers felt strong enough to flex their political muscles and established a council of merchants, landowners and nobles. This self-appointed oligarchy, known as the *veche*, set itself the task of developing Novgorod to the point where the city gradually came to resemble, though not to rival, its European counterparts. In this process, the princes of Novgorod were forced to surrender their rights to raise taxes and to declare war, to participate in the formulation of policy and to tinker with the institutions of their principality. By 1265 they had lost even their titular role as heads of the nascent republic that the state of Novgorod seemed destined to become. Those who are tempted by the 'what if?' school of history might detect in Novgorod the first shoots of what, in other circumstances, might have blossomed into a structure of governance that, as in Europe, might one day have been identified as that of an emergent democracy.

But, unhappily, the circumstances did not lend themselves to such an outcome. The merchants who ran the city reckoned without the resurgent authority of the Orthodox Church. Inexorably, the archbishops of Novgorod gradually managed to acquire more and more control over the temporal as well as the spiritual life of the city, slowly eviscerating the *veche*. Meanwhile, the principality of Muscovy, which had established itself as the most militarily and politically powerful in the Rus, was eyeing Novgorod's wealth with envy. After a succession of skirmishes, the conflict between the two came to a head when Ivan the Great forcibly annexed the city to Muscovy in 1478, removing the last vestiges of the city's autonomy and severing Novgorod's diminishing links with western Europe. The *coup de grâce* was delivered almost a century later when, in 1570, Ivan the Terrible laid waste to the city, massacring tens of thousands of its inhabitants in a frenzy of hatred. Although Novgorod survived as a centre of religious worship and instruction, the city had lost all power and influence.

More than two centuries later, Peter the Great's programme of modernization liberated the great cities of Russia to enjoy the secular arts of western Europe. But he did nothing to lift the cultural yoke of the Orthodox Church from the shoulders of the peasantry. On the contrary. Although he regarded the Church as a parasitical institution, he also saw how the priesthood could usefully be redeployed. In 1721 an ecclesiastical regulation abolished the Patriarchy and replaced it with a Holy Synod, that owed its first loyalty not to God, but to the state, in other words the tsar. Every member of the Holy Synod was required to take an oath, declaring, 'I swear by Almighty God that I resolve and am in duty bound to be a faithful, good and obedient slave and subject to my natural and true Tsar and Sovereign'. Newly ordained priests had to pledge that they would 'defend unsparingly all the powers, rights and prerogatives belonging to the High Autocracy of His Majesty' and his successors. Nothing was to stand in the way of this servitude. Lowly parish priests, often so poorly educated as to be functionally illiterate, were instructed to treat the confidences entrusted to them by their parishioners in the confessional as Peter's personal property. The oath was unequivocal:

> If during confession someone discloses to the priest an unfulfilled but still intended criminal act, especially of treason or rebellion against the Sovereign or the State, or an evil design against the honour or health of the Sovereign and the family of his Majesty...the confessor must not only give him absolution and remission of his openly confessed sins...but must promptly report him at the prescribed places pursuant to the personal decree of His Imperial Majesty...such villains are commanded to be apprehended with all dispatch....

Not least because it suited both parties, Peter's radical 'reform' of the Orthodox Church remained intact until the overthrow of the last tsar, Nicholas II, in the revolution of 1917. In return for mortgaging its soul to the tsar, the Orthodox Church was not only permitted to collect tithes and rents from its huge ecclesiastical holdings, but, of even greater significance, the Church's Faustian pact with the state also protected the priesthood from any challenge to its spiritual hegemony. Free to impose its mystical precepts on the lives of an ignorant and oppressed populace, the unholy alliance further retarded Russia's social and cultural development for another two centuries. As Alexander Solzhenitsyn was to write, the history of Russia would have been 'incomparably more humane and harmonious in the last few centuries if the church had not surrendered its independence'.

Novgorod returned briefly to prominence in the twentieth century when Nazi Germany invaded the Soviet Union in June 1941. Confirming the strategic value placed upon the region by the Vikings more than a thousand years earlier, Hitler's Panzer divisions made a beeline for Novgorod and swiftly occupied the city, driving the Soviet defenders into the countryside beyond. In the battles that ensued over the next two and a half years, both sides were careless of the ancient churches and monasteries. By the time the Germans were finally driven out in January 1944, Novgorod's glorious architectural heritage had been virtually obliterated.

With the end of hostilities, Stalin revealed a quixotic enthusiasm for all Novgorod's historic monuments, not excluding the monasteries, churches and cathedrals that he had persecuted so relentlessly until his attention was diverted by the Great Patriotic War. But the very first beneficiary of Stalin's post-war munificence was a portentous bronze sculpture of massive proportions known as the Millennium Monument of Russia, which had been erected in 1862 to celebrate the thousandth anniversary of Rurik's arrival there. Depicting the great men and women of Russian history, it had evidently been coveted by Hitler, who, in the last days of the occupation of the city, ordered the sculpture to be dismantled and carted back to Berlin where it was destined to be reassembled to celebrate the triumph of German Nazism over Soviet Communism. Happily fate, in the form of defeat, intervened to frustrate Hitler's project.

As I wandered around the base of the Millennium Monument, staring up at a pantheon of heroes that included not only Rurik, but Ivan the Great, Peter the Great, Pushkin, Lermontov and Gogol, not to mention thirty-one custodians of the Orthodox flame, I had the fleeting thought that Stalin must have been overcome by an uncharacteristic bout of self-deprecation. Why else did he forgo the chance during the reconstruction to have his own image insinuated on to the topmost plinth to take his proper place among the heroes of the nation?

Strolling later through the park that surrounds the walls of the kremlin, I watched the weekend life of the city. Hawkers lined the paths with their wares. Garish paintings of the kind that are to be found for sale on the railings that edge Hyde Park jostled for attention with stands selling popcorn, babushka dolls and hamburgers. I declined an invitation to have my photo taken beside a gaunt black crow tied to a wooden perch (which tried to bite me), but I stroked a mangy parrot on a stick (which refused to utter even a squawk in gratitude). There were coffee shops and summer restaurants in abundance. Beyond the kremlin wall a thick slick of fine white sand along the edge of the Volkhov was crowded with sunbathing families, matrons and mothers, small children and babies. Nubile girls in micro-bikinis tanning themselves in the afternoon heat affected to ignore lean youths prancing near them with a football. There were deckchairs and an ice-cream stand. It could almost have been Brighton or Bournemouth.

There was a mismatch, though. As I walked back towards my hotel, passing under a portcullis through an arch of the kremlin wall, the words of the seventeenth-century poet Richard Lovelace came into my mind: 'Stone walls do not a prison make, nor iron bars a cage'. The question of freedom and democracy started nagging me again. Freedom is more a direction of travel than a moment in history. So for me the question is not, 'Is Russia free?' but 'Are the people getting more or less free?' Not only that, but in what ways? And, crucially, who cares either way?

That evening I had a drink in the apartment of a film-maker who also teaches journalism in that dwindling number of colleges that are prepared to pay her to teach heretical – that is to say liberal and demo-cratic – principles. Tatiana was refreshingly scathing about the state of the Russian nation. In Novgorod, she told me, the students in her department were taught both journalism and public relations, but no distinction was made between the two crafts. 'The truth is that they are being taught that their role is to serve those in authority and those with power. This is very dispiriting, but it is true.' She then gave me an example of a losing battle on behalf of the Russian 'fourth estate', which she remains determined to fight until she is sacked. 'In my class I set my students the task of working out how to "break" a news story. But their immediate question to me is always, "Who is paying us? Who is the most powerful person?" What they mean is, "Who do we have to please?" If the story is about the city administration, for example, they want to know what they should say about the mayor or, to be precise, what the mayor wants to have them say about him. If it's the regional governor, it is the same thing: "What does he want to read about himself?" When I criticize this approach, they fight back and they are sometimes quite angry. "You have set conditions for us and we are reacting to those conditions as we know them to be." So I then suggest they write a story simply on the basis of the facts I have given them, as if they were free of any constraint. And the terrible thing is that they simply can't do it. It is psychologically impossible for them. That is freedom for you. And it is getting worse.'

Tatiana was pessimistic. 'I don't think Russia will ever have a genuinely free media. In the Soviet era, when journalists were overtly tools of the state, the media was widely respected. Viewers believed what they saw on television. If a newspaper criticized the chairman of a collective farm, the public noted that a little while later he would be removed from his post. The media was thought to be acting in the interests of the people. Today, when the Kremlin once again controls television – which is much more important than the press – the public still believes the propaganda. It is a state of mind, a psychological fact of the present as it was of the past.' Tatiana was strong-minded but, in the Russian way, she was also resigned. 'Maybe some people will resist, but we will never be strong enough to confront the new elite – which, for the most part, is simply the old elite in new clothing.' T.S. Eliot's perplexing conundrum 'Time present and time past/Are both perhaps present in time future' flashed perversely into my mind. What hope is there for a Russian people who have endured such a past and for whom the present has not yet been redeemed from that past? 'If all time is eternally present/All time is unredeemable.' But perhaps with time, there is hope. 'Only through time time is conquered.'

Moscow

Tula
Yasnaya Polyana

Voronezh

*Volga*

*Volga*

*Volga*

R U S S I A

Astrakhan

Novorossiysk

NORTH
OSSETIA     INGUSHETIA

Pyatigorsk

Kislyar

CABARDINO-
BALKARIA

*R Terek*

Chankayurt

Sochi

Nalchik

Grozny

Makhachkala

Beslan

CHECHNYA

C A S P I A N   S E A

DAGESTAN

B L A C K   S E A

C A U C A S U S   M O U N T A I N S

Route taken

| 0 | | 200 miles |
|---|---|---|
| 0 | | 300 kms |

# PART TWO
# FROM MOSCOW
# TO THE CASPIAN

I walked into my first Russian bath-house with trepidation. Armed only with a leaflet advertising the delights promised inside – which made it sound as though it were run by a gang of torturers' apprentices – I entered through an ornate portico on the corner of a quiet street in the heart of Moscow. Then I ascended wide stone steps that curled around for three flights to a hexagonal ante-chamber that might have come from the rococo interior of an eighteenth-century palace in downtown Vienna. A pair of huge young heavies, with ill-concealed pistols clamped to their *jambon* hips, viewed me with that combination of suspicion and contempt that minders reserve for the weak and impotent. I walked past them, essaying nonchalance, through a set of varnished wooden swing doors into the *banya* itself.

Inside I found a magnificent chamber with an ornately carved wooden ceiling and glass chandeliers. Beneath this splendour, naked male bodies – ghastly bellies sagging shamelessly on to fat thighs – sprawled on their haunches on what looked like pews looted from an English church, except that they were covered in green leather, as if from the cloakroom of a gentlemen's club in St James's. This nostalgic illusion was dispelled by the panelled walls, which were enlivened by erotica – if that is the right term to describe a set of paintings depicting naked women demurely pouring tea for naked men in a fantasy bath-house. Bacchanalia it was not.

Almost all the men – all public *banyas* are segregated – were on their mobiles in animated and, as it seemed to my uncomprehending ear, aggressive dialogue. As I watched this belly-scratching, phone-clasping array of stressed humanity I was graphically reminded that Russia has an alarming death rate from heart disease, and a male life expectancy that, defying the trend of all other developed nations, is not rising but falling. My young guide, a Moscow law student, confirmed that they were indeed conducting rough-and-tough business, adding with distaste, 'They are all crooks and bullies giving orders to their staff.' I remembered the henchmen outside and those reports that the Russian mafia are prone to conduct their business in the *banya* and occasionally to conclude an especially tough deal in the showers, where, as a consequence, white-tiled walls and floors are reputed on occasion to have run pink as warm blood mingled with hot water.

But I should not mock the *banya,* which has an honourable tradition that goes back many centuries and is revered in Russia both as a forum for social intercourse and for its health-enhancing properties. My brochure, written in a delightful Russian equivalent of franglais, promised me 'maximum pleasure...the health and joy of full life, harmony and self-confidence'. This last I lacked entirely. I undressed until, puny and naked – but for an absurd grey felt hat shaped like an upturned flower pot that would supposedly protect my skull from the worst effects of the steam room. Then I advanced into another large chamber, which reminded me of the showers at my boarding school, though it lacked entirely the homo-erotic stimulation that they had nurtured in those long-ago pubescent days. I took a shower, among the other naked bodies, and then, armed only with a bunch of birch twigs, strode self-consciously into the steam room to join some of the giants of Russian commerce at rest. I lay on a hot slab, a minnow among walruses, until, after a lifetime of about ten minutes, I succumbed to the heat and, with globules of sweat pouring down my chest, I made to leave. At this, one of the walruses remonstrated, gesturing to show this foreigner that the ritual of the steam room was not yet complete. Picking up my bunch of soggy birch twigs, he started to flail my back and buttocks. I say 'flail'; in fact it was more of a caress than a flail, and surprisingly soothing.

Next, I hurried out of the steam room and across the shower hall to a mock Roman bath, bracing myself for a plunge into what had been billed as ice-cold water. I made a rush for it and belly-flopped into the pool expecting the worst. In fact, mildly to my disappointment, the water was on the tepid side of cold. I swam around in a circle, wondering if, after all, I was less among walruses than among wimps. I was soon disabused. I had booked a massage and found my way to a row of cubicles, each occupied by a walrus on a slab, groaning with pain or pleasure as a white-towelled masseur pummelled the flab. I clambered on to my allotted slab and my masseur, whose hands, held thumb to thumb, were large enough to span my shoulders, set to his task with relentless expertise. Throwing a bucket of hot water over me and covering my body in soap, he worked his way up and down, back and forth, from head to toe, kneading flesh, muscles and bone until I too yelped and gasped and groaned at that combination of pain and pleasure that connoisseurs describe as sensuous.

Afterwards, more or less purged of impurities, I walked out past the two heavies, daring to essay a 'goodbye' in Russian – a gesture of goodwill that prompted them merely to glance at each other with raised eyebrows as if to say, 'How did he get in?' Had I had enough Russian at my disposal, I would perhaps have been brave enough to tell them that I was off to see Madonna, a prospect that, I suspect, would have transformed their glassy-eyed contempt into envy.

# MADONNA IN MOSCOW

The Madonna-fest was a party organized by the Russian edition of *Vogue* on the eve of her sell-out concert at Moscow's biggest football stadium. We drove to the venue – one of those nondescript post-modern galleries in which post-revolutionary Moscow seems to abound – in heavy traffic on roads laden with Mercedes and Volvos, the occasional Bentley or Maserati, and even one Bugatti, passing designer shops and advertising hoardings that made those of Piccadilly Circus look decidedly dowdy. It was my first visit to Moscow since the headily anarchic days that followed the collapse of the Soviet Union, when everything seemed possible and a fearful freedom prevailed. But in the winter of 1991 the streets were still dark and half empty, the shops indiscernible and gloomy. Advertising – except in the form of redundant slogans promoting this or that virtue of the Central Committee of the Communist Party (the CCCP) – was as yet unknown; and although the Stones had been in town, Madonna had yet to conquer the Russian capital.

But now it could have been New York. A limousine with black-ened windows to spark the curiosity of bystanders swept up to the entrance and, to a ripple of applause from the invited guests, Madonna stepped out surrounded by minders to protect her frail majesty from her adoring fans. A red rope cordoned off a squadron of attendant paparazzi, who crushed each other in their rivalrous attempts to confirm for magazine readers around the world that Madonna was indeed the most important threatened species on the planet. The newspapers and television had been full of her visit, rivalling even the homage that is normally reserved for Vladimir Putin. Her name was on the tip of every tongue. The doorman at my hotel was in despair because he had heard a rumour that she had been stricken by flu and would have to cancel the performance. It was to be a very big event but, even in a city where the glitterati usually hold sway, it was mired in controversy.

After the collapse of Communism former *samizdat* stars like Pink Floyd, the Rolling Stones and, in 2003, Paul McCartney – 'The most important event in the entire history of pop music', as it was billed by the Russian media – had performed in front of adulatory fans. But the arrival of Madonna was different. Her ambiguous sexuality, explicit and provocative, was causing moral apoplexy among social conservatives, while news that her act would include a number in which she would wear a crown of thorns and sing from a crucifix had aroused the wrath of the Orthodox Church. A spokesman, Archpriest Vsevolod Chaplin, declared, 'Madonna exploits the crucifix, statues of the Holy Mother and other religious symbols to illustrate her own passion.' A group calling itself the Union of Orthodox Flag Bearers pronounced a 'Holy Inquisition' against her. Others carried banners demanding 'Madonna Go Home'. The tour organizers were, of course, delighted. Her spokesman noted complacently, 'This is a country where anyone can go into the streets and say they hate Madonna, but we also know that there are thousands of people who are going to come and enjoy her concert.' Commentators noted that even a few years earlier she would have still been *persona non grata* in Russia. Now she had arrived from the airport in a motorcade escorted by police outriders. A protective phalanx of three and a half thousand militiamen, including four hundred riot police and the Moscow bomb squad, were due to be deployed at the Lushniki stadium, where upwards of fifty thousand fans were expected to attend her performance. For them, this was conclusive evidence that Russia really had joined the modern world.

I am an admirer not so much because she is always so sexy, nor because she always manages to reinvent herself just in time, but because one of her staff once told a producer on my ITV Sunday political programme that she admired my work – *my* work – and (we waited with bated breath) she therefore 'very much regretted' that she was unable to grace me with an interview. So near but so impossibly far. Now, in Moscow, as I stood alone, a nobody in the crush, surrounded by glossy models, fashion designers, record producers and chic restaurateurs, all of us swigging sweet champagne or lurid cocktails from plastic glasses, I felt that moment of resentment that is a form of self-important presenters' angst. In London one of the 'event organizers' would at least have had an inkling of who I was, someone would have been attentive to my needs, and, yes, I might have been able to swap a *bon mot* or two with the lady herself. She might even have told me in her own words how very much she had regretted turning down my invitation. Instead, she was whisked in and then whisked out while I wandered disconsolately around the promotional exhibition that she had momentarily graced with her presence. Only her voice remained, singing sulkily in recorded sound-around. I had to make do with elaborately decadent photographs and, on one screen, an animation that contrived to present her writhing with a wild animal in what looked like a fish tank. The beast in me felt envious.

## REMEMBERING GORBACHEV

I first came to Moscow more than a quarter of a century ago. It was 1980, well before Gorbachev – a great man of the last century and, for me, almost on a pedestal with Nelson Mandela – started to rescue the repressive state that he had inherited from collapsing under the weight of its internal contradictions. In those days, with an ailing Leonid Brezhnev presiding over a state paralysed by the political equivalent of senile dementia, a foreign TV reporter was always under observation. I was there to make a six-part ITV series called *The Eagle and the Bear*, in which I sought, in part, to argue that the 'threat' posed by the Other, through which each superpower sought to imprint in the collective psyche of its own citizens the conviction that a nuclear-arms race offered the best hope of delivering them peace and security, was a self-deluding abomination – though, since it was television, I was unable to put the point in quite such terms. We had negotiated in advance a formal contract with the Ministry of Foreign Affairs, an elaborate document that stated where we could travel and to whom we could speak. To breach, or attempt to breach, this 'solemn and binding' agreement would, we had been informed, threaten our entire venture. It had been almost impossible to obtain permission to film outside the capital, let alone in the 'closed' cities with which the Soviet Union was pockmarked. Minders accompanied us wherever we went to make sure we abided by the rules of totalitarianism. Even in Red Square we were forbidden to interview passers-by for fear they might let slip, however discreetly, a doubt about the triumph of Soviet social-ism. In private Muscovites rarely ventured an unorthodox opinion, though, very occasionally, they might venture a knowing smile as if to say, 'You might think so. I could not possibly comment.' As spontane-ity was impossible, we resorted to subterfuge. Since I lack the natural-born killer instinct, it was only professional pride that forced me to become an amateur exponent of cloak-and-dagger derring-do; once or twice, using a subterranean network of contacts, I managed to find my way via a maze of instructions to a meeting with someone brave enough to express openly (but always in disguise) a non-stan-dard opinion. It was a very dispiriting experience.

I had never endorsed President Ronald Reagan's apocalyptic claim that the Soviet Union was 'an evil empire' – or if it was, it seemed to me that, through its own interventions in Vietnam and Latin America, the United States was at the same time open to much the same mean-ingless charge. Nonetheless, while Washington invariably set my pulse racing, Moscow always filled me with gloom. It was not only the drab humiliation of poverty imposed on the morose citizens of the Soviet capital, queuing in the cold for basic foodstuffs or scurrying from one shop to another on the basis of a rumour that shirts or shoes had miraculously defied the upside-down laws of supply and demand to become momentarily available. Nor was it only the sullen plain-clothed KGB officers, in their regulation uniform of shiny suits and scuffed boots, scrutinizing our every move, waiting for an excuse to remove us from this or that arbitrarily forbidden place. Nor was it merely the sense of always being overheard, so that we spoke in whispers in the hotel and searched fruitlessly for hidden microphones that, in our paranoid certainty, we were sure the KGB must have planted to eavesdrop upon our plans to circumvent these asphyxiating constraints. Nor was it only the need to resist the late-night allure of a beautiful Russian woman, posing as a lady of the night but perhaps an agent of the state waiting to compromise you with her body in the service of the state. It was all these things and more that provoked a sense of corruption, decay, drift and failure – and a longing to leave almost as soon as I had arrived.

And then came Gorbachev, ascending the Kremlin throne to usher in *perestroika* and *glasnost* while severing the bonds that imprisoned eastern Europe under Soviet hegemony. In the process, he offered the world a glimpse of what might be: a measured, cautious way out of the dead end into which they had been herded by seventy years of totalitarianism. It took the courage and wisdom of a great statesman to risk his own demise by removing the threat of nuclear Armageddon in Europe when most Russians were persuaded that he had abrogated his responsibility to protect the sovereignty of the Soviet Union over its subject peoples.

A year before Gorbachev's fall, thanks to the persuasive efforts of others, I was granted an interview with the great man. It was the only television interview he gave to any European station (in this case the BBC) while he was still in office and, for me at least, it was a memorable notch on the belt. Margaret Thatcher had arrived in town to 'do business' with the Russian leader. I had interviewed her immediately after her first meeting with Gorbachev, when she showed herself, engagingly, to be in thrall to the magnetic personality of the first Soviet leader in her political lifetime to exhibit more energy and intelligence than a zombie. On this occasion, when they had known each other for four years, there was tough talk, but in an amiable manner. Her consort, Denis, was in tow, but excluded from the private luncheon that the President had laid on for the Prime Minister.

As they chomped their way through a long repast, I waited next door in the grand drawing room of a former palace that had been turned into a guest-house for visiting dignitaries. Suddenly a head peered around the door. It was Denis Thatcher, looking distinctly out of sorts. He wandered into our midst and glanced about disapprovingly. 'What are you doing here?' he barked in my direction. I explained, and he hurrumphed and moved further into the room. Followed by his Russian host, an aide to the President, and accompanied by a translator, he stalked around the room like a connoisseur of nineteenth-century art, inspecting the paintings and sculptures on display. After a while he stopped to examine one of the gilded dining chairs that were ranged along the walls. He fingered the embroidered seat, which depicted a rural idyll, and declared, 'They do this kind of thing much better in the north of England, you know.' This was duly translated to his host, who found himself lost for words. A good job, I thought, that it was his wife who was doing the real business.

A long while later, the President and the Prime Minister emerged from lunch very obviously at ease with each other. She asked the same question of me as her husband and then said, with the hint of a sniff, 'Well, I'd better get out of the way then.' Gorbachev apologized with great charm for being so late and sat down in the chair opposite me. I had been instructed by his press secretary, who, like so many of his kind, was a chameleon – a charmer if the boss is happy and a bully if otherwise – that the President's time was very limited indeed. I was already in trouble with him for ushering Gorbachev to a chair when he had repeatedly insisted that his boss would not have time for a 'sit-down' interview. Now he reminded me once again that we could only talk for five minutes – 'Five minutes, Mr Dimbleby, I insist.' Precisely twenty-eight minutes later the President got up to leave, shaking hands with the BBC team and thanking us warmly for finding the time to see him.

The press secretary was furious. 'Did you not see me making it clear that your time was up?' Indeed I had; it had been impossible to avoid the sight of his hand slicing across the front of his throat, signalling 'Cut, cut, cut'. I had affected not to notice this instruction, but now thought it wise to express my regret – and also my instinct that Gorbachev had enjoyed the encounter. This only provoked a renewed tirade: I was finished, I had broken my word, I would not be welcome ever again. Of course, none of this troubled me unduly because I had my scoop: the BBC would that night splash the 'exclusive' interview all over its bulletins and run it at length on *Newsnight*. Moreover, I had enjoyed the encounter with Gorbachev more than I could ever have imagined. For once it was game, set and match to the reporter; the lackey worsted.

For me it was, and remains, one of the most memorable interviews of my life. It broke no news, it claimed no scalp, and it caused no scandal. It was discursive and exploratory, and Gorbachev proved to be all that I had hoped and expected him to be. The world was emerging from the tomb of the Cold War, thanks as much to him as to his peace-making adversary, the former US President Reagan. Gorbachev was neither triumphant nor self-congratulatory but steely and understated: Communism and capitalism were competing systems, but they could live together. Any change in either should emerge gradually and with consent. On no account would he lead the Russians into a Gadarene rush towards the values of the 'free world'. In any case, he was a Communist who believed in socialism and not in the free market. But peace between the superpowers was essential. In a troubled and dangerous world this required trust and understanding, if not yet a partnership. He spoke quietly, but with intellectual and moral conviction. I thought I had never seen so much wisdom and sadness in one man; he seemed genuinely to be burdened by the weight of history on his shoulders, and resigned to the thought that his middle way might not prevail. I came away exultant and moved and filled with hope. The next morning his press secretary rang and his tone was very different from what it had been the day before. He apologized for his tirade and proffered: 'The President very much enjoyed his conversation with you and hopes you will come back to Russia again soon.' Soon afterwards, history intervened. Gorbachev was gone, derided by the Russian people and placed by them in the ashcan of history.

His successor, the defiant hero of the counter-revolution against the Soviet old guard, who found himself on a tank at a pivotal moment in the collapse of Bolshevism, was clasped to the bosom of cynical Westerners who discerned wrongly that he had the charisma, wisdom and power to bring 'democracy' to Russia, and rightly that he would open the doors to their free market on their terms. I had met Boris Yeltsin briefly inside the Russian parliament, the Duma, in the late eighties. It was a post-prandial encounter and he was not only rude but drunk – an unstable buffoon; the conversation got nowhere fast. Thereafter I could hardly believe the encomiums that greeted his ascendancy. With hindsight, it is hard to exaggerate the baleful impact of his near-decade in power: the oligarchs and the mafia (often one and the same) who stole every asset of any value; the inflation that ruined pensioners and the poor; the corruption that corroded all values and humiliated every decent citizen; and the insecurity that filled everyone with fear and loathing. So much for democracy, the Russians concluded; give us law and order and a sense of national pride.

Thanks in large measure to the Yeltsin years, Russia is both a triumph and a disaster. The nation's wealth is built exclusively on a range and quantity of natural resources – oil, gas, coal, gold, diamonds and platinum – that is unrivalled anywhere else on the planet, and the Russian people are well educated, hard-working and resilient. Yet these resources are owned, directly or indirectly, by a tiny elite of twenty, maybe thirty individuals – the oligarchs – who display no discernible awareness of social or moral obligation to anyone except themselves. The inequalities of wealth and power, which would tear apart other societies, are obscene to anyone with even a minimal sense of fairness and justice. The population, which should be growing, is declining, from 220 million a century ago to under 150 million today and, according to most demographers, on its way down to no more than 120 million by the middle of this century. But a society that should be looking outwards to the rest of the world, inviting immigration to arrest or reverse this alarming demographic trend, is instead becoming more and more introspective. Nationalism (not patriotism) is all the rage, while its twin cousins, xenophobia and racism, are waiting in the wings. All this makes Russia perplexing and unnerving, a wounded giant that wants to flex its muscles but is still flailing.

## THE 'NEW' RUSSIA

All this was in my mind as I meandered through Red Square, relieved to see that the military guard was absent from duty at Lenin's mausoleum, where the moribund leaders of the moribund Soviet Union used to stand at attention to salute the 'evil empire's' weapons of mass destruction as they were trundled loyally past their dais. The Kremlin towered over me, the seat of all power – repressive in the last century, and, I feared, likely to be no better in this. I retreated into the famous department store GUM, transformed by capitalism to a degree that must have had the embalmed corpse of Lenin turning in his catafalque beneath the Kremlin walls. Where once there were gloomy arcades lined by dingy shops, sometimes boarded up, otherwise selling cheap clothes without any show of enthusiasm to a dribble of visitors, GUM is now a shopper's paradise (though by no means the most exclusive in the capital). Gilded avenues filled with rival retail temples display the competing clothes, shoes and perfumes of the world's most desirable brands. Every French, Italian, American or British retailer of note – Versace, Articoli, Mariella Burani, L'Oréal and the rest – has an emporium in GUM to sell their wares. The shops are as international and as elegantly banal as their counterparts in Europe, and no less crowded with window-shoppers, touching, feeling and sometimes even splashing out. As I checked the prices ($3000 for a fur stole, $1500 for a dress, $1500 for a casual jacket, $1200 for a leather handbag), a girl walked by, tall and lean, wearing a black T-shirt with the single word 'RICH' imprinted on her bosom, a triumph of aspiration, I suspected, over reality. It is tempting to mock the nouveau riche of Moscow and, more generally, the vulgarity and garishness of the capital's tinselly new persona, but that would be missing the point. Buy now and live for the moment defines the post-revolutionary culture of young Russians. And why not? It is the flip side of their insecurity: spend now because tomorrow you might not have the chance. And in any case, it is much more attractive than what came before.

Moscow's skyline is all cranes and building sites, tall glass office blocks and apartments, and new six-lane highways radiating out from the centre to suburbs that extend hungrily ever deeper into what was once forest and is now a refuge where the newly rich build their new mansions. Materialism (not of the dialectical variety) rules OK. In the heart of the city, as a pedestrian, you stumble across traffic-jammed streets, weaving a dangerous path through cars and trucks that clog every artery of the city, day and night, undeterred by police sirens that wail with self-important impotence. Your eyes are soon sore with invisible particles of dust, your lungs similarly afflicted. It is all momentarily exhilarating – the bright lights, the hustle, even the aggression – but the anarchy quickly becomes exhausting.

I looked nostalgically at the Bolshoi Theatre where, on the first New Year's Eve of the post-Soviet age, I had taken my family to see *The Nutcracker*, and where, by egalitarian chance, we found ourselves in what had once been the Royal Box. The auditorium was faded and tatty, but the romance had been intoxicating. When we emerged, snow was falling and the city seemed silent, muffled. I indulged myself then with the thought that we should have been clambering into a horse-drawn cab to join some of the characters from *War and Peace* at a French-speaking soirée. As it was, we found a dilapidated taxi and slithered anxiously to a dark apartment block where an old friend, who had been my Soviet interpreter with Gorbachev, had laid on a New Year's dinner for us. Sergey and his wife Katya had prepared a feast, mostly from tins. It was not exactly appetizing, but they had obviously drawn heavily on their savings to entertain this Western family whom they did not even know. Until that evening, despite my best efforts, Sergey had never told me anything about himself or his family. Now he took from under his bed a box that contained a set of dog-eared photographs taken almost a hundred years before. In one of them he pointed out his grandfather, standing in a formal photograph, a young courtier at the time of the last tsar. So for all those years as an official translator for the Soviet state, Sergey had been a closet counter-revolutionary, and for the first time he was now free to admit it. We drank to the future – ours, his and Russia's. I lost touch with him soon afterwards but, a decade and a half later, as I walked past the Bolshoi, now shrouded in plastic sheeting that flapped disconsolately in the wind, I wondered what he must think of the new Russia. Not much, I suspect.

After my wander around Red Square – no snow this time, but a drizzle of clinging rain – I had supper with the Moscow correspondent of *The Economist*, Andrew Miller, a friend who had once worked with me on ITV's self-proclaimed 'flagship' political programme, *Jonathan Dimbleby*. I explained how difficult I found it to understand or like Putin's Russia. He commiserated: 'Putin says he is a democrat. Either he is lying or he means it. The latter is more dangerous than the former. Russia is self-evidently not a democracy. The last elections were a farce. And it will be the same next time round. The Kremlin wields more power now than it did during Soviet times. The President has absolute power. The media that matters – which means the national TV stations and the big-circulation newspapers – are under his control. Putin is at the top of every news bulletin, often for fifteen minutes at a time. Ninety-five per cent of the coverage about him is positive. Ninety-five per cent of the – minimal – coverage given to the official opposition parties is negative. There is no democracy now and there will be less.' And with a late-night flourish he concluded, 'In Russia everything is getting better and everything is getting worse.'

The next morning, as if to confirm this neat paradox, I went to meet the Russian CEO of one of the largest international advertising agencies in Moscow, BBDO. Ella Stewart is an exuberant and forthright boss for whom the term 'blonde bombshell' could have been coined. She breezed in late for our meeting because, yet again, Putin, who lives down the road from her in his fortified compound, had got in her way; or to be precise – she gesticulated with contemptuous frustration – because the daily passage of his motorcade to the Kremlin had, as always, disrupted the notoriously gridlocked traffic flow into the city centre. 'It's really so stupid,' she said. 'Do they know what they are doing? Do they know how much money is being wasted?' She had an air of easy authority that allowed her male colleagues some licence – but not too much – to tease and challenge her.

One of them had compiled a slide show that they were using to market the 'new' Russia to would-be foreign investors. It took the form of a series of visually contrasting images – thens and nows – to highlight the changes that have revolutionized Moscow since the collapse of the Soviet Union. Then the shelves were empty; now they are full. Then people dressed badly; now they wear the latest fashions. Then no one bothered with their hairstyle; now smart salons abound. Then there was only McDonald's and you had to queue around Pushkin Square to buy a burger; now you can eat what you like wherever and whenever you want. Then the streets were deserted; now they are full at all hours of the day or night. Then the old were miserable and tired; now they have a new lease of life. And so on. The images were slick, the presentation sharp, but none of the four young executives around the table really seemed to believe in it. Instead they punctuated the flow of images with mocking asides calculated to show that anyone who accepted these 'then and now' contrasts at face value would believe anything – for instance, the photographic inference that in the Soviet era Russians were gloomy, whereas now, under capitalism, they smile. 'Not so,' Ella said. 'They are still gloomy,' which prompted one of her team to quip, 'Russians only smile when there is a reason to smile – which is not very often. Otherwise they think you are crazy.'

As they started to analyse their own advertising pitch, these clever young people betrayed a degree of uncertainty and anxiety that was oddly reassuring. If the brightest and best in the new Russia are as uneasy about their country as I was feeling, perhaps, I thought, there might be hope. 'If you have money, yes, of course it is a great place,' said Max, an American émigré who had lived and worked in Russia since 1991. 'But there is a dichotomy between the haves and the have nots. If you have the money, you can go to the nightclubs and the restaurants.' He shrugged and paused. 'If not...'

Igor, the most diffident of the quartet, picked up the cue. 'Poverty is our biggest problem – if you are poor, it is really difficult to survive, it is a very hard time.... Yes, of course I am uncomfortable about this – look how much this country earns. The government should do much more to support the people. There is huge money and huge power. What is Putin for if he does nothing about that?' One of his colleagues butted in to tease him. 'But, Igor, you are very socialistic,' to which he responded, 'At least people should have a chance to work. If you kill them with bureaucracy and corruption, they can't.'

Ella half-concurred: 'Of course, it's all right for the young who have money. But the old and the orphans, of which we have huge numbers, suffer badly. You know, BBDO is involved with a charity and we are helping them with advertising. We found out that the government only spends 80 roubles a month per child. It's not even enough for breakfast. It's ridiculous and it's scary. Moscow is a rich city with a lot of rich people. Of course the government should do more. People always talk about the mystery of the Russian soul, and say that we are kind, but actually we had such a hard time for so long that all we ever thought about was our own survival. I think that the culture of sharing and helping is far more developed in the West than here. I saw someone have a heart attack in London, and lots of people came to help and one of them took off his jacket and placed it under the man's head. Here, if the same thing happens, people just walk past, saying, "Oh, another drunkard".'

'But,' Igor interjected, to a nod of general approval, 'the rich, a lot of them, are starting to take notice and to care.' It was a rudimentary analysis, a reminder to me that the very idea of obligation, let alone charity, that is embedded in Western culture is so novel in Russia that the brightest and best, as represented around this advertising agency's boardroom table, were grappling with an alien notion.

So how did these Westernizing Russians deal with the concept of corruption? I wondered. When BBDO set up its Moscow branch in 1994, corruption was already known to be universally endemic. The Russian mafia held terrifying sway; shoot-outs, murders and kidnappings were commonplace. But Ella was persuasively insistent that BBDO employees had never sought or offered bribes at any level; they did not need to do it, she said, and in any case it had been forbidden by head office. Was this unique? Not quite, apparently. 'IKEA also took the same stance.' Another of her colleagues, Ivan, chipped in, 'I was surprised that the mafia didn't move in on the advertising industry. They never controlled it. I remember one day in 1994, when I first joined. A couple of guys came in here and walked straight past reception and into the general manager's office and had a talk. After they left, Bruce – an American – came out red-faced and said, "We need security." The next day a couple of guards carrying pump-action shotguns were placed inside the entrance. A week or so later, the two visitors came again. When they saw the two guards they simply ran out. And we never saw them again. And we never had any more trouble.'

'Today,' Max insisted, 'we don't break any laws, we do everything by the book, we have a lot of lawyers and accountants to make sure that everything we do is above board and legal.' 'And we are still very profitable,' Ella continued. 'It can be done. Perhaps we don't earn as much as some people, perhaps we lose some business, but we are absolutely whiter than white. It's in our blood – and, in any case, we would have been fired by head office.' Ivan had recently been at a seminar for students hoping to go into business. 'There were other speakers there who were running their own companies. I mentioned that at BBDO we all paid our taxes and operated entirely legally. And they looked at me as if I was crazy, like "Why?" There was a German who ran a construction company – you know how they are always considered to do everything by the book? – and he described how it was going to cost him a hundred thousand euros to get legal planning permission. However, by bribing the right official he knew he could get it for ten thousand. It was, he said, obvious what he had to do. I was still quite shocked, but they looked at me as though I was crazy for doing things according to the law.'

And there was another factor that, according to Igor, was rooted deep in Russian history. 'Bribery and corruption have long been a way of getting and keeping power at every level. If you have an official post in the bureaucracy, you have power, and you can use that power to get rich as well and therefore more powerful. That is how it was, and that is how it is.' 'And don't forget,' Ella added, 'salaries are very low. The policeman on the street needs the money.' Max disagreed. 'It's a state of mind. Everyone always convinces themselves they don't have enough money. The billionaires in this country still convince themselves they need more money, so they steal. Corruption is on every level – it's still embedded in this society.'

'I have a friend,' said Ivan, 'who knows that his employees are stealing from him. He does not pay them very much, but he knows they will only steal a certain amount otherwise it would become too obvious, too visible. And he is happy about this because, he says, "They know that I know they are stealing, and they are afraid of me. So I can control them. I can do what I want with them." It is the same at every level. Look at the oil companies. Everyone knew they did not pay taxes. But they were controlled because at any moment they could be arrested and removed from the scene. Corruption is a means of political and social control.' And it goes from top to bottom, from the Kremlin outwards and downwards? Every head nodded in assent. 'Yes, yeah, sure.'

(Later I told another senior advertising executive about BBDO's impressive 'cleaner than clean' stance, and he gave me an old-fashioned look. 'It may be true,' he said, 'but, if so, this company is a remarkable exception to the rule. Of course, the shareholders of any reputable international company expect everything to be above board. But I find it hard to believe that this is possible in Russia, where you can hardly get anything done without bribing your way through the system. For this reason – to my certain knowledge – it is commonplace for foreign businesses to set up an arm's-length local company to do the dirty work for them so that it doesn't show in their books.')

Ella and her colleagues were so engagingly forthcoming that I asked them about their personal behaviour. Had not one of these upright and honourable executives ever offered a bribe? To an official? A bureaucrat? A policeman? Not once? As I teased, they looked at one another gauging how to respond. Would there be collective resistance or a collective breakdown? They opted for the latter, and with a great deal of confessional mirth. Ella weighed in first. 'Oh, a driving licence. Yes, you can still buy them here.' So had all of them acquired theirs by legal means? Max evaded the question, saying that he had an American licence. Igor confessed that he had bought his. Ivan's father had given him his as an eighteenth-birthday present. And Ella? Did she buy hers? She giggled. 'I didn't pass my test.' But she still drove? 'Yes, I do.' So did she have a licence? 'Well...' Ivan stepped in gallantly to her rescue. 'You went to the authorities and you just smiled at them and they gave it to you.' 'Yeah,' said Ella, entirely without shame. Not exactly the Wild West, but a very different culture even among the most European of Russia's sophisticates.

The BBDO team played me a video presentation designed to show that Russia is now a secure haven for investors. Putin was portrayed at a G8 summit, standing alongside George W. Bush – not so much, they explained, to demonstrate that he was a world statesman as, subliminally, to draw a contrast between the new President and his predecessor, a national embarrassment called Boris Yeltsin. Putin by contrast, Max explained, 'is very far from being a buffoon'. 'In Yeltsin's time,' Igor added, 'there was no order. It was crazy – we had Wild West capitalism. Now we are stepping back to become a more controlled country.' And he added his urbane voice to those I had heard in St Petersburg. 'You can't have democracy in a kindergarten. Of course Russia is not a democratic country. The people are not involved, they have no power, they have no access – and they don't want any of it either.' As I listened to these earnest voices, I noted in my diary that the gloating gauntlet laid down by the West before the fledgling Russian Federation – 'Democratize now or die' – was an absurd demand that had done great and possibly irreparable harm to Russia's prospects of transforming itself from a dictatorship into a genuinely open and democratic state. How, I wondered aloud, could any serious Western politician with even a modicum of historical awareness of Europe's own slow trajectory towards parliamentary democracy have believed that a state as fractured and threatened as the new Russian Federation could jump straight from the Communist frying pan into the democratic fire without being badly, if not fatally, burnt?

## TOLSTOY AT HOME

My brain was still in Moscow, but after a few days in a noisy, dirty and aggressive capital my heart had already left for the country, where I hoped to find another Russia – whatever that elusive term might turn out to mean – as opposed to the 'real' Russia that is about you all the time. The brash new shopping malls and grand restaurants are the real Russia, as are the beggars and drunks who litter the streets until the police have moved them on or taken them to a drying-out hostel, where they are required to endure the cold-turkey treatment before they are tipped out again to continue where they left off. Moscow's stations too are the real Russia. As I waited for the train, I looked at the endless flow of people – men and women, young and old – on their way into the capital that sucks them in and spews them out at an almost equal rate. They do not hurry as commuters at a London station, but tread with stolid certainty, carrying bags and cases, resigned but purposeful. For the most part they are plainly dressed in clothes that advertise their poverty and their indifference to appearance. The faces, young and old, do not look healthy, and they lack energy. The young, afflicted by acne and scarred by fights, are suspicious and feral in demeanour. The old, disfigured by a life of labours, are bowed or limping and do not look about them – incuriosity seems to have seized their souls and fatalism shrouds them.

I was heading to the industrial town of Tula, about 125 miles from Moscow, on a train going to the very south of the country. My carriage was packed with long-distance travellers settling in for the journey. They sat on narrow bunks tiered along the carriage, offering just enough space but no privacy. They had already placed bags of food – bread and canned meat predominating – on the small tables that jutted out from under each window. And, some, but by no means all, had started on the vodka and beer. There was a warm smell of bodies. My berth was across the aisle from two young men who turned out to be brothers. The one on the upper bunk was already very drunk. His brother on the lower bunk offered me beer from his half-finished bottle. I accepted and began a ludicrous conversation.

'I going to Tula,' I said in pidgin English as he peered at my paperback, a dog-eared copy of *Anna Karenina*. I tried to explain its authorship. 'You know Tolstoy,' I said, as if the name itself would be enough, pointing at the paperback cover and repeating '*Anna Karenina* ... Great man, great writer.' He nodded but looked blank. I pointed once more at the book and gave it the thumbs up, hoping that my gesture did not send a different cultural message from the one I had intended. He smiled, this time more sagely, and offered me his beer again. To keep the conversation alive, and in the vague hope that he might have heard of the master's famous estate, I added that I was on my way to Yasnaya Polyana, where he wrote both *Anna Karenina* and *War and Peace*. My new friend was uncomprehending, but my hand gesture was clearly in order as he interpreted another thumbs up from me as praise for his beer and I had to have another swig. Our amity thus licensed, he talked away and (now with an interpreter at hand) I understood that he had 'a London sister' whose name was Lena. I summoned interpreting support and went on to discover that he was a migrant labourer on his way home to the Ukraine with his brother (who insisted on waving a drunken arm in front of our faces as if seeking permission to speak, though he was too far gone even to string words together that his sibling could comprehend) after a season of work in Moscow. It would be a twenty-four-hour journey, and he assured me that he intended to drink himself as silly as his brother before he arrived.

Pyotr was a fireman by trade, but he had been in Moscow, like many of his compatriots, working on a building site. These migrants are paid dismally (there is no minimum wage in capitalist Russia) and they live in barracks – in his case, he said, in a dormitory that was teeming with cockroaches. 'Quite normal,' he assured me, as if it genuinely didn't worry him very much. He described the Russian capital as an exciting city with 'lots to do and lots to see, especially the amusement parks and firing ranges'. He told me that he loved karaoke. We then ran out of conversation: too big a gulf of culture and taste and experience and, in any case, too much beer as well. We shook hands amiably, he went to sleep and I returned to *Anna Karenina*.

Levin, the real hero of *Anna Karenina*, has always been my favourite character in all literature: an aristocrat who takes nothing in his life for granted, a landowner who cares for his staff and is passionately committed to agriculture, a radical thinker, a romantic lover, a loving father and yet an outsider, a piece of grit in society's oyster. Of course, Tolstoy's Levin is very like Tolstoy's Tolstoy. And Levin's estate is Tolstoy's Yasnaya Polyana by any other name, where the author lived for most of his long life.

Yasnaya Polyana turned out to be just as I had hoped it would. I entered through modest gates and walked up a long drive towards the house, past a lake on the left and a flower garden on the right. Beyond the lake there was an orchard. In the low evening sun the dark green apples, not yet ripe, were etched against paler leaves, dappled and dancing in a light breeze. There was a scatter of beehives, faded blue by the weather. Two ponies were tethered in the shade of the trees. A labrador was teasing an indifferent cat. All it needed was for a long-haired, bearded man wearing a white smock, on a handsome white horse – Tolstoy on his rounds – to appear round a bend in the farm track that led away towards distant fields to re-create almost to perfection the Yasnaya Polyana of a century ago.

By the standards of his peers, Count Leo Tolstoy lived frugally. His house, which inside and out has been preserved much as it was when he died, is relatively modest – more pavilion than mansion. Only two storeys high, it is painted white and has a blue-grey leaded roof. The south-facing façade is unadorned save for a narrow balcony that looks down over a flower-bed that could have been transplanted from an English cottage garden. Beyond the border a dishevelled lawn disappears informally into a wood of oaks and maples. The simplicity of it all is striking, and the spirit of place is so powerful that I wanted to speak in a whisper as though not to disturb the old man at rest.

Of course, Tolstoy was not always the grandfatherly figure, the revered genius that turn-of-the-twentieth-century writings and photographs depict. Born in 1828 in an upstairs room of what had then been a mansion with forty-eight rooms, he grew to love Yasnaya Polyana with a deep and lasting passion. This love affair did not, however, exclude a youthful interlude during which he might be judged to have gone off the rails – though his rakishness was by no means exceptional among the aristocracy of his day. At university his teachers reported in despair that he was 'both unable and unwilling to learn'. In Moscow and St Petersburg he acquired a well-earned reputation for profligacy and licentiousness. Most alarmingly, like Dostoevsky before him, he became addicted to gambling. So acute was this affliction that in 1855, while serving at the front in the Crimean War, he lost his entire fortune to a fellow officer playing cards. To meet his debts, he was forced to sell his beloved home (to a fellow nobleman who lived near by and carted it off stone by stone, leaving only an annexe of the mansion) and eleven villages. Tolstoy was mortified, writing, 'I'm so disgusted with myself that I'd like to forget about my existence.' However, he soon recovered his zest for life, and, great soul that he was, settled into the annexe, where he lived in a tempestuous marriage that survived to produce no fewer than thirteen children. He planted a stand of birch trees over the ruins of the mansion, where one foundation stone is all that now remains of its former grandeur. It is said that when his grandchildren asked him where he had been born he would point up to the lower branches of one of these trees and say, 'Just there'.

I walked around the estate in something of a trance, guided by a young farm worker, Igor, and his colleague Sasha. Igor lived in a cramped flat in Tula, the grubby industrial town 10 miles away, where he had been born some thirty years ago. When he was a small boy he used to come on frequent excursions to Yasnaya Polyana with his father, and on more formal pilgrimages with his kindergarten (Tolstoy, the anti-state pacifist, had been posthumously resurrected as a hero of the Soviet people, and the estate, which had been requisitioned after the revolution, opened to the public). Igor got to know its fields, its woods and its secret, magical crannies. He was soon bewitched. Tall, intelligent, educated and articulate, Igor had the manner of a teacher, which, like his wife, he could easily have made his calling. Instead, almost reverentially, he laboured on the estate for the grand sum of £25 a week. 'Once you come here,' he said, 'there is no way back. I am a worker, simply a worker,' and added, without any archness, 'I am in the tradition of Tolstoy. My work is physical, and that is what Tolstoy admired – the physical labour with which the peasants feed everyone.'

He seemed almost as entranced as I was by the sense of Tolstoy's immanent presence. He took me to a meadow close by a river. 'In the evening,' he said, 'there is always a mist here and...I do not know whether it is Tolstoy, but you can feel the spirit. It is a disconcerting experience.' The meadow was uneven and parts of it are still mown by scythe, the hay being fed to the horses or given to local peasants for their cattle. I wandered through the grass, quoting aloud for my own delight from one of the most glorious passages in *Anna Karenina*, when Levin tries his hand at haymaking. He watches the peasants – his serfs, the Igors of a century ago – as they cut swathe after swathe of rich meadow grass, wielding their sharpened scythes with rhythmic precision and minimum effort, and then he picks up a scythe for himself and settles alongside them, trying to emulate their easy progress. It is much harder than he had imagined and he quickly falls behind. But, bathed in sweat and aching from the effort, he refuses to contemplate failure. In an extraordinarily detailed and gripping description of Levin's efforts, Tolstoy elevates his eventual triumph at what is superficially a mundane task into a sublime experience: 'The longer Levin mowed, the oftener he experienced those moments of oblivion when it was not his arms that swung the scythe but the scythe seemed to mow of itself, a body full of life and consciousness of its own, and as though by magic, without a thought being given to it, the work did itself regularly and carefully. These were the most blessed moments.' I have always found that last sentence, those six words in that context, to be among the most poignantly beautiful in all Tolstoy's glorious prose, and as I savoured them again in the same meadow that – I like to think – inspired them, I gasped with an intoxication of delight; a moment, so rare for me so far on this journey through Russia, of unequivocal and utter bliss.

Of course Tolstoy himself, like his fictional hero, was the master of all he surveyed. If he fell for a peasant girl, he could exercise his *droit de seigneur* (and he did – frequently); if he wanted to spend time at aristocratic soirées in Moscow or St Petersburg, he was free to do so; if he wanted to play at harvesting, he merely had to pick up a scythe (and, unlike his serfs, cast it aside again). So arid spirits might scoff at Levin's moment of transcendental truth in the hay meadow – though to do so would be to elevate philistinism to an art form. But if it is impossible to scoff at Tolstoy, it is quite valid to mock a pilgrim like me, a one-time and part-time farmer who liked to indulge Levin's own romance. My own farm, in Somerset, was not on the scale of Yasnaya Polyana but, long before I was able to buy it, I used to fantasize myself into Levin's boots and, in my case, it was an indulgence eventually allowed to me by the earnings from my principal trade in broadcasting and books.

I am easily rapt when I watch cows grazing, and I delight in the slurp as they wrap roughened tongues around tufts of grass. When a herd lies in a semi-circle, a conclave of ruminants, regurgitating the wet strands of nutrient from stomach to mouth and back to stomach again – chewing the cud – I allow myself the indulgence that they are 'contented', and, as if by osmosis, I experience that emotion myself. When a ewe strains in labour until the lamb's head finally appears, smeared in mucus and blood, and slithers suddenly on to the straw, and the mother rises at once to lick clean the nostrils and the mouth of her offspring, clearing away the detritus of her own afterbirth, nudging, nuzzling and nickering, until the frail, wet creature shudders into life, I never lose the sense of wonder at that long, tremulous moment until the lamb takes breath and struggles towards the mother's teat. But I like to think that the sentiment is not false. If I delight as a suckling lamb twitches its tail with pleasure, I have also delivered the rotting carcass of a dead lamb from the putrid womb of a dying ewe. If I wonder at the new-born calf, half-buried in straw, steam rising from its flanks as its dam rasps at its wet head, warming and drying with her tongue, I do not forget that the new-born creature is destined for the slaughterhouse, for a moment of final terror before it is hung, drawn and quartered for human consumption. Farming is about life and death, beginnings and endings.

I am aware that it might seem absurd, but as I grapple to understand the emotions that a ripe cornfield or a herd of cows or even a tractor on the skyline provoke in me, I can find no better – or more honest – term than 'love'. Of course, it is not that intensity of feeling that one human being may have for another in the first flush of passion, or later when the fear of loss and the promise of grief over-shadow every shared moment. You do not love a place on the map in the same way that you love a person – or, rather, if you think you do, you are either deficient or deluded. But if you have ever caught your breath at the natural world, if you have ached to be by a favourite stream or meadow, or grieved at the violation of a forest or copse to make way for an airport or housing estate or bypass, if your heart soars when you see a hawk hovering or a skylark on the wing, if the bark of a fox or scream of an owl stops you in your tracks, if you are mesmer-ized by a hoar frost or falling snow, if the moan of a high wind or the muttering from a thunder cloud fills you with awe, then you will understand that the term 'love' in relation to rural England is not as ludicrous as it might at first appear. So, though I do not possess a minute fraction of his genius, I have the temerity to recognize in Tolstoy a kindred spirit, but one blessed with a unique ability both to explore far more profoundly and to express far more vividly than the rest of us can ever hope to emulate those imprecise emotions and longings that the natural world – ordered by hard labour and good husbandry – still arouse in all but the benumbed and benighted. Anyway, I felt at home in Yasnaya Polyana.

Tolstoy's pioneering and revolutionary decision to liberate his own peasants from their chains, which predated the abolition of serfdom in 1861 by two years, combined rare moral sensibility with a romantic vision of the Russian peasantry. The peasants, he wrote, are 'closer to God than we are. They lead moral working lives and their simple wisdom is in many ways superior to all the artifices of our culture and philosophy.' To Tolstoy's fury, Anton Chekhov, who was a doctor as well as a writer, offered a more prosaic and, as the grandson of a serf, perhaps more ironic perspective. In one of his short stories, where events and characters are seen through the eyes of the widow of a Moscow waiter who finds herself marooned in her late husband's village, Chekhov portrays the peasants as 'coarse, dishonest, filthy, drunk, always quarrelling and arguing among themselves, with no respect for one another and living in mutual fear and suspicion'. Tolstoy remonstrated that Chekhov had failed to look beyond the outward appearance into the soul, which he charged was 'a sin before the people'. Commenting on this contretemps between the two writers, Orlando Figes notes with characteristic pertinence in *Natasha's Dance* that 'early Marxists welcomed [Chekhov's shocking depiction] as evidence of exploitation by capitalist classes, and reactionaries also welcomed it because it painted peasants in what they liked to believe were their true colours'. Chekhov was, in truth, not nearly as insensitive as the above extract might suggest. In the same passage his protagonist goes on to note that the peasants 'were still human beings, suffering and weeping like other people, and there was nothing in their lives which did not provide some excuse'. And, as late as 1897, Chekhov empathetically helped collect statistics that offer eloquent testimony to the suffering of the peasantry in tsarist Russia. Only just outside Moscow's city boundary, he was shocked to discover villages in which infant mortality stood at 60 per cent: six out of ten new lives eliminated by poverty before their first birthday.

In *Anna Karenina* Levin tries to translate his own romance with the peasantry into a programme of radical reform. Recognizing that 'the sort of farming he was carrying on was nothing but a cruel and stubborn struggle between him and the labourers', Levin resolves to 'exchange the onerous, idle, artificial, and selfish existence he was leading for that busy, honourable, delightful life of common toil'. Not only would he work alongside his staff, he would introduce profit-sharing as well. He devours the latest European writings on political economy both to inform his own treatise on the salvation of Russian agriculture and, more directly, to help him put his own theories into practice. Tolstoy's unique ability to weave an epic narrative while laying bare the individual souls of his characters transforms the passages in which he explores his vision from the merely didactic and polemical into a personal drama played out on a global canvas. Of course, Levin is ridiculed by his fellow landowners, a boorish gang who not only distrust but fear the consequences of his quasi-anarchist experiment. 'The Russian worker,' one of them declares, 'understands one thing only – how to drink like a hog, and when he is drunk he ruins everything you put in his hands. He will water your horses to death, spoil good harness, barter the tyres off your wheels for a drink, drop a bolt into the thrashing machine so as to break it. He loathes the sight of anything that's not done after his fashion.' Another unburdens himself of the opinion that 'the Russian peasant is a swine and likes swinishness, and that to get him out of his swinishness one must have authority, and [after the 1861 reforms] there is none; one must have the stick, and we have become so liberal that we have all of a sudden replaced the stick that served us for a thousand years.'

Levin is not deterred even when he discovers that, left to their own devices, the freed serfs do bear some resemblance to the contemptuous caricatures of his peers. Intoxicated by his vision of the future, Levin allows himself to imagine a new world order: 'In the place of poverty we must have universal prosperity and contentment; instead of hostility – harmony and unity of interests. In short a bloodless revolution, but a mighty revolution, beginning in the little circle of our district, then reaching the province, Russia, the whole world!'

In the 'real' world of Yasnaya Polyana, Tolstoy summarily sacked his estate foremen and started to run the farm by himself. It was a disaster. Bullying his wife, Sofya, into joining his experiment, he divided up the chores between them. Sofya was to supervise the house, the estate office, the barns, the cattle and the hired labour. She loathed the filth of the farmyard and, as A.N. Wilson observes in his masterly biography *Tolstoy*, 'her efficiency in these areas was not without heroism'. Despite the obedience instilled into young women of her class, the Countess baulked at feeding the pigs. So Tolstoy, who had happily but haplessly taken responsibility for supervising the crops, the forests, the vegetable garden and the beehives, was obliged to take on that task as well. Sacking his swineherd for being drunk, he took sole charge of the piggeries but, like his wife, he soon came to hate the new responsibility with which he had so precipitously saddled himself. So, with a baffling disregard for the welfare of his stock, he deliberately allowed them to die of starvation, even noting with a detachment that is as bizarre as it is cruel, 'I would give the hogs as little food as possible to make them weak. It worked! If the next time I saw them, they were still squeaking, I gave them just a little food. Whenever they became quiet, I knew the end had come.'

Today Yasnaya Polyana is owned by the state but run as an almost self-financing charitable enterprise by the great man's great-great-grandson, Count Vladimir Tolstoy. I liked him at once. He was in his mid-forties with a retreating thatch of straw-coloured hair and an open, ruddy face that knew the outdoors as well as the office desk. He smiled frequently, as well he might, I suppose, given that his reply to my first question about Yasnaya Polyana – 'Does it mean anything more for you than a memorial oasis?' – was 'I love this place. I am one of the happiest men on earth.'

Vladimir is as romantic about Yasnaya Polyana as his great forebear. The land is cultivated with a close regard for the ecology of the whole estate, though not quite on organic lines. I suggested to Vladimir that he should persuade the Prince of Wales to pay a visit as I knew they would have much in common. He was taken aback, slightly awed at the prospect. 'Do you really think he would do that? Prince Charles? Really?' Vladimir was mild in manner but spoke with resolve. 'I would like Yasnaya Polyana to be a symbol of the new Russia, peaceful and full of love. That is my challenge. I have no plans ever to leave here. I want to spread the message. From here, this village, to the district around, maybe to Russia, the whole of Russia. That is my dream. I am an optimist, yes. I am a romantic.'

Vladimir had four children and he was proud of the fact that two of them, Andrey and Ivan, like their great-great-great-grandfather, were born at Yasnaya Polyana. Almost every member of Tolstoy's large family fled Russia after the revolution, and it was not until 1945 that Vladimir's grandfather felt safe enough to return to his homeland –

though not to Yasnaya Polyana, which by then had become a public shrine. But with the collapse of the Soviet Union Vladimir now has a relatively free hand to resurrect the spirit of Tolstoy, though he is constrained by a shortage of funds. Undeterred, he has used his own resources to help to re-establish a kindergarten in the village; it is run by his wife on the guiding principles of his great-great-grandfather, but adapted for the twenty-first century. As part of his vision for a new Russia, Leo Tolstoy had opened a school at Yasnaya Polyana, which he personally oversaw and where the children of the estate were taught for free. He was proud of his own teaching methods, which appeared to have owed much to Socrates and to have mirrored the principles adopted later by radical reformers like A.S. Neill, Rudolf Steiner and Maria Montessori. 'One cannot describe these children,' Tolstoy wrote over a hundred years ago. 'I have never seen the like of them among the children of our own dear rank.... No laziness, no rudeness, no stupid jokes, or distasteful words.' The Minister of Education deplored his methods, which, he reported, were 'spreading ideas which are not only false but dangerously biased'. However, because the state recognized that the famous author was 'above all criminal intention or dishonesty', the government concluded that it was impossible to bring a case against him. His great-great-grandson noted wryly that his wife's teaching methods aroused much the same suspicion in today's educational establishment.

Tolstoy is buried in a glade on the estate under a simple mound of earth covered with turf. I tiptoed towards this hallowed ground, not wanting to disturb the solitude of an evening that was broken only by the crackle of a twig, the flutter of a bird and the rustle of the wind. I stood, more moved by the moment than I had imagined, thinking of the day that he was buried here in 1910. His last hours had been as dramatic and tragic as any that he had devised for his novels.

After almost half a century his marriage to Sofya, which had been cruelly blessed with an early intensity of passion that had enshrined love and hatred in perpetual combat, had by now collapsed into misery and recrimination. Sofya's compulsively painful diaries reveal her to have had a manically depressive, if not disordered, personality, conditions that had been aggravated severely because in old age he had finally rejected her entirely. Her mental state had led into ever more extreme demands and outbursts against him, and he grew colder and colder towards her in consequence. He was, in any case, in retreat from the material world. He had spent the last thirty years of his life in an attempt to live in the sight of God as an ascetic. He had rejected the Orthodox Church and, for his apostasy, had been excommunicated by the Patriarch. He had given up alcohol, meat and tobacco, and even taken to making his own shoes. His religious, political and social iconoclasm had bestowed on him the dubious benefit of ever greater adulation. The more attention he attracted, the more he felt the need to escape into an inner world of contemplation, to wrestle intellectually and spiritually with the ultimate but unanswerable questions of life. But with Sofya in the house, her mood swings ever more unpredictable, this became increasingly difficult to achieve. Her presence, the very sight of her, had started to become intolerable to him. His beloved Yasnaya Polyana, the seat of this unhappiness, now also became unbearable; a prison in which he and Sofya, their love extinguished, had been reduced to that state of permanent warfare that is acknowledged to be a form of living death. He longed both to get away from his wife and to become closer to God.

Early in the morning of 28 October 1910, while Sofya still slept, Tolstoy left the house apparently bound for the Optina Pustyn monastery at Kozelsk, not far from Moscow; his sister, Marya, lived there as a nun at the adjoining convent of Shamardino. The monastery was (and is) a well-spring of Orthodox spirituality. Although Tolstoy had long since rejected the doctrines of the Church – as a young man he had in a moment of ecstasy imagined founding a new religion, 'the religion of Christ but purged of beliefs and mysticism' – the monks at Optina Pustyn did not hesitate to allow the frail old master to rest for the night. After a final meeting with his sister, he left the following

morning, accompanied by his physician, and, with no apparent destination in mind, boarded a train heading south. By now half the world
had heard of his flight from Yasnaya Polyana and, as the reclusive
master made no attempt to disguise his identity, his fellow passengers
recognized him at once and crowded reverently about him. At the
next station, Astapovo, his doctor insisted that Tolstoy disembark
because he was too ill to continue. Weak and shivering with the onset
of a fever, he was taken to the stationmaster's house. The news was
out: Tolstoy was sick. Sensing that the great man was on his deathbed,
journalists, photographers and a cameraman from Pathé News hurried
to Astapovo to record the great man's final hours.

Characteristically, Sofya herself arrived in style, making a grand
entrance in a special train that she had ordered for herself and her
entourage. On discovering that Tolstoy had left Yasnaya Polyana, she
had reacted by rushing from the house declaring, 'I am going to kill
myself', before jumping into a pond that she knew to be only waist-
deep. When Tolstoy was told about this 'drowning' episode, he wrote
coldly, 'Let her know I desire only one thing – freedom from her.'
Partly for this reason, Sofya was not allowed at first to join her husband
at his deathbed in the stationmaster's house. Frantic and apparently
grief-stricken, she paced up and down along the platform, in full sight
of the assembled media, railing against this final outrage. A while later,
Tolstoy, who had not been told of her arrival, roused himself from the
delirium into which he had slumped to ask: 'What is she doing? How
does she feel? Isn't she going to come here?' Eventually she was permitted to enter the room in which he lay dying. But by this time Tolstoy
was beyond reach. She knelt at his bed whispering, 'Forgive me, forgive
me.' Soon afterwards, early in the morning of 7 November, at the age
of eighty-two, Russia's greatest writer drifted quietly into death.

The news provoked an outpouring of grief. There were demonstrations in towns and cities across Russia, confirming that his political
tracts, of which he had written hundreds, had rekindled a latent ardour
for change. In a 1900 essay entitled 'On Anarchy', he had written,

The Anarchists are right in everything; in the negation of the existing order, and in the assertion that, without Authority, there could
not be worse violence than that of Authority under existing conditions. They are mistaken only in thinking that Anarchy can be
instituted by a revolution. But it will be instituted only by there
being more and more people who do not require the protection of
governmental power.... There can only be one permanent revolution – a moral one: the regeneration of the inner man.

For expressing opinions like this any other individual would have been
arrested, but Tolstoy was untouchable; wherever he went he attracted
greater crowds than the tsar. And while his political credo was totally
at odds with the neo-Marxism of the Bolsheviks (which did not stop
them co-opting him – posthumously – to their revolutionary cause a
few years later), it touched a deep chord in the Russian psyche.

Two days after his death, students at St Petersburg University met
to hear a memorial oration from one of their professors. One of those
present recorded the gist of what he said in her diary: 'Tolstoy had
stood alone against the entire established order. He had not crushed
this established order but neither was he crushed by it. Tolstoy had
been open and frank in declaring that he had contempt or scorn for
this or that. Yet those who would never have forgiven such an affront
from anyone else made a pilgrimage to Tolstoy's place.' His words,
placing Tolstoy in a pantheon alongside Martin Luther and Jean-
Jacques Rousseau, so stirred the audience that, according to the
diarist, it remained quite silent when he had finished speaking. This
dangerous reverence for Tolstoy's memory drove the police to break
up other such gatherings, and a detachment of Cossack horsemen –
'shameless, cynical, swearing...whips hissing' – charged into a huge
crowd of students as they left the Armenian church at the end of a
memorial service in Tolstoy's honour. If these repressive measures
were supposed to quench the flame of revolution, they were singularly
unsuccessful: the student diarist, torn between grief and exhilaration,

noted, 'These are days of life and passion, days of anxiety, days on fire, brimming over with thrilling events.'

On the same day Tolstoy's open coffin was taken back to Yasnaya Polyana, borne aloft by his sons and accompanied by a crowd of several thousand mourners. The Church authorities, adamant that his excommunicated soul was now burning in hell, had refused permission for an Orthodox funeral. Any observance by the mourners of the formal rites of burial was therefore a breach of the law. Nonetheless, as his body was placed in the unhallowed ground in the glade that he had selected for his final resting-place, the crowd defied the priesthood and the attendant police officers by chanting traditional Russian funeral hymns. At one point a mourner raised his voice to urge, 'Take off your hats, get down on your knees; take off your hats, get down on your knees.' And the crowd obeyed. Only the police remained standing – until, one by one, they too removed their hats and fell to their knees.

Yasnaya Polyana is still a shrine. I watched a procession of newly-weds, the brides dressed in white chiffon, their scrubbed young husbands in sharp suits and tight shoes, shimmering in the sun as they processed up the long drive towards the house, where they waited in a queue to have their marriage preserved for posterity by a photographer beneath the window of Tolstoy's study. I had by now seen the same ceremony at various Eternal Flames, by statues of Unknown Warriors and under the famous sculpture of Peter the Great in St Petersburg. Somehow this immortalization of these marriages at Yasnaya Polyana was more touching than any I had yet witnessed.

I left Yasnaya Polyana reluctantly. For the first time on my journey I wanted to stay rather than press on; for the first time I felt at ease – almost at home. In part, I know, it was because the estate and the landscape in which it rested had the timeless feel of its English counterpart. But it was more than that. The spirit of Tolstoy is pervasive, his home and estate a shrine not only to his monumental vision and his towering genius, but also to his profound humanity. Yasnaya Polyana belongs to a long historical narrative that has not yet reached its nemesis; it is filled with hope.

This atmosphere, temporarily at least, lifted from my shoulders my perpetual travelling companion, a debilitating dead weight of gloom, a sense of foreboding that makes you want to hide your head under the covers when you wake up in the morning, that drives you to your diary to count how many days, hours, before you will be on the way back home, the mood you have to conceal from those you meet – and, if you are in my trade, from those who may be watching and (I like to believe) listening closely to what you have to say and what you feel. Is this bad faith? I sometimes wonder. Am I deceiving my audience by concealing this angst? I hope not. I hope that the two selves, the one that says, 'Stay out of the limelight or away from the camera at least' and the other that counters, 'This is how I define myself – through work, in presenting, reporting and writing' (and feels the chill when the limelight is switched off), can coexist without being in total contradiction; the private self and public self in tandem, and occasionally even in partnership.

## INDIFFERENCE AND CRUELTY: A RUSSIAN TRAGEDY

We headed on south towards the Black Sea and the Caucasus, travelling to the city of Voronezh in the heart of what is called the Black Earth country – the richest farmland in Russia, indeed in the entire continent. The journey lasted eight hours in a minibus. Before I left for Russia on this leg of the journey, the BBC had provided me with a briefing at which an ex-SAS medical orderly had insisted that the greatest risk to our lives would be not from brigands or terrorists but on the main roads of Russia. He went on to describe the lurid consequences of a head-on collision, when, he advised, heads could be severed and hurled around the inside of the vehicle like clothes in a washing machine. It was, he said, imperative to wear a seat-belt. I

dutifully searched for mine in the minibus. It did not exist. Our security consultant in London had forgotten to add that most Russian
cars do not possess such safety items, that, if they do, they usually
don't work, and that, in any case, it is *de rigueur* not to wear them:
seat-belts are for wimps. But he was right about the mortal threat
posed by Russian roads. I have driven in more than eighty countries
in four continents and in none have I felt so insecure as in Russia.
Russian drivers, however, clearly regard the danger as life-enhancing,
inspired as they must be by an inverted motto: 'Die today because
tomorrow you might live.' Fatalism again. Anyway, without the seat-
belts I spent most of the journey secretly and silently trying to
navigate our car away from one or another close encounter of a final
kind; otherwise I dozed – my mouth open, my head lolling, my body
rolling across a hard seat, my mind wandering and wondering why I
wasn't somewhere else.

We reached Voronezh and – for once – found our hotel without
difficulty. At the bar, where I ordered a large vodka, I was accosted by
a burly man in his thirties with tattoos on his knuckles, who gestured
for me to join him on the plastic sofa. He was with a very young
woman whom I imagined to be his little sister, but turned out to be
his eighteen-year-old girlfriend. He had studied at Bath University,
had been to London no fewer than – he was precise about this –
sixteen times and regarded himself as something of an Anglophile. He
clearly had a lot of money and liked to spend it. Only too happy to
boast of his financial success as a car dealer, or rather as the son of a
car dealer, he quickly left me with the impression that his father was
the brains and he was the brawn of the business. Sales were doing well:
150 Renaults a month and a growing number of Range Rovers. I have
a peculiar aversion to these gas-guzzlers after being too close to them
at too many nasty moments in war zones, when they have been packed
with gun-toting militiamen guarding dodgy local leaders. I have therefore always enjoyed the riddle: 'How can you tell the difference
between a hedgehog and a Range Rover?' Answer: 'With the Range

Rover the pricks are on the inside.' But my host would not have appreciated the slur, so I just listened admiringly to his tale.

Once he had brought me up to date on the motor trade in Voronezh, my car dealer invited me to go clubbing with him and his girlfriend. I declined, explaining that I was tired after a long journey and that I had an early start in the morning. He persisted. I insisted. Not for the first time in Russia I realized that he interpreted my polite rejection as a personal insult, a repudiation of him and all that he might represent (which, in truth, I suppose it was). When he saw that I would not succumb, he swallowed his beer, lifted his bulk from the sofa and, with his girlfriend trotting behind, stalked out of the hotel without another word, to heave his bulk into the very latest, most expensive Range Rover on the market, black-tinted windows and all. I had a sudden image of him transplanted to the Lebanon in battle fatigues with a Kalashnikov in that murderous civil war where playboys killed for the fun of it. I wondered whether his own new-found wealth derived from – how should I put it – the tactical assertiveness of his father in the anarchy of the early nineties, when cities like Voronezh were run by mobsters.

I had better luck at dinner. At the next-door table four young women were in animated conversation and, judging from their gestures, clearly talking about clothes, make-up, hairstyles and men. They were as assured as, but less flashy and somehow more individualistic in style and manner than, the women who grace the coffee shops and restaurants in Moscow, and who seem to have been pressed out of an identically elegant, voguish mould. One of the four, who was dressed alluringly in tight black jeans and long boots, turned around and, in perfect English and with great poise, asked very directly where I came from and why I was there. Then she rattled off her own story. She worked for a tobacco company, earned $2000 a month, owned a Mercedes and had a small flat in a good part of town. But, she said, 'I have a problem. I am twenty-eight years old and I want to get married, but I can't find the right man.' For a moment I thought this piece of information was intended as a proposition, but I swiftly realized from her demeanour that it was simply a statement of fact. I murmured words to the effect that she should not worry, that she was a very attractive woman (which she was) and that the right man would assuredly come along in due course. She was unconvinced and countered, 'My friends, who are married, tell me that it is almost too late.' She then told that me that she had a boyfriend, but unfortunately he lived and worked in Holland. She pre-empted my next question by explaining, 'I can't go and live with him because I must stay here to look after my parents.'

One of the wonders of casual conversation is that a simple aside like that can unexpectedly lead on to illuminate dark recesses, in this case one of the realities of post-Soviet Russia that I had read about, but only in general and statistical terms. 'My father, who is a photographer by profession, is very ill and out of work. My mother, who was a teacher, is also unwell. He has no social security and she has only a tiny pension. They are very poor and very frightened about the future. Of course I will look after them. But this means I can't travel or even leave Voronezh for more than a few days at a time.' As it happened, she had just returned from Moscow and was shocked by what she had seen. 'It is unbelievable how rich people are there. How is it that they can spend so much on just one meal, and yet they do nothing for the poor in the villages who are hungry and have nothing?'

It was the first time I had heard anything like that in Russia – not self-regarding resentment at inequity but moral outrage at the injustice of it. So did she think things would improve? 'I am very worried about the future. I have no hope, no optimism. I think many people are going to suffer.' And what about Putin? 'Things have got a bit better since he came in. He has made other countries respect Russia. Until he took charge, people thought that Russia was just a country of drunks. Now there is respect for us.' And then I asked the Democracy question, by now expecting the answer that she duly delivered: 'Democracy is not right for Russia. We don't need it. If we had it in the European way, it would not work. We need strength.' Yet again, I persevere. What about freedom? 'But I am free. I can say what I like to you.' So did she feel free to say what she wanted about Chechnya? 'What about Chechnya? None of us thinks Chechnya matters. Why do we want Chechnya? Why do we need Chechnya? We have oil enough. If they want to be separate, then let them be. Why are we there? It is a mistake.'

She had made her point; she can indeed say what she wants about the most sensitive political issue in Russia. It was useless for me to bang on, suggesting that she was only free because she was powerless, because there was no democratic structure within which her voice – and those of the millions of fathers, mothers, sons and daughters across Russia who may hold similar views – can even be reflected in parliament or on radio or television; useless for me to say that she could be ignored in a state where the media that matter were obedient to the Kremlin and therefore filtered out all opposing views; useless for me to say that the poverty endured by her parents would persist until concepts like justice and fairness were defined in healthy debate in a democratic forum, where competing parties genuinely vied for election, rather than in the mockery of a parliament that is the Duma; useless for me to say that she was right to be pessimistic about the future but wrong to believe that democracy would make it worse. Instead, we shared a bottle of wine, after which she retreated to her flat, a good woman in a troubled state, and I went to bed to lie awake, dreading the next day.

I have always loathed flying. Once, before it seemed too coy, my *Who's Who* entry contained the phrase, under 'recreations' (which also included tennis, riding and opera), 'postponing departures by air'. My attitude has not changed, except that once I am in the air, knowing once again the plane will indeed crash, I like to think I am a touch more fatalistic than I was – though nowadays, to numb the apprehension, I consume even more vodkas disguised as tomato juice before take-off. The combination of this phobia and a deepening aversion to the worsening misery of modern airports has made it easy for me, when asked, to pledge publicly that – to reduce my carbon footprint of course – I would never again fly for pleasure. On this occasion – business not pleasure – I was in a premature sweat because the following day I was due to fly in an elderly bi-plane in order to survey the Black Earth Country from the air. I had been persuaded that it was by far the best way to appreciate the vast extent of this precious soil, covering, as it does, hundreds of thousands of square miles, Russia's grain basket.

The weather in the morning was clear, so I had no excuse to postpone the flight. I was extremely grumpy. However, the pilot, who reminded me of Douglas Bader but with legs, had an air of breezy competence. Not only was he sober (in Africa I have flown with drunken cowboy pilots), but he reassured me by saying that, although the plane was ancient, he had been flying it and others like it for decades and they were good little aircraft.

Once aloft, I was glad I had not chickened out at the last moment. From the sky, I looked down on a vast chessboard of black earth squares that retreated to the horizon in every direction. Each square I guessed to be more than 100 hectares in area. As we droned over this grand monotony of agricultural land, with its clusters of Lego-like farm buildings and rows of Toytown cottages, I thought of how, by comparison, East Anglia was an agricultural pocket handkerchief, and the farms that surround my home in Devon pointillist dots that would be quite lost in this fertile steppe. An eminent nineteenth-century Russian agronomist, Vasily Dokuchaev, wrote of this black earth that 'it is the Czar of soils, more valuable than oil, more precious than gold'. He was right then and, if you take the long view, his words are equally true today. You can have as much oil and gold as you like, but if you have no soil – no fertile soil – you starve.

It is hard to think of any saga in Russian history that is more terrible – or more dogged by avoidable errors – than the story of the peasantry. It began as a story of ignorance and indifference and, in the twentieth century, developed into one of inexcusable arrogance and persecution. More than eight hundred years earlier, the anonymous author of the epic *The Lay of the Host of Igor* wrote: 'The black earth beneath the hooves was sown with bones and watered with blood: a harvest of sorrow came up over the land of Russia.' Much later, in the closing years of the twentieth century, in his brilliant *Russia under the Old Regime*, the historian Richard Pipes offered a more prosaic but equally devastating insight: 'There is no evidence that the Russian peasant loved the soil; this sentiment is to be found mainly in the imagination of gentry romantics who visited their estates in the summer time.' Pipes's focus was the relationship between property and political power. Although he does not himself use the phrase, it is evident that in a uniquely Russian way this relationship had been dysfunctional from the earliest times. With scholarly precision, Pipes noted that 'the Black Earth has from 2 per cent to 16 per cent humus spread in a layer two to six feet deep. Its surface covers approximately a quarter of a billion acres, which are the centre of Russian agriculture.' This means there is no such vastness as fertile anywhere else on the planet, and that there was no excuse for the catastrophe that for so long has afflicted Russia's rural economy. Other than through turpitude and stupidity, it is hard to explain why this fecund soil should have seen over the centuries so much hunger, starvation and death.

Throughout much of the nineteenth century, Russia's agricultural productivity was lower than in feudal England; both before and after the emancipation of the serfs in 1861 nothing was done to raise the output from this most precious soil. The peasants, liberated from serfdom into penury, still cowered more or less as beasts of burden in hovels, living on a diet of pickled cabbage and cucumber, black bread and vodka. Alcohol (the duty on which was the government's most important source of revenue in the late nineteenth century) insulated the senses, but frequently to such effect that when the peasants staggered out into temperatures that in winter fall to between minus 10 and minus 30 degrees centigrade they would freeze to death in the ice and snow.

Treated bestially, the peasants behaved brutally. The women

suffered most. Required to perform the most menial and exhausting tasks from childhood, they also had to comply with a Russian version of *droit de seigneur*, which obliged them, at puberty, to satisfy on demand the sexual appetites of their fathers-in-law as well as their husbands. If they caused displeasure, and sometimes even if they did not, they endured beatings of such savagery that they sometimes died from their wounds. Orlando Figes has unearthed some horrifying proverbs from this period: 'Hit your wife with the butt of an axe, get down and see if she is breathing. If she is, she is shamming and wants some more'; 'Beat your wife like a fur coat, then there'll be less noise'; and one that neatly sums up the underlying attitude, 'A wife is nice twice – when she is brought into the house and when she is carried out of it to her grave.' Yes, I thought when I read this, Tolstoy was a romantic as well as a seer.

In *Sketches from a Hunter's Diary*, Ivan Turgenev, another of Russia's great masters, writing in the mid-nineteenth century, pre-echoes Thomas Hardy and John Fowles with his evocation of rural life, capturing with precision the harsh contrast between the wonder of the natural world and the cruelty visited upon the peasants. He does so with a grasp of detail and a common humanity that is in places as affecting as Tolstoy. Thus in *Bezhin Lea* he describes a summer's day on the eve of the harvest:

> On such days the heat is very strong and occasionally even 'simmers' along the slopes of the fields. But the wind drives away and disperses the accumulated heat, and whirling dust storms – a sure sign of settled weather – travel in tall white columns along roads through the ploughland. The dry pure air is scented with wormwood, harvested rye and buckwheat. Even an hour before darkness you can feel no dampness. It is just such weather that the farmer wants for harvesting his grain.

By contrast, in *Kasyan from the Beautiful Lands* he describes the passage of a funeral cortège through a very similar landscape:

Of the two women who walked behind the coffin, one was extremely old and pale of face; her motionless features, cruelly contorted with grief, preserved an expression of stern and solemn dignity. She walked in silence, now and then raising a frail hand to her thin, sunken lips. The other woman, of about twenty-five, had eyes that were moist with tears, and her whole face had become swollen from crying. As she drew level with us, she ceased her lament and covered her face with her sleeve. The procession went past us, turning back on to the track once more, and her piteous, heart-rending lament was resumed.

Turgenev does not tell us whether the corpse is that of a husband, a son, a child or a baby, and it does not matter. The power of the passage lies in the universality of its individual pain. In this both Turgenev and Tolstoy are alike: they are at once intoxicated by rural Russia and dismayed by the suffering of those who slaved on the land to feed the nation. Far from ending that suffering, the overthrow of the tsarist dictatorship and its replacement by the 'dictatorship of the proletariat' produced even more of the same, but with a premeditated cruelty that should informally, if not in the legalistic terms required by modern international law, be defined as a crime against humanity.

## A VILLAGE ENCOUNTER

We drove out of Voronezh and, after 10 miles, turned off the main road and entered that other world that I had seen but could not adequately appreciate from the sky. We bumped along a rutted track that led into a straggling village, passing men on bicycles and horses in the shafts of farm carts on the way. The single-storey cottages were made of clapboard in pale blues and soft yellows, their tin roofs glistening in the sun. Some were deserted, but most of the others had front gardens filled with flowers, as if on the lid of an English chocolate box. Goats ate the rough verges. Hens, ducks and geese flapped

out of our way. There was a pond and two wells. In the distance I saw
the ruined tower of an old church. Two little girls dressed, like their
mothers and grandmothers, in traditional scarves stopped their game
of hopscotch to stare at the foreigner. Outside one of the cottages I
saw a weather-beaten babushka, probably in her late sixties but looking ten years older, in a shapeless blue cotton dress patterned with red
and yellow flowers, over which hung a heavy, plum-coloured woollen
cardigan. She was tending the flowers by her front gate, and I asked
her if she knew where I might find Alexander, the leader of the former
collective farm that, after the collapse of the Soviet Union, had been
resurrected as a cooperative. She gestured vaguely back along the way
we had come. Then I noticed her garden, which bloomed with
dahlias, hollyhocks, roses, hostas and chrysanthemums. The old
woman, who said her name was Lena, saw that I was impressed and
invited me in to admire more closely, gesturing proudly at her display
and saying, 'I love my flowers. And we grow grapes. We have an apple
tree. I have done my pickling and salting and bottling – cabbage,
tomatoes and cucumbers.' Bees hovered and hummed, and two duck-
lings scuttled past, watched by an indifferent, plump cat. An old man,
her father or uncle perhaps, was hunched on a bench, a cigarette in his
mouth, looking far away, expressionless, not seeing the stranger. She
went on: 'We have seven pigs, a horse and two cows. We've got chickens and we'll soon be slaughtering a duck.'

Knowing that it is as easy for the twenty-first-century romantic to
be deceived by appearances as were the 'gentry romantics' of the nineteenth century, I asked Lena if life was hard. 'It is hard,' she replied,
'but as long as they pay your pension, all you need in life is your health
and peace.' At that moment, these pleasing sentiments were interrupted by the arrival of a younger, sharper woman, perhaps in her
fifties, wearing a green suede coat and with coiffured hair. She introduced herself as Lena's sister and, explaining that she now lived in the
town, asked bluntly why I was there. I explained that I was on a journey through Russia and that I was particularly interested in seeing

what it was like to live in the countryside. She instantly responded by exhorting me to do something useful: 'Let our President know this is supposed to be the twenty-first century and we are living in the Middle Ages. This is a rich country but we have no gas. There is no gas in the villages. We have no running water. We have to get it all from the well. And have you seen our roads? It is an absolute outrage.' Then, rhetorically, 'Don't you want to come inside the house and see how peasants live?'

She led us through a porch, which could have been painted by Van Gogh in soft hues of blue and yellow, into Lena's kitchen and then through to the living room. Like other simple homes I had already seen, it was sparsely furnished and immaculately tidy. A flower-patterned rug covered most of the unpainted wooden floor, and white net curtains hung over the windows. There was a cabinet with an elderly television set, a few china ornaments in a glass cupboard, two cheap armchairs, a wardrobe and a bright array of artificial flowers in a vase. Even on this mild day there was a chill in the air. Lena noticed that I had clasped my arms about my chest and told me that in winter it would be perishingly cold: 'This year we had lots of snow. It was up to the roofs and it was minus 35 centigrade. That is unusually cold. Most years it is about 25 degrees below.'

I noticed a photo of a young woman hanging on the wall. It was a formal portrait and she was dressed in Sunday best, looking solemnly at the camera. There was a medal pinned to her bosom. Lena explained, 'I was awarded that for being an outstanding milkmaid.' No great pride and no trace of irony, just a statement of fact. On another wall, in contrast, there was a prominent Orthodox icon. She said, 'I was never a Communist, though my late husband was a loyal party member. We used to have terrible rows. Once he said, "You must stop going to church." I said that I would give up the church if he stopped going to party meetings. At that he took one of my icons off the wall and threw it on the floor, smashing the glass and the frame. So I took the picture of Lenin and threw that on the floor, smashing that as well. So he threw another icon on the floor. I seized the picture of Stalin and did the same. He threw another icon. So I followed with Kirov. Soon the floor was littered with smashed frames and broken glass. Then we fought each other. And we both stopped. Neither of us had won. We decided to make up.' She chortled at the memory and said that thereafter they had agreed to differ for the sake of a quiet life. The warring icons – Christian and Soviet – were repaired and rehung in their proper places.

On my way out, I noticed a well half-concealed inside a tin lean-to shed. Beside it, in the open air of the yard, someone had knocked-up a washstand – a small earthenware bowl fitted on a narrow wooden dresser; above the bowl there was a galvanized bucket filled with cold water, at the base of which was a stopper. I pushed the stopper upwards, as you would to release air from the inner tube of a bicycle tyre, and the water splashed round my finger into the bowl below. When I took my hand away, the flow stopped: a simple, ingenious, water-saving device. Beside the bowl there were two worn toothbrushes, a tube of toothpaste and a scabrous bar of soap. It was the Third World in Russia and, as Lena's sister again pointed out, it was not the twenty-first century as they would have liked it to be. When we left, Lena gave me a small bag of marigold seeds, telling me to take them home to my garden in England and plant them there as a memento of our meeting.

I found Alexander, the chairman of the communal farm, in his office, an austere space with an empty table, six upright chairs and a filing cabinet. Nothing seemed to be happening in the dusty offices that surrounded the epicentre of his authority. At first he was gruff to the point of rudeness, extending a formal hand and inviting me to sit opposite him for the kind of briefing that any reporter dreads. I decided to accelerate the procedure by saying that I too was a farmer and asking if he faced the same kind of difficulties that confronted his British counterparts. The atmosphere changed at once. We were very soon at ease together, comparing milk prices, the fluctuating price of grain, and margins so small that they drove decent, hard-working men and women to sell up. He then told me the story of the farm for which he was now responsible. Founded in 1923, it had been one of the oldest collectives in Russia and it was not privatized until 1996 when it joined twenty thousand or more collective farms that had been 'abandoned' to the free market. Today its 4000 hectares of prime land were divided into six hundred nominal units, the shares in which were held by individual families in the village (most of whom also farmed their own small plots).

Alexander himself was very much more than a 'nominal' partner in the business. The collective had once employed more than six hundred workers; he was now responsible for 160, a drastic reduction but, as he knew, still a disastrously inefficient use of labour by the industrial standards of Europe or America. Left to himself, he would have laid off at least two-thirds of the present workforce – some because they were unskilled, others because they were idle, and yet more because they were permanently impaired by alcoholism. But, he gestured emphatically, 'My hands are tied.' Alexander himself was an impressive figure, tall, confident and measured – it was clear why he had been elected leader of the new cooperative. But he had very much less authority than he would need to rescue the business from the edge of bankruptcy, where it now found itself. He was not permitted to lay off workers without the approval of his works council, which included many of those he would have liked to fire. He had no capital to invest and the banks didn't like the look of the books. As he told me this dismal story, his tone was less frustrated than forlorn; resigned rather than resentful.

I asked if we could drive around the farm. He readily agreed, clearly keen to get out of the office and away from those wretched books. We went first to see the dairy herd – three hundred cows in a feeding lot, but between them producing far less milk than the accounts demanded. The milking parlour, which dated back to the seventies, had been modernized, but this brave investment had consumed virtually all the farm's modest credit. The dairy now employed two milkmaids (down from thirteen before privatization), who stood in the mire extracting the last drop of milk from reluctant udders. The herd had made a small profit last year despite the fact that a litre of milk in the supermarket was worth no more than half a litre of bottled water; it was certainly not enough to arrest the apparently irreversible decline of the farm business.

Alexander drove me further into the estate to where a team of labourers, driving machines from the fifties, were harvesting 250 hectares of sugar beet. There was a raw wind blowing and the men were red-faced and haggard. Apart from their rusting, clanking, worn-out machinery, which defined them as belonging to something like the modern world, they could have easily formed a tableau from one of the paintings by the great nineteenth-century artist Ilya Repin: down-trodden, incurious, fatalistic beasts of burden. No wonder, I thought, that they turn to vodka to stay warm and to shut out despair.

Alexander explained in his matter-of-fact way that the sugar-beet crop would lose money this year. There was a glut of sugar, stagnant demand, and as a result the processing firm – the 'big man', as he put it, in Voronezh – which was his only outlet, had him over a barrel. He was planning to give up sugar beet in any case because his beet harvesters broke down the whole time, and the cooperative couldn't raise the funds to replace them. The entire turnover of the business was 30 million roubles; a new harvester bought from Germany would cost 18 million roubles (and he needed three): an impossible equation to resolve. He found it hard to explain any of these immutable laws of the market to his workers. 'They have got used to the idea that manna falls from heaven. That it is always someone else that will take care of it. But it's never them.'

There are large farms in Russia that do make a profit. German and British immigrant farmers, with the capital, the acumen and the entre-preneurial appetite for industrial-scale agriculture, have started to thrive. Tens of thousands of hectares have also been bought by Russian millionaires, hedging against the future but not yet bothering to invest on any significant scale. I asked Alexander what would happen if a big buyer came and offered to take the land off his hands. 'Some of my co-workers – the alcoholics – would want to sell. But most would not let me do it. We have lived on this land for generations. And in the end you can't take the love of the soil away from the peasants. Of course not.' Then, for the first time allowing his despair to show, he burst out, 'This is the best, the richest soil in the world and yet we only get crumbs from it.' Embarrassed by this sudden onrush of emotion, he added with a self-deprecating little laugh, 'What else can I do? I have to laugh. Shall I cry? No one will listen if I cry.'

On the outskirts of the village I came across a group of men and women bent double, harvesting potatoes on their own small plots of private land, which had never been taken from them even by Stalin. I could not help but pick up a clod of the rich soil to filter it through my fingers. One of the women saw me doing this and shouted, 'You wish you had soil like this, yes?' She complained that they were facing a bad crop this year. I asked if she would like me to help. She replied drily, 'The best way you could help would be to send us a potato lifter. It saves you having your bottom up in the air. You try it – you just try it all day.' She joshed and laughed and I allowed myself to believe that, even though hers was a hard life, it was a genuine life of the kind that had so entranced Tolstoy. This welcoming, hard-working, independent peasant woman, mocking my cursory attempt to join her family in picking potatoes, seemed more genuinely rooted, and less unhappy, than any other Russian I had yet met. Closer to God, as Tolstoy would have it, than the rest of us? I doubt it. Closer to life on earth? Of course.

Women like her are crucial to the Russian economy – not in the way of oil or gas, but as 'black earth' peasants. The recent statistics of agricultural production are remarkable. Even in 2005, the small peasant farms and individual plots that occupy no more than 20 per cent of Russia's farmland produced no less than 60 per cent of the state's total agricultural output: 76 per cent of green vegetables, 55 per cent of meat, 67 per cent of milk, and no less than 91 per cent of potatoes. This was not enough to prevent Russia from having to import 33 per cent of its food for the domestic market, which, according to the Agriculture Minister Alexander Gordeyev, 'crosses the line for food security'. With 50 per cent of the rural population living below the poverty line, the government has all manner of schemes to boost output and incomes; but with a rampant black market, rolls of red tape that make the Common Agricultural Policy of the European Union seem like gossamer threads, and an enervating level of bureaucratic corruption, the peasants have every reason to conclude that fine words butter no parsnips.

The past still clings to this village. No one forgets what happened to their relatives or to friends of the family in the worst days of Stalin's rule. The ruined church that I saw as I entered the village did not collapse merely from age and neglect. I was taken to meet a babushka who said she was eighty, though she looked even older. One afternoon when she was a small child her elder brother, who was twelve, took her by the hand and said, 'Come with me, I am going to take you to hear the bells ringing in the church.' He led her close to the foot of the church, where a crowd had gathered. She could see the bells swinging to and fro in the tower and as the solemn notes rang out across the land – 'The bells were famous around here. They could be heard as far as 20 miles away,' she told me – she saw figures clambering along the parapet around the tower. The bells fell silent. There was a struggle. One of the figures toppled over the edge, crashed to the ground and lay still. The dead man was a villager, defiantly protecting his church in the name of God. Those who had pushed him over the edge were young party activists under orders to silence any public manifestation of the Christian faith.

The bells were later hurled to the ground and destroyed, and the church, thenceforth silent, slowly fell into its present state of ruin, a home for crows and roosting pigeons. As the babushka told this story, she seemed to relive it, though how much she saw for herself and how much was passed down to her from her mother was not clear. Nor does it really matter. The essence is true, and is still shocking. It is not hard to picture the villagers, here and in many other places in Russia, watching in dismay, anger and fear as, in the name of Bolshevism, the physical structure of their faith was forcibly denied them, though the faith itself – deep and primitive – endured. Her story told, the old lady fell silent as if there were no more to add save, bizarrely, for the self-contradictory afterthought, 'We need a new Stalin to restore order.'

There are plans to restore the church, but no one yet knows where the money is coming from. It seems unlikely that she will live to see that moment when it is reopened and the bells once more peal across the fields to beckon the faithful to prayer; far more likely that another Stalin, in smooth twenty-first-century style, professing his belief in the Church and in democracy, will once again emerge to 'restore order', thereby ensuring – with their tacit consent – that the Russian people never really emerge from their past to exercise the freedom that they don't really want.

## THE GREAT FAMINE

In Russia the past is all around you, impossible to shake off. There is a tendency for complacent foreigners (as well as those for whom Russia is simply a cornucopia of untapped wealth to be ripped off as quickly as possible) to believe, in effect, that 'the past is another country', that the old want to forget and the young can't remember. That impression seems to me to be remarkably superficial and insensitive; it is more likely that the past, by old and young alike, is suppressed as being too painful and too shameful to recollect in any kind of tranquillity. How is it possible for the people of this region to forget what happened here little more than seven decades ago?

The documents stored with such care in the Russian archives for future generations to wonder at provide more than enough evidence of the crimes committed in the name of the revolution. There is something peculiarly gruesome about the way in which Stalin's pogroms against the peasants were precisely documented by party functionaries as they logged the details of every crime in which they were complicit with the dutiful complacency of tellers in a local bank. In January 1930, at the 7th Plenum of the Central Black Earth Regional Party Committee, a commissar named Vareikis reported on the 'practical measures' that would be implemented around Voronezh 'for the liquidation of the kulaks as a class in connection with the full collectivization' of the region. The kulaks, for whom Stalin and his apparatchiks reserved a peculiarly intense hatred, were middle-income peasants, often employing labourers themselves; by definition, therefore, they were 'reactionaries' and 'counter-revolutionaries' who had to be 'eliminated'.

According to the official records covering the Voronezh region, these 'practical measures' were designed to ensure that 'in the period February to March 1930, between 90,000 and 105,000 households would be dekulakized, between 12,000 and 13,000 kulak families were to be exiled'. Further, Vareikis instructed, in the case of their 'counter-revolutionary' leaders, measures such as 'prison and execution' would be employed. In February of that year, Vareikis sent a telegram to Moscow seeking permission to use Red Army units in the struggle against the peasantry, which was fiercely resisting liquidation. By May he was driven to alert the CCCP to the consequences of his initial success in carrying out Stalin's programme, informing his revolutionary masters: 'There is an absence of bread in all quarters of the region among certain poorer people.... Several cases of malnutrition and illnesses have been registered as a result of not having enough to eat.' In three areas, he reported, half the population had no grain reserves at all.

This creeping starvation across swathes of the Soviet Union was to turn into a man-made mass famine that would dwarf in scale any famine in Africa of any century. It was the direct result of Stalin's instruction that, in addition to the liquidation of the kulaks, the nation's grain baskets should be transferred from the countryside and emptied in cities to feed Russia's urban population. It proved to be more difficult than the great dictator had imagined. Once their 'ringleaders' had been liquidated the peasants began to use the tactic of silent resistance – hoarding their supplies, hiding the grain, and refusing either to sow or to harvest the crops. In October 1930 the head of the Voronezh regional branch of OGPU, the secret police, sent the regional First Secretary a telegram reporting that 'the spring sowing of grain is...still in the fields. The crop is rotting and going to seed.' The situation worsened. Eighteen months later, in the spring of 1932, the First Secretary was forced to send a secret telegram to Stalin to report: 'I think that we are not fulfilling the plan on state procurement', concluding his nervous missive by promising to do better in the months ahead. By May 1933 another secret communiqué from the regional headquarters of OGPU read: 'Fatalities among the population of Borisovsky region are not ceasing.... In just the village of Borisovska more than 1000 people have died of starvation.... In whole numbers of villages the corpses of those who have died are not being collected for long periods...the collective farm workers are abandoning the villages and leaving for the towns.'

Stalin was undeterred. In June, perhaps the most chilling dispatch of all landed on the desk of regional First Secretary Vareikis. It came from the Kremlin: 'I propose that you ensure the first procurement [of grain from the new harvest] whatever it takes...no diversions from the plan...can be contemplated, no mitigating circumstances.' It was signed by Stalin's most trusted lieutenant, Vyacheslav Molotov, chairman of the People's Commissars, the man who was directly responsible for the collectivization of Soviet agriculture (and the party apparatchik who had been described by Leon Trotsky as 'mediocrity personified'). As I read these documents I felt a physical revulsion. Those words 'whatever it takes...no diversion from the plan' seemed to sum up everything that was revolting about the Soviet Union of that era: the indifferent cruelty of men who believed that they could force human beings to bend to their own warped vision of progress.

Of course, the region of Voronezh was but one of many that suffered a similar fate; indeed, it was less stricken than many other parts of Stalin's empire. In 1933, the same year that the Voronezh commissar received his 'whatever it takes' instructions from Molotov, the British journalist Malcolm Muggeridge, then Moscow correspondent of the *Manchester Guardian*, wrote three articles that should have alerted Britain at the least to the reality of Stalin's crimes. Related by marriage to Beatrice Webb, and thus for a time on the periphery of an influential circle of socialists that included like-minded intellectuals, such as Bernard Shaw, Muggeridge was familiar with their enthusiasm for Bolshevism and before he saw it for himself wore relatively red-tinted spectacles as well.

Forty years later, when he was in the autumn of his days, I was befriended by 'St Mugg', as he was mockingly described by his critics, in what turned out to be a fruitless attempt on his part to corral me as a disciple. By then he had become a famous scourge of liberal opinion, who mercilessly pinioned the cant of others – not least where he detected it most, in the pages of the paper by which he had once been employed, now simply the *Guardian*. I was fond of him and greatly entertained. He was clever, mordant and gossipy – and far from immune from the very hypocrisy that he so readily detected in others. When he railed and ranted, he spoke with such mannered eloquence – 'dear boy' would preface such tirades – that it often seemed as though a cultivated mellifluence of style mattered as much to him as the meaning of what he was saying. But even when he was talking nonsense, it was never less than stimulating. In one conversation, though, on a walk in the hills above Nice, he gave vent to his disgust at the Soviet Union with a vituperative violence that made all the 'evil empire' speeches I have heard seem laboured and flaccid by comparison. At that time I knew he had reported from the Soviet Union in the thirties, but I did not realize that he had witnessed the full horror of Stalin's campaign against the kulaks.

In March 1933, in sharp contrast to its earlier coverage (an act of some editorial courage, given the fellow-travelling precepts of many of its readers) the *Manchester Guardian* gave prominence to three brilliant dispatches written by Muggeridge from the epicentre of the famine. In the first of these, under the byline 'An Observer's Notes', he reported from a market town in the Ukraine that, he wrote, 'suggested a military occupation; worse, active war. There were soldiers everywhere – in the railway station, in the streets, every-where...all differing from the civilian population in one respect. They were well fed, and the population was obviously starving, I mean starving in the absolute sense...having had for weeks next to nothing to eat.' He walked around a market where what food he saw was beyond the purse of any peasant. 'How are things with you?' he asked one man, who replied, 'We have nothing, absolutely nothing. They have taken everything away.'

Muggeridge described the wilderness on the outskirts of the town: 'Fields choked with weeds, cattle dead, people starving and dispirited, no horses for ploughing or for transport, not even adequate supplies of seed for the spring sowing. The worst of the class war is that it never stops. First individual kulaks shot and exiled; then groups of peasants; then whole villages.' He went from village to village to provide compelling evidence of the pogrom: 'It is literally true that whole villages have been exiled.... I saw myself a group of 20 peasants being marched off under escort.' In the second article, which contains much similar evidence, Muggeridge asked rhetorically, 'How is it that so many obvious and fundamental facts about Russia are not noticed even by serious and intelligent visitors?' – such as, he might have added, the fellow-travelling aristocracy of the high-brow Left in Bloomsbury and beyond.

On his return to Moscow, Muggeridge drew his readers' attention to a speech in which Stalin had recently declared: 'By developing collective farming we have succeeded in drawing the entire mass of peasants into collective farms.... What does this mean? It means that no less than 20 million of the peasant population have been saved from poverty and ruin, from kulak slavery, and converted, thanks to the collective farms, into people assured of a livelihood. This is a great achievement, comrades. This is such an achievement as the world has never yet known and such as not a single state in the world has ever before secured.' Those words, sounding uncannily like those of Napoleon in *Animal Farm*, turning the truth upside down, were uttered thirteen years before the publication of George Orwell's masterpiece. To persist in denying the truth on which Muggeridge had stumbled, the Bloomsbury intelligentsia and their acolytes must have been either extraordinarily bovine (which seems unlikely) or ideologically (which is worse) purblind. In either case they were accomplices by default in a crime against humanity that not only cost the lives of 6 million peasants, but that had been unsparingly documented by Malcolm Muggeridge and the *Manchester Guardian* before their very eyes in their very own newspaper.

As we left the cooperative, I saw a flock of rooks swooping back and forth over the fields, a permeable black cloud. I imagined them to be the souls of the dead still haunting the souls of the living. Russia can do that to you. A while later, still afflicted by that fanciful image, I found myself in one of those gloomy pine forests where families and lovers like to pick mushrooms and picnic around camp fires drinking vodka. I was trying to find a memorial site that allegedly stood in the trees over a burial ground where, I had been told, lay some ten thousand corpses, local victims of the paranoia that gripped Stalin in the mid-thirties as he set about purging the Soviet Union of any possible threat to his dictatorship.

The regional branch of the NKVD (the successor of OGPU and predecessor of the KGB) had been assiduous in its allotted task, rooting out bourgeois 'elements' – kulaks, priests, bureaucrats and anyone who could not be entirely trusted to follow the party line as it wobbled along behind the latest whim of the dictator. Once they had been condemned in a local kangaroo court, the victims were killed and their remains disposed of in the forest in shallow, unmarked graves. It was an eerie business, walking softly through the evening sunlight and peering through regimented rows of pines in search of I knew not quite what.

I stopped a group of walkers, one of whom spoke a little English. 'Do you know where I can find the memorial?' I asked. 'It has been moved,' he replied, gesturing vaguely into the distance. Then he pointed to the older man standing beside him, saying, matter-of-factly, 'His father was murdered here.' I asked if they too were trying to find the memorial. No, they chorused, they were simply there to pick mushrooms – mushrooms, I could not help but think, had sprouted in the thin soil and been fertilized by the remains of that man's father: dust to dust, ashes to ashes, but with a peculiarly dreadful twist.

Even after Stalin's death it was forbidden to express any public sympathy for the victims of his Terror; for it is merely an embarrassment. There are no memorials to those who died. Perhaps this is because the past is so unspeakably dreadful that most Russians simply want it to be buried. But burial of that kind, a tourniquet applied to the memory, is a form of suppression that poisons the system.

A little deeper into the forest I found a group of young men and women who had collected a large wicker basket full of mushrooms in such a variety of shapes and colours that they looked more like a psychedelic still-life from the brush of an artist intoxicated by their magic properties. They had built a campfire, and as they prepared kebabs, they were downing beer and vodka in liberal quantities; at least three of the six of them were already the worse for it. Once again I asked for directions to the memorial. They looked at me with suspicion, if not hostility – what was this stranger about? – and pointed me deeper into the forest. Anything to get rid of this overly inquisitive foreigner.

I marched on, now determined not to be denied. After about ten minutes, with the sun very low through the trees, the silence was suddenly pierced by the phut-phut of an engine. A motorcycle and sidecar stumbled over the rough ground towards me with three young men perched on it, carrying beer bottles and shouting what I presumed to be mild obscenities in my direction. But perhaps they were simply filled with the joy of life. Here? In this forest? Did they know? Did they care?

At last I saw it. A giant wreath, bigger by far than is encouraged at the Cenotaph in Whitehall, of blood-red artificial flowers, and around it a scatter of small headstones recording the names of that handful of the ten thousand whose corpses had been identified and who had thus recovered their identity and their dignity in death. I stood in front of this forlorn little memorial, moved by the modest intimacy of the evidence. And then I railed aloud, as if in search of atonement, against Stalin and his co-conspiratorial cohorts and against those fellow-travellers in my own country, some of whom I had met, who, at the time and for decades afterwards, averted their gaze from the truth and chose instead to laud the great socialist experiment that, from their comfortable Western eyries, they preferred to detect in the Soviet Union. There is no more creepy a cliché than the tyrants' epigram that 'you can't make an omelette without breaking eggs'.

## A BREAK ON THE BLACK SEA

The train journey from Voronezh to Novorossiysk on the edge of the Black Sea takes eighteen hours. I was beginning to adjust to the trundling pace and the curiously womb-like embrace of this time travel through a no man's landscape of fields that had recently been harvested; rooks searching for spilt grain, a tractor ploughing the stubble. I liked the swathe of space beyond the carriage window and that sense of protected otherness that I had inside the train as it meandered towards our destination, unhurriedly but with purpose. Other trains passed by in the opposite direction, hauling oil, coal and maize, not rushing past in a blur as in Britain but, being half a mile in length, so slowly that you could read the number on each one of forty or fifty wagons. The outside increasingly resembled a cinema screen filled with cameo moments: an old man beside the track, indifferent to the train, bending down, his hand extended, pointing towards the ground, his face set in dismay, but I couldn't see the cause of his distress; four boys in uniform on their way to school, stopping to light their first illicit cigarettes of the day; a woman burning the stalks from a maize crop, shrouded in flames and smoke; a poorly dressed peasant with an axe slicing through a huge chunk of coal that had fallen off a coal wagon, two women in headscarves beside him picking up the pieces; a tall teenage girl, with a Modigliani face and black hair, seductive in a skin-tight black sweater and tan-coloured mini-skirt, picking her way in high heels over the sleepers of the neighbouring track with a shopping bag, heading towards a grizzled labourer with a shovel in his hand; a dun-coloured mongrel scratching the top of its arched back on the underside of a farm cart.

The train lumbered into one small station after another, resting at each to allow more than enough time for travellers to board, lugging boxes and bags and hauling small children, while offering extended farewells to loved ones who stood and waved. At every station there was a welcoming committee of women who walked determinedly along the platform selling food from baskets, elbowing past one another to tempt passengers with rival selections of vodka, beer, buns, eggs, cabbages, onions, gherkins, apples, jars of honey and strings of little smoked fish, each hooked to what looked like a wire coat-hanger. Their sales patter was incomprehensible, but its meaning was clear: 'My produce is better than hers and this is fantastic value for money.' I bought a bottle of beer, an apple and two eggs, and then we were on our way again.

It was far more congenial than the newer, faster trains that exhaust British travellers, who so often find themselves late yet again for a meeting in Leeds or Manchester or Exeter because of some delay that is beyond everyone's control, but for which there is always an excuse that is relayed apologetically through semi-audible speakers by a train 'manager' who is impotent. On Russian trains there is no tannoy and the entire journey is one long delaying tactic so that – in my experience so far – you invariably arrive at your destination on time. It was also a pleasant surprise, just before we reached Novorossiysk, that the superintendent responsible for my carriage, wearing a sharply pressed blue uniform, passed along the corridor wishing everyone farewell, her 'I hope you enjoyed your journey with us' seeming to be more than a formality.

We disembarked into a clear summer day. A voice boomed out from the brightness that half-blinded me, 'Mr Dimbleby, welcome to Novorossiysk.' I walked towards the sound to see a Peter Ustinov lookalike, but in his forties, a face that welcomed more warmly than I had yet experienced in Russia, as wreathed in smiles as it is possible to imagine. This burly apparition, with a voice that seemed more oper-atic Italian than Russian, barely stopped talking for long enough to allow me to discover his name, which turned out to be Igor. He put his arm around my shoulder and frog-marched me affectionately towards a shiny black Land-Rover, on the bonnet of which a Union Jack hung limply in the heat. This diplomatic emblem, Igor told me, signified that I was an official guest of the British Honorary Consul, for whom he worked as a personal assistant and business partner. We set off with vice-regal authority, the flag now fluttering in the breeze, embraced by an illusion of colonial power without responsibility.

Igor did not draw breath as he told me his own life story and that of the city. A raconteur so entertaining that he might indeed have been trained by Ustinov, he tumbled effervescently from one anec-dote to another with a self-deprecatory wit that ensnared me totally in his narrative. But his talent to entertain had a purpose: he believed in Novorossiysk and especially in the surrounding seaside resorts that cluster along this precious Black Sea coast, and he wanted me to real-ize that by reaching this point in my journey I had perchance stumbled upon nirvana. Igor had travelled the oceans of the world as a purser on luxury liners and had been content to stay at sea. Unhappily, his wife had started to suspect that he had formed rather too many liaisons with female passengers (in return for finding them the best berth or a place at the captain's table) and she had insisted that he stay at home or else. 'What could I do?' He spread both palms out in front of him in a theatrically extravagant gesture to suggest that any such suspicion was preposterous but what alternative did he have? Anyway, he had opted for hearth and home and it had been, he confided, a very good decision.

We drove up out of the city around the bay until we had an eagle's-eye view of the harbour while Igor reeled off a barrage of statistics about the port (it was the largest in Russia), the cement works (it produced the best quality in the world), the weather (nowhere else could compete with its balm) and the tourist attractions that draw 12 million Russians to the region for their summer holidays. He conceded that nowadays cheap package flights to Egypt, Cyprus and Turkey offered fierce competition, but the developers had started to fight back, and after a long, slow decline the number of visitors was up once more. Where once members of the Politburo and obedient trade unionists had been rewarded by a month in the sun to disport themselves in the purpose-built sanatoriums that lined the coast towards the resort of Sochi (which will host the 2014 Winter Olympics), now there were five-star hotels, clean beaches, power-boats with water-skis and para-gliders. For those with young families there could be no better, no safer, no more relaxing place anywhere. Like a genial devil promising me the earth, he waved expansively towards the sprawl of beachside hotels, restaurants and amusement parks below us and said, 'Everything I am telling you is true, of that I can assure you.'

Later, as we sat on a pier drinking cold beer under a white awning, watching matrons teaching babies to swim and pretty girls in bikinis flirting with young hunks in bathing briefs, I could see what he meant. It was not as I had imagined the Black Sea resorts, which I had presumed would be like Blackpool, gaudy and garish but irredeemably bleak despite the best efforts of its burghers. This was more Torquay or Bournemouth, but with a guarantee of hot sun and warm water for hotel prices that started at $10 a day and rarely went above $100. Igor's optimism was relentless. 'This place is booming,' he enthused. 'It is the new Monte Carlo of Russia. Over there they are building a summer retreat for Putin and a palace for the Patriarch, who will be his neighbour. Over there, on that headland, they are going to build a new international airport. I tell you, Jonathan, this place has a future. And not just for Russians. I hope that foreigners as well will come here. Can you imagine the growth rate? It has been eightfold in the last four years. I tell you, I am very happy about this. This place is flourishing, it is booming. I hope to stay here and die here, a happy man.' He seemed about to burst with artless, guileless delight.

That evening Igor took me to meet his boss, the Honorary Consul. Clive Rumens turned out to be impressively raffish and blessed with a voice and manner that appeared to have been manufactured either on the playing fields of Eton or, more romantically (if improbably), in some caddish corner of Le Carré land. He explained that he was now the only Honorary Consul left in Russia (his counterpart 7000 miles to the east in Vladivostock recently vacated his post for reasons that Clive did not wish to explore further). In early middle age, when he had yet to succeed in any conventional sphere, Clive had been smart enough to export himself to Russia on the eve of that post-Soviet anarchy of privatization when members of the Soviet nomenclatura turned themselves into oil magnates overnight. Sniffing out a bonanza in the offing, he headed for Novorossiysk, which was already Russia's biggest port on the Black Sea and its most important terminal for the export of crude oil to Europe.

In those days, by his account, Novorossiysk was akin to the Wild West. In the absence of law or order, there were rich pickings to be had – even for people like him, 'small fry', as he put it, but sharp enough to understand the market and with the dash and charm to exploit its possibilities. In those days (as now) it was customary for oil exporters to overstate the tonnage sent down the long pipeline from the east of the Caucasus, while importers invariably understated the quantity that eventually reached them via the tankers that 'trans-shipped' the oil from Novorossiysk across the Black Sea and through the Bosporus into Europe. Clive saw an opening and volunteered himself as a middle-man between the exporters and the importers – an oil inspector or auditor

– bargaining with both sides until they compromised on an agreed figure from which he then took his cut. It was a lucrative little enterprise, and soon Clive was a figure to reckon with. He still is.

That evening the Honorary Consul invited me to dinner. The Land-Rover picked me up at the hotel and, the British flag still resplendent, we set off for a discreet resort a little way up the coast. At his behest we were escorted by a police car, an elderly Lada laden with officers and flashing one of its blue lights (the other was on the blink). We occupied the middle of a quiet main road, driving at a stately pace. Whenever another vehicle had the temerity to approach us on its own side of the road from the opposite direction, the police vehicle veered across towards it, siren wailing, forcing the innocent offender to steer violently on to the rough ground on the far side of the road; not hard, I thought, to appreciate why the police are unloved in Russia. I asked Clive why he had requested a police escort. Unblushingly, he explained that it was a matter of security: there was always the risk of a terrorist attack in this part of the world, he said airily, and he did not want an important visitor to be kidnapped. I resisted the urge to press him further; I could hardly have asked him whether the real reason for our self-important progress had more do with his sense of identity than my security.

The restaurant was deserted but Clive strode in, head high, with me at his side, followed by Igor and his wife. We were greeted obsequiously by the proprietor, who escorted us across the empty dance floor where, undeterred by the lack of any audience, a female crooner bellowed deafeningly into a microphone clasped passionately to her bosom. A table had been arranged for us on a private veranda overlooking the Black Sea. Lights twinkled in the distant night from tankers and fishing boats, the water lapped beneath us, the air was balmy, and there was an abundance of seafood and (courtesy of Clive's own cellar) a delicious choice of wines. Britain's Honorary Consul seemed genuinely honoured to represent Her Majesty in Novorossiysk, though his duties were not exactly onerous. In return for the Union Jack on his Land-Rover, his principal task was to help visitors with lost passports and credit cards, or back-packers arrested for this or that misdemeanour. And his status had by no means been a hindrance to him in business.

Clive regarded himself as a British minnow among Russian sharks, but, blessed with an enviable eye for the main chance, he had cut enough deals in the last fifteen years to make himself a dollar million-aire several times over. He gave me a recent example. In 2004 he had bought a 400-hectare vineyard along the coast for $1.5 million. Two years later he had sold it for five times as much, $7.5 million, to an entrepreneur with the know-how or the cash to secure planning per-mission for a coastal development of offices, shops and apartments on terrain that had been carefully zoned as agricultural land. As the wine flowed, we talked about corruption. Clive was disarmingly forthcom-ing. 'Yes, of course there is corruption here.... I will pay to speed up the system making these facility payments to get the permits and permissions I need. My clients don't understand if they have to wait.' If you didn't pay up, he explained, a permit that should take days would take weeks, and those that should take weeks would take months – by which time someone else would have stepped in, paid up and stolen the deal from under your nose. 'So,' Igor elaborated, 'you open your safe, you get out your banknotes, you put them in an envelope and give them to the bureaucrats. And then you will find your problem settled. And it will be settled very quickly. In this way you can achieve in a fortnight what would otherwise take half a year.' Clive himself was now looking to conquer new territories, moving into Turkmenistan, an absurdly nasty dictatorship that happens to be blessed with an abun-dance of oil and gas. Clive couldn't afford to be fastidious because, he explained, if he didn't snap up the business there 'others will'.

One way and another, he had now made more than enough money to retire, but, he asked rhetorically and with wistful defiance, 'What would I do? There is no place for me in England now.' Although he owns apartments in Moscow (where his girlfriend lives) and London, not to mention a villa in Thailand, Clive exuded an air of disappointment and insecurity, as though he felt himself to be washed up in an outpost of empire, a character, I came to think, more out of Graham Greene than Le Carré. I left Novorossiysk on my way to the Caucasus – 'I wouldn't go there. It's very clannish, very tribal, very dangerous,' Clive warned me kindly – feeling rather sorry for the Honorary Consul, who had been a genial and generous host.

## LERMONTOV'S PLAYGROUND

As we drove for long hours through the featureless flatlands from the edge of the Black Sea into the North Caucasus, I had conflicting emotions. The very names of these mountainous republics – Cabardino-Balkaria, North Ossetia, Ingushetia, Chechnya and Dagestan – were enough to provoke that combination of exhilaration and anxiety associated with wild and dangerous places. As a child in the early fifties, I had been terrified at the prospect of going to Spain, where I knew for certain that every inhabitant was a brigand with a turban and a droopy moustache who carried a cutlass with which to disembowel foreigners. It was now more than fifty years on, and in the meantime I had reported from more than eighty countries and survived to tell the tale, but that trepidation about travel has never left me: that churning of the bowels and an imprecise queasiness that, in this case, as we got closer to our destination, made me wonder again why I hadn't stayed at home instead of embarking on this avoidable escapade.

Throughout history the Caucasus has been synonymous with violent passions, excitement and danger, death and glory. In the back of my mind was a Foreign Office 'advisory' that, in the bureaucratic language of officialdom, painted a picture of the Caucasus as a land peopled by bandits and terrorists, where visitors should only venture at their peril or if their journey was really necessary. The very title of my one-day course in 'hostile regions' training had been enough to conjure up an ominous prospect. Our mentor was an ex-SAS man called Tony, who did not know very much about the Caucasus but knew a great deal about kidnappers and terrorists. As he began his briefing, my mind started to wander. With the vainglory of a once-upon-a-time journalistic 'fireman', I thought back to other 'hazard zones' that I had experienced, and mentally ticked off a list of ventures in Cyprus, Lebanon, the West Bank, Uganda, Ethiopia, Eritrea, Bosnia, Kosovo, Nicaragua, Guatemala and Northern Ireland. What could Tony teach me that I did not know already?

Once or twice I had come under fire, and very occasionally I had been in real danger. I had once even made it on to the front page of the *Sun* newspaper, which is normally a dubious privilege. It was during the Turkish invasion of Cyprus in 1974. I was reporting with an ITV crew from the apparent safety of the British military base at Dhekelia, where we had a grandstand view from which to film forty or more ageing Russian tanks trundling through the plain below us on their way to occupy the seaside resort of Famagusta. Suddenly the tanks came to a halt and swivelled menacingly around until their gun barrels were facing us. Without warning, a burst of tracer fire whistled by our heads. Then came the clunk of an incoming shell, followed by another. I felt an immediate rage, an urge to race towards the invaders, yelling obscenities at these Turks. Instead, in blind panic, I fled, running up the hillside as fast as I could, but slowly, oh, so slowly, as in one of those nightmares when you are trying desperately to run away but your legs refuse to obey the instruction from your brain. You seem to be standing still, paralysed by fear. There was another clunk. Another shell landed somewhere behind me. I kept running, heart pounding, breathless with effort, until I collapsed on the ground, panting and exhausted, and waited. Dimly I heard a siren wailing an alarm. Then there was silence. I was alive.

Later the base commander, Colonel Cartwright, invited me to join him in his Land-Rover and drive down to the plain below us to seek redress. On the way, he told me that he had been within moments of ordering an aerial counter-attack. An embarrassing military skirmish between two NATO allies had been narrowly averted by white-hot phone lines linking Cyprus, London and Ankara. Instead, we had a minor, a very minor, diplomatic incident. The Colonel seemed a little disappointed. When we reached the Turkish position the tank commander, looking gloriously woebegone, saluted his British opposite number and apologized profusely for his error. Colonel Cartwright accepted the apology with grace, but, tongue in cheek, gestured towards me, saying that one of the Turkish tanks had very nearly accounted for a British television reporter. 'You should apologize to Mr Dimbleby as well,' he said sternly. The Turkish commander did as instructed, saluting, apologizing and shaking hands. It was a very British, mini *Scoop*-like moment.

As Tony went on to tell us what we should and should not do if we were stopped by an armed gang, my mind drifted across from Cyprus to Lebanon during the civil war. One day, trying to find our way through the ruins of Beirut, we had driven into the no man's land near the Green Line that separated the west from the east of the city to find ourselves confronted by a group of teenage militiamen who screamed at us in incomprehensible Arabic, furious and frightened. Telling my colleagues to put their equipment away, I smiled apologetically in the general vicinity of the Kalashnikovs pointed in our direction, my hands outstretched in surrender – anything to lower the temperature. Very slowly, still smiling, we got back in the car and backed slowly, very slowly, away from a front line that we had not even known was there.

On several occasions I had also been driven, at top speed, tyres squealing, across the Green Line, knowing that we were in the telescopic sights of a psychotic sniper; I had also seen one of his victims, a corpse splayed bloodily half in and half out of his driving seat, the car door open in a hopeless bid to escape. And there had been several similar incidents in other parts of the world when I had found myself wishing I could believe those beguiling statistics that claim you are more at risk from electrocuting yourself in your own home or driving down the M4 than you are in a conflict zone. In short, I told myself in an attempt to control a surge of remembered fear, I had experienced enough hazards in my trade as a reporter to permit myself a certain insouciance now.

Tony soon put me right. He had been a medical orderly in the SAS and he therefore focused less on the threat that we might or might not have been about to face from terrorists or bandits than on what to do in a medical emergency. To make sure we got the point he showed a batch of grisly videos from Iraq and elsewhere. There were severed arteries, bellies embedded with shrapnel, shattered limbs and broken scalps. He told us what to do in the probable absence of any doctors, nurses or paramedics. He showed us the variety of ways in which to apply a tourniquet, explaining that you bleed to death within a few minutes if you can't staunch the geyser of arterial blood, but that if you leave the tourniquet in place for too long the limb will have to be amputated, adding drily that in these extreme circumstances it was probably 'better to be alive than dead'. He taught us how to resuscitate a cardiac casualty: thirty pumps on the chest followed by mouth-to-mouth – 'two breaths only and don't risk infection' – and assured us that it would be a waste of time if the patient had not been defibrillated within twenty minutes because he would be dead.

It was a useful briefing, but as we headed off into the Caucasus, I found myself remembering that long ago I had vowed that life was too short and too precious to take unnecessary risks again. Now here I was, voluntarily, curiosity battling with dread as we drove through a steppe that stretched endlessly to the horizon, dotted here and there with hamlets and, on the road itself, fast-food outlets and filling stations for the endless convoys of long trucks that worked their way east and west across southern Russia. We were waved through police checkpoints where the trucks were subject to casual inspection by customs officers in search of contraband. There were speed traps too – well signalled by oncoming drivers flashing their lights in warning – manned by jowly, overweight officers hoping to boost a low salary by offering the guilty motorist the option of facing prosecution or opening his wallet there and then in a mutually beneficial but illegal private transaction. Once a military convoy of armoured cars came towards us from the direction of Chechnya; otherwise there was no sign of tension. Along the way we passed peasant women at roadside stalls selling tomatoes, potatoes (washed and waxy in neat pyramid piles), melons, pumpkins and an extravagance of herbs. These mini-traders, shapeless in black woollen sweaters, long skirts, brown stockings and worn-out leather shoes, seemed old before their time. Their faces, nut-brown and wrinkled, half-hidden beneath bright scarves, looked careworn, resigned and impoverished. Were these the guardians of that 'simple wisdom' that Tolstoy believed to be 'in many ways superior to all the artifices of our culture and philosophy'? Perhaps so, but I did not envy them.

After some six hours we began to climb, almost imperceptibly, the fields of sugar beet, sunflowers and maize gradually giving way to upland grazing and then moorland, a wildness of heath that reminded me of Dartmoor but on an apparently eternal scale. And then, through the haze of the late evening, I saw the vague outline of one mountain and then another, twin sugarloafs on a high chaparral, their rounded peaks only just discernible, merging into a grey sky. It was my first sight of the landscape that had inspired three of Russia's greatest writers: Pushkin, Tolstoy and Lermontov. The Caucasus, or more precisely the North Caucasus, was once the border between the Soviet Union and its satellite countries to the south – a mountain range as awesome as any in Europe. Its highest peak, Mount Elbrus (5642 metres), is claimed by Russians to be the highest in Europe, which – if you accept, as some don't, that the Caucasus is indeed in Europe – is true, as Mont Blanc is a mere 4807 metres.

The myriad nations, tribes and clans who inhabit this tortured region have their origins in a past that long predates the emergence of Russia as a nation. For centuries the North Caucasian peoples were renowned as fierce warriors eager to engage in battle with foreign invaders and with each other. Their diverse histories, cultures and languages have long made the Caucasus a cauldron of seething enmities. Since the creation of the Russian state they have been united only in their hostility towards the colonial oppressors: tsarist imperialists who moved south from Moscow to occupy their ancestral lands that had extended deep into the fertile plains to the north of the mountains. Although it has become customary to describe the tribes of the Caucasus as a 'mountain people', most of them were lowland farmers and upland graziers who only retreated into their mountain strongholds when forced to do so by marauders seeking to dispossess them of their crops and animals.

The most significant of these tsarist invaders was Peter the Great, who initiated the imperial drive southwards into the Caucasus in the eighteenth century. Catherine the Great pursued this expansionist strategy, settling all the territory to the north of the mountains from the Black Sea eastwards to the Caspian, a frontier defined by the great rivers that snake along a natural border 400 miles in length. The turbulence of the Caucasus today – the reason why the Foreign Office issues its 'advisories' for the unwary – has its origins in that occupation and the vicious wars that ensued in the middle of the nineteenth century. Although most of the population is Muslim, it is tribalism and nationalism – not religion – that have been the principal source of the turmoil in which the region has been embroiled for so long.

As we rattled our way up towards the spa town of Pyatigorsk, I finished reading Mikhail Lermontov's *A Hero of Our Time*, his only novel but a small masterpiece that depicts the romance and cruelty of the Caucasian conflict through the experiences of his anti-hero, a young Russian cavalry officer called Pechorin. Pechorin is a bounder who appears to be animated by terminal ennui, but his existential swagger disguises – as in Lermontov himself – a hollow sadness of the soul that precisely captures those tragic contradictions by which Russian attitudes towards the Caucasus are still afflicted. The young officer is both captivated by the beauty of the mountains and in thrall to the casual brutality of the human conflict in which he is an enthusiastic participant. Thus he is awed by the Caucasian dawn, by 'the wreaths of mists coiled and twisted like snakes, sliding down the folds of neighbouring cliffs into the abyss, as though they sensed and feared the approach of day', which makes him relish the thought that 'there was peace in heaven and on earth'. But almost in the same breath he says, 'after a month I was so used to the hum of bullets and to being close to death that I honestly took more notice of the mosquitoes'.

Lermontov himself had fallen in love with the mountains when he was sent to stay with relatives in Pyatigorsk during the long, drowsy summers of his teenage years in the 1820s. There he mingled with the elite families of St Petersburg and Moscow, who came to take the spa waters and enjoy the cool mountain air. Sharing Lermontov's romance with a landscape that offered a refreshing contrast to the harsh weather and monotonous flatlands of the Russian steppe, they were indifferent to the suffering imposed on this most beautiful region by an occupation that was – and still is – as resented as it was ruthless.

Unlike most of his peers, Lermontov was a rebel. The trouble with Russia, he once said, was not that 'some people were suffering but that an immense number were suffering without realizing it'. From the age of sixteen, as a student at Moscow University, he produced a cascade of angry poems that poured eloquent contempt on the corruption of the imperial court and which, by inference, implicated the tsar himself. This was to tread in dangerous political territory. In 1837, when Pushkin was killed in a duel, Lermontov wrote an intemperate elegy, in a postscript to which he denounced the tsar's notorious courtiers: 'You, hungry crowd that swarms around the throne,/Butchers of freedom, and genius, and glory.' Describing them as 'parasites of vice', he held them ultimately responsible for goading Pushkin into his fatal challenge to a French diplomat who had allegedly cuckolded the poet. Lermontov's *lèse-majesté* was too much for Nicholas I, who instructed that Pushkin's literary heir be arrested and exiled to the Caucasus, there to serve – like Pushkin before him – in the front line of the imperial struggle against the mountain 'rebels'.

Instead of regarding this edict as a punishment, Lermontov rejoiced to find himself in so glamorous a role. Nor did the experience do anything to tame him. At the age of twenty-six this dandyish genius of a poet, fine horseman and renowned womanizer was an object of admiration and envy, a star of Pyatigorsk's social firmament. Pyatigorsk, he wrote, was Russia's 'Monaco', its streets 'crowded with dancers, gamblers and brawlers; gambling, wine and fighting make us feverish. We are inflamed by women by day and bedbugs by night.' In *A Hero of Our Time* Pechorin, surely expressing the nihilism and despair – the existential angst – of Lermontov's own alter ego, soliloquizes, 'My soul has been corrupted by society. My imagination knows no peace. My heart no satisfaction. Nothing counts for me. I grow used to sorrow as I do to pleasure and my life gets emptier every day.' Turgenev, who had met the young poet in St Petersburg, seemed to detect the ambiguities in his nature, noting 'something sinister and tragic in Lermontov's appearance; a certain gloomy and unkind force, pensive disdain and passion emanated from his swarthy countenance, from his large and steady eyes. Their heavy gaze strangely disagreed with the expression of his almost childishly tender and protruding lips.'

Lermontov evidently viewed the indigenous inhabitants of the Caucasus, against whom he was charged to do battle, with an ambiguous combination of admiration and contempt. In his great poem *Ismail Bey* they are sometimes portrayed as common criminals:

*Nothing to them to steal and cheat*
*Honey and wine their daggers seek*
*Pay with a bullet for their wheat.*

But he also saw them as tribesmen who had once been 'free as the winds' but were now forced to face 'the clank of gold and chains' because 'the sons of autocracy' had chosen to wage war on them to extinguish their ancestral rights. Thus when the 'women of the hills' exact mortal retribution his sympathies lie not with the 'pitiless' Russian invader but with his victims:

> Old men and babes he slaughters, pitiless,
> Young girls and mothers smears with the caress
> Of bloody hands; but the women of the hills
> Are not like women in their souls and wills;
> After a kiss, the dagger flashes high,
> A Russian reels and falls....

Elsewhere, reflecting on the futility of the war, he laments:

> ... O miserable men!
> What do they want? The earth's great plain
> Gives room for all beneath the sky;
> Yet ceaselessly and all in vain,
> Alone, they war for ever – Why?

Lermontov's romance with the Caucasus came to an end in an appropriately spectacular but terrible fashion. One evening at dinner the too-clever-by-half poet goaded a fellow officer with such cruel precision that his victim responded by challenging his tormentor to a duel. At dawn on 27 July 1841 the two young men, armed with pistols, faced each other for the last time. Lermontov was mortally wounded, the brief but frenzied life of one of Russia's greatest poets terminated, like that of his hero Pushkin, by a bullet fired less in anger than from pride. His body was carried back down to the town in secrecy (duelling was outlawed) and laid out in the cottage where he had been billeted, across the garden from where only twenty-four hours earlier he had entertained his fellow officers with such fatal abandon. The news travelled swiftly to St Petersburg, where Nicholas I is reported to have reacted with the words, 'A dog's death for a dog'. However, the tsar's sister persuaded him to amend the public record with an alternative verdict: 'Gentlemen, the man who could have taken Pushkin's place for us has been killed.' Lermontov himself had written, in *A Hero of Our Time*, that 'nothing has any significance in the world. Nature's a simpleton, fate is a goose, and life is but a brass farthing.'

## A SULPHUR BATH

Today Pyatigorsk is a slightly down-at-heel tourist resort that has clearly seen very much better times. However, its location, enfolded by mountains, combines with the weary grandeur of its remaining nineteenth-century buildings to give it a residual dignity and romance. In the municipal gardens young couples wander arm in arm eating ice-creams or posing for photos; pensioners sit in the shade on park benches playing chess, silent and intense; the energetic can climb to the neo-classical Academic Gallery or the Aeolian Harp to read or, if you go higher, to enjoy the glorious view towards 'the tallest mountain in Europe'.

The town tries to promote not only its poetic heritage, but the healing powers of its mineral waters, which can be taken at a dozen sanatoria of competing decrepitude, or in a handful of open-air pools naturally carved out of the rocks on the surrounding hillsides. Indulging myself with the illusion that I was literally following in the footsteps of Lermontov – who, like Pushkin before him and Tolstoy after him, took the waters here – I undressed to my underpants and picked my way over some slippery rocks to descend uneasily into the soft warmth of a sulphurous bath, a natural basin in the rock the size of a very large hot tub. I squeezed my body into what space had been left by the five Russian citizens who already occupied most of it.

As I slipped and skidded into the water, my legs inadvertently found themselves entwined around two of these elderly bodies – an ample woman in a bathing costume that could have graced Brighton beach sixty years ago, and a scrawny septuagenarian who had four gold teeth in the very front of his mouth and wore a smile of vacuous contentment. Extricating myself from their accidental embrace, I lay half-floating in the viscous liquid, watching their silent, almost comatose pleasure as their tired, worn-out bodies, which had laboured for so long in the service of the Soviet Union, felt the benefit. Just above my head a Jimmy Edwards lookalike in black bathing trunks lay immobile under the flow of water from the sulphur spring that drenched his walrus moustache. Nearer where I lay another woman, equally locked into immobility, her skin wrinkled like a prune from lingering too long in the water, was quite expressionless, her mind evidently elsewhere or perhaps nowhere. At first I felt as though I had trespassed upon a ritual to which I had not been invited and at which I was not entirely welcome. But, after scrutinizing me for a minute or two, the Brighton bathing belle – who dwarfed me physically – indulged me with an unexpected smile and, as soon as I confessed that I spoke no Russian, an astonished cackle of laughter. Undeterred, she told me that she had moved to Pyatigorsk from the far north of Russia, where she lived in the Arctic city of Norilsk and had been employed for most of her working life as a welder. She showed me her hands, great plates of worn sinew – 'Bigger and stronger than a man,' she said proudly – and invited me to compare them with mine. The contrast provoked the hitherto silent tableau around me into a burst of laughter – except for old walrus moustache, whose eyes were closed against the streaming water over his head.

My new friend was now in full flow. She told me about her family and how she was homesick for Norilsk, to where she would never now return. As she spoke, her eyes filled with tears at the memories of that lost past, and I found myself leaning forward discreetly to stroke one of her submerged forearms in an attempt at empathy; she looked down with surprise, as though unused to physical contact, and smiled. I felt yet again that surge of warmth that individual Russians so often inspire in me. She was by no means a kindred spirit but, behind that life-toughened and roughened exterior, so often brusque and blunt in Russians, she was endearingly susceptible. I wanted to put my arms around her and say, 'Don't worry. I understand that. I too know about loss and nostalgia.' Instead, being British, I slowly removed my comforting hand and she, regardless, recovered her poise. I volunteered that down here in the south the weather was at least balmier than in the north. She replied with a home-grown aphorism: 'In Norilsk we used to say that we have winter for twelve months and the rest is summer.' The thought seemed to cheer her. After twenty minutes in the sulphur pool (the recommended maximum at any one time if you want to avoid damaging your skin or worse) I extricated myself to genial farewells. Back in the hotel I washed off the sulphur residue, though the faintly noxious smell, like bad drains, remained in my nostrils for several hours.

The following day we drove up into the highlands towards the mountains and Mount Elbrus. It was very soon as intoxicating as Lermontov had led me to suppose. I generally prefer moorland to mountain. I like the thought of men and women managing to eke out a living from the soil with nature and animals, which is virtually impossible in mountains. Tolstoy, Russian literature's other great champion of the Caucasus, wrote a passage in a novella called *The Raid*, in which every sentence of one long paragraph ended, as if in a poem, with the incantation, a sigh of longing '…and the mountains', and I knew what he meant. As we climbed towards the higher peaks, we passed herdsmen bringing their animals down to the shelter of autumn pastures. We were also moving against the flow of a succession of elderly trucks and puffing tractors pulling antiquated trailers, all alarmingly overloaded, hauling stacks of hay mown on the high meadows to feed the livestock in winter. At one point I asked my driver to stop so that I could breathe in the air and the view – a milky blue-green landscape in the haze, hanging valleys and great ravines. An eagle, circling intently above us searching for prey, allowed itself to be carried up in the eddies of warm air, pirouetting towards the heavens.

A herd of cows wandered by, driven by a herdsman on a fine black horse. A big man, wrapped in a leather jerkin and wearing a turban, he had a face coarsened by weather and his eyes were half-buried in the creases of his skin. He had black hair, a thick moustache and broken teeth. On a whim I stopped him. 'Could I ride your horse?' I asked. I knew the animal to be a Cabardine stallion, a breed that is fast and hardy and now much in demand internationally for endurance trials, as they are tireless over very long distances. Without a moment's demur, the herdsman dismounted and gave me a leg-up. I felt that surge of delight that wide open spaces, fresh air and a good horse invariably provoke. Within a few moments, I was galloping away from the road, away from the herdsman, away from his cattle, up higher and higher it seemed, the wind whipping at my face, the horse's long mane flying. It was a moment of intense exhilaration; I knew what it was to be 'on top of the world'. After a while I stopped and stared about me. I could see for miles in every direction. There was not one building, not one other person, only the sigh of the wind and my horse's heaving breath. I sat there motionless, watching and listening, momentarily at peace with the natural world. When I rode back down to the road the herdsman was still there, perfectly at ease, although his cattle were out of sight. He nodded as I returned his horse, as if a foreigner wanting a ride were an everyday occurrence. Then, slinging himself aboard, he gave a roar of encouragement to the horse and galloped off after his meandering herd. He was soon a distant figure shrouded in the mountain mist – 'and the mountains'.

## A WEDDING IN THE CAUCASUS

I had been invited to a Caucasian wedding in a village not far from Nalchik, the capital of Cabardino-Balkaria. Ahmed and Anzar, two friends of the couple, had been deputed to drive me the ninety-minute journey from Pyatigorsk into the rural heart of the Caucasus. That neither of them was Russian was at once evident: they were open-faced, charming and debonair with, on the surface at least, a lightness of being that was as refreshing as the mountain air. They were both handsome men in their late thirties or early forties, energetic and considerate. Ahmed was a dental technician and Anzar had been trained as a lawyer. Well informed and communicative, they were anxious for me to understand that they were patriots – but not, I should be clear, 'Russian' patriots. Dispensing swiftly with small talk about wives and children, they moved to the only topic that seemed really to matter to them, speaking with an intensity that only semi-concealed a kind of desperation, as though I might disappear before they had finished what they had to tell me. Their apparent lightness of being gave way to a sombreness, in which pride, the offspring of ancient sorrows and persistent injustices became their dominant theme.

'We are not Russians,' Ahmed insisted. 'We are Cabardine people, Cabardians.' 'So if a foreigner asks you where you come from, what do you tell them?' I asked. 'I tell them that we are from the Caucasus. Not Russia. Never Russia.' To a degree that became almost obsessive, they explained that their national identity was affirmed by clinging on to the Cabardine language and by attempting to revive other aspects of an ancient culture. In their case, this meant weaponry. 'We are fighters by tradition,' they both asserted, each finishing the other's sentences to fill salient gaps in the story. Ahmed owned a facsimile of the Cabardine sabre, which, he insisted, was the finest in the world, even better than its Japanese equivalent. He was learning to master the skills required to wield it with the same murderous effect as his ancestors had deployed in their struggle to repel the Russian invaders in Lermontov's time. 'Unfortunately, only a few of us understand how to use these weapons. But we have to re-create these skills and traditions. We have to study the books and ask our elders. The dance movements that you will see at the wedding are warrior steps. We have to resurrect the art of fighting.' Then, as if I might have inferred from his passion that the viper of terrorism could be nurtured in the revival of the martial arts, he was anxious that I should understand the distinction between patriotism and nationalism. 'We are not nationalists,' they both insisted, aware that 'nationalist', at least when the term was used by Russians in reference to the Caucasus, was more or less synonymous with 'terrorist'.

Cabardino-Balkaria is unstable and combustible. Long contested between the Russian and Ottoman empires, the region was eventually wrested from his Turkish rival by Tsar Nicholas I in the first half of the nineteenth century. Any irredentist tendency among the Cabardians was suppressed by force. After the Bolshevik revolution, in what was 'spun' by the Kremlin as a recognition of their historic rights, their 'occupied' territory was designated an 'autonomous' region – a sleight of hand that, from the perspective of Ahmed and Anzar, meant almost as little under Putin as it meant under Stalin. They were at one about the futility of terrorism, but their antipathy to the Russian occupation of their land was unequivocal. 'Of course we are a proud people. The tsars did everything they could to wipe us off the map. Then came the Communists. When we were children in the Soviet Union "nationalism" was forbidden. Nationalism for us did not mean terrorism, but being proud of our history and our traditions, our language, our customs and our religion. But as schoolchildren we were not even allowed to speak our own language. Our teachers were Russian, and they made us speak in Russian. If they heard us speaking to each other in our Cabardine language, they ordered us to stop. Once I asked why this was so. The teacher replied, "Because I need to understand everything you are saying."'

After the collapse of the Soviet Union it was inevitable that the struggle for Chechen independence would eventually spill over into neighbouring Cabardino-Balkaria. In October 2005 Nalchik, where both Ahmed and Anzar live with their respective families, was besieged by insurgents. Armed with automatic weapons and grenade launchers, they attacked the Russian Interior Ministry, three city police stations and the republic's 'anti-terrorism' centre. It was a futile enterprise that was instantly crushed by the Russian security forces. At least sixty insurgents were killed, but not before they had accounted for twenty-four police officers. Whether the rebels were Islamists or separatists or nationalists (and there is continuing debate about this), whether they were led locally or by militants from other Caucasian republics, they had clearly relied on inside knowledge; for months afterwards the citizens of Nalchik cowered under a stern and sometimes brutal Russian investigation.

Before the attack, Ahmed had already suspected that one of his friends had been involved in some kind of conspiracy and had done his best to dissuade him from resorting to terrorism. Urging him to realize that to take on the endemic brutality of the security services would only provoke more of the same and worse, he argued that independence from Russia would only ever be possible through negotiation. To use force was to indulge a self-indulgent and self-destructive folly. When he realized that his advice would be ignored, Ahmed made sure to exclude himself from the company of anyone he feared might be involved in the plot. But, since he was a Cabardine patriot, it would have been inconceivable for him to report his suspicions to the police.

Ahmed's apprehension has proved to be well founded. Since the 2005 uprising, the Russian authorities have tightened the security screws in Nalchik. Believing that the nationalist insurrection had been fuelled by Islamic fundamentalism, they punished the faithful by closing the mosques in this mainly Muslim city. And, in an act of peculiarly cruel vengeance, they have refused to return the corpses of the insurgents to their grieving families for burial. Since then, for month after month, on one day of every week the mothers of the 'disappeared' have stood in vigil outside the City Hall demanding the return of their dead children so that they can buried according to the rites of the Muslim faith. So far this dignified plea has been to no avail. No better way, as Anzar noted with quiet despair, to store up hatred and nurture future terrorism.

At that point we came to a roadblock, one of scores in the Caucasus, which are manned (I saw no women employed on these duties) by Russian police officers and customs officials who are notoriously lax and corrupt. If you have committed an infraction of the law (a licence that is out of date, some papers missing, a malfunctioning sidelight), you have two options: to face the full rigour of the law, or bribe your way out of trouble whatever your nationality. Most choose the latter course. But, according to Anzar, 'If your vehicle has Caucasian number plates, you are certain to be stopped and hassled, even if your papers are in order.' 'What are these checkpoints for?' Ahmed demanded. 'Any terrorist can get round them, so they are useless as security barriers. They are simply there to show us who's who and to make money, or maybe to get another medal on your chest.' Anzar picked up, 'You know, Jonathan, we don't go to Moscow now. The Russian police are always on our backs just because we are from the Caucasus and the Russian people don't like us. They call us "blacks".'

I was reminded of a conversation I had had at the British Honorary Consul's dinner table by the Black Sea. Igor's wife was complaining about the cost of food and especially about the prices, which had risen sharply in her local market. 'Why is that?' I had asked, prompting her to reply, 'Because our market has been taken over by the blacks.' As I had not seen any black people in Novorossiysk, I asked to whom she was referring. 'The Caucasians,' she explained in a matter-of-fact way – but she had used the term 'black' in precisely the same tone that several decades earlier I had heard white racists in Alabama talk about 'niggers'. Linguistic ironies abound: that the ethnographical use of the phrase 'white Caucasian male' is a contradiction in Russian terms because Caucasians are 'black'; and that the term 'nationalist' is used self-referentially by all (but not only) Russian racists, although when they apply the term to Caucasians it means 'terrorist'.

Once we were through the checkpoint, Ahmed picked up his theme: 'Of course I do not hide the fact that I want our people to have our own sovereign state, but only through constitutional means. The Chechen militants are crazy. Do they not realize that you can't win against the power of the Russian state? They don't have the money, the weapons or the manpower. Do they expect the Russians to get out of Chechnya? If they did that, they would lose the entire North Caucasus –

the whole lot would crumble. The Russians would never do it.' We talked about the oil pipelines that run through the Caucasus and the oil that lies underground in Chechnya. We reminded ourselves of the fact that the states to the south and west, which had once been satellites of the Soviet Union and a buffer against NATO during the Cold War, were now independent nations and therefore that the mountains had become the only physical border guarding the southern perimeter of the Russian Federation. It was naive, we concurred, to suppose even for a moment that an insecure but resurgent Kremlin would willingly surrender the North Caucasus to its indigenous peoples, whose ancient internal rivalries ran almost as deep as their shared loathing of Russian hegemony. To reinforce the last point, Anzar added contemptuously, 'If we were to drive into Chechnya, the two of us would be killed and you would be kidnapped and held for ransom.' The Foreign Office 'advisory' suddenly acquired a new significance.

We arrived at our destination soon after midday, by which time the wedding celebration had already started. A confusion of festivity – cars bedecked with balloons, ribbons and flowers, and laden with presents – immediately identified the bridegroom's family home. A group of young men, the bridegroom's party, made a show of preventing any car entering until their occupants had paid a ransom. After a brief show of resistance and much tooting of horns, the guests handed over a few rouble notes and the gates were thrown open to allow them inside. In the boot of one car a live sheep, trussed in ropes and with a green ribbon around its neck, groaned with what seemed like foreboding. One of the men lifted it out and dragged it away to the orchard behind the house where, out of sight of the guests, he slit its throat with one swift swipe of a sharp knife. Soon the smell of mutton, cooking in a cauldron on an open fire, wafted across the courtyard. Ahmed and Anzar raised their rifles and fired repeated shots into the air. The sound of the shots, an ear-splitting crackle, cut through the insistent beat of the traditional Cabardine music, updated for a twenty-first-century electronic organ, which pulsated with ancient warrior energy.

Very soon, unable to resist the pull of the dance, one, then two, then three young men, dark-eyed, black-haired, olive-skinned and wearing snappy black suits with winkle-picker shoes, took centre stage in the dusty yard. They were surrounded by young women, sisters and girlfriends, some dressed in T-shirts and jeans, others more formally in flowery summer frocks, who formed a circle around the men, clapping in time to the music. Turning and twisting, advancing and retreating, their feet hardly on the ground, the dancers were as self-absorbed as matadors preparing to face the bull. Then a sinister apparition appeared from the crowd. A monkey mask hid his face and he had a sheepskin fez on his head. He carried a walking stick, around which he skipped and pirouetted as he sauntered in and out of the circling dancers, who made way for him, a threatening fool who caused gasps of fearful mirth.

The courtyard was enclosed by a single-storey family house, painted white, and an L-shaped veranda, which combined to provide the homestead with privacy from the prying eyes of outsiders beyond the front gates. Under the shade of this veranda, the elders of the community sat watching the proceedings. At one table were the men, two of them wearing black bowler hats shiny with age; at the other the women, widows, wives and sisters, all in their Sunday best. The men barely spoke, but stared wistfully at the dancers as they remembered their lost youth, while the women gossiped with urgent intensity. Each group seemed to inhabit a quite different world from the other. Both tables were laden for the feast – mutton stew, polenta, pasta, sweetcorn, rice, beetroot, carrots, lettuce, cabbage, cucumbers and potatoes, delicately chopped up and elaborately arranged in a seductive display of colour, taste and texture by the women of the family. Only the peas, I noticed, came from a tin. A turkey cock watched, puffed up and gobbling with indignation at this human invasion of his territory. An indifferent chicken wandered through the throng picking up pieces of waste food.

For the most part the Muslims of Cabardino-Balkaria take a relaxed view of alcohol, and as the afternoon wore on, still with no sign of bride or groom (who had both departed earlier for the mayor's office to solemnize in law a marriage that had already been blessed by the local imam), the beer and vodka started to flow in abundance. Faces began to glow and smiles lasted longer, inhibition and formality gradually yielding to a mood of prospective recklessness. One toast followed another, and I soon found myself embraced as though I had long been a member of the bridegroom's extended family. Summoned by their men, the women began to dance as well, prettily but without the flamboyance of their peacock suitors. I was seized by one of the dancers, who insisted on teaching me the rudiments of the dance. My arms flailing lumpenly, my feet tied to the earth, I was a source of embarrassment to myself, but evidently of affectionate entertainment to the onlookers, whom I hoped were saying to one another, 'He's making rather a fool of himself, but at least he's trying.'

After I had escaped, exhausted, Ahmed took me to one side to explain the ritual. By tradition, a proposal of marriage was made by the groom's family who, by appointment, would visit the prospective bride's house for the purpose. The girl's family would never agree at once; three such visits were required before her father and mother would consent to barter their daughter away. In upper-class families, as recently as the second half of the twentieth century, the two young people might not even have set eyes on each other until the third visit. This was not to say that the two principals in this ritual were entirely irrelevant to the process. In a decorous, symbolic way the girl's parents would find out if she could imagine sleeping with her suitor, asking a question designed to elicit the response, 'There are many stars in the sky tonight' if she wished to reject the prospect. Silence signalled consent. Similarly, the groom, having inspected his prospective bride, would pick up his hat from the sideboard. To replace it on his head back to front signified rejection. To claim her, on the other hand, he would plunge his dagger into the table or scratch his arm with it until he drew blood. Under no circumstances would either of them say 'yes' or 'no' directly.

Today that tradition has finally died out, although a 'good' marriage is still coveted, and echoes of the marriage ritual persist. As the tempo of this celebration became more insistent, the bride, Nishasha, finally appeared dressed in white, her head veiled. She stood in the midst of the assembly, modest and nervous, as one by one grandmother, mother, aunts and cousins approached her in line, looking as though they were about to receive Holy Communion, but in fact to kiss her on both cheeks and mutter a private blessing. Then her mother lifted the veil to reveal a genuinely blushing bride. She was not beautiful in any conventional way, but her demurely downcast eyes and shy smile gave her a luminous innocence that enchanted everyone.

A few minutes later, a tumult of disruptive noise announced the arrival of the bridegroom, all swagger and show, surrounded by his friends and led by his brother. He advanced to claim his bride. But it was not so simple. There was a ransom to be paid first: the bride's mother had to be compensated because her future son-in-law had (as custom dictates) 'kidnapped' her daughter and seduced her into accepting his hand in marriage without her mother's consent. Eventually a deal was struck. The bridegroom stuffed more and more notes into his mother-in-law's hands until she finally agreed that the marriage could be consummated. But even that was not quite the end of it. Suddenly there was a roar from the wedding party as the bride's brothers and cousins, helped now by his own friends, seized the bridegroom and threw him to the ground where they proceeded to give him a good (mock) kicking. At this point I rather lost the plot and retreated to the old men's table, where I was pressed to have another vodka followed by another and another. From this vantage point I watched indulgently as the shadows lengthened and the evening drifted into night, the music still pulsing, the winkle-pickers still twirling – a culture refusing to die.

# BESLAN

The next morning I succumbed once more to gloom. It was a beautiful day, with a low sun above the mountains, a river sparkling in the light and the water from the melted snows gurgling through a sheen of whitened boulders. Only the very jaundiced indeed could be immune. And yet I found myself noting in my diary, 'I have seen other mountains and rivers no less spectacular elsewhere in the world and I can no longer gasp in awe. I am sixty-two and I see mortality around the corner. The question of "purpose" becomes pressing. I shall make no impact on Russia, make no footprint, no mark. So what I am doing here? I should be at home.' As I wrote those words I knew it was self-indulgent, but that is what happens when the black crow settles on my shoulder. 'Pull yourself together,' I told myself before returning to the edge of depression and writing, 'The truth is I am lost. Nothing shocks me, nothing surprises me, nothing touches me. Where has my curiosity gone? Why don't I have the courage to call a halt? To give up the perpetual round of meetings, contracts, editorial battles, e-mails, long journeys, uncomfortable hotels, the nerves, the anxiety about meeting new people?' When I read those words back to myself later, the immersion in self-pity disgusted me. But it was how I felt at that moment and for a while the mood embraced me in its vice, draining me of energy and resolve. I know that these periods of deep gloom will pass; and, mercifully, that I am not trapped perpetually in the dangerous underworld that genuine depressives have to endure. Even so, here in Russia I have too often found myself wanting to cower under the covers instead of getting up and on with the day. The mood generally evaporates under the pressure and stimulation of work, and in this case I wonder in retrospect whether this particular slough of despond was caused as much by the nuptial vodka as by the prospect of the day ahead.

I did not relish the thought of my visit to School Number One in the town of Beslan. I had a vivid image in my mind of the charred and broken bodies of the little children in the ruins of the school gymnasium; of their parents, demented by shock and grief; of the terrorists waving their weapons; and of the Russian soldiers coldly but wildly ending the siege on the orders of a remote and uncaring Kremlin. On one day, 3 September 2004, 334 hostages, 186 of them children, died in the battle. Hundreds more were wounded.

I had read Tolstoy's short masterpiece *Hadji Murat*, in which he lays bare the inner truths of the nineteenth-century conflict between the guerrilla fighters of the Caucasus and their imperial Russian enemy. He wrote of the 'insuperable revulsion, contempt, disgust and hatred for all Russians' in the heart of a Chechen warlord, and of the 'cruel, senseless and dishonourable imperial will' of the tsar, who had licensed his military commanders and their men to regard the Chechens as a subhuman species against whom no vengeance, however terrible, was to be regarded as an atrocity. And as I walked towards the school, his lament, echoing Lermontov's *Ismail Bey*, from a short story called '*The Raid*', passed and repassed through my mind: 'Is it possible that there is not room for all men on this beautiful earth? Can it be that amidst this enchanting nature feelings of hatred, vengeance, and the desire to exterminate their fellow beings can endure in the souls of men?' In a sense this made all further comment redundant. And yet I knew I had to go on, and that to pass by on the other side would be an act of moral cowardice, a failure to bear witness – like visiting Jerusalem but avoiding the Holocaust Museum. The particularity and universality of this horror gave me no right to make a detour around such implacable evidence of humanity's inhumanity.

You approach the ruined gymnasium up a concrete path through the rough grass of what was once a playground. It was quite silent, but you can hear the echoes of children, shouting, quarrelling and laughing, who are now dead. Wreaths of plastic flowers, garish but loving, line what is now the shell of the building. Inside, it is open to the sky; what remains of the roof are rusting struts and girders. The walls are scorched and peeling. At either end a twisted hoop of metal reminds you that the children used to play basketball here. A simple wooden

Orthodox cross has been erected in the middle of this otherwise deserted space. It is surrounded by a circle of plastic water bottles, both a reminder that the children suffered terrible thirst and a symbol of the belief that, in their afterlife, even heavenly souls need refreshment. On the walls along each side of the gymnasium the little faces stare out at you from fading photographs, side by side in long rows: the smiling, the proud, the hopeful, the shy, the recalcitrant, the beautiful and the plain; their immortalized lives a permanent rebuke.

As I took this in, blinking back the tears, I saw a boy walk into the gymnasium and walk up to one of these photographs. He must have been about twelve years old. Oblivious of my presence, he stared at the image – a brother? a friend? – for a full minute. Then he turned away, shaking his head as if in disbelief, and walked out again without looking to left or right. And then I wept. For him, for them, and, I suppose, for myself as well.

Outside the school a woman walked up to me, wearing a purple dress to her ankles. She was thin and worn, her face still beautiful but prematurely aged. She had a grubby package under her arm that, at her behest, I unwrapped. Inside there was a photo, grimy from constant handling. It was of a barely recognizable corpse, the charred body of a child. Her child. 'I look at this every day,' she said. 'My life has stopped. They tell me lies. I want the truth.' What truth? Whose truth? Why had her child died? Whose weapon? Whose decision? What madness? I knew what she meant and I also know that she will never know, that she will never be told, and that this implacable fact will torment her to the grave. Her sorrow was terrible to witness. I stroked her arm, wanting to hug her frail, small body to mine, but fearing that this would be an intrusion that her culture could not bear. But even my modest gesture of sympathy was enough to cause the tears to pour down her cheeks. She turned away, inconsolable, shaking her head, demented with grief. She needed care and counselling, but when I asked if the survivors of the massacre could access such support, a sympathetic official shrugged. The answer, of course, was 'no'.

They have built a new school in Beslan, where the pupils from School Number One are taught with other children of the town who were not so directly affected by the trauma. I met one of their teachers, Elena, a startlingly beautiful woman in her mid-thirties, elegantly dressed in a lime-green skirt and orange sweater. Her eyes were a deep brown, brimming with intelligence and strength. 'There is no happy ending for the children,' she said. 'Sometimes they suddenly close in on themselves, they become very pensive, it is very hard to draw them out. We try to give them psychological support, but we don't talk about it much. The best thing is time. Time will heal.'

The last thought was not very convincing, and the less so when she added, 'It is hard for the teachers as well because days go by and we don't talk about this act of terrorism. Once the Caucasus was associated with everything that was beautiful. It was proud. It was great. People wanted to see the fantastic scenery. It is so sad for us that the word "Caucasus" is now only associated with war, conflict and death. But, you know, we are teachers. We have to hope. We have to believe, and the only way to be good teachers is to help our children to believe, to believe there is something good, that their future holds something positive.' She sounded so wistful that I asked her what she thought might happen. 'Some people want this struggle to continue – they make money out if it. Once we used to cross the border quite freely. Now we are fearful even to look in the direction of Chechnya.' She said this without any hint of melodrama, but rather in a tone of finality. At that moment a small boy ran up to her – her son, who was one of the survivors of the siege. She hugged him and they walked off together out of the new school courtyard into the street, her words still hanging in the air.

In the cemetery on the outskirts of Beslan there is a section for the children who died in the massacre: six long rows of identical red and black marble graves, but made touchingly personal both by the haunting photographs of the victims engraved formally on each headstone and by a favourite toy placed reverently at the base of every one – a grey-green Maserati, a teddy bear, a plastic Batman without Robin, a crushed rubber football, a once-loved hairless doll. I watched a young women tending the fresh flowers laid on her son's grave. She wept as she worked, distractedly, as if unable to leave the spot. The boy's name was Boris Gurieva. When she finally wandered away, I read the inscription under the photo of this twelve year old: 'You were the man in our house. A support for the family. Forgive us that we did not protect you.' And on another, to a girl named Veira, 'You were a light for us. Our light has disappeared. The world around us is in darkness.'

## IN THE MOUNTAINS OF DAGESTAN

At the border between North Ossetia and Dagestan I had to say goodbye to Ahmed and Anzar, taking their advice that it would be wiser for us to find another guide and protector in this fearsomely clannish region where they were both strangers. I had opted to skirt Chechnya. Although we had been given formal permission by the Ministry of Foreign Affairs to enter that combat zone, we would have been obliged to travel under military escort and the very watchful eye of the FSB. I would have had little chance to meet any Chechen foolhardy enough to tell me the truth about the current occupation. However, I did make an attempt to sound out local people to see if anyone would take us in by one of the many unofficial routes that bypass the few heavily fortified main roads into Chechnya. One braggart assured us that there would be 'no problem' and that the Cossack community, of which he was a member, would find us a guide. But the closer we got to the agreed date for the trip, the more elusive became our guide. In the end we gave up. With Ahmed's and Anzar's warnings fresh in my mind, I was not unduly disappointed.

As we drove through Dagestan past one of the few official crossing points into Chechnya – a forest of barricades in steel and wire, with guardposts and a roadblock all bristling with antennae and bedecked with searchlights, and patrolled by soldiers and police in armoured cars –

I was reminded of the words written by Anna Politkovskaya, the famous Russian reporter, about Putin's man in Chechnya. President Ramzan Kadyrov, she wrote, was a 'psychopath' who had told her that his favourite pastime was 'fighting', warning for good measure that 'those who do not surrender we shall exterminate'. I was glad that I was not to have the privilege of his acquaintance. And, as it happened, I was to discover what I thought was as much, if not more, about the historic hatreds that fuel the Chechen secessionists in Dagestan as I would have done had I defied the advice of Ahmed and Anzar.

Over the last decade or more I had followed the brutal story of the Chechen tragedy spasmodically from the safety of a radio or television studio in London, wondering at the courage of colleagues who braved the front line to tell it how it was. The 'first' Chechen war started in 1994, following the republic's declaration of independence from Russia three years earlier in the chaotic days after the collapse of the Soviet Union. Between 1991 and 1994 Chechnya had been stricken by a level of instability and violence that virtually amounted to civil war. In the course of this continuing upheaval, some three hundred thousand ethnically non-Chechen citizens fled the republic. In the prevailing anarchy, President Boris Yeltsin issued an ultimatum to the warring factions, but it was ignored. The Russian invasion of Chechnya began in December 1994. The Kremlin had convinced itself that its superior military might would ensure a short, sharp victory over the rebels. Instead the Russian troops found themselves bogged down in a military campaign that lasted two gruesome years. Around a hundred thousand people, at least half of them civilians, are thought to have been killed in the war, notably in the sustained aerial bombardment of the Chechen capital, Grozny, by the Russian air force and in their indiscriminate terror bombing elsewhere.

Despite this barbarity, the Russian armed forces did not prevail, and in 1996 Yeltsin was forced to call a halt to the slaughter. It was a humiliating defeat for what had so recently been the world's other superpower, and an extraordinary victory for the Chechen guerrillas, who appeared, for a moment, to have won their struggle for independence. But in 1999, following a wave of insurgent attacks against military and police targets in Chechnya and a succession of mysterious terrorist atrocities directed at civilians within Russia, which were attributed – rightly or wrongly – to Chechen Islamists, Yeltsin's newly appointed prime minister, Vladimir Putin, ordered the troops into battle once again. This time, after a winter siege of the capital in which yet again tens of thousands of civilians died, the might of the Russian army prevailed.

But there has been no peace. Instead, terror begat terror in a downward spiral of horror that was barely reported in the outside world, though it has been captured in print with brilliance and courage by Anna Politkovskaya, who illuminated in unsparing detail the medieval savagery unleashed by the Kremlin upon the people of Chechnya. Her accounts of the rape, torture, murder, misery and starvation inflicted on an entire population by Putin's brutalized conscripts alerted human-rights organizations both inside and outside Russia, but to very little avail. The chancelleries of the Western world, the advocates of freedom and democracy around the world, remained stubbornly indifferent, blind and deaf to the entreaties of the victims in Chechnya. After the destruction of the Twin Towers on 11 September 2001, Putin cunningly reminded his Western 'partners' in Washington and the chancelleries of Europe that in Chechnya he was merely assisting their global struggle in the worldwide 'war on terror' – and in this war, as they clearly appreciated, almost anything goes.

In Dagestan I was in the wise and knowledgeable hands of a Dagestani professor of ethnography, Magamed Khan, who looked like the mountain tribesman that he is. Swarthy and weatherbeaten, at first glance he could have been mistaken for a local guide but the appearance deceives. Khan is renowned internationally as a scholar and, among aficionados, for the delicately woven carpets that are handmade in the traditional style in Dagestani villages and that he exports to Europe and the United States. His academic credentials are beyond dispute, but he combines clinical detachment with a deep passion for his land and his people that I have never encountered in Europe. I could not have found a better companion to steer me through this troubled republic. I felt immediately secure in his company and quickly forgot about the Foreign Office 'advisory' and the reports of abduction and murder, which over the last few years have emanated from this wild and mountainous terrain.

Khan wanted me to understand better the origins of the Chechen conflict, which historically had been inextricably entwined with the fate of Dagestan. He took me first to a village close to the official border with Chechnya. Chankayurt was at the very end of the line, down a long road on the edge of the steppe, just beneath the mountains that lour in the distance. At first glance, the village was indistinguishable from the scores of others in the region. Sleepy in the afternoon sun, it displayed little physical charm or character, nothing to mark it out as in any way special. There was the usual motley collection of dogs and chickens, a man digging a drain, a boy mending a bike, but otherwise nothing to be seen except single-storey, tin-roofed houses sheltering behind corrugated iron fencing. But Chankayurt had a story to tell that put my aesthetic jaundice to shame.

As we walked down the dusty street that ran through the village, in my case feeling as though we had lost the five other members of the Magnificent Seven, Khan explained the background to the story of Chankayurt. The borders between the Caucasian republics had not been drawn on a map but were perpetually contested by rival clans and tribes until eventually, in the early nineteenth century, a kind of order, a modus vivendi, emerged. In this process Chechnya spilled into Dagestan (and vice versa) so that there were now 120,000 Chechens living in Dagestan, where they freely intermingled and intermarried with their fellow Caucasians. However, Chankayurt was exclusively populated by Chechens. This anomaly – this accident of history – helped illuminate an unforgotten and unforgiven past.

In the mid-nineteenth century, the Chechens and Dagestanis had fought together against the tsarist occupation. After a war that lasted twenty-five years, the rebels were finally defeated. For more than half a century, until 1917, they endured Russian hegemony, crushed but resentful. But any hopes they might have held that the 'autonomy' promised to them by the Bolshevik revolution might liberate them from the tsarist yoke were swiftly dispelled by Stalin. Their religion, Islam, was as reprehensible to their Soviet masters as Christianity, while their myriad tribal distinctions, their scores of mutually incomprehensible languages, were a violation of the Soviet vision, an anachronism to be eliminated. Indeed, Stalin soon made their persecution at the hands of Tsar Nicholas I seem positively benign. For the Chechens, and therefore for the villagers of Chankayurt, the rendezvous with catastrophe came in February 1944.

Khan took me to meet some of the village elders who had been boys at that time. As a friend of Khan, I was welcomed and embraced with the traditional Chechen greeting, 'May you be neither hungry nor cold.' We sat in an orchard under a cherry tree, as idyllic as a Chekhovian stage set, while they produced photographs of their families and told their tale with that concentrated fluency that flows from the repetition of great anguish. On 23 February 1944 the police arrived and instructed the men of the village to gather in the mosque. Once they were inside, the doors were locked and they were given their instructions. They should return to their homes, collect their belongings and report with their families for a long journey. Then, at gunpoint, the entire village – more than a thousand men, women and children – were loaded like animals into twelve Studebaker trucks (which had been sent by the Americans to assist the Russian front against the Nazis) and driven to the railhead at Khasavyurt. There the villagers were herded into cattle trucks for a train journey to an unknown destination. It was snowing, it was cold, and they were very frightened.

The elders looked at me intently as one of them spoke, willing me to understand the enormity of what I was being told. 'We were freezing,' one of them said, his old eyes still burning with the intensity of remembered feeling. 'It was February, remember – winter, and there was no heating. And we had no food. We were so tightly packed together that we could hardly breathe. People died, and we had to throw them out of the truck for dogs and birds to devour.' One of the elders then took me to meet an old woman who had been fifteen at the time of this deportation. She elaborated on their experience, speaking in Chechen, which her daughter-in-law translated into Russian. 'The snowstorm was so severe that we could hardly keep our eyes open. My mother had been so scared that she was unable to gather any of our belongings in time. So we had nothing at all except a little flour or corn for the children. Everyone was crying. It was terrible.' She paused at the enormity of it, her eyes brimming with tears, before repeating, 'It was terrible. We did not know where we were going. The journey took fifteen days, but there was real hunger and many people died.' She paused again. After a long silence, I asked what her feelings were now. 'Of course,' she replied, 'the memories are still very bitter.'

It was only when they reached the remote Central Asian republic of Kyrgyzstan that they discovered that they were not alone, that under Stalin's orders the entire population of Chechnya, some hundreds of thousands of families, had been deported as well: their ancestral homeland had been emptied almost overnight. To this day no one knows what inspired Stalin to this dreadful crime. Ostensibly it was alleged that the Chechens had collaborated with Hitler; that they had become informers helping to sabotage and subvert the Soviet defence of the Caucasus from the Nazis. But the evidence is so scanty as to be incredible and even if some Chechens had collaborated with the Germans, it was scarcely justification for the punishment and deportation of an entire nation.

Whatever the explanation for Stalin's paranoid cruelty, the suffering of the Chechen people was far from over. Once in Kyrgyzstan, the families were distributed among the collective farms in the region, where they lived in appalling, slave-like conditions and with very little means of subsistence. The old woman in Chankayurt picked up the threads of her story: 'I was too weak to help when members of my family started to die. We had to carry their bodies out of the house and try to cover them with soil, but it was only a light covering. But we had to get them out of the house.' When she arrived in Kyrgyzstan, she was the youngest of five. Within two years she was the only one left alive, a seventeen-year-old girl alone in an alien land.

In 1956, three years after he succeeded Stalin as First Secretary, Nikita Khrushchev announced that the Chechen deportees would be allowed to return to their homes. The news came to the exiles from Chankayurt via a radio broadcast. And that was all. No regrets. No apology. No inquiry. Nor did the state authorities provide any assistance, funds or transport to help with their repatriation. According to the elders of Chankayurt, most of the Chechens simply sold or abandoned their possessions, and one by one made the long trek back from Central Asia to their homeland. Everyone in Chankayurt seems to have a memory of the Return. They found that the village had been pillaged, their possessions stolen, their livestock sold and their homes requisitioned. 'We had to start our lives again,' one of them explained. 'We had nothing.' I offered what sympathy I could, telling the old lady that their experiences were too dreadful for most people even to imagine. She replied, 'There is nothing for us to do but to cry.' Although she had heard the story many times before, her daughter-in-law was clearly distressed. I asked if her generation was still affected by what had happened. She replied, 'When my mother-in-law tells us these stories she cries and we cry too. It is terrible and it is painful.' From one generation to the next, I thought – the memories of the parents passed on to the children, neither forgotten nor forgiven. It helped put the atrocity at Beslan into historical, though not moral, perspective.

I asked the old men what they thought of the crisis in Chechnya today. 'They are our brothers, and what is happening there causes us a great deal of sadness and unhappiness,' the senior figure among them said as his friends nodded in agreement. 'During the war

Chechen refugees found their way to our village and we "adopted" their village inside Chechnya. But many of them who stayed there died. There is no trace of what happened to them – we do not even know where they are buried. It is a disease, and it the same for us here as it is for our brothers in Chechnya.' I asked if this 'disease' made them angry. Mindful perhaps of the long reach of the FSB, they did not answer directly, but one eventually replied, 'You have to remember the deportation and then this war. There has been no attempt to communicate, no attempt at dialogue.' Then, at a tangent, he added, 'There are seven hundred police officers in this district. You know how many of them are Chechen? Not one.' What explanation did they have for this discrimination? I wondered. 'It is stupidity, stupidity, the absence of intelligence,' one of them answered. So do the Chechen people have any responsibility for the horror and the misery of the past decade? The answer came back, short and swift and final: 'No.'

The second Chechen war, which lasted for only a few months from late 1999 until the spring of 2000, was partly obscured by the 'Dagestan War', a brief but bloody battle in the autumn of 1999, which took place in the mountains that form the border with Chechnya. The trigger for this conflict was the 'invasion' of Dagestan by the Chechen warlord Shamil Basayev. He crossed over with a thousand or more fighters to support a small force of Dagestani separatists who, following the 1991 Chechen *démarche*, had proclaimed the independence of Dagestan too. But Dagestan was not Chechnya, and the Russians used maximum firepower on land and from the air to rout the Dagestani insurgents. Scores of fighters and many hundreds of civilians died in the onslaught, while the Russians admitted to suffering 1200 casualties, including 279 dead. The Dagestani separatists, supported by Basayev's guerrillas and, it is rumoured, a contingent of foreign Islamists and mercenaries, lacked popular support, even from among those who aspired to independence. Today the remnants of that insurgency, a small guerrilla force of Dagestani Islamists, is scattered in the mountains, unable to make headway with what the overwhelming majority of their compatriots evidently regard as a wild and desperate cause.

The critical events in Tolstoy's last novel, *Hadji Murat*, took place in those self-same mountains at the height of an epic twenty-five-year struggle for independence, which lasted from 1833 to 1858. The leading protagonists were the notoriously quixotic and cruel Tsar Nicholas I and a charismatic warlord, Sheik Shamil, who had, for the first – and last – time, managed to unite the disparate peoples of the Caucasus against the Russian enemy. 'I am fascinated,' wrote Tolstoy in the foreword to *Hadji Murat*, 'by the parallel between the two main figures pitted against each other: Shamil and Nicholas I. They represent two poles of absolutism – Asiatic and European.' Such is Tolstoy's genius that *Hadji Murat* – making allowances for changes in military technology – reflects precisely the attitudes and motives that so poison the Caucasus today: the romance, the duplicity, the hatred, the nobility, the tyranny and the self-delusion.

Hadji Murat, Tolstoy's eponymous hero, is one of Sheik Shamil's most senior lieutenants, but finds himself trapped between the twin despotisms referred to by Tolstoy and tortured by competing loyalties and passions. Although he has 'an insuperable revulsion for all Russians', he is also locked into a tribal blood feud with his own leader, whom he loathes beyond all measure. As an officer in the imperial army who had served on the Caucasus front, Tolstoy was exceptionally well placed to explore the forces by which the conflict was animated and to present them through the dramatic prism of Hadji Murat's private torment.

In skirmishes that – aside from the weapons available to either side (they are, of course, very much more destructive and indiscriminate today) – are uncannily reminiscent of the twenty-first-century kind, Russian officers lead light cavalry charges against a more or less invisible enemy, firing vaguely in the direction of a guerrilla force that immediately melts away into the safety of the forest. It is a hit and, more often, miss affair – 'a cannonball flew by, with ominous whistling and, ploughing up the earth, hit the middle of a string of carts in the maize field along the road'. However, such haphazard encounters do not prevent the Russian soldiers returning triumphantly 'in the most cheerful frame of mind' to their headquarters, from where their general sends back exaggerated reports of their 'victory' to Moscow. In the meantime, the rebels steal back to the vantage point from which they had been momentarily dislodged.

To punish one particularly recalcitrant rebel stronghold the Russian troops enter a village, killing, plundering, torching huts and poisoning the water supply. To add further insult they defile the mosque before riding off with their booty of cattle and grain. Afterwards the elders gather in the village square. One of them has lost his son, bayoneted in the back; his wife is weeping over the corpse. They feel, in one of Tolstoy's telling phrases, 'bewilderment before the ridiculous cruelty of these beings'. Consumed by feelings that are 'stronger than anger' for these 'rats, poisonous spiders and wolves', they know that one day they will wreak vengeance on their Russian tormentors. As portrayed by Tolstoy, Shamil, their military and spiritual leader, rules like a despot, presiding whimsically, if not psychopathically, over the decisions of a shariah court that distributes 'Islamic' justice with chilling imperturbability – 'two were to be condemned to have their hands chopped off for thieving, one to be beheaded for murder, three were pardoned'. Even though his followers have to endure unspeakable reprisals at the hands of the Russians, Shamil rallies the waverers with his fiery eloquence, promising them (in words that have a disconcerting twenty-first-century resonance): 'If you are not rewarded in this life, then you will receive your reward in the next.'

Tolstoy's portrait of Shamil (*Hadji Murat* was completed in 1901, almost half a century after his own experiences at the front line – though not published until two years after his death in 1910) is consistent with the historical record, but far more vivid and illuminating in both psychological insight and close observation. Shamil was indeed an inspiration on the battlefield, blessed with daring and cunning. For year after year, he outwitted and eluded the might of the imperial army, and the manner of his eventual capture (which fell outside the timeframe of Tolstoy's novel) is recorded with pride in the histories of the region, as though his defeat had been their victory. Perhaps in a sense it was: today Tsar Nicholas I is universally reviled in Russia, while Shamil has become a legendary figure who inspires nostalgic reverence not only among insurgents but throughout the otherwise divided peoples of the Caucasus as well.

My guide, Khan, did not precisely share that reverence but was determined that I should see the exact spot where Shamil and his dwindling band of fighters were allegedly cornered and driven to surrender. We drove up through high, lush valleys, which grew vegetables on a commercial scale – cabbages in every direction – into the uplands, which were breathtakingly like the Yorkshire Dales. Soon we were above the tree line on the edge of a remote and forbidding range of mountains, granite-grey as though a vast herd of giant elephants had lain down one behind the other, undulating and fat to the far horizon. As we went further into this other-worldly terrain, we passed great gorges and canyons and whorls of rock in tiered balconies and natural amphitheatres, seeming to anticipate a heavenly audience for a performance of *Götterdämmerung*. The scale of these surroundings filled me with an exhilarating stupefaction so that I almost expected to see Wotan appear from behind a garrison of rock to berate us earthlings for daring to trespass into the Kingdom of the Gods.

And then, like pirates searching for treasure – 'X marks the spot' – we found the tiny, half-ruined hamlet where Sheik Shamil had made his last stand, perched in a cleft of rock, protected from the wind but not from the imperial troops hunting him down. With his small group of followers, a few score fighters, his wife and children, he was surrounded. According to the legend (to which *Hadji Murat* makes no reference), Shamil wanted to fight to the end, but his son implored him to surrender. Eventually, after protracted negotiations – the Russians knew very well that to kill him would further fuel the irredentist fires they were trying to extinguish – he left the cottage where he had taken refuge and, head held high, began to stride down the mountain to where his adversary, the Russian general, was bivouacked a mile or so away. As he passed the victorious Russian soldiers, who stood on either side of the mountain track, they began to mock and jeer at their captive. Almost immediately Shamil halted. Declaring that he would rather die in one last battle than face such humiliation, he made as if to retrace his steps. Hearing this, the Russian general at once dispatched an order to his men instructing them to remain silent and respectful in victory. They obeyed, and on 29 August 1859, now flanked by a guard of honour, Sheik Shamil formally offered his surrender.

You might have expected this 'terrorist' to be deported to Siberia, if not tortured and executed. Instead, so great was the romantic attachment to his name in St Petersburg and Moscow that Tsar Nicholas provided him with a palace in which he was incarcerated with all the splendour of an exotic bird in a gilded cage. Twelve years later, now an old man, he was allowed to leave Russia for Mecca to participate in the haj, but before reaching his destination he collapsed and died in the holy city of Medina. It is said that he was buried in a grave close by that of the Prophet Mohammed, a posthumous conjunction that served only to strengthen the hold he still has over the imagination of Muslims in the Caucasus and Islamists elsewhere.

Following Shamil's defeat, hundreds of thousands of his followers were forced to flee. They settled in parts of Turkey and the Middle East, and today form a diaspora in which their mythic leader is still revered. I even found a website that virtually deifies the 'Caucasian Eagle Imam Sheik Shamil who fights for victory carrying the Koran in one hand and a sword in the other'. Nonetheless it was startling to see a mosaic on the front wall of a modern municipal office in the centre of the village of Gunin, where Shamil was held after his surrender and before his deportation from the Caucasus, and an equally recent fresco on a great slab of rock on the mountainside overlooking the main square, both depicting the great imam in heroic pose. In

*Hadji Murat*, Tolstoy describes Shamil riding on a white Arab horse, 'wearing a fur coat covered with brown cloth with black fur showing around the neck and the sleeves.... On his head he wore a tall, flat-topped sheepskin hat...with a white turban wound round it.... His pale face, fringed with a trimmed red beard, with its small eyes constantly screwed up, was like stone, utterly immobile.' The crafts-men of Gunin might have found their inspiration in Tolstoy's words; his description is precisely replicated in both portraits as he stares down sternly at the children playing football and the old men sitting on benches catching the last of the evening sun. Another reminder for me that, in the Caucasus, the past is the continuous present.

Later, over a glass and more of vodka – Khan is a Muslim but, like many in the Caucasus, resists the pressure to eschew alcohol – the professor of ethnology told me that blood feuds of the kind that mortified Hadji Murat still persist in the remoter villages of Dagestan. As he explained it, crimes like murder, rape or burglary do not neces-sarily provoke a 'blood feud' but may precipitate an 'honour killing'. In such cases the criminal's family will endorse the appropriate act of revenge without demur. If the elders decree the death sentence, it will be carried out by the victim's family. If a child is raped, the villagers will together beat the offender until he is dead; the mutilated corpse will then be cremated in shame, not buried in decency. A 'blood feud' is generated when one family is set against another as a result of an unprovoked assault for which guilt is not admitted or when adequate recompense has not been offered. The crime has to be avenged. This obligation falls to the victim's family, to brothers or cousins who are required in honour to execute the perpetrator of the alleged crime. If the latter's family persists in rejecting the allegation, they will retaliate in similar fashion. Thus a blood feud is carried down from one gener-ation to another.

Sometimes the village elders will attempt to mediate, to call a halt to this tit-for-tat killing. If they are successful, the warring families will participate in a ceremony of reconciliation: a formal handshake to bury the past, followed by a communal feast to celebrate the end of the feud. Often the elders fail in their task and the killings continue. As he told me this, Khan spoke in the present tense. So I double-checked. Was he talking about the past or the present? 'The present,' he insisted. 'The present.' And this, I thought, in a modern state where the rule of law is supposed to reach every part of the Russian Federation. When I made this point, Khan shrugged. 'You know, even if a murderer is found guilty in the law courts and is, let us say, sentenced to fifteen years' imprisonment, it may be that his punishment is not enough to satisfy the victim's family. In such cases they may arrange for him to be killed in jail or, alternatively, when he is finally released he may simply "disappear". Everyone will know who has done it and why, but no one will speak of it.'

Khan was an enchanting companion, but the communal behaviour that he described with such detachment belonged to a culture that was so alien to my own that I wondered whether he found himself in some kind of cultural limbo. How did this academic, immersed in Western precepts and methodologies, reconcile the behaviour of his fellow Dagestanis with his own values? He was not at all disconcerted at this question but told me, 'You can't change things. They will change in their own time and their own way. It is better to describe than to judge.' I realized that, despite his professorship, his excellent English and his companionability, Khan – the clan elder – empathized more easily with the mountain culture of the Caucasus from which he has sprung than I had presumed.

After another drink, we moved on to the topic of sex. In the Dagestani villages, Khan said, sex before marriage is strictly forbidden. However, there is a way round the problem of sexual frustration – at least for the male of the species. A man is permitted to sleep with a divorcee who has 'the same needs', but only so long as she comes from another village. In these cases their friends and families will affect not to notice the liaison, which must be conducted in secret. It is, though, generally forbidden for a man to marry a divorcee as the latter cannot be a virgin – although this 'virginity' principle is not absolute; a widow, for example, would be treated as though she were a virgin and is therefore allowed to remarry.

'Dagestani families still have great authority,' Khan went on, 'and this means that if two people want to marry – no one, incidentally, is forced to marry – they will be subjected to very close scrutiny by their respective parents. If there is anything disreputable or dishonourable that is discovered in the past of either family, then the marriage will not be permitted.' Even if they love one another? I wondered. Khan nodded but qualified, 'If there is a dispute about this, then an elder – a "big man" – may be asked to intervene by, for instance, trying to persuade a bridegroom's father who has rejected his son's choice of bride to change his mind. If he fails, the marriage cannot go ahead.' I suggested that the rules he had described meant there must be a great many frustrated young men in Dagestan. 'That is true,' Khan agreed, 'but we have prostitutes for them – at least for the lower class of people, alcoholics and others. And since 1991 we have saunas that men may go to for the same purpose.' Khan said this with an air of such disdain that I had to resist asking him if he had ever availed himself of either facility.

Instead I tiptoed into even more delicate territory. Homosexuality is taboo in Islamic culture, an unpardonable sin, so what would happen, I asked, if someone was discovered to be 'gay'? Khan replied, as if explaining a phenomenon with which I must be unfamiliar, 'A homosexual – you know, a man who touches another man – brings shame on a family. His own brothers will deal with it. For example, they will say to him, "We need the horse that is up on the mountain. Please will you go and fetch it for us?" The horse will have been taken to graze some hours away from their home. Later they will follow him. Some time afterwards his body will be found. The family will pretend to grieve. No one must know the truth. They will treat his death as a riding accident.' I asked Khan what he thought of this practice, expecting him to share my horror. Instead he shrugged again, as if to say, 'Stuff happens'.

That evening Khan invited me to have supper with some friends in Makhachkala, the capital of Dagestan, which is a major port on the Caspian Sea. I had hoped the place would have a distinctly Caucasian feel, but architecturally at least it turned out to be indistinguishable from any of the other monochrome cities bequeathed to Russia by the Soviet Union. We drove through a forest of apartment blocks, each identical to the other, until we reached an unkempt courtyard. Khan guided me through a heavy metal security door and up a flight of concrete steps until we reached his friend's apartment.

Inside it was warm and cheerful. Our host was a policeman, who welcomed us by embracing Khan and putting his arm around my shoulder. We joined three other men, also friends of Khan, who were already seated at a table laden with cold meats, sausages, salad, wine, beer and vodka. The five of us drank one toast after another and ate freely, while the policeman's wife and his two daughters, heads bowed demurely, served us in silence. None of my companions addressed a single word to the women, except, from time to time, to issue an instruction to bring in more food. After a while I asked if I could thank his womenfolk for the delicious dinner they had prepared. They were duly summoned and, as Khan explained, were 'granted the right' to join us. Momentarily liberated, the children (who looked to be about twelve and ten) talked brightly and easily about their school. Their mother, a confident and articulate woman in her late thirties, told me about her job as a mathematics teacher with an authority that her earlier deference had entirely concealed. They had evidently been allocated a five-minute slot with the men. Time up, they retreated to the kitchen, leaving me with the distinct impression that they were not greatly distressed to get away from a table of noisy men who displayed a greater interest in each other's sporting anecdotes than in what the womenfolk had to say.

Khan told us about an academic term he had spent at Cambridge, Massachusetts, in 1995. One evening he went to a rough-looking bar called the Blue Café for a late meal. Once inside, he discovered that it was filled with what he called 'pederasts'. 'You mean it was a gay bar?' I asked. 'Yes,' he replied. 'And you know what happened? One of these pederasts came up to me and tried to touch me. I was horrified and told the man to go away. I then finished my meal as fast as I could and went to leave. But as I was going out of the door they started to push me about. I escaped and went away down the road feeling very bruised. And then, remembering that I am a Dagestani, I felt even more bruised. So I turned round and went back into the café and started to lay about me with my fists. I scored some hits, but they ganged up and really beat me up. I was literally thrown out into the street.' He paused to observe the effect his story had had on the table, and then turned to me. 'Jonathan, can you tell me, how are pederasts allowed to have such power in America?' I was reminded of Sacha Baron Cohen in *Borat*, but with Khan's friends nodding in sympathy I realized that they were scandalized less at the kicking than at the fact that Americans (for the most part) do not believe that all gays are pederasts or that homosexuality is a mortal sin. So instead of expressing my own views on the subject, I took the coward's way and simply shrugged as if to say, 'Beats me'. We drank some more and talked about women instead.

The following day Khan took me to the largest market in Dagestan. It was set in a dustbowl in the scrubby foothills of the surrounding mountains, filling an area that could accommodate at least forty football pitches. Farmers, driving their herds and flocks towards their final hour, walked at a steady pace down from the mountains, sending small dust clouds up into the breeze. The early arrivals were already tethered or hobbled for would-be purchasers to select, a process that requires much prodding and spitting and arguing. Once selected for slaughter, the animal was goaded into an outdoor killing ground that stank of blood and offal and buzzed with flies, there to be dispatched by skilled butchers with long, sharp, knives who set about their business with clinical precision. The animal bleated its last and within minutes was skinned, hung, drawn and quartered in full view of the next victim.

In nearby tented alleyways, sun-weathered women, dressed in multi-coloured skirts that reached to the ground, sat in long rows, competing to sell fruit, vegetables, eggs, nuts, spices and flowers. It was much less raucous than I had imagined, and lacked the mysterious and faintly intimidating buzz of an Arab souk or a Moroccan bazaar. I reminded Khan of the Foreign Office 'advisory' suggesting that it was unwise to travel through his republic. 'Well, right now you are in one of the most dangerous places in Dagestan,' he replied with an ironic twinkle. 'You might be kidnapped by one of these traders, by these ladies sitting on the ground here. And their business here is very dangerous. You should watch out.'

As we walked and talked, I noticed that while most of the men were dressed in Western style – sweatshirts and jeans predominating – a few of the younger men were wearing the long white cotton robes of Islam. Were they merely choosing to dress in the traditional manner for reasons of taste and style, or were they asserting their religious 'fundamentalism'? Khan said it was impossible to know, but that of course the Islamists had not been eliminated from Dagestan. I asked him if they posed any threat, if he had any anxieties about security. 'Of course, I am anxious about the Wahhabis. Everyone is,' he replied. From their hide-outs in the mountains, the Wahhabis – the Islamists who still defy the Russian 'occupation' – have conducted a spasmodic campaign of attacks against government targets. It is not on a scale to disrupt everyday life, but more than enough to keep the police on edge. Khan insisted that the Wahhabis have no popular base in Dagestan. 'Yes, most Dagestanis aspire to independence from Russia, but they know it is only possible through political means. And you should also remember that Islam in Dagestan has long had a tradition of moderation. The Wahhabis do not represent any Dagestani village, nor even any Dagestani hamlet. They are outcasts.' So he did fear them? 'Yes, of course I am afraid of them. I fear for my children. That is why I believe we should treat them as ordinary criminals.' His tone left me with the impression that the Dagestani Islamists may have rather more influence underground and in secret than he, or most of his compatriots, like to acknowledge.

## FEASTING WITH THE COSSACKS

It is impossible to travel through the Caucasus without discovering the Cossacks. Lionized by Tolstoy, used as cannon fodder by imperial Russia and persecuted by the Soviet Union, they have a folkloric status as adventurers and warriors and dancers that defies reality. I met Pyotr, an *ataman* or leader who was a Terek Cossack. He lived on a *stanitza*, a smallholding in the heart of his commune on the edge of the town of Kislyar from where, almost a century ago, tens of thousands of his forebears had been deported to Siberia as 'reactionaries' who had fought on for the Whites and against the Reds in the Civil War. Pyotr, who beamed me a welcome that was irresistible, was a politician with a seat in the Dagestani parliament, where he represented the Cossack community. Today, though, he was off duty. Dressed in military fatigues, he was making the final preparations for a fishing, shooting and camping weekend with a group of his best friends, all similarly attired. Pyotr, who was very much in charge but gentle in manner, invited me to join them.

Before setting off he led me round his little estate – the vegetable patch, the flower garden, the pond, the dogs, the hens, the ducks and the beehives. He had far too many creatures for such a small plot, and the muddy paths along which we slithered were covered with feathers and faeces. But Pyotr's face was lit with a pride so utterly disarming that I felt a twinge of guilt for allowing myself to notice any of the estate's shortcomings. Here, I realized, and doubtless on countless other plots of similar size, Pyotr and his fellows expressed their essence as Cossacks, albeit in romantic miniature.

Unlike the tribes of the Caucasus against whom they were pitted by the imperial army, the Cossacks had no ethnic or geographical roots in the Russian Empire. With roots that can be spasmodically traced back to medieval times, they were originally regarded as vagabonds – escaped serfs, outlaws and adventurers – who were press-ganged into military service or volunteered themselves as mercenaries, plundering on all sides, but earning grudging respect as fighters. In the process, they gradually established an identity for themselves. By the sixteenth century their larger clans were even regarded by some contemporary historians as 'sovereign nations'. Although they possessed no territory, they had become a law unto themselves; so much so that in 1549 Ivan the Terrible is said to have responded to a plea from the Turkish Sultan to stop the Don Cossacks from marauding through the Ottoman Empire with the words, 'The Cossacks do not swear allegiance to me and they live as they themselves please.' Their reputation as warriors went before them. Ottoman chronicles of the seventeenth century record that 'one can safely say that in the entire world one cannot find a people more careless for their lives or having less fear of death'.

By this time they had come to regard themselves as a united 'nation' although, scattered as they were through Russia and eastern Europe, they were more realistically regarded merely as 'organizations'. Accordingly, they slowly lost their influence until, in the eighteenth century, even this identity was stripped from them by Catherine the Great. Nevertheless, the eleven separate Cossack groupings in Russia managed to retain a remarkable degree of autonomy. In the territory that bounded their *stanitzas* they were free to arrange their own affairs and collect their own taxes. In return for this licence, all adult males had to serve in Cossack squadrons attached to the imperial army for a minimum of twenty years. The army supplied their weapons, but they were required to buy their own uniforms and equipment. The arrangement suited both sides; by the turn of the nineteenth century there were over 2.5 million Cossacks living in this dependent but remunerative relationship with the imperial state. Owning a total of some 228,000 square miles of land, they were provident farmers, breeding cattle and horses, planting vineyards, producing honey, hunting and fishing and producing enough surplus

With a migrant labourer on his way home
from Moscow. He was on a twenty-four-
hour journey and he intended to drink
himself silly before he arrived.

Tolstoy in the grounds of Yasnaya
Polyana. Today his estate is a shrine
to this greatest of Russia's writers.

The annexe of the old mansion at
Yasnaya Polyana, where Tolstoy lived in
a tempestuous marriage that survived to
produce no fewer than thirteen children.

*The view of Russia's Black Earth country –*
*'the tsar of soils, more valuable than oil' –*
*from an elderly biplane.*

*Pyatigorsk is a slightly down-at-heel tourist resort,*
*but its remaining nineteenth-century buildings*
*give it a residual dignity and romance.*

In a sulphur pool at Pyatigorsk 'I lay half-floating in the viscous liquid, watching their silent, almost comatose pleasure ...'

A wedding in the Caucasus:
'I was seized by one of the dancers
... My arms flailing lumpenly,
my feet tied to the earth ...'

In the mountains of
the Caucasus 'a herd
of cows wandered by
driven by a herdsman
on a fine black horse ...'

*The school gymnasium in Beslan,*
*where 'the little children stare out*
*at you from fading photographs ... their*
*immortalized lives a permanent rebuke'.*

'We sat in an orchard under a cherry tree ...' A group of Chechen villagers describe their 'rendezvous with catastrophe' at the hands of Stalin.

President Gorbachev with British Prime Minister Margaret Thatcher, in Moscow to 'do business' with the Russian leader.

'Boris Yeltsin was clasped to the bosom of cynical Westerners who discerned wrongly that he had the charisma, wisdom and power to bring "democracy" to Russia.'

Yeltsin's successor, Vladimir Putin, 'has abandoned any pretence of international bonhomie. In its place, the Russian president has sounded belligerent and resentful ...'

A market in the Caucasus: 'Right now you are in one of the most dangerous places in Dagestan. You might be kidnapped ...'

Oleg One and Oleg Two who used to poach sturgeon from the River Volga: 'We steal and we think nothing of stealing because everyone is stealing.'

A roadside stall on the way to Volgograd, where a small plastic pot of black caviar is sold (illegally) for £10 – 'cheap at the price'.

to finance schools and colleges that were widely held to be of a higher standard than in the rest of imperial Russia.

And then came the revolution of 1917. With their traditional opportunism, the Cossacks found themselves fighting variously on both sides in the civil war that followed – with calamitous results. After the defeat of the White Army, the Bolsheviks came to regard all Cossacks as a threat, regardless of where their transient loyalties had lain during the fighting. In accord with the policy of 'Decossackization', they were dispossessed of their lands, and in this process at least three hundred thousand and perhaps five hundred thousand of their number were killed or deported. Their status and influence broken, the remaining Cossacks lived resentfully in their scattered communities, fearful of arbitrary reprisal in Stalin's Russia. Nonetheless, in the Great Patriotic War of 1941–5 most of them, while abhorring Communism, fought – often heroically – on the side of the Motherland against the Nazi invaders. Unhappily, a minority – perhaps twenty-five thousand warriors – deserted from the Soviet army and put their services at the disposal of the Germans. This treachery did little to rehabilitate the reputation of the Cossack community, which continued to be regarded by the Soviet authorities with distrust and disdain. Although they were not persecuted more than other citizens, their organizations were proscribed as illegal groupings, and it was only with the collapse of the Soviet Union that they have been allowed (and sometimes encouraged) to reassert their identity.

Scattered along what was once the Russian side of the front line through the Caucasus, guardians of the tsarist empire, the various Cossack clans have set about their reincarnation in somewhat different ways and with varying degrees of success. To the west, the Don Cossacks have now emerged as a significant political force. Exploiting Russia's latent xenophobia, they have re-established their own schools devoted to patriotism, discipline and commitment to the Orthodox Church. Further along the old front line to the east the Kuban Cossacks, while sharing the same values, are altogether cruder in their approach, forming a movement with which the British National Front would have found common cause. They openly intimidate those ethnic and religious minorities – Turks, Greeks, Muslims – who have had the temerity to move out of their own historic ghettos into territory that the Cossacks have chosen to define as 'pure' Russia. In some cases this extreme nationalism is reportedly encouraged by the regional police, who sympathize with their values but cannot be seen to use their methods. Still further to the east, however, the Terek Cossacks (so named from the river of that name) – Pyotr's people – are altogether less alarming, though they remain proud of their past and determined to cling on to the identity that a romantic version of history has bestowed on them.

It was that identity – as warriors and farmers, proud servants of the imperial army, with fierce passions and stern rules – that so entranced the young Tolstoy when, serving as a volunteer in the imperial army, he saw the Terek Cossacks under his command at close quarters. In another of his great novels, *The Cossacks*, he describes a *stanitza* at the end of day as the moon rises:

> The last lights had been put out in the huts. The last sounds had died away in the village. The wattle fences and the cattle gleaming white in the yards, the roofs of the houses and the stately poplars, all seemed to be sleeping the labourers' healthy peaceful sleep.... In the east the stars were growing fewer and fewer and seemed to be melting in the increasing light but overhead they were denser and deeper than before.

Tolstoy's romance is Pyotr's nostalgia. We sat together for a long, large breakfast at a table in the courtyard surrounded by cats, dogs and mosquitoes. Afterwards, Pyotr and his friends loaded their ex-army people carrier with tents, rugs, sleeping bags, guns, fishing rods, saucepans, food and vodka (in gargantuan quantities) for the outing to the Terek delta. Once under way, Pyotr and his four friends fortified

themselves with vodka and began to sing a rollicking round of traditional Cossack songs, in which I was required to add my voice. I did
my best but had a sudden fellow feeling for the Conservative MP John
Redwood, who tried valiantly but failed hopelessly to mouth the
words of the Welsh National Anthem in front of the television cameras
at a public event when he was Secretary of State for the principality.

One song struck me more than the rest: it sounded like a dirge,
funereal, doleful, and they sang it in a hushed tone. I asked Pyotr to tell
me about it. He gave me a long and elaborate reply, during which we
all had to refuel ourselves with vodka, and from which I gleaned only
that it was about a Cossack fighter who had a dream in which, after
much derring-do, he found he had lost his helmet. When he woke up
he wanted to know what his dream had portended. He consulted a wise
old man, a seer, who told him, 'It means you are going to die.' This
was such a bathetic denouement that I could not resist pointing out –
incautiously – that in the long run the old seer would almost certainly
be proved right, even if our hero *was* a Cossack.

There was a silence as they looked at each other, and for an instant
I was alarmed. What if I had caused offence? Would they decide to
show this insipid foreigner what it really means to be a Cossack? An
image floated into my mind of a colleague who had been beaten up by
a posse of high-spirited Don Cossacks apparently resolved to demonstrate to him that they were not yet a spent force. Mercifully, the
silence of my companions yielded to a collective guffaw of apprecia-
tion. One of them clapped me on the back. To cement our amity I
decided to ingratiate myself with my host. As we lurched along a dirt
track for mile after mile, getting further and further from what had
passed for civilization, I said, 'Pyotr, there is no doubt you are the
Placido Domingo of the Cossacks.' He replied, 'Domingo is nothing
in comparison with me.' He started to sing again. I relaxed.

Pyotr the Cossack and Khan the Caucasian were ostensibly fellow
citizens of the republic of Dagestan. They were both leading figures in
their own communities, but beyond that they had almost nothing in

common. Pyotr regretted that the Cossacks of Dagestan were in decline, numerically, economically and politically, while Khan was reassured by the statistical evidence that they were a spent force. Pyotr also resented the growing presence of the 'mountain people' in and around what had once been Cossack territory. 'The mountain people, the Caucasian people, are here now. They have taken over. But they are different. We are farmers and fighters. And the Causasians? Well, I can't even take them fishing. They know nothing about fishing. They have different customs. Their religion is different.'

Khan, on the other hand, was disconcerted by the Cossack festivals that provide Pyotr and his compatriots with a chance to revive their traditional songs and dances, to display their prowess on horseback and with sabres, to dress up in traditional costume, and therewith to recall the glory days when they had fought in the front line at the emperor's behest against Khan's forefathers, Shamil and his followers, in the mountains of Dagestan. 'Why do they dress up? Why the horses, the saddles and guns? Why all this performance? Why bring all this back? Is it really necessary? I know it is part of their military culture, but is it really necessary? Yes, they have the right to enact these rituals, but it would not be so easy if this started to interfere in our social and political life. What do they want from us? They seem to be saying, "We are the oldest here. We have the deepest roots." This is an unacceptable nationalism and it could become a big problem. It is very chauvinistic.'

I detected no sign that Pyotr and his friends harboured any resurgent longings. 'I am a Russian nationalist and I believe in equality for everyone. And I don't like the oligarchs. Why does [Ramon] Abramovich invest his money in Chelsea Football Club and not in Russia? Why doesn't he support our clubs and buy the players for Russian clubs?' So was it just a hobby being a Cossack, I wondered. I had provoked him. He answered with an unexpected intensity. 'Being a Cossack is my life, my birthright. I am sixth generation. To be a Cossack is my very existence.' And then, after a pause, 'But we are weaker than we were.

There is no hope of recovery. It is not possible. Even over the last ten years, in our *stanitza*, our numbers have fallen fourfold. Most of the farmers used to produce wine. We used to pass the skills on from one generation to another. But in the last fifteen years we have fallen from 8000 hectares of production to no more than 200. *In fifteen years.* Once in this district of Kislyar we were 100 per cent in control. Now we are not.' Pyotr was wistfully admiring of the Don and Kuban Cossacks, who were not in such sharp decline. 'They are still a dominant force, who can determine the choice of mayors and governors. They can dominate the regional councils, and therefore they can vote for laws that are historically needed for their survival. But in our case, with only 20 per cent of the population?' His expression said there was no more to be said; in Dagestan, the Cossacks were a spent force.

As we neared their camping ground on the edge of their beloved Terek River, Pyotr's spirits revived. He and his friends might be a political side-show in Dagestan, but they were still free to live out their Tolstoyan romance, reaching back to folk memories of what was and what might have been. Their weekend expedition was not just one of those male-bonding assertions that 'real men' do with fishing rods and guns, but an expression of their true nature, reconnecting with their past, with their essence, with what made them different and proud. As I listened to their voices still singing, raucous and tuneless but happy, I felt sorry for them. They were, after all, not threatening but faintly pathetic – the remnants, though not the dregs, of a culture whose time has passed. As we drove closer to the mouth of the Terek where it enters the Caspian Sea, they ceased singing and instead looked out expectantly at the passing wasteland of sand and reeds. Then I corrected myself: they were not so much pathetic as poignant.

We reached a spit of sand in the wetlands. It was quiet. Only the ripple of waves lapping on the beach and the rustle of dry reeds in the sea breeze disturbed the silence. The Cossacks surveyed their demesne and without talking set about their allotted tasks – unloading the van, preparing a fire and erecting the tents, their bivouacs. Two of them rowed off in a rubber dinghy in search of fish for supper. Pyotr slipped away with his gun, wading into the water in thigh boots and striding out across the lagoon with the water waist-high, then almost to his neck, heading towards an island of reeds perhaps half a mile away. Soon, in a scene that could have come straight from *Anna Karenina*, he was almost out of sight. There was a long silence. He raised his gun, dark against the water behind him. A flock of ducks rose into the air, the seagulls wheeled, and we heard the sound of the shot, muffled by the breeze. Then there was silence again. Pyotr disappeared from sight. There was another shot and then another. Again the birds flew into the air and flapped mournfully out of range. A few minutes later, Pyotr reappeared. He waded triumphantly towards us, his gun in one hand, three ducks held aloft in the other.

A while later the fishing party returned, collecting their catch from the nets that they had strung out the previous weekend. They had two large fish, like bass, perhaps 3.5 kilos in weight, still thrashing in search of escape. Nicolai, the Cossack chef, who towered over us all and had hands like hams and a face coarsened by work and drink, scaled them while they were still alive, oblivious to their suffering. Then, gutting them with dexterity, he chopped them into steak-sized chunks and threw these into a bubbling cauldron. As he prepared his feast, his friends, now back on the vodka and renewed in spirit, urged me to ask him about the Cossacks, saying that he would 'tell it like it really is', that he never minced his words. 'Are you a proud Cossack?' I asked. 'Yes,' he replied, waving his knife with vigour. 'And what is it to be a Cossack?' 'To know how to run your household, to control your wife and to keep your cock hard.' He gestured in case I had misunderstood. I ploughed on. 'And you have faith in Mother Russia?' 'Yes, of course. One day the Bear will wake up and everything will be in its right place again, a united Russia, a true Russia.' 'And what is the true Russia?' I ventured. 'Russia is the Russian people.' He repeated this phrase, thrusting his wide jaw towards me as though daring me to challenge him. I wanted to recoil, but instead clapped Nicolai on the shoulder in false but shameless bonhomie to signal that I had no intention of picking an argument.

The evening had suddenly lost its innocence and its charm. Nostalgia is a most perfidious elixir. I drank more vodka, smiled weakly and raised my glass to the Cossacks, suddenly wishing I was elsewhere.

Route taken

N

*Volga*

Moscow

Perm

URAL MOUNTAINS

Kazan

Samara
Chapaevsk

*Volga*

R  U  S  S  I  A

0          200 miles
0          300 kms

Volgograd

*Akhtuba*

*Volga*

Sarai

Astrakhan

Novorossiysk

CASPIAN SEA

Makhachkala

BLACK SEA

CAUCASUS MOUNTAINS

# PART THREE
# FROM ASTRAKHAN
# TO THE URALS

Astrakhan is indelibly associated for me with the elegant, fur-collared topcoats worn by aristocratic bounders carrying silver-topped canes in romantic English novels set in the Victorian and Edwardian eras. Arriving in the city itself, I wondered if I would see the real thing – but as I looked around at the wind-chilled February faces of the workers hurrying grimly to overheated offices, I saw only black leather jackets or anoraks. Astrakhan has suffered grievously since the glory days when it was a great entrepôt on the Volga, some 60 miles upstream from where Russia's most renowned river enters the Caspian Sea. At first sight 'Mother Volga', as the river has long been known in Russia on account of its fecundity as a source of fish, is a disappointment. At 2290 miles from source to mouth, it was once a vital artery curving like a sickle through the nation; but today, concealed by a decaying dockyard, a stumpery of dilapidated factories and the detritus of unfinished building projects – a wasteland of concrete piles, coils of rusting wire, oil drums, broken fences and tin sheds – the Volga reveals itself as a grey and sluggish slick of water, fouled by submerged hulks and plastic bottles. Astrakhan may once have throbbed with maritime energy, but I could see little sign of activity, none of that organized confusion of ferries, lighters and freighters that makes a commercial port so enticing. It was at once evident that Astrakhan, celebrating its 450th anniversary, had seen better days.

The city's origins go back many hundreds of years. From the ninth century, if not earlier, it was the capital of the mighty Khazar Empire, which covered a swathe of what is now southern Russia, Kazakhstan, the eastern Ukraine and large portions of the Caucasus and the Crimea. Known then as Khadzhi-Tarhan, the city was a vibrant trading post linking east to west and north to south. Astrakhan, as it became known later, was on the line of the Silk Route from China to Europe. Cloth, spices, herbs and perfumes came from Persia and India, furs from the Baltic. In the early thirteenth century, when the Mongols invaded and conquered Rus, establishing in the region a mighty khanate known as the Golden Horde, Astrakhan diminished in status. But three hundred years later, with the Mongols in retreat across Europe and Asia, the city became their final stronghold in Russia. Not for long.

In 1556 – the year from which Astrakhan dates its Russian origins – the remnants of the Golden Horde, once an apparently invincible colonial power, were ousted from the city and slipped away to the east, offering little resistance to the forces of Ivan IV, the notorious Ivan the Terrible. To ensure that Russia should never again face such humiliation – especially from one or other of the resurgent Turkish or Persian empires – the first Russian leader to proclaim himself tsar ordered a fortress to be built on high ground dominating the Volga. The remains of Ivan the Terrible's fortress form the foundation of what today is a spacious white stone kremlin, which retains an austere simplicity, despite some nineteenth-century embellishments. Aside from two baroque cathedrals, it is now virtually the only building of note that remains in the city.

During the seventeenth century, Astrakhan became Europe's gateway to the Orient as French, German, British and Dutch diplomatic emissaries settled in the city, using Mother Volga as an essential and, for the citizens of Astrakhan, a lucrative means of transport between their two worlds. In the nineteenth century the city became famous for the soft skins of newborn lambs from a local breed of sheep, the curly-wooled karakul. This was the 'fur' from which tailors made both the astrakhan collars worn by the rich of those times and the chimney-pot hats that were later favoured by the Soviet Politburo.

But by this time the city had become even better known throughout Russia and Europe for harvesting that edible treasure from the Caspian known as Beluga caviar. As the caviar merchants prospered, so the city acquired a decidedly cosmopolitan and cultivated mien. The Sapozhnikov family, for instance, which became exceedingly rich on the sturgeon's roe, lived in the grand manner. The walls of their city mansion were adorned with fine paintings, including Leonardo da Vinci's *Madonna of the Flowers*, which remained in the family until the Bolshevik revolution and now hangs in the Hermitage in St Petersburg, where it is known as the 'Benois Madonna'.

## IN SEARCH OF THE ELUSIVE BELUGA

With such images of past grandeur in my mind, I wandered through the potholed streets in search of the fish market where, until a decade or so ago, you could buy Beluga caviar by the scoopful even on a worker's pay. Today, though, the principal market, Selenskiye Sady, is a dispiriting place and the fish not enticing: the carp, perch, catfish, razorfish and eel are laid out on rows of identical stalls differentiated only by the individual raw-faced women with roughened hands who wait resignedly to sell their sorry produce. There is no caviar, not even – as I had been told there might be – a whispered promise that, like an illicit drug, it could be found for me if I were willing to pay the price. Until recently the Caspian and the Volga, where the sturgeon spawn, contained by far the highest concentration of sturgeon in the world. So why is there no caviar? The question leads you down a tortuous path from the laws of supply and demand, via poaching, prison and corruption, to an environmental crisis accelerated by the collapse of the Soviet Union.

The sturgeon is not a pretty creature; in fact it is exceedingly ugly. It has a ferocious appearance, thin, scaly and stickle-backed, with a platypus snout concealing a mouth that is in fact toothless but looks as though it belongs to a shark. Indeed, it is believed that the sturgeon evolved from the shark some 350 million years ago. In evolutionary terms the fish is decidedly backward, though entirely harmless except to crayfish, snails and other small creatures, which it hoovers up from the seabed, sucking them into its belly through protuberant fleshy lips.

The northern reaches of the Caspian provide an ideal habitat for the sturgeon, being not only salty but, in the shallows, warm as well. Of the three main sub-species that populate the Caspian, the Beluga, which grows to more than 5 metres in length and can live for over a century, is the rarest, the largest, the most valuable and therefore the most threatened. The roe of the female Beluga is regarded by gour- mets as a heavenly delicacy that – judging from the way they write about the texture on the tongue of one small, soft, black salty egg, the thrill of bursting it gently against the roof of your mouth and thereby seducing the silky liquid into slithering down your throat – provides for them an experience so ecstatic as to exceed by far the joys of sex. Because black caviar is such a fashionable elixir, the sturgeon has been fished almost to the point of extinction, which is why it is now illegal to sell it in Russia, except through a limited number of designated stores – which means that it is unavailable, except to the deepest pock- ets. It is also the reason why there is an international ban on the export of black caviar – a ban policed with much the same resolve as the ban on ivory from Africa and with the same limited effect. In Selenskiye Sady market a pair of police officers sauntered through the almost deserted aisles, stopping periodically for a word with the fishwives and presumably noting that the only sturgeon on sale here were of a kind that does not produce black caviar. About 30 centimetres in length, they had been smoked to a wrinkled, rusty brown. 'No caviar?' I asked innocently. '*Nyet*,' came the answer.

In the 'Soviet era', as most Russians prefer to call those totalitarian years, the production and sale of black caviar was controlled by the state and the decline in fish stocks was gradual. But in the anarchy of the market economy in the early nineties, the trade became a free-for-all. Sharply rising demand around the world exceeded the dwindling supply, and as a result the black market in black caviar became a multi-million-dollar business, controlled by the Russian mafia allegedly in cahoots with some of the most powerful individuals in regional and central government. This allegation has been strenuously denied and, of course, will never be tested in the courts.

Today the government insists that it is taking every possible step to eliminate the illegal trade and to restore the depleted stocks of sturgeon. On paper, you have to believe this is a serious commitment. According to the law, poaching for caviar is as serious a crime as gun-running or drug-dealing, with penalties that range from heavy fines to long prison sentences. The authorities have closed down every processing plant except one, and a flotilla of fast boats polices the Caspian. But cynics, which in Russia means most of the people most of the time, believe that the illicit caviar market is merely being more subtly managed than it was a decade ago by what one of them described to me as 'those bandits in Moscow'. As my informant, himself a former poacher, confided, 'The big boys who poach the sea pay big bribes, the little men who poach the river pay little bribes.' The ill-gotten proceeds run into many millions of dollars and, he insisted, find their way up to the very apex of power in Russia.

In an attempt to demonstrate that the cynics were wrong, the head of the Astrakhan customs authority invited me to join one of its inshore vessels patrolling the lower reaches of the Volga. As it was early in the season they did not expect to find any poachers, but, he assured me, I would get a sense of how they tried to crack down on these criminals. It was a bitterly cold day, and though I was wrapped in every kind of thermal clothing, I was chilled even before we set off. I had expected a motor yacht bristling with antennae and even a popgun or two on the forward deck, but the craft turned out to be a 60-metre open speedboat with a great 200 horsepower outboard engine mounted on the stern. Artur, who led the patrol, was a massive man, so large inside his cold-weather gear that he reminded me of a giant ham that had been granted large sausages for fingers. But his physique belied his demeanour: for a state official, he was uncharacteristically open and welcoming. He was also a skilled boatman. As we sliced downriver towards the open sea, through white-crested wavelets whipped up by the wind from Siberia, we passed low reed banks on either side that, Artur explained, could easily conceal a poacher's inflatable. Above the roar of the outboard engine and through chattering teeth – the wind chill factor must have reduced the apparent temperature to at least minus 20 degrees centigrade – I asked him about the allegations that everyone involved in the caviar supply chain, including his own customs authority, was on the take. He vehemently denied this, insisting that poaching was a very serious offence: 'If you are caught poaching just one fish with your own rod, you face up to two years in jail. Last year my patrol made thirty-five arrests. You must understand that the governor [of the Astrakhan province] is very committed to stamping this out. And on the river we are winning the battle. Of course it is different at sea, where it is big business.' After three hours on the watery wastes of the Volga delta we returned, chilled to the marrow, to the customs depot. No poachers, no catch.

Aware of the developing crisis, the Soviet authorities had begun the slow process of restocking the Caspian in the eighties, but it has been a fitful and half-hearted process. Artur told me that the new governor was resolved to make better progress. To prove his point there are several fishponds around Astrakhan where Beluga sturgeon are reared in safety and then released into the sea as young adults.

However, it takes at least eighteen years for the sturgeon to reach maturity and – given the level of poaching not only by Russian gangs but by Azerbaijanis, Kazakhstanis and Turkmenistanis (who are rarely disturbed about their business by their own dysfunctional regimes) – no one is optimistic that the sturgeon will escape from the list of endangered species. What an irony that its very means of reproduction – coupled, of course, with human greed – should be the cause of its demise.

The next day I was driven out of Astrakhan to a fishing lodge on a tributary of the Volga to meet Oleg Sarana, a passionate fisherman and the co-presenter of a regional television programme devoted to hunting, shooting and fishing. He was not the archetype for this role. Slight, wispy-haired, whey-faced and saturnine, he had been unkindly blessed with a receding chin. But I soon discovered that he had a sharp mind, an open nature and a dry sense of humour. His opening gambit was: 'If you want to talk about poaching and the caviar crisis, you have to talk about politics.' By way of preamble he told me that in the late Soviet era he had been a career officer in one of the best army units, but that in 1989 he had decided to resign his commission. 'My superiors could not understand why I wanted to leave. They told me I was a good officer and due for promotion. But I wanted more opportunities than you can get in the army. So I became a street trader. I used to drive to Moscow and buy cigarettes, chewing gum and chocolate, which I would sell at a kiosk I had rented in Astrakhan. With the proceeds I bought meat and took it to Moscow and sold it there. Before long I had enough capital to buy a warehouse, and because I had been trained as an engineer I went into the metallurgy trade. But it is poaching that really got me where I am now. That's how I really collected the capital. And it is the same with Oleg.' He gestured at his friend, who had joined him in the bar and was listening with benign assent. Oleg Two, as I called him, played Eric to Oleg One's Ernie.

Oleg Two was burly, smiling and boastful, but so innocently that he was rather endearing. He told me that he owned a building supplies firm, which was booming. To prove it, he showed me his Special Edition Land-Rover of which he was obviously very proud. Between them the two Olegs explained that only the very wealthy could afford caviar nowadays and that anyone who caught – or rather poached – sturgeon never ate the caviar because they needed the money from selling it on the black market. Oleg Two elaborated. 'You know that when things were at their worst you could get the equivalent of one month's salary by selling one small jar of black caviar. In one day you could earn one hundred times your monthly wage. That was *perestroika* money.'

'Who's to blame?' asked Oleg One rhetorically, finally coming to the politics of poaching. 'Of course we could blame the government and we could blame our leaders, but I reckon we have to blame ourselves – him [pointing at Oleg Two], me and millions of Russians. Why? Because we don't vote, we don't believe in anything, we don't believe that it will make any difference. We get the leaders we deserve. We steal, and we think nothing of stealing because everyone is stealing.'

From what they had gleaned from titbits of gossip with friends in the coastguard and customs service, they believed that on any given day there were some five hundred powerboats in the Caspian poaching for sturgeon. 'Five hundred? And they can't stop them?' I asked. They shrugged: 'The governor can't fight it. He may want to, but it is not possible. If the federal authorities really want to act decisively, they could use helicopters to pinpoint the location of the speedboats and catch them that way. They could catch them today, tomorrow, any time. But the poachers work in big gangs and they are protected at the very highest level, the highest echelons of power. So, as with everything else – not just poaching – the authorities give the impression that they are fighting the poachers, but in fact they are making money from them.'

The only hope, they said without much hope, was that the stocks would become so depleted that it would no longer be a commercial proposition to fish for them and the poachers would then move on to something else. 'Fifteen years ago we could have shown you the sturgeon all along these banks. They made the water boil, there were so many of them, and they were up to 30 kilos in weight. You caught them like that.' (Oleg One mimicked hanging a rod over the water and catching a fish immediately.) 'But now, even if you go out with big nets, you find nothing.' At this they raised their glasses for a lugubrious toast (though Oleg One, as a recovering alcoholic who used to drink several bottles of vodka a day, drank only Coca-Cola): 'To the sturgeon. Let there be more. If not in our lifetime, then one day.'

I asked them about the customs officers in the speedboats that policed the Volga delta, who had seemed to me sincere enough. The two Olegs begged to differ. 'If they tell you they have the poachers on the run, they can't all be telling the truth. It goes on, and they know it does. If you know who to pay, you can fish as much as you like. It is like a club, a secret club. Members don't pay. Non-members do. You should ask the crews of the government patrol boats how they manage to buy their two-storey houses and their new cars. It certainly isn't from their pay packets.' But the two Olegs, who had emerged from their poaching stage to become anxious environmentalists, were careful not to condemn this level of corruption. 'It is the system, and they are simply working the system. That's how it is.' So where should the buck stop? Oleg One answered that President Putin turned a blind eye to the problem of poaching. Oleg Two added, 'We have a system of oligarchical capitalism in Russia, where all our natural resources have been taken and divided among twenty people. Of course Putin condemns the poachers and he speaks eloquently, but I am not sure he means what he says.'

By the time we had finished it was close to midnight, but the two Olegs were going to be up early the next morning to go fishing. They asked me to join them, saying that they would be leaving before dawn. I went to bed filled with good intentions, but by the time I woke they were long gone. I caught up with them later, tracing their route in a little hired speedboat. As soon as they saw me coming, they stood up in their boat, holding their catch in the air with a look of inexpressible satisfaction. They had caught eight fat fish, which looked like trout and bream (they were certainly not sturgeon) and which, they said, weighed between 2 and 4 kilos apiece. We rowed ashore, collected driftwood for a fire and crouched down out of a piercing wind to warm ourselves in front of the flames.

Passing around the vodka (it was eleven o'clock in the morning by now), the two Olegs spoke rhapsodically about the delights of fishing and hunting, stalking boar in the reeds and wolves on the steppe. Absorbed in the lore of the hunt, they told me that wolves were exceptionally cunning animals that killed in pairs. To illustrate their point, they told me a story that they assured me was true in every detail. 'Two wolves approach a flock of sheep. One of them makes sure to stay hidden while the other goes out of its way to make its presence known to the shepherd. As soon as the shepherd reacts by raising his gun to shoot it, this "decoy" wolf affects to flee. The shepherd follows on horseback, but his prey is fast enough to stay just out of range. Gradually the shepherd is drawn further and further away from his flock. Eventually he decides to give up the chase and hurries back, only to discover that there are no sheep to be seen. He casts around in furious anxiety, but when he eventually catches up with his exhausted animals he discovers that up to a dozen of them are dead, killed by the other wolf. Disconsolate, he leads the surviving animals back to their night shelter. As soon as he is gone, the entire pack of wolves moves in to feast on the kill.'

There were more such stories and more vodka and, as I watched the two Olegs reliving moments of excitement, disappointment and sometimes danger, I felt that on my journey so far I had not been with two such genuinely contented individuals. They could have been characters out of Tolstoy or Turgenev; the steppe – the wide expanse of gently undulating, arid land that characterizes almost all southern Russia – was as much their home as the apartments where they lived in urban Astrakhan. Yes, one was a television presenter and the other a car dealer, but if there is a uniquely Russian soul, I felt had come close to discovering it here on a river bank where, apart from their quiet voices and happy faces, there was only the sound of firewood spitting and crackling as the deep flow of water eddied past. We sat looking across the river to an eternal distance of steppe and forest, a haze of smoke rising above the flames; overhead a steel-grey sky framed a landscape where man – Russian man – has for centuries forgotten the tortures of the past and the nastiness of the present, and feels himself to be in his element, an innocent out of time.

## MONGOL RICHES

We chose an exceptionally cold day for my next stop, a corner of nowhere that is not marked on most maps and is hardly known even to the people of the Astrakhan region. Sarai belongs to an almost forgotten past but, in the thirteenth century it was the capital of the Mongol Empire in the Lower Volga delta, a teeming international city, vibrant with power and energy, surplanting Astrakhan in the process. Yet if we hadn't been told where to go and where to look – on the high plain overlooking the River Akhtuba, just outside a modest village called Selitrennoe – it would have been impossible to distinguish this medieval seat of power from the rest of the bleak steppe that surrounds it.

The nomadic tribes that stormed off the steppe at the end of the twelfth century were exceptionally fierce warriors led by a military genius, Genghis Khan. The wars of expansion that he instigated were to yield for the Mongol 'hordes' the largest contiguous land empire the world has ever known. Within fifty years they had colonized China and Persia, and had swept like a tornado across Russia. In 1237 they besieged and sacked Moscow. Three years later they meted out the same punishment to Kiev, which was then the capital of Rus. Not content with this astonishing, panzer-like progress, their front-line fighters advanced even further west until they had established toeholds in Poland, Bohemia and Hungary. It was an amazing military venture.

News of their conquests swept through the chancelleries of Europe, inspiring horror and fear. 'This race of people is wild, outlawed and ignorant of the laws of humanity,' wrote the Holy Roman Emperor, Frederick II, to the King of England. Tales of their bestiality flowed from the pens of contemporary chroniclers – though how much of what they recounted had any basis in fact is unclear. 'The old and ugly women were given to their dog-headed cannibals,' one of these scribes wrote. 'Those who were beautiful [were] saved alive to be stifled and overwhelmed by the number of their ravishers.... Virgins were deflowered until they died of exhaustion, when their breasts were cut off to be kept as dainties for their chiefs and their bodies furnished a jovial banquet to the savages.'

In 1227, more than a decade before the sack of Kiev, Genghis Khan died after a fall from his horse, but as an astute dynast he had already been careful to divide his rapidly growing empire among his descendants. His grandson Batu, the leader of the Golden Horde, inherited the Russian front. Following his subjugation of Rus, Batu chose Sarai as his military headquarters, from where he would rule his vast Russian demesne. Explaining this decision, he wrote of the Volga delta that 'it is the place where the air is freshest, the water most pure, and the pastures most nourishing'.

I had imagined that Sarai might resemble the ruins of Xanadu, the summer capital of Kublai Khan's Mongol Empire to the north of Beijing, where the remnants of that thirteenth-century 'stately pleasure dome' may still be seen. But of Sarai there was nothing to meet the eye except wasteland stretching to the horizon. And yet by the mid-fourteenth century the population of Sarai was estimated to have been 75,000 – only a little smaller than that of London had been before the onset of the Black Death at this time. One thirteenth-century traveller, an Arab from North Africa, described it as 'one of the most beautiful cities, one which has achieved extraordinary size, filled to overflowing with people, handsome markets and broad streets'. Riding through the place, which took him and his retinue half a day, he counted thirteen large mosques and thirteen cathedrals, numerous bazaars and bath-houses. And it was cosmopolitan as well. In addition to the 'masters', as he described the Mongol rulers, he saw Russians, Caucasians and many 'merchants and strangers' from as far afield as Iraq, Egypt, Syria and Greece, 'each nation living in its own quarter'. An Egyptian writer from the same era, al-Omari, drew on various accounts to describe the Sultan's 'place of sojourn' as 'a great palace, upon the highest point of which there is a golden crescent [weighing] two Egyptian quintals…surrounded by walls, towers and houses, in which his emirs live'.

I had hoped to meet Professor Pigarev, who has been doggedly excavating the site at Sarai for many years, but, as it is too cold to dig except in the short summer season, he was away when I arrived. In his place I was shown around by Sasha, Sarai's part-time custodian. Sasha lives in Selitrennoe, dreaming that Sarai may one day be recognized as a World Heritage Site and that, as a result, prosperity may transform his impoverished little village. He showed me where Pigarev and his small team of volunteers had been digging over the last decade, but as a mere traveller I was unable to glean any meaning from the small piles of disturbed earth and rock on one corner of the site, the only tangible evidence of the professor's endeavours. It was tantalizing and frustrating to know that there must be so many secrets buried there in the steppe, and yet to see no evidence of what had once been a complex and sophisticated civilization. I wished that I had Pigarev's interpretive genius. He has discerned evidence not only of Sarai's wealth of public and private buildings and the materials from which they were built, but also of the social structures they defined, describing the 'big rectangular dug-outs' that came complete with earth bunks along two or three walls as being for better-off families, while even the dug-outs owned by 'poor but free' people had heating systems, ovens for baking bread, plastered walls and wash basins. The rich, he has concluded, lived in large brick houses with 'multiple rooms...and sometimes a little covered patio'.

As in so many European 'histories', so it is in Russia: the Mongol invaders have long been vilified as marauding barbarians – an ignorant and inferior sub-species of the human race – who subjected the Motherland to brutal oppression for almost three centuries. The facts are evidently otherwise. There is ample evidence that the colonial administration established by the Golden Horde was cannily pragmatic. Far from either laying waste to the land on which their own herds grazed or pillaging the communities over which they held sway, they allowed their subject peoples to continue their traditional way of life and to retain their culture. It may still rankle in the collective Russian memory, but the Mongols astutely offered the princes and nobles of Rus a deal they could hardly refuse: the retention of their feudal rights and privileges in return for the payment of tithes and taxes to fill the coffers of the khanate. This arrangement served the needs of both victor and vanquished – even if it reveals the latter in a less than heroic light. Perhaps this is why, more than half a millennium later, Russia still seems reluctant to give the Golden Horde its historic due. As Orlando Figes has noted in *Natasha's Dance*, the Russians have long preferred the myth of the Mongols as a culturally backward people who, in Pushkin's phrase, brought to the Motherland 'neither Algebra nor Aristotle'. As it is, the cultural legacy of the Mongols – whom Russians like to believe plunged their nation into a 'dark age' – is more or less still buried and forgotten under the barren soil of Sarai.

Yet Russians recall with pride how rapidly the Mongol 'rule of terror' disintegrated, an event that they are prone to attribute more to their own prowess than to the self-destructive impulse that, as with so many other empires before and since, brought the invaders' hegemony to a premature end. Barely two hundred years after defeating Rus, the Golden Horde found itself dangerously over-extended, stricken by internal conflict and exhausted by conquest. By the end of the fifteenth century, Ivan III, known as Ivan the Great, had prized the

Mongol grip from Moscow and torn up the charter that had bound Rus to servitude for more than two centuries. But the *coup de grâce* was not delivered for another hundred years, when Ivan the Terrible ordered the fading city of Sarai to be dismantled and transported downstream, red brick by red brick, to rebuild Astrakhan as an important military garrison on the southern perimeter of his new Russian Empire. In doing so he ensured that Sarai would be erased from the face of the steppe and from Russia's collective memory.

Sarai was not rediscovered until the nineteenth century, and serious excavations did not begin until the third decade of the twentieth. These have unearthed a well, a kiln, an underground mausoleum and a number of villas. Later, archaeologists also discovered a complex of workshops that had produced ceramic vessels and ornaments, bone carvings and jewellery made from semi-precious stones. So far, however, these excavations have barely scraped the surface of one corner of a site that covers more than 7 square miles.

Sasha led me to a little outhouse hidden away behind a wooden palisade in the middle of Selitrennoe village. This was where Professor Pigarev stored his treasure trove of Mongol artefacts. Earthenware pots, vases for oil and water, a brooch and a ring were arrayed on a dusty wooden table in the corner of the ill-lit hut. The tools of the archaeological trade – soft brushes, pincers, scissors and magnifying glasses – hung neatly on the walls. I was about to leave when I saw an old red and black striped mattress and, resting on it like a macabre crown on a kingly cushion, a human skull that had, Sasha told me, been dated to the middle of the fourteenth century, when the Mongol Empire was at its zenith.

## NOT A STEP BACK

After a long trundle across a snow-swept steppe we reached the outskirts of Volgograd where our people carrier was pulled over brusquely by a police officer at a customs post on the bridge that forms the main crossing point over the river into the city. He peered into the vehicle and then asked casually, 'Have you got any caviar?' It seemed an odd question. It clearly wasn't just a polite enquiry, but if he was suspicious, why didn't he search the vehicle? And then I realized that he was merely cutting to the chase. His question was a demand, a statement to the effect that if we did have any caviar about our persons, we should pay him the customary bribe by means of which all manner of contraband is permitted passage through the Russian Federation. As it happened, we were a caviar-free zone and our driver answered with a nonchalant, '*Nyet.*' The officer shrugged, slammed the door shut and waved us on our way.

Later we stopped at a roadside fish market. The car park was full of cars and trucks that had disgorged businessmen, long-distance hauliers and couples with children, all now drinking coffee and Coca-Cola and buying dried fish for the journey. As I wandered from stall to stall, I noticed two white plastic cups filled with the precious black caviar openly on display. I asked the woman behind the counter where she had bought it. She smiled, but with some discomfort, before saying vaguely, 'I am not sure exactly – it is given to us to sell.' She wanted me to buy a cupful. 'It's only 600 roubles.' It was, at £10, cheap at the price. I told her that I was tempted, but that I also knew it was illegal to buy or sell caviar like this. She looked perplexed and said, 'Well, if you change your mind you will buy from me and not anyone else?' Instead I bought a piece of dried fish, which she gutted for me. It was juicy and delicious. 'Eat and be healthy,' she said. I left uttering a grateful '*Do svidaniya*' in farewell, which prompted her to an unexpected '*Auf wiedersehen*'.

At first glimpse Volgograd looks much like a prosperous nineteenth-century city in the north of England, a Leeds or a Manchester, solid, assured and just a little self-satisfied. The impression is misleading. Volgograd is a twentieth-century creation, a neo-classical reconstruction out of the rubble of World War II when it was known as Stalingrad. I had read Anthony Beevor's coruscating history of the epic struggle between Hitler and Stalin, which reached its decisive climax in the streets of the city between August 1942 and February 1943. I had also seen the dreadful carnage of those days from grainy newsreels, but nonetheless I had somehow allowed myself to assume that, as elsewhere in Russia, in this city the past would have become another country. I could not have been more wrong. Psychologically at least, Volgograd is still fundamentally Stalingrad.

On a chill morning with an unremitting wind from the east slicing through the city and driving flurries of snow before it, I stood in the main square near the Grand Café. As most of the citizens scurried by, heads down, a clutch of bystanders watched with rapt attention as five teenagers, three boys and two girls dressed in military uniform, stood at attention immobile and in silence, forming a guard of honour before the city's Eternal Flame. One of the onlookers, a man of about my own age, his face raw in the cold, looked on with an expression so kindly and so approving that I went up to him. Andrey Vosdievsky turned out to be a teacher from Middle School 13, and it was his pupils, whom he had trained, who were performing today's ritual. 'I am very proud of them,' he said. 'It is so important that this history is passed down from generation to generation. When I was a child in the same class I did this, and now, as their teacher, seeing my pupils standing here doing this very honourable task just fills me with pride. Of course I worry that they do it properly. It is a very big responsibility because all the children doing this duty have someone in their own family who died during the Battle of Stalingrad, a grandfather or a grandmother. You should see them when they put on this uniform. They feel the weight of responsibility. They become different people – you can see it, you feel it.'

After forty-five minutes, his students changed the guard with the same precision that you might admire outside Buckingham Palace. Their young faces stern and impassive, they slow-marched away from the War Memorial, goose-stepping in perfect time, their boots crunching on the snow-covered avenue. When they were allowed to fall out,

Andrey went across to congratulate them and then, leaving his charges to be embraced by their families, he came over to tell me, 'You know, Volgograd is now the only city in Russia to maintain this tradition. It happens every day between ten and two.'

Near the waterfront is the Museum of the Battle of Stalingrad. The detritus of war on display was as depressing as I find all such collections: guns, badges and uniforms that testify so blandly to the mortal struggle of war. They seem not to touch the horror but to distance us from the bodies blown apart, the innards scattered on blood-soaked ground, the noise, the terror, the courage and the futility. I was feeling thoroughly indifferent as I wandered through Volgograd's collection of such memorabilia until I climbed a set of spiral stairs to discover a huge 360-degree mural around the cylindrical centre of the domed building. It depicted the battle at the moment of greatest crisis. I was suddenly hooked.

From the onlooker's perspective, the artist appears to have been standing in the middle of the city with a panoramic view of the front line and the encircling German troops. It was painted in the neo-realist style inflicted on the Soviet people by Stalinism, but for once, so far from diminishing the impact, its crudely detailed observation – though bowdlerized to glorify the Russian defenders and vilify the Nazi invaders – was quite extraordinarily powerful. The enemy troops were fighting hand-to-hand, their forward positions over-run. Prisoners were pulled out of secret foxholes, their bodies butchered by bayonets. Mangled tanks lay grotesquely at the bottom of snowy ravines. Luftwaffe planes spiralled out of control. A German general was led away, abject in surrender. The mural's panoramic grip on the known facts of the battle may be tenuous, but as a vision of victorious torment on the icy steppe it imprinted itself on my mind – as it clearly did on the party of schoolchildren that had arrived just before me to be reminded of what their grandparents had endured on their behalf.

By August 1942 the German Panzer divisions had advanced rapidly across the steppe from the west driving the Soviet armies back towards the Volga. The Russians were soon forced to retreat into the city itself but under orders – at all costs – to prevent the enemy reaching the heavy industrial plants that were strung out along the west bank of the river and that were in flat-out production to sustain the war effort. But the Nazi onslaught by land and air was so ferocious that, despite rushing reinforcements across the river from the east bank, the Russian high command was unable to prevent the German front-line soldiers from penetrating to the very heart of the city.

The crude statistics of the Battle of Stalingrad – the numbers of corpses and the casualties on each side in this charnel house – have no reality that I can grasp, but hearing individual testimonies from those who experienced the siege and survived is a searing experience even sixty-five years on. I met Vladislav Mamontov on a piece of hallowed ground near the river beside what everyone calls simply the Flour Mill, which had been battered but not entirely destroyed by the German bombardment. It is now preserved as an eloquent monument, its gaping windows seeming to echo a primeval scream of suffering. Vladislav walked across the snow to me, helped along by a friend to stop him slipping. A slight figure, wrapped in gloves and a scarf but not at all frail of mind, this semi-retired professor of archaeology at Volgograd University is blessed with a memory so precise that you almost forget he was only six years old when the German onslaught began.

'I remember the twenty-third of August. It was the most terrible day. There had been bombing before in the industrial zone – the Tractor factory and the Red October [steel] plant. And people had been quite calm when the air-raid signals went off. But on the twenty-third, in the middle of the day there was another warning. And people didn't really take any notice. People at work, I suppose, doing their laundry, filling in their ration cards. Then the German planes came over and dropped leaflets. We weren't allowed to pick them up, but we did. They were blood-red and they showed Soviet machines and guns in the middle and German tanks surrounding them. And the slogan on it said, "Surrender, surrender".

'Then came the bombers, layer upon layer of fighters and bombers coming from that direction' – he pointed into the sky towards the west – 'and the bombs fell. Explosions. Whistling. A terrible noise. It was carpet bombing. It was absolutely terrifying. The grown-ups covered me with their bodies to protect me from flying fragments of metal. And there was smoke, a terrible taste in the mouth. And I was crying because my mother wasn't with me. She had gone out to pick up one of the leaflets and I thought she must have been buried alive.

'Later there was a lull in the bombing and we climbed out, and we could not recognize our own city. There was nothing. It was completely bombed. No buildings. Nothing. There were bodies everywhere. We stumbled over the corpses. And we saw great flames from the fuel depots. In one ravine there must have been fifteen bodies, all killed in one moment. There were just tears, tears, tears. And then I saw my mother – she must have jumped into a foxhole or something. She was weeping because I was alive. After that there was no life. No food. No water. All the water pipes were broken. We had to find water where we could, from the ravines....

'And then the Germans arrived. We were living underground in what shelter we could find. We saw them walking overhead. The old people started to cross themselves, to pray to God and ask, "How will the Germans treat us?" It was terrifying.... After a while they let us out, but they took everything we had and anything we were able to find.... They were always looking for people. "Are there any Jews here?" We hid an elderly Jewish couple, but someone must have reported seeing two strangers because the soldiers came kicking every-where, searching. They did not discover them. But the German commandant said that no one would be hurt, so the next morning the couple came out and gave themselves up. They were marched away. I now think they must have died in a concentration camp somewhere.'

Vladislav's tone was measured but he spoke as though he were reporting live from Armageddon, in shock at what he had witnessed but determined to get the facts right for the record. I asked if he still lived with the horror of what had happened. 'Yes,' he replied. 'Sometimes they show old films about Stalingrad and my wife says, "I don't want to watch it," but I do. I knew the town as it was, and I want to see it again. The Germans didn't even treat us like people....' His words died away as though there were both too much and yet nothing more to be said.

By November 1942 almost all the city had fallen into German hands. But Stalin had issued Order 227, *Ni Shagu Nazad* – 'not a step back' – which instructed his generals that 'each position, each metre of Soviet territory must be stubbornly defended, to the last drop of blood'. Under no circumstances should the German Sixth Army be permitted to cross the Volga. The survival of the Motherland was at stake and there could be no retreat – and every Russian soldier knew that he had a Soviet gun to his back just as merciless as the German gun to his front. As it happened, Hitler, like the Mongols and Napoleon before him, had over-reached himself. Appalling weather, a 1200-mile-long supply line from Berlin, shortages of clothing, equipment, fuel and ammunition, and the failure of the Luftwaffe to supply sufficient air cover or food supplies steadily wore down his troops at the front. A brilliant Russian counter-attack later in the month broke the siege by encircling and imprisoning the Germans inside the city that they had only just captured. They could neither retreat nor advance without terrible loss of life and, given the terrain and the river, they had little prospect of success. But Hitler was as indifferent to human life as Stalin. When his generals sought permission to break free of the Russian stranglehold by opening a corridor down which to make a tactical retreat, he ordered them to remain in their place and turn Stalingrad into a German 'fortress'.

In October 1942 Vladimir Akharchenkov was sixteen, the youngest member of the battalion defending the Red October factory, a steel plant on the edge of the Volga, which, though severely damaged, was still in production as the Germans fought their way metre by metre towards the river. Today, as then, the factory belches flames and molten metal in a cacophony of clanking, groaning and whining machinery – an inferno from the industrial revolution producing a million tonnes of steel a year. As Vladimir showed me the spot where he had stood and fought hand-to-hand with the enemy sixty-five years earlier, his tired old eyes came alive not in triumph but with remembered horror. Of the ten thousand Russian troops belonging to the 193rd Artillery Division deployed in the factory, five hundred emerged alive at the end of the hundred-day battle.

'There were flames everywhere – you couldn't see anybody. The water of the Volga was hot with burning oil and debris. Gradually we were being pressed further and further towards the river. We were only a few metres from each other. If you saw one of them first, you'd kill him; if they saw you first, they'd get you.

'One day, after I'd been sent across the river to get food and ammunition from our dumps on the other side, I was walking along carrying a box full of ammunition weighing 32 kilos. I was with my mate. Suddenly we heard a German voice: "*Halt*, hands up!" We dropped the box and the German shot me in the shoulder. My mate fired back and killed him. I was wounded twice, but I was lucky.

'The Germans were bombarding us all the time, but we had the metal furnaces over there' – he pointed to some waste ground 200 metres from the factory itself – 'and whenever there was bombing or shelling we hid inside them. They had such thick walls that nothing could pierce them. But the noise was terrible, and when we came out we were totally disorientated. The Germans got control of at least half the plant, but they were running short of supplies. They became desperate to get to the Volga, not to get across the river, but for water – they were parched with thirst.

'Soon it became like a meat-grinder right where we are standing now. There were bodies everywhere. You could not move without standing on a body – theirs and ours. The Germans kept coming and we kept killing them. There were bodies everywhere. What else could we do?' As he said that, the flow of memory stopped and he looked at me as if the question had been not rhetorical but a genuine enquiry. No bitterness, no hatred, only a deep, deep sorrow at the waste of so many lives. And then, his pride swelling in the memory of the final triumph, he opened his greatcoat to show me row upon row of medals, proving that he was a Soviet hero of this and that battle during four years of perpetual warfare that had taken him from Stalingrad to Berlin and back again; an old man, glad to have defended the Motherland in its moment of greatest peril, his finest hour.

The enemy was driven back from the Volga but had nowhere to turn. By the middle of December 1942, Hitler's troops were trapped, starving and starting to be killed by the cold in large numbers. On Christmas Day alone 1500 soldiers died of frostbite and exposure. But as the death toll mounted, Hitler remained obdurate, rejecting outright a Russian offer to negotiate terms of surrender that might have given a small measure of relief to his broken troops. By now the Führer's insane posturing was impossible to obey. With his men dying all about him – frequently by their own hand to escape the torment – the German commander-in-chief, General Paulus, had no choice but to order his forces to retreat. It soon became a rout. Of the 90,000 Axis soldiers who managed to free themselves from the Russian vice, 5000 survived to return home. The remaining 85,000 men were either mown down as they fled or died from starvation, cold and disease. According to the most authoritative statistics, the total military losses at the Battle of Stalingrad approached 2 million, of whom 1.1 million were Russian troops and the remainder from the German, Italian, Hungarian and Romanian soldiers who had formed the Axis front line. These figures, of course, exclude the many scores of thousands of Russian civilians who were killed by the indiscriminate German aerial bombardment, which by February 1943 had razed Stalingrad to the ground.

Iraida was only six when the battle began. 'A child's memory is very sharp,' she told me in her tiny office, where she still patiently, obsessively, collates testimonies of the war from other survivors and their families. 'I remember my grandmother telling me, "It will be terrible if your mother dies, if your sisters die, if I die, so pray to God that we are spared."' Iraida spent the entire six months of the battle in a troglodyte world, deep underground in what she describes as 'a dug-out where we did not know whether it was day or night'. In February, when the guns finally fell silent, she heard the loudspeakers. 'They told us, "The battle is over. You must come out now," and I remember it was absolutely freezing. We were cold and hungry and I remember saying to my granny, "I want to go to school tomorrow, I want to go to school."

'I remember one day especially. There were no people around. I was with my grandmother and we saw a deep pit, and in it there was this pile of bodies as high as a two-storey house in layers on top of one another, German, Russian, German all piled up together. And this man gave my grandmother a rope and showed her how to tie it to the ankle of a dead body. I saw her joining them and helping to drag a body with a rope over her shoulder and then dropping it in another big pit. Then she untied the rope and went back for another body....'

At the end of the war a census showed the population of the ruined city to be 43,000 citizens and 285,000 prisoners of war. Only 203 buildings had survived, all of which are now memorial monuments. Although some of the city's original 350,000 inhabitants had managed to escape the bombardment, many perished. There are no precise figures, but to this day there are thousands, perhaps tens of thousands, of corpses still buried under the new city of Volgograd. Not a week passes without the discovery of a wartime corpse. Construction workers digging the foundations for a new office block or householders building an extension to their homes routinely unearth uniformed skeletons buried where they fell more than sixty years ago. 'Last summer,' I was told by the mayor's office, 'the bodies of ninety-two soldiers that had been uncovered in previous months were given a formal reburial in the War Memorial Cemetery near the village at Rossoshki. It is an annual ceremony. The Russian reburials are on 15 May; the German reburials take place a few days later.'

The cemetery is some 20 miles from the city centre on what was once the battlefield and where the dead still seem to be in contention. It must be one of the bleakest places on earth. On one side of the road are the graves of Russian soldiers with small identical tombstones, each with a Soviet helmet resting on top. On the other side, some 500 metres away, a cylindrical stone-faced mass grave covered in grass contains the corpses of 60,000 German soldiers. Leading away from this great, featureless tomb are scores of rectangular granite blocks, each some 2 metres in height and shaped like military pillboxes that have been dropped from the heavens and scattered on the steppe as if to form a modish sculpture park. Only when you get very close do you see that each slab of granite is covered with the names of 120,000 young men who died for Hitler's vainglory. It is so desolate a place, so haunting, so final a solution, that all you can do is stand and despair.

## STALIN'S CITY STILL

In Volgograd today it is virtually impossible to bypass the Battle of Stalingrad. Aside from the Flour Mill, the Red October steel plant and the Tractor factory there is a grand Avenue of Heroes, along which raised tablets of stone display the names of hundreds of those who were awarded military decorations of the highest order – Hero of the Soviet Union and Order of Glory. Above all this, towering over the city on a hill named Mamaev Kurgan, is Rodina Mat ('The Motherland is Calling'), which is Volgograd's answer to the Statue of Liberty (and 3 metres taller). This colossal figure, a giantess holding a sword of vengeance, leans forward as though into the teeth of the gale, protecting the city from any further assault. It is massive, but without dignity or delicacy or gentleness or sorrow; Rodina Mat seems only to rage against the world. But it is much loved by the citizens of Volgograd, who climb up in all weathers to stand at its base and photograph the city beneath, especially the view down to the Red October factory and the Volga beyond.

Stalin is Volgograd's undisputed hero. It was he who oversaw the transformation of a backwater port into a great industrial city stretching for 40 miles along the western bank of the river. It was his 'not a step back' that saved the city from Nazism. And it was Stalin who ordered that the city that bore his name should be rebuilt out of the ruins as a celebration of classicism, an imitation of ancient empire, of Greece and Rome – and regardless of cost. As a result, you will hear hardly a word against Uncle Joe in this nostalgic city. Conversely, the city's *bête noire* is Stalin's successor, Khrushchev, who followed his 1956 denunciation of Stalin's 'cult of personality' by ordering that Stalingrad be renamed Volgograd.

In the process of de-Stalinization, orders were given that a vulgar mosaic of the great dictator – dressed in pure white as a Soviet Admiral of the Fleet and posing against a background of shimmering gold – which then dominated the inner atrium of the city's neo-classical planetarium, should be concealed from public view. He was duly plastered into oblivion. But three years ago, when the decorators were in, they scraped at the atrium walls to reveal the mosaic once again, an unbowed Buddha, re-emerging like a pompous Cheshire Cat, as self-satisfied as ever. Far from ordering his re-suffocation, the city authorities – by popular demand – had him restored to his former glory. Today he is once again on show for schoolchildren and loyal Stalinists to wonder at as they ascend to view other stars of the firmament from the viewing platform under the glazed roof of the planetarium.

One of Stalin's most loyal latter-day followers turned out to be the deputy director of the Stalingrad museum, where she had been a dominant force for twenty-five years. Svetlana Argastseva, who had already steered me around her beloved city, seemed never to pause for breath and rarely brooked interruption. A stout platinum blonde, expensively dressed, bejewelled and pancaked with an excess of powder and lipstick, she strode through Volgograd bestowing goodwill on the citizenry with an air of absolute authority. That she had an encyclopedic knowledge of her city was without doubt, but I was taken aback to discover how unequivocally she hero-worshipped the tyrant responsible for its renaissance. Steering me into the planetarium, she led me directly to the Stalin mosaic, where she stopped in reverence before the heavily bemedalled admiral. For a moment I thought she was about to genuflect or make the sign of the cross or demand a minute's silence. Thus bathed in his glory, we stood incongruously beneath the portrait while she extolled Stalin's multiplicity of virtues.

When she had finished, I said, 'Svetlana, this is very disconcerting. In fact it is rather appalling, because like many other people I think of the deportations, the Gulag, the show trials, the terror, the millions of Russian men and women who died because of him – and yet you regard him as some kind of hero.' She was imperturbable. 'He is a hero not just for me but for many, many other people too, and even for people throughout the world, and even for people who hated the Soviet Union, who hated Communism. Even Churchill said, "Little people make little mistakes, big people make big mistakes." And I would like to say that the numbers that you say died in the Gulag and so on – millions and millions – is very much exaggerated. And that it wasn't Stalin alone who was to blame for these things. There were other people who were in his entourage, and many people went to the Gulag only because of one another. You must know that it was a revolutionary period. It was a time of turbulence, and these things were part of that time that Stalin gave his name to.' 'Only because of one another' in 'a time of turbulence': one way, I supposed, of describing the ubiquitous and iniquitous practice of 'denunciation'.

Doubting that anything I might say would puncture her certainties, I tried a simple rebuke. 'But that's the kind of thing that apologists for Hitler say about Nazism.' It had no effect. 'Fascism under Hitler and socialism under Stalin were not the same. You shouldn't compare them. Churchill said that when Stalin came to power, he found a country in the Middle Ages. He left this country with heavy industry, a space programme and the atom bomb. He did marvellous things for this country. Of course there were mistakes, and of course there were things that shouldn't have happened, but every leader has made mistakes. The fact is that there is a movement to rename this city as Stalingrad. It just shows, you know, how much he did.'

I tried once more. 'I find it dismaying that people want to call this city Stalingrad again because when I look up there at that figure I'm afraid I see someone who was a monster.' Svetlana countered, 'When one thousand people showed up at the opening of the museum where I work, I asked for a show of hands. "How many people in your family have a relative who was persecuted under Stalin?" And I looked around and, believe me, 90 per cent didn't have anybody in their family who had suffered at the hands of Stalin. It makes me think that all these figures might be exaggerated. I think this history really needs to be very carefully looked at again. And don't forget that if the people of the country he ruled over love him as much as they do, he couldn't have been such a monster.'

By now I was floundering. 'So you would really like another Stalin to rule this country?' 'Stalin or not Stalin, I don't know, but I would like to see our country as it was when Stalin ruled over it: economically strong, beautiful, with people who are happy, who have a future, whose children have a future, who have something that they can believe in and that will continue.'

Svetlana had responded to my challenge as imperturbably as a well-trained psychiatric nurse handling a recalcitrant patient. Thwarted, I went off in search of the railway station, where her nostalgia for Stalin's version of the way, the truth and the light is vividly affirmed in the murals and friezes with which it is adorned. For those who enjoy counterfeit culture, this grandiose terminus is a fine example of neo-classical Stalinism. Inside, its domed ceiling is painted an azure blue, below which lies a sun-kissed, Stalin-blessed Soviet Union. Healthy boys and girls disport themselves innocently, singing and dancing in Arcadian bliss. A courting couple – he dressed neatly in a grey, pin-striped suit with an overcoat folded neatly over his arm, she in a summer frock and carrying a bunch of white roses – stride confidently into a land of future plenty. Near them, mothers and fathers stand at a dockside. Some are waving a proud farewell to sons in military fatigues on their way to protect the Motherland. Others welcome home a loved one, back from yet another Soviet victory at the front. Near by, a huddle of architects and builders, carpenters and masons are busily shaping the city of Stalin's dreams. Over them all, the Red Flag flies protectively in the breeze from the top of an imperial arch. Everyone is smiling, everyone is happy, and all is evidently for the best in the best of all possible worlds. Perhaps, I thought, Svetlana and the many who think like her really believe that this is how it was.

Before I left Volgograd I went for a drink in the Grand Café, which has about it the feel of one of those Parisian tourist traps on the Champs Elysées – much glass and many posters, tables of dark polished wood and pretty waitresses in retro-uniforms hurrying to serve. But it was a relief to rejoin the twenty-first century, to have a half-decent cappuccino and to watch the new world order, the international order of the young – here, as in the West, sweeping all before them. Noisy, casual, confident, glued to iPods or mobiles, bantering, arguing and flirting, always on the move from table to table, careless and fearless. Surely, I wondered, these young people who have discovered a kind of freedom would never permit the Russian clock to be turned back, nor contemplate the re-emergence of that 'strong, beautiful and happy' Russia of Svetlana's fond false memory. Surely not.

My reverie was interrupted by the arrival of a smartly dressed woman in her thirties. I had spoken to her briefly a day earlier and she had said she wanted to talk to me about the city. Like Svetlana she was blonde, but unlike the museum deputy director she did not behave as if she owned the place. Her smile was modest and her manner reticent. But when she laughed it was full-throatedly and her eyes had a mischief that – I indulged myself – was mildly flirtatious. In another age, I fantasized, this beautiful woman would have made a more than passable Mata Hari. I shall call her merely Olga because after we had exchanged pleasantries it was clear that she feared to speak openly. She worked for the government and was anxious to tell me about the plight of the mayor of Volgograd, Yevgeny Ishchenko.

She lowered her voice, and I had to lean towards her to catch her words as she explained that he had been elected in 2003 but had now been in jail, detained without charge or trial, for over a year. It had been alleged by his enemies – whom Olga described as 'business people, politicians and criminals whom I dare not name even in confidence' – that he had used his mayoral office corruptly in order to benefit himself. The allegations, she said, were without foundation. 'The issue is land. There is fierce competition for development land between rival groups in this city. If you give permission to the "wrong" person you are in big trouble. These are very dangerous times.' The mayor had chosen the 'wrong' people and, having done so, refused to be intimidated by the 'right' people, who had lost out on a lucrative deal.

'He fought them for two years,' Olga continued, 'but he underestimated their strength and so they had him arrested. This is easy in Russia because the system is so corrupt. They knew that he was a rich man before he became mayor, and they also knew there was no evidence at all that he enriched himself in office. Under the law the police are supposed to lay charges after twenty-four hours, but of course they had no evidence. So they kept him in jail for ten days and then refused to give him bail. And now he is still there, and there is still no trial. The case was brought to court, but because the evidence against him was so flimsy the trial was suspended. Since then there has been silence. And he has been inside for more than a year. His family has not been allowed to see him, not even the archbishop who is his spiritual father.'

So what happens next? 'No one knows,' Olga replied. 'I think they want to keep him inside until it is too late for him to mobilize support for the next elections. He still has strong support in the state Duma, and one or two newspapers are on his side. Otherwise, despite the lack of evidence, he would have been convicted by now. But I never expected such a thing to happen in this city.' I looked around again at the young Saturday-evening crowd circling each other, on the go, preparing for the clubs to open, the dancing to begin. Surely, if they knew of this case, they would care? About human rights? About the separation of powers? About an independent judiciary? About the rule of law? About the very bedrock of a free society? Surely? Or only perhaps? Or even perhaps not?

## BACK TO MOSCOW

I left Volgograd by sleeper in a first-class compartment, all lace and velvet and pressed linen. As we creaked out of the station, an immaculately tailored attendant, dressed in a blue uniform and wearing a dark tie with a Windsor knot, came to take my order for dinner, which he informed me I could take at any time between 5.15 p.m. and 10 p.m. As I waited for what turned out to be a delicious feast – solyanka soup made from ham, chicken and beef stirred in with pickled cucumber, sautéed onions, potatoes, tomato sauce, olives and lemon, all laced with sour cream – I gave myself a break from Russia and read Philip Roth's masterly *American Pastoral*. I noted down a passage that went straight to my heart. 'He had learned the worst lesson that life can teach – that it makes no sense. And when that happens the happiness is never spontaneous again. It is artificial and, even then, bought at the price of an obstinate estrangement from oneself and one's history.' I was transfixed by a thought that seemed at once so specific and yet so universal. Moved by such an intense expression of personal loss, I found myself at the same time wondering if an 'obstinate estrangement from oneself and one's history' is not the existential threat facing all Russians, young and old, strong and weak, nostalgic and forgetful; that in both abandoning and denying the past, they would be doomed to sleepwalk their way back to yet another version of that intractable fate by which their nation has always been cursed.

It was to be a twenty-four-hour trundle to Moscow, plenty of time for conundrums. But as I drifted into reverie, I realized that slowly, perilously slowly, my feelings about Russia were altering. I noted in my diary: 'It seems pathetic, even as I write the words, but I am less daunted, less intimidated by the scale of the challenge. I am less fearful of the people and not so demoralized by their brutalism. I am starting to see beneath the carapace, the veneer of distrust, the absence of a smile. I still can't speak a useful word – except for hello, goodbye, good day and thank you – but this no longer grinds me down towards despair. I have been touched and embraced by kindness and generosity that is the more affecting because it is without self-regard and it seeks no reciprocity.' There had been the manager in the canteen at the Red October plant, who saw that I was chilled by the Siberian wind cutting across the Volga and clasped me firmly by the hands, rubbing them warm, fussing about me until I had eaten my bread and borscht, which she brought to my table with a maternal bustle. And there had been Elena, a government official who had met me on my first day in the city, who had hurried to the station and boarded the train before I left to make sure that I was comfortable. 'I hope you enjoyed your stay in our city. I hope you will come again,' she had said as she jumped back on to the platform, waving until we were out of sight.

And there was another thing that lifted my spirits. I was on my way to Moscow and from there to England, where I was to be married in three weeks' time and without telling anyone except my immediate family. From the moment of Sue's death in September 2003, one or two tabloid newspapers had decided – in the public interest, of course – to take a closer than usual interest in my private life. Perhaps speculation and gossip about bereavement and its consequences are the stuff of life, but this relentless prurience seemed gratuitous and had been painful as well. When they discovered that their sixty-two-year-old prey had begun a relationship with a woman half his age, their concern for the public good had become positively priapic. They did not rest until they had first tracked down Jessica and then secured a paparazzi photo of the two of us together. We had felt violated by their intrusiveness and by the semi-leering gossip that accompanied the image. So we were determined that no reporter would learn about our wedding; there would be no stolen photos of our private celebration. Until now, despite the fact that, as the law requires, our banns had been published in Totnes and Islington, our 'secret' was intact. I was grateful to the local stringers, who so far had either been too sleepy or too kind to pass it up the line to their journalist colleagues.

Now, as the Moscow train rumbled its way north, I felt a sudden elation, a rush of joy, and I scribbled in my diary,

> I feel, finally, I have a new beginning, a fresh start – those cliché terms we use as we try to grasp shifts in time and place, and fix them for a moment. For the first time in three years, I feel a calmness, no perturbation, no inner turmoil. I am blessed by love – by the love of my children and still of Bel, who has adapted so generously to an upheaval that neither of us had sought or expected. And – how can this be possible? – I am now blessed by a new and wonderful love which I could never have expected. For the first time since Sue died I can now look forward to the future. Perhaps this is why Russia holds no terrors for me now. I hope that it remains so.

## THE WOUNDED BEAR

I returned to Russia in May 2007, flying into the city of Samara in a renewed state of misery and dread. Jessica and I had been married in March, quietly in Devon, without any unwanted attention, and our child was due to be born in eight weeks' time. Everything in me cried out to stay at home. 'Would not a responsible husband stay at home and nurture his new wife?' I asked myself lugubriously. Although Jessica is stalwart and resourceful, I knew that she too had dreaded my departure. And with that, my stomach once again churned with anxiety at the prospect of continuing my remorseless journey through what once again seemed an alien land.

An alien land? The new Russia? Boris Yeltsin had just died, an event that provoked a torrent of sentimental panegyrics in the Western media. Yeltsin, I had always thought, had been an almost unmitigated disaster. Inheriting the chalice at a most delicate moment of transition, he had hurled it to the ground with a breathtaking disdain both for the recent history of Russia and for the fragile structure of a dysfunctional society. Cheered on by international economists of the monetarist school, he had ushered in an era of unbounded greed and corruption, of insecurity and fear, of unemployment and inflation. In the process he had also poisoned the wellspring of democracy that had been slowly and carefully cultivated by his predecessor, the infinitely greater Mikhail Gorbachev. Proclaiming that his people would now be free to drink their fill of this elixir, he promptly turned the tanks on the elected representatives of the people when he was faced with defeat in the Duma. To their disgrace, this suspension of democracy was greeted with scarcely a murmur of protest from his allies in the West. He had gone on to hold a fraudulent referendum that more or less assured his re-election in 1995, urged on by a malleable media that, for the most part, had yet to discover the basic distinction between subservience and independence.

His chosen successor, a former officer in the KGB and then head of its 'democratic' successor, the FSB, restored a measure of order to the economic and social anarchy over which Yeltsin presided. Shielded by the autocratic constitution bequeathed him by Yeltsin, Putin found himself free to maintain the outward forms of democratic accountability while draining them of any inner meaning. Under him the Kremlin has accumulated even more power than it exercised in the Soviet era. The Russian Federation is constructed on a constitutional fraud, with all key appointments, notably those of the regional governors, now directly or indirectly in the hands of Moscow. The television stations, or all those that matter, are in the hands of the state and duly regurgitate the Kremlin's propaganda. With few exceptions, every newspaper that counts is owned by Kremlin acolytes. Far from providing any kind of 'fourth estate' to counter the baleful influence of an increasingly authoritarian Kremlin and a supine parliament – whose members have only reached their constitutional and legislative eminence through a gerrymandered electoral system – the media is now muzzled to the service of the state. The seeds of democracy that had been nurtured by Gorbachev's *glasnost*, and had sprouted momentarily during Yeltsin's anarchy, are now parched and withering on the stem. Those individual writers or lawyers who have dared to stand up against this perfidy have been harassed, persecuted and, in some cases, murdered for their pains. The most notable of the latter was the reporter Anna Politkovskaya, whose coruscating dispatches from the charnel house of Chechnya for *Novaya Gazeta* – which remains uniquely brave and independent – had infuriated the authorities in Moscow and Chechnya itself. For this *lèse-majesté* she was gunned down at the door of her apartment in the Russian capital. A murder investigation was launched and the alleged conspirators were found, but in Putin's Russia the close links they were widely presumed to have had with the Chechen president, Kadyrov, have not been the subject of official inquiry – even though it is generally presumed that Politkovskaya was murdered on his orders.

A little under a year before, in July 2006, Putin had welcomed the leaders of the G8 to St Petersburg for the first Russian summit. In the interest of progress on a range of international issues – energy supplies, Africa, climate change and terrorism – his fellow heads of state and prime ministers had contrived to avert their collective gaze from their host's tsarist tendencies at home. Were his guests briefed by their embassies that, before their arrival, the streets of the city had been swept clear of the halt, the lame and the hungry – many of them conscripts returning from the Chechen front line – or that the police had banned demonstrations in the city while arbitrarily arresting, detaining or expelling those suspected of dissenting views? If they had been so briefed, Messrs Bush, Blair and the rest studiously avoided mentioning it in public.

At a remarkably cosy press conference after the event, the Russian leader had congratulated his colleagues for allowing the G8 to become 'more democratic and open'. In response to a softball question lobbed by a Russian TV journalist about The Other Russia, a small political grouping, but a troublesome thorn in the Kremlin's side led by the former world chess champion Garry Kasparov, Putin opined that its very existence 'was another sign that democratic processes are developing normally here and that we have a functioning opposition. As is the role of the opposition, it criticizes the authorities. There is always reason to criticize the authorities.... If the opposition says some constructive things, it is really our duty, in my view, to take these opinions into account.' Less than a year later Kasparov was arrested, along with 170 others, and fined for seeking to participate in a banned demonstration in Pushkin Square.

Putin himself is supremely confident and calculating, far colder and probably cleverer than any of his peers on the world stage. Most of his ministers and senior officials, generally co-opted by him from the security services, have been appointed to strategically sensitive posts as chairmen of the state-owned or renationalized industries that exploit Russia's natural resources and from which the country's new-found wealth is extracted. Putin's cronies are very big cheeses in gas and oil, gold, diamonds, coal, nuclear energy, air transport and mobile phones, working closely with those twenty or thirty oligarchs who among them own most of the country's wealth, and who understand that they can enjoy their pre-eminence indefinitely as long as they don't interfere in politics or challenge the President's authority. Russia is, in effect, an autarchy: it has the trappings of democracy, but in every relevant respect its institutions mock the essential principles of a democratic society. To protect the apparatus that he has constructed about his presidency Putin has trebled the budget of his Alma Mater, the FSB, which is itself largely staffed by former members of the KGB. Putin's achievement is to have carried through a secret putsch, a peaceful coup – the first in Russia's history – that leaves the Kremlin with more absolute power than has been wielded by any of his predecessors. 'Our strategic mission is accomplished – we have seized power,' he is said to have joked with his friends in the FSB. Whether he said it or not, it is true enough.

Since the St Petersburg summit Putin has abandoned any pretence of international bonhomie. In its place he has sounded belligerent and resentful, a tone that ill disguises a deep-seated and long-standing national inferiority complex. However, when he says that it is 'pernicious' that America 'has created a unipolar world in which there is one master, one sovereign' you can see his point. It may be far-fetched to claim, as Russia's Foreign Minister, Sergey Lavrov, has done, that the United States is using NATO to encircle and contain Russia militarily (by 'swallowing up' Poland, Estonia, Latvia, Lithuania and soon, possibly, Georgia). It may be that the USA's unilateral decision to tear up the Anti-Ballistic Missile treaty that the two superpowers signed in 1972, and to plant ABM missiles within a few hundred miles of the Russian border, has no other motive than to deter an ill-defined and unexplained nuclear threat from a terrorist or 'rogue state'. But it is incredible to presume that the White House would have responded with equanimity to similar moves by Russia in America's own 'backyard'. Nor should it surprise any serious observer that Putin would retaliate by threatening to withdraw from the INF (Intermediate-Range Nuclear Forces) treaty that the two sides signed in 1987 and whose purpose was to eliminate all ground-launched nuclear missiles, such as Cruise and Pershing, from the European 'theatre'. Disconcerting but, under the circumstances, not surprising.

The Kremlin's belligerent tone has led some excitable commentators to predict a new Cold War. But to view Russia's resurgence through the prism of the twentieth-century rivalry between the two superpowers is to miss the point; it is to mistake form for substance, appearance for reality. Russia no longer even pretends to be a military superpower (its spending on defence may rival that of the UK, but it is no more than, and probably well under, 10 per cent of the Pentagon budget). Nor can the Kremlin contemplate for a moment a military confrontation with NATO; even if the new Russian president carries out Putin's threat to rewrite or withdraw from one or more arms treaties negotiated before and after the end of the Cold War, it would have far more 'declaratory' than strategic impact. In military terms the Russian leadership speaks from a position of weakness, not strength, which surely in part explains Putin's sour exasperation.

Of course, there is a deepening chill in the atmosphere. Russia is sorely bruised: bruised by NATO's refusal to contemplate a serious partnership in the nineties, bruised by the patronizing tone so often adopted by its former adversaries, and bruised by the 'ingratitude' of its former allies in eastern Europe. More important than the resurgence of this pathology, though, is the degree to which Moscow is bruised by the apparent disregard of the West for its claim to be a very big player and even partner in the post-superpower world. This claim is not only valid but is bound to become even more insistent. In a world where supplies of oil and gas are shrinking and where demand, which is still growing rapidly, promises to outstrip supply sooner rather than later, Russia's massive reserves of these two vital commodities give the Kremlin an increasingly powerful economic weapon that is of far greater significance than all the military hardware in the world. With energy prices soaring, GDP rising steadily at almost 7 per cent a year, a 'stabilization' fund of $80 billion in the Kremlin's back pocket and reserves valued at $250 billion, Putin has been delivered an unprecedented degree of macro-economic security at home that should be taken far more seriously abroad. A bear that is resentful but powerful may not be a pretty sight, but you slight it at your peril.

## BIG BUSINESS IN NEW RUSSIA

All this was running through my mind as I stared down at the Russian steppe, trying to avoid noticing the threadbare condition of the ancient Tupolev jet to which I had entrusted my life and that belonged to one of the many little airlines spawned in the post-Soviet free-for-all, owned by companies boasting safety records that do not bear close examination. To confirm my anxieties I had in front of me a newspaper article about the proposed merger of five regional airline companies. The words that glared back at me were: 'After a slew of crashes last year....' I stopped reading and looked miserably out of the window again. As if on cue, the roar and shudder of the plane's engines suddenly yielded to a murmur and we began a sharp descent. I looked at my watch and saw that we were barely an hour into a flight that had left Moscow more or less on time at 8 p.m. and was due to arrive at 10 p.m. I craned my neck forward and looked out to see dark clouds ahead. A storm? Was the pilot taking avoiding action? We continued the descent, none of my fellow passengers apparently aware that anything was amiss. I felt a sudden surge of resentment. Why are the Russians so fatalistic? Do they want to die? And then the pilot spoke over a crackly Tannoy. Although I could not understand a word, he sounded resolute and calm. But then pilots always sound like that. A steward walked slowly down the aisle, checking left and right that our seat-belts were fastened. Everyone was still remarkably unperturbed, while I was imagining what the fireball would look like from outside – the flames on the steppe and the incinerated corpses, mine among them. But, determined to keep a stiff upper lip, I summoned a steward who spoke a few words of English and asked, as nonchalantly as possible, 'How long before we reach Samara?' She looked at her watch and replied soothingly, 'We have twenty minutes to landing.' What? How was this possible? And then a sudden realization. My schedule had omitted to mention that between Moscow and Samara we would cross from one time zone to another – my watch was an hour behind local time. We landed safely, and with a surge of relief I walked across the tarmac, picked up my bags, and strode out of the airport into a balmy spring evening, a born-again traveller filled with what felt like boundless energy.

The euphoria did not last long. The next morning I sat in the breakfast room of my modest hotel staring at the plate that had been placed in front of me. There was a 'croissant' in a plastic bag with the words '7 days' and 'with vanilla cream filling' stamped on it, a slice of processed cheese, a dab of jam (also in a tiny plastic bag), a bar of Nesquik chocolate, two slices of processed white bread, a plastic pot of artificially flavoured yoghurt and an apple. I ate one slice of the apple, which tasted like cotton wool, and contemplated a cup of instant coffee. My spirits sank. I was most certainly back in Russia.

I thought back a quarter of a century, when I was with a colleague in Moscow where we were working on a television series about the Cold War. In those days the food in the hotels was uniformly dreadful and the service surly. In our hotel the crush bar provided the only evidence of human animation. It was filled with very pretty women, skimpily dressed. The mood was indiscreet and the atmosphere provocative but – despite the flow of vodka – it was all the easier to resist temptation because I indulged myself with the fear that in this Le Carré world I would be ensnared in a KGB 'honey trap' if I succumbed.

One evening, to guard against any loss of self-restraint, we decided to escape the hotel and went off in search of a restaurant, of which Moscow then boasted only a handful. The best were reserved for members of the nomenclatura or for foreigners with dollars to spare. We eventually found a Georgian restaurant, tucked away up a side street near Red Square. There was a long queue outside and it was bitterly cold. We stood for a while stamping our feet and rubbing our hands until the doorman saw that we were foreigners. He ushered us in and we were directed to a table where we seated ourselves opposite a grizzled hulk of a man who had a half-empty bottle of vodka in front of him. He gestured roughly at us to have a glass with him – it was less an invitation than an order. We drank. The same thing happened again. He summoned another bottle and repeated the unsmiling ritual. Staring at us, red-faced, long-haired and aggressive, he did not relent until we had yet again done his bidding. After four or five glasses I remonstrated, signalling that I had drunk enough. This infuriated him. Gripping my wrist in his huge fist, he made as if to clamp the glass to my lips. Filled with a sudden surge of Dutch courage, I resisted. The vodka splashed out of the glass and I yelled at him in English, 'That's enough – fuck off!' He got the message, and to my surprise immediately left us alone.

However, it took a long time to persuade a waiter to bring us a menu, and when it did come neither of us could unravel it. Although the quality of Georgian food is renowned, a glance around at other tables suggested a certain lack of variety. Everyone seemed to be eating chicken. Scrawny legs all round. We summoned the waiter once more, and, pointing to a couple chewing off the last of the meat from the bones, tried to explain that we too would have chicken. Our waiter failed to comprehend. Unabashed, my colleague decided to use sign language, drawing the outline of a chicken in the air. Our waiter looked bemused. He tried again and I joined in, flapping our arms like chicken wings and clucking like broody hens. The restaurant fell silent in bemusement. But the waiter understood. Dramatically invigorated by our manic efforts, he sped away to the kichen. A few minutes later he returned triumphantly bearing two hard-boiled eggs, one for each of us, on an otherwise empty plate. We gave up. Our former drinking companion was asleep.

Reminding myself of those dark days in Moscow when your every move was under scrutiny from an invisible KGB, I tried to struggle free of the gathering cloud of gloom that had started to hover over me in Samara, telling myself that it was all very much better today. As if to mock the thought, a cover version of 'Hotel California' started to pipe its way into the room to remind me that 'You can check out any time you like, but you can never leave'. A waitress brought me a cup of hot water to mix with my sachet of instant coffee. I asked for some milk to go with it. She brought me sugar. I tried again, pulling at the imaginary teats of a cow, hoping she would not think I was making an obscene proposal. It worked. Her hitherto solemn face collapsed into giggles and she returned, still giggling, with a glass of milk. I began to wonder if my gesture had a double entendre in Russia as well. As I left, she said, 'Have a good day.' I would, I told myself.

Samara is a city that is attempting to reinvent itself. Before *perestroika* it was entirely closed to foreigners. The centre was criss-crossed by high walls topped with barbed wire that concealed cities within a city, complete with long boulevards, avenues of trees and garden squares built around the heart of the Soviet Union's answer to America's military–industrial complex. Armaments factories produced all manner of weaponry from supersonic rockets to anti-chemical warfare equipment and high explosives – the material required to sustain a superpower's military rivalry. Samara's Aviation College was a training and recruitment centre for the aeronautical industry and the Soviet Space programme. Thirty-seven metres underground, the city also concealed Stalin's wartime bunker, though there is no evidence that he ever used it. Today, in the spirit of the new age, the bunker has been opened to the public and the city welcomes foreigners to a post-modern industrial and commercial complex. Only a few of the old wire-topped walls remain, while Cold War factories have been turned into leisure centres and the ideologues have been replaced by entrepreneurs.

One of the few factories that from the outside still looks as though it belongs to the Soviet era is now owned by the Samara Aviation Corporation, Aviacor. Established in 1935, the original plant had been the saving of the Soviet Union during World War II. At the height of that conflict, it turned out a squadron of fighters every day for four years, 35,000 planes in all. It was an astonishing achievement. Later, Antonovs and Tupolevs of all shapes and sizes continued to roll off the assembly lines. The most famous of these was the TU-114, the Soviet Union's first airliner capable of flying non-stop from Russia to the

United States. Khrushchev used it in 1959 for his first transatlantic flight, after which he delivered his infamous shoe-banging performance at the United Nations. Then came the TU-95 long-range bomber, a rival to the B52; and the mid-range TU-154, Russia's answer to the Boeing 727 and the workhorse of the Russian civilian fleet.

In those days this huge aircraft factory employed 27,000 workers. Today there are only 4000. Most of the production lines have been closed down. Birds fly in and out of the broken windows in roofs that shield the silent factory floors below only from the worst of the weather. The ill-kempt open spaces reminded me of the dismal collective farms that had littered my journey across Russia, all twisted metal, wrecked machinery, deserted cattle yards and weeds. At Aviacor, however, I was greeted by a young woman who spoke good English and was efficiently polite. She was straight out of university and was already half in charge of public relations. She led me through a succession of creaking wooden doors, up some stairs and into a long panelled corridor, dimly illuminated by occasional light bulbs. On either side of us were closed doors and silent offices. The only sound was our footfall on the worn linoleum.

She knocked on a door and I was ushered into an office as big as the boardroom of a merchant bank in the City of London. At one end stood a large desk and, sitting behind a computer but – *mirabile dictu* – looking up with a smile as we entered, a dapper, dark-suited man, whom I judged to be in his late thirties. He strode down the expanse of his office to greet me, walking with that semi-swagger adopted by George W. Bush and copied by Tony Blair when he was contriving to look equally presidential (I think modern leaders must employ body-language coaches as well as spin-doctors). Sergey Likharev greeted me with suave courtesy. Speaking in faultless English, he told me that he was a graduate of Moscow University, where he had got a top degree in physics. But, as with thousands of other scientists, it had proved impossible to find research work after the collapse of the Soviet Union. Deciding he had no choice but to enter what he called 'the commercial sector', he found a job in a meat-packing plant, which allowed him to save up enough for a spell in the United States, where he obtained an MBA at Cornell University. 'Sergey's our sausage-making physicist,' his fellow students teased. Back in Russia he moved from job to job, rising up through the ranks in a variety of sales and marketing teams, but earning a valuable reputation as a trouble-shooter in the process. 'That is how I came here,' he said, with a candour as engaging as it was unexpected. 'In 2004 this business was just half a step from bankruptcy – for the third time. I have been brought in to rescue this place, and I think we might just do it.'

'Who owns the company?' I asked. 'Aviacor is a 100 per cent private-enterprise business, and we have a lot of problems,' he replied. Then, with a brevity that is unusual in Russia, he outlined the story. 'After the collapse of the Soviet Union, this place was in terrible trouble. There were no jobs. But the governor of Samara was worried about unemployment and social stability. He was also passionate about aviation. He believed that a Russian market for airplanes would emerge in due course, as there was an alarming deficit of new planes. But this was not enough in itself to get a production line going.' In the mid-nineties the factory secured a few contracts overhauling, reconditioning and modernizing Russia's ageing fleet of TU-154s. At the same time, the state governor managed to win the production contract for a new forty-seater turbo-prop passenger jet, the Antonov-40, which had been developed in Ukraine. As it turned out, this coup had a price. 'The company had to take out huge commercial loans, and the level of sales was not enough to repay them. In 1998 it was bankrupt. And then Mr Deripaska stepped in.' 'Deripaska? You mean *the* Deripaska?' I asked. 'Yes, he bought the company and put his own money into it.'

Oleg Deripaska is estimated to be even richer than Roman Abramovich, which makes him the richest man in Russia – and one of the richest men in the world. 'How much do you think he is worth?' I asked Sergey, thinking he would demur. He was unabashed. 'I should say – I don't know for sure, as it is a private company – but I would say about $20 billion.' Latest estimates put his wealth nearer $40 billion. As with every oligarch who got rich very quickly indeed in the early nineties, rumours and allegations abound: how did such a young man acquire so much wealth so fast?

Encouraged by Sergey's openness, I pressed on. 'Is your boss a straight guy in his business dealings?' He did not blink. 'Yes, he is a straight guy. It is true that there have been a lot of rumours about him in the past, but people are changing. Remember the USA when it was the Wild West? Well, we all have to go through that phase, and unfortunately we are no different.' I probed a little more. 'There were a great many rumours about him?' 'Yes, that's true. But now we are trying to be – how do you say – more transparent, more open, more honest, more straightforward than the Russian environment sometimes allows. Somebody has to start.'

The allegations about Deripaska have their origins in the 'aluminium wars' of the nineties when he was in his mid-twenties. Starting as a metal trader in the anarchy of Yeltsin's free-for-all market economy, he bought a small stake in a Siberian smelting plant. This was the Wild West untamed. Corpses and body parts littered a battlefield where competing mafia gangs fought for control of this massively lucrative industry. It is reported that at one point Deripaska, who had a reputation for being a very hard nut indeed, narrowly avoided being blown apart by a grenade launcher – a story he denies. One way or another, though, he emerged as master of all he surveyed, the owner of United Russia Aluminium, the world's biggest producer of the metal. Since then, Sergey reminded me, Deripaska has used his virtual monopoly over the aluminium market to branch out into the oil and gas industries; he owns the Volga car company and Gazelle bus company, not to mention finance companies, civil-construction enterprises and a host of other interlocking industries. Counting all this up, Sergey revised his estimate of Deripaska's wealth. 'Maybe it is more than $20 billion. It must be more like $25 billion.' As if that were not enough, Deripaska also enjoys a privileged status enjoyed by no other oligarch:

he is married to a member of the Putin clan, within which he is a trusted member of the dynasty and a close friend of the President. For so long as Putin has influence he will be untouchable.

I pressed again. 'You'll forgive me, Sergey, if I sound patronizing – but you seem to me to be a new kind of Russian, trained as a scientist, a technocrat, trying to salvage a business and make it work. But anywhere in the world now, the world "oligarch" means stealing the nation's wealth, corruption on a massive scale, and the mafia.' I expected him to bridle, but he replied, 'Unfortunately, and very painfully for me, what you are saying is not without reason. It was like this, and in some cases it is still like this. But I won't operate in this way, although it causes problems for us. Sometimes we lose business because of it, but we are looking to the future and we want to reach Western standards. That is what our major shareholder wants us to be. It is a pain sometimes because, to speak frankly, he is losing money here at the moment. But he sees it as the way ahead. We have to look ahead.'

Sergey hoped that the Antonov-140 would help turn Aviacor's fortunes around. 'I think it has a real future. It is quiet, fuel-efficient, the only Russian plane to meet Chapter 4 noise-emission standards in the European Union.' After all manner of false starts and delays the first plane had been delivered in 2006 and a second was now in final assembly. Sergey showed me inside the fuselage of this salvation aircraft, a tangle of wires that confirmed my own belief that a fear of flying is a rational response to an irrational means of transport. Sergey reassured me. 'In the forty years since the first Tupolev went into service we have not had a single case of a catastrophe caused by technical malfunction. We have had terrorist attacks, control-tower errors, pilot errors, servicing errors, bad weather – but nothing wrong with the equipment or the construction of the plane.' Very reassuring.

Before I left, Sergey gave me some glossy brochures promoting the Antonov-140 as Russia's answer to the Dash 300 but, candid as he had been, he somehow omitted to tell me about the day that the first new plane off the assembly line was unveiled at a glitzy ceremony in front of the television cameras and a pack of expectant reporters. The governor of Samara announced that the plane was almost ready to make its first test flight. However, closer inspection by an unusually inquisitive journalist revealed that this particular Antonov-140 had yet to be fitted with an engine. He wrote up the story in his newspaper to the great embarrassment of the governor and Aviacor. But revelations of this kind have long been the stock-in-trade of the city's least biddable journalist, Sergey Kurt-Khadjiev, who edits the Samara edition of *Novaya Gazeta*, whose star reporter Anna Koslovskeya (as I mentioned earlier) was murdered for showing the kind of indomitable resolve that the paper inspires in its staff.

I met Kurt-Khadjiev at Samara's journalists' club, where he had invited me to talk to a group of his colleagues about our common trade. I had expected an informal meeting; instead I found myself sitting beside Sergey at the head of an oval table facing twenty young reporters, all with their notebooks at the ready. How did I find Samara? What were the best things about the city? Were there any bad things? Why was I in Russia? What did I think of Russia? Was I free to write what I liked? They noted assiduously every word I uttered, a disconcerting experience as I hedged a few bets in case the FSB had planted an informer at the meeting. However, rather pompously, I did allow myself to deliver a brief homily on the virtues – as well as the vices – of a free press. In particular I said, 'I don't know about you, but I would find it humiliating to live in an environment where reporters are shadowed by the FSB and where your proprietors and the government make it difficult, if not impossible, for you to tell the truth, where if you peer too closely into the darker recesses of life in Russia, you may find yourself unable to work, your permits withdrawn, your requests refused. It is demeaning and it is wrong.' At this point, I noticed, most of my interrogators laid down their pens and pencils, and the radio reporter withdrew her microphone.

Nonetheless these young men and women were – in private – both engaging and engaged by issues of freedom and responsibility, ownership and accountability. I felt sorry for them; had I been among their number, I like to think I would have resisted the self-censorship they impose in order to survive – but I doubt if I would have had the courage. Nor, I suspect, would I have been as resolute as Sergey, who had convened the meeting in the hope that his young colleagues would imbibe some of the attitudes and ideas that it was so easy for me to express.

Sergey did not look or talk like a sleuth. Rather, he had the reflective, vaguely sceptical manner of a middle-aged academic who knows precisely what he thinks, but listens with care as you ask him a question and weighs his answers carefully to demonstrate that he is not a man to overstate his case. But behind the reserved manner, the grey hair and the thick glasses there was an unmistakable resolution, a steeliness, an obstinate tenacity that I have noticed before in exceptionally independent characters and that must infuriate his many enemies among the rich and powerful of Samara. I asked him about his editorial stance. 'Mostly we write about issues that other journalists won't touch,' he replied matter-of-factly, 'and for quite objective reasons. Either economic or financial reasons. It is just not profitable for them to write such exposés. And it could be fear as well.' Fear? 'I mean perfectly ordinary human fear for yourself, for the people close to you. Not necessarily fear for your life, but you might be beaten up for it. You might have court orders and proceedings brought against you. It is simple, psychological fear. You know, I have around five court cases against me in any year.' Sergey has been bullied, threatened and beaten up; he has had his computer removed by the police and his disks destroyed; and he has been arrested and held without charge. But he has not yet succumbed.

I told him about a curious encounter I'd had earlier in the day at one of Samara's new leisure centres, carved out of a former Cold War factory that manufactured gas masks. Kin Up, as it was now called, was an up-to-the-minute sort of place of the kind you might find in any Western city. Lithe young women in leotards contorted themselves into obscenely provocative shapes; young male athletes pumped iron, their biceps and buttocks taut with effort; older men and women tried slavishly to recover their lost youth, striding and jogging on treadmills or cross-trainers, looking into the distance – in this case over the Volga – focused but unseeing. There was an indoor tennis court, a clutch of billiard tables and a swimming pool. But most of the area was covered by a state-of-the-art bowling alley. Kin Up's manager told me that full membership cost $1000 a year and that they were getting busier by the week catering for Samara's emerging middle class.

You could hire the bowling alley by the hour, and when I was there family groups and friends clustered around small tables behind each alley, intent on the video screens that recorded their hit rates as tabletop monitors simultaneously computed their scores. One family invited me to try my hand. My first throw disappeared into the left-hand gutter and my second into the right-hand gutter. Greatly amused, they insisted I join them for a drink. They poured me a size-able vodka and demanded that I down it in one, explaining amidst much kindly laughter that this would make all the difference to my hitherto lamentable performance. I did as instructed, picked a fresh ball, ran forward and released it at precisely the right moment, perfectly balanced, mind and body coordinated. True to their promise, the ball flowed smoothly from my hand to steer a perfect course – well, to be precise an almost perfect course – and eight pins fell in a single, glorious clatter.

My new friends cheered enthusiastically and pressed me to another vodka. Not for the first time, I wondered whether such generosity of spirit to a stranger would be reciprocated in my own country. I mentioned this to the manager, who was touchingly pleased that I had noted that the Russians are not invariably as boorish as they are often thought to be. We chatted affably about the leisure industry, and just before I left I asked him who owned the business. At once his demeanour changed: 'I don't think we should talk about that,' he replied. I thought at first he was joking or had misunderstood. 'I mean,' I went on, 'is it owned by a private individual? A company? Is

Kin Up part of a chain?' He looked even more uncomfortable and repeated with finality, 'I don't think we should talk about this.' He was clearly anxious for me to leave. He had pressing business to attend to; our conversation was over. I was intrigued. What had I stumbled on? Why such secrecy? Was an oligarch involved? Or an oligarch's wife? A mobster? Was it laundered money? Drug money?

When I reported this to Sergey, he said, 'That is a very common conversation in Samara. If you look carefully into who owns what here, you will find that there are companies registered in the names of dead people and tramps. The real money is hidden. Just see how many tax inspectors there are who officially earn 20,000 roubles and yet own a fantastic estate of houses – an estate that is registered in the name of a son. No, unfortunately, most of the big money in Russia is in the shadows – and until it comes out into the open we won't have proper order here. Everywhere – not just in Samara – everywhere it is corruption and bribery.'

The amounts thus expended are enormous. Authoritative figures suggest that private citizens pay out almost $3 billion in bribes every year. But, as Alena V. Ledeneva has described in her excellent *How Russia Really Works*, that sum represents no more than 10 per cent of the 'corruption market'; it is estimated that some $30 billion a year is spent by companies, both national and international, to secure export licences, quotas and tax transfers, and to avoid customs duties. In short, the entire system is rotten from top to bottom. Corruption in Samara is, as Sergey had made clear, the tip of a very large and very dirty iceberg.

'I know a great deal about Samara,' Sergey went on, 'but it is very difficult to write about it because unless I have the documents and people who are ready to talk I risk being taken to court. And I'll lose the case because I can't prove it – even though everyone knows it to be true.' When I suggested that, if he was correct, the apartment blocks, the glass offices, the atrium-hearted hotels, the restaurants with international cuisine and the leisure centres that I had seen sprouting across the city formed the glossy surface that concealed the seamy underbelly of Putin's Russia, he replied simply, 'Yes.' So what drove Sergey to persist against such odds, I wondered. He did not answer directly but said, with that obstinate defiance that I had detected earlier, 'What am I supposed to do? Can I leave? Can I get out? Can I go to England or Germany?' A lawyer's answer to his questions would have been 'Yes, yes and yes again,' but that wasn't the point. 'This is my town, this is where I live. And I want my children to live here and my grandchildren. And it is a question of "us" or "them". I am a man' – 'In the sense that you are not a mouse?' I almost interjected – 'and this is where I am going to live, and this is my job and my task, and I will stay here.' In short, Sergey Kurt-Khadjiev is not a quitter.

## A CHEMICAL DISASTER ZONE

Sergey had urged me to visit the town of Chapaevsk, some 45 miles from Samara. It was, he said, a very good example of a place where 'everyone knows the truth…but everyone is afraid to say it out loud. Knowledge is not the issue – it is saying it out loud.' The approach to Chapaevsk does not inspire confidence. In the distance you see a profusion of factories and chimneys stretching across the skyline, and yet there is almost no sign of human activity. As you approach the city boundary, you are greeted at a roundabout by a squat column built of concrete with what appears to be a giant hand grenade carved on one face: Chapaevsk, it seems to say, means weapons of war. The further you penetrate towards the centre of the town, the more you feel this chemical megapolis is very probably as sinister as its history would lead you to suspect. It straggles over an area of 72 square miles, more than half of which is covered by antiquated industrial plants, most of them out of commission, boarded up and falling down; a wasteland of weeds and rubbish and barbed wire and broken bottles and toxic waste. And these factories are not isolated from the community, but set in its midst. Rather as British coalminers used to live beside the local pit, so the families of Chapaevsk live huddled beneath the factories in which they once laboured for the Soviet Union.

The town was founded early in the twentieth century to produce shells and gunpowder for tsarist Russia. In the thirties it was developed into one huge chemical plant, called Middle Volga, producing mustard gas and lewisite. After the war Middle Volga continued this product line, but now as a counter-threat to the United States, which at that time possessed and manufactured similar Weapons of Mass Destruction (as they would very soon be officially labelled). Both mustard gas and lewisite cause rapid and severe blisters, which are not usually fatal but inflict lasting damage on the skin, eyes, respiratory tract and internal organs. In 1967 production of these WMD was halted as each superpower concentrated instead on developing ever more potent nuclear weapons. For the next twenty years Middle Volga produced highly toxic chemicals for civilian use, notably hexachlorine and its derivatives, including lindane, a carcinogenic pesticide (which has only recently been banned in Europe and the United States). Although the hexachlorine plant was decommissioned in 1987, Middle Volga continued to manufacture a wide range of other toxic chlorine compounds. This twentieth-century concoction of chemical poisons has bequeathed Chapaevsk an environment so lethal that in any other developed country the population would have been evacuated long ago and the area sealed off until it had been thoroughly decontaminated. But this is not Europe or America, and Chapaevsk is today still populated by seventy thousand souls imprisoned in homes that no one wants to buy and from which they cannot afford to escape.

I was taken around the town by a local writer, Yevgeny Sartinov, a member of Sergey's informal network of friends and contacts, and an eyewitness to Chapaevsk's history over the last thirty years. It was a profoundly disturbing experience. He showed me ample and poignant evidence of a regular spate of dreadful industrial accidents that began in the early twentieth century and lasted until well into the eighties. It is a record of gigantic explosions, raging fires, accidental poisoning and an official indifference to public safety, resulting in the killing and maiming of thousands of Soviet citizens.

The evidence lies in the town cemeteries, where the victims lie buried in neat rows, one beside the other. They are remembered simply as individuals, young men and women, who – you are invited to believe – merely happened to die on the same day. In its character-istically callous way, the Soviet state did not honour them formally in any way; they have no collective memorial stone or monument, not a single plaque to commemorate their unnecessary deaths. Only the identical dates on identical headstones disclose that they must have perished in an industrial disaster.

Yevgeny was himself witness to one such fatal incident. 'It was in 1985 and I remember it vividly. I was 5 miles away from the epicen-tre. It was 12.30 a.m. and the room I was in started to sway. The first thought in my head was that a nuclear war had begun. The force was so great that not only the windows, but the entire window frames of the nearby flats were blown out. It soon emerged that the explosion had destroyed an entire factory floor and killed eleven people – though they could not find the bodies, only the body parts…. But this was not an isolated incident. You must know that this kind of thing was a regular occurrence in our town. Of course, the authorities always tried to cover up what had happened. No inquiry. No explanation. The entire population of the town used to turn up in the main square to follow the funeral cortège to the cemetery, but not a word about it would be reported in the newspapers.'

Under the Chemical Weapons Convention, which was eventually signed in 1993, the stockpiles of mustard gas and lewisite should by now have been destroyed, but – like the USA – Russia is well behind schedule. Yevgeny pointed out two tall red-brick buildings in which these genocidal weapons were produced, and which he said were still dangerously contaminated. Seven years ago the media was summoned to Chapaevsk to witness the start of the decommissioning process. The television cameras dutifully recorded a team of demolition specialists, luridly dressed from head to toe in protective clothing and wearing gas masks, apparently preparing to set about their hazardous task. But when the film crews and the reporters departed so did the demolition team and, according to Yevgeny, they have yet to return. You might expect this cynical exercise in public relations to have provoked a response from the people of Chapaevsk. But the community appears to have been so exploited for so long, to have become so ground down and so fatalistic, that there has been no significant protest about this shameful and shameless breach of faith and duty. As Tolstoy observed in *Anna Karenina*, 'There are no conditions of life to which a man cannot get accustomed, especially if he sees them accepted by everyone around him.'

Meanwhile, a 'high-security' perimeter fence is supposed to keep the public safely away from any WMD residue or other hazardous waste that may be stored in Middle Volga. But the fence is buckled and rusting; in one or two places it has been trampled to the ground to provide a shortcut across the contaminated ground or access to a decrepit pillbox or guard-house that sits in the middle of the waste ground that surrounds the plant. Without quite knowing where I was, I walked through this 'security barrier' and towards the edge of the factory complex for at least 100 metres before being mildly shooed away by a dozy guard in military fatigues. How many children, I wondered, had preceded me into this poisonous playground? And how many others, with less innocent intent, might have been able to breach this perimeter if they wished? Yevgeny shrugged his shoulders in the Russian way as if to say, 'This is Russia.'

Then, even worse, there is dioxin, which is the principal waste product of the chemical factories that have been polluting Chapaevsk since the late sixties. In the virulence of its effect on human beings, dioxin almost rivals radioactive waste. Dioxin 'congeners', as they are called in the unemotive terminology of scientific jargon, are 'extremely stable, both to environmental and biological degradation, leading to their persistence in the environment and accumulation in the food chain'. What this means in practice is that from the late sixties for a further quarter of a century the soil, water and air in and around Chapaevsk were heavily polluted, year in, year out, by hundreds of tonnes of poisonous waste that has been ingested by scores of thousands of the townspeople via the vegetables they grow, the animals they rear and, most alarmingly, the water they drink. Because dioxin is so 'stable' people are still being poisoned today, even though the waste that still leaches from the few remaining chemical plants in Middle Volga is very low in volume and, in any case, is supposed to be safely contained.

Yevgeny took me to a lake on the outskirts of the town. A faded notice, a relic of Soviet times, proclaimed the waterside to be a 'Park of Culture and Recreation'. At first glance it looked enchanting. Hidden from the view of factories and furnaces by reeds and willows rustling in the breeze, the water was ruffled into whitecaps. But the lake has been so badly contaminated by dioxin and other waste products that for more than a decade it has been far too dangerous to use for any form of recreation: no boating, no swimming no paddling. Two years before my arrival the Chapaevsk authorities tried restocking the lake with crayfish, which are especially sensitive to pollution. A week later, all were found dead on the surface of the water or flapping their last on the shoreline. Notwithstanding this evidence, the authorities decided to try once more, and the following summer, Yevgeny told me, the lake was tentatively opened to swimmers. This non-scientific experiment lasted precisely a week. By that time those children who had taken up the invitation had developed sores on their bodies and lesions on their lips. The lake was once more put out of bounds.

Dioxin is arguably the 'dirtiest' pollutant that has yet to be eliminated under an international treaty called the Stockholm Convention. It is still pumped into the atmosphere all over the world by a wide range of chemical processes – in the manufacture of PVC , in smelting and recycling plants – but, it is claimed, only at levels of toxicity that do not threaten human health. Today in Chapaevsk, dioxin is present at between two and seven times the levels 'permitted' in Russia, which are themselves much higher than the limits set in Europe.

The precise relationship between dioxin contamination and human health is still a matter of research and contention. However, there is no significant dissent from the prevailing view that this toxin is closely associated with a wide range of cancers, diabetes, spontaneous abortions, congenital abnormalities and childhood ailments. The most recent statistical data for Chapaevsk, compiled in 2001, state that its residents 'experience substantially higher rates of cancer, cardiovascular diseases, spontaneous abortions, pre-term deliveries and congenital malformations, as compared to the average rates for Samara province and Russia'.

In an open society with a free media, Chapaevsk would be a national scandal. Long ago large areas of the town would have been declared unfit for human habitation. Over a wider zone, the meat, milk, cheese, fruit and vegetables produced from the contaminated soil would have been declared unfit for human consumption, while the water supply would have been sealed off and replaced by an unpolluted source. But I saw men and women tilling backyard plots of vegetables. Dairy cows roamed freely within a few hundred metres of the chemical factories. I also observed an elderly man and then a child filling up pails of water from one of the standpipes in the middle of town, which are still the only source of drinking water for many families. And this despite the fact that, when the water supply was last tested (in 1997), it contained 140 times the levels of dioxin permitted in Europe. As though all this were not enough, Yevgeny told me that there had been a plan to bring in a new pipeline with fresh water drawn from reservoirs well away from Chapaevsk. But, although the money had been allocated, there had been no sign of the new pipeline. The funds had mysteriously evaporated.

You might expect that even in Russia the most cynical politicians would want to publicize the continuing threat to the townspeople, but I found it extraordinarily difficult to discover the health status of the local population. Officials and doctors who had promised to talk to me became difficult to contact and then, inexplicably, one by one, they became 'unavailable for comment'. Yevgeny had an explanation. Apparently the FSB had issued instructions that no one should discuss the problems of Chapaevsk with this visiting foreigner. Despite this, I was eventually introduced to a doctor who had been explicitly informed that if she defied this order she would be fired and that the state funds for her hospital would be at risk. Irena Lyubavina had much to lose. As deputy director of Chapaevsk's psycho-neurological hospital, she ran a project exploring the impact of dioxin poisoning on young children and she did not want to put that precious funding at risk. She also had a young family to rear and she needed to earn a living. But these factors did not weigh with her as heavily as her hope that by talking to me she might be able to mobilize further international support for her clinical research. Torn between succumbing to blackmail and missing a rare chance to make her case, she opted to speak out.

As we walked through a dilapidated playground on an impoverished housing estate less than half a mile from the chemical plant, we paused to watch two little girls cavorting on a swing. Irena smiled in their direction and, in a tone that was in no obvious way rebellious, defiant or even exasperated, outlined the risks faced by those children. 'I can't give you precise figures because we don't have them. But you will know that mortality rates and sickness rates are the two key indicators of the health status of a population. If I tell you that the mortality rate for Chapaevsk is between 30 and 35 per cent higher than for the rest of the Samara region, and that for children it is 50 per cent higher, you will know we have a very serious problem indeed. Back in 1992 or 1993, one of our scientific-research institutions carried out tests to determine the levels of dioxin in Chapaevsk. In this process they tested the breast milk in our maternity wards and found very significantly high levels. We can say, almost for certain, that the 'under-five' mortality and sickness rates for children have been affected by the dioxin in their mothers' milk. We know for sure that the dioxin in the water, the soil, the vegetables and the mothers' milk has led to all kinds of birth defects and mental retardation. The level of sickness in our children is 70 per cent higher than the regional average.'

Irena delivered this evidence quite calmly, as if the facts themselves should be enough to compel attention. But there was resignation in her voice as well; deep down she knew that, in Russia at least, no one with power or influence really cared quite enough. It had been brave of her to speak to me, and the effort seemed to have deflated her; she looked suddenly woebegone. But I persisted, 'And the mothers of these children playing here...?' Realizing the futility of what I was about to say, I let my question tail away; but Irena sensed precisely what was in my mind and replied, 'Yes, absolutely. We ask people not to eat fish caught in the reservoirs around here, not to drink the water, not to eat the meat from the cattle, nor the vegetables, the carrots and the beetroot, not to give these things to their children.' 'But they ignore you?' She nodded, explaining that, in the absence of any public campaign, most of the town's residents were still unaware of the threat. As an afterthought she concluded, bathetically, 'Of course, it is no secret that Chapaevsk is a very unhealthy place to live.'

I felt a renewed surge of disgust at the authoritarian, dishonest and indifferent elite that holds sway in Russia today. 'How is it,' I wanted to rage, 'that in 2007 this can be possible? The lies. The deceit. The wilful neglect.' Then I forced myself to remember Yevgeny's fatalistic 'This is Russia' and, reminding myself that such self-indulgent diatribes were a waste of my energy and Irena's time, I said nothing. But I still wanted to find out why the FSB had been so intrusive. What was at stake? Why had they instructed the medical authorities not to speak to me? The town is no longer closed off to foreigners. Scientists and epidemiologists had sampled, recorded and analysed Chapaevsk's predicament. So what was there to hide? Once again Yevgeny had the answer. The warning by the FSB to the hospital doctors had been explicit: 'Ignore us and your funding will be at risk.' 'But why?' they had asked. The answer: 'Any exposure of the problems facing Chapaevsk at this juncture would interfere with the forthcoming elections.' 'But surely that is precisely what elections are supposed to be about?' I said. Once again Yevgeny had to remind me that I was in Russia. 'You know that five hundred thousand roubles was allocated a decade ago to start bringing clean water to Chapaevsk. Every year since then, more than half a million has been allocated. Now it amounts to several millions. But there is still no pipeline. And that is not all. Ten years ago they promised to build a new children's hospital. The money was allocated, but the hospital still hasn't opened.'

Although he does not say so explicitly, the inference is obvious. Chapaevsk is a graveyard of scandal that no official wants to disinter. Most, if not all, of them have been on the take and, as ever, it has fallen to the FSB – Putin's very own FSB – to muzzle the truth. As Yevgeny says, 'This is Russia.'

I arrived back in Samara to hear that Sergey Kurt-Khadjiev had been arrested. We hurried down to the police station to find out what had happened. As we pulled up, I saw him emerge on to the street. I crossed the road towards him just as two large officers emerged from a police van and, with a scowling glance in my direction, walked stolidly into their headquarters with that bulging-belly, big-arsed, gun-in-the holster, self-important swagger affected by those with petty but absolute authority. 'That was the guy who arrested me,' said Sergey laconically, pointing at the more senior of the two men. It had all started, he explained, a few days earlier. The police had raided his office and, on the eve of publication of that week's edition of *Novaya Gazeta*, removed his computer. They told him he was under suspicion for using pirated software – an offence so routine in Russia that the courts would be clogged for a century if every alleged miscreant were brought to justice. But as he and everyone else in Russia is aware, the law is an ass – though a very dangerous, Kafkaesque ass. It is virtually impossible to survive, let alone prosper, either in business or in private life without knowingly committing one or another criminal offence on a regular basis. As a result, while the law and its officers are held in widespread contempt, they are also a permanent source of anxiety – weaponry at the disposal of the rich and powerful to threaten or destroy any challenge to their hegemony. Sergey is repeatedly targeted by the police as, on behalf of their powerful clients in business and politics, they try to harass him into greater compliance.

On this occasion, Sergey's computer was returned and no charge was laid against him. But on the eve of my arrival in Samara his daughter, a feisty twenty-one year old who shares her father's iconoclastic temperament, had signed a petition requesting the right to hold a rally at the EU summit that was due to be held in Samara on 18 May (and that had already been billed in Europe as an unproductive stand-off between President Putin and the new German Chancellor, Angela Merkel). For her impertinent urge to exercise her constitutional right of peaceful protest, Sergey's daughter was arrested and taken into custody on suspicion of forging the signature of the deputy mayor on her petition – an allegation of which she protested her innocence. Eventually, in an absurd development of the kind that Gogol would have relished, it emerged that the arresting officers had failed to check their facts with their principal witness, the deputy mayor himself. Unable or unwilling to contemplate perjury, he confirmed that he had indeed signed the petition. The police had no choice but to release her. According to Sergey, she had been arrested for only one reason: to intimidate him.

But that was not quite the end of the episode. While I was in Chapaevsk, he was subjected to entirely unwarranted attention from the police yet again. 'I was strolling near my home when a police van drew up. This major in police uniform came and grabbed me without any kind of explanation,' Sergey said. 'But they had no evidence, so, after three hours, they had no choice but to release me.' I asked him if he had been worn down by such persistent harassment. 'It does wear you down. It is very unpleasant, and it wastes a lot of time. But they can't intimidate an entire nation. And in our case it will simply strengthen our resolve to tell the truth.'

## REMEMBERING THE FALLEN

In Russia, 9 May is Victory Day. The television monitor in the hotel lobby was relaying images from across the nation as it prepared to honour those who had died to save the Soviet Union in the Great Patriotic War. The young woman at the front desk addressed me in English with an enchanting formality. 'If you are interested in our history and our culture, then I advise you to watch Channel One. It has many memories of the war. If you see me crying, I hope you will understand.' Outside in the streets, Samara was preparing for the big day. Police lined every road leading up to the vast parade ground near the city centre. A military band prepared its drums, trumpets and horns; platoons of soldiers took up their positions under the stern gaze of a company sergeant major bellowing in the best British tradition; and a modest crowd, braving the bitter wind and driving rain, waited patiently under their umbrellas, glad to be there. One by one the dignitaries arrived. In the VIP section retired generals and old comrades, weighed down by medals of honour worn proudly on wheezing chests squeezed into neatly pressed uniforms, embraced one another in the bear-hug way. Then the mayor and the governor arrived almost simultaneously, neither anxious to cede precedence to the other. They looked around complacently towards the crowd before taking up their positions on the dais that faced the parade ground. Finally, just before the witching hour of 11 a.m., a trio of jeeps, each importantly separated from the next by an expectant pause of a minute or so, entered stage right. Each vehicle contained a commanding offi-cer, standing at attention, eyes front, stomach thrust forward, the dignity of one of them fatally imperilled by an unexpected jolt that threatened to topple him like a felled waxwork from Madame Tussauds. Two young women conscripts standing beside me in the crowd clearly saw the moment as well; they looked at the general and then at each other, raising their eyebrows in mirth before collapsing into insubordinate giggles.

On the stroke of eleven, the band began to play and the march-past began. It was an impressive drill, well up to British standards: every soldier faultlessly in time, every goose-step high up to the regulation distance from the ground, a military ballet up and past, eyes right, eyes front, rank after rank, solemn and triumphant. The march-past accomplished, the three battalions stood to attention, motionless as one of the three generals on the dais, invisible to most of the spectators, reminded his men of the great victory of 1945. 'Remember it was the Soviet Union that liberated Russia and the world from the tyranny of Nazism. Let us salute the heroes and the victors. Their courage represented the heroic victory of the Soviet people.' Then, less stridently, 'Not everybody lived to see that day. Half a million died in this region alone. We must honour their memory, the lives they gave for their country.' As he finished each paragraph, he intoned, like a priest reading from the liturgy, 'Long live the independence of our Motherland.' As he did so, the voices of the young soldiers facing him echoed as one back across the parade ground, 'Long live the independence of our Motherland.'

The band struck up again and played the national anthem of the Russian Federation. I noticed that almost no one was singing the words, though everyone seemed to be mouthing something. A woman beside me in the crowd, who spoke some English, whispered, 'We used to have the Soviet anthem, but no one knew the words to that either. Then they brought in a new anthem with new words. This time no one knew the tune either, let alone the words. So they went back to the old Soviet anthem but kept the new words – but still no one knows them.'

The formal proceedings accomplished, Victory Day turned into a kind of Military Open Day. Soldiers helped little children to clamber aboard tanks and on to the barrels of long-range artillery weapons and rocket launchers, posing innocently and waving much as their grandparents had done after the liberation of the Soviet Union almost seven decades earlier. Old comrades stood and reminisced, weighed down by memories embalmed in dog-eared documents and campaign medals that they showed me with pride, rheumy eyes glistening. One of them, who must have been in his mid-eighties but was still ramrod-upright, produced his old CCCP party card. 'I am still a Communist. Things were much better then, before Yeltsin arrived.' Pensioners queued in orderly lines for a free bowl of buckwheat porridge, and, for the old soldiers only, a half bottle of vodka. The conversation flowed.

I watched a quartet of young conscripts, raw-faced and acne-streaked, looking uncomfortable in ill-fitting uniforms as they were shepherded through the mêlée by a colonel who repeatedly posed self-importantly to have his photograph taken for a family album, organizing his young charges around him like a clucking hen. Only when he was fully satisfied that they were all present and correct did he signal to a hapless mother that he was ready to be digitally immortalized for her benefit. He then embarked on an impromptu speech to his men about pride and duty and honour. They didn't look too impressed. I waited for him to finish, which took a while, and then went up to ask him about his own career, which gave him an opportunity for another homily, the gist of which was: 'I am proud to be with these young men. I have served in the army for twenty-nine years. I have completed three tours of duty in Chechnya, and I have returned from there with these soldiers. These men are ready to follow me to any hotspot, to any war.' Then, apropos of nothing in particular, he said in halting English, 'The Queen of your country was in Washington recently and I saw that she laid a wreath on the tomb of the Unknown Warrior. She was a fighter herself in the war. It pleased me.' On cue, the rain cleared and a warm sun shone on the gathering.

In the afternoon, I went to the main cemetery on the outskirts of the city where the families of the fallen remember their loved ones. The mood here was subtly different, more reflective than celebratory, though they carried garishly cheerful bouquets of freshly minted artificial carnations and gladioli in purples, blues, yellows and mauves as they paraded down long, winding avenues under the protective canopy of trees that shelters this hallowed ground. They sat in small groups, ones and twos and threes – more women than men, more old than young – facing the family tombstone, each one segregated within a square of ground with its own protective fence; a bewilderment of railings, like so many playpens, but made of rusty iron. They unpacked bread, sausages, cheese and chocolate, and sometimes a bottle of vodka. Scattered throughout the cemetery, these little groups talked softly but in such numbers that, as I wandered past, their voices sounded like a rustling from the obscuring trees that offered them a little privacy for their feelings. Some sat in silence, and in one corner I saw a woman stooped over a grave, weeping.

I walked on through the cemetery until I was far away from the sound of traffic. There I came upon a high memorial cross to those who had fallen in the Great Patriotic War. Close by, an ancient babushka, tears streaming down her face, looked in dismay at a vandalized headstone. 'See what they have done! See what they have done!' she cried out, pointing at the damage, bewildered that anyone could do such a thing to the memory of her grandfather who had been a general in the Soviet army. 'See what they have done,' she repeated. 'They are out of control.' Then, comforted by her daughter, she recovered herself. Gathering that I was English, she took me by the elbow, and, gesturing to the clear, late afternoon sky, said, 'May the sun always shine on our two countries. We are friends – we have always been friends.' Not for the first time, I was both struck by the intensity of goodwill that elderly Russian men and women have for their wartime allies and chastened by the realization that any reciprocal affection that may be felt by their peers in Britain so rarely finds similar expression. I clasped her hands and nodded vigorously in agreement. She barely noticed and was soon on her way, limping on tired old legs, helped by her daughter, deep in her own thoughts.

As the sun began to fade, one by one, group by group, the families packed up and walked slowly back out of the peace of the cemetery into the noise of the city. A mother and daughter passed me, the older woman soberly dressed in dark skirt and white blouse, the younger in tight white jeans, on which was printed in red capitals on her ample backside, the English word 'JUICY'. It was the only discordant note of the day.

## SERVING THE MOTHERLAND

'Spine-chilling' is an over-used term. But it was the first phrase that came to mind when I saw the video that, following a tip-off, I downloaded in a busy internet café near Samara's city centre. The seven-minute tape was technically sophisticated, but editorially crude almost beyond belief. It took the form of an animated cartoon depicting American imperialism on the rampage – black octopus tentacles reaching out from Washington across the globe, planting missiles on surrogate soil, encircling the Motherland and parachuting US marines into the remotest parts of Russia to suppress the local population before planting the Stars and Stripes on Russian soil. An urgent and alarmist soundtrack heightened the sense of an imminent threat to the nation, which required an urgent patriotic response.

The USA is a big fat guy who has eaten too much and now can't stop gobbling up more and more. You can find the food America wants all over the world – oil, gas, metals, people. Without all this America will simply die. And a significant part of the food that America wants is in Russia – and that's bad for us. To the Americans we are like hicks from the backwoods. A little bear with a bottle of moonshine vodka....

They have a choice. Either to eat less and less and in the end stop growing and die. Or to come and get the food. They will come and get it...every single American wants his car to be powerful, his clothes fashionable, his house bigger, his lights brighter.

And they are already close at hand. They're in the Baltic states. In Ukraine. In Georgia. They have their military bases there, their missiles. Guess who they are aimed at? There is only one thing that will stop America going to war with us – if our army is at the very least no weaker than theirs...otherwise under the slightest pretext they'll swallow us up.

The images and sentiments were so crass that for a while I thought they must have been intended as a satire on paranoia or, alternatively, that the video had been produced by a handful of xenophobic internet nuts. But it was in fact part of a state-authorized recruitment campaign urging young men and women to rally to the cause, to sign on and do their duty by serving the nation as military conscripts. According to the commentary, too many of them had taken to making 'dishonest' and 'treasonable' excuses to avoid defending the Motherland in her hour of need. Compiled by a Kremlin-inspired youth movement called Nashi – which translates literally as 'Ours' – the video expressed, in very much cruder terms, an attitude towards the West that could have been written by the President himself.

Nashi's members, now in the tens of thousands, are urged to be clean-cut and clean-living; at their annual summer camp they cut their hair short, don identical red T-shirts and wave patriotic flags. But boy scouts and girl guides they are not. Skilfully managed by the movement's leader, Vasily Yakimenko, who belongs to the Kremlin establishment and has recently been appointed chairman of the State Committee on Youth of the Russian Federation (a kind of Minister for Youth Affairs), Nashi claims to be internationalist and anti-racist while its pronouncements seem calculated to stoke the flames of nationalism and xenophobia. While Nashi is encouraged to take to the streets to celebrate the President's birthday, it has also been given the power to obstruct the regime's democratic opponents when they seek to exercise similar rights to peaceful demonstration. In an Orwellian intervention, one of the Kremlin's trusted advisers, Gleb Pavlovsky, has even called upon Nashi to stand by to 'break up fascist demonstrations and to prevent with force any attempt to overthrow the constitution'. Putin's shock troops, but in red shirts rather than black or brown? As its critics like to point out, the words 'Nashi' and 'Nazi' are disconcertingly similar – and their nasty little video does precious little to invalidate the comparison.

The over-riding message of the Nashi video is 'Your Country Needs You' – and it has a rather desperate air about it. Russia's conscript army is short of recruits and low in morale. Those who have the resources or contacts to do so generally manage to bribe or talk their way out of an eighteen-month obligation that is universally associated as much with penal servitude as with national service. With this in mind, I got myself invited to a farewell party for a young recruit the night before he was due to sign on. Although I had been forewarned that such occasions are invariably fuelled by alcohol and charged by the anguish of separation, I was not prepared for the intensity of suppressed emotion I was about to witness.

Vitaly's family lived in a run-down working-class suburb, on the fifth floor of one of those identical Soviet blocks from which middle-class Westerners like myself shrink in dismay. Their apartment was cramped but welcoming and very crowded. In addition to his mother and father and two sisters, not to mention his grandmothers and an aunt or two, he had invited half a dozen of his best friends, all of whom seemed to have been at school with him. To my embarrassment, Vitaly insisted I sit by his side. As soon as I had clambered into my place, he proposed a toast to all his guests. The evening was under way in earnest. His mother, a buxom woman with platinum hair and a harassed smile, hovered dotingly to replenish a table that was heavily laden with meats and salads and beer and vodka.

Vitaly was twenty years old. Tall and broad-shouldered, he was open-faced and disarmingly gentle, a smile hovering all the time. I asked him if he was as happy as he seemed to be about the prospect of life in the army. Was he really looking forward to being away from his home and family for the year and a half? 'Yes,' he replied, but with a slight note of defiance, as though trying to convince himself that he meant what he was saying. Wasn't he worried about army rules and regulations? 'No' – but again said with an air of bravura that was not entirely convincing. Then he clasped me in a bear-hug and poured me another glass of vodka as if to say, 'Let's forget about these things – let's drink instead.'

The television set was relaying a pop concert from another world: a nightclub in St Petersburg packed with young people gyrating to an insistent beat – stick insects under strobe lighting – while a trio of semi-naked dancers slithered up and down a pole on stage in simulation of sexual passion. Two of Vitaly's friends decided to cross the divide of distance and culture, squeezing themselves into the tiny space between the dining table and the TV to join the dance, staring fixedly at the screen to help them along. One pointed at the writhing women on screen and said in English, with unfeigned admiration, 'Look, *Russian* girls!' – with the emphasis on the second word.

Vitaly's mother, affecting not to notice this incongruity in her very proper little parlour, became more anxious than ever as the evening wore on. She repeatedly stuck out her lower lip, not pouting but to blow cooling air on to her forehead, her blonde fringe wisping up into the air as she did so. Finally, clearly steeling herself for the effort, she clapped her hands for attention. Addressing herself directly to her son, she said, 'I want you to be a worthy soldier. I want you to serve honestly, and I want you to defend not just yourself but everybody. And you must know that we will be waiting for you when you come back.' It was brief and dignified. For a moment everyone was silent and solemn. And then they raised their glasses to her sacrificial lamb. This, I realized, was an important ritual, a rite of unwanted passage.

Her public words clearly belied her private feelings as she retreated to her place beside the television barely able to restrain her tears. Next to her Vitaly's grandmother wept openly. I asked his mother if she was as distressed as I felt her to be. She nodded. Was it because her son was leaving home, or because the army was known to be 'a difficult life'? She replied, 'I am worried because of the stories you hear, and I am worried about what goes on there. You hear things. But you have to do your duty. It is the duty of every man to defend Russia.' Then, filling a glass with vodka, she offered a private toast, which she clearly did not want him to hear and which seemed more like a prayer: 'To Vitaly – that he comes back alive and healthy. We love him and we will be waiting for him.' I did not press to know what she meant by the 'stories you hear' because I knew she knew I knew. It is the subject that you don't talk about, and in this particular room on this particular evening it was a very big elephant indeed.

A recent Human Rights Watch report, *Inhuman and Degrading Treatment of New Recruits in the Russian Armed Forces*, has documented in detail the catalogue of routine and ritual abuse to which new recruits are likely to be subjected when they sign on. It describes a system called *dedovshchina*, 'rule of the grandfathers', which allows second-year conscripts, unsupervised by their superiors, to impose on new recruits 'a year-long state of pointless servitude…to punish them violently for any infractions of official or informal rules… [and] to abuse them gratuitously'. Using official documents and first-hand testimony as the principal sources for its allegations, the report further states that 'dozens of conscripts are killed every year as a result of these abuses, and thousands sustain serious – and often permanent – damage to their physical and mental health. Hundreds commit or attempt suicide and thousands run away from their units.' (*Human Rights Watch*, vol. 16, No. 8(D), p. 2.)

The researchers cite a convincing array of supporting evidence drawn from letters and from interviews with conscripts and their families, conducted either by their own researchers or by Russian academics of impeccable credentials. Some of these are heart-rending. One conscript writes to his mother, fearful that he will become so indoctrinated that he too will become a 'grandfather' – the abused as abuser – and either turn into what he calls a 'psycho' or go 'crazy'. And then he continues, 'I am not a bastard, I can't beat a person for no reason, just like that, take him and beat him.… Mother, here you can become a bastard, a beast, they are almost like animals here.... I am afraid that I may become like them.'

If second-year recruits risk becoming 'psychos', first-year recruits find themselves turned into what one of them describes as 'slaves' at the mercy of their 'grandfathers' and only 'eligible' to eat, wash, relax, sleep, be sick or even keep track of time with their consent. To acquire these 'rights', they are obliged to perform menial tasks at the behest of the second-year recruits: cleaning their equipment, washing their clothes and mending their collars. To disobey an 'order', however absurd, demeaning or outrageous it may be, is to court severe punishment. Beatings with batons, sticks, chair legs or any other offensive weapon that might be at hand are commonplace, and may also be meted out to those who merely fail to meet the arbitrary but exacting standards set by their 'grandfathers'. Such punishments are reported to be so severe that first-year recruits are routinely hospitalized as a result, and dozens of them are known to have died from their injuries.

One annual rite, known as *stodnevka*, obliges each first-year recruit to procure cigarettes for his 'grandfather'. In 2002, in a case cited by Human Rights Watch, a new recruit, Dmitri Samsonov, wrote home on 27 May– three weeks before the start of *stodnevka* – with an urgent request for money and cigarettes. Explaining why he needed them, he ended his letter with the words, 'Mama, don't forget to send this immediately. Immediately!' He heard nothing. On 19 June he wrote again: 'Today the *stodnevka* is starting and I haven't received anything from you.... I don't know what to do.... I wrote to you, begged you...but nobody responded. You just don't understand how impor-tant it was for me....' And he added a footnote: 'I love you very much and miss you but I don't know how I am going to survive now.' His letters arrived too late. On 13 July he wrote again, this time from a military hospital, to report that he had suffered a broken wrist. 'I am not going to explain how it happened...I just wanted to inform you that I survived the beginning of the *stodnevka*.' Nine days later his parents received a telegram informing them that their son was dead.

Later they were told that Dmitri had slit his veins. His commanding officer recorded yet another suicide.

This kind of horror may be routine, but it is not inevitable. Human Rights Watch is careful to report that, where military commanders are intolerant of such barbarity, the practice is swiftly eliminated. But too often *dedovshchina* is condoned or ignored by an officer class that is either indifferent to the suffering or appears to believe that such 'Wrongs of Passage', as Human Rights Watch subheads its report, are an effective way of establishing *esprit de corps* and military discipline.

How is it, I wondered as I read my way through this ghastly evidence, that President Putin has not yet insisted that this grotesque violation of human rights is stamped out? And then I read an interview with the Russian Defence Minister, Sergei Ivanov (one of his most loyal lieutenants), which happened to have been conducted two months after Dmitri Samsonov's 'suicide': in it Ivanov declared that the most recent intake of army recruits had been 'a pathetic lot, afflicted with drug addiction, psychological problems and malnutrition'. Since that oafish comment, little appears to have changed – except that the length of service for conscripts in Russia's armed forces has been reduced from two years to eighteen months and is due to fall again in the coming years. For a moment I indulged myself by wondering why the Russian media was not on the warpath, running campaigns, demanding inquiries, challenging the government. Were so many television and newspaper editors really purblind or intimidated? Were they really so self-censorious or muzzled? And then I reminded myself which country I was in.

All that evidence from Human Rights Watch, had she been aware of it, would have done little more than confirm Vitaly's mother's fears. Word of mouth had already told her much of it. Before I left the party one of his young friends, who had finished his military service a year earlier, whispered to me in broken English that he had been beaten up twice by the 'grandfathers'. I asked him why. 'Because I did not obey an order.' Both times he had had to be taken by stretcher to the military hospital. On the first occasion the doctors had diagnosed several broken ribs and internal bruising; on the second they had delivered the same diagnosis, but this time the punishment had been so severe that he had been put out of action for four months. Astonishingly, he showed no great resentment at the memory. 'Stuff happens,' he seemed to be saying, before confiding with a look of sudden concern, 'I hope Vitaly will be all right. He is a very gentle person, so he might not be noticed if he is careful and does what he is told. But he is a strong character, and they might pick on him to break his will.' I looked across at Vitaly. He was laughing and joking, quite drunk by now but affable and affectionate. Before I left he gave me another bear-hug and I said lamely, 'Look after yourself.' I knew he knew what I meant.

## KAZAN: WHERE TWO WORLDS MEET

The journey by road from Samara to Kazan, in an arc north and then west, was due to last eight hours. Once we had escaped the suburbs, we were again in the steppe, that unrelenting pattern of huge square fields, stretching to the horizon in every direction, that soon numbs the senses. To ward off the gloom that started to encircle me I forced myself to look more closely at the passing landscape with a semi-professional farmer's eye – and I was at once absorbed, noting some sharp contrasts along the way. In some places the fields on either side were well groomed, neatly tilled and planted. They had been bordered with new hedges and young trees, silver birch or fir, which would soon grow to protect the precious loam from the driving easterlies. Here and there an array of glossy farm machinery – ploughs, harrows, drills and combine harvesters from Germany and the United States – reminded me of the American Midwest. Someone – some company, some entrepreneur, some oligarch – had invested serious money in this fertile bowl of black earth. Perhaps they had been advised that a century ago, before the revolution, the output in this region, coupled with that of Ukraine, had made Russia the world's largest exporter of grain. In those days winter wheat, rye, oats, barley and millet were taken by horse and cart from this land and stored along the banks of the Volga, where the grain was loaded on to barges and cargo vessels for sale to all parts of the world. But this air of promise was conspicuously limited to the environs of Samara. As we drove further from the city, the countryside began to look very much less prosperous. Instead of shiny new equipment, the landscape was littered with rusting machinery, crumbling farm buildings and woebegone villages. Between these apparently lifeless outposts of human habitation the fields were mean, either half-tilled or left fallow and filled with weeds – lasting evidence of that ruinous scheme to collectivize food production throughout the Soviet Union.

The route we had chosen between Samara and Kazan looked like a shortcut, a hypotenuse on the map. It was a minor road that, our driver advised, would reduce our journey by two hours. For several miles ours was the only vehicle on the road. We soon saw why. The asphalt surface became more and more uneven and eventually so potholed that we had to drive through an obstacle course of craters, some of which looked almost deep enough to bury a car. In places chunks of asphalt had erupted to form crazed tarmac sculptures. Finally, one of these craters proved impossible to negotiate and we were obliged to retrace our steps and find our way by another, much longer route.

The gloom returned. Yet more hours cooped up in a people carrier in an alien land with too much time for reflection. To stop the rot, I buried myself in *Far from the Madding Crowd* (for at least the fifth time – its power never diminishes) and imagined myself to be in Thomas Hardy's Wessex among the hills and valleys and moors, the small towns and villages of my own 'Motherland'. I could almost smell the patter of rain on English trees and hear the birds in the woods. After a while, in the twilight, I let myself drift into reverie until I found myself quite at home in rural England. I woke some time later as we entered the outskirts of Kazan, capital of the federal republic of Tatarstan.

It was dark by this time, but to my surprise the city was brightly lit and our route was lined with video-active advertising hoardings, just as in any Western city. As we drove closer to the centre we passed new apartment blocks and office buildings, all glass and porticos of the reach-me-down kind that British also-ran architects have exported so successfully from Guildford and Croydon to the Gulf – and now, evidently, to Kazan as well. But by comparison with the bleak anti-aesthetic that has governed so much Russian architecture of the last fifty years, these serried ranks of neo-Georgian sandstone, complete with Corinthian columns and atriums glazed in green or black to guard against the raging of the sun, are, en masse, genuinely impos-ing. They speak of corporate imperialism, self-confidence and wealth – which is a measure of the clever opportunism with which Tatarstan has weathered the economic storms that have assailed the Russian Federation since the collapse of Communism.

On 30 August 1990, in the near anarchy following that event, Tatarstan declared itself an independent sovereign state in a constitu-tional *coup d'état* similar to that essayed so catastrophically by Chechnya. The following year a referendum confirming the declara-tion was endorsed by 62 per cent of those who voted. But when the Kremlin exerted intense pressure on the governor to avert secession he was astute enough to acquiesce, settling for an imprecise but substan-tial degree of 'autonomy' within the framework of the Russian Federation. In sharp contrast to Chechnya, where emotions ran far deeper, Tatarstan has since interpreted the raft of accords reached with the Kremlin with the kind of constructive ambiguity that allows the elites on both sides to claim a constitutional and political triumph – to the benefit of both parties. But there is self-delusion on the Tatarstani side. The republic is not 'autonomous' to any significant degree, and is likely to become less so.

Elections in Tatarstan have thus acquired a pronounced *Alice Through the Looking Glass* quality, with voters encouraged to believe that their 'autonomous' vote has some meaning. This political sleight of hand is facilitated by the fact that the republic is prosperous and, by comparison with the rest of Russia, highly developed. Oil and gas pipelines, chemical plants, machine- and truck-building factories have combined with an unusually well-developed transport infrastructure (which includes four major rivers) to place Tatarstan second only to the Samara region in the Russian league table of industrial production. But Tatarstan's 'President', Mintimer Shaymiev, who has been re-elected every four years since 1991, now depends on the benevolence of the almighty Kremlin to survive in office. As power is drained from the regions to the centre, there is no exemption for Tatarstan from the federal decree that all governors and presidents are to be appointed by Moscow. So far, Shaymiev has done nothing to earn the fatal *nyet* from the Kremlin.

The region's ethnic majority, which today forms a little over 50 per cent of the 3.7 million population, are the descendants of the Volga Bulgars, a Turkic people who became known collectively as Tatars. After the invasion and occupation of the region by the Mongols in the early thirteenth century, the Bulgars and their Mongol overlords lived in relative amity, assimilating to the point where Russians came to use the terms 'Tatar' and 'Mongol' inter-changeably (until later they dropped the word 'Mongol' from their everyday vocabulary almost entirely).

In medieval times Kazan flourished as a mercantile city and centre of learning. But in 1552 Ivan the Terrible, intent on his mission to expel the Mongols from Russian soil, descended on the city and, after an exceptionally bloody struggle, evicted the Golden Horde from its political and military stronghold on the edge of the Volga. In a prequel to his much easier victory in Astrakhan the following year, Ivan ordered the construction of a new kremlin in Kazan, which was to become a citadel against all invaders. Instructing that a cathedral be built within its precincts, he encouraged the forcible conversion of Muslims to the Orthodox Church. By the end of the sixteenth century not one mosque remained in what is now Tatarstan, although the overwhelming majority of the indigenous population had been followers of Islam since the tenth century.

It was not until the reign of Catherine the Great, almost two hundred years later, that the Tatars of Kazan were once more allowed to build mosques and practise their faith. For the most part they subsequently lived in harmony with their imperial overlords. By the nineteenth century Kazan's skyline was dotted with mosques and churches flourishing side by side, or rather quarter by quarter, since Tatars and Russians retained their separate social and cultural traditions. Alexander Herzen, the eminent nineteenth-century writer and political philosopher, noted that 'the significance of Kazan is very great: it is where two worlds meet. It has two origins, the West and the East, and you can see them at every crossroads; here they lived in amity as a result of continuous interaction and began to create something quite original.'

Today, 170 years later, Herzen's valediction appears still to hold true. Despite Stalin's attempt to expunge all vestiges of religion from the secular soil of Russia – which, in the case of Kazan, required the destruction or abolition of sixty-nine cathedrals and nineteen mosques (although, in that haphazardly cruel way that marked the system, one church was allowed to remain open) – the faithful of both religions gloriously refused to surrender their spiritual identity. There are now more than a thousand religious buildings in Tatarstan, and the capital is once more an oasis of competing faiths. Despite its tormented past, Kazan has a reassuringly complaisant air, as if it is peopled by citizens who know where they have come from and where they want to go. In contrast to the cauldron of the Caucasus, the political temperature in Tatarstan is very far from boiling point.

The modern kremlin is, for the most part, a nineteenth-century version of Ivan the Terrible's original conception and as imposing as Russia's first tsar would have wished. The President's new palace, his regal guest-house, the government offices, a new mosque, the ancient cathedral and a clutch of smaller ecclesiastical buildings are all set within its white-painted stone walls and intersected by manicured gardens in which red tulips bloom and neatly trimmed paths offer grandstand views over the confluence of the Volga and Kazanka rivers. Its effect is to suggest a secure political establishment, albeit of a far grander kind than you would expect for a population of less than 4 million. But it looks good and, on a fine, late spring day, it feels good as well.

I wandered through the old city that huddles beneath the walls of the kremlin, admiring the elegant nineteenth-century apartments still preserved amidst the cranes and diggers that testify to Kazan's post-Soviet resurrection. Downtown, in the cosmopolitan shopping centre, where Western cafés jostle with ethnic restaurants, Tatars and Russians mingle comfortably, the former barely distinguishable from the latter except perhaps that their skin is less pallid, their hair more uniformly dark and the older men tend to favour the traditional black fez (though without the tassel) and, in one or two cases, flowing white pantaloon trousers. In the main the young of both religions dress interchangeably and would, in this anthropological sense, look equally at home in any British city.

But it was neither Kazan's historic past nor its embrace of the present that had tempted me here. I had come principally to rediscover Maxim Gorky, whom – as it were – I had left in disgrace on the Gulag archipelago of Solovki in the far northwest at the beginning of my journey. But Bolshevism's grand apologist, the revolutionary student of the underbelly of tsarist Russia, is a hero in Kazan. The 'lower depths' of life in this city were, he later insisted, the inspiration for all his work. The alumni of Kazan University – which in status has always ranked alongside the best in Russia – include both Tolstoy and Lenin. As an impoverished orphan, however, Gorky lacked both the funds and the formal qualifications required to attend such an august institution.

He had been brought up by his doting grandmother in the city of Nizhni Novgorod, but at the age of eleven he evidently decided to make his own way in the world. Heading for Kazan – a journey of some 200 miles – he arrived there in 1879 and at once joined its small army of street urchins, scavenging for food and taking work wherever he could find it. The brutality and squalor by which he was now surrounded disgusted him. It also became his inspiration; the 'loathsome truth', as he would write, 'a truth which must be known down to its very roots, so that by tearing them up it can be entirely erased from the memory, from the soul of man, from our whole oppressive and shameful life'.

He found casual work in the docks, sometimes as a stevedore, sometimes as a deckhand on the barges that plied Mother Volga. And here, for the first time, he discovered enchantment, a balm for his anger and resentment. He wrote lyrically about the river: at night the moon 'made a streak of light to the meadows on shore. The old reddish steamer, with a white band around her smokestack, moved unhurriedly. Her paddlewheel flailed at the silvery water with uneven movements. The dark banks came towards her, casting their shadows on the water, dotted with red lights from the windows of peasant houses…' and he went on, 'The beauty of the night moved me to tears.'

That beauty is still evident but – to my eyes – only at night, when the hydro-electric plants, the dams and the sour-smelling, orange smoke-belching factories are transformed into a twinkle of lights that conceal the unspeakable ugliness of Soviet utilitarianism run riot. Describing this desecration, Lesley Chamberlain has written with eloquent despair in *Volga Volga* of the Soviet 're-birth' of the river as an 'artificial, irreverent, man-centred creation in defiance of nature' that has been 'immensely painful to all surrounding life, animal and vegetable. The fish have almost disappeared, the riverside lands have been drastically diminished, the landscape is blighted and the bathing dirty….'

In Gorky's time, there was a dark side to the work of the river as well. A freighter on which he found a job for a while, the *Dobry* (the 'Good One'), used to tow barges. One of these had an iron cage on its deck, which, he wrote, was full of convicts sentenced to penal colonies or hard labour. A sentry's bayonet shone on the bows like a candle and the tiny stars in the blue sky glinted like candles as well. No noise came from the barge and it was brightly illuminated by the moon. Behind metal bars I could see dim, round grey figures – these were convicts looking at the Volga. The water sobbed and seemed to be crying and then quietly laughing....

And this was – yet how could it be – the same Gorky who fifty years later found himself providing his seal of approval to Stalin's Solovki.

The young Gorky was clearly a very remarkable boy – so much so that his prodigious and precocious intellect came to the attention of a group of radical students at the Kazan Gymnasium. They not only befriended the clever and eccentric newcomer, but even tried – in vain – to find him a place at the university. Instead he found a job in a bakery; it was a seminal experience. He worked in a broiling, humid basement that he later described in a short story called 'Twenty-six Men and One Girl': 'We found it oppressive and nauseating...in a suffocating, smelly atmosphere we parted dough and twisted the pretzels, moistening them with our sweat. We hated our work with such a fierce hatred that we never ate that which was made by our own hands, preferring black bread.' Writing many years later, he averred 'I am a Marxist! Yes, I am! But a Marxist not according to Marx....Better than any books, Marxism was taught to me by the Kazan baker, Semenov.'

He was rescued from that inferno by his student friends, who found him a job in another bakery that doubled as a grocery store. The business was run by an enlightened radical, Andrey Dorenkov, who had turned his private rooms above the store into a secret library of forbidden works. Here old revolutionaries and young students used to gather and explore the competing ideological passions that offered theoretical alternatives to tsarist despotism. Gorky worked a fourteen-hour day in the bakery, but made sure to attend these gatherings. He listened intently and read voraciously. But he was careful to keep his distance, to remain an observer and never to join either the crowd or any particular movement. By his own account he was a very confused young man: 'I lived with neither the workers nor the students. I was spinning like a top, while a strong unknown hand vigorously lashed me with a whip.'

In 1887 this mental confusion brought on an attack of severe depression, and at the age of nineteen he decided to kill himself. Buying an old army pistol, he walked down to the edge of the Kazanka River and shot himself in the chest. Miraculously, the bullet missed his heart but pierced a lung and lodged in his back. At the hospital he was given little chance of survival. However, despite the fact that the operation to remove the bullet was performed by a young and inexperienced surgeon, it was a success. In attempting to commit suicide Gorky had committed a crime against the doctrines of the Orthodox Church and he was duly summoned to the ecclesiastical authorities, who gave him a severe reprimand. Gorky was impenitent: 'Next time I'll hang myself from your gates,' he retorted.

Mercifully, it did not come to that. In 1888 he left Kazan and, after a misadventure or two, made his way to Samara, where at last he found himself a job more suited to his talent and his temperament as a columnist on the *Samara Gazeta*. There he began to write the slew of essays, novels and plays that were to make his reputation as a great proletarian writer, Russia's first 'social realist'. Later he returned to the city of his birth, Nizhni Novgorod. By now he was not only admired by Lenin, but by Russia's two literary lions, Tolstoy and Chekhov, both of whom found time to meet him, clearly intrigued and perhaps entertained by the angry young man of Russian letters. Chekhov even played a part in his rapid rise to fame, urging him to write *The Lower Depths*, which is probably his most famous work. But Gorky was never content, never at ease.

His self-imposed exile in Switzerland and eventual return to Russia were to give him material comfort, but no spiritual respite from that torment that had led to his attempted suicide as a very young man. In a memorable pen portrait the Communist writer, Victor Serge described seeing him at the age of sixty:

> Leaning back alone, in the rear seat of a big Lincoln car, he seemed remote from the street, remote from the life of Moscow, reduced to an algebraic cipher of himself. He had not aged, but rather thinned and dried, his head bony and cropped inside a Turkish skull-cap, his nose and cheek bones jutting, his eye-sockets hollow like a skeleton's. Here was an ascetic, emaciated figure, with nothing alive in it except the will to exist and think...
>
> But this 'will to think' seemed to be either absent or stricken by bad faith. Feted as a hero of the revolution, he found himself manipulated by Stalin to the point where he became no more than a propagandist for tyranny. Paraded as a model of Soviet creativity – most of Gorky's peers had chosen exile rather than submission – he enjoined younger writers to fulfil their obligation to the state in their prime role as 'engineers of human souls'.

Yet, towards the end, he seems to have sought redemption. In 1935, the year before his death, he invited the French writer Romain Rolland to stay with him in his grace-and-favour Moscow apartment. His guest detected in Gorky a belated distress at the trap that he realized Stalin had set for him. As the prisoner of an ideology that had run out of control and for which he no longer evinced any sympathy, 'the old bear', Rolland observed, had found himself with 'a ring in his nose'. There is further evidence that Gorky did not entirely surrender his soul. After his death, during the murky terror of the show trials, it emerged that Gorky had probably allied himself with Nikolay Bukharin and Sergey Kirov in their plot against Stalin. Much later, his wife Ekaterina wrote of her conviction that her husband had not died of natural causes but had been murdered on the orders of the Soviet leader.

I found myself more and more fascinated by Gorky's tortuous and tortured life; by his righteous passion and the frailty of character that led him to become a traitor to the very cause that had first inspired him: the acute suffering of the Russian people in whom he seemed to detect a tragic flaw. 'To Russians,' he wrote, 'through the poverty and squalor of their lives, suffering comes as a diversion, is turned into a game and they play it like children and rarely feel ashamed of their misfortune. In this monotony of everyday existence grief comes as a holiday and a fire is an entertainment. A scratch embellishes an empty face.' Unlike much of his writing, this dreadful insight seems to me to travel very well through time to sum up the fatalism that still corrodes the Russian character.

## THE TRUTH ABOUT RURAL LIFE

As we set off to the northeast, heading towards the Ural mountains on the final leg of this part of my journey, Gorky remained very much in my mind. He knew this land and its people more intimately than many of his peers, and his reaction to the steppe lacked any hint of romance; instead, he detected in its endless horizons a 'poisonous' quality. 'The peasant has only to go out past the bounds of the village and look at the emptiness around him to feel that this emptiness is creeping into his very soul...', he wrote. 'Round about lie endless plains and in the centre of them, insignificant, tiny man abandoned on this dull earth for penal labour....' I forced myself to focus more sharply on the passing landscape and particularly at the villages: mean wooden houses, bungalow-size, many of them boarded up and surrounded by rank grass, with weeds settling in broken gutters; cart tracks for main streets; chickens pecking at dusty soil; mongrel dogs scratching for fleas; a listless horse standing in the shafts of a cart; an old man hunched on a bench; a small child carrying a stick, meandering from rut to rut. The images trapped in my mind were not of the twenty-first century – or certainly not the guide-book version. This was rural life in the raw, without varnish. We could not have been further from St Petersburg or Moscow or Samara or Kazan.

Deciding to look even more closely, we turned down a rough track and after half a mile or so pulled up in a deserted farmyard. Eight rusting combine harvesters, partly covered in flapping and torn tarpaulin, stood as if waiting for the knacker's yard. A wreckage of buildings, windows broken, slates missing, paid tribute to the disaster that had befallen this community. Before the fall of Communism, the now long-empty yard that ran down one side of this forlorn complex had housed row upon row of cows producing their annual quota of milk according to the artificial laws of supply, not demand. In the neighbouring barns, grain had been piled high to meet the same objectives. On paper, as a theoretical system of production, it worked. Year after year Stalin and his successors hailed the output figures as a triumph of socialist planning. But, as they must have known, collectivization was in reality an unmitigated failure. The system was grotesquely unproductive, so much so that, as Lesley Chamberlain notes in *Volga Volga*, between 1913 and 1973 Russia went from being the world's largest exporter of grain to a 'superpower in need'. But no one with any level of responsibility for this economic catastrophe seemed to care; venality and fear held sway. Throughout the Soviet Union, the managers of individual collective farms would almost infallibly reach their allotted targets by cooking the books; their superiors in the region re-cooked the cooked figures; and in Moscow the most superior of their superiors further recooked those cooked figures to publish statistics of production that were designed to astound the world but that bore no relationship to the true facts. Moreover, no one in authority even knew the true facts; they knew only that the 'facts' as published were lies. The system was bound to implode.

As I wandered around the ruins of this farmyard, three workers emerged from the tangle of rotting buildings, scrap metal and rampant weeds. Their faces were corrugated by weather and, in two cases, by drink as well. They were among the residual shareholders in what was clearly a bankrupt business, a post-Soviet cooperative in which they had virtually nothing over which to cooperate. They still jointly owned some five hundred cows, and they grew corn as well (the combine harvesters that I had supposed to be wrecks were apparently still able to wheeze, shake and rattle their way very slowly over the steppe), but with the price of milk at 8 roubles a litre at the farm gate and diesel for the machines at 16 roubles a litre, the cooperative workers were in Micawberland, running at a loss with no respite around the corner, but hoping that something might turn up. They told me this without anger or bitterness, but simply as a matter of fact.

One of them, a bright-eyed leprechaun of a man with a surprisingly chirpy smile, sporting an outsize bushy moustache and aged rubber boots at least two sizes too big, offered to show me around. We wallowed through the mud that formed the village street, passing a row of wooden shacks on either side, some in a state of terminal decay, others kept up with evident pride, each with its plot of land producing fruit and vegetables and eggs for the house. At first glance on a fine day, it could be confused for a rural idyll. But though the village had electricity, there was no gas for cooking or heating, and mains water was piped only to a communal well; all right for a 'back to basics' holiday, but hardly to be expected in one of the major G8 nations in the twenty-first century.

Two little girls played in the grass by the track but the village had a desolate, deserted feel, as though there had been an exodus and they had somehow got left behind. My guide pointed to a cluster of buildings a quarter of a mile or so from the village. It had once been the school, but was now disused and tumbling down. When they grew older the children would have to board away from home during the school week, and it would cost 800 roubles a month for the privilege, which was more than their parents could afford. A little boy, dressed warmly in a woollen jacket and grey jeans with huge turn-ups to allow for growth, stared at us intently. What future for him? I wondered. 'The forest, the forest,' my leprechaun replied, shaking his head. The forest? 'Yes, a dark future.' Were the old days better? Would he like them back again? *'Da, da, da, da, da.'* Because? 'Then we were wanted. We were in demand. There was demand for our labour. And now we are left by the wayside.' Those who can – who have the skill or the energy – have moved away in search of work.

My guide introduced me to the local policeman, who told me that he was responsible for six similar villages. I asked him about crime. 'Our worst problem is domestic violence. The men get drunk, and they come home and beat their wives. But I can only intervene if the woman complains, or if she is so badly beaten that she has to be taken to hospital.' I was reminded once more of Gorky, who had himself been beaten unconscious when he tried to intercede on behalf of a woman who had been stripped naked and, in the words of the historian Orlando Figes, was in the throes of being 'horsewhipped by her husband and a howling mob after being found guilty of adultery'. That was in 1891.

In 2007 a local policeman at his level was paid 9000 roubles a month, he informed me, which had allowed him to buy a satellite television – but, since he was required to provide his own car to patrol his scattered beat, he had no money left to save. But he said that his life was better than most: 'I don't have a wife or children,' he said with no apparent regret. However, he worried about the fate of the village in which he had lived all his life. 'The President said that our homes would be repaired, but it hasn't happened.' 'Why is that, do you think?' I asked. He shrugged as if to say, 'What else would you expect?' So was life for him today better or worse than it had been in the Soviet era? He echoed my leprechaun. 'It never changes for the better, and it is worse than it was a generation ago.' Such bleakness.

As I drove out of this dying village – a here today, gone tomorrow scavenger of fleeting impressions – I felt a surge of guilt, the reporter's angst. All over the world I have trespassed into the lives of others, exploiting them so that I can tell my story. Of course I have liked to believe that it would spread a message about injustice or poverty or war or famine, but the process of enquiry nonetheless steals something, sucks something from those lives that I have pinioned with my notebook or a camera like collector's specimens; their recompense – if any – is general, not specific. I have walked into and out of the other's world, recording intimate hopes and fears, beachcombing for a national psyche but not touching an individual soul. The faces of the men I had just met stayed with me. Long-suffering is their over-riding quality. They are not quite Tolstoy's paragons, nor Chekhov's oafs, nor Gorky's broken tribe, but they endure, they survive. No one cares very much about them. They have no future, and their past is despised. They eke out a living from the soil and they know nothing else.

## THE BUREAUCRACY OF CRUELTY

My next destination, the last on this leg of my journey, had been cursed with a chillingly bland name: PERM 36. I wondered where PERMs 1, 2, 3 and all the rest might have been, but they have long since been razed to the ground if not quite erased from the mind. The route to PERM 36, which is not marked on the map, took us from the city of Perm for 80 miles, until we turned off the main road down a lane that ran through tranquil pastureland. We drove past a clutch of wooden cottages and a bus stop, guided by an innocent signpost to the village of Kuchino, which lies in the foothills of the Ural mountains. As we entered the village, still heading for PERM 36, we passed small groups of men shuffling lamely along the verge. One man carried a bucket filled with potatoes, others pulled handcarts laden with sacks of flour or a heap of cabbages and, in one case, a pile of washing. They smiled amiably in our direction but with a disconcerting vacancy of expression. It was only when our mini-bus came to a halt that it was possible to see for certain that they all suffered from some form of physical or mental handicap. Most of them had congenital deformities: a misshapen head, a severe limp or a humped back.

The scene reminded me of my own experience in Beirut in 1975 during the early days of the civil war, when each side committed the most foul atrocities against the other. I had been taken to see a pile of stinking, mutilated corpses in a malfunctioning deep-freeze in the morgue of a lunatic asylum. As I walked down the stairs into the morgue, I was surrounded by a group of maniacal inmates, leering at me and grabbing at my clothes, slobbering with unnatural excitement. It was an unnerving experience, seared in my memory by their uniformed male 'nurses' who cleared a path for me by laying about them indiscriminately (but to little effect) with rubber truncheons. Now, more than thirty years later in this Russian village, I feared that I had arrived at the precincts of another such institution. In this case, however, the patients seemed to be in a state of soporific ecstasy, as though each one had been drugged into his own little nirvana. We drew up by what was unmistakably a psychiatric hospital, where some of the inmates sat listlessly in the sun. The eeriness of the atmosphere was compounded by a non-stop barrage of Euro-pop on a loop, which boomed out from loudspeakers fixed to a couple of the barrack-room walls that surrounded the compound. But I was not there to visit the hospital (where, incidentally, I had no reason to believe the patients were treated other than in a kindly way). Followed by the treacly tones of 'Sweet Dreams (Are Made of This)', which ricocheted mockingly from every surrounding building, I walked across the road and pushed at a heavy metal door: the entrance to PERM 36, the last surviving monument to a tyranny that lasted from the days of Stalin until, and including, the early years of Gorbachev's reign as the last leader of the Soviet Union.

The origins of PERM 36 go back to the years following the Great Patriotic War. By the late forties, thousands of similar concentration camps had been built throughout the Soviet Union, to play their part in the Gulag network that had been prototyped at Solovki, and in which at any one time, according to Anne Applebaum's authoritative *Gulag*, 'more than two million people were imprisoned...most having never committed a crime'. By the time of Stalin's death, some 18 million people had passed through the system. Slaves in the service of the Soviet economy, they played a critical part in the exploitation of Russia's natural resources. They worked in the mines, on building sites, in factories, on roads and railways, on farms and – in the case of PERM 36, which was opened in 1946 as one of several hundred logging camps in the region – as lumberjacks, felling timber in the surrounding forest. The wood was then floated down a network of rivers to the Volga, and thence transported to industrial powerhouses elsewhere in the Soviet Union. A small plaque by the entrance commemorates that great crime against humanity with the words, in Russian and English, 'The former corrective labour colony ITK-6 of the Molotovsky UITLK NKVD ITK VS389/36'. I imagined a clerk in some dingy NKVD office diligently recording the names and numbers of the victims both as they entered and as they left, alive or dead.

As the door clanged shut behind me, I found myself in a narrow passageway that led via a grilled turnstile into a guard-house, where prisoners used to sign in, and then into the compound itself, which – despite the false promises pounding out from the loudspeakers on the other side of the perimeter wall within which I was now imprisoned – emanated a terrible ghostliness, so that, as in a cemetery, I walked around slowly and as quietly as possible so as not to disturb the past.

After the collapse of the Soviet Union, the wooden huts in which the prisoners lived, the refectory and the store rooms that all but filled the compound were systematically vandalized by the KGB in an apparent attempt to conceal their secrets from any inquisitive outsider. The perimeter fence of thick wooden palisades, painted white and topped by razor wire, was bulldozed. But despite this, the evidence at PERM 36 has not been entirely obliterated. Thanks primarily to members of the human-rights organization Memorial, which was set up in the days of *glasnost* to ensure that no Russians need forget their past, the camp is gradually being reconstructed to help those who want to know what it was like to be a slave labourer in the Soviet Union. The walls have been resurrected, as has the barbed wire, the sentry boxes at each corner overlooking the compound and three of the dormitory blocks.

It is virtually the only physical evidence of the Gulag system that survives, and certainly the most damning.

Today the compound has a faintly antiseptic air, like a film set for a remake of *Colditz*, but if you stand still for a moment and listen to the sigh of the wind in the trees and the song of the birds, you swiftly find yourself carried back half a century. You can imagine the prisoners, five thousand of them, ill clothed and ill fed, shuffling out of their poorly heated huts to be lined up in the snow, their names ticked off, before being marched into the frozen forest to work until they dropped, too weak to obey. In summer the temperature rose to 40 degrees centigrade; in winter it fell to minus 25 degrees centigrade and sometimes as low as minus 50 degrees centigrade. As in the other work camps of the Gulag, the dictum 'From each according to his means, to each according to his needs' acquired a new meaning at PERM 36, where the prisoners were fed according to the level of output they were able to achieve in the day. In Applebaum's words, 'The elderly and the ill died quickly. Those who survived did so because they were younger and stronger – or because they had learned how to treat the brigadiers and guards who measured their effort.'

The economic folly of the Gulag system – though not its intrinsic evil – was eventually recognized by the Kremlin and it was dismantled. But this did not signal the end of PERM 36. In 1972, under conditions of strict secrecy, the camp was given a new lease as a correction facility in which to incarcerate political prisoners, who were held to be among the most dangerous and hardened 'criminals' in the Soviet Union. In those paranoid days, when the Kremlin feared a surge of anti-Communist agitation that might shake the very foundations of the state, the courts meted out punishments of the utmost severity. PERM 36 soon held four hundred 'subversives' housed in two prison blocks. Famous among the many writers, poets, scientists and scholars who endured this barbarity were dissidents like Vladimir Bukovsky, Yury Orlov, Anatoly Sharansky and Sergey Kovalev, who acquired international renown.

Sergey Kovalev is one of the few survivors of PERM 36 still living in Russia. Prominent as a biophysicist, the author of more than sixty scientific papers, he was the founder, in the late sixties, of the Initiative Group for the Defence of Human Rights in the USSR. In this role he contributed to *samizdat* publications circulating in Moscow, the most prominent of which was *The Chronicle of Current Events*. As a result, he was charged with 'anti-Soviet agitation and propaganda' and in 1974, at the age forty-four, sentenced to seven years' imprisonment to be followed by three years of internal exile. He soon found himself in PERM 36 and now, more than thirty years on, he was prepared to show me round the site of his long ordeal.

Kovalev is now an old man, weary and worn, his eyes rheumy and sad behind thick-rimmed glasses, but his voice is strong and his memories are sharp. He led me into the punishment block, where those who challenged the prison governor were dispatched for up to six weeks of solitary confinement on starvation rations. It was a warm day, but as we stepped down into the subterranean cells we both shivered in the chill. In a single moment we seemed to have been transported back three decades to the time when he was often locked up here for fifteen days at a stretch. He led me into one, where a sliver of sunlight from a tiny window pierced the gloom to illuminate a small concrete table, a hole-in-the floor toilet and a wooden-slatted bunk where he used to sleep on the bare boards with one thin blanket to cover him.

Even in winter he was allowed to wear only the regulation cotton jacket, cotton trousers and a pair of slippers over his bare feet. The cold, he said, had been far worse than the hunger. 'The call would come that you were allowed to rest. You would lie on these boards and put your slippers under your head. You would fall asleep immediately. And then in an hour you would wake again, suffering from an unbearable trembling. You would jump up and try to work your limbs, wrapping yourself around the heating pipe like this.' He demonstrated what he meant by crouching on the concrete floor and rubbing his back up and down on the pipe that ran along the outer wall of the cell. 'When you were slightly revived you would fall back on your bunk again. During the night you would wake up every hour – seven or eight times – and that was a real punishment.'

In the oddly Soviet way, there was a set of regulations designed to safeguard the basic rights of even 'dangerous' criminals like Kovalev. For instance, if the temperature in the punishment block fell towards freezing, inmates were entitled to be offered a quilted jacket. This rule gave the warders the chance to play a peculiarly cruel joke on their charges. 'If you asked them to check the temperature, an officer would come in with a round metallic thermometer which he would place here on the table. And he would look at it and say, "It is exactly 14 degrees, so there is nothing I can do. I am afraid you are not entitled to a quilted jacket." But whatever the temperature in the cell, however far it fell, the thermometer never budged up or down from 14 degrees.'

As he said this, Kovalev half-smiled at the memory. 'You make light of it,' I said. 'I can't understand that.' He replied, 'You could not live every minute if you felt yourself to be a wretched prisoner. You would have to hang yourself. When you think of yourself as a martyr, it always ends up very badly. I know many cases where that happened. Yes, prison can break people, but it can also give you strength. In my own case, let me tell you, I was never as free as I was when I was in here. In here, you think more deeply about the moral standards you want to set yourself and, with all your soul, you think about how you would like life to be for all the people who are around you. You think far more deeply about these things than you do in the outside world.'

When we came out of that dungeon, Kovalev went to warm up in the Memorial offices and I wandered into what had been the maximum-security unit. Built in 1977 to house those defined as being 'particularly dangerous recidivists' – dissidents who had been convicted more than once for the crime of 'anti-Soviet propaganda' – it offered conditions just marginally less dreadful than in the punishment block. Confined in two-man cells, but otherwise isolated from their fellow dissidents for up to ten years, maximum-security prisoners were allowed forty-five minutes of exercise a day. The 'exercise block' consisted of a cube measuring 3 metres square. Except for some strands of barbed wire running across the top, it was open to the sky; but the tin-lined solid walls made it impossible to see out into the prison compound or towards the landscape beyond, let alone to catch a glimpse of any other living soul. I walked round and round this tiny space – it took eight paces to complete one circumference – and thought that had I been there for ten days, let alone ten years, I would have been driven insane. I have visited prison yards in Third World countries where political prisoners are held for years at a time and where conditions are grim, but I have never witnessed evidence of quite such a bureaucracy of cruelty as that meted out to the inmates at PERM 36.

Thanks to the work of Memorial and a number of Russian and international donors, PERM 36 is now a museum. Its director confirmed to me that, while no political prisoner died of hunger in those years, they were tortured by boredom – by a routine that kept them locked in their cells for twenty-three hours a day assembling or repairing electrical goods and similar mind-numbing tasks. The historian Robert Skidelsky did not exaggerate when, after his own researches and a visit to PERM 36, he judged that 'the prisoners were subjected to psychological torture and extreme physical hardship'.

I noticed that the block that housed the latrines was one of the few buildings to survive the KGB's attempt to bury the past in rubble. The date of its construction, 1972, remained just as it had been neatly inscribed by a plasterer on the wall at the entrance. More tellingly, on the path leading up to the entrance someone – presumably a prisoner – had used a forefinger to mark another date in the wet concrete: 1986. This was the year after Gorbachev came to power, promising that the Soviet Union would henceforth conform with Article VII of the Helsinki Accord (which Brezhnev had signed a decade earlier and which committed all parties to 'Respect for Human Rights and fundamental freedoms, including the freedom of thought, conscience, religion and belief'); and the year after he had specifically announced that the Soviet Union no longer held any political prisoners or prisoners of conscience. Perhaps he had overlooked the little matter of PERM 36, or perhaps his officials had forgotten to tell him. If so, he must have been reminded at some point later because the last political prisoner finally walked out of the camp, a free man, in December 1987.

A year earlier Kovalev, who had served his full sentence in PERM 36 and its sister camps in the region, followed by three years of internal exile in Siberia, had been given permission to return to Moscow. Unrepentant and undaunted, he immediately allied himself with Andrey Sakharov, working closely with him to fan the flames of freedom in the final years of the Soviet Union. He helped found Memorial and the Moscow branch of Amnesty International. In 1989, at Sakharov's suggestion, he became co-director of what later became known as the Russian–American Human Rights Group. After the collapse of the Soviet Union he was, by common consent, arguably the most important human-rights activist in Russia. Responsible, at Yeltsin's request, for drafting the 'Rights and Liberties' section of the new constitution, he became a member of the Praesidium of the Supreme Council of the Russian Federation and was appointed by Yeltsin to chair the President's Human Rights Commission. This galvanized him to greater efforts, but he resigned the post in 1996 in frustration at the obstacles put in the way of reform. He was horrified by the slaughter in Chechnya, and his outspoken criticism of the Kremlin touched a nerve in Russian opinion. In 2002 he set up a public commission to investigate the mysterious circumstances of the Moscow apartment bombings, but when, in the following year, one of its members was assassinated and another poisoned with thallium, he felt obliged to abandon the project. He ought to be a hero of the state, but in Putin's Russia he has become a pariah, a voice crying in the wilderness.

As we wandered down a leafy avenue running through the centre of PERM 36, I asked him about state freedom and democracy in Russia today. He suddenly erupted in a blaze of frustration, turning towards me and shaking his head in despair at how purblind the world has allowed itself to become. 'You in the West are fools. You think there is a problem with democracy in Russia but you say to one another, "At least they have elections there." Do you not understand we have sham elections? Today's Russia is like a kingdom of falsifiers – we are ruled by falsifiers. The legal framework of the state, the constitution, is not worth the paper it is written on. It is called a Federation. But where else in the world are the governors of the members of the Federation appointed by the central power? There is no division of power in Russia. Our judiciary brazenly serves the executive. We have a servile, parasitic, slave-like parliament that gives the impression of being a parliament but is nothing of the sort. The state today is even more powerful – much more powerful – than it was in the time of the Soviet Union. Indeed, it was better under Stalin because at least then everyone knew it was a sham.'

I saw the despair in the face of this great old campaigner, now a bitter and disappointed man, whose life's work had been brought – in his mind – to nothing. I felt a surge of sympathy and wanted to embrace him. Instead I blundered on to ask about the future. 'I am afraid,' he said. 'In fact I am convinced now that our government will never be changed through the electoral system.' So was there no hope? 'My hope is in Solidarity.' 'You mean as in Poland?' 'Yes, they forced the government to understand.' Unhelpfully, I then suggested that the Russian people were not at all like the Poles, that they were far more acquiescent. Kovalev, the fire dying down, sighed. 'Yes, it is more difficult than in Poland. You remember that in Germany people wanted no one but Hitler.' Our conversation was at an end. He was tired and I had nothing further to ask.

I left PERM 36 with Kovalev's pessimism ringing in my ears. It is misleading to equate the Russian Gulag system that gave birth to

PERM 36 with the Nazi Holocaust; comparisons between the twin evils have a tendency to obfuscate the distinctive horror of each. But in one respect at least a comparison is illuminating. I have been to both Belsen and Buchenwald, and both have long been 'lest we forget' monuments. In Germany the Holocaust is still a source of sorrow and shame, and no political leader from the first post-war Chancellor, Konrad Adenauer, onwards has failed to offer apology and atonement for Nazism's atrocities. Those who deny or diminish the Holocaust are treated as pariahs, if not criminals. But in Russia, since the collapse of the Soviet Union, there has been no such search for forgiveness, no public declaration of shame or sorrow. PERM 36 may be a memorial, but it is not a place of pilgrimage. It has received not a single visit from any senior emissary from Moscow, let alone the head of state. There has been no effort to begin any process of Truth and Reconciliation, the means by which grief and anger can be mediated and assuaged. The Russian leadership and many millions, if not most, of the Russian people seem to be in denial, either not knowing about the crimes perpetrated by the Soviet Union or not wanting to know. And, unlike some of the Nazi concentration camps, PERM 36 exists; yet this, the last surviving memorial, has no support from the Russian state. Instead, President Putin has ordained that 'history should be positive'.

Leaving the prison camp, our driver, an affable soul who was working hard to build his little taxi business in the city of Perm, said that he had never heard of PERM 36 before. When I told him about the crimes that had been perpetrated there, he was genuinely baffled. 'But they were opposed to the system, weren't they? They were trying to subvert it.' Precisely.

Later, as our mini-bus climbed steadily from Perm towards the Urals, Kovalev's crystallizing analysis stayed with me. My disconcerting experiences in Putin's Russia until then had often tempted me to write the word 'fascist' in my diary, but I had not yet done so because it seemed like an expletive that emptied the word of meaning. 'Fascist' is much over-used as a term of gratuitous abuse in general, and far too often employed as a weapon with which to assail political opponents in free societies – which is not to say that free societies are free of fascists. I did not think that Russia was a fascist state yet, but in those last few weeks I often found myself wrestling with the thought that I might be travelling through a sort of 'pre-fascist' state without realizing it. So, dredging my memory (as an erstwhile philosophy student who had forgotten most of what I had learned almost forty years ago), I spent much of the drive staring at the passing forest and trying to separate the wood from the trees in my head.

A great many political scientists have wrestled with the concept of fascism, trying to identify its distinguishing features, its necessary and sufficient conditions. Authoritarianism is, of course, a defining characteristic. So too are the elevation of nationalism to the status of a cardinal virtue; the manipulation of the electoral system to preserve the outward forms of democracy while strangling its meaning; an intolerance of opposition, and, crucially, the emergence of a strong leader supported by a powerful vanguard drawn from the business elite or the leaders of what is often called 'corporate capitalism'. To express it as crudely as I put in my diary, 'Putin's Russia ticks all those boxes.'

And yet I still held back. I did not want to offer gratuitous insults to those in Russia whose grandparents saved the free world from Nazism and fascism. Moreover, in recent years genuine, committed fascists in many parts of the world had generally liked to parade and promote their distorted vision of humanity's aspirations. By contrast – aside from a few irrelevant skinheads – no one in Russia overtly promoted fascism. But perhaps it is possible to drift into fascism, to be so lulled by its promise of security as to ignore its commitment to tyranny.

In a famous TV debate at the 1968 Democratic Convention in Chicago, when the values of a free society were sorely tested by the excesses of Mayor Richard J. Daley and his storm-trooping police force, Gore Vidal allowed himself to abuse his adversary, the conservative columnist Bill Buckley, by describing him as a Nazi. Afterwards he withdrew the slander and said that he should have used the term 'crypto-fascist' instead. This must have been of precious little comfort to Buckley, but it may be a pertinent way of describing a nation that is drifting into fascism but in a state of denial about it. Perhaps, I mused as we climbed above the tree line, I was right to see Russia as a 'pre-fascist' or, better, a 'crypto-fascist' state. It was not an encouraging thought as I headed in the direction of Siberia.

## SIBERIA: EXILES AND PIONEERS

The air became much cooler as we nudged towards the lower peaks of the Urals. Although it was already early summer, the larger snowdrifts had yet to melt. But it was exhilarating to see the expanse of hills to left and right, yielding slowly to mountains shrouded in haze, with a ribbon of snow running along the distant skyline. After PERM 36 it was refreshing, cleansing, to emerge into a natural world that was untouched and unadulterated. Like the Cairngorms, the Urals are neither startling nor disappointing. As with the Scottish range, which forms Britain's largest national park, there are no soaring peaks in the Urals. The highest, Mount Narodnaya, is, at 1895 metres, not much higher than Ben Nevis at 1343 metres, but the Urals, which run from the Arctic Circle south to the Aral Sea, a distance of more than 1500 miles, are on a far greater scale than their Scottish rivals.

Geologically, the range marks a physical collision, some 250–300 million years ago, of Europe with Asia. With its unique mix of European and Asian conifers, spruces, larches and, under their protective canopy, Siberian reindeer and sable alongside European hare, polecat and mink, the Urals are of rare ecological value. But they are also a source of astonishing natural wealth in the form of gold, platinum, silver, nickel, copper, potash and coal, not to mention precious stones like emerald, topaz and amethyst. The exploitation of these resources, from the days of Peter the Great onwards, has pockmarked the Urals with underground workings and chemical plants that belch violently into the heavens, degrading the environment and threatening the habitats of the mammals and birds that cling to this precious eco-region.

But it is as a psychological barrier between West and East – between western Russia and Siberia – that the Urals really capture the imagination. In *Natasha's Dance* Orlando Figes writes of how in the eighteenth-century imagination 'the Urals were built up into a vast mountain range, as if shaped by God on the middle of the steppe to mark the eastern limit of the civilized world. The Russians on the western side of these mountains were Christian in their ways, whereas the Asians on the eastern side were described by Russian travellers as "savages" who needed to be tamed.' The nineteenth-century American explorer George Kennan, in his *Across the American Frontier*, published in 1891, described the 'multitude of broken people' – peasants expelled by the tsar as criminals – who were allowed to pause at the border 'for rest and for a last good-bye to home and country...some gave way to unrestrained grief; some comforted the weeping; some knelt and pressed their faces to the loved soil of their native country, and collected a little earth to take with them into exile'. In the twentieth century, Stalin's slave labourers were dispatched from the West to the East in their millions to transform the wasteland of Siberia into a massive economic powerhouse that was supposed both to provide the energy to fuel the Soviet economic miracle and to confirm unequivocally that, in Siberia, Moscow ruled as absolutely as in any other part of the Russian Empire.

But in addition to the forlorn movement of exiles and prisoners 'sent to Siberia' there were also pioneers and romantics, individuals for whom Siberia represented a test of will or an opportunity, challenging the patriotic Russian to explore and exploit. And this vision of Siberia has lodged in the Russian imagination. Although he had exposed the dreadful means used by Stalin to exploit Siberia's wealth, Alexander Solzhenitsyn clearly believed in the ends. 'These boundless expanses, senselessly left stagnant and barren for four centuries, await our hands, our sacrifices, our zeal and our love,' he wrote some twenty years after the publication of *The Gulag Archipelago*. And at the turn of this century, in uncharacteristically emotive terms, one of Moscow's most respected think-tanks, the Council on Foreign and Defence Policy, argued in a major strategic analysis, 'Siberia and the Far East are not only Russia's "strength" but her very destiny.'

Peering across into Siberia from a modest mountain top, I felt myself to be both an exile and a pioneer. With some 4500 miles already accomplished, but more than 6000 still to go before I reached my final destination, I felt a *frisson* of both satisfaction and dread. Did I have the resolve and the energy to explore this entirely unknown territory with its extremes of distance and climate? Or would I simply feel further from home than ever? As I crossed, like so many before me, from one side of a monument on the main road that formally marks the border between Europe and Asia, I comforted myself with the thought that, though I had not exactly conquered a psychological Mount Everest in the Urals, I had reached something of a milestone on my journey across Russia.

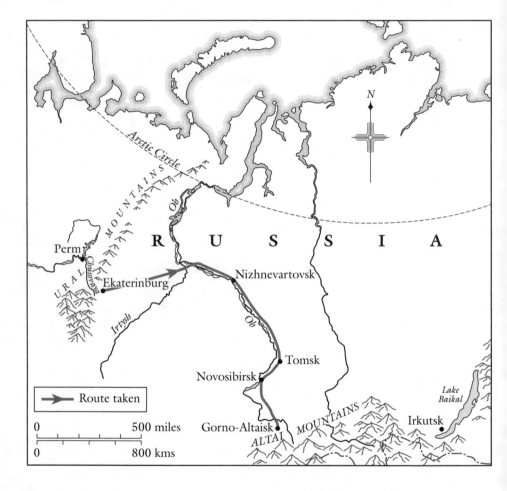

N

Arctic Circle

U R A L   M O U N T A I N S

RUSSIA

Perm

Chusovaya

Ob

Irtysh

Ekaterinburg

Nizhnevartovsk

Ob

Tomsk

Novosibirsk

Lake Baikal

Gorno-Altaisk

ALTAI   MOUNTAINS

Irkutsk

Route taken

0          500 miles

0          800 kms

# PART FOUR

# FROM EKATERINBURG TO THE ALTAI MOUNTAINS

The sheer size of Siberia – it encompasses 77 per cent of the Russian Federation and by itself would be much the largest country in the world – is a challenge. How does one begin to assimilate, let alone embrace, a region that runs from the Urals in the west to the Pacific in the east, and from the Arctic in the north to Kazakhstan, Mongolia and China in the south – and covers 5 million square miles of land? Then there is its extreme climate, which in summer can send the thermometer soaring towards 50 degrees centigrade and in winter may drive it down to minus 50 degrees centigrade: Oymyakon, where the temperature once fell to minus 71 degrees centigrade, has the dubious privilege of being the coldest town on the planet. As for the landscape, every photograph I had seen suggested that aside from one or two spectacular exceptions, such as Lake Baikal, Siberia would be as featureless as it is endless. A cruel land and a harsh climate: no wonder Siberia was an Elsewhere place to which the Unforgiven were sent to be forgotten, wiped from the map of civilization. And yet I was also aware that Siberia is now of incalculable importance to Russia. According to the official figures, this enormous region holds around 80 per cent of the country's oil, gas and coal resources, a similar percentage of its precious metals, and over 40 per cent of its timber. Without Siberia – the nation's economic heartland – it is hardly an exaggeration to say that Russia would soon be bankrupt.

None of these statistics, important and awe-inspiring though they were, had managed to kindle in me that anticipatory thrill that would have made the next stage of my 4000-mile journey through Russia seem more than an endurance test. Instead I found myself empathizing strongly – if self-indulgently – with the poor wretches who had been driven over the Urals like cattle in the nineteenth and twentieth centuries to exploit, as slave labourers, the great wealth on which their persecutors grew fat. Although I made sure to read Colin Thubron's matchless *In Siberia*, even his graceful descriptions of a land where 'white cranes dance on the permafrost; where a great city floats lost among the ice floes; where mammoths sleep under glaciers' merely drove me further towards the arms of melancholy.

My mood was exacerbated by the fact that this time I had to say goodbye not only to Jessica but to our six-week-old daughter, Daisy. Leaving the house was horrible and it fuelled an absurd resentment. Why go? Why not chuck it all in? What if I die, if I never see them again? I scanned a host of mental images – a plane crash, a car accident, a heart attack – that coalesced into a kaleidoscope of loss and missed opportunities. On the plane to Ekaterinburg, this inner turmoil was compounded by the accidental conjunction of two imminent dates. First, 4 September would mark the fourth anniversary of Sue's death. I tried but failed to stop myself from reliving her final hours: the involuntary refusal of her strong lungs to surrender; the ghastly, shuddering breaths – only one or two in a minute – that racked her body for one excruciating hour after another, each seeming to be the last; the regular hiss of the syringe drivers that pumped more and more morphine into her bloodstream and that insulated her, I prayed, from further physical suffering; the waiting at her bedside, holding her cool hand and whispering words designed to be of comfort (because it is the hearing that goes last) but fearing I might be irritating her final hours; and then, in the last moments, as she slipped away, the light, shallow panting that ceased precisely at four minutes past four on that September afternoon. Four years on, the memory consumed me.

The other date was not an anniversary but a wedding that was the indirect consequence of my grief for Sue. On 8 September Bel, to whom I had been married for thirty-six years, was herself about to be remarried and to someone who had been almost part of our family for much of the last two decades. Robin had been both a fixture and a fitting in our lives, and although I wished them happiness together, I was nonetheless stricken by an implacable nostalgia for all that had been lost between two people who had not ceased to love one another despite it all. In the privacy of my seat as we headed towards the Urals, I put my face to the aircraft window and stared into the void. Would the ghosts and demons never leave me, I despaired? After a while, eyes sore with tears, I fell asleep.

I woke up and rummaged in my briefcase to open a little home-made book of photos put together by Jessica, with words of love written on Daisy's behalf: mother and daughter within minutes of the birth; Daisy cuddled by her half-siblings, my children Dan and Kitty; Daisy on my ninety-four-year-old mother's lap; Daisy lying on my chest in bed. In a moment the remembered sorrows and losses that had so recently competed to obliterate joy were dispelled, their place taken by an elation of love and hope.

The young Russian sitting beside me, travelling with his wife and small son on the plane from Moscow to Ekaterinburg, looked affable and clearly wanted to talk. His name was Igor and he was thirty-nine years old. He told me that, after a spell at the Ekaterinburg Military Academy, he had gone on to study finance and economics at the city's university. In the 'crazy' world of the early nineties he had become a financial go-between, linking a quartet of new Moscow banks with their counterparts in Siberia and forging deals that would have been impossible a few years before. The sums involved, he said with evident relish, were 'in the billions of dollars. It was easy money. My cut was 6 per cent of every deal.' Soon he had acquired the capital to buy his way into the motor trade. He now imported Pirelli tyres, Castrol oils and Japanese cars, and employed 450 staff. He had been in London to visit his daughter, who was a student at St Martin's College of Art.

Despite his entrepreneurial success, Igor was far from enthusiastic about the state of Russia. 'I don't like Putin. I liked Yeltsin, the free press and democracy. Today it is crazy. The whole country is run by a hundred people. There is too much of the KGB in Putin. He is too...' he paused, and then ground his thumb into the armrest to signify that his President's instincts were repressive. But Igor himself was doing pretty well, I suggested. 'Yes, the economy in Siberia is doing well. My company is growing fast. But I belong to the bourgeoisie, to the middle class, and I know that it is not possible for a country to go on like this in the hands of so few people. Do you know that the administrators in every region – every Oblast – are now appointed by Putin? No one gets into power without his approval. In our Oblast, he is not only appointing the big bosses but he is asking, "Who are the administrators?" in every city and every town.' So what would happen? 'It can't go on like this,' he replied. Did he mean that people like him, the middle classes, would demand greater accountability from the Kremlin? More rights? He nodded. 'Of course, of course. And maybe there will be change. Perhaps in ten years.' Did he feel free to say such things openly? 'I say it to my friends whom I trust. We talk about it naturally. But I would not say this publicly. You know, it might cause some trouble for me and my business.' I liked Igor and told him, 'I hope you are the voice of the future.' He replied, 'Enjoy Siberia.' I told him I would.

## RICHES BEYOND THE URALS

In Russian folklore the conquest of Siberia was begun by a Cossack adventurer called Ermak in the mid-sixteenth century. According to the legend that clings as tenaciously as bindweed to the available facts, Ermak Timofeevich was, in the words of his only chronicler, 'most courageous, shrewd and humane, well-favoured and endowed with every kind of wisdom; flat-faced, black of beard with curly hair, of medium stature and thick-set and broad-shouldered'. He had been hired by the powerful Stroganoff dynasty to advance into the no man's land of Siberia to crush the marauding tribes on the far side of the Urals. The purpose was to protect the family's existing demesnes within Russia and to open up the lucrative forests of Siberia in the name of the Tsar, Ivan the Terrible. Ermak and 840 followers crossed the Urals and sailed up the Chusovaya River in search of the enemy. Although the vision had yet to be formulated, this piratical raiding party became, in effect, the advance guard of an imperial drive into Siberia that would eventually reach the Pacific Ocean some 5000 miles away.

Courtesy of a company that specialized in expeditions to the Urals, I immersed myself briefly in Ermak's world. Our group was led by Dmitry Voroshchuk, a bearded, bespectacled, thirty-four-year-old graduate of the local Mining Institute, who had transferred his academic expertise into a profitable little enterprise escorting like-minded enthusiasts through the geological and ecological wonders of the Urals. We drove out of Ekaterinburg along a minor road until we came to a rough track that led to a clearing overlooking the Chusovaya. Then we clambered some 200 metres down a steep and slippery wooded bank, carrying a couple of inflated catamaran rafts that would take us downriver for the afternoon. Once launched, we paddled gently in Ermak's wake. In spring the river becomes a dangerous torrent; in the autumn sunlight it was reassuringly benign, though it occasionally bubbled and boiled as it accelerated over a shoal of mini-rapids that threatened to ground us ignominiously in the middle of the river. On either side the trees crowded from the skyline to the water's edge, making way only for the occasional slab of grey-white perpendicular rock at 30 metres or more in height – the Urals undressed – which ran down into the water, a natural fortress against the invaders.

On 26 October 1582 Ermak, crossing from the Chusovaya to the Irtysh, made contact with a force of Tatar tribesmen. The result was a foregone conclusion. The Tatars charged Ermak's militia with spears and shields; the invaders responded with musket fire. After the rout, Ermak and his men celebrated what, in mythology, became known as 'the conquest of Siberia' and then set about pillaging the Tatar capital at Isker, where they divided among themselves the great store of pelts and furs piled high in the vaults of the treasury. According to W. Bruce Lincoln in *The Conquest of a Continent: Siberia and the Russians*, Ermak – who now 'claimed' this vast region in the name of Ivan the Terrible – at once sent back to Moscow a royal tribute. 'At a time when a prime sable pelt sold for ten times what a peasant family could earn in a year and a black fox fetched up to ten times the price of a sable, Ermak's Cossacks carried the pelts of twenty-four hundred prime sable, eight hundred black fox, and two thousand beaver.' But, as Lincoln points out, even this hoard was 'only the tiniest fraction of what the Russians would take from Siberia in the years ahead'.

Ermak himself advanced slowly eastwards, harried by the Tatars and indigenous tribes through whose ancestral lands he and his men passed. They soon found themselves in urgent need of reinforcements and supplies, which eventually arrived – in nugatory quantities – a year later than they had been promised. By the start of their second winter in Siberia, Ermak's men were in a desperate plight. Stricken by hunger and disease, many of them died, a later chronicler reporting that 'his men were forced to eat the bodies of their companions'. The Tatar ambushes became bolder and more effective. On the night of 5 August 1585, less than three years after their 'conquest', Ermak and his exhausted men fell asleep but failed to post any guards to protect their encampment. The Tatars fell upon them and killed most of the Cossack invaders. But, so the legend runs, Ermak managed to escape and ran down to one of the boats that was moored by the shore. He leapt, missed his footing and fell into the water, where he was dragged to the bottom by the weight of the royal chain-mail in which he was clad – his final reward from Ivan the Terrible for planting the imperial flag on Siberian soil.

But Ermak's end was only the beginning. The occupation of Siberia soon became a permanent presence. The Stroganoff family had not only funded Ermak's expedition, but had promised Moscow to resource the process of colonization. To this end they undertook to raise the military force needed to suppress the indigenous peoples, to plant crops on their tribal lands and, where there had been only forest, to build fine cities and churches that would both honour the Tsar and promote Russian culture. It was an enticing vista and Moscow was suitably grateful. By 1588, according to the family records, the Stroganoffs had been granted nearly 3.5 million hectares of Siberia to occupy and exploit. It was not only the insatiable demand for pelts and furs that swelled the family coffers; there were also salt, gold, semi-precious stones (malachite, marble, topaz, tourmaline and cornelian), emeralds and river pearls. Exempted from taxation for twenty years, apparently to encourage further settlement in Siberia, the Stroganoffs were also allowed to smelt iron ore and to explore for lead, sulphur, silver, gold, copper and tin. By comparison, even the grotesque wealth of today's oligarchs fades into relative insignificance.

## THE BIRTHPLACE OF SOVIET ROCK

The city of Ekaterinburg is an ugly but impressive monument to the industrial exploitation of the Urals. Founded by Peter the Great in 1723 and named after his consort, Catherine, it was built as a fortress around an iron foundry, the first of some twenty-six iron-casting plants to be built in the southern Urals by the middle of the century. Soon afterwards came the imperial mint that supplied the nation with copper coins, and, in 1726, the first gem-processing works. In 1745 the first copper plant was opened by the Tverdushev brothers, who owned more than five hundred copper mines. Then, in abundance, came gold and emeralds. Symbolic of Siberia's growing importance, the Empire's greatest highway, built on the orders of Catherine the Great, passed through the city. Ekaterinburg was pivotal: to the West it was known as the Moscow Highway and to the East as the Great Siberian Highway.

Today this self-styled 'capital of the Urals' is the third-largest city in Siberia, a status it owes to Stalin and his successors. After the revolution, Ekaterinburg was renamed Sverdlovsk in honour of the Bolshevik party leader of that name. To conceal the scale of industrialization needed to produce the civil and military equipment required to realize the Soviet vision, it became a 'closed' city, a secretive status it had to endure until 1990. Now that the veil is lifted and the original name has been restored, Ekaterinburg likes to boast that it is a thoroughly international centre (with international flights direct from Europe) that welcomes foreigners and is eager to become a magnet for global investment. But although it remains at the productive epicentre of Russia's great source of natural wealth, the city cannot quite shake off a dated, provincial air. Of course it has its hotels, theatres, discos, nightclubs and restaurants, but 'sophistication' – that dubiously seductive quality – is not immediately discernible along either side of the broad but traffic-clogged avenues that drive a depressing swathe through the brutalist buildings of the late Soviet era.

On my first evening in the city I had supper in a small restaurant concealed inside one of these monstrosities. It was called the Dacha, and had been constructed in wood to reproduce something of the atmosphere of a forest hideaway with the aim of impressing innocent foreigners. Its pine walls and floors seemed thoroughly Scandinavian. A jazz pianist (every musician I have heard in Russia's bars and restaurants has far exceeded in talent his European counterparts) lulled me into the illusion that I was at the heart of a new cosmopolis. As evidence of their internationalist aspirations – and as in so many other parts of Russia – the owners had made an admirable effort to translate the Russian menu into English. Among the dishes on offer: 'guts chicken with simplicity executions' and 'meat of a deer from the North, under oil from an overseas white truffle'. I chose 'meat of the rabbit house' because I approved of the ungarnished truth of the description. I also chose 'root of a vegetable at women of fashion popular,' which turned out, disappointingly, to be a chunk of beetroot. I kept the menu as a souvenir, not to patronize but to amuse.

Later I went to the opening night of a new club. Called the KGB, it is a self-conscious raspberry blown back at the Soviet era and, in the case of the owner and his friends, it was heartfelt retribution. Vladimir Shakhrin (who co-owns the KGB with the director of Ekaterinburg's annual rock festival, Evgeny Gorenburg) is a big star in Russia, the leader of a rock group called Chaif. 'When I go to Moscow and say I am from Ekaterinburg, they say simply, "Oh! Chaif,"' one of Vladimir's fans told me in the densely crowded cellar bar. The KGB was refreshingly anti-authoritarian in decor, though – from a modish European perspective – would probably be regarded as being trapped in the eighties rather than retro. The ceiling was painted black, the chairs decorated in red, white and blue interspersed with stars and – no, not stripes – the hammer and sickle. Worn-out guitars and steam radios adorned the recesses, and the walls were covered with mocking memorabilia of the bad old days – grim black and white photographs of long-dead Soviet persecutors.

The overall effect was somehow to suggest that Vladimir's values were as much about today as yesterday. If you chose to substitute the letters FSB for KGB, the young fans were gently invited to conclude, you wouldn't be far off the mark. You should always think subversively, the price of freedom being eternal vigilance. Vladimir himself presided over his new venture with a delightfully anarchic uncertainty, taking to the tiny stage to declare, 'This is new, an experiment, we don't know how to do it and we don't know how it will work.' He then yielded the microphone to a young singer, dressed as though he would have been more at home in a folk club, but who went into Elvis (this being anniversary time), singing some of the King's early heavy-duty numbers that had so thrilled my generation forty years ago. The KGB fans, mostly in their twenties and respectably middle class in dress and demeanour, filled every cramped square metre of the floor space, moving and shaking to the beat.

Vladimir joined me at the bar, bubbling with satisfaction. A small man in his mid-fifties, he did not look like a rock star, even a superannuated one. He was dressed neatly in well-pressed chinos and a red shirt that hung loose and thereby almost disguised a small paunch. He showed no evidence of youthful excess, no haggardness; only a bright-eyed, round-faced happiness that reminded me of those smiling Frenchmen of my childhood who used to cycle about England selling strings of onions. Was it really true, I asked him, that Ekaterinburg had been the rock capital of the Soviet Union a quarter of a century earlier? He did not answer the question directly but instead told me, in an enchantingly unassuming way, about the origins of rock music in Ekaterinburg. 'Remember that one of the first atomic power stations was here in Sverdlovsk. So you might say that there was a lot of radiation and we are all kind of mutants. But to be more serious: this was a place of exile in the nineteenth century. So it has had a long tradition of free-thinking. Then, during the Second World War, the scientific and artistic elite was evacuated here. So there was also a high degree of intellectual life as well.'

Vladimir and his friends, mutating from that inheritance, were dissidents without an ideology, rebels with only one cause: to confront the cultural behemoths in Moscow who had for so long either smothered the creative energy of the young or sought to channel it towards their own 'proletarian' dead end. 'Of course you know how wonderful life was in the Soviet Union? How glorious everything was then?' Vladimir said with cheery contempt. 'I think it was just a question of being in the right place at the right time. People wanted to hear music that was written in Russian and that was about Russians, about themselves, instead of the pompous and banal lyrics that were churned out on the official radio stations. Well, our songs, even our simple love songs, rang true.' But it was not easy to perform or to hear their music. 'We really took it in the neck from the KGB. They would follow us and question us. I can't pretend that I was a great victim of persecution myself because I was just an ordinary worker on a building site, and there is not much you can do to ruin the career of a labourer. But it was a much more serious threat for my friends because their careers, their whole lives were at risk. So this club is, if you like, one in the eye for the KGB.' Vladimir smiled almost lasciviously at the sheer impertinence of that thought. Somehow managing to tiptoe along the margins of the law, he and his friends had rapidly defined themselves as an anti-establishment challenge to the values of the Soviet Union. As Vladimir told his tale, it seemed to me that Chaif's music-making had been, above all, a primeval *cri de coeur* from a late twentieth-century version of Gorky's *The Lower Depths*, a challenge from a generation that felt itself to be suffocating.

In those *samizdat* days, their music was passed secretly from hand to hand to be heard in communal flats and apartment blocks. 'It was a time when the deficit was total. You had to find a way round everything. If you wanted to eat, there was nothing to eat. You had to find a way of getting food. If you wanted to read a good book and it wasn't for sale in the official shop, you had to find another means of getting hold of it. And if you wanted to listen to good music, it was the same. People just found a way. We really didn't do very much ourselves. We got hold of a tape recorder and we'd make five copies of an album and within a week they were all over the Soviet Union from Leningrad to Vladivostok. I really don't know how it happened. But of course it had to be good music.' Vladimir paused, as though still bemused by his band's subversive triumph.

With the arrival of *glasnost* they were able to surface into the public arena, where they were at once greeted with popular acclaim and critical success. Although the focus of Russian rock music has since shifted to Moscow, Chaif remains a star attraction on the national circuit. Ekaterinburg's annual festival of rock still draws the best in the business, while the city is renowned for nurturing new talent and helping to sustain the integrity of a movement that Chaif pioneered. Vladimir is such a force that there was a rumour that he had been invited to the Kremlin when President Putin asked him to use his status and influence to combat the malign potential of Ukraine's Orange Revolution to gain a toehold in Russia. Disappointingly, he insisted that the story was entirely false. But was he still a rebel in Putin's Russia as he had been in the days of the Soviet Union, or had he become part of the new establishment? 'I'd love to think I hadn't changed, that I was still the same guy doing all the things I did and believed in,' he replied disarmingly, 'but it wouldn't be true to say that nothing has changed. I am the co-owner of this club. I have a pretty good car outside the door and with my wife we go off and tour Italy. So I have become somewhat bourgeois – though I like to think that I haven't wholly succumbed, that I haven't trans-gressed into the vulgarity of a bourgeois life. That I am still on the right side of that.'

The sound of Elvis ceased and the young singer, one of Vladimir's protégés joined us. 'Hi! My name is Vova. I love music. Rock and blues. That is my life,' he said loudly in English, the adrenalin still pumping. He repeated the sentiment so many times, jerking his head around as if awaiting an urgent summons from elsewhere in the club, that for a moment I wondered whether he was on speed. 'I don't do drugs,' he volunteered suddenly – though I had not in fact mentioned my suspicion. 'Drugs and rock music don't mix.' I raised my eyebrows. 'You can't do drugs and sing well,' he continued. 'All my friends at school – I am twenty-eight – who took drugs, they are all dead.' He was absolutely focused now and intent. I looked around at his fans. All of them were young, but not one seemed drunk or drugged. There was no raucousness, and none of that befuddled but intimidating cockiness that has become the hallmark of a British night on the town. Later, as I left, I saw a teenage girl, a leggy blonde dressed in a white trouser suit and wearing black and white leather boots with winkle-picker toes. She was with her boyfriend, who had imprisoned himself in a tight bronze-tinted linen suit. Their provincial chic was touching, and became all the more so the moment he collected her coat from the cloakroom and placed it solicitously around her shoulders before escorting her out into the night. Such old-world courtesy from a teenager in a rock club? As others had said to me in very different circumstances, 'This is Russia.' Yes, I thought, adding, like any grumpy old man, 'And, for once, a very good thing too.'

## THE ALCOHOL PROBLEM

Ekaterinburg sees the other end of the spectrum too. The Russian phrase for it is *Trezvy Gorod*. It means literally Sober City, and it is the name of a charity, itself a rarity in Russia, that has been set up to combat the sale of illicit alcohol. It is run by a former alcoholic called Evgeny Malyonkin, who is as ardent as any convert about the evils of drink. A transport manager by profession, he doubles as an aide to a local politician, Leonid Roizman, who became known as Ekaterinburg's 'Mr Drugs-Buster' after he established a 'City without Drugs' initiative, which has had significant success in cutting the number of deaths from drug abuse. Evgeny has adapted Roizman's formula to alcohol poisoning. He invited me to join him on a police raid – a sting – against one of the many petty criminals at the bottom of a lucrative supply chain as corrupt and vicious as any controlled by the drug baronies that pollute Russia.

As we drove out of the city centre towards one of the dreary and impoverished satellite towns around Ekaterinburg, I reminded myself of the terrifying statistics. In a country where life expectancy for men of working age has fallen to fifty-nine years and in which, according to the World Health Organization, alcohol abuse is linked to 75 per cent of all murders and more than 40 per cent of all suicides, the government's own statistics confirm that alcohol is the direct cause of death of between 550,000 and 700,000 Russian citizens each year. More than 2 million Russians are registered as alcoholics, of whom 65,000 are children below the age of fourteen and under treatment for 'uncontrollable' addiction to the bottle. However, since registration usually involves commitment to an unpopular 'cold turkey' regime, it is generally assumed that the real problem is very much greater.

And there is worse: at least 20,000 people die each year from being poisoned by fake vodka distilled from household-cleaning products, medicines and the liquid waste from industrial processes. These very low-quality spirits are diluted and bottled in underground workshops. Local printing shops provide the labels (without feeling the necessity to inform the police of any suspicions they may harbour), and the final product is sold in twenty-four-hour kiosks, dodgy little shops whose owners know very well that they are participating in a murderous scam and even private apartments. Once again the statistics show that this human tragedy is also an economic disaster: almost 50 per cent of all deaths among men of working age are caused by drinking bootleg alcohol. So why, I asked Evgeny, why – in heaven's name – don't these alcoholics take more care about what they buy? It was a naive question. 'It is simple. They can't afford it. They don't have the money to buy good vodka.' And he went on to explain that young men and old men alike – it is almost invariably men – drank to obliterate the world about them. They tend to be poor and unemployed, their diet is atrocious and they live in filthy, overcrowded apartments. They have no prospects and no hope. Drinking cheap 'vodka' – even if it meant poisoning themselves to death – is a means of escape from life.

Evgeny had a map of the 'drunken' city, heavily pockmarked with red dots showing the areas most afflicted by the sale of counterfeit alcohol. In the last two years his 'citizens' initiative', as he called it, had managed to confiscate 670 tonnes of illicit alcohol with a street value of $2 million. As a result, there had been a slight fall in the number of deaths directly attributed to alcohol poisoning. It had not been an easy process. As his mentor Leonid Roizman had discovered when he started to combat the drugs menace, some very powerful people had done their best to frustrate the Sober City enterprise. A little over a year before Evgeny established the project, a group of doctors from twenty-three regional hospitals had tried to set up a similar programme – but it had foundered on the threatened wrath of the local mafia, who were themselves 'protected' by senior police officers. It was a very lucrative business. Even today, when the police were ostensibly committed to stamping out the sale of illicit alcohol, they frequently displayed a marked reluctance to take any initiative on their own behalf. Without the commitment of Evgeny and the streetwise intelligence of his team of volunteers – themselves also ex-addicts – the police in Ekaterinburg would not only avoid confronting the criminals who peddled the poison, but continue to share in this region's share of a nationwide 'protection' racket. So why did he persist? Why his crusade? 'I am a patriot. If I don't do something, who will?'

We reached the outskirts of a miserable housing estate: dilapidated tenement blocks in serried ranks, flanked by desultory trees. An elderly couple sat on a bench in the late afternoon sun. A woman wheeled a baby in a decrepit pram. A dog scratched itself. And we waited and waited, concealed inside our van, watching the windows of an apartment on the third floor. Evgeny was on his phone, coordinating the operation with the police, who had arrived separately and taken up positions around the block. We saw no movement, but, Evgeny assured me, they knew a bootleg vendor operated from there and she was inside at that moment. She? 'Yes. Many of them are women, often pensioners. They buy their supplies from further up the chain and they do it to eke out their pensions. Although I hate what they do, I have some sympathy for them. They are simply trying to survive. Their lives are very hard.'

One of Evgeny's Sober City volunteers, carrying a plastic bag, sauntered into the building and disappeared from view. He had already been given a wad of rouble notes, each one of which had been photo-copied by the police, and he was wired. The sting depended on him. Some weeks before this raid he had befriended his 'supplier', overcoming her suspicion, gaining her trust and then buying her poisonous product. His task now was to exchange the marked roubles for a further supply of alcohol and to signal the police immediately the transaction had been completed. At this point the trap would be sprung.

After fifteen minutes he emerged again, his bag filled with several bottles. On cue, three plain-clothed officers ran into the building and, taking the stairs two at a time, arrived panting at the suspect's door. They banged once, then again, and more loudly a third time. After a moment the door opened to reveal a crumpled little woman who must have been in her mid-seventies, her eyes wide with apparent bewilderment. 'Whatever can this be about?' she seemed to gesture. 'Please come on in.' The three officers, accompanied by Evgeny and his 'plant', began their search for evidence. Her humble 'How can I help you?' manner was remarkably convincing: how could a poor old woman, me, a pensioner, have done anything that might be against the law? You think I sell illicit alcohol? Me? The police ignored this ingratiation and set about their task with thoroughness. They opened cupboards, looked under the bed, felt behind the cooker. Even the fridge was empty. They seemed flummoxed. I began to wonder whether they had the wrong woman. Or had she been too clever for them? Too quick? Had she somehow emptied the bottles and hidden the money? I looked more closely at her and watched her eyes furtively darting about the room, following every move.

One of the police tried to open a door into another room. It was locked. Inside, a dog growled. The old woman explained that the room belonged to her son. She did not have a key. The police persisted. On second thoughts, she did have a key after all. She unlocked the door and scolded the dog into silence before shutting the creature in a broom cupboard, where he continued to whine and growl. One officer went to a fridge where he found three small, tonic-sized bottles.

Meanwhile, in the living room another officer discovered a small metal box, hidden in a drawer, with rouble notes inside it. The old woman began to cross herself. In the name of the Almighty she swore that she had committed no offence; that she did not deal in illicit alcohol and that she had been given the roubles by Evgeny's 'plant' – gesturing towards him – as a present. But the numbers on the notes matched those on the photocopies, and the police had discovered a stash of bottles, a plastic bag filled with bottle caps, and a measuring jug. The old woman suddenly crumbled and began to wheedle. 'I am sorry. This is the first time. I will not do it again. In the name of the Lord.' She crossed herself repeatedly as she spoke, praying to the Almighty for aid. Evgeny, who had been quietly impassive throughout the search, now began to interrogate her. It was impressive to watch: a do-gooder, who until now had seemed so gentle in manner though not in conviction, now revealed a steely, quiet anger. Why did she sell this poison to young people? Had she no shame? Where was her humanity? She repeated again and again – as, from the experience of scores of similar encounters, Evgeny knew she would – that she only did it because her pension was too small, that she had no choice, but that she would not do it again. Evincing not a glimmer of sympathy for her, he persisted, grinding her down with magisterial and righteous contempt. The old woman was so pathetic that after a while I intervened to ease the pressure on her: 'But you must know that what you are selling kills people?' I asked reproachfully. This time she replied with a chilling defiance: 'But people die all the time.' The sympathy I had just mustered vanished at once.

The police collected up the evidence, the detritus of her disgusting little enterprise. She signed a document, laboriously compiled in longhand, and then we left. She would go to court and she would be convicted but what, I asked Evgeny, had really been achieved? So much effort and time for so little. 'Of course,' he replied, 'there are thousands and thousands like her. But we hope that she will lead us up the chain to dealers, and then up to the really powerful people who are running this racket. But even if we don't succeed, you should remember that every bottle kills.' The old woman's offence, he added, carried a maximum jail sentence of five years, but because this would be her first conviction she would almost certainly escape with a fine.

## IN THE EMERALD MINE

In Moscow the rich think nothing of paying upwards of $30,000 for a decent emerald. The chances are that such translucent beauty will have come from the Malyshev mine, some three hours by road from Ekaterinburg. To reach the mine, you pass through the suburbs and out into the forest on the edge of the Urals. The route is itself a journey through the city's industrial decline, fall and resurrection. We passed a dilapidated chemical plant still puffing out its poisonous fumes and, a little further on, wreckage of factories where weed-covered railway lines traversed deserted concrete storage and loading areas. Broken windows, buckled girders and gaping roofs stood in forlorn tribute to the past. It was hard to tell which factories still operated and which had collapsed with the end of the Soviet Union; there was nothing modernist or post-modern about what was once a power-house city of the Soviet Union. And then we found ourselves on a new dual carriageway, where the decrepitude gave way to row upon row of individually designed houses – very 'des. res.' executive homes on the Ascot or Wimbledon model – complete with spacious patios and plenty of space for the third car. These estates ooze new money, and more are going up all the time.

Once past this new suburbia, we turned off the highway on to a familiarly potholed road that led deeper into the forest. We passed hamlets and villages until we reached a collection of shabby industrial buildings in the middle of a semi-derelict site that declared itself modestly to be the head office of the Malyshev mine. The mine was opened in 1832 after geologists had discovered an emerald-rich seam of rock, 15 miles long by 1.5 miles wide. Since then, for generation after generation, men have been digging for emeralds here. There was an interregnum between 1956 and 1990, during which, in conditions of great secrecy, the search for emeralds was diverted to the mining of beryllium that was locked in this huge seam. Beryllium was a critical component in the construction of the nuclear reactors needed to expand a Soviet atomic-weapons programme to rival that of NATO. For the duration, emeralds and alexandrites – the translucent stone named after the tsar who was on the throne when the mine was opened, Alexander II – were treated as accidental by-products.

After the collapse of the Soviet Union, the mine was 'moth-balled' until 2005, when – after a complex series of buy-outs and take-overs – the once-again famous Malyshev emerald mine was bought by a Canadian company, which, with anachronistic flair, calls itself the Tsar Emerald Corporation. Their lease does not cover the entire emerald seam, but is thought to contain 80 per cent of all its known reserves. The first emeralds were brought to the surface in 2006 and, even after a sizeable capital investment to restore the mineshafts and the surrounding plant, the Canadians are already making a great deal of money.

I had been down a mine only once before. It was some thirty years ago and I was the guest of the Yorkshire miners' leader, Arthur Scargill, who had invited me and other notable 'subversives' like the broadcaster Joan Bakewell to attend the annual gala of the Yorkshire miners. My task was first to judge a variety of competitions involving fancy dress, and then to enjoy a fine dinner with even finer wines, courtesy of the Yorkshire branch of the National Union of Mineworkers. The following morning I was taken underground: in the cage, surrounded by pale faces half-concealed under pit helmets as we accelerated down the mineshaft to the bottom, the sour-smelling wind damp on my face; at the bottom, in semi-darkness, voices rico-cheting through the tunnel, stumbling, heads bowed, towards the coalface; the incomprehensible shriek and whine of machinery, the echoes eerily magnified; the blackened faces of miners covered with dust, the stabbing and pounding of the drill against the rock, the dull vibration shaking the ground and invading my bowels.

When I emerged some three hours later – bruised and cold, coughing up black dust, and aching with the effort of crawling along a final seam so narrow that I could hardly raise my body on to my elbows without grazing my back – I was relieved to be out of it, but aghast at the conditions in which we required human beings to work in order to keep the rest of us warm and mobile and prosperous. I drew two instant conclusions: first, that the miners were disgracefully exploited by the state on our behalf, and, second, that the sooner all pits were closed, the miners profitably redeployed elsewhere, the better for them and for us. (Some time later, when Scargill was arrested for an alleged breach of the peace following his participation in a 'flying picket' during the 1984 strike, I was phoned by a tabloid newspaper. Would I stand bail for the Red Demon if asked to do so? I replied that I thought this would be unnecessary for a variety of reasons, but that, yes, if bail were required and if the NUM or others were not willing to find the money, then I would indeed come to the rescue. The next day a headline blazoned: 'Dimbleby supports Scargill'.)

Suitably attired in overalls, boots and, for the second time in my life, pit helmet, I once more entered the cage and within a couple of minutes we were 250 metres underground. But instead of encountering gloom and dust, we entered a well-lit chamber giving on to several tunnels that were hardly smaller than those of the London Underground and had been sealed with a concrete skim that had once – in the Cold War – been painted white. We strode along on duckboards (underground springs seep through the rock and the water has to be pumped away) for about half a mile, following a narrow-gauge railway track, until we reached the rockface. By contrast with any coalmine, there was no risk of explosion. I watched a miner drilling into the rock, half-hoping that I might see emeralds cascading forth like coins from a slot machine. I was, of course, disappointed. The great chunks of rock that are gouged out of the seam have to be

*Students in Volgograd guard the city's Eternal Flame: 'It is so important that history is passed down from generation to generation.'*

*The Red October factory in Volgograd was at the epicentre of the Battle of Stalingrad: 'Soon it became like a meat-grinder. There were bodies everywhere.'*

*Vladimir Akharchenkov, who at the age of sixteen fought in hand-to-hand combat at the Battle of Stalingrad, shows off his wartime medals.*

*Rodina Mat ('The Motherland is Calling') is a memorial to those who died to save Stalingrad. Taller than the Statue of Liberty, it towers over the modern city.*

*A recently restored mosaic of Joseph Stalin in the Volgograd Planetarium – 'an unbowed Buddha, re-emerging as a pompous Cheshire Cat' – on public display for children to admire.*

*'The significance of Kazan is very great: it is where two worlds meet.' The new kremlin, adapted from Ivan the Terrible's original conception, is on the grand scale.*

*Sergei Kovalev, a former inmate of PERM 36, is a human rights activist. 'In Putin's Russia he has become a pariah.'*

*PERM 36, one of Stalin's Gulag labour camps, where later some of the Soviet Union's most famous political dissidents were imprisoned. It was not closed until 1987.*

*A vodka-inspired triumph at a bowling alley in Samara. But who owns it? 'I don't think we should talk about that.'*

*Victory Day in Samara, where pensioners are anxious to share their memories of the Great Patriotic War against Nazi Germany.*

*The Tupolev factory in Samara is owned by Russia's richest oligarch, Oleg Deripaska. 'He is losing money here at the moment ...'*

*Tsar Nicholas II and his family –*
*the last of the Romanovs – were*
*murdered by the Bolsheviks on the*
*night of 16–17 July 1918.*

*Sergey Pogorelov leads the*
*archaeological team searching for*
*further evidence of the murdered*
*royal family: 'What we found here*
*are the holy relics of saints.'*

*Rafting in the Ural mountains, following*
*the route taken by the first Russians to*
*'invade' Siberia in the sixteenth century.*

*Siberia holds around 80 per cent of Russia's oil, gas and coal resources, a similar percentage of its precious metals, and over 40 per cent of its timber. Without Siberia it is hardly an exaggeration to say that Russia would soon be bankrupt.*

*Like Marlon Brando and the Wild Bunch,
oil executive Dmitri Orlov (right) with his
daughter, the author and fellow bikers after
a burn-up through Nizhenvartovsk.*

At a logging camp outside Tomsk 'Boreal Boris' (left) explains, 'I love the forest … but the forest has to be cut.' Professor of biology Sergey Kirpotkin (centre) replies, 'We are facing an ecological landslide.'

In 2007 'Boreal Boris' and his team felled 750,000 trees from this part of the Tomsk forest. 'A ferocious destruction,' according to Professor Kirpotkin.

Vladimir and his wife on their way back home from the forest, where they had been collecting pine nuts. Once processed, their haul (in the trailer) will be worth £200.

broken and crushed before they reveal their wealth. Nonetheless, with the miners earning only 10,000–15,000 roubles (£200–300) a month, pilfering gems, one of which could easily be worth twice the higher amount on the emerald black market, is not a petty matter. Despite a variety of security measures, light-fingered workers cost the Canadians several thousand dollars a month.

I was shown round by the manager, a white Zimbabwean expatriate who could be described, politely, as a 'rough diamond'. He was small and stout and, for my benefit, adopted a pugnacious manner that, so far as I was able to discern, did not conceal any other character trait than an urge to demonstrate that he was very definitely in charge of everyone about him. But then Jimmy Wilde had spent the last quarter of a century roughing it and toughing it around the mines of the world, and his colonial sinews had only been toughened by the experience. He was prone to make the kind of jokes about homosexuals that doubtless went down well in the company he kept in those days. He also boasted to me that his Russian employees had finally become accustomed to his use of words like 'fuck' – the adjectival version of which certainly peppered his conversation with me. But, after two years in Russia, he was still unable to communicate with his colleagues except in English. His interpreter, a pert young Russian woman who skilfully concealed any distaste she may have felt for his manners, was always at his side.

I got the impression that, aside from her, Wilde was profoundly frustrated by most of the team over which he presided. Russians, he seemed to think, were arrogant enough to believe that they were better than anyone else at everything to which they turned their hand, that they had all the answers, and that foreigners were in some way significantly inferior. Wilde's experience appeared to have left him with the opposite impression of his host nation. Either way, the gulf of personality and culture between him and his colleagues was immediately evident over the buffet lunch that the Tsar Emerald Corporation had generously provided, and at which he presided in one corner while they kept their distance on the other side of a heavily laden table. The bonds between them were clearly entirely professional and not at all personal.

That Wilde was an effective manager was not in doubt. I had thought that I would not be greatly interested in emeralds except as jewellery to admire on beautiful necks and fingers. But as he rattled off the statistics, I began to appreciate the astonishing human effort required to produce such exquisite gems. The previous year the miners had excavated 204,000 tonnes of rock, he told me, which would rise to 340,000 tonnes this year. After the rock had been brought to the surface, it was crushed, washed and then hand-sorted by women labourers who were paid 10,500 roubles (£210) a month. They drudged under constant scrutiny from CCTV cameras and security guards waiting to pounce on any pilferers. Last year the mine had yielded up some 3 million carats of emeralds. At 5 carats to the gram, this equated roughly to 600,000 grams or 6 tonnes; 6 tonnes of emeralds from 204,000 tonnes of rock, or 34,000 tonnes of rock for every tonne of emeralds.

Wilde led me into the dealers' room, passing through three locked doors until I found myself under scrutiny from at least three CCTV cameras and two security guards. I was instructed to stand far enough back from the table to ensure that I could not secrete away a single gem. Then one of the security guards poured out a pouch full of emeralds for my perusal. Pliny once wrote that the emerald gladdens the eye without tiring it. The tones and shades of green in the uncut stone, some milky pale, others vividly deep and translucent, some no bigger than a baby's fingernail, others (less valuably) the size of a hazelnut, were a glitter of acquisitive delight. I longed to run them though my fingers, but was told that this was forbidden. Could I hold one of them? Sorry, that too was impossible. I felt an onrush of desire, that folly of greed, an urge to possess. For the first time I understood why the rich will pay hundreds of thousands of dollars for that desirable, one-in-a-million rarity, a 'perfect' – unblemished – emerald.

Not to be thwarted, I asked if I could buy an emerald. Of course, I was told, of course. I chose a small stone of the deepest, most vivid green. I had chosen well. Too well. It weighed 3 carats and I offered $500 for it. It would cost me more, much more. How much more? Well, once it had been cut and polished it would sell for at least $25,000. The deal collapsed.

Wilde told me that his Canadian bosses were preparing to float their asset on the London Stock Exchange to raise £15 million for further investment in the Malyshev mine. 'We now have four hundred and fifty workers underground and we will soon increase that to more than seven hundred,' he said with evident pride. 'We are bringing this community back to life.' His own experience of this rejuvenating process had not been easy. He lived in the nearby village, but for the first year his neighbours did not even raise their eyes to greet him in the street. It was a lonely life. In the short weeks of early summer, when it was not too hot and the mosquitoes less violent, he could at least go for long walks. In the long, harsh winter, when it was too cold to stay outside, he lived in front of his television screen playing DVDs – 'It's shit, man,' he said reflectively. This admission of loneliness and isolation from such a rough-edged character finally touched me. So why, I wondered, did he force himself to endure such privation? Was he really in it for the money? He told me that mining was his life – it was all he knew. He would move on in a while to another place and another challenge, and would continue to do so until he was past it. He was, I concluded with reluctant admiration, a genuine buccaneer. A pretty lowly figure in the hierarchy of the global market, he was easily dispensable, but psychologically he was a pioneer, a descendant of those Russians who came to Siberia in the tracks of Ermak, prospecting for treasure untold. Jimmy Wilde was very far from being sorry for himself, but as I drove away I felt as though I was leaving behind a lost soul washed up in an alien land.

## RELICS FROM THE PAST

If Ekaterinburg means emeralds to some, it means murder to many. It was here on the night of 16–17 July 1918 that the last tsar, Nicholas II, his wife, the Empress Alexandra, and their five children were executed in a place and a manner that constituted a peculiarly cruel end to Russia's imperial history. The revolutionary fervour that had gripped Russia following the humiliation of its defeat in the 1905 war against Japan, and the attempted assassination of the Tsar in the same year, had been severely repressed but not strangled. Within a decade, the dire impact of World War I – terrible losses on the battlefield and acute shortages of basic foodstuffs caused by the mass call-up of the peasantry – fuelled the flames of anger and bitterness against the regime. By February 1917 the Russian Empire was on the brink of collapse. In freezing weather, supplies of flour and fuel all but ran out in the capital, St Petersburg. As the crisis worsened, police opened fire on rioters and looters searching for food. At the same time a spate of strikes by workers and mutiny in the armed forces produced near anarchy. Obstinately clinging on to power and physically isolated from the crisis, from his military staff headquarters in Mogilev some 400 miles away the Tsar ordered the popular uprising to be crushed.

On Sunday, 11 March, the populace defied an imperial order to stay in their homes. Vast crowds took to the streets and only dispersed when around two hundred people had been shot dead. But this imperial 'victory' was short-lived. By the end of the day, regiment after regiment had mutinied, and at least sixty thousand troops joined the revolution. By nightfall the city was in the hands of the insurgents. Abandoned by his generals, his civilian advisers and parliament, the Tsar finally acknowledged the inevitable and abdicated three days later. It is hard to exaggerate the seismic and malign impact of the collapse of tsarism in Russia on the tormented history of the twentieth century. At the time it was welcomed by liberals and democrats throughout Europe and in the United States. Only reactionaries in both continents deplored the downfall of an antiquated autocracy. No one foresaw the rise of Stalin or the replacement of national rivalries within Europe by a global struggle between two nuclear-tipped superpowers that would only end with the triumph of American capitalism over Soviet Communism – a triumph that would eventually be grotesquely misdescribed as the victory of 'good' over 'evil'.

In the early, chaotic months of the revolution the victors treated the imperial family, the Romanovs, with surprising lenience. There was no lynch mob to string them up and no summary execution. Instead, they and their entourage were held in conditions that the historian Orlando Figes, in *A People's Tragedy*, has compared to a 'long Edwardian house party'. Tennis, dominoes and prayers filled their time as Nicholas awaited his undetermined fate. But later in the year, apparently amidst growing concern for their safety at the hands of the mob, the imperial family was removed to the town of Tobolsk in Siberia. There they stayed until the summer of 1918, when, in a ferment of revolutionary feuding over their fate, they were removed to Ekaterinburg. They were held here in a mansion commandeered from a rich merchant called Ipatiev. By now Trotsky was planning a show trial for the Tsar in which he would play the lead role as public prosecutor and was reported to have decided that 'the proceedings would be broadcast to the nation by radio'.

But events conspired to forestall even this rudimentary experiment in popular 'justice'. Trotsky's plan was scuppered by a combination of the pressure from an inflamed populace and the insistence of his revolutionary rivals that a swift and final solution was required. Early in July the order came secretly from Moscow, where the Bolsheviks had established their capital, that the entire family should be executed forthwith. In the early hours of the seventeenth, Tsar Nicholas, his wife Alexandra, their daughters – Olga (twenty-three), Tatiana (twenty-one), Maria (nineteen), Anastasia (seventeen) – and the heir to the throne, fourteen-year-old Alexei, accompanied by their doctor, a cook and two servants, were herded down to the small cellar, where they were ranged along a wall as though for a family photograph. One of their captors read out the formal order for their execution. There was a volley of shots that filled the cramped space with ricocheting bullets and acrid smoke. When it was clear enough to examine their handiwork, the killers saw that Alexei was still alive; they finished him off with two shots to the head. His sister Anastasia also showed signs of life. Bemused by this, the assassins untied her bodice to discover that some of the family's most precious jewels had been secreted in the cloth and that these had partially protected her from the indiscriminate spray of bullets. They put her out of her misery by stabbing her to death with a bayonet.

The royal remains were then removed secretly by truck to the forest on the outskirts of the city, where, to conceal what they had done, the killers mutilated the corpses and buried them beneath a canopy of fir trees in a shallow grave formed by a disused mineshaft. As Orlando Figes has noted – against those who have argued that the murder of the Romanovs was a mere footnote in the history of a mass revolution – the political significance of this single atrocity was that it constituted 'a declaration of the Terror'. Trotsky had once said, 'We must put an end once and for all to the papist-Quaker babble about the sanctity of human life.' In the decades to come, many millions of Russians were to pay the price for this Bolshevik value-system with their blood.

The scene of the murders – the Ipatiev House, as it was subsequently known – was soon turned into a museum to celebrate the Bolshevik revolution and the demise of tsarism. A while later it was reclassified as a Museum of Atheism. But in 1977, sixty years after the incarceration of the imperial family there, the head of the regional party committee, Boris Yeltsin – mindful perhaps that history would not look so kindly on the 'necessary' murder of these representatives of the *ancien régime* – ordered the Ipatiev House to be demolished. But the crime was not forgotten or forgiven.

In 1991, following the collapse of the Soviet Union, a team of archaeologists exhumed five of the bodies: those of the Tsar, his wife and three of their daughters. The whereabouts of his son Alexei and his third daughter, Maria, remained unknown. Seven years later, on 17 July 1998, the eightieth anniversary of the murders, the same Boris Yeltsin, now reinvented as his nation's democratic president, found himself in the place of honour at a funeral service in St Petersburg, where (minus the two missing corpses) the remains of the last of the Romanovs were reburied in the crypt of the St Catherine Chapel inside the St Peter and Paul Cathedral, alongside those of every tsar since Peter the Great. 'Today is a historic day for Russia,' the President intoned. 'For many years we kept quiet about this monstrous crime, but the truth has to be spoken.' Unhappily, this belated act of national reconciliation was somewhat marred by the refusal of the Patriarch, Alexei II, to attend the obsequies on the grounds that the scientific evidence had not proved conclusively that the corpses found in the Ekaterinburg forest were those of the imperial family.

Notwithstanding this controversy, the Tsar, his wife and all his children have since been canonized by the Russian Orthodox Church. This sanctification – a reassertion of what had for so long been an unholy alliance between the Orthodox Church and the imperial family – has now metamorphosed into a grandiose monastery that is nearing completion in the forest beside the disused mineshaft in which most of the bodies were initially dumped. The undertaking has been financed by a local oligarch, Andrey Kozitsyn, who now owns the mine that still produces abundant supplies of copper. I had expected to be impressed, but a notice at the entrance to the monastery inviting me – or rather instructing me – to be overawed had the opposite effect. 'In this beautiful forest' the souls of the imperial family had 'ascended into the heavens from where they shone through the gloom of atheism,' I read. 'We stand here transfixed into adoration before the unbelievable miracle of the holiness which becomes apparent to all those who visit this heavenly and earthly beauty and who are blessed by it.... When pilgrims visit the monastery they feel the divine will of God, as everything here is touched by the invisible holy relics of the tsarist martyrs.' There was more of the same; rather too much for an iconoclast to stomach easily.

So I meandered around this amphitheatre in the forest, wondering at the spiritual devotion – not to mention the roubles – required to create this shrine to an autocratic dynasty that, in the atavistic person of Nicholas II, had clung on to earthly power long after his time was up, and was still claiming, even in the twentieth century, that he ruled by divine right. Via a network of neat gravel paths a devotional pilgrim can walk from one royal chapel to another – seven in all, one for each of the murdered Romanovs. They are finely built in timber hewn from the forest, and the smell of freshly cut pine trees wafted through the glade. Golden onion domes shimmering in the late sun, soft green-tiled roofs and the blue sky canopying this newly consecrated land formed a magnificent vista, but the impact on me was somehow less than its creators might have hoped. It seemed not so much a shrine as a 'stately pleasure dome' decreed by a twenty-first-century triple alliance of the Orthodox Church, a neo-imperial state and the oligarchs who collectively order the temporal and spiritual affairs of the nation with an authoritarian grip that Nicholas II would have envied.

One of the monks, draped in dark robes, a full black beard framing a white face, led me into the church of the Holy Royal Martyrs. His demeanour was remote, austere and effortlessly sepulchral, his eyes focused on some far horizon beyond his uninvited guest. With a reverence that I did not doubt but that seemed decidedly idolatrous, he produced a large key from the folds of his cassock and unlocked a casket to produce a heavy golden crucifix encrusted in precious stones, which, he said, had once belonged to the Tsar. He looked at it longingly and did not speak. 'What is it worth?' I interrupted crassly. He glanced at me with distaste before replying coldly: 'It is beyond value. I do not measure or think about such considerations.' He replaced it in the casket and bade me a very detached farewell. I could hardly blame him.

Behind the church there was a raised covered walkway around an oval depression in the ground. A notice in English stated baldly: 'After July 17th 1918, near this mine No. 7, the bodies of the Holy Royal Martyrs of Russia were burned with the use of petrol and then destroyed by sulphuric acid.' Near by, overlooking the sunken memorial, there was a small wooden cross. It was surrounded by half a dozen bouquets, artificial flowers left by pilgrims. Pinned to the cross – haphazardly, as if an afterthought – I noticed a fading photograph protected by a tattered plastic folder. It showed the Romanov family posing for an official photograph. They stared out at the camera: Tsar Nicholas in military fatigues, the Empress wearing a small tiara, and, like her four daughters, strikingly beautiful in a plain white dress flowing to the ground. But it was Alexei, the haemophiliac heir to the throne, who caught my eye. Pale and frail, he was dressed in a sailor-boy's uniform, seeming to stare out with resignation at a future he would never know.

With that solemn little tableau in my mind, I found my way to another glade in the forest, where the murderers – who had in fact failed to destroy the evidence with either petrol or sulphuric acid – finally buried the scorched remains of the imperial family. They must have hoped that this would be their victims' final resting place, lost in the forest, never to be revealed. Today the shallow grave in which the Tsar, his wife and three of their daughters were dumped, is overgrown, marked only by a square of white stones and a cross to which someone has affixed a small brass plate on which are inscribed the words, 'Goodnight children. God bless you. Sleep tight.' I turned away, my eyes pricking with sudden tears at such tenderness.

A little further on I saw a large khaki tent in front of which smoke wafted into the trees from a fire that was heating a cauldron of stew. A girl was shaking herbs and pine nuts into the mixture, stirring it from time to time. She was preparing lunch for a squad of young men and women who were carefully excavating the thin soil with trowels, searching methodically for further evidence of the crime. Each square metre of ground was neatly pegged out and sealed off with string. So far the team had uncovered pieces of pottery and the rusty metal clasp and charred wood from a crate that had contained the jars of sulphuric acid. A fortnight before my arrival their labours had hit the Russian headlines because they had uncovered the bones of a young woman and a teenage boy, some of which had been semi-smashed with a pick-axe. Initial analysis suggested, and it was later confirmed beyond reasonable doubt, that these belonged to the other two royal children: the little sailor-boy and his sister Maria.

For many Russians the reports of this bleak discovery finally – well, almost finally – closed a long and tormented chapter in the history of their nation. But the painstaking dig in the forest will continue until every centimetre of ground has been combed for further evidence of what the archaeologist in charge, Sergey Pogorelov, described to me as 'this incredibly bloody and terrible crime'. As he sifted through the photographs he had taken as his team removed each bone, one by one, from the shallow ground, this mild-mannered scholar expressed his revulsion: 'Look at this. The bones you can see there – that skull has been hacked to pieces with what must have been sharpened spades – hacked and cut up as best they could into small pieces.'

Why, though, I wondered had he devoted so much – unpaid – time to a task that he obviously found gruesome? 'This site is not just archaeologically important, it is not just historically important,' he replied. 'It has religious and spiritual significance as well. You know that the Tsar and his family have been canonized. So what we found here are the holy relics of saints.' Did he believe that himself? 'I am not a religious man. I am an atheist. But I think a scientist, a professional like myself, should understand and respect the beliefs of all people.'

## A CONVERSATION WITH A DISSIDENT

The train journey from Ekaterinburg to Nizhnevartovsk, BP's oil capital in Siberia, a distance of some 1000 miles, was due to take thirty hours. I had relished the prospect of entering again that out-of-time, out-of-place bubble that is an escape from reality. It did not quite turn out like that. Before I left Ekaterinburg I had arranged to meet a former Russian dissident, Maria Vovchok. But our timetables clashed and I had to catch the train or miss my rendezvous with a BP oil rig. Happily, Maria said she would come part of the way with me. I had never met her before, but I recognized her at once. Tall and poised, she had elegantly coiffed blonde hair that framed a pale, delicate but resourceful face, the eyes set wide apart, not so much innocent as lacking all wariness. She had applied only the lightest touch of make-up, which suggested an understated sense of self that is rare in provincial Russia. I thought she must be in her early fifties, but later discovered that she was a few years older. She could easily have passed for a European émigrée, fresh from a salon in London or Paris or Rome. And – I indulged myself the small romance – she had about her a hint of the mysterious, as though she could have stepped out of *Smiley's People* or maybe *Birdsong*.

As the train lurched away from the station, we sat in my compartment with a cup of herbal tea each and she told me her story. 'It really started when I was a child. I was brought up here in Ekaterinburg – which was a closed city – where my parents were both university professors. They were liberals, typical members of the intelligentsia. And at home they talked about the regime quite openly, so that we grew up knowing that we were surrounded by lies. I never believed the Soviet system or the victory of Communism or any such nonsense – even though I took the precaution of joining the Komsomol [the youth wing of the Communist Party]. I was intensely bored. I felt the atmosphere was stifling. I wasn't free to move where I wanted or to say what I wanted. I was very fed up.

'Then I got a place at Leningrad State University to study English, hoping that one day I would be able to find work outside Russia. I just wanted to get out. Meanwhile, I worked as an interpreter for a branch of Intourist [the Russian tourist agency] in my spare time. And then in 1971, two months before I was due to graduate, I was asked to go on a delegation to Manchester with two other students, both of whom were senior members of the Komsomol. We arrived in Manchester as guests of the mayor. We were due to stay for a week. But three nights before we were due to leave, at 2.30 a.m. I got dressed, slipped out of my room, walked downstairs and out into the street. After a bit I saw a policeman. So I went up to him and said, "I am from Russia. I want to stay here. Please will you take me to the police station." He looked very surprised.

'At the station they were very friendly, but they seemed rather perplexed. They didn't seem to know what they should do. However, it was very cosy. They were drinking cups of tea and they were very enthusiastic because, I think, I was unexpected entertainment on their night shift. After a while someone made the decision to keep me in custody to protect me from the KGB. So I spent two days with them, sleeping in the doctor's office near the cells. On the third day a man arrived from London. He called himself Charles Wadworth. He told me that the Russian embassy in London had been alerted to my defection and that the KGB would be hunting for me. I had to get into his Jaguar, and he told me to lie on the back floor with a rug over me so that no one would see me. Once we got to London, they put me up in a bedsit in Putney – which was presumably a "safe house".'

Over the course of the next three months, she was taken twice a week to a building near the Ministry of Defence, where, over tea and biscuits, she was closely interrogated by officials from what she presumed to be the intelligence services. 'I was very impressed. Obviously I was an unusual case. I was young and I was female. It was clear they wanted to establish that I was not a "plant". They would show me photographs – Russian cityscapes and people – and I was asked to identify them. One of them was my biology teacher at school, another was a fellow student, others were friends and colleagues of my parents. I recognized most of them. MI6 clearly had a very good operation in Russia.'

Eventually the British government satisfied itself that Maria was genuine, and in March 1971 she was given a visa and a work permit. A few days later the Whitehall official, Charles Wadworth, took her to the offices of the BBC World Service at Bush House in the Strand. After passing a series of language and translation tests she was given a job in the Russian service, where she stayed for five years. From the BBC she moved to the Cold War propaganda station Radio Free Europe in Oxford Street as London Editor. Soon after that she moved to another arm of Western propaganda, beamed at the Eastern bloc from Munich, to work in the Russian service of Radio Liberty. She remained there until the station closed in 1995. A 'victim' of the collapse of the Soviet Union, she eventually found casual employment. But in 2003, alone in Germany following her divorce, she decided to return to her home-land. Although her family still lived in Ekaterinburg, it was not an easy decision and it had not been an easy re-immersion.

'It is exciting here. Life is very intense, so one really lives. But Russians are so rude. They are insensitive and sometimes they are cruel. So living here is not pleasant, it is not easy – it is hard.' And, for Maria, it was getting harder. Soon after her return she found a job working for the US Consul-General in Ekaterinburg as Assistant for Political and Economic Affairs. But her new appointment coincided with Russia's born-again assertiveness in foreign policy and with an ugly authoritarianism at home. 'Putin has been rolling back democ-racy. The NGOs that have been working in this field find it increasingly difficult to get grants; Russian NGOs haven't got any money, and their foreign partners find it virtually impossible now to get registered. Then there is the media. I find it deeply saddening that, after the wonderfully fresh and intrepid television reportage we had after *perestroika*, it is all over. We are back to the Soviet days again. It is vulgar and it is bland. And it is the same thing with the printed media. One or two papers say things in a veiled sort of way. But the rest....' She had spoken quietly, almost confidentially, but at this point her voice tailed away, defeated by the implacability of Putin's Russia.

Maria's work took her back and forth across the Ekaterinburg region to meet politicians and political analysts from across Russia's attenuated political spectrum. In the run-up to the December 2007 elections to the Duma, her job had become increasingly difficult. The steady deterioration in US–Soviet relations and Putin's strident nationalism meant that her contacts now regarded her with deepening suspicion. It was once again not politic for an aspiring party hack to be seen consorting with an 'agent' of the erstwhile adversary. Maria found this disconcerting and dangerous in a world where it is very important that major powers are able to communicate with one another on an informal basis. 'How can America understand Russia better without learning through the conversations I have – in private, off-the-record – with politicians and officials what really matters to them? It is the essence of diplomacy, the basis of trust and understanding. I mean, I am not a spy trying to get secret information. In the course of my work I have to talk with people.'

I wondered if her Russian contacts had come to regard her as some kind of fifth-columnist. She replied unhesitatingly: 'Yes, that is so. And I can tell you that people are becoming more and more fearful of dealing with us. People who used to come to consular receptions and who used to enjoy talking to the staff of the consulate have started to avoid such meetings. As it happens, I don't like Bush and I disapprove of his policies, but all this stuff from the Kremlin about "We are a super power once more" – all this jingoism – is having an effect. The Americans are "those Yanks" again, and I don't like it one little bit. And what is more, we have got our priorities all wrong. We have terrible social problems. The gap between the rich and the poor. Unwanted children discarded. Old people who practically starve because their pensions are so low. These should be the priorities. This concentration on our former glory is a false priority.'

As I listened to Maria's bleak analysis, I wondered why she did not 'defect' for a second time. 'It would be easier for me to live in the West,' she replied wistfully, looking out of the carriage window that, in the dusk, now reflected her image back at her, 'and I don't just mean in the material sense, but spiritually. However, I feel a sense of duty. I skipped a lot of contemporary Russian history. I wasn't there when things were happening, when the Soviet Union collapsed. I have to compensate for that. I can't do very much, but I can try. I think my place is here for the moment.'

We were more than three hours into the journey, and she would be leaving me at the next station. 'Maria,' I said, 'on my journey through Russia I have tried to understand. I see the authoritarian state that people either conspire with or ignore. I see the free press suppressed. I see the rule of law that doesn't function. I see endemic corruption. I see the powerful and the rich in cahoots with the Kremlin and the army and the security services. For me that is a pretty good description of a fascist state. Does that make sense to you?' She replied with the caveat that had hitherto stopped me asking that question. 'Well, for me there are different connotations with that term because, after all, I grew up in the Soviet Union, and for us fascists were Nazis. So this is different for us. I would not put it in those terms. But, yes, it is definitely authoritarian and it is getting worse. And if it goes on like this, everything will have been in vain.' She paused and then said, with unintended bathos, 'And that would be a pity.'

The train came to a halt. We embraced lightly and she stepped carefully down on to the platform. I watched her fade into the gloom, a resolute but saddened woman, set apart from her fellow passengers, who by comparison seemed to slouch from the station, burdened and tired, a stranger in her own land, an émigrée who would never be at home. 'And that,' I thought as she was swallowed up in the dark, 'would indeed be a pity.'

That night I slept fitfully, thoughts racing through my head about the nature of the Russian beast that Maria had described to me. Once, when the train jolted to a halt, I peered out of the window to see that we were at a small junction, deserted except for a station master and a handful of passengers laden with cases and boxes waiting to board.

Otherwise we seemed to be in the middle of a Siberian nowhere. Sometimes we even stopped in this nowhere, arrested between stations with nothing to be seen outside except those sentinel pines and above them the stars. Then it was silent except for the creak and occasional clang of metal from somewhere along the track. On one occasion I noted that we halted for twenty-seven minutes like this for no apparent reason. No wonder our average speed would be no more than 40 mph.

I reached for the cabin light and, flicking through my invaluable guide book, found some nuggets of history about the Russian railways. The first 15-mile stretch of track had been opened in 1836, when British steam engines were used to link St Petersburg to the Tsar's summer palace in Tsarskoe Selo. Fifty-five years later the first stone of the Trans-Siberian Railway was laid in Vladivostok, more than 5500 miles from Moscow, by the then heir to the throne, the ill-fated Nicholas II. The potted history also answered my nagging question about the timetable: why did we wait so long between stations and yet trains were never late at their destination? As I later confirmed with a helpful railway official, the reason is really very simple. Russia's vast and complex rail network has one over-riding operating principle: that trains should always be on time, that they should arrive on time and they should depart on time. This target is achieved by the simple device – subsequently adapted surreptitiously but with much less success by British rail operators – of drawing up a timetable that allows far more time than is needed to get from point to point. We were waiting in the wilderness to ensure that we did not arrive too early at the next station: we would duly arrive on time and we would leave on time. To sustain this punctuality principle, every train driver receives a bonus for keeping to schedule and a penalty for being either early or late. On this thirty-hour journey the system seemed to be working exceptionally well. I drifted back to sleep reassured that these matters were beyond my control, that these 'delays' – unlike those that make travelling by rail in Britain such an uncertain enterprise – were all part of the plan. As so much that is Russian, I mused, it was both remarkably efficient and totally inefficient.

## THE POLITICS OF OIL

By the next morning, fifteen hours into the journey, the landscape had perceptibly altered. The arable farms of the Ekaterinburg region – the fields of harvested corn and round bales of straw – had yielded to a colder, wilder terrain. Here the railway had been laid across the huge swamp that covers much of western Siberia. In winter this quagmire freezes, but in autumn it reveals itself in the form of lakes and ponds surrounded by scrubland interspersed with forest. The yellow, gold and russet of the birch leaves rustling to the ground in the chill wind driving from the east reminded me of Vermont in the fall, but on a much larger scale and – because the variety of trees is so much narrower – of an inferior splendour.

Feeling hungry, I negotiated my way down the corridor towards the restaurant car, sidling past female attendants, all of whom seemed to have been selected on account of their great girth to discourage any movement from one carriage to another and who looked at me with evident disapproval. I made way for other passengers, who likewise failed to respond with even a vestige of gratitude. Only once was it otherwise. When I pretended to fall down as a small boy fired his toy machine-gun at me, his father responded with a brief but collusive smile, momentarily bridging that cultural divide between the smilers and the non-smilers that makes it so easy to defame the Russian people for boorishness merely because they fail to copy our Western ways.

As if to confirm this self-rebuke, I was stopped between carriages by an overweight, bullet-headed young man wearing a bright orange T-shirt. He wanted to talk. Boasting that he had already consumed fifteen cans of lager, he was effusive and repetitive, but still quite cogent. Discovering that I was English, he said that he supported Arsenal. I told him that from where I lived in London, I could hear the roar when his team had scored. (I refrained from adding that match days were a purgatory of closed roads and police officers.) 'Are you a footballer?' I asked, looking at his spreading paunch. He replied without answering: 'I used to be very thin.' He asked for an American cigarette. I told him I did not smoke. He said he smoked twenty-five a day. With that intake of beer and cigarettes he seemed destined for entry into the statistics of premature death that alarm the demographers, so I said rather pompously, 'You'll kill yourself.' He replied, 'I started smoking when I was in the army. I was in Chechnya. You have your Iraq. We have Chechnya.' No more to be said. He put out his hand. 'My name is Radic.'

He was joined by a friend, who was no less effusively friendly, and they started to reminisce about their experience as conscripts when they served on the Chechen front in 2003. Interrupting each other frequently to add a detail or contradict a memory, they told me, 'What they tell you is not true. They say the government provides the conscripts with food, clothes and ammunition. But that is not true. The food is terrible and the pay – 4000 roubles a month – is not enough. And the regular soldiers, the professionals, who aren't paid that much more are driven to sell their weapons to the militants, to the enemy. You know what we ended up thinking? That the militants, the Muslims, are fighting for freedom, for the independence of their lands. And that the best of them become suicide bombers.

'Do you know what we have seen? Russian soldiers laundering money, ripping off the local economy. And they are killing kids. If my phone battery was working' – this was Radic speaking – 'I could show you the photos.' They continued almost in unison: 'If a Russian was killed, they would kill a Chechen in reprisal. They kill militants and civilians. They don't care. They bomb villages. It is a war against partisans.' Except for the weaponry now available, they could have been describing – like Tolstóy but without his insight – the conflict in the Caucasus a century and a half earlier. Radic's friend told me his name. 'I am Murzadin and I come from Dagestan.

You ask me, "Why are the Russians in Chechnya?" I ask you, "Why are the Americans in Iraq?"'

Radic and Murzadan were migrant workers on their way from southern Russia to Nizhnevartovsk. They were skilled welders, but there was no work at home and the oil boom in Siberia provided plenty of jobs. 'My life is typical,' said Radic. 'I come here for three months at a time. It is exhausting work, welding pipes and tubes. We don't get that much money, and we have to work a twelve-hour shift which starts at 6 a.m. It is dirt and it is sweat. I live in a dormitory. It is a very hard life. And I miss my family. If I could get work near home, I wouldn't leave them. But I have to do it. I have to earn the money.' As he said that, his eyes reddened and moistened. I was not sure whether it was from emotion or because of the smoke from his cigarette, which curled and wreathed round his head.

We arrived at the new but nondescript station of Nizhnevartovsk precisely on time, thirty hours after our departure from Ekaterinburg. It was just after midnight, it was raining and it took a long time for a surly taxi driver to decide that our custom was other than an unwarranted intrusion into his privacy. It was not the welcome for which I had hoped from one of the great oil cities of the modern world. Anyway, for once the hotel had a bath with a plug. I clambered into the hot water and soaked myself. Then, for the first time in two days, I slept like the ageing sybarite I sometimes imagine myself to be.

I had expected Nizhnevartovsk to reflect its Wild West, pioneering reputation as a 'black gold' Klondike. But the main street had no such identity, though it did seem to run in a straight line from nowhere to nowhere. On either side rows of blandly modern apartment blocks faced one another across a broad avenue. On one side, then the other, I saw a city hall, a shopping mall, an amusement park with go-carts, bars, restaurants and fast-food cafés. Nizhnevartovsk looked orderly and prosperous and entirely free of character, a here today, gone tomorrow sort of place without a story to tell. A lone orange flame burning off gas from an oil well, bright against a lowering sky in the distance, was the most, the only, visual hint that the city had a purpose. So much for first impressions.

Nizhnevartovsk does indeed have a 'back story', and a remarkable one at that; nor is it without that Wild West *frisson* for which I had hoped. Until the early years of the twentieth century the region was populated only by the indigenous Khati people, who lived by herding reindeer, hunting and fishing. It was not until 1909 that the first pioneering Russians, hunters and traders, settled here. They built a village of wooden huts in the swamp and a landing stage on the edge of the great river, the Ob, that they had navigated to reach this outback. Within fifteen years, there were enough settlers in this trading post for the village to be formally designated an identifiable 'soviet'. By the fifties it had been elevated to the status of a 'workers' village', home to a growing army of geologists, engineers and technicians, all of whom, according to state propaganda, had arrived in this desolate region as 'volunteers' for the greater good of the Soviet Union. This was not an accidental caravanserai. Preliminary surveys had suggested that the rock type and strata in the region would almost certainly yield an apparently limitless supply of oil. The geologists were proved right, and in September 1965 the prospectors were able to report to Moscow that the first geyser was on tap, spouting oil to the surface at the rate of 300 cubic metres a day. Today the city's PR people like to proclaim that the famous Samotlor oilfield, the largest in Russia, is still 'the biggest pearl' in the region's 'oil necklace'.

Over the last forty years Nizhnevartovsk has grown from a collection of wooden shacks into a city of a quarter of a million people, almost all of them prospering directly or indirectly from oil. And, though in the nature of the business it is bound to be a transient prosperity, the oil bosses have the unfeigned pride of genuine prospectors. They reel off statistics as if they were personally responsible for the geology of the region of which they are the industrious beneficiaries. At its peak in the mid-eighties, Samotlor yielded an annual 150 million tonnes of crude oil, which met more than 50 per cent of demand in the Soviet Union. So far, the accumulated total is 2.3 billion tonnes. In 2003 Samotlor changed hands thanks to a well-timed and canny move by Lord Browne, chief executive of the British oil giant, BP. Working closely with Blair and Putin, when relations between Britain and Russia were far more cordial, Browne constructed an elaborate deal with three Russian oligarchs (the joint owners of an amalgamated company called Alfa Access Renova) to form a fifty-fifty partnership called TNK-BP. The new company, in which BP invested $6.75 billion, was now the third-biggest oil producer in Russia and Samotlor was TNK-BP's 'pearl'. Although production from Samotlor has fallen sharply since the geyser-gushing days of the eighties to an annual 22 million tonnes, it remains the major source of Russian oil.

Accompanied by a posse of TNK-BP minders, who were far more attentive than the FSB had yet shown itself to be, I was escorted into one corner of Samotlor. We bounced down long mud tracks gouged out of the forest. Here and there small groups of workers, heavily muffled against a cutting wind, were using 'nodding donkeys' to suck the dregs of 'black gold' from the older wells. So if Samotlor were running out, I wondered, what did the future hold? My minders were – from the company's perspective – immensely reassuring. Apparently, as one seam runs dry the geologists discover yet more. Informally, they insisted that TNK-BP's assets in the region contained enough reserves – perhaps another billion tonnes – to keep Nizhnevartovsk afloat for at least another half century.

This figure sat a little uncomfortably with TNK-BP's publicly audited claim in 2006 that it possessed 'proved' reserves of just over a billion tonnes in total from all four of its Russian oilfields, located elsewhere in the region and in eastern Siberia. But when I pressed further, TNK-BP's most senior local officials became remarkably coy. Perhaps the precise figures are a commercial secret, perhaps – like so many producers – they cannot help but inflate the figures to reassure an ever more volatile and anxious market, or perhaps they simply didn't know.

When I asked Oleg Nam, the softly spoken and delightfully non-baronial regional boss of TNK-BP, if Nizhnevartovsk were living on borrowed time, he offered me a tour of the city by way of an answer. 'Look around you,' he riposted as we drove through the heavy flow of traffic – 4×4s in the ascendant – up and down and across the grid of avenues that make up the heart of the city. 'Look at the new church, look at the Palace of Arts, look at our puppet theatre, look at the new apartment blocks. Does it look as though it is a temporary place? We have good roads, clean drinking water, a centralized heating and hot-water system, which means that even in the coldest winter – and it can be very cold – we can live in comfort.'

I soon felt rebuked by Oleg's attachment to Nizhnevartovsk; once again ashamed of my instinctive sneer at the city's dreary consumerism. I asked him why he cared so much. 'This is the first place and the first time that my family has been able to imagine a settled future,' he replied. 'I am the child of refugee parents. My grandparents were victims of Stalin.' As Soviet citizens of Korean origin, they had been deported from Russia in 1936 to what is now Kazakhstan. It was during one of the periodic bouts of tension between the Soviet Union and the Japanese Empire. According to Oleg, Stalin feared that the Koreans in Russia would ally themselves with the enemy. 'So anyone with Korean features was exiled. The entire civilian population. My grandparents were given two hours to collect their belongings. They had eight children. My mother was six years old. In Kazakhstan they had nothing. Many of them were soon afterwards transported from Kazakhstan to Uzbekistan. There they were organized into "work units" and sent to labour in the uranium mines. They were always under suspicion. Many people died, especially the children. Can you imagine what it must have been like? To be taken from your traditional home? Not to speak the language, to have nothing?'

His family settled in Tashkent, where Oleg was born in 1953, the year of Stalin's death. He performed poorly at school. 'I had problems with Russian grammar but I was not allowed to speak Korean, so I was not at all academic.' In 1971, after his grandparents had died, his parents decided to 'emigrate' to Nizhnevartovsk. 'I remember very clearly when we had no roads here. We had to wade through the mud in thigh-boots. At the well-head itself we were up to our waist in mud – but look at our city now.' It was said with pride and affection.

TNK-BP not only provides most of the jobs in the town, but is also its principal charitable benefactor. Not surprisingly, therefore, Oleg is also a leading member of the town council. 'We have an international city here now. A new railway station and a new airport. People have come here from all over the Soviet Union, and now they come from all over the world. So we have an internationalist spirit here. Of course you may say that they came for the money, but many of them have stayed and that is because they had big hearts as well. People would not stay here just for the pay packet. And our population is still growing. So we are building more nursery schools, for example.' He paused for breath and, rather ungraciously, I repeated my earlier question: how long would it all last? This time he answered directly: 'If you take into account only the reserves we have now, then if we extract thirty million tonnes a year the town will flourish for at least another thirty years. But we are not going to rely on that and shrug our shoulders, because the exploration will continue. I am sure that we will discover new reserves. So I think the city could flourish for another seventy years, perhaps even more.' I felt that for him this vision of the future was as much about his roots – the new roots that he and his family had managed to put down in this unstable swamp that was now their home – as it was about oil.

There was another side to the story of Nizhnevartovsk and I heard it from a very reliable source, a Western oil man, who – for reasons that soon became clear – asked me not to name him. 'This town was indeed a Wild West sort of place, and until very recently. Until a few years ago, it was run by five rival gangs and they were ruthless. Fifteen years ago this was murder alley. It was crazy. Hardly a day went by without a mobster's killing. All the gangs were run by businessmen growing fat on oil. A new mayor was brought in to stamp out crime and to bring order to the town. In the process, of course, he upset a few people. One day he stepped out of his car and it blew up in his face. Literally. He recovered, but he has lost half his face. He was unable to continue as mayor, but his compensation – if that is the right term – is that he was appointed to the role of deputy. Now four of the gangs have been eliminated by the fifth, which now runs the place. And that is very much better for Nizhnevartovsk.'

Even so, security remains tight. When the head of TNK-BP 'upstream', Sergey Brezitsky, who has overall responsibility for the company's drilling operations, is in town, he stays in a company apartment in a new block near the centre of the city. 'Everyone knows when he is here because he is accompanied by a phalanx of body-guards at all times. They are on guard twenty-four hours a day at the entrance to his apartment.' Old scores still to be settled? 'No one of real power can afford to take the risk. The most powerful business-man in Nizhnevartovsk – I won't name him – now owns all the supermarkets. He builds sports complexes and he virtually runs the regional Olympic teams. And they say he is after the nightclubs as well. You should see what it is like when *he* is town. He always stays at the Pearl of Siberia – the grandest hotel in town.

'Wherever he goes he is accompanied by three "chase" cars and an army of bodyguards. I happened to be at the hotel once when he was coming out. I was looking out of a window. Suddenly one of them looked up and saw me. He pulled out his gun, and within moments there were four or five of them pointing their guns at me. Then he hurried out. He was bundled into the back of one of the limousines and roared off. That's how it is. Go into any of the grander restaurants in town – Imperial Plus, for example – and you will have to run a gauntlet of ten heavies if any of the city's big players have dropped in for dinner.' So, I mused, it was like the Wild West after all, but mani-cured to meet the needs of the twenty-first century – 'traditional values in a modern setting'.

The next day I met Dmitry Orlov, who had recently been promoted from his role as a managing director with TNK-BP to become the chief executive of one of the smaller companies that shelter under the TNK-BP umbrella. He was a walking caricature of an oil man; not so large as a stereotypical Texan, but just as formidable. He invited me to join him on the River Ob in a speedboat so that I could admire his city from the water. We zoomed up and down at 40 knots while he pointed out the same sights that Oleg Nam had shown me from his car. At that speed – the city stretches for about 4 miles along the foreshore – our trip did not take long. But it was impressive. And Dmitry was just as smitten by the city as Oleg. He had arrived here with his parents at the age of five in the seventies. After school he had joined the Soviet air force in the belief that he was officer material. But it was soon clear to his superiors that he was an unsuitable candidate and he was duly expelled from the service. 'I suppose,' he said with a swagger of hindsight, 'I was just not the kind of person to take orders from others.' He had blue eyes and he did not smile, but his manner was so cocky that he might easily have modelled himself on Marlon Brando in *The Wild Bunch*.

This impression was reinforced when he suggested I ride pillion on his motorbike for an evening's joyride with some friends. Saying 'boys' toys' to myself in a superior fashion, I accepted his invitation. There were six bikers in all, each one an oil executive with little better to do than race through the streets of Nizhnevartovsk at speeds up to 80 mph. It was anarchic, irresponsible, lawless and – perhaps therefore – an exhilarating if nerve-racking experience. Then I noticed Dmitry's precocious nine-year-old daughter (to whom he had given a quad bike for her birthday) riding pillion beside me on a Honda Gold Wing. She had refused to wear a helmet and her long blonde hair flew wildly about her head. Motorists kept a respectful distance from our posse or took avoiding action, but the cows that bizarrely threaded their way through the city streets showed a contemptuous indifference to our antics – which, in the case of one of our number, included the performance of 'wheelies' as he careered in and out of a bewildered flow of night-time traffic. I was told later that a shortage of fodder in the surrounding swampland drives the cows into the city centre, where they graze on the grass verges and in the public gardens. Another touch of the Wild West.

The next day I saw Dmitry again. No longer the middle-aged rebel without a cause in biker gear, he was now a hard-headed executive in a hard hat. We had endured a mud-spattered, four-wheeled drive along a rough track through the swamp to one of the scores of TNK-BP oil rigs that pockmark the wilderness. To make these tracks passable they have had to pour millions of tonnes of sand, dredged from the Ob, on to the surface of the swamp to soak up the surface water. This produces a thick slurry, which is in turn topped with tree trunks and branches on which they lay a hardcore surface. But nature is always rebelling; the tracks are always sinking. Trucks, diggers and graders are perpetually in motion to keep the roads open and the oil flowing.

It was raining and it was cold. We were standing in boots and over-alls bearing the TNK-BP company insignia in a forlorn, mud-covered clearing that must have been about 8 hectares in area. The rig stood in isolated splendour from the trucks, mobile canteens and offices that lined the perimeter. Like a rocket launcher bedecked by bright lights, it seemed to be awaiting the moment of lift-off. Figures ghostly in the murky light went purposefully about their business, measuring, cali-brating, loading, joining, assessing and checking. I was led up a long ladder into the innards of the rig, a chaos of cogs, wires and wheels. A clunking and clanging, whirring and whining of machinery made speech and comprehension impossible. I watched three men in a protective booth surrounded by dials and knobs. They did not speak to each other but concentrated intently, making small adjustments to their computerized controls as they electronically lowered a succession of hollow steel tubes, one on top of the other, deep into the drilled rock and along a sloping tunnel for a quarter of a mile until they could be immersed in the precious oil lake beneath, there to slake an insatiable thirst with the thick hot liquid that has seeped into the soul of our civilization. I imagined all the other rigs all over the world similarly slurping and sucking in the bowels of the earth until one day, like an old wet nurse with withered dugs, the source runs dry.

I climbed out on to a platform where it was suddenly quiet, and looked down at the fetid swamp and the broken, blackened trees that had been felled to make way for this oil moonscape. In the distance an orange flare glowed in the sky. I have always had a fantasy about New York – that one day tour buses will take visitors around the deserted archipelago of skyscrapers of that evacuated city. The tourists will wonder aloud, 'Did people really live here like that?' and the guide will answer, 'Yes, this is where our forebears used to live.' Now, on the rig, I similarly imagined the future after all the oil has gone. The roads will disappear, consumed by the bog. Bushes and shrubs will once again cover the ground, and the last vestiges of humanity's speculative footprint will be expunged for ever. In centuries to come archaeologists, using satellite imagery and other devices as yet unknown, will explore the site with wonder. They will discover that there was once a man-made 'field' in the wilderness, an outpost of an old civilization that produced billions of litres of a black liquid that was used to sustain every aspect of life on earth. Adventure tourists, dependent for their own lives on other technologies of which our generation has not yet dreamed, will scramble through the swamp to discover for themselves what had once been a wonder of the world – and they will themselves wonder at the ingenuity of primitive man.... Meanwhile, as I stood on the platform, the surviving trees, precious guardians of the planet's delicate ecology, seemed quietly to offer nature's rebuke to this greedy invasion. The autumn yellows and golds that fringed this industrial amphitheatre glittered in a sharpening wind, nodding and shaking and swaying. One day soon, its task fulfilled, the rig will be dismantled and the oil men's caravanserai will move on.

There is an unnerving paradox in Russia's self-proclaimed status as an 'energy superpower'. At its heart are two doom-laden words, 'Peak

Oil', which refer to that moment, which will assuredly arrive sooner than later, when demand for oil has not only outstripped supply, but the reserves are known to be running out. No one quite knows what will then happen. Will there be panic? Will oil prices break all barriers? Will there be a world recession? Will it be worse than that? A number of sober analysts predict a crash so severe as to usher in a new Dark Age almost as devastating in its impact as a nuclear holocaust. And if we are somehow spared this outcome, a severe disruption to the global economy is still widely assumed to be inevitable. Even a rush into alternative sources of energy – accelerated by fears about global warming – could not possibly be of the scale required to avert the crisis.

For the moment, 'Peak Oil' is still a term used mainly by energy 'anoraks'. In private, though, every thoughtful energy executive shivers at the prospect. It might appear that in such circumstances the world's self-proclaimed 'energy superpower' would, for a while, find itself in possession of a priceless resource, a hoard of black gold, to eke out at maximum profit. But if there were a slump or a crash, Russia would be no more immune from its devastating impact than any other nation. Black gold would be fool's gold. But that is in the future.

Dmitry is a man of today and likes to think of himself as a realist. As we stood beside the rig – 'The preliminary prediction is that it will be pumping out about five hundred tonnes a day,' he noted with satisfaction – I asked him whether he felt that this oil belonged to Russia or to TNK-BP. 'The oil is Russian oil – it is beneath Russian earth until it is exploited. Then you have the rigs and you process the oil. That is done by the companies. They pay tax and they create jobs. And most of the oil – so far as I know – stays in Russia. If it is exported, then there are more taxes to be paid. So it works very well.' But I was after a slightly different point. What did he think about Russia's new status as an 'energy superpower'? Did it give him pride? 'Of course I am proud that Russia has great wealth beneath our land. If we are sensible in the way it is exploited and in the way it is used, then it is something to be proud of.'

Dmitry's sentiment is widely shared; it is an emotional seam that the Kremlin has tapped with brutal resolve and from which, like other international prospectors, TNK-BP has not emerged unscathed. Putin's early enthusiasm for Western investment in Russia's strategic resources slowly evaporated. In a challenge to the White House's assertive foreign policy, he clearly decided to reassert Russia's national identity on the world stage. His strategic weapon, an immensely powerful one, was not of the military kind but lay under the surface of the Motherland. Massive reserves of oil and gas would both resurrect the domestic economy and be deployed at the front line to service Russian revanchism. In crude terms, Putin wanted the world to know that Russia intended once again to become a superpower and the world had better not forget it.

The Kremlin's volte-face began when Putin turned on Yukos, the company owned by Mikhail Khodorkovsky, the richest of all the oligarchs, who had dared to challenge the political hegemony of the Kremlin (for his *lèse-majesté*, he is now serving a long prison sentence in Siberia on a series of trumped-up 'fraud' charges). Yukos was subsequently declared bankrupt and its assets were sold off to its former rivals. Soon after that Shell was arbitrarily forced out of its oil- and gasfields off the island of Sakhalin in Russia's Far East, allegedly for breaching 'environmental' standards. Then came BP's turn. In June 2007 TNK-BP was arm-twisted into selling its controlling stake in Kovykta, one of the world's largest undeveloped gasfields, to Gazprom. This giant conglomerate has become one of the world's most powerful companies, with a valuation of more than $300 billion. It controls more than 90 per cent of all gas production in Russia (which has the largest gas reserves in the world); it controls more than 17 per cent of the world's known gas supplies, and it provides 25 per cent of the European Union's consumption of natural gas. Even more to the point, Gazprom's majority shareholder is the Russian Federation, which means in effect that the company is controlled by whoever is in charge in the Kremlin.

That the authorities in Moscow intended to humiliate TNK-BP became starkly clear when Putin criticized BP in public for 'doing nothing' at the Kovykta field – although he must have known that TNK-BP had in fact been unable to meet its agreed production targets because his very own Gazprom, which has a monopoly on gas exports, had failed to develop the necessary pipelines. The delivery of the *coup de grâce*, sanctioned and devised by the Kremlin, was given to Dmitry Medvedev – who happened to double as one of Putin's deputy prime ministers at the same time and in December 2007 was anointed by him as his successor. BP executives affected nonchalance at the forced sale to Gazprom, releasing banal public statements like 'We look forward to broadening our relationship with Gazprom' – as the fox might have said to the hound. At the suggestion that at some future date TNK-BP might be allowed to buy back a minority shareholding in Gazprom's Kovykta investment, Medvedev riposted patronizingly: 'To remain in a monastery one has to leave it, be purged of sin and return to it.' So much for BP.

No one believes that the Kremlin has finished its aggressive rena-tionalization of Russia's energy resources. Rumours abound, not least in Nizhnevartovsk, that in due course the state will also move to divest BP of its oil investments by another means of forced sale either to Gazprom or, more probably, to the other state-owned energy giant, Rosneft. When I asked Oleg Nam about this prospect, he answered valiantly, 'I don't think it will happen. At TNK-BP we are better at our jobs than Gazprom. Our job is to exploit our reserves as cheaply as we can and then sell the oil as expensively as we can. And if we do this well, then the government does well. You know, you can put forward all sorts of theo-ries, but my feeling is that there is no need for the government to have more control. I can't see anything to give us cause for fear.' When I put the same question to Dmitry he was more circumspect. 'That', he said, 'is a political issue. I have no comment.' Quite so.

After my day at the well-head, I found sanctuary back at Nizhnevartovsk in the company of a Glaswegian oil man called Colin

McCaffery, the only British expatriate working for TNK-BP in the region. A chemist by training who used to work for the Ministry of Defence, travelling the world on the nation's behalf as a member of the 'quality control directorate', Colin was headhunted by BP and now did the same for them. He had been married since 2005 to Johanna, a gentle and quiet Indonesian some twenty years younger than himself, whom he had met there seven years ago on one of his more than fifty 'troubleshooting' assignments for BP. I had seen similar people elsewhere: expatriates insulating themselves from the isolation of another culture with every kind of modern technology. Their spacious apartment in the centre of Nizhnevartovsk boasted not just video cameras but cameras of the webcam sort to communicate directly with friends and family in the Far East and Europe, a giant plasma TV screen on which to watch Celtic beat Rangers (or was it the other way round?), a stash of DVD players and VCR machines (most of which were about ready to be dumped on eBay) and of course a surround-sound system to rival the very best. Otherwise there were three plump sofas, some memorabilia from various oil platforms around the world, a cluster of framed photographs, one of which depicted a lifeboat, the *Queen Mother*, travelling at speed with Colin at the helm (he used to serve in the RNLI), and a drinks cabinet heavily laden with a careful selection of malt whiskies. The impression was that their residence here was temporary; it was not a home.

Colin himself was a delight: round-faced, bespectacled, gentle and blessed with a warm smile and a quick sense of humour in a city where it had struck me that there was very little to smile about – unless, of course, gushing oil in a ruined landscape has that effect on you. But Colin had the gift of making light of every travail and, in a *Life of Brian* sort of way, managing to look on the bright side of life even in Nizhnevartovsk. He was also very much his own man in a corporate world that was excessively secretive and jumpy. He started by telling me that, as I was a journalist, he had felt it his duty to inform the PR people at BP's head office in London that he proposed to meet me.

He had been urged not to divulge his thoughts and feelings about either BP or Russia, an injunction he clearly intended to ignore. He poured two sizeable whiskies and then invited me on a *tour d'horizon* of life in Nizhnevartovsk and with BP.

As it happened, he thought that BP was an exemplary employer. 'I get very well paid. You get enhancements for being abroad, and I get frequent breaks. In fact the company realizes that it is impossible to stay here for long without feeling the pressure. The temperature went down to minus 54 degrees centigrade one time last winter. And once it goes below minus 35 you can't go outside. I tried it once, walking by the river when it was minus 38, wanting to get some exercise. I lasted for thirty minutes and then my legs were gone. It was really painful. You can get numb in Scotland, but this was really pretty bad. So in winter we have to stay indoors. But BP helps to make it bearable. It's a company rule that all expatriates working in Siberia must leave the country for a vacation at least four times a year. I even have to produce the ticket stubs for both of us to prove that we've done it. It's a great bonus. The company pays and we get to go to Indonesia twice a year and to Scotland.'

Colin manages the production-loss team, a role that is simple to describe. 'My job is to deliver improved production. Better performance. More barrels of oil.' But it is less easy to achieve. 'My biggest task is to convince people who have been working in the same way for twenty, thirty, forty years that there is another, better way. You can understand it. Suddenly Colin McCaffery walks in from Scotland and has all the answers. So it's very hard to get that message across. Russians tend to operate in a command-and-control environment, where people are told exactly what to do and when to do it. But I can't just tell them. My job is done more by influence and encouragement. And that's quite a challenge.'

TNK-BP's PR team at the company's regional headquarters in Nizhnevartovsk – as hapless a duo as it is possible to imagine – had told me that I would not see any flares from the rigs on the Samotlor oilfield because the company was no longer expelling waste gas into the atmosphere (as they do in the Gulf). Colin sighed when I told him this. 'Of course you see gas flares. We are wasting millions of tonnes a year like this. BP wants to capture this gas as it provides all the energy needs of each oil rig, but TNK aren't used to thinking like this. It will take time.' And he added, 'You can't change a culture overnight. It's just not going to happen. You know, you can't have the audacity to come into someone else's country and try to change the way they've been living for a thousand years.'

Colin's cultural sensitivity was in such marked contrast to his expatriate counterpart at the emerald mine outside Ekaterinburg that I wondered whether, unlike Jimmy Wilde, he and his wife had been able to forge any friendships after almost a year in Nizhnevartovsk. 'At first, here as anywhere else in the world, you don't feel comfortable. New city. New people. It makes you apprehensive. But I'm learning with age you have to force yourself to get into it as quickly as possible. The more you try to blend in with the locals, the more accepted you become, and then you find people go out of their way to help you. When I arrived here for the first time I was, as ever, pretty frightened. You hear media stories, but you don't know what to expect. It took me at least a month to settle in.'

And? 'Well, it hasn't been at all easy. It's terrible to have to say it, but we stay in most of the time, watching DVDs or playing computer games. When we go out together people stare at us – not just because of the age difference, but because Johanna comes from Indonesia.' I knew that what he could not quite bring himself to say was that a good many Russians are not merely nationalistic but xenophobic if not racist as well. Instead he lowered his voice, as if he did not want Johanna to hear, and told me that they hardly went out to dinner in restaurants now – and for precisely the reason I had supposed. 'Once we were at a very good restaurant and we had a table just across the way from a Russian couple. I noticed that the man kept looking across at us, staring at Johanna. He was drinking heavily. Eventually he called to me and asked if I would join them for a moment. I went over to his table and in front of his wife, who looked very uncomfortable, he said to me in broken English, "I've been to Thailand. I know what the women there are like. You can have a lot of fun. I like Thai girls." And then he said, "We are staying here in…" – he named the hotel – "and I wonder if your girlfriend would like to come back with us and have some fun?" It was horrible' – Colin cringed at the memory – 'but I just turned around and walked away. He became abusive and said some very offensive things about Johanna. And then they left. I don't think that my wife would like you to know what has happened, but it did. Since then we haven't gone out very much, though each week Johanna does go to the International Women's Club for lunch.'

The more Colin told me, the more grisly his life in Siberia seemed to be. But he was remarkably resilient, without becoming – as so many in this very tough environment – coarsened by hardship. He returned to the challenges facing BP. Among his responsibilities he had to monitor TNK-BP's health-and-safety procedures – an exceptionally sensitive issue for BP itself after its lamentable record of the last few years. The explosion at a plant in Texas that killed fifteen workers in 2005, together with a ruptured pipeline in Alaska that caused a major oil spillage, followed by a number of explosions, flare-ups and fires have all had a catastrophic effect on BP's carefully nurtured image as a responsible global corporation.

Before his departure as chief executive, Lord Browne felt obliged to tell shareholders that 'safety' had been put at the top of the company's business. If Colin were right, BP had heeded that admirable commitment but to a gloriously ludicrous degree. Not content with introducing new procedures at BP drilling rigs, the company had initiated a safety programme in which everyone was obliged to participate. It was called STOP, and required every employee to warn a colleague, wherever they were, if he or she was observed taking even a minor risk with their own or another's safety. This warning is administered publicly by raising one hand in the air in the manner of a traffic policeman and saying, 'Stop'. In Nizhnevartovsk, according to Colin, the directive had been interpreted with such attention to detail that a poster rolled up on a shelf above head height was now regarded as a 'safety hazard'. 'Why?' I asked. 'Because it could fall off.' And then what? 'It might hit you in the eye.' Was he serious? 'Yes, absolutely.'

Every TNK-BP employee was issued with a Stop Card at the rate of two a month or twenty-four a year. 'This is of course an insane procedure,' Colin chortled. 'You have to fill in the card – which is really no more than a box-ticking exercise – to prove that you have stopped a colleague at least once in the prescribed period from taking a health or safety risk.' I asked for an example. 'Well, under the STOP rules you aren't supposed to walk downstairs – for instance, at head office where I'm based – without holding the banister with one hand. You mustn't read as you walk, nor use a mobile phone, nor carry any item that can't be held in one hand. If you do, someone will stop you and you will be "booked".'

And that is not the end of it. TNK-BP has recently introduced a new 'positive' Stop Card. 'One day I was walking down the stairs at head office, very carefully obeying the rules, when a cleaner stopped me at the bottom.' Colin chuckled with renewed hilarity. 'She had her "positive" Stop Card with her and she said, "I want to congratulate you for walking safely down the stairs."' I wondered if anyone else shared his mirth at the way in which a sound policy can be taken to ridiculous extremes. Not, it appeared, in Nizhnevartovsk. Later I decided to test the rules for myself. I walked down the main staircase at TNK-BP's HQ brazenly carrying a briefcase in one hand and speaking into a mobile phone that I was cradling in the other. To my disappointment, no one stopped me. Either standards were slipping or they knew I didn't count.

I was eager to leave Nizhnevartovsk, but I said goodbye to Colin with real regret. He had moral strength, tolerance and stamina – all of which, it seemed to me, he would need in abundance to survive his assignment there. But he had no doubts. 'We came out prepared to do two years. But I'm now settling in and I think I'd be happy to do three years – though I'd have to discuss that with my wife first. But it will take me three years to complete the job I'm doing, and I'd hate to walk away from it before it's finished.' I was quite certain that, given the choice, Johanna would return to her family in Jakarta (where both of them intend to settle one day), but equally sure that she was so devoted to Colin that she would never gainsay him. Three years it would be. I did not envy either of them.

## A JOURNEY ON THE OB

On a grey morning just after dawn I waited at the main landing stage to board the daily hydrofoil for the 300-mile trip down the River Ob from Nizhnevartovsk towards the ancient city of Tomsk. It was pouring with rain, but my spirits were high. I have been romantic about rivers ever since I had to learn the names of the most famous of them in geography lessons at school. The Ob is not one of the most famous rivers of the world, but it is the seventh longest. It flows north and west from high in the Altai mountains in China through Russia until it reaches the Arctic Ocean, 3360 miles from its source. I was only going to cover one-tenth of that distance, and it would take me ten hours at a cruising speed of 50 knots. There was a full complement of passengers, men and women with young children and babies, all looking tired and worn-down, the men haggard, the women overweight. They neither smiled nor talked as they struggled aboard, laden with awkward parcels and bulging cases. They were poorly dressed and their faces very often blotched by poor diets and too much vodka. It was clear that the prospect of this journey, which exhilarated me, was for them a routine discomfort that they would wish to have avoided, could they afford it, by taking a plane.

We pulled slowly away from the mist-shrouded city skyline and then the engines heaved and the hydrofoil lifted itself from the water, accelerating on to the plane like a prototype prehistoric monster. As we sped over the water, I sat by a window, peering through the Perspex and wiping away the condensation created by the fug of humanity around me, crammed into bucket-shop airline seats and hemmed in by the piles of luggage that littered the central aisle. Through the blur the Ob was a grey slick of water moving sluggishly if at all. I could just make out, perhaps half a mile away, a long, low bank edging a featureless and evidently deserted plain beyond. It was not the Dart, my home river, and to me the most beautiful in England, but the Ob did have a grim grandeur, a slow and majestic purpose that held me in thrall.

My mind drifted back to what I had read about the pioneers who had opened up Siberia in the eighteenth and early nineteenth centuries: to the buccaneers, explorers and adventurers; the hunters, trappers and traders; the botanists, geologists and topographers; the peasants, hungry for land or escaping serfdom; and the criminals and conmen who followed in their footsteps. They had done for the Wild East what their counterparts in America later did for the Wild West. Collectively they formed a nation of immigrants navigating and settling a barren land that, though they did not know it at the time, was greater in size than the entire United States and western Europe combined. As they advanced eastwards, they established forts and outposts that became towns that later turned into cities. And, as in America, they were distressingly careless about the rights of the indigenous tribes through whose ancestral lands they tramped with purposeful abandon. But by the mid-eighteenth century the new cities that they built boasted public libraries, museums, colleges, clubs and theatres. The well-to-do had established themselves in airy, spacious houses and – while the serfs in western Russia still endured unspeak-able hardship – the peasants in western and southern Siberia had food to spare and to sell. So, although the continental climate was extreme, the living was not, apparently, quite as harsh as the image I had always had; it was not merely a place of punishment into which you did not venture unless you had been 'sent' to Siberia.

Indeed, according to one renowned traveller writing in 1861, Siberia was very far from being beyond the pale of civilization. 'I was fascinated at every step by the cordiality and hospitality I met everywhere. I was fascinated by the richness and the abundance. Everywhere we were received as if we were in a friendly country, everywhere we were fed well, and when I asked how much I owed them, they didn't want to take anything, saying "Light a candle to God".' This account is the more telling because it was written by Polina Annenkova, the wife of one of the Decembrists, who had accompanied her husband into exile following the group's thwarted uprising against the Tsar in 1825. This is not to say that the Decembrists and their families lived off the fat of the land. The hard labour to which they had been sentenced in the early years of their incarceration took a dreadful toll. Some died of exhaustion and disease, others suffered such psychological trauma that it drove them insane. But many of those who survived their ordeal adapted to the privations and even flourished. The entrancing monotony beyond my porthole confirmed the point: that Siberia is remote and challenging and extreme, but what makes it dark and forbidding is not its topography or its climate but its history – the use to which this innocent vastness has been put by Russia's rulers and, most terribly of all, not by the tsars but by Stalin.

The Gulag system that Lenin had pioneered at Solovki reached its hideous apotheosis in Siberia. The precise figures are disputed, and in the end the numbers lose all meaning, but by the mid-thirties some 5 million Soviet citizens were incarcerated in forced-labour camps at any one time. By the time of Stalin's death in 1953, untold millions of these Soviet slaves had perished from disease and starvation. Hardened criminals, petty crooks, purged party members, prisoners of war, ethnic minorities suspected of disloyalty, dissident intellectuals – anyone who had been sentenced, however arbitrarily, to three years or more – entered the Gulag. In Siberia they not only worked in the mines, factories and farms, but, of even greater importance, they built much of the infrastructure – roads, railways, canals and dams – that makes economic and social life possible in this inhospitable region today. It is not an exaggeration, though it may seem cruel to mention it, but the citizens of modern Siberia owe much to the Gulag.

The system was dismantled in the late fifties, but the drive to develop and populate Siberia was undiminished. Huge industrial and construction projects, including the world's largest aluminium plant, attracted workers in their millions. They were joined by an army of 'youth' activists, members of the Komsomol, apparently inspired to realize the Soviet vision as volunteers. In return for their willingness to endure severe privation they were lionized as pioneers who were 'conquering new lands' and, perhaps rather more alluringly, the workers (but not the Komsomol) were paid higher wages and given special privileges for their families. During the Cold War the population of Siberia continued to grow as the Soviet leadership not only built more and more factories and processing plants near to the sources of energy and raw materials, but based a significant proportion of its army and air force in eastern Siberia on the military front line against the presumed threat from China. Siberia was very far from being the freezing, snow-covered desert of my imagination.

Every so often on our voyage up the Ob, the engines would be throttled back and the hydrofoil would lower itself plumply into the water. On the first occasion I thought for a moment we had been stricken by engine failure. I could still see only water and the vague outline of a wasteland through the blur of my window. Then, out of the murk, I saw a wooden landing stage with a huddle of people sheltering from the rain and waiting to board. Meanwhile, a handful of our passengers were waiting to disembark. The gangplank was lowered and there was a sudden rush in either direction. One of the two deckhands swiftly restored order, and I watched as the gaggle of departing passengers, men and women with their bags (supplies purchased in Nizhnevartovsk, I presumed), toiled up a steep mud bank, slipping and sliding on a stairway of waterlogged duckboards. They disappeared into the mist towards one of the many remote hamlets dotted along the Ob, back to their hand-to-mouth existence on their peasant holdings and as trappers and hunters.

The newcomers were a bedraggled bunch, pushing their way into the cabin for fear of losing a place. Their anxiety was justified; there were not enough seats. Two disconsolate passengers accepted the inevitable and retreated to the landing stage, resigned to waiting for the next boat, which would arrive two days later. But another, a young man who had evidently warded off the effects of the chill air with more than a tot of vodka, refused to accept defeat. He complained vehemently and tried to elbow his way below. As he stood precariously in the companionway, the skipper carefully edged his craft away from the landing stage until, at precisely the right moment – not too soon and not too late – the deckhand gave the unwary interloper a hefty but carefully calibrated shove in the chest. It was enough both to propel him ashore without danger and to ensure that he would fall into the water if he tried to reboard the craft, which now accelerated away, leaving him to gesticulate forlornly as we disappeared from view.

I invited myself into the wheelhouse where the skipper, Andrey Lukashin, attired in a well-pressed uniform with a peaked cap, gave me a warm welcome of the 'What brings you to this part of the world?' variety. 'So what do you think of Russia?' he asked. I countered by asking him the same question. 'We have lost more than we have gained,' was his immediate response, ticking off a familiar list of issues. 'We have lost our free education, we have lost our free healthcare and our social security has got worse.' 'Since when?' I enquired with faux-naive innocence. 'Since the end of the Soviet Union,' he replied, as by now I knew he would. He was thirty-three and for a moment I wondered whether he was indulging a premature nostalgia for the 'good old days' imbibed from his parents. But the collapse of the Soviet Union had been visited upon him at an impressionable age, when absolute security was suddenly replaced by total anarchy. Moreover, to him the history of the twentieth century was the story of another country that was far away and about which he had been taught virtually nothing: Stalin was a war hero and the Soviet Union a benign imperium, nothing more, nothing less. In any case, the present and the future were what mattered. And Andrey had real anxieties: where would he find the money to guarantee his son a place at the best state school? What would happen if one of his family became seriously ill? And what about his parents, whose pensions were now worth a fraction of what they been promised? How would he care for them?

And yet Andrey was not at all resentful. On the contrary, he appeared to relish his life afloat. He wore his authority as captain lightly, but had a natural assurance. As the windscreen wipers fought a losing battle with the rain, he pored over his charts, pointing out the shoals and hidden rocks – carefully marked, but hard to see in bad weather – that demand sound navigational skills and constant attention. Once he discovered that I liked messing about in boats, we shared notes like two water-rat conspirators. 'I have a romance with this river,' he said, 'and I know every twist and turn. I must have been up and down this stretch more than one hundred times. And it is a satisfying life. I provide an important service to the people who live in this region. At this time of year, boats are the only means of transport. There are no roads, no airstrips and no railway. It is swamp and sparsely inhabited. So I am the only means of contact that people have.' He pointed out a tug that approached on our port side. Slowing down, he brought the hydrofoil neatly alongside and one of our passengers disembarked, stepping carefully on to the grimy deck of the river workhorse at what was obviously a pre-arranged rendezvous. Andrey also handed his counterpart on the tug a letter. 'So you are a postman as well?' I asked. 'Yes, I am,' he smiled, 'but only in the summer.'

In the second half of October the hydrofoil service is suspended until the following May, as by then the Ob starts to freeze over and is too dangerous to navigate. But, from the point of view of the inhabitants along the route, all is very much not lost. On the contrary, the ice is soon a metre thick and the Ob becomes strong enough to carry heavy trucks. For a moment I had visions of a huge ice rink, an adventure playground with purpose. But it is not quite like that. The river does not freeze evenly or uniformly but is corrugated by irregular frozen waves. Graders and levellers are brought in to scrape a highway through the ice, which then has to be navigated with almost as much care as the river in full flood. As Andrey explained all this, we entered a patch of choppy water. The hydrofoil started to judder and bounce, and he reduced speed until the motion was once again comfortable. I looked at the whitecaps whipped up by the wind on the waves and, as all sailors do, imagined really bad weather. Andrey confirmed my guess-work. 'Oh, yes. Sometimes we have violent storms with huge waves up to two metres in height. It is impossible to plane in this kind of weather. We have to crawl forward, hardly making any progress at all. Sometimes we arrive several hours late, and occasionally not until the next day.' After ten hours of uneventful navigation, I thanked our skip-per for getting me to my destination on time. 'It's a pleasure,' he replied, adding a sentiment that I had not heard before from any public servant in Russia. 'We are always pleased to have guests on board.'

We had arrived at another little waterside settlement. It was six o'clock in the evening, and still raining as steadily as it had been twelve hours earlier. I climbed up the duckboards over the mud and found the bus that was to take us to Tomsk. Seven hours later, most of it along an unmade road, we reached the highway on the outskirts of this old Siberian city.

Tomsk feels like a backwater, and none the worse for that. I took a tram downtown, past a well-kept park and a succession of neat little formal gardens that edged a scatter of theatres, museums and churches and found my way to a leafy enclave of wooden houses in the very heart of the city. Many of these had obviously been restored to remind the visitor of the glory days when Tomsk was a centre of culture and learning, home of Siberia's first university, opened in 1878. There is a prevailing myth that the city owes its relative gentility to the late nine-teenth-century city fathers who refused to accommodate the new Trans-Siberian Railway, which was due to pass through Tomsk. The truth is more prosaic: the width of the river and the depth of the swamp on either side of the Ob would have made the engineering feat required to span the two banks here uneconomic. Instead, the course of the railway was diverted 30 miles to the south, where the river is much narrower. Nonetheless the citizens of this ancient city – in 2004 it celebrated the four hundreth anniversary of its foundation by Tsar Boris Godunov – do seem to relish its reputation for being out of the mainstream. Although Tomsk is an industrial centre that benefits from a plutonium production and uranium enrichment plant some 10 miles to the south, its burghers prefer to draw the visitor's attention to the manufacture of matches, furniture, pencils, paints and dyes for which Tomsk is renowned.

In this reassuringly provincial setting I was startled to see a large poster that bore, in capital letters, the two words 'LED ZEPPELIN'. It seemed gloriously out of place and time, but the sight of it gave me a sudden nostalgic *frisson*. Almost four decades ago, I had found myself, rather by accident, at the Bath Blues Festival. The event took place without great fanfare in June 1970, but those who were 'in attendance' – it now seems like a royal occasion – will reminisce about that momentous weekend into their dotage because it was there that Led Zeppelin made its first appearance in Britain in front of a crowd of 150,000. I must have been the only BBC journalist on site, because I got a message that the *Today* programme, in the person of its anchorman Jack de Manio, wished to interview me at 7.15 a.m. the following day. The event had hit the tabloid headlines with lurid reports of running battles between Hell's Angels and drug-crazed fans. Inevitably, therefore, De Manio's first gravel-toned questions were about the presumed chaos. Could I describe what had been going on? How bad was it? As I had been wholly seduced by the music and had witnessed no violence at all, I diverted the interview into what I like to think was a vivid description of the scene around me: the fans now asleep, lovers entwined, the tents submerged in the mud, the embers of a thousand campfires and the drift of wood smoke. The scene was, I reported with a hyperbole that now makes me wince, 'like a Roman encampment of peace'. Afterwards *Today*'s producer thanked me so curtly that I presumed he had concluded that I had dosed myself to the eyeballs with cannabis or worse (which I hadn't), but I had clearly done nothing to advance my career. Yet the following day I had a call from the editor of *The World at One*, renowned at Broadcasting House for being a troublesome iconoclast and a contemptuous adversary of the rival *Today* programme. 'Hello, Jonathan,' Andrew Boyle said. 'I heard you at that festival. How would you like to come and work for *The World at One*?' I packed my bags a few days later on my way to what I hoped would be a glittering future, ever grateful to Led Zeppelin and a fan for life.

Unhappily, I soon discovered that Tomsk was not about to host a Siberian warm-up concert by my heroes as a prequel to their imminent reunion in London. The poster was merely advertising the group's decision to make its entire backlist (much in demand in Russia) available for fans to purchase online. So instead of rushing in search of the Sports Palace, where they would have filled the stadium, I sat near the river in the late afternoon, watching the sun sink over the water, and reminded myself of a facet of the city's past that, I soon discovered, did not sit comfortably with the congenial provincialism by which, until that moment, I had felt myself to be surrounded.

In the late nineteenth century Tomsk, already establishing its reputation as a centre of excellence, had also become a staging post and dumping ground for a forlorn exodus from western Russia of both common criminals and political dissidents – the latter convicted as felons and sentenced to exile in Siberia without right of appeal and often in ignorance of the charges laid against them. After sentence these 'nihilists, terrorists, and malcontents', as one contemporary apologist described them, were dispatched from Moscow or St Petersburg to Kazan, on the 'Russian' side of the Urals. There they were herded on to trains or barges (similar to those on which Gorky found work as a deckhand) for the journey to Tiumen, the westernmost city in Siberia.

In the summer of 1885 the American traveller George Kennan witnessed at first hand the atrocious conditions in which they were held there. In one cell he counted 160 men in an area measuring 10.7 by 7.6 metres. 'Every cubic foot of it had apparently been respired over and over again until it did not contain an atom of oxygen,' he wrote later. 'It was laden with fever germs from the unventilated hospital wards, fetid odors from diseased human lungs and unclean human bodies, and the stench arising from unemptied excrement buckets.' According to the historian W. Bruce Lincoln in *The Conquest of a Continent*, some fifteen thousand prisoners a year, often accompanied by their wives and children, were reputed to have passed through Tiumen on their way into exile. But one-third of them died before they could be dispatched deeper into Siberia. 'Tiumen's death rate during the 1870s and 1880s,' he noted, 'was twice that of London during the Great Plague of 1665 and higher, even, than the death rate of the bubonic plague that decimated a quarter of Europe in the fourteenth century.' The survivors continued their dolorous journey by barge along the very same stretch of the Ob by which, I reflected ruefully, I had been so ignorantly entranced on my hydrofoil trip.

When they reached Tomsk, the prisoners were once again herded into transit camps that smelt as foul and were as filthy as those they had left ten days earlier in Tiumen. According to Kennan's first-hand testimony, one of the hurriedly erected sheds in which they were confined 'was surrounded by a foul ditch half full of filth, into which water or urine was dripping from the floor which had given way here and there and the inmates had used the holes as places into which to throw refuse and pour slops and excrement.' For the prisoners and their families it must have been a relief to escape these degrading conditions, even though that meant a further three-month journey on foot to the city of Irkutsk, 1000 miles to the east, where they would finally be dispersed to the work camps or places of exile to which they had been assigned. Of course, Siberia was also a pioneers' paradise and, for runaway or liberated serfs, a place of refuge, not exile. But, as so often in Russia's past, you turn over stones of hope and reveal despair.

## THE PLUNDERING OF THE TAIGA

On the promenade at the edge of the Ob there is a bronze statue of one of Russia's great writers, Anton Chekhov. The sculptor clearly had a sense of humour: the author is depicted wearing a large floppy hat and carrying an umbrella. Yet the eye is drawn not to his head but to his feet, which are abnormally large. The effect is to make the great man appear as quaintly ridiculous as a circus clown. It was explained to me that the perspective was intentionally that of a drunk lying in the gutter. The work was apparently commissioned as a tongue-in-cheek retaliation for Chekhov's notoriously unflattering account of Siberia's citadel of intellectual ferment. In 1890 he passed through Tomsk on a long and gruelling journey to the notorious penal colony on the island of Sakhalin in the Russian Far East on the edge of the Pacific. There, in an excoriating denunciation of the Empire's penal system, he wrote of his experience of witnessing the 'extreme limits of degradation'. But the holding camps in Tomsk had evidently escaped his attention. 'Tomsk is a very dull town,' he wrote to his sister, 'to judge from the drunkards whose acquaintance I have made, and from the intellectual people who have come to the hotel to pay their respects to me, the inhabitants are very dull too.'

Times have clearly changed. The professor of biology who came to greet me at my hotel the next day was very far from dull. Sergey Kirpotin is an ecologist of international repute and a very worried scientist indeed. He speaks excellent English and became my delightful companion for a seven-hour journey deep into the forest. Our destination was a logging camp run by one of the largest timber firms operating out of Tomsk. Some three hours from the city the road became too rough for any but an off-road vehicle, so we transferred to a four-wheel-drive bus that reminded me of the yellow 'ducks' that take tourists up and down and around the River Thames to see the sights of London. The next stage of our journey was like driving through a battlefield: the forest razed and burnt, the ground gouged by bulldozers, shallow craters filled with fetid water, tree stumps breaking through the surface as if struggling for oxygen, branches torn from their trunks but too small to be of any economic use piled up haphazardly like funeral pyres, and, at the perimeter of this destruction, trees at drunken angles, wounded but not felled by the grim reaper scything through the forest.

Sergey observed this ecological genocide with dismay, taking photos through the side window to bear witness. I felt myself to be with a kindred spirit. In a modest way I have long been on the periphery of the environmental debate and I am also one of those who are prone to be mocked by philistines – the Prince of Wales is chastised with particular venom – for having the urge and sometimes the irrepressible need to 'hug' a tree. In this respect the firs and pines in this part of the forest did not compete for my attentions with the English oak, ash or beech, but they had been there for more than a century and they did have the nobility of age as well as a crucial role in sustaining our life on earth. I shared these feelings with Sergey, who confirmed my impression that for him too trees had a spiritual as well as an economic and an ecological value. It is, though, the latter two characteristics that most immediately concern Sergey and other scientists in Russia and around the world.

Almost 70 per cent of Russia's total land area is forested; this vast expanse is about the same size as the landmass of the United States and contains approximately 20 per cent of the world's timber. Most of this wealth is situated in the Siberian taiga – the belt of poor, thin, cold, acidic soil sandwiched between the tundra to the north and the steppe to the south. It is hard to exaggerate the environmental and economic importance of the larch, spruce, pine and birch that form this precious forest. According to the World Resources Institute, the accelerating destruction of the world's forests (at the rate of 16 billion hectares a year, by the most recent count) is 'brutally degrading' the ecosystems that depend upon them. In Siberia's case, this means not only bears, wolves, lynx, racoons, foxes and weasels; not only golden eagles, rough-legged buzzards, grouse, white-throated sparrows, black-throated green warblers and the Siberian thrush; but, from the top to the bottom of the food chain, more than 70 per cent of the world's most endangered species of mammals, 40 per cent of birds, 55 per cent of amphibians and almost 70 per cent of reptiles that depend upon an ecosystem that is itself crucial to sustaining the global environment on which all life on earth ultimately depends.

Siberia's so-called 'frontier' forests (those that have never been harvested) are also 'carbon sinks', sequestering some 435 billion tonnes of carbon. This is more than the global total of carbon that would be emitted over the next sixty-five years by burning fossil fuels and manufacturing cement at the present rate. Leaving aside humanity's need for wild spaces, these statistics highlight the crucial – but widely underestimated – role of the Siberian forest in combating climate change. But this resource is under threat. The demand for timber, not only from within Russia but also from China, Japan and Korea, has been growing rapidly. In the nineties one of Russia's leading specialists, Alexey Grigoriev, complained, 'We are in the grip of a mafia economy that sells these resources in order to import such necessities as Mars and Snickers,' neatly pointing out that the value of exported Siberian timber was roughly equivalent to the $2 billion that Russia spent on the import of Western chocolates and sweets. At the 2002 Earth Summit delegates heard in detail about the impact of the economic anarchy that followed the collapse of Communism. For most of the nineties the newly privatized logging companies were permitted to operate without constraint over vast swathes of virgin taiga, the 'rights' to this serial degradation sold off to them by a cash-strapped central government. Export controls were lifted and corrupt officials 'licensed' illegal logging on a grand scale. Virtually all Soviet controls that had been introduced to protect the forest wilderness were lifted or ignored. In the last few years this wilful abuse has supposedly been confronted by a stricter adherence to the pre-existing laws, but the planet's Siberian heritage remains under severe threat.

On our way deeper into the forest we passed the ruins of a deserted village, one of many strewn throughout the taiga. All we could see from our wildly swaying bus were the remnants of houses, roofs stoved in, and garden plots over-run by undergrowth and freshly sprouting birch trees. Before the revolution these villages had thrived. Their inhabitants, many of them 'Old Believers' – Christian dissidents escaping the persecution of the Orthodox Church – lived in the forest, clearing enough land to grow vegetables and raise a few cows, pigs and chickens. They were hunters and fishermen who also harvested the 'fruits' of the forest – berries, nuts, honey and mushrooms – to sell in local markets. But after the revolution, the Kremlin's tentacles eventually reached even into this remote region. The peasants were corralled into collective farms, and the delicate structure of an independent and sustainable life on the margins of the money economy imploded. Despite the new schools and health clinics that the Soviet ideologues had contrived to believe would establish a Communist nirvana in this untamed land, the population started to fall. The erosion accelerated over the decades, and by time the Soviet Union was in its death throes only a handful of old people – with admirable obstinacy – clung on, choosing to end their days where their parents had been born and they had been reared.

After three hours jolting along an increasingly treacherous mud track that threatened to suck our 'duck' under, we reached a logging depot where forty or more flatbed timber lorries were lined up as though at the start of a truckers' Derby. Here we transferred to a tracked vehicle that looked very much like a British Scorpion tank. The engine whined and roared and spluttered, carbon fumes belching from a chimney set low on the snub-nosed bonnet of our terrain-busting vehicle – but it was clearly the only way of surmounting the broken tree trunks and branches, cavernous ruts and deep, glutinous mud through which we had to pass. After a spine-crunching journey of a further two hours, our chain-smoking driver navigated us into a clearing, where two rows of wooden huts, painted incongruously in pink with windows picked out in pale blue, heralded our arrival at the loggers' camp.

From there we walked for a mile or more to the front line, following a rough path hacked through the trees, which opened to reveal a new wasteland of fallen firs. The smell of newly cut wood and pine needles wafted towards us. In the distance we could see the outline of two large machines, wheeling, advancing and retreating in a macabre gavotte on the edge of the clearing. A pine tree at least 30 metres high suddenly appeared to detach itself from its fellows, rising into the air, its upper branches swaying, and then glided sideways across the edge of the forest. It stopped, it hovered and then it keeled over like a guardsman fainting on parade, falling to the ground with a terminal crash. As we got closer to the two machines, I began to make out the meaning of the dance. One of them was a giant JCB-lookalike, an American monster. But instead of a jointed arm with an earth-scooping bucket at the bottom, it had one arm taller than a telegraph pole and bolted upright to the chassis. Attached to this were three robot arms, one above the other some 2 metres apart, ready to clasp their victim in a deathly embrace. At the base of the machine was a high-speed circular saw about 60 centimetres in diameter.

As we watched, the machine positioned itself in front of a tree that had a girth of about 1.25 metres. It nudged towards it until the three open arms were in place around the trunk. The saw, shiny and sharp, lightly touched the base of the tree about 20 centimetres from the ground. High in his cab the driver engaged a lever and eased forward, pressing against the trunk, the saw spinning at high speed and entering the flesh of the wood. The tree shivered and paused for a moment, as if undecided, before toppling forward to be gripped tightly by the mechanical arms, like a monster with a maiden flailing her arms in impotent distress. The machine backed away, turned around and dumped the severed trunk on to a growing pile of felled timber. The entire operation had taken no more than thirty seconds. As the machine reversed towards its next victim, the second machine arrived to chain itself to four of the felled trees. It towed them away to another area, where the branches were stripped until the trunks were naked and ready to be dragged away by a third vehicle, resembling a giant quad bike, to be laid out, like so many corpses piled on top of one another, waiting for the winter trucks that would cart them away to be turned into chipboard for sale to Uzbekistan and Kazakhstan. This year, for this purpose, this company alone would fell 750,000 trees.

Sergey looked on in dismay, familiar with the process, but far from reconciled to it. 'This is a ravaged land. The management is poor. The ground despoiled. It is a ferocious destruction of the forest. It is sad to see that there has been no replanting. So the forest will disappear altogether,' he said with the bleak acceptance of someone who knows that it is folly, but that it is also the way of the world. We were accompanied by the deputy director of the logging company, a large, heavy, weatherbeaten lumberjack, whose broad, crevassed face reminded me of the furrowed track along which we had bumped and tumbled to reach this killing field. I was disposed to dislike him not so much because his demeanour was forbidding, but because of what he represented. But that evening over supper in the canteen I found myself warming to him, and I don't think it was just the vodka. His name, appropriately, was Boris – Boreal Boris, I nicknamed him to myself. I asked him whether he cared about the forest. 'I love the forest. I grew up here. Of course I love the forest,' he replied, and he clearly meant it. 'But the forest has to be cut. If it is cut, we get a salary and we get the wood that we all need. Of course the forest is exploited, but not so very much.' 'Don't you ever feel you are destroying something?' I asked, thinking of the hundreds of thousands, soon millions, of doomed trees in his own small patch. 'We understand nature,' he replied, 'and we know that this wood would rot and fall and do even more damage to nature than if we cut it down.' The sincerity but paucity of this response finally provoked Sergey, who had hitherto kept his counsel. 'I have different feelings because I feel that trees are living organisms and if we cut them, I feel in my heart that what is happening is wrong. But what we need is a better system of forestry management. With a better system of management we could even improve our forests.' So how bad was the management here? 'It is not bad by Russian standards, but it is not good by world standards or by comparison with Scandinavia.' Boris did not react except to repeat that his business was conducted on sound, if not flawless, principles.

'This work is an extreme challenge for both people and equipment,' he continued, changing the subject. 'We can only cut at the most for six months of the year. For the rest of the time it is too cold. And that is also why you saw the timber piled up. The trucks can't get through the bog to get here – you know what it is like. They have to wait until the ground is snow-covered and frozen. Once the surface of the bog is frozen solid, when the temperature is down to minus twenty or even lower, we grade the track that you came along, and the trucks come in and out one after the other, driving fully loaded, at 50 miles an hour' – I raised my eyebrows – ' yes, on the ice with special tyres that speed is quite possible. And they have no choice. They have to drive at speed to get the timber out of here before the thaw. So you see our work is very extreme, very intense.'

I had read a report produced by Greenpeace that suggested that up to 50 per cent of the timber felled in Siberia is harvested illegally by unlicensed operators. 'Of course we have problems, even here in Tomsk,' Boris conceded, 'but it is not nearly so bad as further east, especially near the border with China. There people are cutting down trees that should be saved. And it is very wrong.' 'And they bribe officials?' I asked, rubbing my thumb against my fingers in the universal gesture. 'Yes, of course, and they trade under false names as well.' 'So why doesn't anyone stop it?' Boris shrugged his shoulders to imply that that was how things were in Russia, beyond his control. The situation was, Sergey and I agreed, deeply depressing. Boris nodded,

Eeyore-like, ruminating on fate. Then, unexpectedly, he started to hold forth, revealing far deeper feelings than I had supposed him to possess. The federal authorities, he insisted, were really making some effort to conserve the forests, but the odds in the marketplace were stacked against them. Chinese timber brokers were among the worst offenders. They had moved into Siberia, usually carrying false passports or temporary business visas. They negotiated local deals to export huge quantities of raw timber across the border to northern China, where Beijing had forbidden all logging. These Chinese merchants now controlled much of the timber trade in Siberia, Boris explained, selecting and harvesting the most valuable wood with no care at all for sustainability. Organized crime, in the form of the Chinese Triads, was deeply embedded in this illicit business.

On a smaller scale, he continued, there were any number of other scams. It was common, for example, for exporters to label high-quality timber as pulp-grade logs that attracted lower export taxes. The true value of the timber was negotiated in secret, and an under-the-counter price agreed to the mutual benefit of buyer and seller. Another ploy was arson, rife in the Tomsk region as elsewhere in the taiga. Under the existing regulations, timber merchants could acquire a logging licence at a significantly lower price if it were to clear a fire-damaged area of forest. The temptation was obvious, and many yielded. Boris, who had earlier been so stolidly fatalistic, now shook his head and said with quiet vehemence, 'It is a very great shame.' He then added, 'It was very much better in Soviet times – far more controlled.'

I proposed a toast. The following day was Foresters' Day, which meant that the machines would be silent and no trees would be felled. 'To the Forest and the Foresters,' I declared. We clinked glasses and drained the last of the vodka and stumbled off to bed.

The next morning, Sergey led me off to look more closely at the natural ecology of the forest. We walked down a steep track, tripping over roots and assailed even on a cool autumn day by mosquitoes, through firs and pines, aspens and birches, trees that had last been harvested while Nicholas II was still apparently secure on the imperial throne over a hundred years earlier. A weak sun had just managed to pierce through the protective canopy to illuminate the differing soft tones of green that distinguished one species from another. Sergey explained that in the taiga the faster-growing birches and aspens protected the firs and the pines, which were the more valuable crop. And he gave me one of those Siberian statistics that boggle the mind. 'The Tomsk region, which is one-tenth the area of western Siberia, is approximately the size of France and sixty per cent of this land is covered by forest. Scientists used to believe that the tropical forests were more important than the Siberian forest, but they now realize that the converse is true. Tropical forests produce oxygen by day but a huge amount of carbon dioxide by night. The Siberian forest has a different balance, and overall expels much more oxygen into the atmosphere. This is very, very important for combating global warming. They are sinks for carbon dioxide, which has been sequestrated here over thousands of years.'

I followed Sergey further down the slope until we reached the edge of a bog in which stunted trees stood drunkenly in hideous array as he elaborated, 'You know that this too is important. It is not beautiful to you, perhaps, but it is important. The trees are small and thin because they are growing on peat, and I think it is quite a deep layer of peat. This process began after the last ice age, more than ten thousand years ago. In that time western Siberia was covered by a wide variety of bogs. As peat accumulates, it sequestrates carbon dioxide from the atmosphere. Gradually the peat rises and the trees drown. If the process is left to nature, new trees will grow eventually to replace those that have drowned in the bog. These bogs form a crucial part of the world's carbon sink.' 'How crucial?' I asked. 'We believe that the bog ecosystems in western Siberia contain about twenty-six per cent of the carbon dioxide that has been sequestrated by the world's terrestrial ecosystems.'

That was not all. 'We have growing evidence that the bogs in the northern parts of Siberia are quite different from those in the southern part where we are now. There, in the north, it is a huge area of permafrost covered by frozen bogs. And what is happening to these bogs is very, very disturbing.' Sergey now became visibly, and uncharacteristically, agitated. 'Do you know that, about five or six years ago, the process of permafrost melting started in this area? You know why that matters?' He hurried on, not waiting for a reply. 'Methane is bubbling to the surface of the bog as it melts and is being expelled into the atmosphere. This is really very dangerous. The process has already been identified in eastern Siberia, where scientists have recorded the emissions from methane "hotspots" as the gas bubbles up from the bottom of lakes. But to my mind – I am sure of this – we have very many more such hotspots in western Siberia. The problem is that they are extremely difficult to find because during the winter the bog is covered by snow. At the moment, therefore, our statistics suggest a very low rate of emission, when I believe it is very high. We have got to change our methods of measuring this.'

According to Sergey, the evidence is overwhelming: far more methane (which is twenty times as damaging as carbon dioxide) is being pumped into the atmosphere than is yet generally acknowledged by the scientific community. The impact on climate change is calamitous. Methane escaping from the melting permafrost is accelerating global warming, which itself hastens the melting of the permafrost, a vicious circle from which it seems virtually impossible to escape. 'It is a kind of trigger that has already started and that becomes irreversible. We are facing a kind of ecological landslide.'

Sergey has not quite been a lone voice. He has addressed international symposiums and argued his corner in papers and articles, and his views are heard with respect – but, so far, to little avail. 'I fear that we can no longer stop global warming, but we can slow the process down. However, we do not have very much time. I would say five, ten, twenty years, maybe fifty at the outside – though I believe it likely to be nearer five than fifty. Too many scientists keep saying that we don't yet have enough evidence to act, but to my mind we don't have any time to waste. We have to find solutions urgently.' 'So what would happen if all your peers were to share your analysis?' I asked. 'I think it would make a dramatic difference. We would remodel our projections for global warming to take account of the fact that far more methane is coming from the Siberian bog than scientists have so far estimated. Climate change is happening much faster than we like to think.'

## A KIND OF HAPPINESS

On our way back to Tomsk, our bus was held up by a small covered wagon pulled by an elderly tractor. A woman, half hidden by the tarpaulin, sat in the back with a lurcher dog. She stared back at us, incuriously. The little group could have been mistaken for refugees from war or famine; or maybe travellers, tinkers or gypsies, wandering the great Siberian forest in search of work and sustenance. Eventually we were able to overtake and I stopped the bus to find out more. I introduced myself to the tractor driver, whose name was Vladimir, a nut-brown-faced, mustachioed peasant who smiled in bemusement that a foreigner could be in any way interested in him. 'Where have you come from and where are you going?' I asked, sounding to myself like a character from one of Thomas Hardy's Wessex novels. 'I have been in the forest with my wife picking pine nuts to sell at the market,' Vladimir replied. 'We have been out for three days and we are just on our way home. We have had a successful time. Once we have processed the nuts, I think they will be worth about twelve thousand roubles [over £200].'

The forest is an astonishing source of natural wealth. The statistics for the Tomsk region alone beggar the imagination: hidden in and among the trees there is an estimated annual crop of 55,000 tonnes of berries, 50,000 tonnes of pine nuts and 58,000 tonnes of wild mushrooms. They are a huge source of income both for the rural poor, like Vladimir, and the small businesses that process this harvest. In 2006 the total yield from the forests in the Tomsk region was no less than 700 million roubles (£16 million). I doubt that Vladimir was aware of these statistics, but he was only too pleased to show me his contribution to this triumph of enterprise and effort. Walking round to the back of his wagon, he flung back the tarpaulin, causing his wife to shrink back into the darkness away from the intrusive stranger. He told her to open one of the bulging hessian sacks piled about her, and removed a handful of pine cones. Prising one of them open, he extracted a single, tiny nut, which he cracked with his teeth, swallowing the soft pulp inside. Invited to follow suit, I succeeded only in masticating the entire nut, which tasted exceedingly bitter.

Vladimir growled another instruction to his wife. She obediently removed the lid of an old galvanized milk churn, dipped a tin mug into it and passed it out to Vladimir, who offered it to me. Expecting a mug of milk, I was disconcerted to see an oily, clear liquid inside. Noticing this, Vladimir said triumphantly, 'Vodka!' I had repeatedly been warned not to drink vodka unless I knew its provenance. But it was too late. His hospitality was quite impossible to refuse. I swallowed. He swallowed. She topped us up. I drank. He drank.

Thus fortified, Vladimir told me that when they started to haul the timber from the forest he would get work as a driver, but that his principal source of income was the forest: not only pine nuts, berries and mushrooms, but game birds, squirrels (for their fur) and deer; he also had a plot of land on which they grew vegetables and kept a few animals. As he and his wife (who by this time had summoned the courage to emerge from tarpaulin purdah) waved farewell and set off for home, I indulged the thought that at last, here in the Siberian forest, I had found an example of truly sustainable stewardship. But I also knew that even to harbour the thought was to spit in the wind of 'progress'.

Back in Chekhov's 'very dull town', I went to meet a local historian who again proved to be very far from dull. Eduard Maidanyuk and his wife Alla lived in an apartment in one of the old wooden houses that I had noticed on my arrival. Eduard met me in the street halfway along a leafy avenue of elegant buildings, each different from the other, each designed to meet the individual tastes of the well-to-do merchants and public servants who lived there at the turn of the nineteenth century. The style was reminiscent of the wooden houses that are fashionable in the Georgetown district of Washington, but these were much larger and more obviously Victorian Gothic. Nor were they built entirely in clapboard. The ground-floor walls were made of timber from the forest, smoothly turned tree trunks (aspen, because it is so hard, facing north, pine or fir on the other three sides), while the upper floors were clad in unpainted wooden planking from the same source. This simplicity was offset by scrolled ornamentation, elaborately but not fussily carved, flowing barge boards, 'gingerbread' trims, and windows decorated with fleur-de-lis encrustations or, in several cases, a fish-head staring down at the visitor. They were painted in a variety of colours – blues, greys and pinks, but all subtly chosen in the heritage way. Taste, you are given to understand, has long meant something in Tomsk and it still does.

Eduard and Alla were both in their seventies and had lived in their apartment for almost thirty-five years. They led me up a wide, once grand but now worn and rickety, staircase past shelves that were haphazardly laden with dusty books, papers and photographs that I assumed at first to be the detritus of a long life together. Eduard corrected me. They were precious artefacts, the history of the twentieth century in Tomsk, which in a country that likes to forget the past formed a precious record of daily life. He pointed out the sit-up-and-beg bicycle that hung on the wall out of reach above us, and inside the apartment, with the curatorial passion of a serious collector, heap upon heap of books and boxes, and a chest filled with postcards and antique gramophone records, including a collection of arias sung by the great operatic bass of the first half of the twentieth century, Fyodor Shaliapin. There were Soviet radios in mock mahogany, an upright piano from the forties, and an accordion. The walls were adorned with old family photographs – great-grandparents, grandparents and parents from both sides of the family, all upstanding citizens, comfortable burghers, staring at the camera with confidence but without a smile. The only objects in the entire apartment that clearly belonged to the twenty-first century were a new kettle and their son's laptop, which had found a place for itself among a scatter of documents piled high on a table in the corner, just behind an antimacassar-covered settee.

Alla had the absent-minded air of a slightly dotty resident of Bloomsbury in the twenties or thirties. Her hair was dishevelled, she dressed without concern for what others might think, and she bustled about her business with a distracted air. 'Would you like a cup of tea?' she asked, explaining that she had available a range of English teas, including Earl Grey. 'Which would you prefer?' I settled for the Earl Grey. Scooping three teaspoonfuls of tea from a tin caddy and tipping them carefully into a pink, flower-patterned china teapot (which she had taken care to warm on an electric stove that must have been manufactured at least fifty years earlier), she added boiling water, stirred the brew and – after precisely three minutes – poured the liquid through a silver strainer into my matching china cup. The precision with which she accomplished this afternoon ritual belonged more to the world of *The Forsyte Saga* than twenty-first-century Russia. And there was a reason. 'I am an Anglophile,' she explained. 'I love Galsworthy and Dickens and Peter Sellers. Not a month goes by without me reading one or other of the novelists or watching a Peter Sellers film.' Errol Flynn, however, was her great heart-throb, and to prove it she hurried out of the sitting room into a study as full of memorabilia as the rest of the apartment, returning with a brown envelope stuffed with faded photographs of her swashbuckling pin-up and yellowing printed articles that I admired with due reverence.

When Alla left the room to busy herself in the kitchen, Eduard – who had been meekly waiting his turn – seized his chance. 'I grew up in my grandparents' house. There they are on the wall up there. It was a wooden house with a vegetable plot, and it was a wonderful childhood. When I was a student in Tomsk we once celebrated New Year in this very flat (though it did not then belong to my family) and it was simply wonderful. It was beautifully done with a Christmas – or rather a New Year – tree with old toys and decorations on it. After that I always thought it would be good to live in an old building like this. So when I saw a small advertisement in a newspaper from some-one wanting to swap, my wife and I thought, "It's just made for us". Of course, some of our friends thought it was a very bad idea to give up a modern flat in a block in the great city of Novosibirsk, where we then lived, for an old wooden house that probably needed a great deal of work on it. But others understood.'

The sceptics had a point. The date was 1973 and, according to Eduard, 'These old houses were regarded then as just a pile of old logs. No point in repairing them. Who would want to live in them anyway? When we arrived here the roof was leaking and the whole building needed a major overhaul. There was supposed to be a reno-vation scheme, but five years later, in 1978, we were still asking for the repairs to be done. It took a long time. But this place means every-thing to us. We have an expression in Russian, "Your hearth belongs to your family", and that is how it is for us. My children were brought up here. My grandchildren were brought up here. They have now gone to different places, but this hearth draws them back. To have a home and a hearth is very important. My wife and I can't imagine what it would be like if we didn't live in this house, and sometimes we worry what would happen if they pulled it down. Because that is happening to a lot of these old houses in Tomsk.'

'What?' I interrupted. 'They are pulling these houses down? Don't they have preservation orders?' I should have known better. 'Yes,' Eduard said in the resigned tone that I had heard so often on my jour-ney. 'There are rules and there are regulations. But people are very crafty at getting round them. Investors and property developers want to pull them down and put up multi-storey apartment blocks. They simply say that the building is too old or dilapidated to repair, or that it is unsafe for habitation. And they get away with it.' Bribery yet again? Backhanders to officials? Percentage deals? 'Yes, money changes hands. Money decides all these things.' He shook his head despondently. 'It is a very great shame because people come here for the beauty of this city. It is perhaps the only city in Russia that has whole neighbourhoods of these old houses, and they are unique. If they were only kept in good order and made to look like they once were, you would even get Hollywood producers wanting to come and film here. You know, when these houses were built it was during Tomsk's Golden Age. The city was a centre for science, trade, culture and academic excellence. And though the Trans-Siberian Railway bypassed us, their offices were here. Two thousand engineers, technicians and managers moved in here. Aside from their professional skills, they were a very cultivated group. They knew music and literature. That was Tomsk in those days.'

Eduard's 'dream' is to raise the funds to create a local museum out of his collection of memorabilia from the last century. It would have three rooms. 'One would be in the style of my grandparents, another in the pre-war style of my parents' generation, and the third would be a reflection of how we lived when we were younger in the second half of the century.' I enquired as gently as possible whether his accumulation of memorabilia would really meet any public demand. It was, I suggested, a very 'eclectic' mix. What was the unifying theme? 'The thing that unites them,' he replied with a certainty that was engagingly obsessive, 'the thing that unites it all is that everything is about friends and family, and it goes from the start of the twentieth century to the end. They are all reminders of the time that people I knew lived through. And even though they might seem at times to be ephemeral or useless, they actually speak to us about those times. I would really like to turn this house into the museum. But there isn't enough room, because we live here as well. So everything just piles up, box upon box, pile upon pile. There just isn't enough space. So my problem is that I have nowhere to show these exhibits.' He gestured around the room, not defeated but frustrated.

By this time Alla had rejoined us. I asked them both what they thought of their city today. 'Money,' I reminded them, was, in Eduard's words, 'at the root of everything.' But they clearly lived modestly. They lived with their ideas and with their dreams, which – I almost added – were inhabited by nostalgia. So what made them happy? Eduard's reply was touchingly guileless: 'I am so glad you understand us. That you've put your finger on what we are like. The thing is that the people who have money actually lead a very crazy lifestyle. They are the ones who make the noise, they are the ones who – superficially – catch your eye and stand out. But here in Tomsk there are still quite a number of people who have different values and who still – even though we might be a dying generation – have normal human attitudes. We represent the generation that put spiritual things before material things.'

Tomsk likes to pride itself on its independent spirit, acquired both from the dissidents who were dumped here before the revolution and from the intellectual distinction of its first university, now one of five institutions of higher education in the city. On the face of it there is evidence for this in the results of the 2005 local elections. It had been expected that Putin's creation, United Russia, would cruise to a comfortable victory, but the party was beaten into second place by the Pensioners' Party. However, there was less to this apparently stunning local challenge to the Kremlin's iron grip on power than met the eye. In the smoke-and-mirrors world of Russian politics, the leader of the Pensioners' Party at that time was one of Putin's long-standing allies and had campaigned for him in the 2000 presidential election. Since the 2005 elections in Tomsk, this alliance has become even more overt. In 2006 the Pensioners' Party merged with two other small parties to form Just Russia, which has been welcomed by Putin as the 'official' opposition to his own political creature, United Russia. Apologists for this sleight of hand like to compare the relationship between United Russia and Just Russia with that of the Democrats and Republicans in the United States. However, Congress is very frequently not only at war with itself but with the White House as well. By contrast, the new leader of Just Russia, Sergey Mironov, has sworn unswerving fealty to the Kremlin, declaring in his inaugural speech in October 2006, 'We will follow the course of President Vladimir Putin and will not allow anyone to veer from it after he leaves office in 2008.' If the pensioners of Tomsk derive any benefit from their 'victory' over United Russia in the 2005 elections, it will only be because it is so willed by the Kremlin.

Eduard and Alla were truly independent spirits, so I suspected they might be not only anti-materialists but political dissidents, well aware of the democratic deceptions so shamelessly perpetrated on them by the Kremlin. I could not have been more wrong. 'We have lost a lot since the end of the Soviet Union, but there are many pluses as well,' Eduard said. So what about Putin? Alla replied, 'I feel positive about him,' and Eduard finished her thought: 'We have seen a move back towards normality.' 'And,' they added in chorus, 'we are now very much more respected on the international level.' Eduard went on, 'We don't really get involved in politics. I don't read the papers, I don't watch television and I don't listen to the radio.' In Britain such detachment would seem irritatingly whimsical or irresponsible. But as I left Eduard and Alla, I wondered if my own attitudes towards freedom and democracy had failed to accommodate an unpalatable fact about Putin's Russia: that if you are outside the system, if you are not a member of the new nomenclatura, then even – perhaps especially – for the intelligentsia, political ignorance allows a measure of personal bliss.

## A CENTRE OF ACADEMIC EXCELLENCE

When Tomsk was enjoying its 'golden years' the city of Novosibirsk, 450 miles and ten hours by road to the southwest, was hardly more than a village. Today it is the third-largest city in Russia (after Moscow and St Petersburg), with a population of 1.5 million. It is an important financial, mercantile and industrial hub, and its imposing avenues and neo-classical public buildings are designed to assert its status. Among its cultural centres, it boasts the biggest opera house in Russia (beating the Bolshoi in Moscow) and the biggest library in Siberia. But the city feels soulless, too grand in conception and on too great a scale for its inhabitants, who looked to me to be dwarfed, like figures dislocated in a Lowry landscape. After the charm of Tomsk, to drive into Novosibirsk was to return to one of those lookalike Soviet cities that, in my memory, blur easily into a single megalopolis, devoid of individual character. There is little to disdain but, unless you have business there, nothing to detain you either. There is one exception: the city's main station is an absurd but glorious monument to the Trans-Siberian Railway, a feat of nineteenth-century engineering and political will that is truly astonishing. The main façade of this, the largest of all the TranSib stations, is at least as long as that of the National Gallery in Trafalgar Square (including the Sainsbury Wing), but is unhappily painted in a seasick-including olive green. The bilious effect is not quite camouflaged even by the elegant eaves-to-floor windows that run along its entire length, or by the magnificent portico with giant Doric columns, each one picked out in white. Inside, there are grand stairways, marble columns, cut-glass chandeliers and Grecian urns filled with an overflowing abundance of green foliage. But, to me, the electronic departures and arrivals board was even more impressive. A romantic fantasy of travel, it invites you into a Victorian world of distant destinations: from Vladivostok to Moscow and Moscow to Vladivostok, seven days in either direction, or from Novosibirsk to almost anywhere in Russia. Sadly, I was only there to board a commuter train to a stop in the suburbs, Akademgorodok.

The place is set pleasantly enough on the banks of the Ob, and laid out with parks, gardens and meandering avenues. It is, however, famous in Russia not for its location, but for the vision that inspired its creation out of virgin forest no more than half a century ago. Akademgorodok was the brainchild of an eminent mathematician, Academician Mikhail Lavrentiev, who personally persuaded the Soviet leader, Nikita Khrushchev, that Siberia needed a centre of academic excellence to rival any in the West. His pitch fell on fertile soil in the Kremlin. It was decided that Akademgorodok would not only become the world's most illustrious centre of pure research in all fields of science, but would also apply this research to the better exploitation of Siberia's vast mineral resources, which far exceeded those immediately available in the United States. Within a decade of this Soviet proclamation, forty-five thousand scientists had descended on the embryo garden city to take up posts at the state university and at thirty-five other research institutes. For once they came voluntarily, for reasons of scholarship and for the relatively sybaritic lifestyle offered to them by way of inducement. Although their salaries were modest, they were given access to special retail outlets that provided them with an abundant source of basic foodstuffs that were rationed and difficult to obtain elsewhere. Members of the illustrious Soviet Academy of Sciences were offered houses to live in rather than the multi-apartment tenement blocks endured by lesser mortals. No less attractive, at least to those who felt stifled by totalitarianism, Akademgorodok was open to visitors from outside, even though its residents were pioneering breakthroughs in mathematics, nuclear physics, geology and computer science. At its peak, in the seventies, the population of scientists in the city had risen to sixty-five thousand (which gave Akademgorodok a place in the *Guinness Book of Records*).

But as the campus grew in status, a model of Soviet planning, so a culture of independence, even dissidence, began to emerge in the collaborative atmosphere fostered by Lavrentiev. In cafés with bizarre names like Under Integral and the Coffee and Cybernetics Club, talk was free and open. So was the music: the dissident film-maker, poet, song-writer and bard Alexander Galich – who had fallen so foul of the regime by 1974 that he was expelled from the Writers' Union and three years later fled into exile – performed openly in the city in 1968. It has even been claimed that the critical mass of human intelligence gathered together in this one place was instrumental in nurturing the seeds of *perestroika*. Ironically, it was *perestroika* that almost brought about the end of Akademgorodok. A year after the collapse of the Soviet Union, the Russian government slashed spending on the university to 10 per cent of its 1991 level. The community was suddenly in tatters. The best young scientists fled to Europe and the United States in search of employment. Those who remained entered the deepest slough of despond.

After the fall, the writer Colin Thubron dropped in on Akadem-gorodok, where he chanced to meet the General Secretary of the Praesidium, who 'loomed big and surly behind his desk'. At the end of a surreal conversation (related with relish in his *In Siberia*), the author pressed his interlocutor about a new city that, it had been promised, would 'astound the world' but that had yet to be built. This madcap scheme had been dreamt up by Lavrentiev and his fellow scientific pioneers, who had convinced themselves they could harness nuclear power to melt the Siberian permafrost. As a result a frozen waste would be transformed, becoming 'ideally suitable for human habitation'. As Thubron persisted with his mischievous enquiry, the General Secretary suddenly became very angry – not with Thubron, as the author at first suspected, but with Boris Yeltsin, who was at that time still in office. 'We have one over-riding problem here. Money,' the General Secretary stormed. 'We receive no money for new equipment, hardly enough for our salaries. There are people here who haven't been paid for six months. This year we requested funds for six or seven different programmes! Not one has been accepted by the government. Science is now as cut off from the state as the Church used to be. As far as I can see, everything's run by mafia.' Thubron asked about the future. 'The future?' he said. 'When we have a government that realizes no country can do without science, Akademgorodok will flourish again.'

I was curious to see what had happened in the intervening decade. To imbibe the atmosphere of academia more fully, I biked along the cycle tracks that thread their way from one scientific institute to another. Hardly a rival to Cambridge or the Massachusetts Institute of

Technology, this giant campus nonetheless had a certain grandeur and was certainly less offensive on the eye than so many of the campus buildings constructed by the architectural brutalists of the same era in the United Kingdom. But from the outside at least, Akademgorodok did seem dormant, a cul-de-sac, a campus out of season – as if the scientists had indeed fled for warmer climes. It was very clearly no longer the vibrant centre of world science that its founder – who stared down at passing bicycles from a plinth overlooking the main thoroughfare – had hoped for.

My impression that the past must have been better than the present – if not the future – was reinforced when I walked through the long, ill-lit, deserted corridors of the Praesidium building, past locked doors and empty rooms that had once been at the epicentre of that Soviet ferment of intellectual energy. I was there to meet the late Professor Lavrentiev's son, who is also called Mikhail and is also a professor of mathematics. But Lavrentiev the Younger was also chairman of an IT company called Computer Graphics Software that makes video games for the American market. Mikhail led me into a computer room where a silent conclave of clever young men stared intently at their screens, inhabiting a virtual world that Lavrentiev the Elder could not even have imagined. At one terminal his son showed me a video game that his team had been sub-contracted to manufacture by an American firm to 'sell into' the US market. In its own way it was a triumph of computer graphics: an American gasoline truck careering along the coastal highway north of San Diego on its way to Santa Barbara being chased by speed cops that – when I took the controls – jack-knifed on a bend, killing the occupants of the police car before cascading into the ocean with me still at the wheel. Professor Lavrentiev explained that the acute intellectual and technical challenge involved in creating this video game promised great rewards for his company as it sought to penetrate further into the highly competitive US market. I wondered what his late father would have thought of his son's venture.

Whether or not Akademgorodok's founder would have been aghast, Lavrentiev the Younger is merely adapting the Elder's original vision to the realities of post-Soviet Russia. The academic institutions have been slimmed down to meet the needs of a different age. The mathematicians, physicists, chemists, even doubtless the philosophers and philologists, not to mention the cytologists and geneticists, who still inhabit these august corridors of scientific excellence would once have relied entirely on central government to give practical purpose to their theoretical breakthroughs. Now, like their peers in America and Europe, they look to the marketplace for funds. Mikhail Lavrentiev believed he had the best team in the world. 'We are very close to the scientific community. We use the really high end of science in all our products and all our developments. And we are creating the technologies of the future.' Excuse me – video games? Mikhail was unabashed. 'That game was created principally as a teaching aid, a simulator, for US truck drivers. And that is still its main purpose. The video game is a spin-off.'

To emphasize his point, he took me across to another terminal where a young man was working on a graphic of immense complexity, some beauty and indubitable utility. 'This is a simulator designed for the Russian Space Agency to help astronauts to perfect their technique for docking a space capsule with its orbiting base station,' Mikhail explained as his designer steered the astronauts' capsule towards the space station. 'This is a government contract that we are now adapting for the European space programme. And, Jonathan, in modified form it will also be available soon as a video game.'

Since Colin Thubron's visit, Akademgorodok has not exactly threatened to emulate Silicon Valley, but there is renewed confidence. International companies like Intel, Schlumberger, Microsoft and Hewlett-Packard have opened offices, tapping into the local IT talent. There are upwards of a hundred small and medium-sized companies like Mikhail's. In 2006 private investment in Akademgorodok reached $150 million a year (up from $10 million a decade ago), and a programme to develop nano-technology in the form of a laser systems laboratory has just won a government grant of $3 million.

Most ambitiously of all, there is a grand scheme to create a federally funded Technopark, comprising research facilities, offices, production plants and an international trade centre – all of which is designed to attract many more foreign investors. The planned investment is $670 million and, the enthusiasts insist, this project really will restore Akademgorodok to its proper role as an international centre of research, innovation and design in almost every field of science and technology. But – there is always a but – at the moment, like Lavrentiev the Elder's ghost city, the Technopark in which Lavrentiev the Younger invests such faith exists only in the mind. Work on the site was supposed to have started in September 2007, but the various stakeholders are at war with one another over how the government's bounty should be spent. As a result, the project is on hold. Lavrentiev refuses to be disheartened. 'We hope that the Technopark will be launched here. And I strongly believe that the project will succeed. The global market needs us. Remember the old joke? If you want a run-of-the-mill job, ask the Indians. If it is difficult, ask the Chinese. If it is impossible, call in the Russians. The truth is that we bear comparison with any other IT centre in the world.'

Akademgorodok's immediate challenge is to stop the haemorrhage of talent to the West. The brain drain of scientific brilliance that sapped the Soviet Union in its last years became a torrent in the nineties, and the outflow has not yet been stemmed. Lavrentiev, who moonlights energetically as Dean of the Information Technologies Department at the university, finds himself torn between boasting that 'at least four hundred of our graduates are working in Silicon Valley' and lamenting the fact that he can't keep them in Akademgorodok. 'We are still losing very good students and PhD students. We can't compete with Microsoft salaries.' I suggested it must be exceedingly frustrating. 'It is. But we struggle against it by promoting this community as a friendly environment. And you must have noticed that we have a very special atmosphere. We are intellectuals. We use our minds. We are more friendly here. Less hurried. Definitely less aggressive.' I was quite prepared to believe him but, as Mikhail conceded, Akademgorodok's 'unique selling point' has yet to turn the tide.

'Only last month, one of my second-year PhD students faced me with the fact that he has been hired by Microsoft in Canada and that he is going to leave his course without completing his studies.' 'What did you say to him? Did you call him a traitor or wish him good luck?' 'Somewhere between the two,' Lavrentiev replied. 'I told him that in one year he would have earned his PhD and that his future career in Microsoft would then be even brighter. He didn't believe me.' I suggested that unless he, Lavrentiev, could attract and keep the cleverest students, Akademgorodok would find it hard to achieve the critical mass that his father knew to be necessary for it to become a global centre of excellence to rival any other. 'You are right,' he replied, 'but it will happen. Basic salaries for scientists have been very low. But they are now starting to improve. So the trend is upwards. But of course we don't know long this will last. We still have to fight to get the best students to opt for science.' 'And if you fail,' I said unhelpfully, 'your dream will unravel.' 'Yes, you are right. We are still in danger, but we are hopeful.'

I found some grounds for Lavrentiev's optimism at the local high school, where one of the staff, an International Resources teacher called Nina, introduced me to some of the very brightest and best of her pupils. Almost all of them were the offspring of Akademgorodok's present scientific elite. These hothouse children were delightfully guileless. Gifted pupils and articulate in English, they were refreshingly innocent and unselfconsciously old-fashioned. Apparently untouched by the vulgarity of the Russian media, with its cult of individualism and an obsession with celebrity every bit as shallow as that which poisons British culture, these teenagers wanted to talk about morality and patriotism. When I asked what was important to them – expecting to hear about pop stars, clothes, football teams, cars and good money – Anna, who wanted to be a travel agent, set the tone. 'In my life it is important to be a good person and to make other people happy and not to do things that I will be sorry for.' Elizabeth, an aspiring opera singer, chipped in. 'I think people must think about their neighbours. They should want to change the lives of other people and make their lives better. And then their lives will get better as well.' Antion, who starred at volleyball, picked up the theme. 'For me it is important to have many friends, to be a good person in society, and I will be happy if I am a good person throughout my life and have no sins.'

When I asked them whether they would stay in Russia or, like so many of the generation before them, emigrate in search of a better life, they almost all answered in terms that Putin would have relished. Not for them a soft life in the West, but, as patriots, their desire and their duty was to serve the Motherland; their future lay in Russia. There was only one mildly dissenting voice. Dmitry, a would-be physicist, said, 'I will make up my mind later. I don't know what I shall do at the moment. I don't know what Russia will be like by the time I leave university. Time will show.'

Nina took me to meet the head teacher. Sergey was a historian by training but seemed more like a young army officer – clean-cut, direct and precise. With President Putin's ominous demand that 'history should be positive' in mind, I asked him how he set about teaching the history of 'the Soviet era' to his pupils. Did he teach 'positive' history? He answered without any hesitation. 'Yes, I think that Putin is right. He is very concerned about the curriculum in history.' 'But,' I asked, 'how can you dictate by fiat that history will be "positive"? What does it mean? History is about the interpretation of evidence. It shouldn't set out to be either positive or negative. Do you really think Putin is right?' Sergey countered indirectly. 'First of all, it is very difficult to interpret, and interpretation is changing and improving all the time. It is not an exact science.' By now I was really irritated. 'But that is precisely why you should not distort the evidence to make history "positive".' Sergei was unmoved. 'My way of looking at it,' he replied, 'is that the Russian people have had a burden placed on them by history. But there have always been moments of heroism. And those we should emphasize.' 'Why is that?' I persevered. 'Because we are still in a critical situation,' he replied. 'You have to make children aware that there are ways of improving their lot, that people have overcome crises in the past. That it is possible.' This seemed to me to be an alarming conflation of historical truth and civic duty that came perilously close to brainwashing – and I said so. He remained quite unmoved, trumping my pedantic insistence on the distinction between truth and propaganda with a resounding non sequitur: 'The thing is that Putin has optimism and he conveys it. And this is very important to our students because they really feel it because he transmits it to them.' I was reminded simultaneously of Alan Bennett's *Forty Years On* and Monty Python's *Life of Brian*: the past was another country where they did things differently, and in the meantime we should always look on the bright side of life.

The high school was hugely oversubscribed. As Nina explained the admissions system, I realized why so many of those good men and women I had met along the way were in despair about a system that purports to offer a free education to all but does nothing of the sort. In Akademgorodok's most sought-after secondary school only 50 per cent of the pupils have a genuinely free place. The rest, by one means or another, have to pay for their education. The best students are awarded scholarships and their parents pay nothing, while the rest have to find around $1500 a year. At first I could not detect whether Nina approved of this two-tier structure or whether, as an exceptional teacher from the Soviet era who now advised central government, she deplored it. She simply gave me the facts. Although the school was required to take 75 per cent of its pupils from the local catchment area, the other 25 per cent of places were open to competition. 'The demand is so great,' Nina said, 'that we even have grandparents coming here at the start of the school year and queuing outside the administration building on the day before we are open for applications. But we also have parents producing documents that are obviously false to prove that their child is resident here. And there are other pressures as well. This year we had one family where the father said, "If you don't accept my son I shall move to Moscow."' And what did they do? 'We accepted him.'

Nina had been so forthcoming that I asked whether it was true that even those pupils who were ostensibly given free places had to pay up to $1000 to guarantee a place at a good state school. 'Yes. But this is a voluntary foundation to which parents can contribute to help with the upkeep of the school. And parents want to do that. At this school we have some rich parents who give very generously indeed.' Then she added, with no hint of irony, 'But no one is forced to pay. If they don't want to pay, they can take their child to another school.' Nina was an award-winning teacher, which made it even more disconcerting that she had no qualms about an education system calculated to separate sheep from goats so crudely and arbitrarily as to make the historic distinction in Britain between grammar schools and secondary moderns appear positively progressive. But, of course, I also knew that if I were a Russian parent, I would want Nina and her colleagues to teach my child and that, *faute de mieux*, I would do everything in my power to achieve it. Not very honourable, but I would defend my position with a native shrug and remind myself that this was how things worked in Russia.

## THE ALTAI MOUNTAINS

It was to be a twelve-hour drive, following the course of the River Ob southeast from Akademgorodok into the Altai mountains. The range extends for some 1200 miles from northwest to southeast and forms Russia's natural border with Mongolia, China and Kazakhstan. As we drove south, the landscape changed perceptibly, the forests of birch and pine giving way to open arable land, gently undulating fields where combine harvesters were snatching the last of the autumn crops before winter set in. The sky was quite clear of clouds, and a huge dome of pale blue translucence arched around us, creating a magnificent amphitheatre that was deserted except for the distant red machines that crawled across the yellow corn, trailing dust clouds that swirled away in the breeze. A glimpse of a lake behind a stand of birch trees provided me with the nostalgic illusion that Capability Brown must have been hired by a Russian nobleman to create a monumental copy of that pastoral splendour with which he graced the grand estates of eighteenth-century England. But there was no Blenheim Palace or Harewood House in this elegant no man's land of agricultural hard labour.

However, even elegance can become monotonous. To ward off drowsiness I focused on passing moments: a man huddled on the verge with his back to the road, a bucket of carrots by his side; a middle-of-nowhere roadside stall, where a peasant couple waited to sell pine nuts, berries, honey and birch twigs for the *banya*; an army truck in front of us, filled with pinch-faced, disconsolate conscripts, that lurched and bounced on the pitted asphalt; an allotment in a village where a small child was helping a bowed old man – his grandfather? – to carry cabbages across the rough ground of an allotment; a couple skinning a dead sheep at the roadside. I wondered what had brought them to this other-worldly Siberia. They seemed to have drifted into the frame by chance, accidental inhabitants of nowhere in particular, eking out an existence on the margins of the money economy. As we drove further south, the landscape became balmier still. I saw sunflowers, their blackened heads drooping as they awaited the harvest. A herd of Friesian cows, black and white dots on an oasis of greensward, meandered among round bales of straw and traditional stooks of hay. A peasant woman on a sit-up-and-beg bicycle steered a cow and her calf along a track towards the horizon, presumably heading towards an unseen homestead: a universal symbol of patience and endurance.

It has been argued by a number of Western analysts with impeccable credentials that Russia should 'shrink' – contracting not its physical
territory but its economic geography – in order to compete effectively
in the global market. The economic case, made for instance by the
authors of *The Siberian Curse*, seems – in its own terms – remarkably
persuasive. The Soviet industrialization of this vast territory, they argue,
was in conscious defiance of the logic of the marketplace, and this
'misallocation' of resources – principally through the agency of the
millions of slave labourers who worked in the Gulag – led to the
production of the wrong things in the wrong way by people who were
educated with the wrong skills. The legacy is that Russia is being
drained of its economic wealth by a lethally adverse combination of
communications and climate. Communications by road, rail and air
among the major population centres are so poor that they hobble
efforts to promote trade and to develop markets. But even to invest the
billions required to bring them up to competitive standards – itself a
further drain of resources – would be insufficient to combat the
economic impact of the world's cruellest climate. Too many of Siberia's
cities have temperatures that dip so low for many months of the year
that huge central-government subsidies for fuel and food are required
in order to sustain human life. As a result of these and other factors, the
authors have calculated that the real cost of living is up to four times
higher in Siberia than elsewhere in the Russian Federation. State subsidies for domestic heating and the cost of transporting winter fuel (at an
annual cost of well over $700 million) are a further drain on the excheq-
uer. To 'shrink' successfully, the authors insist, 'people in Russia need to
move to warmer, more productive places, closer to markets and away
from the cold, distant cities placed by the Gulag and the communist
planners in Siberia'. As in other parts of the world where the conditions
of life are extreme, only those citizens needed to extract Siberia's wealth
and to maintain the transport infrastructure would remain.

Theirs is a twenty-first-century variation on the 'On your bike' or
'Go west, young man' injunction, and doubtless makes great theoret-

ical sense. But as I glanced out at the passing landscape – the occasional settlement, a military camp, an oil depot and later a factory belching fumes, and an interminable march of pylons and electric cables into the distance – I thought that in historical, political, social, psychological and even spiritual terms, *The Siberian Curse* inhabits not only another continent, but another planet. Its proposal – however commonsensical it may appear on paper – simply won't be realized. Siberia has been conquered and settled over centuries of terrible hardship, but it has become a Motherland that is every bit as precious to its inhabitants as any other part of Russia. Of course, if the economy falters, the population of Siberia may 'shrink' by default (as it has done in the past) but it is inconceivable that even the most authoritarian neo-tsar will produce a strategy for emptying Siberia of its economically redundant population.

When we were some 300 miles from Akademgorodok, I noticed a blue-grey blur in the distant haze. It slowly emerged, breathtakingly silhouetted against the sun, like a mirage in the plain, until, in a moment, it revealed itself as a mountain, the first I had seen for thousands of miles. Gradually others appeared, and soon I could discern on the skyline a long line of peaks seeming to block our way south. Gradually, almost imperceptibly, we began to climb towards the foothills of the Altai mountains. The corn and the cows gave way again to birch trees and firs. A broad, shallow river, a tributary of the Ob, leapt and gurgled around white boulders, the water sparkling in the afternoon sun. Soon we were in an Alpine landscape, with bright yellow flowers and giant Michaelmas daisies whispering in the grass, and bright fields running up to the very edge of an escarpment where firs clung with improbable tenacity to the vertiginous edge of granite rock. This was tourist territory. A roadside hoarding advertised a ski resort, another a host of 'adventure' holidays, from white-water rafting to hiking and pony trekking. There were new hotels and, just visible between the trees by the water's edge, several magnificent chalets, each surrounded by a high-security fence – summer homes for the regional rich. Along the side of the road an orderly row of souvenir stalls, most of them already closed for the winter but one or two still hoping to catch the stragglers, confirmed what I had been told in Akademgorodok: that the Altai mountains are Siberia's paradise.

Further on and higher still, we entered a high plateau edged by mountains on either side, one hanging valley after another. We were now in the heart of the Altai Republic, in a remote land where one-third of the two hundred thousand inhabitants are members of an indigenous race, the descendants of Bronze Age nomadic tribes now known collectively as Pazyrik people, who roamed the high plateaux with their herds and flocks, trading their footsure mountain horses with merchants as far away as India, Persia and Mongolia. The Altai tombs or barrows – called *kurgans* – have recently yielded an invaluable insight into an ancient civilization about which Herodotus, writing almost two and a half thousand years ago, had hitherto been the most reliable source. According to the archaeologists who have excavated these sites over the last half century, we have the peculiar climatic conditions in the Altai to thank for the survival of a cultural treasure trove that dates from the fifth century BC. Evidently, water had seeped into the burial chambers, where it froze, mummifying their contents in a protective shield of ice.

The wonders of ancient daily life that they have extracted from these frozen tombs include the oldest woven carpet in the world, felt hangings and saddle cloths, all intricately patterned in vivid colours and elaborate designs. Even more astonishing are the perfectly preserved remains of horses buried alongside a chieftain to hasten his journey into the Other World. There are human corpses as well, their bodies tattooed with monsters and other fantastical creatures from land and sea, potent evocations of an ancient animist faith. But by common consent, the most spectacular find of all is the embalmed body of a young woman who is known today as the Ice Maiden. Discovered in 1993, she is 1.7 metres tall. She has blonde hair and her delicate body is tattooed with a deer-like creature that has flower-like horns or antlers. In the last few years she has become the focus of bitter controversy, the symbol of a cultural fissure between the Altai people and their Russian overlords. For the former her burial place, like every other *kurgan*, is a sacred tomb. They bitterly resent the fact that she was disinterred and removed to a museum in Novosibirsk, 450 miles to the north. Their leaders insist that until she is reinterred the Altai people will be dogged by ill fortune. But the Russian scientists responsible for preserving her remains, and the archaeologists for whom the Ice Maiden and their excavations in some 150 *kurgans* are a means of reconstructing the history of the Pazyrik people, claim (in the words of one of their number) that they would become 'an international laughing stock' if they surrendered to such primitive atavism. So far in this stand-off science has prevailed.

One of the very few ethnic groups to survive both tsarist invasion and Soviet repression without losing their cultural identity, the people of the Altai are set apart from their fellow Russian citizens (who only invaded these mountain lands three centuries ago) by history, culture and language. The villagers who glanced up at us as we drove through the scattered settlements that edged the road were shrouded in thick coats against the cold. Generally slight in stature, they were strong and wiry with broad, flat faces, high cheekbones and eyes so deep-set as to be half-lost in crinkles of skin ravaged by harsh weather and bright sun. Helped by the fact that my mind had started to drift after ten hours on the road, it took little imagination to picture their ancestors advancing through the mountains, foot soldiers in the service of the Golden Horde that swept north and west from Mongolia to conquer Rus more than seven hundred years earlier. Even today, vestiges of that past remain. In every backyard along the side of the road I noticed not only a cluster of pigs, ducks, geese, dogs and cats, but, either hobbled or tethered to a rail, one or sometimes two horses. The horse is as iconic and utilitarian today in the Altai as the camel in the desert. Similarly, almost every homestead contained a simple yurt-like wooden structure, the traditional nomadic dwelling known to the

Altai people as an *ail*. The construction of these emblematic dwellings (more often used today as outhouses) had been discouraged during the decades of Soviet repression, but since the nineties they have made a comeback as the people of the Altai reassert their traditional rights.

The dusk gave way to night. Soon it was pitch-black, with no moon to light the shadows, and as we penetrated deeper into the mountains, only the occasional pinpoint of light from the very few settlements we passed reminded us that we had not entirely escaped the vestiges of twenty-first-century civilization. Just before midnight our headlights picked out a huddle of sheds. We pulled into an unlit farmyard, where I could just discern a collection of modern agricultural implements, three horses tied to a rail, and two Land Cruisers looking opulently out of place. We had reached the edge of a huge estate belonging to one of the Altai's most prominent entrepreneurs, who had invited me to visit his mountain ranch. We changed vehicles and set off again across the kind of terrain that really does require a horse, a tractor or (if you are rich enough) a top-of-the-range 4×4 – though somehow our van managed to slither along in our wake. Sometimes we were on mud tracks and sometimes on rock. We forded streams and drove along dried-up river beds. We climbed precipitous mountain tracks and inched down boulder-strewn pathways through the forest. Once the headlights illuminated the outline of a herd of horses grazing wild on the upland. They raised their heads as we advanced towards them, their eyes glinting in the headlights, before turning to trot away into the darkness.

Our host, Alexander Kulakov, drove with practised ease. He was squat and corpulent, his features unequivocally Mongolian. Good living had not been a friend to his physique. His head sat on his shoulders with no visible sign of a neck, enfolded in protective layers of flesh like a Michelin man; his eyes were almost lost in the folds of surrounding skin. But he exuded power and authority, a big player who was accustomed to giving orders and expecting them to be obeyed. He did not smile but, as we twisted our way for some two hours through the empty night, spoke guilelessly, almost garrulously, rattling off the relevant data about himself and his achievements. 'I bought my first ranch in 1996. It had been a collective farm, but after the end of the Soviet Union it was turned into a cooperative. But it never thrived and it was not hard for me to buy it. I now own three ranches, a total of four and a half thousand hectares – that's more than ten thousand acres. I am taking you to the largest ranch, which is 25 miles in circumference, all of which is fenced to a height of two and a half metres. It takes between four and five days to circumnavigate my estate, which rises from the meadows through forested mountain slopes to a height of more than eighteen hundred metres. All of it has to be patrolled to keep poachers at bay. I have a very productive business – much more efficient than my neighbours'. I have four thousand sheep, a thousand cows, six hundred horses and two and a half thousand marals.'

The maral is often referred to as a reindeer, but Alexander insisted that it was unique to the Altai. Once this fine species of deer roamed freely through the mountains, but for at least a hundred years they have been reared commercially. They are valued less for the venison than for their horns, which are widely regarded in Asia as the source of an incomparable elixir. The young antlers of the stag are 'harvested' in the early summer before the horn has hardened. Alexander explained. 'We round up the stags and drive them into holding pens. They are then driven into a crush, where they are unable to move. Then we saw off the antlers.' It is, by his account, a gruesome and bloody procedure. As I already knew, the antler is not like the horn of a horse's hoof, insensate and easy to trim, but live tissue; to hack through an antler with a saw is much like amputating a limb. Without an anaesthetic, the pain is exquisite. But anaesthetics are expensive and eat into profits. On this very efficient ranch, they do not use anaesthetics.

Alexander was far more concerned to tell me about the restorative properties of the maral antler. 'They help strengthen the immune system and also,' he gave me a sharp glance and winked knowingly,

'I think this would be very useful to you, Jonathan: they increase sexual potency. They have the same effect on a man as Viagra.' I tried to reply in kind, 'Well, Alexander,' I said archly, 'I suppose you must be the world's living expert about that.' For the first time he smiled and then gave a short laugh; my leaden riposte had obviously passed some sort of virility test. Before they are in a condition to render such traditional services to humanity, the severed antlers have to be dipped in boiling brine to cleanse them of blood and other impurities. They are then hung on racks to dry out in the summer air. By early autumn they are ready to be sold to merchants, who arrange for their delivery into an Asian market where demand far exceeds supply. 'We sell to China, Korea and Thailand, where they grind the horn to produce a powder that is sold by pharmacies all over Asia and even in Europe. There is a big demand, especially in Germany.' Later I looked up the sales pitch made by the online dealers: 'We are proud to present 100 per cent natural Altai Antler Velvet products...combat fatigue...support your immune system...rejuvenate...lipid and fat metabolism.... You want to stay mentally, physically and sexually active.... Here finally you have discovered the source of Health and Longevity...stunning performance enhancers....' This snake-oil salesmanship is evidently very persuasive. 'We sell the dried antlers from here for about three hundred and fifty dollars a kilo,' Alexander said, 'but by the time it reaches the shops it is much, much more expensive. And that is because everyone knows that the Altai antlers are the best in the world.'

It long after midnight as we crossed the last stream and entered Alexander's compound. There was a row of wooden huts that served as dormitories, an outside washstand, a *banya* and a newly built *ail* that served as kitchen and dining room. Alexander invited me to join him for a bowl of hot stew. He was not only a farmer but a developer as well. 'I have constructed at least ten per cent of the buildings in Gorno-Altaisk [the capital of the Altai Republic], which has a population of seventy thousand. I have won contracts to build private homes, schools and other public buildings.' One way and another, it soon emerged, he was a force to be reckoned with throughout the Altai. Behind his bland, almost opaque demeanour I sensed a streak of ruthlessness and political cunning that sat uneasily with my romantic vision of the Altai. Alexander was very careful to nurture close relationships with the regional authorities, the politicians and planners. He entertained them in the hotel he owned in the town, and he brought them to the ranch, where they could hunt for the bears and wolves that abounded in the forest. 'You must be a rich man?' I asked. 'No. I am just a normal person.' I decided not to enquire any further into the precise character of his dealings with the various planners, customs officials and tax inspectors who have the power to make or break any business, and Alexander showed little sign of wanting to elaborate. Although he was a generous host, his eyes gave nothing away; I sensed a wariness, not quite as strong as suspicion, but enough to make me tread carefully.

In Soviet times, Alexander had worked as an engineer elsewhere in the country. Since then he had managed to accumulate enough money (I did not ask how) to return to his beloved Altai mountains and put his wealth to good purpose. He 'looked after' sixty members of his extended family, many of whom had jobs in the family businesses, and he delighted in his godfatherly role. 'When my son was married, I decided to invite only the family. That meant four hundred guests.' I asked him if he was a happy man. 'Yes,' he replied simply. 'I love this land and these mountains. I spend most of my time in Gorno-Altaisk and I travel for work and recreation, but I always come back here. I am happy here in the mountains. This is where I am at home.' I believed him.

In the early hours I stood in the cold, looking at the vague outline of distant peaks. I could hear the tumble of a nearby stream. Otherwise the silence was punctuated only by the occasional high-pitched, other-worldly roar of the maral stags, not in pain but – this being the rutting season – in competitive lust. Then, after fourteen hours on the road and my lungs filled with mountain air, I collapsed on to my dormitory bed and slept.

The next morning Alexander took me on a tour of his estate by horseback. With five of his herdsmen alongside, we set off towards the mountains accompanied by a small pack of mongrel hounds. It was cold and the sky was heavy with the promise of snow, but it was immediately exhilarating. A long time ago I used to ride horses professionally, and I have always liked to think that I am a competent horseman. I have jumped five-barred gates, I have been pushed hard against a wall by what straw-chewing old-timers like to call 'a bad 'un', and I have learned to stay on an 'unbroken' animal even when it rears dangerously towards the vertical or bucks in back-jolting circles in a desperate attempt to unseat the alien from its back. Anyway, on this day in the Altai I was, in the words of Philip Larkin's 'Show Saturday', 'all saddle-swank'. The horses were really no more than ponies, strong, lean and agile, with long, entangled manes, but as we jogged across the plateau American-style, sitting deep in the saddle, I imagined myself as one of the Magnificent Seven, heading into the Wild West. It was totally childish and quite glorious.

Alexander's herdsmen were well suited to their animals. Slight and wiry, they rode with the ease and grace that you expect from men for whom horses are both a livelihood and the principal means of transport. We did not talk as we climbed towards the forest and the roar of stags competing for hinds. The ground was strewn with tree stumps and boulders, but I soon realized that my horse would find its way without any interference from me. Above the tree line I could see snow dusting the mountains, forbiddingly bleak. We were at 1800 metres, where the temperature ranges from plus 40 degrees to minus 40 degrees centigrade. Higher up, where the peaks rise towards 3600 metres (the highest mountain in the range is just over 4200 metres), it gets even colder. I had never ridden in such wild terrain before.

After a while one of the herdsman, Grigory, signalled to his team to spread out. Riding straight up the steep mountainside, they disappeared into the harsh undergrowth. Alexander and I followed by what was supposed to be a more circuitous and safer route. I was not sure whether he was looking after me or himself, but, in either case, we were soon scrambling up a vertiginous mountain path of loose stones and slabs of rock, leaning forward as far as possible to avoid falling backwards. In the distance we could hear Grigory and his men whistling to one another or to their dogs as they began to round up the deer that were grazing high in the forest.

A horse responds to a rider and if you are calm and competent, you build a rapport, a primitive sense of mutual dependency. We had started to traverse the mountain along a path no more than 30 centimetres wide, with sheer rock above and a precipice below. Almost any other horse would have refused the risk, either freezing into mulish immobility or rushing backwards in panic. One slip on my part could easily have sent both of us crashing over the edge. I had to resist a *frisson* of fear as my horse, to whom I murmured blandishments, placed its feet with delicate precision on the broken ground as though we were merely doing a round in Rotten Row. We emerged on to a narrow slab of smooth rock, tilted at a sharp angle towards the base of the mountain and my horse halted, his head hung low. Peering over his shoulder, I could see why. There was now nothing in front of us, only the precipice. It would have been hazardous to yank the animal's head around, hoping that he would about-turn on the spot with me still in the saddle. My weight would have been certain to topple us both. I dismounted or, rather, stepped sideways from the saddle on to the edge of the rock, too focused to be afraid. Of its own volition, my little horse at once swivelled around on his hind legs and waited for me to remount. Alexander's animal performed the same manoeuvre and we retraced our steps.

By this time the herdsmen had started to drive the marals down towards the plateau. Alexander signalled to me to help cut them off before they U-turned up into the forest again. I followed him down the slope at a perilous pace, urging my horse forward with the crazed exhilaration that kills people in the hunting field. I drove forward, faster and faster, determined to reach the bottom before the great beasts had thundered away out of sight. Then I saw them, leaping and bounding to outpace the herdsmen. A breakaway group was racing along the hillside trying to escape into the safety of the forest. I drove my horse until I was neck and neck, and then just in front of the animals, but strategically higher up the slope. We were 40 metres away from each other. I turned my horse down towards the leading stag. He saw me and veered off with his followers to rejoin the main herd. With a surge of triumph I halted my horse, his flanks now heaving with the effort, and watched as the herd thundered down into the valley; fifty, one hundred, then two hundred animals, racing away from these predatory humans, their tormentors.

After they had passed, I rode down the slope to rejoin Alexander. Rather pathetically I hoped that he and his team had witnessed my exploit and might offer a word of praise for my horsemanship. I should have known better. Either he hadn't noticed or, like the horse dealer for whom I once worked, he wasn't going to waste his breath on flattery. I said that it had been a moment of real drama on the rock, hoping that he would at least concede this point. Again I should have known my man better. Alexander was not the sort to indulge any illusion. 'I was careful to take you by the safest route,' he said bluntly. 'It is really dangerous further up the mountain.' Suitably chastened, I rode with him back to the compound in silence. It had started to rain, a steady, relentless rain that promised worse weather to come.

The following evening the herdsmen invited me to drink tea with them in the nearby village where one or two of them lived. On the way Eduard, one of the herdsmen who had been sent to collect me, told me about his life. I asked the simple question: 'Do you enjoy your job?' Eduard did not seem to understand and replied 'It is what I do – it is normal.' I realized that he had never been asked such a soft twenty-first-century question before. If you are born in the Altai mountains, you either leave for the city in search of work or you find a job on a ranch. This was not a choice in which 'enjoyment' played any part. 'If you are lazy, that is not good and of course you get nowhere,' Eduard observed. I persisted. 'But it is a hard life?' 'It is normal,' he replied. I felt properly put in my place. He told me that he worked a shift pattern, ten days on followed by a week off. But in the summer he was used to working seven days a week for weeks on end because his boss, Alexander, brought guests to the ranch and there were tourists as well.

The visitors come for the walking, the climbing and the hunting, and to bathe in antler 'juice'. I had noticed a line of six chipped enamel baths in a shed. They reminded me of my boarding school, where we had been compelled to bath in cold water on two early mornings a week. I could never appreciate this barbarity, especially once I realized that it was almost certainly intended – ineffectually, as it happens – to freeze the adolescent libido rather than to toughen our moral sinew. I now pictured a row of sallow, naked people soaking silently in antler 'juice', faintly disappointed that the elixir did not spring them into life, and wondering bleakly how long it would be before they started to feel the benefit. Eduard must have detected my scepticism because he said proudly, 'You know, we have guests from as far away as Moscow and Nizhnevartovsk.'

The *ail* in which Grigory and his men had gathered was hexagonal, about 7 metres in diameter. A pitched roof rose to a peak about 5 metres from the ground. In the centre, a kettle bubbled on a spit over a crackling log fire, the smoke from which eddied up and out into the evening air through a hole in the roof. Ranged along the walls of the *ail* were a bed and a sofa, both worn beyond redemption, a churn of buttermilk, and a sideboard bearing kitchen utensils and china plates and cups, all of which hung higgledy-piggledy from rusty nails. The herdsmen were sitting on rickety wooden benches in a circle around the fire.

I had intended, as custom entails, to bring a bottle of vodka with me, but we had run out the day before. Shamefacedly, I produced a bottle of Chilean Cabernet Sauvignon instead. It appeared not to matter. We sat for a while until Grigory poured a liberal sprinkling of wine on the flames, which sizzled and spat at us in response. He explained quietly that he was 'making an offering to the fire', a ritual without which no social gathering could proceed. I presumed that this rite of passage was more form than content. I was swiftly disabused. Noticing that a log was about to fall back from the flames, I kicked it back into the fire with my foot. Everyone stared at me and one of the younger men shook his finger at me in rebuke, saying sharply, 'You have not shown respect for the fire. You may move the log with your hand, but not with your feet.' I apologized.

Grigory then explained that the fire was sacred and that the rituals that they practised around it were deeply rooted in their national culture. All libations must be passed clockwise around the fire. Grigory sipped the wine and then passed it to me. I drank and handed it back to him. He replenished the cup and passed it to the neighbour on my left, and so on until everyone had tasted. The ritual reminded me a little of Holy Communion. By this time the kettle had boiled and we moved on to tea. Although Grigory and his colleagues spoke fluent Russian, they talked to each other in their own language. Grigory explained, 'We speak Altai to each other. It is our mother tongue.' He went on, eloquent and articulate. 'The Altai is my motherland. It is the centre of the world, and, as one of our famous writers said, "The Altai mountains are the cradle of humanity." It is not so much that we praise the Altai. It is simply that we respect and admire it. It gives us oxygen, and it gives us the natural world in which we live. We are a small nation, but we are a great nation. There have been wars, there has been Hitler and fascism, but we are still here. You English live all over the world – you live in Canada, you live in America, you live everywhere – but the Altai people only live in the Altai.'

This was said with such a wondrous combination of simplicity and intelligence that I felt encouraged to go further. Why the offering to the fire? Was it just a traditional ritual, or did it have a greater significance?' 'Let me tell you. We worship fire, water, air, the sun and the moon. They are all gods. They are nature, and we are part of nature.

Our religion is a little like Buddhism and a little like the beliefs of the American Indians.' I asked him how he practised his faith. 'Every day and anywhere,' he replied. 'When we ride through a mountain pass I may pray to the mountain. We worship nature. We are part of nature. We are children of nature.'

Christians decry such belief as 'primitive' or 'pagan'. Evangelicals would want to save Grigory's soul for Christ. They would want him to believe in a Holy Trinity, an Immaculate Conception and a Resurrection. They would insist that their cosmology was grounded in the unassailable 'truths' of monotheism, while his belief was rooted in superstition. What arrogance, what purblind arrogance, I thought, as I listened to this quiet homily in a plain little tent in the middle of a Siberian nowhere while we passed cups of tea one to another around the fire. Grigory spoke again. 'Everyone has to travel their own life and then to teach their children how to travel it. Wherever you are, that is the fate of man.'

Later that night, unable to sleep, I stood on the veranda of my dormitory. The rain had turned to snow, large flakes that at first dissolved as they hit the ground, but gradually began to settle. The grass started to turn white, and then the outdoor washstand and the roofs of the compound were similarly laced with snow. It was quite silent in the thickening fall. For a while I felt at peace, at home with nature. And then a sudden anxiety: what if it snowed so hard that we would be unable to leave? I would be trapped here when I should be driving to the nearest airport, twelve hours away, to fly home to my family. Then I cursed the snow, or, more precisely, I begged – I know not to what or to whom – that it might melt away by dawn. I went inside and tried to sleep, but kept tweaking the curtain and saw that the snow was still falling. By the small hours, raging with impotent resentment, I knew that I was done for, that I would never escape. Alexander had left the previous evening in his Land Cruiser. So I cursed him for good measure as well. My romance with the Altai was over.

The next morning it was still snowing. But as I packed my bags, I could hear a tractor cough and splutter into life. Like a shipwrecked sailor I hurried out to make sure that this life-saver was heading in our direction. A surge of relief. Grigory was at the wheel, ready to tow our van towards civilization. We lurched and skidded for an hour or so until we found firmer ground, when I thanked Grigory and he set off back to the compound. Before we moved on I looked around at the dazzling beauty of the mountains and the forest, catching my breath with delight at a scene that had not changed in centuries. I thought of Grigory's wise words from the evening before: 'We are part of nature. We are children of nature.'

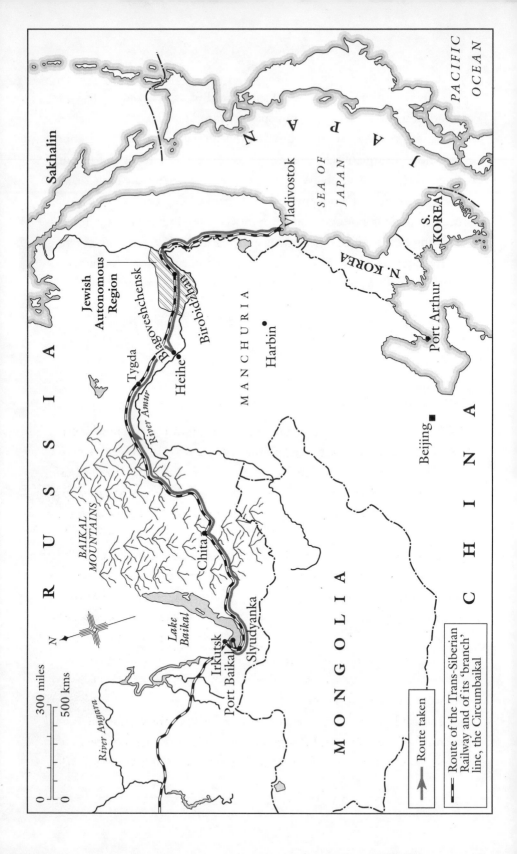

PACIFIC
OCEAN

Sakhalin

J A P A N

Vladivostok

SEA OF
JAPAN

S.
KOREA

N. KOREA

Port Arthur

Jewish
Autonomous
Region

Blagoveshchensk

Birobidzhan

Tygda

Heihe

MANCHURIA

Harbin

River Amur

Beijing

C H I N A

R U S S I A

BAIKAL
MOUNTAINS

Chita

Slyudyanka

Lake
Baikal

MONGOLIA

N

Irkutsk
Port Baikal

River Angara

300 miles

500 kms

0

0

Route taken

Route of the Trans-Siberian
Railway and of its 'branch'
line, the Circumbaikal

# PART FIVE
# FROM IRKUTSK
# TO VLADIVOSTOK

The thermometer on the veranda of the hunting lodge in which I had spent the night read minus 18 degrees centigrade. I was dressed as though for the Arctic, with a fur coat that made me look as though I had been given a bit part in *Dr Zhivago* but did not stop the hair in my nostrils crinkling in the cold. It was a cloudless blue-sky day: the mountains all around were covered with snow and glistened in the early morning sun. Everything was exhilaratingly silent until two layka hunting dogs suddenly began to bark at me in hostile unison. The layka looks a little like a husky, but is local to this region of Siberia and is distinguished by three twists to its tail. As laykas are renowned for confronting bear and boar as well as elk, sable and the three types of fox – black, red and polar – that frequent the surrounding wilderness, I was relieved to discover that the pair facing me were all bark and no bite.

I walked up the snow-covered road away from the compound, an assembly of log cabins and eco-green roofs, with the sound of the two guard dogs retreating into silence behind me. I felt the thrill of absolute solitude, sharpened by the suspicion that every twig that crackled and every bough that swayed concealed a hungry brown bear. The only animal I saw, however, was a tethered horse, the snow frozen on its back. Otherwise I was in a genuine wonderland of winter, glorying at the implacable, interminable scale of Siberia. I still had the best part of 3000 miles to go before reaching my final destination, Vladivostok on the Pacific coast, but for the first time, with more than 7000 miles now accomplished since leaving Murmansk in the far northwest, I felt no shiver of homesickness but only a surge of delight.

On my journey so far I felt as though I had been on two parallel voyages of discovery, one of places and people, the other of myself. So far, the exterior journey had been by turns fascinating, illuminating, entertaining, disturbing, challenging, frustrating, frightening, infuriating, saddening and at times heart-warming as well. My interior journey had too often been troubled, miserable and lonely even to the point of despair; not only a test of character (which I had often failed), but a test of endurance, psychological rather than physical, from which I now realized I was emerging, if not triumphant, at least unvanquished. I knew myself to be stronger than I had been for more than four years; that the waves of misery that rolled up without warning now engulfed me far less often; that I was far less frequently battered by gloom; that I could once again stride, not skulk, into the future; and that I could now at last – or once again – identify and embrace the important certainties in my life.

Of course, I still had feelings of sadness and loss – who doesn't? – but I had rediscovered happiness; not only those moments of joy that are a form of emotional intoxication, but a sustained, quiet optimism, a renewed sense of purpose that permits one to give an almost unequivocal answer to the question 'Are you happy?' In large measure I owed this to family and friends, but it was overwhelmingly due to the love and strength of Jessica, who had endured my bouts of self-absorption, despair and misery yet had never once complained. But I also knew that my long, long journey through Russia had, paradoxically, been my road to recovery, a real and metaphorical cushion – albeit a firm cushion – on which to rest a troubled psyche in need of reflection and restoration. Now, standing alone in the snow-waste, I rejoiced.

## AN ENCOUNTER WITH A SHAMAN

I had reached a remote part of southeastern Siberia called the Buryat Republic. It is easy, once you start to cover very long distances, to become blasé about it. Even here, I had to remind myself that Great Britain could be folded into the Buryat Republic almost twice over, although the British population is more than sixty times that of this relatively small land, which has fewer than 1 million inhabitants. I was on my way to meet Valentin Khagdaev, a shaman. 'More showman than shaman' someone had said sourly when I mentioned my destination. But, knowing very little about the ancient religion of shamanism, I was intrigued both by Valentin's faith and by the man himself. I had assumed that shamanism was some kind of religious cult that had died out except as a tourist attraction for spiritual romantics of the Glastonbury school of paganism; I came to repent my superciliousness.

I found Valentin in a middle-of-nowhere village called Yelantsi, where he lives in a modest two-storey house (but the only one of its size in the community) with his wife and his young son. At first sight he was not a prepossessing figure. A broad Mongolian face, topped by a fluffy tangle of black hair clasped in a ponytail, seemed to be perched uncomfortably on a body that was so rotund as to be almost obese. Short arms and stubby fingers accentuated a squat physique. But at least he was dressed for the part of a holy man, resplendent in a shaman's coat of many colours in which, as he put it, 'the eternal blue of the Mongolian sky' predominated.

As Valentin led me through his kitchen into the sitting room, I initially had to resist the thought that he could be a clown who had escaped from a travelling circus. Embroidered in green silk ('repre-senting the earth') and with black silk cuffs ('representing eternal wisdom'), the coat was laden with charms that hung about his person like a tinker's utensils. But as he explained their symbolism, I soon found myself entranced. There was a mirror ('to reverse the flight of an incoming enemy's arrow and to deflect hostile feelings'); a bronze eagle ('that protects all shamans'); a bronze shield decorated with wild and fantastic animals – a horse, a snake and a dragon – that encircled an engraved portrait of two human figures, male and female ('to represent our belief in ancestor-worship'); a little three-edged sword in silver ('to pierce the darkness of ignorance'); and, low over his belly, a medallion depicting Genghis Khan ('our great leader'). Valentin had described this confusing cornucopia with such seriousness and evident sincerity that I did not interrupt his flow until this point. 'Genghis Khan?' I asked quizzically. 'Yes, he led us to this land. The Buryat people are his descendants and we owe him everything.'

Valentin sat me down on a worn-out sofa and went to a sideboard that was covered with photographs. He scooped these up and brought across a garishly decorated plastic photo album as well. With a pride that was entirely free of false modesty, he pointed out his unmistakable bulk in each one, posing with government officials, priests of the Catholic and Orthodox Churches, Buddhist lamas, Muslim imams and Jewish elders. He had travelled all over Russia and widely in Asia and the United States. In one photo he was in the middle of a group of Native Americans in Arizona, who had given him the dangle of coloured beads that now hung about his neck. 'The Buryat people have a great deal in common with other indigenous peoples,' he explained. 'We are losing our language and our religious traditions and our history. We have much to discuss and try to find ways of solving our problems.' In another picture he was sitting incongruously astride a quad bike presented to him by the chairman of an energy corporation, ostensibly to facilitate his way from one holy place to the next across rough terrain, but, I suspected, in reality to ingratiate the donor with an influential figure in the community to whom many of the Buryat people looked for guidance. And there was a host of photographs in which Valentin stood on open ground surrounded by a group of evidently credulous tourists who sat enraptured as he delivered a seminar on the history and practices of shamanism.

Valentin was not at all embarrassed by the 'showman' jibe: the more people wanted to know about his religion, the better. He was a spiritual teacher schooled from birth in the rites and rituals of shamanism and, though he abhorred evangelism, he wanted his religion to thrive and prosper after a long period of persecution by the state. He practised both as a priest and, very occasionally, as a healer, applying traditional remedies alongside conventional medicine – which, in general, he believed to be far more effective. He came from a long line of shamans, a role that is generally passed down the family lineage though it very often jumps many generations. His grandfather had been a leading Buryat shaman, but under Stalin, hundreds of shamans (as well as Buddhist lamas) had been arrested, tortured and killed in an effort to stamp out their 'primitive' pagan beliefs. Valentin's father decided to conceal his religious identity and even joined the Communist Party. 'In those days it was too dangerous to be a shaman. My father was captured by the Germans in the war, and for that reason and that reason only he was imprisoned in the Gulag for three years. When he was released he found his way back to this village, and I was born here. When I was a child all religions were being persecuted, but I was still brought up in the shaman tradition, which was preserved despite the Soviet Union.'

Valentin was born with a double or split right thumb, which he called his 'second thumb' or 'sixth finger' and which, complete with its nail, sprouted branch-like from just above the joint. This 'deformity' – an extra bone in his body – immediately marked him out as an earthly conduit between the spirit world and the human world. At first he resisted the pressure to take on his allotted role, but eventually, following a series of signs and portents that he felt unable to resist, he succumbed to what he came to accept as his vocation. Today he is both master and student: the author of a postgraduate thesis on the history of shamanism, and a holy man who guides the faithful and treats the sick.

We drove out of the village along a snow-covered road towards the mountains to visit Valentin's favourite shrine. Along the way he talked about the Buryat people's origins in Mongolia that go back thousands of years and of their close but distrustful and sometimes combative links to China; of their ancient language, alphabet and script ('the Soviet authorities declared it to be feudal and forbade its use, but now I am teaching my son how to write in it'); of their great courage ('inherited from Genghis Khan'); and of their skill as horsemen and horse-breeders, hunters and fishermen, and later as farmers. His sense of national identity, preserved against the odds in the twentieth century, was clearly bound intimately to his religion: shamanism, though it reaches far beyond the confines of the Buryat Republic, is still one of the two 'national' faiths of his people, the other being Buddhism.

We turned off the road, driving on virgin snow, climbing up between outcrops of rock until we came to open ground high on the mountainside. 'We have arrived,' Valentin said, 'and this' – he spread his arms to the heavens – 'this is my cathedral.' We were surrounded by mountains, all white, their peaks blessed by a deep blue, cloudless sky. It was as pure and simple as the soul could ever seek, and as only a Matisse could ever transpose on to canvas. No photograph or film could quite convey the utter purity of the place. A hundred metres from where we stood an isolated conical rock, perhaps 4 metres high, protruded from the snow, patches of yellow lichen clinging to its rough edges. A vertical fissure ran through the granite, and somehow a delicate silver birch had managed to root there so that it appeared to have had the supernatural strength to force its way through the rock from which it had emerged, frail but triumphant, to reach for the sky. The surrounding mountain showed no other sign of life for as far as I could see to the distant horizon. 'This is a holy place and this is where I worship,' Valentin explained. 'I always feel the presence of the spirits here, and I feel a kind of awe when I am here. Let us go there.'

Valentin's simplicity of language, his certainties and the beauty of the landscape all around us made the terms used by Western scholars in their efforts to distil the essence of his religion seem unduly patronizing. To those whose culture has been nurtured by the 'great' monotheist religions, pantheism and animism are ostensibly neutral terms but are subconsciously laden with cultural baggage across which is emblazoned the word 'primitive'. *The Oxford English Dictionary* definition of shamanism is characteristic: 'The primitive religion...in which all the good and evil of life are thought to be brought about by spirits who can be influenced only by the shamans...the beliefs, rituals, techniques, etc., associated with a shaman, the general pattern of which is found almost universally in primitive cultures at the food-gathering stage of social development.' This may be factually correct, but 'primitive' is a slippery term for which the word 'backward' – as well as 'ancient' – is a common synonym. The pejorative implication is that developed societies, by virtue of education and progress, discard animist faiths for more 'advanced' or 'modern' religions like Christianity – as if the tenets of the latter are in some way superior to those of the former. This has always seemed to me a particularly absurd assertion of cultural superiority. Nonetheless, perhaps because I am infected with the prevailing attitudes of the West, I felt a deep unease as I walked beside Valentin to his shrine. Was I about to participate from good manners but in bad faith in a voodoo ritual (from which I instinctively recoiled)? 'Do you really want me to join you?' I asked, hoping to escape. Valentine nodded, 'Please. Anyone can come here – from all faiths and none. Let me tell you about this rock and this tree.' He spoke so gently that I had no choice.

'The sky is the ceiling of our temple. The ground is our house. In our prayers we say, "The high skies are our father and the wide ground is our mother." The tree unites the sky and the earth, and through its roots it reaches to the underground. The underworld, the middle world and the upper world. And here we pay tribute to the spirits that are in all three worlds. We can also make a wish and the wind will carry our wishes to their destination.' I followed Valentin up to the rock like a novice monk, copying his every move. We hugged the rock, 'to show our reverence for all the spirits of the three worlds'. We caressed the twigs on the lower branches of the silver birch, holding them to our faces, 'to ask the gods to bless us'. Numerous strips of white cloth, like bandannas, fluttered in the breeze from the branches to which previous pilgrims had tied them, 'symbolizing our gifts to the gods'. He produced two such strips from the folds of his robe and gave one to me. We pressed these to our foreheads and paused to make a wish, after which we tied them to the tree, 'asking the wind to take our wishes to the spirits'.

As we stepped back from the tree I half-expected him to make the sign of the cross, but after a pause he turned away. We walked down over a small ridge towards a little group of people who were standing around a crudely constructed bench, behind which there was a pole suspended horizontally from two uprights about 2 metres off the ground, which Valentin called a 'stall'. It reminded me of those stands that gamekeepers erect to hang out dead weasels and crows and rats and other pheasant-threatening vermin, but, like the tree, it too was bedecked with ribbons. It is called a *sarge* and was to form the centrepiece of another ritual, this time enacted with his family, his wife, their son and three other relatives who had joined us for the ceremony. His son had laid a fire and Valentin put a match to it. 'Christians light candles in their cathedrals – we light fires in the open,' he explained. His wife had brought a shopping bag with her from which she unearthed a half bottle of vodka, a packet of tea and some wrapped sweets that were to form part of the ritual. 'This is our family's place. I feel more at home here than anywhere else. I am the leader of my clan, which has more than four hundred family members, and they all come here to worship. We owe our existence to a Creator, a dear Creator – we do not use the word God – who gives life and death, wealth and poverty, all that exists. All faiths have their vision of hell and nirvana. We have a cult of our ancestors, the guardians of eternal life. We pray to them, telling them what is happening on earth in our lives, and then they can tell us how to reach heaven. When that happens, we will be united with the creative light.'

By this time the fire was glowing fiercely and the water had boiled. Valentin produced a tambourine and lined his family up facing the *sarge*. Beating a slow rhythm on the tambourine while his son poured most of the vodka on to the fire, which produced a sudden flare of flames, he walked round the *sarge* in a circle, round and round, like a Pied Piper, with his family following behind. After a few circumnavigations, they came to a halt. Valentin told his son to fetch the kettle of tea, which he carefully poured along the base of the *sarge*. His wife did the same with the sweets, laying each one down to form a row as though she were planting out potatoes. The propitiation of their ancestors thus accomplished, they started to circle the *sarge* yet again. The ceremony lasted for some thirty minutes, but was conducted so casually that I only realized it had come to an end when I was invited to help drink the remains of the vodka (discarding the bottle on a small pile beside the *sarge*) and to eat one of the sweets. Then, without ceremony, we departed, leaving only the glowing fire and empty bottles of vodka as the evidence of our presence at this holy place in the mountains.

Valentin's reverence for the natural world made him anxious about the future. 'We have to live in harmony with nature and with each other and then all would be well. Nature is like a long stick with two ends. If we break the stick at one end it will hit us with the other. We now have a wild capitalism. They cut down the forests and send the timber to China. The next generation will find there is no forest. In Lake Baikal there will be less water and fewer fish. And future generations will blame us.' I thought of Boris who presided over the desecration of the forest outside Tomsk as he continued, 'Every tree has its soul, so it should only be cut for a good purpose. We perform a rite to the gods before we cut. But the logging companies don't respect that rite. They just cut them and cut them. And that is why we have so many natural disasters. When trees are cut down, the rivers dry out and there is drought. And then people wonder why they don't have enough fish. We need to understand that we are all citizens of this earth and we need to take care of our planet – otherwise we will destroy it. I think that mankind is at the last step, on the edge. We have to make a choice. Everything in nature is linked.'

Valentin spoke with passion, like a teacher who really cares but needs to explain in language that no pupil could possibly misunderstand. To an instinctive Gaian, like myself, his words seemed both spiritually compelling and scientifically sound. So when he added, 'There was a lake where there were many ducks, and people came to shoot the ducks. And the lake dried through grief,' I found myself carried along to the point where, had I remained in Buryat, I might well have become a disciple, learning to speak in parables and waging peaceful war against global warming with arguably greater effect than a Western campaigner would ever achieve. 'Yes,' I thought as we parted, 'everything in nature is linked,' adding to myself, 'That is all we know and all we need to know.'

## THE AIDS CAPITAL OF RUSSIA

Irkutsk, which bills itself as the 'gateway to the East', the capital city of eastern Siberia, offered a very sharp contrast indeed. It was founded in 1661 as a garrison town against the marauding Buryat tribesman, or – from the marauders' alternative perspective – as a fortress from which to launch punitive raids against the indigenous peoples of the region who were resisting the inexorable occupation of their lands by the expanding Russian Empire. At the confluence of the Irkut and Angara rivers, it straddled the trade route between Russia and China via Mongolia, and grew rich and important. By the end of the nineteenth century the city, as it had become, was both opulent and blowzy, elegant and vulgar. Heralded as the 'Paris of Siberia', Irkutsk, with its fine avenues and grand apartments, was richly endowed with hospitals, schools and libraries, and dignified by lavish provincial balls that sought to emulate the grander versions that were fashionable in St Petersburg. But it had a darker side too.

As a major administrative and commercial centre, Irkutsk not only stood on a lucrative trade route, but was a foul junction on the sorry one-way system along which tsarist convicts and exiles were driven from West to East into servitude. In addition to these unhappy immigrants, the town attracted gold miners, merchants and traders, as well as criminals of every class and variety. Colin Thubron's *In Siberia* has vividly captured the spirit of those cruel but buccaneering days. 'A nightlife of merriment and debauchery was sharpened by rampant crime.... The nights were bedevilled by professional garrotters; and sledgers would gallop out in blizzards to lasso lone pedestrians and murder them up side-alleys. Nobody interfered. The police were helpless.' By the turn of the twentieth century, its reputation had hardly improved. *Bradshaw's Through Routes to the Chief Cities of the World* warned that in Irkutsk the garrotters were still about their business and the police were still helpless; moreover, 'escaped convicts and ticket-of-leave criminals are many...the stranger should not walk after dark...be careful in making crossings, and do not stop, or the immense mongrel mastiffs, turned loose in the streets as guards, will attack'.

In those days, Irkutsk was known as the 'murder capital' of Russia. A century later that unenviable baton has been passed to Moscow, and Irkutsk has acquired a new and equally unwelcome sobriquet: the 'AIDS capital' of the nation. To find out more, I joined a team of Red Cross volunteers as they went out on one of their nightly visits to the street corners where prostitutes ply for business and the sink estates where addicts congregate to share drugs and needles. On the surface, modern Irkutsk seemed modestly prosperous but mildly dilapidated, like an old biddy trying against the odds to keep up appearances. But as soon as you peer under that peeling carapace, you find yourself in a netherworld of deprivation and decline. As we drove through the dim streets into the suburbs, I listened to what was – at one level – a familiar story. Sexual intercourse and shared needles are the main means of HIV transmission; 'drug users' and 'street workers' – the terms preferred by the Red Cross – are two of the hardest 'target groups' to reach. Alienated almost by definition, fearful of the authorities and profoundly ignorant of the Russian-roulette risks with which they live every day, the most 'at-risk' groups are as fatalistic about life and death as Rudyard Kipling thought we should all be about triumph and disaster. But HIV is not an imposter.

We pulled up in a dark courtyard surrounded by tenement blocks, switched off the headlights of the Red Cross people carrier and waited. After a while, a young man appeared from the gloom and came up to the van. The door opened and he entered. He had come to exchange his used needles for a new supply for himself and his friends. 'How many do you want?' 'Two hundred and fifty,' (enough to last them for a week). The Red Cross outreach workers on this shift were themselves ex-addicts, and it was at once clear that, as soon as he had seen that their arrival had not been secretly tracked by the police, they had a bond of shared experience that swiftly broke through any barriers of mistrust.

Their conversation soon became technical, with talk about Red Hats ('I'm not shooting up with Red Hats – I don't need them at the moment'), Doubles ('Give us some Doubles', 'OK – I'll give you one pack of Doubles and some needles') and Fivers ('I bring some next week'). Then there were the wipes ('You must use them before and after shooting up') and a supply of sanitary towels for the girls ('How many girls have you got there?' 'I don't know – four, maybe five'). After ten minutes he prepared to get out of the van, promising to show up next week when the Red Cross would be on site with an HIV blood-testing kit, so saving him and his friends from a trek to the clinic. He disappeared into the night with his bag of vital goodies – one sad young man who, with luck, will not infect others in future. I wondered at the skill and patience of his Red Cross mentor. In a city so heavily stricken by drug addiction, he knew that success could be measured only on a small scale, yet he persevered, undaunted by the statistics.

The Red Cross team leader was a young woman doctor, plump, elegantly coiffured, with disconcertingly long black eyelashes, laden with mascara, that tilted upwards like Bambi's. But she was not at all soft-centred – her tone was matter-of-fact. 'When the epidemic really took hold, in 1998, it was drug users sharing needles who passed it to each other. They made up ninety-seven per cent of the HIV cases in the city.' Apparently, they concocted their own drugs, often injecting cannabis, mixed with blood, intravenously to secure an instant 'high'. 'Now it is different. They are almost all on heroin, which they buy from middlemen, and it is of very poor quality. Recently they have started to add other substances like eye-drops to the heroin in the belief that it will conceal their addiction from the authorities by dilating their pupils.' 'How does the heroin get into the city?' I asked. 'Remember that Irkutsk has always been a crossroads. Now it is drug-traffickers bringing it from Afghanistan via Mongolia.' 'Is the situation getting worse?' She sighed, paused, looking uncomfortable, and then said, 'Not according to the official figures. Let's not talk about that. I am not authorized to discuss the statistics.'

A few miles further on we turned off a main road and pulled up under a lamp that filtered a yellow light on to the truck-blackened snow that had been scraped up into neat heaps in the gutter. I noticed a line of washing hanging from a ground-floor balcony – a pair of trousers, shirts, socks and underwear, frozen and cracked, a line of snow along the top of each garment – and I suddenly felt the chill of a minus 10 degrees night-time temperature. 'Mild for the time of year,' I was told. We had reached a regular rendezvous and, a few minutes after our arrival, a young woman hurried over to the van. Serti was twenty-one years old and had been on the game for two years. She charged 150 roubles for oral sex and 500 for full intercourse. She needed to earn upwards of 1500 roubles a night, enough for the ten small doses of very low-quality heroin with which she injected herself every day. Under the lamp-post she looked much younger than I had expected. She wore a fawn woolly hat prettily embroidered with beads and a thick scarf around her neck so that she seemed more child than adult. Her long, fur-collared leather coat completed a picture of vulnerable modesty; though her face was embalmed in make-up, she was round-faced and pretty in an English rose way. It was only when I looked more closely that I saw her broken teeth and the sores around her mouth that she had pathetically tried to conceal with a smear of scarlet lipstick.

'Most of the girls are between twenty and thirty. We give them condoms, a pregnancy testing kit and tissues for cleaning themselves after sex,' one of the Red Cross team explained, 'and of course we offer counselling as well.' Serti was now a regular client, and they had hopes she would soon go into voluntary rehab. I asked her about her future. She replied in a flat monotone, but with more clarity than I had thought likely. 'The Red Cross has helped me. They are very good people. They are all former users of intravenous drugs and now they are normal people. I want to be a normal person, so I am going into rehab, but before that I have to go back into hospital. I've been inject-ing myself, and I have shot up my veins so badly that on Saturday I was practically at death's door. My veins had to be operated on and now I can barely walk. It is very painful. On Wednesday they are going to take my stitches out. I have to start thinking about my life very hard – I mean, how much of this can your body take?'

Her inspiration – her hope against hope – was one of the Red Cross team whom she had known when she too was on heroin. 'She had been injecting herself for eight years. I lost touch with her, and the next time I saw her she was working with the Red Cross. I did not recognize her – she had changed completely. But she recognized me. "Look at the state you are in," she said to me. "Look what has happened to you!" And I thought that if she could make herself better, then I could cure myself as well. I'm a strong person. I am just twenty-one and I can be like her.' She did not seem at all strong and

I will never know whether she succeeds in becoming a 'normal' person again, but her courage of that moment and the empathetic tenacity of the Red Cross team will stay with me.

I had seen other outreach workers in other countries, so, admirable though they were, I knew that the Red Cross volunteers were part of a worldwide effort by similar teams, often working in even more demanding conditions, to combat the pandemic. I had spent time in hospitals in several African countries where the beds were overflowing with patients dying of full-blown AIDS. I had witnessed dreadful suffering and shared the frustration of doctors and nurses denied access to basic drugs, let alone the anti-retrovirals that were (long before the turn of the last century) routinely available in the West. I met the mothers who were fatally infected and their soon-to-be-orphaned little children in earth-floored hovels in filthy townships where they had no food, let alone medicine. And, to uncertain avail, I had railed in public – in articles, speeches, interviews and TV films – that the world's fail-ure to provide the resources available to help the victims to 'live' with AIDS was properly, if not technically, a crime against humanity. But even in the poorest countries in Africa – Ethiopia, Malawi, Zambia and Uganda – I had not witnessed quite such an inexcusably avoidable disaster as that which now afflicts Irkutsk.

When I tried to find out why HIV was so disproportionately rampant in the city, I was at first told only part of the story – though Dr Yulia Raikana, who runs the AIDS Unit in Irkutsk's decrepit nineteenth-century Hospital for Infectious Diseases, was impressively brisk and clear-minded. She has worked devotedly in the Russian equivalent of the NHS for twenty-five years and was clearly a frustrated woman, who gave me the impression that she wanted to be even more forthright than her official position allowed. She told me about patients who – catastrophi-cally – stop taking their drugs as soon as they feel better, and about young people 'who think they have for ever so that by the time they come to us it is too late'. Many others simply ignore the government's 'safe-sex' messages and, according to Dr Raikana, 'very often they don't even have the money to buy condoms' in any case. As a result, not only is the incidence of HIV increasing but, through 'vertical transmission', a growing number of infants are infected with the virus.

The city's predicament is further complicated by its forlorn history as a place of punishment and exile. 'We have so many prisons in the region, and TB is endemic in them. When the convicts are released they have nothing, so they live on the streets, in alleys, sleeping on the heating grids to keep warm. The disease spreads fast. It is the principal opportunistic infection among HIV/AIDS patients – at least fifty per cent of them contract TB as well.' Because the onset of the pandemic is so recent, most of Dr Raikana's patients are not yet aware of what it is like to experience full-blown AIDS. This gives a degree of cold comfort. 'When people see the fatalities that we are going to have in very large numbers, we may be able to convince them that they must play safe and they must take their drugs.' As she said that, she looked as bleak as her words sounded.

The prospect is as grim as it is possible to imagine. According to the official figures, twenty thousand people are registered as HIV-positive in the Irkutsk region – four times the national average. 'But,' Dr Raikana cautioned, 'our epidemiological analysis shows that the real figure is three or four times that – between seventy and eighty thousand.' In a country where the official statistics show the number of cases to be increasing at a rate of 12 per cent a year, Irkutsk's epidemic is on a truly alarming path. But what is really shocking is how little was done to combat the disease after the first case in the city was revealed in 1991, eight years after the World Health Organization had alerted the international community to the threat posed by the AIDS virus. The explanation for this failure is highly sensitive and, in microcosm, it tells you a great deal about the nature and structure of power and politics in post-Soviet Russia. I only stumbled on the truth in a meeting with the head of the Red Cross in Irkutsk, Marina Akulova.

We had started to discuss the organization's unique position in a country that the Kremlin has encouraged to become institutionally paranoid about non-governmental organizations, especially those that are based abroad, when she startled me by saying, 'If we did not have the international status that being the Red Cross gives us, our HIV outreach programme would have been closed down long ago. It would have been killed by the Drug Control authorities.' 'What?' I said in disbelief. 'Yes. You have to know that until very recently, until eighteen months ago, the authorities in Irkutsk had ignored the problem. Non-profit organizations were scared to tackle the problem, scared to raise awareness, fearing that they would become *persona non grata*.' 'But why? How could this be?' I persisted. 'The authorities were in denial – they just didn't want to know. It may be hard to believe, but even in the late nineties the statistics were concealed by the authorities. They took their cue from the governor, and the governor refused even to meet us to discuss the issue. It was ostrich politics.'

I began to understand why everyone I had met so far seemed so reluctant to explain how an outbreak of HIV in a very small group of drug addicts had so rapidly exploded into a full-scale epidemic. Marina only felt free to speak like this because she was protected by the shield of the Red Cross, which gives her a quasi-diplomatic immunity, an advantage that none of her peers could presume upon. This did not detract from her courage – others in her position might well have judged it politic to keep their counsel – but it did mean that her voice could not be smothered. She picked up her story. 'Two years ago we had a new governor in office, but he also took a long time to recognize the scale of the problem. No one around him wanted to discuss it. Then Vladimir Posner came here with his programme *Time to Live*, and everything changed.'

Vladimir Posner? My mind went back more than two decades to a time when the same Posner was a familiar voice from Moscow in the eighties, a smooth apologist for the Soviet Union, with a disarming manner and a mastery of the English language, which he spoke with a faultless Harvard accent. I had met him on a couple of occasions and had always doubted his sincerity – though not his charm. It was not at all surprising to discover that he was now born again as a television star for the post-Soviet age. Posner's producers had packed the *Time to Live* studio with drug users and representatives of local charities. 'The governor was interviewed by Posner, and it was soon clear that he knew nothing about the HIV epidemic in Irkutsk. Posner gave him a really rough ride and he was obviously very embarrassed. Even today when I say the word "Posner" to the authorities it is like a red rag to a bull.' Marina smiled with relived pleasure. 'It is much better now. We still don't have enough education, and we still don't have the resources to reach out beyond the city to the region, where there is still a total failure to understand the problem and how to prevent it. But at least the bureaucracy, which has been appalling, is now facing in the right direction.'

And there have been results. In 2006 the government unfolded a $125 million national AIDS initiative, which, given the scale of the challenge, is a very modest sum – but it is a start, and some of this money has already reached Irkutsk. 'The situation is changing. Our prophylactic programmes are beginning to have an effect. Among our target groups, there is more "peer to peer" counselling. The official figures show that where we now focus our work, in schools and colleges, the number of HIV infections is falling,' Marina said. 'But it should never have reached this point,' I interrupted. 'If the governor had acted on what he knew, rather than ignoring the problem, it could have been contained.' 'Yes, that is true. We could have worked far earlier with the intravenous drug users, the high-risk group. The epidemic had started by 1999, but it wasn't for another three years that a serious programme was got under way. The moment was missed, and the disease spread out to the rest of the population.'

I followed her logic to its implicit conclusion. 'So there is very little excuse for the authorities. They knew what was happening, but they chose to ignore it. As a result, a lot of people are going to get full-blown AIDS and will die unnecessarily.' For a moment, the enormity of how she was about to respond flummoxed her. She said nothing for a full thirty seconds. Then, hesitantly, 'You want me to take quite a serious step here, don't you?' she said, evidently struggling to reconcile her deep feelings with the need to preserve the Red Cross's relationship with an administration that she so clearly despised. I nodded. She tiptoed into an answer that almost achieved her purpose. 'Er, well, if you like, I think the, er, authorities are, er, responsible for what happens in any region, for their, er, style of governance and, er, in any number of questions it is the responsibility of the authorities. Um, perhaps that is an answer?' She looked at me with an expression that implored me not to be crass enough to press the point. I nodded, thinking that I had not yet met anyone in Russia more tenacious or more caring than this slight woman with her delicate features but indomitable spirit. She looked at me gratefully and a moment later said, in quiet parenthesis, 'I live in Irkutsk and I love this place. It is very sad.'

## NATURAL AND MAN-MADE WONDERS

We left Irkutsk before dawn, scudding out of the city on dry, crunchy snow that blew in coils around the car. A convoy of snow ploughs, yellow lights twittering in the dark, was already at work, but we were soon in front of them, driving fast towards Lake Baikal with a ferry to catch. In Britain, where 'severe weather' warnings are given whenever there is a rainstorm in the offing, the concept has lost almost all credibility. But this was by any standards – except Russian – severe weather. Nevertheless, our driver – and those in the occasional car that loomed out of the darkness towards us at a similar speed, giving a combined collision-course speed of around 75 mph – was clearly indifferent to the threat of imminent oblivion. And yet, although our vehicle had no chains or snow tyres, in conditions that would have brought all traffic to a standstill in 'unless your journey is really necessary' Britain, the tyres didn't spin and we didn't swerve or skid once in a two-hour journey uphill and downhill on a bed of snow at least 10 centimetres deep. After a while I even began to enjoy the thrill of the risk.

The road itself was as straight as though it had been built by the Romans, switchbacking through the forest and over the hills towards Port Baikal. Its construction is said to have been ordered by Khrushchev half a century ago so that President Dwight D. Eisenhower could be whisked from Irkutsk to see the wonder of Lake Baikal. In the late fifties, during a brief Cold War thaw, the Russian leader held out an olive branch to the West, which he labelled 'Peaceful Co-existence'. In 1959 he was rewarded with a personal visit to the United States, where he was refused admission to Disneyland on the grounds of 'national security', but was granted an audience with his American counterpart at Camp David. Eisenhower was due to make a return visit the following year. Then fate intervened in the form of the U2 spy-plane incident, when the American pilot Gary Powers was shot down over Ekaterinburg (then known as Sverdlovsk), and the visit was cancelled. But, unlike the course of US–Soviet relations, the development of the road on which we now careered towards the famous lake proceeded smoothly on its way.

By the time we reached the little jetty at the edge of Lake Baikal just outside the village of Listvyanka, it was dawn and the sun was peeping over the water. A strong wind had built this corner of the lake into white-capped waves, and there was no sign of the ferry that was to take us across the mouth of the Angara River that flows out of Lake Baikal. It was very cold, with a wind chill factor that made minus 10 degrees centigrade seem very much worse. Eventually a boat, a little larger than a wartime landing craft, emerged from a headland on the other side of the entrance to the river and lurched slowly towards us. I had a momentary *frisson* as I remembered the storm on the White Sea some 6000 miles behind me, but the wind had begun to fall away and by the time the ferry had docked safely under the lee of the land, the whitecaps had all but disappeared. On the way across to Port Baikal I stood in the open, the wind in my face, stamping my feet, looking out across the lake to the Baikal mountains to the east, their tips now illuminated by the rising sun.

I had allowed myself to believe that Port Baikal would be a busy terminal with freighters and pleasure craft, cranes and derricks, dockers and harbourmasters. In fact there was no movement on the water and very little on the land. A trio of deserted tugs and four elderly pleasure steamers, streaked yellow with rust and mothballed for the winter, were moored alongside a crumbling jetty. Otherwise the harbour was no more than a graveyard for a disorderly array of abandoned hulks, long stripped of reusable gear and tackle. Whatever commercial utility Port Baikal might once have had was impossible to discern in this forlorn wreckage. There weren't even any seagulls.

But I hadn't come to Port Baikal for the boats – I was intending to catch a train. And as soon as I went ashore I saw it. Tucked behind a collection of tumbledown sheds was a spruce little station and, waiting for us, the single turbo-carriage that was to take us for a 100-mile ride along the edge of the lake. The route had once formed part of the Trans-Siberian Railway, linking Port Baikal to the town of Slyudyanka southwest of Irkutsk. It was at once clear that the Circumbaikal Line, as it is now known, was an astonishing feat of engineering. The mountains fall steeply to the water, in some places leaving only just enough space for the track so that, as it snaked its way around the lake, our little train seemed sometimes to overhang the water. We twisted around headlands and across ravines. Where it had proved impossible to circumnavigate the cliffs, the engineers had punched a way through the rock. As we trundled from sunlight into the pitch-darkness, I soon lost count of the neatly chiselled tunnels, but not my wonder at the ambition of the enterprise.

Originally the Trans-Siberian ran from Moscow to Irkutsk (a distance of just over 3000 miles), and then from Irkutsk along the eastern bank of the Angara River to Port Baikal. The government had resolved in 1893 that from there, in the summer months, the trains would be ferried directly across to the eastern side of the lake by ship; in winter they would take the same route, but each carriage would be pulled by draught horses along rail tracks laid on the ice. At the time it seemed an imaginative and financially prudent way of bypassing the impenetrable mountains to the south of the lake. Accordingly, in 1895 a British company based in Newcastle-upon-Tyne won the contract to supply two ice-breaking ferries. Six months later the two vessels duly arrived on the shores of Lake Baikal, packed in boxes, every part neatly marked. There they were unpacked and reassembled. For the next five years the two ferries, named the *Angara* and the *Baikal*, plied their way back and forth across the southern end of the lake.

But it very soon became evident that the unpredictable weather patterns over Baikal – which brought winds of hurricane strength, great storms and impenetrable fogs – would fatally disrupt what had been designed as the strategically vital link between Moscow and the Trans-Siberian's final destination, Vladivostok. This port city, a further 2500 miles across Siberia, had been established forty years earlier as the Pacific base for the Russian Imperial Navy. Rising fears about the expansionist dreams of the Japanese Empire forced the tsar's hand, and in 1899 work started on the construction of the Circumbaikal Line. It was a monumental undertaking. As there was no way across the mountains, all materials, supplies and equipment had to be brought by barges across the lake. Upwards of thirteen thousand men, most of them convicts, laboured in atrocious conditions to hack their way through the rock, building more than fifty tunnels and over two hundred bridges and viaducts, as well as artificial embankments to protect the track from landslides on either side. As one of the leaders of the project noted, the construction of the Circumbaikal Line 'surpassed in difficulty and amount of work all those constructed in the Russian Empire up to the present'.

The urgency of the task was dramatically confirmed in February 1904 when the Japanese launched a surprise torpedo attack on the Russian fleet at Port Arthur (Lu-Shun), precipitating the Russo-Japanese War in the Pacific. In *To the Great Ocean*, Harmon Tupper has vividly described the crippling impact of the Lake Baikal bottleneck as the Russians rushed men and material across the Urals to confront the

Japanese in Manchuria. 'The chaos of congestion reached its peak in the spring and summer of 1904 at Irkutsk where whole regiments piled up awaiting passage on the *Baikal* and the *Angara*, which together could manage no more than four daily round trips when not delayed by fog and mechanical breakdowns.' Seven months later the line was opened, but with so many defects that, according to Tupper, 'the first train derailed ten times [and] failed to pass through one of the tunnels until the tops of the car-roof ventilators were removed'.

By now it was far too late for the Circumbaikal Line to play a significant role in the war. After several sea battles and a long siege, the commander of the base at Port Arthur surrendered in January 1905. Desperate attempts by Russian naval squadrons to reach Vladivostok, their only other port in the Pacific, failed. After a further fifteen battles, in which the Russians lost two of their three naval fleets, St Petersburg was forced to sue for peace. Following mediation by President Theodore Roosevelt (for which he was awarded a Nobel Peace Prize), Russia was obliged to cede southern Manchuria to Japan – and thereby what the Russians had regarded as a vital sphere of influence in that region. The international prestige of the Japanese Empire rose sharply and that of the Russian Empire fell in equal measure; the balance of power in eastern Asia had been transformed.

The impact of the war on opinion in Russia was profound. The revolution of 1905 was not caused by the Empire's humiliation at the hands of the Japanese, but it coincided with the string of defeats in the Pacific and fuelled the resentment of the populace against the tsar. On 9 January, as Nicholas II allegedly played cards at home with his family, his troops fired at a crowd of more than one hundred thousand peaceful demonstrators who had taken to the streets of St Petersburg carrying a petition for the tsar that pleaded: 'We are beggars, we are oppressed and overburdened with work, we are not looked on as human beings but as slaves. The moment has come for us when death would be better for us than the prolongation of our intolerable sufferings. We are seeking here our last salvation. Do not refuse to help your people.' News of the massacre, in which around a thousand demonstrators were killed and a further five thousand wounded, spread rapidly. Sailors on the battleship *Potemkin* mutinied. Strikes and disruption spread. The tsar attempted conciliation with his October Manifesto, but two months later deployed loyal troops, back from the Pacific front, to crush strikers in Moscow and to restore order in the countryside.

Although he had belatedly held out the offer of political and social reform, the seeds of the 1917 Bolshevik revolution had been sown and, with them, the fate of the last of the Romanovs. As the American consul in Odessa wrote presciently, 'The present ruler has absolutely lost the affection of the Russian people, and whatever the future may hold in store for the dynasty, the present Czar will never again be safe in the midst of his people.'

As my little train ambled along the Circumbaikal, I indulged in a little counter-factual speculation. What if the bottleneck at Lake Baikal had been relieved earlier? What if the Trans-Siberian loop around the lake had been opened six months before? What if the supplies had reached Vladivostok? Would Russia have been spared defeat in the Pacific? Would the peasants and workers in St Petersburg have found themselves bound to the tsar by renewed patriotic fervour? Would the revolution have been postponed or even cancelled? Would Germany have hesitated before declaring war on Russia in August 1914? Would we have been spared Hitler and Stalin? Would the history of the world have taken an entirely different course? The answer, of course, was very probably 'no' all round, but as we wound our way along the tranquil edge of Lake Baikal, one of the great natural wonders of our planet, my own mental meanderings did not seem entirely absurd.

Almost 400 miles in length and 50 miles wide, Lake Baikal is the oldest and deepest lake in the world. In fact it is so old and so deep that more than a thousand of its two thousand species are unique to the lake – a mystery of evolution that goes back 25 million years. With a depth of over 1600 metres, Baikal contains one-fifth of the planet's supply of fresh water, which is as much as you will find in all five of the

Great Lakes of America combined; it has been calculated that if the entire population of the world started to use water at the highest current rate of urban consumption, the lake would supply all our needs for fifty years. It is a real wonder of the world.

Lake Baikal is magnificent but it is far from benign. Unexpected hurricanes and storms, transforming a placid surface into a cauldron of boiling water within minutes, have claimed the lives of countless fishermen, sailors and travellers. It is no less ferocious when winter arrives and the water turns to ice several metres deep. Then, with an unpredictable violence that is enough to make even a rational being shiver in primitive terror, the ice is prone to crack, opening up fissures up to 2 metres wide and nearly 20 miles in length. Horses, camels, sledges, carts, trucks, cars and even a locomotive have been sucked into the abyss along with their drivers and passengers, all frozen to death within moments. Not surprisingly, the Buryat people have long regarded the lake with fear and awe. I looked back towards the Bay of Ecstasy and Cape Burkhan, both of which Valentin the shaman had described to me as sacred, home to the holy spirits of Baikal. By now the sun was low in the sky and the water was ruffled only by catspaws scudding across the surface. It was beautiful, still and eerie, as if all the secrets of the world might be hidden in its depths.

## CHITA, CITY OF EXILES

At Slyudyanka, a Trans-Siberian junction on the route from Irkutsk, we caught a night train heading for Chita, 650 miles further along the way to Vladivostok. At last I was on the great railway for real. Disappointingly, my train seemed to have no features that would distinguish it from the multitude that had seen me most of the way thus far from my starting point in Murmansk. However, with a seventeen-hour journey ahead of me I soon settled contentedly into what was by now a familiar ritual: pulling down my pillow, blankets and sheets from the rack above the sliding door into my compartment, fetching tea from the samovar, and settling myself in a corner with blinds drawn, first to read and, very soon after that, lulled by the rhythmic swaying of the train, to sleep.

As it happened, I kept sleep at bay on this occasion by reading about the history of the Trans-Siberian Railway. I have never been a railway buff, let alone a train-spotter, but the story of the track over which we now trundled swiftly broke my resistance. Although it is often described as the longest railway in the world, that prize belongs jointly to the Moscow–Pyongyang and the Kiev–Vladivostok lines, both of which are precisely 6380 miles in length. At 5771 miles, the Trans-Siberian comes a mere third in the hierarchy. But from Russia's perspective it is by the far most important. Until the last decade of the nineteenth century, steamboats on rivers and sledges on ice were the principal means of transport through Siberia; the long, unpaved high-way known as the Great Siberian Route, which was commissioned in the late seventeenth century but took almost two hundred years to complete, was clearly 'not fit for purpose' by the closing decades of the nineteenth century.

Approved by Tsar Alexander II, the early construction of the Trans-Siberian was supervised by his son, Alexander III. The work started simultaneously in the west and the east in 1891, and it took a mere twenty-four years to complete (though most of it was finished within the first fifteen). Its impact was immediate. Land-hungry peas-ants pouring eastwards over the Urals into Siberia, a total of 2.5 million people between 1895 and 1916, were only the first wave of a mass migration in the early years of the twentieth century that led to a transformation of the Siberian economy that could not have been contemplated without the Trans-Siberian. Today, despite a modest growth of road and air transport, this rail link is still by far the most important east–west artery in the nation. Without it, life in the Russian Federation, let alone Siberia, would be severely, if not fatally, disrupted. The raw data – the inventory of trains, carriages and wagons, the number of staff and passengers, the variety, weight and value of goods, the proportion of imports and exports, the movement of soldiers and weapons – testify to its critical social, economic and strategic importance even in the twenty-first century. Pop-eyed and mind-boggled at the scale and complexity of an endeavour that is even more important today than it was a century ago, I eventually fell asleep with the statistics still in my hands, rocked by the gentle sway of my carriage and the diggedy-dig of wheels on rails.

The next morning I made my way to the restaurant car for break-fast. It did not bear close comparison with, say, the Orient Express, let alone the Brighton Belle, but the pale blue curtains and table-cloths, the vases of artificial flowers and an aspirational menu made a promising combination. A pretty teenage waitress, dressed neatly in a black uniform and a pinafore of the kind favoured by traditional French restaurants, smiled a welcome. I had in mind a breakfast of the all-day kind. Eggs, bacon, toast and coffee. Did they have eggs? She smiled and shook her head. Did they have bacon? '*Niet.*' Toast? '*Niet.*' Coffee? '*Da.*' 'Coffee with milk, please,' I said. 'Sorry, no milk,' she smiled. I settled for black tea and asked her what she could offer me to eat. She went away to return with a cold, minced-lamb pasty, which she described, in English, as a pizza. I settled for a cut piece of dry rye bread.

Knowing that she worked long hours for a pittance even by Russian standards, I asked her about her future. What was her ambi-tion? 'I learnt English at school,' she replied wistfully and with that constraint of vocabulary that makes intense feelings sound even more powerful, 'but I don't know what will happen. At the moment the future is only a dream. What I can do, I will do.' When she had finished serving me, she walked down to the end of the carriage, where I had noticed a pale, open-faced youth with large brown eyes and a brooding demeanour. He wore a black sweater and black cap and, apart from the bubble gum that kept popping from between his lips, he could have walked off the set of any film depicting the roman-tic realism of the Russian working class at any time in the twentieth century: perfect fodder for Eisenstein or Godard. Quite unfazed by the customers around them, the waitress and the worker (that I presumed him to be) embraced passionately. She then draped herself around him, affectionately stroking his hair, while he resumed his previous posture, staring out in sultry detachment through the half-iced window at the snow-covered flatlands that passed by unchanging and eternal, like a looped reel of film.

Back in my compartment I listened to a BBC Radio 4 recording of *War and Peace*. I was inspired to return to this epic by Orlando Figes's *Natasha's Dance*, where it is suggested that Tolstoy's inspiration for the fictional character of Prince Andrey Bolkonsky was his distant cousin, Prince Sergey Volkonsky, a member of an aristocratic family to which Tolstoy was connected through his mother's line. Whether or not this was the case – Tolstoy himself insisted that 'Andrey Bolkonsky is NOBODY just like any character invented by a novelist' – he most certainly admired his relative with some fervour. 'He is an enthusiast, a mystic and a Christian, with high ideals for the new Russia,' Tolstoy wrote after meeting Volkonsky in 1859. By this time Volkonsky was revered by young radicals for his role as one the leaders of the Decembrist uprising against the tsar in 1825. Although Tolstoy restructured and relocated his novel (which was to have been called *The Decembrists*) once he came to appreciate that the intellectual and moral roots of the Decembrist movement lay in the 1812 war against France, it remains easy to see why Volkonsky's extraordinary story might have been his original inspiration. Volkonsky was not only a revolutionary mutineer but, along with 120 other conspirators, was sentenced to prison and exile in Siberia, where he revealed a zeal for social reform that became a lodestar for any Russian anxious for an end to feudalism.

The Decembrists had spent the early years of their sentence in Chita, which was one of the reasons for making it our next stop. I wanted to find out whether their heroism still resonated in what is still widely known as 'the city of exiles'. We arrived there on time in the middle of the afternoon as the sun was edging towards the horizon.

The city is an administrative capital, its neo-classical main square wide enough and long enough to accommodate even the largest Soviet parade of military hardware. The red, white and blue flags of the Russian Federation fluttered strategically from the elegant Victorian lamp-posts along either side of what is still called Red Square. A few minutes' drive away from this portentousness, half-hidden behind a large apartment block, I found the little wooden chapel where Volkonsky and his fellow Decembrists had once attended Mass in the days when Chita was a settlement of only a few hundred people, a primitive outpost without any of the trappings of what then passed for 'modern civilization'. The chapel is now a museum dedicated to the memory of the Decembrists, the walls covered with paintings and drawings depicting the history of the principal characters from the point of their mutiny against the tsar to the lives they made for themselves in Chita and later in other parts of Siberia.

Their uprising sprang from several causes. The boneheaded failure of Tsar Alexander I to appreciate or reward the patriotism and sacrifice of the peasants in the War of 1812 against Napoleon distressed the younger and more progressive officers. They were also shocked by the reactionary attitudes of the Empire's most senior generals, who appeared to believe it was they, not the ordinary soldiers, who had driven the French out of Moscow, and who continued to brutalize their men despite their heroic defence of the country. And, not least (as Richard Pipes points out in *Russian Conservatism and Its Critics*), the three-year occupation by the Russian armies in Germany and France after the victory had given them a chance to taste life in the West at first hand. In Europe one of the future Decembrists, Nicholas Turgenev, wrote in 1814 that 'it was possible to have civic order and flourishing kingdoms without slavery'. And, returning from Europe to Russia, Volkonsky wrote that it 'felt like going back to a pre-historic past'.

Such sentiments were profoundly affected by the comradely alliance established on the battlefield between this new breed of officers and their men. 'We rejected the harsh discipline of the old system,'

Volkonsky said later, 'and tried through fellowship with our men to win their love and trust.' Another Decembrist wrote, 'We were the children of 1812.' After the war, these young officers returned to their estates, where progressive noblemen like Volkonsky, foreshadowing Tolstoy's own radical compassion, began to pay for the upkeep of children orphaned by the war and to finance the education of their serfs who had (in the words of Orlando Figes) 'shown their potential in the ranks of 1812'. The Decembrists now found themselves intellectually and morally in fundamental opposition to serfdom, which soon led them to challenge the entire social and economic structure of the tsarist state.

In verses intended for, but not included in, his great verse-novel *Eugene Onegin*, which he wrote very soon after the 1825 uprising, Pushkin wrote somewhat dismissively of the Decembrists, many of whom had been his friends and companions, suggesting that their 'plots' were 'hatched between claret and champagne to the accompaniment of satirical songs and friendly arguments...deep in their hearts, there was no revolutionary intent. It all came out of boredom....' But Paul Pestel, the most radical and intellectually driven of the plotters, had a far more serious purpose than Pushkin allowed. After his arrest and before his show trial, at which he was sentenced to death by hanging, he wrote in radical terms of his conversion to republicanism. Rejecting the European 'constitutional' monarchies and the 'smoke-screens' of the two-chamber parliamentary systems over which they presided, he concluded, 'It seems to me that the main striving of our age is the struggle between the masses and the aristocracy of every kind, whether based on wealth or on hereditary rights. I judged that these aristocracies will, in the end, become mightier than the monarch himself, as had happened in England, and that they are the obstacle to the state's well-being and that they can be removed only by the republican form of government.' These were not the dilettante meanderings of a salon rebel – unless Lenin is to be similarly discounted.

Whatever its intellectual or moral underpinning, the uprising itself was a dismal military failure, ineptly organized and swiftly crushed. On

14 December 1825, when soldiers from the St Petersburg garrisons were assembled to declare their loyalty to the new tsar, Nicholas I, only three thousand out of a possible twenty thousand refused to swear the oath. These rebels marched instead to Senate Square, where they assembled under *The Bronze Horseman* to demand a new constitution. Five hours later Nicholas I, who took personal command of the majority of soldiers still loyal to him, ordered his men to fire at the mutineers. Sixty were killed; the rest scattered. Within days some five hundred Decembrists were arrested. Five of the ringleaders, whose names were already known to the security services, were executed (with such cruel incompetence that one of their number is said to have cried out, 'What a wretched country! They don't even know how to hang properly.') Along with that of a hundred other fellow conspirators, Volkonsky's life was spared, and in 1827 he was transported in chains to the Siberian silver mine at Nerchinsk, near the Chinese border, where he was to spend the first of the fifteen years of hard labour to which he had been sentenced.

It is hard to exaggerate the extent to which exile in Siberia was generally regarded in Russia as a living death. In Colin Thubron's telling phrase, Siberia was 'a rural waste into which were cast the bacilli infecting the state body'. On hearing that he was to be sent into exile, the Decembrist Nikolay Basargin wrote, 'I ceased to consider myself an inhabitant of this world.' In 1828 twelve of the Decembrists, including Volkonsky, were moved from Nerchinsk to Chita, where they were permitted to fend rather more for themselves. Not the least heroic aspect of this phase of their incarceration was the way in which they managed to overcome adversity, preserving their integrity against the odds, and, to a remarkable degree, helping to transform for the better the lives of the impoverished peasants on whose behalf they had been exiled.

I had been put in touch with Dmitry Yakushkin, the great-great-great-great-grandson of one of the leading Decembrists, Ivan Yakushkin. A former press aide to Yeltsin, Dmitry was now the publicaffairs director of a gold-mining business. He invited me to join him for dinner at the guest-house that the company maintains on the edge of Chita (which is only a day's drive from one of its mines). Dmitry does not flaunt his aristocratic credentials, but is a proud scion of the family and – speaking fluent English – retains a faintly patrician courtesy; I could easily picture him at his ease in front of a roaring log fire in the great hall of a grand country mansion not too far from St Petersburg. As it was, we were served by a housekeeper and her husband with an abundance of food, vodka and wine while Dmitry talked about his great forebear and the relevance of the Decembrists in modern Russia.

'You see, they never lost their moral strength. There were no recriminations, no settling of scores, no blame for what had gone wrong. They were cut off from their homes and families, and the conditions were harsh. They could so easily have succumbed to depression, a downward spiral. Instead they created a life for themselves and for others. They got hold of books on medicine, books in German and English, and they studied. They established schools and they worked as doctors. One of them was an architect and planner who drew up plans for the development of Chita and, in fact, you can see that they were incorporated into the original design for the town. They had spirit. They fought back. They are a lesson for all of us.'

As the evening progressed, it became clear that Dmitry was deeply troubled by the state of Russia today. 'We spend all our time looking back to the past. We can't do anything or say anything without looking back. We cherish our past, and maybe that is because we don't like our present. I am very frustrated – it really depresses me. My past is a burden to me. I have a coat of arms, but I don't look at it. I am not interested in the servants we had or the land we owned. After the revolution, my grandfather was put in prison basically because he had belonged to the nobility. But I used to be a Communist. I really believed. I was offended when my brother-in-law once compared Stalin to Hitler. I was in the Komsomol and we enjoyed ourselves. But there is more to it than that. In those days teachers and doctors were respected – they were special because they knew things that we didn't know: public service really meant something. But who wants to be a teacher today? They have no status and the job is very badly paid. Society has lost its roots.

'Today young people can do anything and go where they want. They look at their parents who are highly qualified, but they have no money. So why should they think about becoming a teacher? And they lose respect for their parents as well. Instead they watch television and see the beautiful girls, the fashion models, the stars, the restaurants. And, of course, their ambition is to go to Moscow to share in that life.'

The thought of the capital city triggered a renewed torrent of dismay. 'The other day I was crossing from Red Square using the underpass on my way to the Ritz-Carlton Hotel. It was desperate. The forgotten people gathered there, the people who have nothing. And then I went into the Ritz-Carlton where others have everything. Maybe I am too emotional, but I am offended too that in Moscow you now have an "English pub" and a pizza parlour that have been built only twenty metres from the Tomb of the Unknown Soldier. They look out at the Eternal Flame, at a sacred place. How can this be? In London you fight against these things because you have a civil society. We have nothing. In the time of Peter the Great the people around him served the state first and stole from the people second; Putin's people steal from the people first and then serve the state.'

Dmitry paused in mid-flow, long enough for me to suggest that his former boss, Yeltsin, had much to answer for – that he had unleashed the deluge that Dmitry so deplored. 'It pains me to admit it, but yes, you are right. Yeltsin inherited a country on the verge of starvation and he had no plan. So our society self-destructed.' 'And now you have Putin?' 'Yes. And, the other day, three weeks before the Duma elections I saw this great electronic banner that read, "Moscow is voting for Putin". It was not a campaign slogan but a statement of fact. You can see why I say that the Decembrists are a lesson to all of us. And why we look back, not forward.'

The moral challenge faced by the Decembrists was greater because they were not only physically expelled; Prince Volkonsky was also stripped of his titles and honours and estates. Even worse, his own mother, Princess Alexandra, a favourite at court, was so outraged by her son's act of treason that she disowned him as well. 'I only hope that there will be no other monsters in the family,' she would say to those who visited her to commiserate, '*Il n'ya plus de Sergey.*' Many years later, a little before his death in 1865, Volkonsky wrote, 'These words haunted me throughout my life in exile.'

There was compensation, however. No less impressive than the stoicism shown by the Decembrists was the example set by their wives. Either from devotion or duty, many of them followed their husbands into exile, often bringing their children as well. It was an arduous journey that took several months by carriage or cart in dreadful conditions across a most inhospitable and dangerous terrain. Having put loyalty to their partners before loyalty to the tsar, they too were expunged from the collective psyche of St Petersburg's polite society and stripped of their right to return. Undaunted, they settled themselves in houses around the prison, which were built for them by their husbands, and set about creating a new life in this back-of-beyond outpost. It is hard to imagine a greater contrast than that offered by Chita to the grand life of the court and the salon to which they had been accustomed in the capital, some 3700 miles away in another world. In a moving account of Maria Volkonsky's decision to follow her husband into exile, Orlando Figes records that a year after her arrival, her baby boy died. 'Maria never ceased to grieve for him. At the end of her long life, after thirty years of penal exile, when someone asked her how she felt about Russia, she gave this reply: "The only homeland that I know is the patch of grass where my son lies in the ground."' The graves of some of those exiles who perished, young and old, still exist, carefully tended under the hallowed turf immediately around the chapel.

A particularly striking painting in the chapel–museum depicts one of the cells in the Decembrists' prison in Chita. The scene is deceptively civilized. There is a supply of books piled on a table in the middle of the room. Four truckle beds line the walls. Fur hats and cloaks are hung on a hook by a dresser. Volkonsky and three of his fellow convicts are shown in various poses. One is sitting at a bench reading, another lounges on his bed, two others stand casually, almost foppishly, in the foreground, deep in thoughtful conversation, cigarettes held aloft in the Noël Coward style. They are dressed in frock coats, as well-tailored as men of rank would expect to appear in public. It could almost be the library of a gentlemen's club until you look more carefully and notice that all four men are encased in leg irons. They remained thus incarcerated, slave-labouring by day, imprisoned by night, for most of the next decade.

A short walk from the chapel, I went to visit the sole surviving house of the original Decembrist settlement. A one-storey wooden shack, it had belonged to Elizabeth Narishkina, whose husband, Mikhail, was been incarcerated with Volkonsky. It is now a library much in need of repair but, perhaps for that reason, it easily rekindles the atmosphere of that time. When I arrived the final preparations were under way, in what had been her sitting room, for a concert to celebrate Elizabeth's memory. One of the organizers, Olga Fleshler, an elderly but wonderfully passionate professor of English and an ardent student of the Decembrists, told me that it had taken Elizabeth ten months to get permission to follow her husband to Chita. On her arrival, after a terrible journey lasting over two months, she wrote home, 'I am excited and overjoyed. I am so happy. But when I saw my husband in leg irons, I could not believe it. I fainted.' An accomplished pianist among whose favourite composers were Beethoven and Chopin (whose early reputation had already reached St Petersburg), she had arranged for her piano to be transported by cart from St Petersburg.

The concert was to open, appropriately, with Beethoven's 'Für Elise'. The room had been made ready, with six or seven small plastic tables and chairs at one end, a piano and space for a singer and readers at the other. Cakes and teacups were brought in and laid out carefully on the tables with paper napkins beside them. The audience started to arrive, crowding in to take their seats. A very real sense of anticipation rippled through the grey-cardigan and blue-stocking audience. An engagingly anachronistic air of bohemia – as though the Bloomsbury Group had booked Betty's Tea Rooms in Harrogate – pervaded the atmosphere. At a sign from the chief librarian a pianist took her place, adjusting her stool nervously. Beside her, a soprano (who was to have trouble with her top notes) stood magnificently upright, an ageing Brunhilde, to sing light Russian ballads. There was a narrator who only stumbled when she took her eye off her text (which she did less often as the hour progressed); and there were three drama students, two boys and a girl, back home from Moscow, dressed in period costume and flushed with nerves. It had the potential to be a ghastly evening of amateur dramatics. But despite its technical flaws, the high seriousness and romantic import of the text combined with a spirited choice of Russian and European music to produce an unexpectedly seductive performance. The audience remained rapt throughout.

Afterwards I ate cake and drank tea with Olga and a fellow academic, Tatiana Khanova. 'Was this concert merely an exercise in nostalgia, or do the Decembrists have a message for today and tomorrow?' I asked. 'It is both,' said Olga. 'Nostalgia because those days have gone, but for the future because we have to educate our young people, our students, about their noble spirit.' Tatiana added, 'Our young people have a great thirst for these noble values. We have so little at present. They embodied integrity, and we have so little of that now.' 'The Decembrists did not know what it was to have double standards,' said Olga, 'but that is a phenomenon that is only too widespread today. Look at our present elite. They say noble things about how they want to serve the people and how they will break their backs to make us happy. But nothing happens because they say one thing and do another.' Tatiana added, 'We revere their memory and I think that their spirit endures. When people come to Chita they notice the very special atmosphere here, and I think that dates back to the influence of the Decembrists.' Tatiana had brought six of her teenage students, who during the concert had concentrated as fervently as their elders and now listened intently to our conversation. 'For my students, the Decembrists set an example. They help them distinguish what is fake from what is real. And that gives us hope for the future.' The girls nodded in agreement. In Chita, I thought, at least a candle still flickers for the Decembrists.

Back in my hotel room I turned on the television to discover that, with less than a week to go before the Duma state elections, Garry Kasparov, as one of the leaders of The Other Russia (which, unlike almost every other 'opposition' party, is genuinely and deeply opposed to the Kremlin), had just been arrested for participating in a rally and then marching on the Election Commission building in Moscow. He was summarily sentenced to five days in prison, which effectively isolated him from the remainder of the campaign. As he was being bundled into the police van, he said, 'Once again they have demonstrated that the only language they can use with their own people is the language of violence, truncheons and riot police.' In this 'city of exile' this nasty little episode, so characteristic of Putin's Russia, seemed to be an appropriately ironic symbol that Volkonsky and his fellow insurrectionists would have appreciated.

Even after thirty years of exile, Volkonsky did not falter. After his liberation he wrote, 'Falsehood. This is the sickness of the Russian state. Falsehood and its sisters, hypocricy and cynicism, Russia could not exist without them. Yet surely the point is not to exist but to exist with dignity. And if we want to be honest with ourselves, then we must recognise that if Russia cannot exist otherwise than she existed in the past, then she does not deserve to exist.' The words could have been written by Tolstoy himself, and they echo sadly down the intervening years with as much pertinence today as they had 150 years ago.

No individual better represents the truth of Volkonsky's passionate sentiments than Mikhail Khodorkovsky, the oligarch who fell foul of President Putin and who, as a result, has become Chita's most famous 'resident'. He is moved from high-security jail to high-security jail in and around Chita and no one can confidently say where he is at any one time – but he is only two years into a seven-year sentence. Like Volkonsky before him, Khodorkovsky is the most prominent convict of his age and, without pushing the ironies or the parallels too far, both men – the nineteenth-century landed aristocrat and the twenty-first-century billionaire – have been victims of their unyielding commitment to the belief that, in the former's phrase, 'Russia cannot exist otherwise than she existed in the past.' Things had to change. In Khodorkovsky's case this meant using his wealth to challenge the Kremlin's secretive autocracy. From Putin's perspective, the pushy oligarch had failed to obey the rules of the Russian power game: that he could get as filthy rich as he wanted so long as he did not dabble in politics. But as chairman and CEO of the Yukos oil company, Khodorkovsky was not disposed merely to flourish in obedient obscurity, famous only as the richest man in Russia. Influenced by the global financier George Soros, who had used his own money to pioneer democratic values in Russia and elsewhere through his Open Society Institute, Khodorkovsky had made Yukos what the *Financial Times* judged to be 'Russia's most transparent, best-governed company'. Together with Soros, he built on his reputation as Russia's straightest oligarch to fund the Open Russia Foundation, which worked to create genuine multi-party democracy and to strengthen civic institutions like an independent judiciary, a free press and independent think-tanks. This was clearly too much for the Kremlin, which wanted to dismantle Yukos and appeared to believe that Khodorkovsky, who was by this time financing several liberal-democratic parties in the run-up to the December 2003 parliamentary elections, had designs on the presidency as well.

In October 2003 Khodorkovksy was arrested and charged with tax evasion, fraud and embezzlement (and, to push the point home, Soros's Open Society Institute was expelled from Russia a few days

*Tomsk's famous nineteenth-century wooden buildings are under threat: 'Property developers want to pull them down and put up multi-storey apartment blocks.' Bribery yet again? 'Yes, money changes hands. Money decides everything. It is a very great shame.'*

*Russian trains trundle slowly but they invariably depart and arrive on time. Like so much in Russia, the system 'is both remarkably efficient and totally inefficient'.*

In Russia's purpose-built science and technology city, Academgorodok, where IT specialists make virtual simulators for the government and then turn them into computer games for the American market.

At 1800 metres in the Altai mountains: 'I imagined myself as one of the Magnificent Seven. It was totally childish and quite glorious.'

*Valentin Khagdaev is a shaman who believes that spirits inhabit the rock and the tree where he worships in the mountains near Lake Baikal. A spiritual leader of the Buryat people, he is also revered as a healer. His status as a shaman is confirmed by his 'double' thumb, which marks him out as a holy man.*

*Irkutsk bills itself as 'the gateway to the East'. In the nineteenth-century the city was known as the 'murder capital' of Russia. It is now the 'AIDS capital' of the nation.*

Lake Baikal is the oldest and deepest lake in the world. 'If the entire population of the world started to use water at the current rate of urban consumption, the lake would supply all our needs for fifty years.'

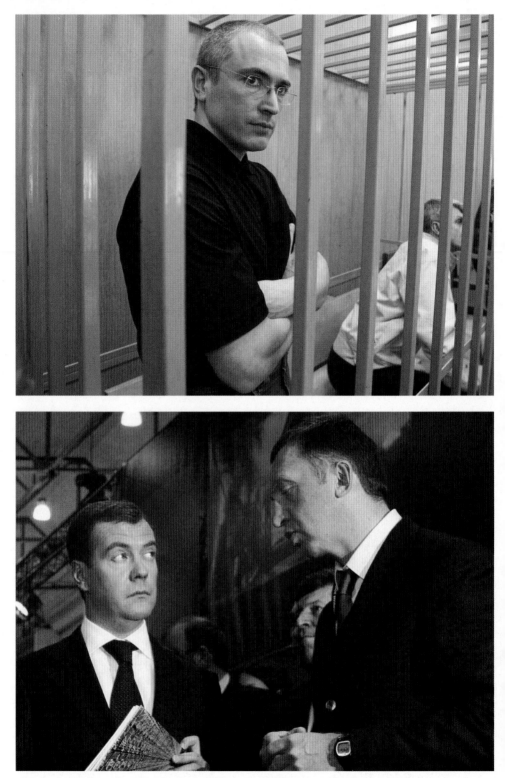

*A tale of two oligarchs: Oleg Deripaska (above, in the blue tie, with President-elect Dmitry Medvedev) is the richest man in Russia. Mikhail Khodorkovsky (top) was the richest man in Russia until he fell foul of President Putin. He is now in jail.*

Tatiana Khanova and Olga Fleshler are ardent students of Russia's first revolutionaries, the Decembrists. 'We have to educate our young people about their noble spirit … They embodied integrity and we have so little of that now.'

My final destination, Vladivostok: 'Like Keats's "stout Cortès", I looked down on the port and felt some of the "wild surmise" that, in the poet's imagination, the conquistador's men had experienced as they saw the Pacific for the first time.'

*Re-reading the great works of nineteenth-century
Russian literature was one of the delights of my
journey across Russia.*

later). The trial opened on 16 June 2004 and lasted until 31 May the following year. There was never any doubt that Khodorkovsky would be found guilty as charged; moreover it would be surprising if Yukos – like every other major company in Russia – had not from time to time bent the law to its advantage. Nor should it be supposed that Khodorkovsky was above reproach in other respects; persistent allegations that his company's 'security service' was responsible for several extra-judicial killings in the anarchic nineties cannot be entirely dismissed as a crude attempt by his enemies to destroy an unblemished reputation. But that is beside the point in a country where every oligarch could be similarly held to account. It is beyond reasonable doubt that the sole reason for his arrest and conviction was that Putin, in the manner of King Henry II, had murmured, 'Who will rid me of this turbulent oligarch?' and that a panel of compliant judges had duly taken the hint. Khodorkovsky was sentenced to eight years' imprisonment, reduced to seven on appeal. It is a dispiriting measure of the extent to which corruption has eaten into the very soul of the judiciary that today even those who are relieved that he has been taken out of circulation rarely bother to dispute this analysis; they merely observe that he should have known better than to challenge the Kremlin.

The fallen oligarch was transferred to Chita in October 2005. Human-rights organizations and the International Commission of Jurists still campaign on his behalf, but to no avail. As the courts prepare new charges against him, which could lengthen his stay in jail by a further fifteen years, his supporters and lawyers have been harassed and intimidated at every turn. But for most Russians Khodorkovsky, like Volkonsky before him, is already history, and, like so much in their history, they want him to be forgotten, not disinterred. But Olga, the champion of the Decembrists, is not so wittingly purblind. 'Of course the formal reason for his arrest was fraud or whatever,' she said. 'The real reason, everyone knows, is politics. Khodorkovsky saw himself – and many people saw him – as fit for high office. He is rich, he is handsome and he is charismatic. And when he was asked, he did not deny that he might enter politics. It was too much....' She faltered momentarily. 'What you are saying,' I prompted, 'is that he is here in prison because Putin and those around Putin decided they could not take the threat that he posed to their power?' 'That is what we mean,' she said, nodding decidedly.

Later that evening I took a taxi and drove past one of the prisons in which Khodorkovsky is frequently incarcerated. I could see no lights inside. The watchtowers looked deserted, and I could only discern the razor-wire above the high concrete wall when it was momentarily caught in the beam of our headlights. I pictured Khodorkovsky alone in his cell, where he is reported by his supporters to be cooped up for most of the day. In my mind's eye he was reading and writing and had found some solace thereby. I hoped that, like Volkonsky, he was able to combat the injustice he has to endure by using the time now at his disposal to good purpose. But even as I had the thought, it seemed toe-curlingly sepulchral; as we drove away I half-waved in the direction of the jail in feeble commiseration.

## WORKERS FROM CHINA

On the train to Chita, I had walked through one carriage entirely filled with Chinese workers. By comparison with the 'Russian' carriages, theirs was neat, orderly and quiet. They played cards or talked in low voices, with only the occasional burst of communal laughter to suggest their collective mood. I asked one of them, who said he was a chef in Moscow, where they were heading. 'We are going home,' he said happily. 'For good?' I asked. 'No,' he replied, explaining that from all over Russia at this time Chinese migrant workers return to their towns and villages to join their families for a break over the New Year. Of course they were happy, he added: 'We will see our wives and our children, and we will take them the money we have earned here in Russia.' About 60 miles beyond Chita the Trans-Siberian divides, the upper route to the east heading for

Vladivostok, the lower route heading into China through Manchuria and thence via Harbin to the capital, Beijing. Chita's pivotal position near this junction has led to a surge of Chinese immigrants to the city: refugees from unemployment in northern China, eager to work as labourers, who plug a large gap in the job market.

Because of the region's border with China, Chita has long been a heavily fortified military zone. During the Cold War and especially during the Cultural Revolution, nuclear missiles were based here, aimed not only at the United States, but at the People's Republic as well. At that time Olga Fleshler used to listen to a Russian-language station broadcasting from Beijing that used to round off its evening programmes with the words, 'Goodnight, dear Siberians, temporarily living in our territory.' At the time Olga was already head of the English Department at the Pedagogical University, where her Chinese husband-to-be was working as a boilerman in the bowels of the central-heating unit. He had been allowed to cross the border into Russia because he had left school early without any academic qualifications – as a mere labourer he was not regarded as a potential threat to the Maoist revolution. He went on to matriculate in Modern Languages in Chita, eventually graduating from the Pedagogical University with a degree in Chinese. As a result of these links, Olga became the first Soviet citizen to be invited – as an individual – to visit Beijing. Later, in 1988, she had a spell as a lecturer at Beijing University. Wandering around Chita today, it is hard to realize how novel, and perhaps disconcerting, the rapprochement between the two great powers must seem to those who only a few decades ago lived under the shadow of their mutual hostility. Today there are Chinese restaurants in abundance and Chinese workers on every building site.

I had arranged to meet one of Chita's best-known entrepreneurs, a property developer called Vera Shavrova, who is the beneficiary of a mini-boom in the city and has a reputation for being formidably tough and direct. Beforehand, one of her staff took me on a tour of her various projects. I could not detect any architectural originality or merit among the scatter of apartment blocks, offices and commercial buildings that, at her behest, had started to sprout into the blue Chita sky. Judging by their design and location, concepts like zoning, let alone town planning, are as alien to Chita as they are to so many other towns and cities in Russia. The unwritten rules are pretty straightforward: if you can acquire the land, you can build on it – unless you fall foul of the planning authorities, which usually means unless you fail to grease the appropriate palms with the right amount of cash. But by whatever means, licit or illicit, you acquire the land or get the planning permission, you still have to find the workers to put up the buildings. And when Vera Shavrova first went into business on her own account they were not easy to find.

After the collapse of the Soviet Union, the Russian construction industry fell apart as well. By the mid-nineties a surge in unemployment led to an exodus of labour into other industries and to alcoholism. Chita was especially hard-hit. So when the local economy began to recover, and along with it a demand for new homes and offices, it proved almost impossible to hire Russian labourers. Some disdained the work, others lacked even the basic skills required as masons and carpenters, and yet more had moved to other parts of the Federation. Vera looked elsewhere for a solution and found it across the border, where impoverished workers were only too ready to flee from high unemployment in subsistence villages in China to a living wage in Russia. Now almost all her employees are Chinese migrants.

I watched a group of them at work in the open on a day when the wind chill factor had sent the temperature swooping below minus 10 degrees centigrade. Although they were protected by leather jerkins and Balaclava helmets, their faces looked pinched by the cold. They were digging the foundations of a new office block. The only Russian among them was the driver of a large excavator that scooped their shovel-work out of the pit into a pile of spoil, to be carted away by a succession of dumper trucks. I peered inside one of the wooden dormitories, where they slept twenty to a room on hard bunks with only their blankets for privacy. In an adjoining hut one of them, deputed to be chef, was preparing vegetables for the wok.

At another site a team of masons was constructing a retaining wall made of large concrete blocks. The wall was far from straight and would certainly have been rejected by any British building inspector, but it was going up at a rate that any British contractor would envy. Vera's trusted foreman, who was also Chinese, was evidently unperturbed by that or any similar imperfections: the bricks on the face of one wall were so uneven, with quantities of redundant mortar oozing from every join, that they might have been laid by a child using Plasticine; radiators inside the block hung haphazardly off the horizontal; and the water pipes, ostensibly plumbed securely into the heating system, dripped ominously on to the floor of what was destined to become an 'executive' apartment.

I asked the foreman, Chou, what had brought him to Chita. 'It is very simple. They need us and we need them. They want labour and we work fast and well. And for us the wages are higher. We can earn thirty per cent more here than at home.' 'But you must miss your families – you are away from them for a year at a time.' 'Of course we miss our wives and our children. But it will soon be the New Year, and then we will be going back home to see them again. And I will have money with me – for the whole family, my old parents as well as my wife and children.' So saying, he was summoned away to inspect the wobbly wall.

Vera Shavrova joined us at one of her new developments where she had already installed herself in a first-floor flat – '*pour encourager les autres*', I presumed. She arrived in a chauffeur-driven 4×4 and emerged power-dressed from top to toe in black. I thought of Honor Blackman playing opposite Sean Connery in *Goldfinger*. Vera lived up to her billing, neither wasting time nor mincing words. 'I prefer the Chinese worker to the Russian worker. The Chinese are disciplined. They come here and they really try to work very, very hard. At the moment Russian workers are not as disciplined and they don't have the same attitude to work. I only use Russians when I have to – for specialist tasks like welding and plumbing, for example. That's how it is.' 'There must be some resentment among the Russians in Chita?' I suggested. She did not prevaricate. 'Yes, and there is bound to be. It is only natural. It happens in any society. I will give you an example. I was walking down the street not so long ago just down there' – she pointed to where her Chinese labourers were at work – 'and I saw a Russian woman who had been drinking. She had a baby in her arms. She was shouting and swearing at my Chinese labourers and being very offensive to them. She was drunk and they were still at work, hard at work, working long hours. That was the situation. It happens.'

There are strict controls on migrant labour, a quota system to limit the inflow from China, and within China there is sharp competition for Russian jobs. Vera regularly sends one of her staff, a Chinese speaker, as far as the south of the country to recruit new workers, explaining to me that this serves as a useful reminder to her employees that their jobs are always under threat, that there is always a competitor for their place. As it is, migrants are only permitted to remain in Russia for eleven months without both employer and employee becoming subject to federal taxes; all contracts are therefore terminated at that cut-off date. 'We are very careful to observe the rules and regulations. If the workers overstay their permit, they are forcibly deported, transported back to the border in buses. Employers who collude in this are subject to a pretty hefty fine, which can be up to several hundred thousand roubles. So we are careful to observe the laws and we haven't yet been fined once. We make sure they go in time.' With that she leapt back into her 4×4 and was driven off to her next appointment. I went to catch my train.

## GOLD IN RUSSIA'S FAR EAST

Even at 2 a.m. it was still unseasonably warm, a mere minus 9 degrees in the dark. I stood on the platform, stamping my feet and counting the number of freight trains that rumbled through Chita laden with coal, timber and cement from other parts of Siberia, and with containers from Vladivostok filled with consumer goods imported from China and Japan: twenty, forty, fifty and once sixty wagons, rattling, groaning and shaking the ground beneath our feet before they disappeared into the silence of the night. A company of young conscripts, shaven-headed and raw-faced, was lined up waiting for the same train, laden with kit-bags and ration boxes, little platoons of acne-spotted teenagers on their way deeper into Siberia to serve the Motherland. The officer in charge, lean and chisel-faced but relaxed in manner, steered them to a trio of carriages that had been set aside for their use. When our train arrived there was some shunting and jolting – Thomas the Tank Engine, but on a mighty scale – and we were on our way. Twenty-five hours of travelling lay ahead of us on this leg.

The next morning, a little after dawn, the sky was what I had by now started to regard as perpetual blue. A papery half-moon had yet to disappear over one horizon as the sun came up over the other. There was no more than a shiver of snow on the ground that fell away from the train, flat and open, for 2 miles or more before rising gently into the hills, seemingly whisked into whorls of granite to form an ever-undulating backdrop to this *mise-en-scène*. In places the wind had blown away the snow-dust to reveal a delicacy of green and brown ground cover lightly iced with hoar-frost. Visitors often describe the Siberian landscape as featureless. This is not quite right. For sure, it is not as dauntingly dramatic as the Andes or the Rift Valley that runs down the spine of Africa, nor is it as conventionally beautiful to European eyes as the Loire Valley or the Yorkshire Dales. But if you drive out from London westwards along the M4, you will find yourself, near Swindon, climbing towards the top of the Downs until the road suddenly crests a modest summit to reveal a wide, shallow plateau that seems to promise a limitless space of opportunities. In summer, when the corn is turning to gold and the sun is low in the sky, the half-truth of that promise never ceases to take my breath away. Of course, by comparison with other landscapes around Britain, let alone the rest of the world, it is very far from being sensational. Yet it has a kind of liberating grandeur, born of contour, simplicity and scale. For me, eastern Siberia, which is on an almost unimaginably greater scale and far wilder, had begun to have a similar effect.

The surface of the earth looked primeval. I could not see even the suggestion of any fields beneath the snow, no livestock and no people. The only evidence of human life – aside from the train itself and the station settlements through which we passed – was a meander of cart-tracks and a very occasional line of pylons taking power to a far-off, hidden settlement where today's pioneers drill for gas or oil or precious metals and where, in one or two places, the hunter–gatherers of another age still cling on to their traditional ways. The rivers may sparkle in summer; in winter they were white slicks of powdery snow on solid ice. Once I saw a fur-hatted man, burly in a greatcoat, riding his elderly motorbike and sidecar along the course of the frozen river, followed by two lurcher dogs. He had a shotgun slung across his back, but I could see no birds or beasts for him to track or shoot. Otherwise I saw virtually no sign of human activity for more than 600 miles.

In the restaurant car I had a bowl of goulash soup, a very tired salad and some soggy chips. A handful of the recruits I had seen on Chita station wandered to and fro past my table. Most of them were as sober as military regulations required, but one or two of them had clearly filled the vacant hours with alcohol. One had allowed himself to be so carried away that he had removed his shirt, exposing a narrow, pinched chest that he would have done well to conceal. They bantered with each other, until one of them was prompted to come over to where I was sitting. He stopped and smiled, leaning benignly over the swaying table as he tried to reorder his lips to form the words that might express some of the thoughts or feelings that lurked somewhere within but refused to emerge from the recesses of his sodden brain. He had a livid scar down his left cheek, which had been so crudely stitched that the tissue had bubbled up in places, exacerbating the ugliness.

'What happened?' I asked with careful sympathy. 'I had a car accident,' he said, glassily focused for a moment. Isn't it a knife wound? Or a bottle perhaps? 'It was a car accident,' he repeated. Then, putting his arm round my shoulder, he relapsed, embracing me with that soggy camaraderie that only a disintegrating drunk feels able to share.

Across the compartment another party, this time of older men, was equally close to disintegration. One of them, sensing that I was beginning to feel both over- and underwhelmed by the attentions of my would-be soulmate, lurched across and told the young soldier to leave me alone. He then introduced himself by pulling an ID card from an inside pocket. 'I am a police captain from Irkutsk,' he announced, showing me his insignia of office to prove the point. In broken, slurred English he managed to convey the fact that he was on his way to Vladivostok to buy a car that he would drive the 2000-mile journey back home. 'Nissan, no good. Toyota, no good,' he volunteered. 'Mitsubishi, good.' It transpired that he was going to buy a 4×4 and that almost every person in the compartment was similarly bound for the huge secondhand car market in Vladivostok, to buy Japanese cars either for themselves or to sell again at a small profit in central and western Siberia, where the appetite for these vehicles is insatiable. The train manager told me that many of his passengers were regular commuters, earning their livelihood by making this punishing 4000- or even 6000-mile round trip week after week, month after month. 'It must be very boring,' I suggested. 'Yes, it is, of course. But they just drink themselves into a stupor until the day before the train reaches Vladivostok. They then sober up so that they can buy a car and drive back to where they came from. It's a job.'

Despite the flow of alcohol, the atmosphere was quite free from the threat of violence. On a British train the manager would by this stage have ordered at least three of the passengers to leave the train at the next stop, the transport police would have been summoned to meet them, arrests would have been made, and, somewhere along the line, violence would most surely have erupted. On this journey at least, despite the alarming quantities of alcohol, the waitress was in complete control of the restaurant car. When she remonstrated with one passenger who had half-fallen off his seat into the aisle, his companion apologized at once and hauled him back into an upright position. When another passenger, one of the few who were more or less sober, saw that my police captain had overstayed his welcome, he beckoned him to leave me and return to his place – which he did without demur.

We had entered what the Russians know simply, and confusingly for Europeans, as the Far East. It covers the remotest part of what we call Siberia and embraces a third of the entire Russian Federation. But its population is little more than 6.5 million people, which, in terms of density, equates to 250 acres of land for every single one of them: it is as sparsely inhabited as anywhere on the planet. In the early hours of the morning the train halted at a tiny junction called Tygda, which is really a nowhere kind of place. But it has a goldmine, one of the very richest in Russia, and we hurried to disembark before the train pulled out again.

I have always been perplexed by our obsession with gold. Ever since the final collapse of the gold standard in 1971, which at the time looked as though it would herald an age of great financial turbulence but in fact ushered in a period of relative stability, no government has undertaken to redeem paper notes to a specified weight of gold, which means that, as a hedge against inflation, its value is purely a matter of faith. I know that, when alloyed with metals like copper, gold still has a use in dentistry, electronics and a range of other industrial processes. But, unlike oil or gas, it is not a vital commodity whose market value fluctuates according to the global laws of supply and demand. Of course, as a decorative metal it has been used to create surpassing beauty in temples and mosques, in paintings and manuscripts, and, of course, in jewellery – even though, as a 'must have' accessory for the twenty-first century, the latter has become irredeemably associated with the vulgarity of 'bling'. Yet none of that explains why gold remains an international harbinger of mankind's fate; why it is that when the rich are fearful the price rises, and that when they are carefree it falls. Ultimately, if I am right, gold is no more than a talisman, a lucky charm that, if you can afford it, you store in a psychological vault constructed from a pack of speculative cards.

None of that matters very much to the men who work in the Pokrovskiy mine, which is a forty-minute drive out of Tygda. They dig for gold around the clock, so that as we arrived in the main compound, an orderly row of wooden huts where the miners live, the sky was ablaze with distant arc lights where diggers and trucks were excavating the rock at a rate of production that, in the mining world, has made the very word Pokrovskiy synonymous with large and rapidly growing profits. It is one of three owned by Peter Hambro Mining (PHM), whose eponymous chairman, a scion of the banking family, was due to visit the mine while I was there. Judging by the anticipatory thrill that ran through his staff, it was to be something of a state visit; Peter Hambro was clearly revered. At a health-and-safety briefing laid on for our benefit, I noticed that his employees wore PHM hats and, embroidered on their overalls, the family coat of arms, which depicts a coronet with a sprightly lion walking gingerly around its rim and carrying a heraldic stave. In a feebly subversive attempt to puncture the prevailing mood, I joked that the coat of arms depicted their chairman walking all over the Queen of England. No one even smiled. One of them, clearly shocked, waved his finger, saying, 'No, not Peter Hambro. Oh, no!' Peter Hambro, I concluded, was not to be lightly dismissed.

The gold at Pokrovskiy is excavated from the surface. There are no mineshafts or tunnels, only a ruin of landscape in what was virgin land little more than a decade ago. Today it looks much like a gravel pit but on a grand Siberian scale; a Devil's Punchbowl gouged out of the bowels of the earth's upper crust. It is hideous, but it is also mightily impressive. From a vantage point on the edge of the mine I looked down at a fleet of bright yellow 4×4 trucks, each capable of carrying

45 tonnes of rock, descending in orderly file down a steep track until they reached the floor of the mine. There they were reversed up to a giant excavator that clanked and roared in perpetual movement, digging into the crumbling rock face and swivelling around to pile its precious load neatly and swiftly into one truck after another. The steady movement of these trucks climbing in and out of the mine looked as though an unseen child wielding a remote control were playing a game with Dinky toys. In fact the operation is precisely timed from inside a modern control centre, where a bank of monitors and computers tracks the movement of every vehicle on the site, and can relay instructions to ensure that the entire process – from the moment when the rock is blasted by explosive until the melted gold is poured into ingots – continues without let or hindrance for twenty-four hours a day on every day of the year.

Perhaps because I had an image of gnarled prospectors panning for gold in the Klondike, I had envisaged seeing the occasional yellow nugget embedded in a chunk of rock. No such luck: the seams of Pokrovskiy gold are invisible to the naked eye, and they have no discernible colour until the rock has been crushed, rolled and baked, when, at a temperature of more than 1000 degrees centigrade, the tiny slivers of gold melt and separate, enabling them to be poured off and purified. Technically, this process is not complex, but it requires expertise and an enormous mechanical effort. In 2006 the diggers extracted 6.5 million tonnes of ore, of which less than 25 per cent – 1.5 million tonnes – contained gold; every tonne of ore yields on average just 3.5 grams of gold. I did a rough calculation, on the basis of which I concluded that each yellow truck hauling itself out of the bottom of the mine contained on average 38 grams of gold, enough to make one necklace. Then I did a further calculation: with the price at around $850 an ounce ($30 a gram and rising), each yellow truck was also removing, from this little oasis in the Siberian steppe, the equivalent in value of rather more than $4000 worth of gold. As PHM is on course to extract a million ounces (28,000 kilograms) of gold a year by 2009, I had no reason to doubt that Peter Hambro would be as buoyant as his company reports. I was not disappointed.

The boss arrived in the company's new helicopter from the regional airport at Blagoveshchensk, where he had arrived in a private jet after an overnight flight from London via Moscow. He should have looked drained after some fifteen hours in the air. Instead he strode about his demesne, raffishly elegant in a tweed jacket, blue shirt and pale yellow cord trousers, a combination that, aside from a topcoat trimmed with fur and his woolly hat, would have been at home on a country estate in Norfolk. He looked and sounded like a caricature of an English aristocrat; nor did he entirely lack that self-deprecatory nonchalance that so often masks the ruthless drive of his class. But he was engagingly candid about himself and his business. 'I have always loved gold,' he enthused with a boyish delight that I found hard to resist. 'You mean you love it because it's used to make beautiful jewellery, or because you can make a killing – albeit at high risk?' I asked. Instead of denying the vulgar impulse to 'make a killing', he replied disarmingly that, in truth, his venture had been 'pretty low risk'. Low-risk? 'Well, gold is the hedge against those things that you don't know you need to hedge against. It's its own store of value, its own guarantee – it's no one else's promise. It's real.' So much for my scepticism about gold, I thought. If his own passionate metaphysic is as widely shared as the market suggests, then he was right and I was wrong. Moreover, his faith has yielded him a dividend that even Beelzebub would envy.

Hambro's father and grandfather served in the army, offspring of the famous banking family who arrived in Britain from Denmark in the nineteenth century. Peter started his career in the bank but was very soon bored by the City. Dazzled by the lure of gold, he joined one of the world's largest gold traders, McGatter and Goldsmith, negotiating with producers to handle their product on the world market. In the early eighties he was sent to see if he could secure a deal in Moscow. The meeting with the Soviet gold commissars, which took place around a large oblong table, soon collapsed into a mammoth drinking session, by the end of which Hambro had passed out. He woke up in his hotel room, relieved to find no evidence of any compromising behaviour that could make him vulnerable to blackmail. He returned to London, entirely forgetful of what, if anything, had been agreed with the Soviet authorities. But, as he tells it – and I suspect that he rarely fails to embroider a good anecdote – he went into the office with a dreadful hangover to find himself surrounded by colleagues clamouring to congratulate him. 'Peter, how did you do it?' they kept asking. As he had no recollection of what he had achieved, he was at a loss to give a coherent answer. Did he not realize, they told him, that he had secured the right to handle the international trading of almost every ingot of Soviet gold? It had been a triumph.

After the collapse of the Soviet Union, Hambro was thus well placed to get into the gold business on his own account. He tells another colourful story about how he found his way to his present fortune. It included long journeys across the Siberian wastes, visiting one run-down goldmine after another, all of which were hopeless prospects, getting lost off-road in freezing white-outs, and a mysterious blonde woman of remarkable facial beauty but a very large bottom who managed to persuade him, when he had all but given up, to visit one last goldmine. It was Pokrovskiy.

As a natural-born deal maker, Hambro fell in with a former member of the Soviet nomenclatura who had turned himself into a post-Soviet entrepreneur. Pavel Maslovsky shared Hambro's buccaneering spirit, and his sharp eye for the main chance. More importantly, they also liked and trusted one another almost at first sight. Pokrovskiy was virtually derelict, but the geological evidence was unequivocal: it was rich, very rich, in gold. All it needed was the licence, the capital, the know-how and the labour. In 1994 they were granted the licence. Hambro put in £5 million of his own money ('I bet the farm, but the opportunity was so fantastic that I thought even I couldn't make a mess of it') and they raised the rest from the venture-capital market.

Meanwhile, Maslovsky used his network of contacts to put together a Russian management team and labour force. Soon the bulldozers moved in to clear what Hambro describes as 'absolutely virgin territory'. They built roads, brought in electricity supplies, constructed a new processing plant, and within months had established a virtually self-sustaining village that now houses 1500 workers in the kind of comfort – subsidized food, constant hot water, comfortable dormitories, a shop, a health centre – that most Russian workers could only dream about.

The first gold came out of the ground in 1999. Within five years PHM's shares were trading on the London stock market. Today the company is the second-largest producer of gold in Russia and is valued at over £1 billion. With 7 per cent of the shares in his own name, Hambro's 'I bet the farm' investment of £5 million is now worth at least twenty times that – and, he forecast, gold will soon be $1000 an ounce and will go on up to $1500 in the months ahead. As we stood overlooking the mine from my vantage point of the previous day, he could not restrain his elation. 'It gives me a sense of absolute amazement. It never occurred to me when we started that it would be as big and as powerful as it has become. To have achieved that in thirteen years is quite extraordinary.' I could hardly disagree.

Tygda itself is something of a company town. Until the arrival of the mine it was – like so many other small settlements in Siberia – on its uppers. Aside from the state railway (the principal employer in every community along the route of the Trans-Siberian), it had few prospects, and those were diminishing. The only other significant source of work, aside from the school, the hospital, the post office, the fire station and the police, had been a logging and timber collective that had collapsed soon after the fall of the Soviet Union. For a while Tygda became a staging post, a supply depot for a hydro-electric plant being constructed deeper in the interior, but when the building work was finished the depot was closed and the workers lost their jobs. PHM came to the rescue. Although most of its employees come from other parts of Siberia and beyond, it has recruited some two hundred workers locally – labourers, watchmen, security guards, drivers, cooks, cleaners and clerical staff. The company was also careful to demonstrate a sense of civic duty, helping to rebuild the fire station, supporting a sports hall and contributing funds to the village school.

The school has 390 pupils aged from six to seventeen, only a little over half the roll-call before the fall. According to the head teacher, PHM has made a real difference. 'Before the mine many of the parents were unemployed and had no money even for the basics. Our children had no decent clothes. Now they are dressed properly. And the mine helps us out.' When the water purifier broke down, PHM sent an engineer to fix the motor. When the carpentry classes had to be suspended because they had no tools or wood, PHM provided both. The intensity of gratitude with which she described what seemed to me to be pocket money from the vaults of a multi-million-dollar business had an air of desperate deference. Why, I wondered, was PHM so important? Her answer was straightforward. 'We have no one else to turn to, no one else to ask.'

PHM's management team had been determined that I should appreciate the company's reputation as an outstanding employer with a genuine concern for the welfare of their workers. After staying comfortably in the compound and eating well at the canteen, I was able to confirm to them that their standards were indeed as high as they claimed – and far higher than some of the hotels and lodgings in which I had stayed during my journey. After watching and talking to some of the workers about their wages and shift pattern – fifteen days on, fifteen days off – I was also able to confirm that morale seemed to be was as high as PHM hoped, and far higher than I have seen in many other parts of the world. But that was not all. They were equally anxious for me to appreciate that they cared for their employees' offspring as well. One of the management team, Boris, a powerful political figure in Tygda, had accompanied me to the school. He listened carefully to the head teacher as she told me that when the

Pokrovskiy children graduate from school they are presented with a certificate and given a present by the mine. Far more importantly, PHM sponsors the next stage of their education, subsidizing their fees at college or university.

But what about the other children, I wondered; was there not a danger that they would feel themselves to be second-class students of second-class parents? For the first time, she faltered. However, her colleague Galina, a far more volatile character, interrupted to say, 'Of course you are right. And we have requested the mine, "Please help the other families as well. Don't leave them out." But so far...' She shrugged and looked at their benefactor, who was evidently less than pleased at this disclosure. She went on to explain that only seventeen of that year's forty-four school-leavers had gone into higher education. 'The parents cannot afford it. It costs thirty-five thousand roubles a year to send a student to the State University. There are free places, but there is great competition for them, so many parents have to pay. And many of our parents simply don't have the money.' At this point, suddenly emboldened, she turned directly to Boris and urged him to give more support. For a few moments he listened and then, clearly irritated at her refusal to take his noncommittal response as an answer, abruptly put his hand in the air and, like the party apparatchik he had once been, instructed her, 'That is enough' – in a tone that clearly meant, 'Watch it – remember who's in charge here.' She subsided at once. It was an ugly little reminder of the realities of the underlying relationship between the benefactor and the beneficiary, the powerful and the powerless in such a small and dependent community.

But Galina had too much spirit to surrender entirely. Later, out of Boris's hearing, she reiterated, 'The mine is very good to us, of course. But it is awful for us as teachers – who are responsible for all the children – to see this differentiation where the children of the miners have a special status. We would like to see the mine support all the children equally.' Then, after a pause, 'We will have to demand and demand and fight and fight.' Later I mentioned her plea to Hambro himself, who nodded sympathetically. Perhaps, I thought, when the value of gold rises to $1000 an ounce, PHM will find the resources needed to help send all the eligible children in Tygda to higher education and all with their special PHM certificates of merit.

Back at the compound I was invited to join Peter and his son Jay (who runs one of PHM's several offshoot companies) in the company's board room for dinner. Pavel Maslovsky was there too, a tall, fit, handsome figure dressed impeccably by Savile Row, who wore an air of easy authority. He spoke with a clipped English accent, and it did not surprise me to discover that he has turned himself into something of an upper-class Englishman, with a country house in the west of England and membership of one of Pall Mall's grander gentlemen's clubs; the following weekend he was joining Peter Hambro for a shoot in Norfolk. The baleful Boris was also there, at the other end of the table, where he contrived to be both deferential to his bosses and boisterously domineering towards the rest of the company. And there was another diner, a mysterious personage to whom I was not introduced.

Beside Boris at the top of the table a gargantuan figure eased himself into his chair, expending such effort in the process as to cause him near apoplexy; his little eyes bulged, his porcine face turned scarlet and he gasped for breath. For most of the meal he kept his head lowered, his jowls almost touching the top of the table, merely raising a fat flipper of a hand to summon more food. I found myself horribly fascinated as mountainous quantities of a fine feast found their way into his belly: caviar, soup, lobster, fish, chicken pieces, minced lamb, lamb shanks in a rich stew, potatoes, cabbage, fruit, puddings and sweets, all washed down with glass after glass of vodka. His gluttony was of a mesmerizing order. More intriguingly, though, when he did raise his head to survey the room everyone, not excluding Hambro himself, paid attention, and on the very few occasions that he spoke the whole table fell silent. Peter explained to me why this grotesque man exerted such authority. He was the mastermind behind the layout and construction of the site, the organizing genius who had devised and still oversaw a production network that had helped give PHM one of the lowest operating costs of any goldmine in the world (around $135 an ounce/$5 a gram) at Pokrovskiy. He had also played a similarly crucial role in the design and development of a new mine near by. Called Pioneer, it was an investment that would very soon be rivalling Pokrovskiy as a source of massive wealth for PHM.

I now realized why this unnerving gargoyle of a man held such sway over the company, why it was that when he smiled, with a slow, commanding leer, everyone beamed, and when he allowed himself a soft, indulgent laugh, everyone guffawed. This momentary expression of powerful feeling was provoked by one of Boris's many excruciatingly long-winded and sexist 'jokes', of which mercifully only one lodged in my mind: 'A husband spent all his time fishing, weekend after weekend. His wife did not like this. So one evening when he had gone out drinking, she went to the room where he kept his fishing rod and she broke it in pieces. She then went to sleep. The next morning she was found dead in her bed.' It is just possible that I misheard the punchline or that my own sense of humour is deficient because the denouement provoked an uproar of belly laughs and clinking glasses at his end of the table.

Peter Hambro is not a man to have qualms about anything. A little before he left office, a wishful-thinking Tony Blair had warned Putin that unless Russia adopted Western values there would be a backlash from the international business community. For his naivety, the then prime minister was roundly rebuked by those on whose behalf he had presumed to speak. Among them, Peter Hambro was the most forthright, saying bluntly that Blair's position was 'very different from that of business' and that his comments ran the risk of 'damaging' British interests in Russia. I was curious to know, therefore, whether the values of transparency, accountability, freedom and the rule of law – which Western politicians insist are crucial to global capitalism – meant anything at all to Peter Hambro. He was airily dismissive. 'I've spent quite a lot of time talking to people in Whitehall. They make a huge song and dance, but nothing happens on the ground here at all. Life goes on.' But did it matter to him that Putin's Russia is authoritarian and autocratic? 'Well, when I first came here it was a run-down Soviet state. It has transformed itself into a capitalist country, and I think it will continue to transform itself and become just like the rest of the major world states.' 'But,' I said, 'Russia is not going forward in terms of democracy, openness, transparency and the rule of law – it's going backwards.' 'It's hard really to say that,' he replied with equanimity. 'I mean, it's not like California. It's Russia, and it's needed to curb some of the madnesses of the Yeltsin years. I mean, the Yeltsin years were fantastic. He's my hero – one of the bravest men I have ever come across. But it got chaotic. The place was a complete shambles when we came here... Putin is a much tougher manager.'

To reinforce his point Hambro offered his own version of the omelette metaphor. 'Gorbachev was the guy who broke the eggs, Yeltsin whipped them up and Putin has cooked them.' I did not pursue the metaphor to suggest that the eggs that had been fresh were now rotten, or that the omelette had congealed to the point when it was inedible. Instead I said, 'You provide jobs here, but you don't seem to feel any responsibility towards those values that you are able to enjoy at home and that are absent in this country, where the press is muzzled and elections are a sham.' Hambro was unruffled, answering with practised urbanity, 'I'm not a politician, I'm a businessman. I'm not sure a businessman has any right to tell any country how it should run itself. The present administration is hugely popular and Russia is a very proud country. If they want to do it their way, they have a right to that, and I don't think I have much of a right to interfere.'

I wanted to persist, to enter the realms of moral philosophy, to recall for him that it is neither intellectually nor morally valid to split one's identity by saying, for example, 'Personally I deplore capital punishment, but as a hangman I am content to execute this man'; that such a stance – however common it may be – is either incoherent or adopted in bad faith. I wanted to bang on, insisting that it is similarly

invalid to declare – in effect – that 'As an individual I am committed
to democracy and human rights but as a businessman I am willing to
collude in their suppression'. I had witnessed such bad faith many
times before – from American investors who worked closely with some
of the nastiest dictatorships in Latin America during the seventies, to
British bankers in Hong Kong in the early nineties – and I had found
it abhorrent. In Britain's last colony I had observed in close-up some
of the powerful expatriates doing all they could to thwart the very
same principles of democracy that they took for granted whenever
they boarded their first-class flights to London – and I had been
ashamed of my compatriots. Putin's Russia is a different case, but I still
wanted to challenge Peter Hambro – partly because I liked him, and
partly because I hoped that he might advance a more persuasive justification than he had so far advanced. I thought of goading him by
asking if there were any country in which he would refuse to invest on
principle. Today's Burma? Yesterday's Cambodia? The day before
yesterday's Germany? Of course, even in relation to Putin's Russia that
would have been to push my point to an extreme – though I suspect
he would nonetheless have engaged me with his customary breeziness.
As it was, I drew back, fearing that it would seem both boorish and an
abuse of hospitality to persist. In any case, I would have found myself
up against Her Majesty the Queen, who in 2006 was 'graciously
pleased' to confer one of her awards upon Peter Hambro Mining for
its 'outstanding achievements in international trade'. And who could
quarrel with that?

## THE CHINESE INFLUENCE

We left the mine early for the five-hour journey to Blagoveshchensk,
driving very fast on snow-covered roads in a fleet of Toyota 4×4s
provided by PHM. We arrived in good time to walk down to the edge
of the River Amur, where I looked across at the Chinese city of Heihe
on the other bank. The river here is not much wider than the lower

reaches of the Thames, narrow enough for loudspeakers on the Chinese side to have broadcast the thoughts of Chairman Mao across the water for the delectation of the Soviet citizenry during the Cultural Revolution. On the Russian side there are still look-out posts and pill-boxes (now disused and crumbling), and rolls of barbed wire along the beach, where border guards in white shell-suits still patrol in pairs to prevent illegal incursions. Today these patrols are little more than a formality, a statement of national identity rather than a real effort to repel illegal immigrants. The Amur was frozen. Half a dozen little hovercraft were skimming noisily back and forth across the river, skid-ding and sliding and sometimes turning in circles, as though they were partners in a dodgem car ballet, unable to steer a direct course on the slippery surface. On board were day-trippers from Blagoveshchensk on their way to and from the supermarkets of Heihe; empty-handed on the outward crossing, they return heavily laden with bags, baskets and boxes. This perpetual hover-shuttle is now as routine as the day-traffic between Dover and Calais, but even twenty years ago it would have been an unimaginable prospect.

The once-contested border between Russia and China is more than 2500 miles in length, and the major part of it that is formed by the Amur had been a source of friction between the two Communist powers for most of the latter half of the twentieth century. Until the collapse of the Soviet Union the border was closed to virtually all civil-ian movement, hermetically sealing one Communist power from the other. It was not until the spring of 2005 that Moscow and Beijing finally repaired the damage by signing an agreement that formally ended a dispute that had its origins in claims and counter-claims about a series of treaties forced upon the Qing Dynasty by tsarist Russia in the second half of the nineteenth century. Specifically, when in 1858 China had been defeated in the Second Opium War, the tsar authorized the annexation of Chinese territory on the north bank of the Amur – oblig-ing Beijing to acquiesce in one of several such 'unequal treaties' that the 'sick man' of Asia had been forced to accept in that period.

In 1890, on his famous pilgrimage to report on the horrifying conditions in the penal colony on Sakhalin Island on the Russian Empire's Pacific seaboard, Anton Chekhov travelled eastwards in a steamship along the Amur, pausing *en route* in Blagoveshchensk. His letters from on board describe an untroubled and beautiful region that rendered him almost speechless with delight. 'It is quite beyond my powers to describe the beauties of the banks of the Amur; I can but throw up my hands and confess my inadequacy,' he wrote to his friend Alexey Suvorin, before going on to describe 'the crags, cliffs, forests, thousands of ducks, herons and all kinds of fowl with viciously long bills, and wilderness all around'. By now he had sailed more than 2000 miles along the river that divided the two empires, noting that 'China is as wild and deserted as Russia: you can sometimes see villages and guard huts, but not very often... I'm in love with the Amur and would be happy to stay here for a couple of years.'

He was no less entranced by the atmosphere in his little floating home. Writing to his family, he enthused:

> The air on board is red-hot from all the talking. Out here no one worries about saying what he thinks. There's no one to arrest you and nowhere to exile people to, so you can be as liberal as you please. The people grow ever more independent, self-sufficient and understanding.... There's no culture of denouncing people here. A political prisoner on the run can take a steamer all the way to the ocean, without fearing the captain will turn him in. In part this can be explained by a complete indifference to what goes on in Russia. Everybody would say 'What has that got to do with me?'

The conversation on board always turned to gold. 'Gold, gold – nothing else,' he reported to Alexey Suvorin and to his family. 'Every peasant in Pokrovskoe [the region in which Peter Hambro now mines his millions], even the priests, is out prospecting for gold. So are the exiles, who can get rich here as quickly as they can get poor. There are some nouveaux riches who won't drink anything but champagne.'

Blagoveshchensk, which had evolved from a fortress into a substantial trading centre, was more to his taste than Irkutsk. Visitors from other parts of Russia, from England, France and Germany came here to trade in furs, timber, diamonds, coal and, of course, gold. But most conspicuously in evidence were the Chinese. According to Chekhov, they were everywhere, 'more numerous than flies'. But they were agreeably, indeed 'astonishingly' polite. He described a meeting with one 'Chinaman' whom he invited to join him for a glass of vodka. 'He held the glass out to me, to the barman and to the waiters before drinking it,' embracing them all in his toast. 'This a Chinese formality,' Chekhov noted solemnly, like an anthropologist recording the habits of an unknown tribe, recording, 'He did not drink it down in one go, as we do, but in sips, nibbling something after each sip.'

I found my way to the old square on the edge of the river, which, aside from a ghastly Soviet war memorial, has been preserved more or less intact from those days when, with a population of thirty thousand, it was a more important entrepôt than Vladivostok. In the summer months the quayside was frantically busy accommodating the stream of ships and barges offloading their international cargo of passengers and goods. It must have seethed with mercantile energy. Today Ploshchad Pobedy, as the square is called, has a grandeur that still retains an echo of those days, though it is now almost deserted, a lifeless heritage site where only a bust of Chekhov on the wall of the apartment block where he took lodgings reminds the visitor that this city was once styled by its inhabitants 'the New York of Siberia'.

But Chekhov was also politically prescient. 'There is no doubt,' he wrote, 'that the Chinese are going to take the Amur from us.... The people who live along the Amur are a very sardonic lot; they find it highly amusing that Russia is so exercised about Bulgaria, which isn't worth a brass farthing, and pays no attention whatever to the Amur. It is an improvident and foolish attitude to take.' It did not quite happen as Chekhov had predicted, partly because of paranoia about the 'Yellow Peril', which had long infected the Russian people and which Chekhov had clearly detected. This reached an ugly nadir in 1900, when troops from the Cossack garrison in Blagoveshchensk – allegedly fired upon from the other shore and, in any case, determined to avenge their losses at the hands of the Chinese in the Boxer Rebellion – rounded up every member of the Chinese community they could find and drove them into the river at bayonet point. Five thousand victims of this pogrom, men, women and children, died in the icy water before they could reach the safety of the other shore. This atrocity provoked an international outcry but, aside from ordering the transfer of the commander of the Blagoveshchensk garrison to another post, the Russian authorities did nothing.

Although official relations were gradually repaired, the doubts and suspicions that each side harboured about the other endured throughout most of the first half of the twentieth century even as – in their own ways and at very different speeds – the two empires dissolved themselves into an apparent unity of revolutionary brotherhood. Thus in 1938 Stalin ordered a clampdown on the dwindling number of Chinese immigrants, so that a late nineteenth-century population of 90,000 gradually fell to almost zero, as many of Russia's unwelcome guests made their way back across the border into China. After 1950, with the emergence of the People's Republic of China, each looked briefly to the other for support against the surrounding threat from the international 'conspiracy' of the capitalist nations. But the fear of that Western Other was not strong enough either to forge the bonds that might have genuinely posed a mutually protective girdle around the two giant Communist states or to conceal their own deep cultural and ideological divisions.

The mistrust turned to animosity as each side started to build up troop levels along their shared border. By the mid-sixties, with more than 800,000 Soviet and almost 700,000 Chinese soldiers facing each other across the Amur, the two nuclear states were at risk of reaching the point of no return. Despite a belated diplomatic attempt to avoid a calamitous conflict, the stand-off led to an escalating series of skirmishes along the disputed border that, in the spring of 1969, caused at least 1000 casualties, most of them Chinese. At this point both Moscow and Beijing recognized that unless they drew back they would only too easily be drawn down into a vortex with incalculable consequences. In September 1969 the Soviet Prime Minister, Aleksey Kosygin, who was on his way back to Moscow from the funeral of the Vietnamese leader Ho Chi Minh, met his counterpart, Zhou Enlai, for talks at Beijing airport. They agreed to restore diplomatic relations and negotiate a solution to the border dispute, but little further was done to achieve this stated aim.

Cleverly exploiting the mutual distrust between the two Communist neighbours, President Richard Nixon, through the agency of his National Security Adviser, Henry Kissinger, moved swiftly to open negotiations with China. This 'ping-pong' diplomatic initiative culminated in the American leader's 1972 visit to Beijing for an historic meeting with Chairman Mao. As China tilted towards America, the Cold War between the superpowers accelerated the seismic shift in the balance of global power towards the West. Only with the imminent collapse of the Soviet Union did the latent tension between Moscow and Beijing seem finally to evaporate.

Today, after no more than two decades, their rapprochement – at a diplomatic level – appears to be unequivocal; it is knitted into every aspect of their strategic and economic relationship, where expressions of mutual amity fall like petals over newly-weds. Commercial relations have blossomed, with bilateral trade in 2006 worth more than $30 billion a year. Although the trade balance hugely favours the People's Republic, China still needs Russian military hardware, oil, gas and huge quantities of timber, the receipts from which help finance the import of a rapidly growing range of Chinese consumer products and its limitless supply of cheap labour. The demand for Chinese labour is insatiable: despite a post-millennial economic boom, Russia's Far East

has suffered a precipitous decline in population since the collapse of
the Soviet Union – from over 8 million to 6.5 million at the latest
count. It is projected by some analysts to fall further, to 4.5 million,
over the next decade. At the moment Chinese immigrants, many of
them with temporary work permits and many more of them illegal
residents, are guesstimated to form around 4 per cent of the regional
population; their numbers would increase dramatically if the Russian
population continues to fall as sharply as projected and they were
permitted to replace the departing workforce. There are at least 100
million Chinese living across the border, many of whom would be
only too willing to fill the vacuum and – in the imaginations of many
Russians – to reclaim the lands once inhabited by their forebears.

It is this suspicion that seems to have fuelled the xenophobia that
has encouraged some extreme Russian nationalists once more to talk
openly and in racist terms of the 'Yellow Peril' – a widespread sentiment
that, a little over a year before my arrival in Blagoveshchensk, provoked
the director of the Federal Service for Migration to declare, with silky
menace, 'Neighbourhoods of the Chinatown type are unacceptable for
Russia and we won't have them.' To make good this commitment, in
the spring of 2007 the new quota system was introduced to restrict the
number of migrant workers, a move that has frustrated many employers in the Russian Far East, where demand for skilled, hard-working
and sober labourers far outweighs any residual fears they might share
about an eventual Chinese 'takeover' of the region.

Blagoveshchensk has a population of a little over 200,000 and, as
a city that trades freely across the border, is host to a higher concentration of Chinese than almost anywhere else in the Russian
Federation. No one knows the precise number of immigrants, but as
I wandered around the city I did not detect any ethnic tension, even
though there is more than one neighbourhood 'of the Chinatown
type'. The central market has a large Chinese section, where merchants compete to sell the Russian customers as familiar an assembly
of cheap goods – brightly coloured clothes, children's toys, mobile

phones – as you would find almost anywhere in the world. Despite a supposed crackdown on Chinese street traders, the formal and illicit markets in which they operate appeared to cohabit without discrimination by the police. Nor, judging by the number of Chinese visitors who cross the river to indulge themselves in the city's free-market supply of casinos and prostitutes, is there much discernible antipathy towards this tawdry tourist trade. In Blagoveshchensk, as elsewhere throughout the Russian Far East, Chinese businessmen working in partnership with Russians have invested not only in gambling and brothels, but in hotels, transport, commerce and the construction industry. The scale of this investment is growing to the point where, in entrepreneurial terms, the Chinese are surging ahead at the expense of their Russian counterparts – despite the protectionist quota restrictions imposed by the government, which are designed to slow, if not impede, their progress.

The day after my arrival I joined a queue of Russians shoppers waiting to board a hovercraft for a day trip across the river to Heihe. The hovercraft was a vintage machine that looked as though it would have failed a Health and Safety inspection for use on the Serpentine. But although it twice turned a full 180 degrees regardless of the helmsman's efforts, we were soon on the other side. On leaving Blagoveshchensk we had been given a tourists' briefing in terms that reminded me of my earlier 'hazard zone' warnings about the Caucasus – a list of 'dos and don'ts' that left the impression that China was a Third World nation of footpads and thieves who had not yet escaped from the streetwise rules of Dickensian London. However, from the moment we walked into the spacious immigration department on the Chinese side every visitor was treated with great courtesy. We were swiftly out into the city itself, where the influx of shoppers is obviously helping Heihe's economic boom – the taxi drivers competing for our custom had a smile even when they lost out.

The contrast between the Russian city and its Chinese counterpart could not be sharper. The former is grubby and dilapidated, the latter clean and fresh. In the former, the snow is piled haphazardly on the side of the road; in the latter, it is swept into neat piles and removed by tractor and trailer. In the former the shops are – with a few exceptions – gloomily utilitarian; in the latter they are equally utilitarian, but brash and lively. In the former the same goods are more expensive than in the latter; in the latter the standard of service is much higher than in the former. Of course these comparisons are unfair: the Russian city was founded in 1856, whereas the Chinese one is only twenty years old. Blagoveshchensk has much that is ugly, but also some fine public buildings that date from the turn of the twentieth century and give the city a feeling of rooted provincialism. Heihe's arcades and apartment blocks, all glass and concrete, are entirely lacking in architectural merit. Even in these limited terms, it is therefore easy to see why the Russians prefer to shop in the Chinese city but would never want to live there.

I had tagged on to a Russian family who invited me to accompany them on their outing. Roman was the manager of a construction company, his wife Angelina a part-time bookkeeper, and their ten-year-old son, Daniel, a Chelsea fan. Angelina was very much in charge. Tall and graceful, she had long black hair and wore a full-length black mink coat and black boots, her striking allure increased by the streaks of white fur on her black mink hat. She looked as though she might have walked out of an exclusive Paris couturier's, but in fact she had bought the entire outfit – very cheap at the price – in one of Heihe's many emporia. As she led the way from one shopping mall to another, with a purposeful stride that brooked no objection, Roman and Daniel trotted along dutifully in her wake.

Angelina knew exactly what she intended to buy: 'A beautiful new outfit for the New Year. And I want to dress my men – find nice clothes for them. There are souvenirs as New Year presents because we have lots of family and relatives to buy for.' Daniel said he wanted to buy a pair of football gloves and a football. Roman did not really buy anything at all, but under pressure conceded that he might buy a strimmer for their dacha. 'Do you like shopping?' I asked him. 'I don't like it at all. I really don't like shopping,' he replied. 'I seem to have come to this town seven hundred times since 1995 and I have seen it all. There are three streets filled with shops. After an hour my legs give up.' However, despite this confirmation of the Venus and Mars principle, he was clearly besotted with his wife and obeyed her without demur, solemnly assenting to all her ideas and all her decisions.

My legs began to give up in sympathy with Roman as we marched down one long aisle and into another, up and down escalators, from this level to the other, past cheek-by-jowl counters with eager young salespeople demanding our attention for every kind of consumer product. We were bombarded by choice: clothes for every purpose, children's toys, LCD screens, generators, kettles, computers, binoculars, chainsaws, Chinese-made Russian dolls, power drills, sex aids, an electronically animated Father Christmas rock group, two second-hand Toyota people carriers, a bus and, finally, a counter selling lawn mowers and strimmers. Roman investigated the options with as much thoroughness as Angelina had shown when selecting her own New Year dress and Daniel's sweater and gloves, but it took far longer because he cross-questioned the resolutely smiling Chinese salesman with a graceless suspicion that amply demonstrated that national stereotypes are not always invalid.

Finally, laden with clothes, the strimmer and Daniel's football, we went to have lunch in one of the many Chinese restaurants that line Heihe's principal avenues. Inside, samples of the lunchtime options were laid out on a long counter with as much dainty artistry as I have seen anywhere. Delicate in design, subtle in colour, inventive in choice, the variety of tastes on offer was calculated to bedazzle – and it did. There were multi-coloured fish, lobsters, crabs and terrapin waiting their turn in glass water tanks; shellfish laid out prettily on a bed of ice; and, more exotically, the living, writhing pupae of silkworms, ready to be boiled alive. There were fresh vegetables and green salads, curds, sweetmeats and – the restaurant's *pièce de résistance* – a spit laden with ducks, already golden-brown, turning slowly in an open charcoal oven. After we had made our choices a waitress, one of five who had stood by the door to bow their heads in greeting as we entered, escorted us upstairs to one of a dozen private dining rooms, where we sat at a round table and where the reality – especially the Peking duck – fully lived up to the downstairs appearance.

Angelina was an aficionado. 'I love the way the Chinese prepare the food,' she enthused. 'I love the way they cook it on a great open fire. The sauces, the spices, everything. We just love it, which is why we always come here.' So which did she prefer, I wondered, Russian or Chinese food? 'Chinese. My great-great-grandfather was Chinese – perhaps it is in my roots, in my blood.' So, since she preferred the shops here, could she imagine coming over to live on the Chinese side of the border? 'No. I love my own country, I love my Motherland. I have my family there. I couldn't live here. You would always feel like a stranger here.'

I asked Roman the 'Chinese question', about the numbers of Chinese who come across to work and live in Russia. He looked uncomfortable, but answered bluntly, 'There are enough of them on our side. Let them stay here on their side. I am happier to visit them rather than the other way round.' Angelina had a subtler reaction. 'We have a lot of Chinese living in Russia. They study in Russia, sometimes they work in Russia, and they like it. They like to come to Russia as we like going to China – and I think it should continue on this basis.' His wife's insouciance provoked Roman. 'They are elbowing us out. They have a cheap labour force, their goods are cheap. I think it would be better if we started to get our own workforce going so that we won't go on being edged out by the Chinese. I don't like the way in which they are elbowing us out all the time.'

As in Europe, and not least in the United Kingdom, such feelings are only too easy to orchestrate or exploit. Roman was simply saying aloud – after a couple of glasses of beer – what many Russians, not only the lumpenproletariat, are known to feel about the Chinese 'threat'; all the available research confirms that xenophobia among the obsessively nationalistic Russian people lurks only a little beneath the surface. There is resentment and insecurity, a collective inferiority complex – a touchpaper that could easily be set alight. No wonder that immigration – in a country increasingly short of skilled labour – has become so sensitive an issue that a government minister is driven to promise that no more Chinatowns will be permitted to take root. As it transpired, however, Roman's own attitudes were not quite so crude as they had at first seemed. When I asked him directly, 'Do you fear, deep down, the Yellow Peril?' he shook his head. 'No, I don't see it as that kind of threat any more. What we are facing is a peaceful conquest because of the quality of their goods and markets. And it is not just us, it is everywhere. And don't forget, in this region there have long been friendly relations. We have a friend who is Chinese. He is married to a Russian woman and they now have a child. And they live together in harmony. There are many stories like that.' We returned to the Russian hovercraft laden, according to Roman's calculation, with $300 worth of purchases, and within ten minutes were safely back in the bosom of the Motherland.

## ELECTIONS RUSSIAN-STYLE

It was election day in Russia on 2 December. The result was a foregone conclusion in Blagoveshchensk as everywhere else in the Federation. The Kremlin's elaborate corruption of the political process had already emptied the term 'election' of almost all meaning unless prefixed by the word 'sham'. The state's control of the media, its harassment of genuine opposition candidates and parties, and its iron-like grip on the administrative structure of every region had already made it practically certain that almost every genuinely independent voice would be excluded from the State Duma. According to the freshly minted rules of Putin's 'sovereign' democracy – a Brave New World concept that defies rational analysis – only three or four parties (of the eleven that were qualified to stand) would have any chance of surmounting the elaborately constructed constitutional hurdles that had been erected around this rubber-stamp parliament to protect the Kremlin from even the slightest challenge to its absolute authority. And even these parties – with the exception of the Communists, who occasionally offer a nominal critique of the Kremlin – were Putin's own creation. Thus, in the procedures of the Duma, he had more or less preserved the shell of a liberal democracy but had sucked it of all life. This brutal theft of Russia's nascent democracy has been elaborately conceived and brilliantly executed. As a result, in the run-up to the Big Day the voters seemed either to have been deluded into the belief that the ballot box would fairly reflect the democratically expressed will of the nation or, more disconcertingly, they knew the electoral process had been a sham but did not care: Putin was their man and the ballot box would prove it.

I went to a polling station near the centre of town to watch the voters about their business. For months the Russian government and the Organization for Security and Cooperation in Europe (OSCE) had been wrangling over the terms and conditions under which this international 'watchdog' (of which Russia is a leading member) would be permitted to monitor the election. With a little over two weeks to go, the Kremlin's delaying tactics led the OSCE to announce that it had no choice but to abandon its plans because it would be impossible to establish the proper monitoring procedures in the time now available. In the event, the OSCE agreed to contribute a number of its officials to an international team of four hundred monitors, who arrived at the last minute to observe the voting procedures at a tiny proportion of the 95,000 polling stations scattered across the largest country in the world. Against that background I decided that I should do my bit for democracy: I would monitor 'my' polling station with due diligence.

I joined a trickle of voters on their way into the foyer of a Blagoveshchensk concert hall, immediately to discover that the trappings of liberal democracy had been studiously mimicked. Along one side, a row of tellers ticked off voters' names from the electoral register for this downtown ward and steered each elector to a voting booth on the other side of the foyer. There, in curtained privacy, the good men and women of Blagoveshchensk marked their ballot papers, folded them in half, and emerged to deposit them into one of two red ballot boxes in the centre of the room. The voters were young and old, sometimes in family groups, sometimes alone, and they clearly took their responsibilities with high seriousness. They rarely spoke, and even then in subdued tones, as though they were in a place and participating in a process worthy of respect. Once they had fulfilled their democratic duty, they filed out into the cold of the night, leaving me with a twinge of guilt at my cynicism, which was, however, swiftly followed by a surge of contempt for the conspiracy of deceit by which they had been duped.

The ballot closed at 8 p.m. and the tellers got into a huddle at one end of the room. I was at once suspicious. What were they up to? Rigging the results already? When I went over to watch more closely I discovered that they were simply totting up the number of electors in the ward who had cast a vote. I asked the presiding officer for the figures. She double-checked her arithmetic and then said authoritatively, 'Eleven hundred and thirty-seven votes have been cast out of a possible sixteen hundred and fifty-two.' 'A good turnout,' I said. 'Must be over sixty per cent.' She nodded appreciatively. (I did a back-of-an-envelope calculation a few minutes later; the turnout was in fact over 65 per cent, a good showing by comparison with the 61 per cent turnout at the last British general election.)

Once the tellers had confirmed the turnout, their tables were carried to the middle of the foyer and rearranged into a large square. The ballot boxes were emptied on to the table. The presiding officer picked each ballot paper up one by one and, with the help of her colleagues, distributed them around the table according to party. I was free to go up to the table and scrutinize the process in close-up, duly noting that the ballot papers were clearly marked and properly distributed. It was very soon clear that there would be no surprises in this little corner of Blagoveshchensk. I watched as the United Russia pile grew rapidly, with the Communist Party some way behind in second place and the remaining nine parties nowhere.

At midnight the votes were counted by hand and, so far as I could tell, accurately. The tellers would not give me the figures (which had to be confirmed by Moscow) but Putin's very own United Russia seemed to have comfortably secured over 60 per cent of the vote. The Communists, who huff and puff in a policy-free zone of formal 'opposition' but, stricken by nostalgia, are relevant principally for the role they play as Putin's patriotic drum-majors, were second with about 15 per cent. And then, a long way behind, came the far right Liberal Democrats (who are unswervingly loyal to the Kremlin and also bang the patriotic drum but even more crudely; one of their candidates, successful as it transpired, was Andrey Lugovoi, wanted in Britain for the murder of Alexander Litvinenko) and Just Russia (a party conjured out of nowhere by Putin himself) – both securing the 7 per cent share of the vote needed to give them an acquiescent place in Putin's Duma. The tellers had fulfilled their allotted task with admirable dispatch and efficiency, but as they packed up to leave, there was no hint of celebration, no victorious candidates, no party faithful, no banners, no congratulations, no cheers – just one caretaker to ensure that the lights were switched out and the doors locked. It was a dispiriting moment.

In a measured critique, the OSCE and the Council of Europe subsequently concluded that the election had been 'unfair' because it had taken place in 'an atmosphere which seriously limited political competition'. Others, with greater access, were less reticent. A host of independent critics detected a systematic campaign of threats, intimidation and coercion orchestrated by the Kremlin and its regional satraps in the run-up to the election, not to mention malpractice and fraud on the day itself. Even the Communist Party and the ultra-nationalist Vladimir Zhirinovsky, leader of the Liberal Democrats, felt obliged to challenge the results, complaining of vote-rigging and ballot-stuffing in several regions, including Chechnya and Dagestan. In another Caucasian republic, Ingushetia, the results showed that 98.35 per cent of the electorate had turned out, of whom an astonishing 98.72 per cent had apparently cast their vote for United Russia. In the light of these remarkable figures the proprietor of an independent website, Ingushetiya.ru, began a campaign to establish whether – against all the anecdotal evidence – the turnout had really been so overwhelming. So far, more than 85,000 residents of Ingushetia, who constitute more than 54 per cent of the little republic's eligible voters – have signed statements saying that they had refused to go to the polls, many of them in protest against the corruption and economic incompetence of their Kremlin-approved president.

In its customary manner, the Central Election Commission of Russia announced emolliently that 'all complaints and allegations will be carefully examined'. But by this time a spokesman for the Kremlin had already told CNN that the complaints were 'groundless'. President Putin doubtless drew comfort from the fact that official monitors from the Shanghai Cooperation Organization (whose members include such freedom-loving nations as China, Kazakhstan, Kyrgyzstan, Tajikistan and Uzbekistan) had inspected thirty precincts in the electoral district of Moscow and taken a very different view from the OSCE. At the conclusion of their work they issued a statement reporting that 'in the election district observed by the Mission' the election had been 'legitimate, free and open, and [had] basically conformed to the requirements of the national legislation of the Russian Federation and its international obligations'.

But an opinion poll taken in the week following the election must have been even more heart-warming to the Kremlin. Conducted in 153 locations scattered over 46 regions of the Federation by the reputable Russian Public Opinion Research Centre, the poll showed that 53 per cent of the Russian people believed the election to have been free, democratic and fair; only 19 per cent took the opposite view. In a depressing way, this finding was not only predictable but explicable. Only the most naive or brainwashed voter could have thought the election to have been anything more than a convoluted plebiscite on the President who had restored order, stability and national pride. His overwhelming popularity was not in question, and, as most electors were perfectly well aware, the political parties for which they were ostensibly voting were quite irrelevant to the business of government. As the results of the election confirmed the desired outcome, it must have been tempting to conclude, despite the over-whelming evidence to the contrary, that the process itself had been as 'free, democratic and fair' as any fair-minded observer could wish. For the record, United Russia is credited with securing 64.3 per cent of the vote, the Communist Party 11.6 per cent, the Liberal Democrats 8.1 per cent, and Just Russia 7.7 per cent. This gave Putin's party 341 of the 450 seats in the Duma. No wonder that in 2007 the Russian President, like Stalin before him, was chosen as *Time* magazine's Man of the Year.

On my way to the station, I noticed a new 4×4 Land Cruiser. Written along one side in silver lettering were the words, in English, 'I move where my heart takes me. I am not bound to anything. I run in the fields. I cross over mountain tops. I pass through a lot of great places in this immense earth.' It was, absurdly enough, a marketing ploy by the local Toyota dealer. But I felt very glad indeed that, like the 4×4 fantasy, I was not electorally bound to Blagoveshchensk or Russia or Vladimir Putin.

## STALIN'S JEWISH HOMELAND

I was now little more than 600 miles – or some thirty Trans-Siberian hours – from Vladivostok. Although I was now in a hurry to reach my final destination, it was impossible to bypass one of the most intriguing and least-known curiosities in all Russia: the Jewish Autonomous Region (JAR). When I heard the term I wanted to repeat aloud, music-hall fashion, 'The Jewish Autonomous Region? In Russia? What do you mean? Is it a ghetto? Is there "another" Israel?' I looked on the map. Sure enough there it was, located even further along the Amur River, on the border with China. So, fifteen hours out of Blagoveshchensk, I left the train at yet another station but that, unlike any other, had its name, Birobidzhan, blazoned over the main concourse in Yiddish.

It was the eve of Hanukkah. The lights shone out from a synagogue, a short walk from the main square. As I got close, I could just hear the lilting chant of a Jewish catechism. Inside, I tiptoed up to the balcony in what was obviously a very new building, all white paint and natural woodwork. I looked down on the gentlest of rituals: a young Orthodox rabbi, bearded and cloaked, was standing at a lectern, reading at characteristically breakneck speed from the Talmud, bowing back and forth in reverence before the holy words. In the pews behind him some twenty men, all skullcapped, played their part, uttering their formal responses and bowing with practised certainty towards the lectern in their turn. I judged their average age to be above sixty. One or two were clearly much older, perhaps eighty or more. But there were also a couple of youths and a young boy (who turned out to be the rabbi's son).

With the informality that characterizes the religious rites of Orthodox Jewry, the service was suddenly over. The men removed their skullcaps, donned the wide-brimmed hats favoured by their sect, dressed themselves against the evening cold and processed towards the main square. One or two of the old men cavorted with joy like little leprechauns. A few of them burst into a cackle of discordant song. The sound began to swell, caught its rhythm, and soon they were almost a choir. But then they faltered, losing their way through the words, and the singing stopped abruptly. I followed as they processed into the main square, where a small crowd of onlookers had arrived to watch the annual ceremony of Hanukkah. We gathered around a plinth where the rabbi delivered a brief address and a blessing before he lit the first of the nine candles on the menorah, a simple gas-fuelled candelabrum suspended a metre or so above his head. Afterwards the women passed around hot unleavened doughnuts filled with jam, and the men offered vodka. The combination, in what was now a very cold (minus 10 degrees centigrade) night, was unexpectedly delicious.

Breaking off frequently to greet friends and relatives from the town's Jewish community, the rabbi, who introduced himself as Mordechai Shayler, told me the version of the Hanukkah story favoured by most Hassidic Jews. He spoke earnestly, as if to convey the literal truth of a miracle. In the latter half of the second century BC, when the Jews finally liberated the Second Temple in Jerusalem from the Syrian monarchy, the elders wanted to light the menorah to celebrate. But they could only find enough olive oil to light its eight lamps for one night. Miraculously, however, the lamps continued to burn for eight days. The ninth candle is used to light the others at a rate of one a day. Hanukkah entered the Jewish calendar as both a memorial and a celebration. Watching the faithful friends together reliving this myth, I sensed a poignancy in the atmosphere, a pervasive spirit of meditation and reflection, not so much joyous as sombre.

Perhaps I was being over-lugubrious, reading too much into the occasion. However, my feelings were immediately reinforced by the arrival of three of the oldest members of the congregation. I asked them how long they had lived in Birobidzhan. The eldest of the elders took the lead. 'I arrived when there was nothing here. It was in the thirties. It was just a swamp. We were the new settlers and there were no proper houses. Nothing. We were brought here in trucks. There were no cars, only horses. We were taken to a collective farm by cart and slowly began to settle the land. It was a very hard life. There were only Chinese people, there were ninety of them, and they were the ones who used to feed us because we couldn't yet grow anything. We tried to grow things, but it just wasn't happening for us.' As he spoke he looked at me, one of his eyes watering in the sharp wind, with a ferocious intensity, seeming to revisit every moment of those days. 'It was terrible, terrible cold weather. Terrible severe frosts. We tried....' And then he glanced away, lost in contemplation, before picking up his train of thought once more. 'Later, specialists came to help and we slowly got to grow our own food. But to start with it was just the Chinese. In the middle of town here, you could see the tents they lived in.'

Until 1917, since the days of Catherine the Great in the eighteenth century most Russian Jews had been confined to what was called the Pale, a region in the far west of the Empire that embraced parts of what is now Lithuania, Belarus, Poland, Moldova and Ukraine. But in the early years of the Bolshevik revolution the 2.5 million Jews living under Soviet rule enjoyed an unprecedented degree of freedom – which meant in practice that they were granted the same civil and political rights as every other member of the new proletariat. Many of the Jewish intelligentsia were avowed Communists who had given fervent support to the revolution, while the strong stance against anti-Semitism adopted by the Bolshevik leadership offered further hope of genuine emancipation. These hopes were buttressed when Stalin declared the Jews to be a 'nationality group' with a right to receive a territorial slice of the Soviet Union in which their autonomy would be protected and enhanced. Although Communist ideologues believed that such national identities would eventually disappear along with their accompanying religious convictions, it appears – from a paucity of available evidence – that Stalin was genuinely convinced that, at this stage in their cultural development, the Jews required their own homeland in Russia. Whether or not the Soviet leader was also animated by a desire to divert the attention of Russian Jewry – who at that time were treated as valued citizens by the Communist hierarchy – from the growing Zionist clamour for a homeland in Palestine is a matter for speculation. Either way, in March 1928 the regime issued a decree designating the district around Birobidzhan for the settlement of Jews willing to work the land.

The Kremlin could not have selected a more remote or difficult region in which to settle a people who were experienced in finance, commerce, trade and retail, and skilled as artisans, blacksmiths and tailors, but who had been forbidden to own land and discouraged from engaging in agricultural production; they were townspeople, not peasants. Much of the land around Birobidzhan was an inhospitable, swampy waste, oppressively sultry in the summer heat and heavily infested by mosquitoes, but bitterly cold in winter. These physical conditions did not feature prominently in the propaganda campaign to persuade Russian Jews and those living elsewhere in the Diaspora to find their destiny in this eldorado promised for them in the Russian Far East. That they came at all is testament less to their naivety than to a profound urge to affirm their Jewish identity within a Russian homeland. But even the most skilled agriculturalists would have had an uphill struggle to turn the swamp into productive land suitable for collective cultivation. And since the first pioneers lacked not only the basic skills, but very frequently also the equipment, the tools, the barns and the potable water needed to rear livestock, they faced a sisyphean task to make the Jewish Autonomous Region habitable.

In *Stalin's Forgotten Zion*, Robert Weinberg has written a memorable account of their travails.

> Wagons became mired in impassable, muddy roads, and the settlers had to haggle with officials over their land allotments; all contended with particularly fierce mosquitos until the land was drained and reclaimed; everyone had to make do with livestock stricken with a variety of diseases. Primitive medical facilities were frequently located miles away from the new settlements. And to make matters worse, massive floods covered the J.A.R. in 1928 and 1932, destroying crops and forcing some collective and state farms to start anew.

A Soviet journalist who arrived at the fledgling settlement of Birobidzhan wrote scathingly of the makeshift barracks around the station that 'would put prisons to shame'. He concluded magisterially that 'the colonization of Birobidzhan was begun and executed without preparation, planning and study. All the misfortunes are due to the hasty manner in which the Birobidzhan project was implemented.'

Nonetheless, the Jewish Autonomous Region of Birobidzhan, which was formally established in May 1934, slowly emerged as a functioning, constituent part of the USSR, with not only collective farms but textile factories, furniture-making guilds, newspapers and schools. Nor was there any let-up in the propaganda. A Yiddish novelist, David Begelman, writing romantically of the pioneers, described how they chopped down primeval forests, drained swamps, built roads, houses and schools, and then – as it were on the seventh day – allowed themselves to bask in a glorious environment where 'the snow lies smooth as a counterpane' and where 'the sun, above you, below you, on the hillocks and in the sky is so bright that your spirits soar with the sheer joy of life on earth'. There was more such romantic drivel in films like *Seekers of Happiness* (1936), of which one of the co-directors, Vladimir Korsh-Sablin, wrote, 'I have straightened up the stooping Jews, shaved off their beards and cut their hair and have shown them as healthy, good-looking people, full of life and energy.'

But even at its peak the Jewish population of the JAR never rose above 32,000, and by the mid-thirties it was already starting to decline as thousands of disillusioned immigrants retreated to the European side of the Urals. Despite a small influx of non-Soviet Jews lured by the same propaganda as the first pioneers, the Jewish population was soon heavily outnumbered by a rapidly growing influx of Russian Gentiles, attracted by the job prospects promised in Stalin's Second Five-Year Plan. In consequence, the non-Jewish immigrants soon outnumbered the Jewish settlers by a ratio of 4:1. The founding vision was starting to fade, and before long it would be obliterated entirely.

In the early years, the use of Yiddish was officially encouraged as, in Weinberg's words, 'the bedrock of a secular, proletarian Soviet Jewish culture and community'. But by the same token religious observation was discouraged and with increasing severity. In the absence of a synagogue, those who wanted to practise their faith by celebrating the Sabbath in Birobidzhan had to meet discreetly in a private apartment in order to avoid the attentions of the regional League of the Militant Godless, which at Passover campaigned noisily against the Jewish faith, arguing that socialism and religion were incompatible. Then, in 1936, came the Stalin purges and a paranoid persecution from which the JAR was no more excused than anywhere else in the Soviet Union. Along with thousands of their peers elsewhere, leading members of the Jewish community in Birobidzhan were arrested, imprisoned and, in several cases, executed.

By the end of the thirties, Stalin's homicidal tendencies had helped to reduce the number of Jews in the JAR to just over 17,500, a mere 16 per cent of the 100,000 inhabitants of the region. Although their numbers were briefly swollen by an influx of Jewish refugees escaping the disruption and dislocation caused by the Great Patriotic War, the dream was already dead. In 1948, with a capriciousness that was as cruel as it was inexplicable, Stalin once more turned on Russian Jewry. Their leaders in the JAR were variously accused of 'bourgeois nationalism' and 'rootless cosmopolitanism', while all contact between the Jews of the JAR and non-Soviet Jewry was forbidden. And, as if to obliterate their very identity, the state moved against their institutions as well. Not only the synagogue in Birobidzhan but the Jewish theatre, and almost every Yiddish school, were forcibly closed down.

Had Stalin detected the contradictions at the core of his original policy? Or was he impatient at the failure of the Jews to fuse their cultural identity into that of a common Soviet culture as rapidly as he had intended? Or did he simply change his mind? Whatever the case, he was merciless. In Birobidzhan the psychological cataclysm of those days is still remembered with horror. 'It was terrible. People would go to work and they would not know whether they would return in the evening,' one of the elders told me, gripping my arm with the insistence of an Ancient Mariner. 'I remember one Party Secretary who was summoned to Moscow and he never came back. They arrested our intelligentsia. Many people in our community were simply wiped out.

Our schools were annihilated. And they burnt our books. It was terrible. It was terrible.' He did not exaggerate. In an approach that was reminiscent of Nazi Germany, albeit on a far smaller scale, the authorities ordered that the Jewish section in the town's museum be dismantled and, in the most symbolic act of all, local party officials removed some thirty thousand books from the Judaica collection in the public library and destroyed them in a funeral pyre. To all intents and purposes the distinctive identity of the Jewish Autonomous Region, Stalin's 'Soviet Zion', had been obliterated.

It was not until Gorbachev introduced his twin policies of *glasnost* and *perestroika* in the second half of the eighties that the surviving members of the Jewish community in the JAR were allowed, little by little, to replant the seeds of their cultural identity. By the nineties these seeds had started to flower. Yiddish became the official language of the JAR once again, an enterprising editor started a Yiddish newspaper, the local college provided students with the opportunity to study Yiddish, and a local radio station broadcast a weekly programme in Yiddish. Although it was too late to prevent a rapid exodus of Jews from the region (even today, Jews make up less than 2 per cent of the JAR's population), this cultural renaissance was given a new dimension by the arrival of Rabbi Shayler and the construction of the new synagogue where, as the leader of the Chabad Hassidic sect in the region, he has become a pivotal figure among the remnants of the Orthodox community. With his help, like prisoners released from the dark into a bright light, the 'chosen ones' have sought to rebuild the foundations of their ancient faith whose practices and doctrines had virtually been erased from the collective memory.

The rabbi invited me to his apartment to meet his wife and six children. Esther and one of her daughters were making yet more doughnuts in a tiny kitchen that was filled with the smell of baking. As an Orthodox woman, she was not permitted to have any physical contact with me, so when I put my hand out she shook her head, rebuffing my gesture but with a self-deprecating smile. At first her husband did the talking while she and her daughter worked in diligent silence. Mordechai not only took his religious role seriously but was prone to speak at inordinate and didactic length, his demeanour so solemn as to suggest that he had long ago been subjected to a sense-of-humour bypass. So I teased him. 'I see, the women do all the work and the men sit around?' He did not smile but replied, 'Every one has their own role. I work, but at my job and in my own way.' And then he added, with a hint of aggression, 'I know what is in hiding behind your question: you are trying to say that there are religious beliefs that say men should do one kind of work and women should do another kind of work' – in truth I had intended no such inference – 'but what I want to say is that the Being who created the world had a better understanding than all of us about who should do what work. And it is written in the Torah about what should be woman's work and what should be man's work. And that it is very much better for peace and harmony that there is variety on earth – that we shouldn't all be the same and that men and women have different tasks and that they complement one another.' To which I felt an infantile urge to respond by saying, 'And so say all of us.'

Instead I changed the subject to ask what it was like for an Israeli rabbi of Russian descent to return to the country where his grandfather and his father had endured persecution under Stalin. This time he surprised me with a moment of practical candour rather than the sepulchral complacency that had hitherto afflicted him. 'Well, the climate wasn't a problem. We just wore more clothes. But there were a lot of other problems. A lot of strangeness. People didn't understand that for us certain things really were a matter of principle. For instance, kosher food. When we moved here, this kitchen didn't even have the proper division between meat and milk. So we couldn't cook here until it was rearranged for us in the proper kosher fashion. We ate out of suitcases for a month. Luckily we had brought enough kosher food for a year. And it had to last because we would only feed the children on kosher food.'

This memory emboldened Esther to join our conversation. Although she had produced six children (and, according to the rules of her faith, was happy to bear as many more as God wished), she looked as slight and fragile as the delicate stem of a hothouse flower. Only her lustrous eyes, azure blue and deep-set in a narrow, dark face, suggested the strength of character that she must have had to uproot herself from Israel to live in Birobidzhan as handmaiden to her husband. 'It was difficult. There was the different language and there is a different mentality here. And I have my family in Israel – it was my home. But I have got used to it now. People have been very kind and hospitable. Now when I go back to Israel I feel that I am going on a visit. I feel like a guest and that my home is here in Birobidzhan. And my husband has found his place here. He fits this community like a glove. There were many things that people here did not know about their religion – about the doctrine and the practices – and he explains and he teaches and he is wonderful at it. This is his place.'

Mordechai remained impassive through this wifely tribute. So I asked him if he felt as much at home here in Russia's Far East as his wife did. 'No, I couldn't say that,' he replied carefully. 'I don't feel that Russia is my home. In every way Israel is my home. Although I am fine here and like it very much, Israel is my home.' So what, I wondered, would constitute success or failure in his mission to the Jews of the JAR? 'That is a very difficult question to answer,' he replied laboriously, adopting once more the sepulchral tone that seemed to fit him only too comfortably. 'Every day I ask myself, "What more can I do? What other things can I bring here?" It's a question I am always asking myself: "What more can I can bring to this community."' It was impossible not to respect Mordechai Shayler's learning or his sincerity, but to keep his company for long, I concluded, would be like swimming in treacle. Despite the family's generous hospitality, I could not help feeling a surge of relief as I made my excuses and bid Rabbi Shayler farewell.

The secular Jews of the JAR, who are hugely in the numerical ascendancy, might well have offered their own irreverent answer to the rabbi's rhetorical question. 'You could try and get God to bring us the Bridge.' The Bridge is the brainchild of the ever-inventive Peter Hambro and his partner Pavel Maslovsky, whose interests extend well beyond their goldmines. Through a sister company, Aricom, which is run (under their supervision) by Jay Hambro, they have started to extract iron ore, manganese and graphite in rapidly growing quantities from a number of sites in the Amur region and in the barely exploited JAR. Before I left the Pokrovskiy mine Maslovsky had unrolled a large map of the Russian Far East, poring over it like a general inspecting the deployment of his troops on a Napoleonic battlefield, to show me how the bridge, which is planned to link Russia with China across the Amur River, would not only revolutionize their own business but transform the economy of the entire region. The consortium put together by Peter Hambro Mining and Aricom to build the bridge is – inevitably – called Rubicon.

With a total span of just over 2100 metres, the bridge will be significantly shorter than the Forth Road Bridge, and in any other location would hardly raise an eyebrow. But this bridge is a hugely ambitious project that has great symbolic as well as practical significance. As the only permanent link between Russia and China along a 2160-mile stretch of their common border between Chita and Vladivostok, *The Bridge on the Amur* (as I imagined the title of the epic film devoted to the venture) would have an incalculable impact on the relationship between the two neighbours. Maslovsky's eyes seemed to glow with suppressed excitement as he described how Aricom's almost limitless supply of ore would soon – within three years – be trundling over the bridge to be deposited in China's 'Black Hole', as he described the insatiable demand for steel in a Chinese economy growing at an annual rate of over 11 per cent.

From Aricom's perspective this prospect would make the new toll bridge cheap at almost any price, even though, with the cost of building and of upgrading a 70-mile rail link from the Trans-Siberian line to the crossing point on the Amur, it will cost upwards of $800 million. Aricom had already 'committed' to a 50 per cent investment; the rest was to be financed by the Russian and the Chinese governments. According to Maslovsky, the formal contracts had just been approved in principle by both Moscow and Beijing and, he added, there were now only some 'technical issues' still to be resolved between the two sides. 'Only "technical issues"?' I had murmured dubiously, the pooper at the party. 'It will happen. It will happen. I assure you it will happen,' he insisted. As I had expected, Peter Hambro had been no less bullish as he happily totted up the financial rewards that would come their way from this ambitious project. 'The bridge will last for at least fifty years. It will take only three years for us to recover our investment. But the capacity is far greater than we will need. Others will want to use it and we will have our share of the income from the tolls they will pay.' He smiled with satisfaction, not like a stockbroker or banker smiles, with complacency, but as a genuine buccaneer prospecting for gold of whatever kind and wherever it may be found and always keen to cross yet another frontier. It was hard to resist their enthusiasm.

In Birobidzhan the bridge was virtually the only topic of conversation among the regional power-brokers. At the hotel one evening I was treated to a kosher feast complete with kosher vodka, at which Hambro's man in the Rubicon hot seat, Sergey Lavrentiev, was joined by various local Jewish luminaries, most notably Viktor Kireev, who used to be a member of the nomenclatura in the Soviet period when he rose to hold almost every important position in the JAR except that of governor. Between them Sergey (himself a former Soviet regional boss) and Viktor carry real clout in the region. Sergey was even more ebullient than Hambro and Maslovsky. 'It is a massive project that requires the coordination of permissions and agreements from dozens of different ministries and departments, not to mention the cooperation between Russia and China.' So if it all goes wrong? He gestured dismissively. 'I'm not just a hundred per cent sure it will be successful,

I'm a thousand per cent sure. It is just a matter of technical procedures and the document will be signed.' Those 'technical' issues again.

But Sergey's enthusiasm was seductive. As he listed the benefits that Aricom would bring, my scepticism evaporated and I almost began to believe that the bridge might reverse the exodus that has seen the population of the JAR fall from 220,000 fifteen years ago to 170,000 today. 'If you come back here to this town in five years, or certainly in ten years, you won't recognize it or the area around. It is starting to happen already. As you know, the Jews left here in large numbers after the fall of the Soviet Union. But now some of them are coming back and the area is getting more prosperous. This will accelerate even more rapidly in the next few years.' He seemed to be imagining a land flowing with milk and honey, which reminded me of the British Honorary Consul's assistant Igor at the Black Sea port of Novorossiysk. 'Of course we are a long way from paradise, but we are doing this for the people. And it has to be a joint enterprise between business and government. It is the only way you will improve people's lives. And it is happening. It will just get better and better. And if you do things for people, the people will pay you back. They will work harder and they will be happier. They will want to contribute their labour, and that is for the good of everyone.' For a moment he sounded like a nineteenth-century American philanthropist, rather than a twenty-first-century project director for Aricom's money-spinning bridge – and I liked him all the better for it.

Viktor weighed in. Brought up in a community that had been ravaged by Stalin's vendettas, he had been left without any knowledge of Jewish culture. 'We didn't observe the Jewish festivals. We couldn't tell the difference between the menorah and the Hanukkah candles. And we had no idea about the teachings of the Talmud. But in the eighties, when we began to see the awakening of democracy, the Jewish community started to revive. Then, of course, in the nineties there was a great exodus. Now we hope the Jews will return. Quite a few have already come back, and we have created for them the right

conditions where they can observe their cultural life and their traditions and follow their faith.'

I noticed that he used the word 'they' rather than 'we', and asked
him why it was so important for the Jews to return. Confirming that,
as a secular Jew, it made no difference to him whether the region's
urgent economic needs were met by Jews or Gentiles, Viktor avowed
that the policy of the government had not changed since the establishment of the JAR; then, as now, the region was a home for 'the nation
of Jews', but the administration itself was devoid of any 'national' or
'religious' identity. So why was it important specifically to attract Jews?
'The region is short of specialists, and among the Jews there are always
skilled people, especially in the professions,' he replied, but added, to
make sure I got the point, 'They might be Jews, but we are very happy
to welcome non-Jews as well. What matters is that they are good
people.' In truth, the original concept enshrined in the constitutional
entity known as the Jewish Autonomous Region is virtually as mean-
ingless today as it was seventy years ago, but for quite different reasons;
in a nation where Jews are now free to practise their faith and celebrate
their culture anywhere they wish, the JAR is a touching anachronism.

Everyone around the table was in a position of authority and influence. I wondered therefore what they thought about one of Putin's
most egregious constitutional 'reforms', which had been approved by
a supine Duma but sucked power away from the regions into the
Kremlin. Did they approve of Putin's tsarist diktat that in future
regional governors would not be elected by the voters but be
appointed by the Kremlin? Viktor answered for them all. 'I think it is
a good initiative, a good idea,' he replied, offering quite the most
bizarre justification for autocracy that I had yet heard. 'If you are
elected, then you can only be removed in an election,' he explained.
'Yes,' I murmured as he continued, 'and there is a great deal of opportunity for wrong-doing for which you can only be removed at an
election.' I wanted to intervene, but he was in full flow. 'If governors
are appointed, they have to take into account that they could be

removed at any time. And the same applies to their teams. For this reason they will perform their tasks more effectively.' Baffled by this Byzantine exegesis, I half-joked, 'But that is an argument for getting rid of all elections, isn't it?' Viktor was unmoved. 'I don't think that will happen,' he replied judiciously, and perhaps with a hint of regret as well. 'The democratic process is now in place.'

As I left Birobidzhan, the 'technical issues' bedevilling the Bridge over the Amur had yet to be resolved; the project was supposed to be finished by 2010, but by the end of 2007 it had yet to be started. I feared that the people of the Jewish Autonomous Region had invested rather too many of their dreams in Peter Hambro's vision. But on my way to the station to catch the train for Vladivostok I passed a life-size sculpture that depicted a family of Jewish pioneers from the twenties, who had reached Birobidzhan in a horse and trap with nothing but a few personal belongings and their dreams. I hoped I was wrong about the bridge and that Peter Hambro et al. were right.

## VLADIVOSTOK: FINAL DESTINATION

The journey from Birobidzhan to Vladivostok was due to last a mere fifteen hours – the last fifteen hours of my trans-Russian adventure. To my intense surprise I found myself gripped by a wave of regret that my days in Russia were numbered, that I was nearly at the end of the line. For so long I had anticipated the relief of achieving my final destination, and yet now I wanted the train to linger. It was not that the view was in any way so dramatic as to make the heart race. On the contrary, I had already come to the conclusion that anyone simply seeking spectacular scenery should avoid the Trans-Siberian; far better to go on the Canadian Pacific through the Rockies or take the train from Cape Town to Johannesburg or, indeed, the line from Edinburgh to Inverness. No, the wonder of this journey through Siberia is the sheer size and scale – I almost want to write unnatural or inhuman scale – of the landscape. Its very monotony embraces you

– you become curiously enfolded by it, not dwarfed but enslaved. You submit and become passive, entranced by the slowly altering features as the flatlands drift into hills and back again. Entranced is perhaps the word, literally. I have never been high on drugs, nor has transcendental meditation played any part in my life, but as I stared out of the window for hour after hour, I almost hallucinated: the hills became hedgehogs, the fir trees their prickles; the blue sky (it had been like that for day after day) untouched by a single cloud, without perspective or definition, seemed to beckon me towards infinity – as though, like a child, I merely had to assent to this promise and I would find myself borne aloft towards the heavens. It was so mesmeric that it was unnerving; and, as in that demi-world between sleep and wakening – that half-dream state that you can almost control and from which you don't want to escape – I had to pull myself by a force of will to return to what passes for reality.

No, the regret was not that I would never see the steppe again but that the journey itself was about to hit the buffers. I had seen so much and yet so little. I had discovered a great deal but I still had so very much still to learn. Had I been able to stay here and there, in this village or that town, for longer (which I had never wanted to do), had I observed more closely and listened more intently, I would, I knew, have been in a much better position now to reach a conclusion, not only of the journey, but about Russia and the Russians. As the train trundled along at its regulation 50 mph (I calculated that if it had been a TGV or a Japanese bullet train, or even an elderly 125, the trans-Siberian part of the journey could have been accomplished in little more than a third of the time it had in fact taken), it seemed to be accelerating towards Vladivostok with unnecessary haste. 'Slow down, slow down,' I wanted to say. 'I need more time.'

About forty-five minutes out from Vladivostok, the hills on the right of the train gave way to a long, wide waterway that at first I thought was the open sea, but that the map showed to be a large inlet, a bay to the southeast of the city. As I stared at it into the glare of the sun, I thought at first that I must be having a genuine hallucination: I saw that the bay was covered in what looked like a layer of sugary icing, as though a demented chef had run riot with his piping bag and then topped off the confection by planting an army of little penguins on it. I stared even more intently through the frost-streaked carriage window until I realized that the bay was simply frozen, totally frozen, and that the penguins were people, sitting in rows like a conclave of cardinals, in seeming meditation, though with a fishing rod rather than a stave in their hands, staring down through the neat hole that each of them had drilled through the ice towards their prey. There were scores of them sprinkled out from very close to the shoreline to a distance of a third of a mile or so towards the middle of the bay. For some reason the combination of this surreal image with the very practical purpose on which the fishermen were engaged filled me with such delight that I gasped and grinned and looked around, hoping that others on the train were as excited by the scene as I was. But my fellow passengers, or those whom I could see along the corridor, were either entirely untouched by the moment or far better at containing their feelings.

My elation stayed with me as the train pulled into the station and as I walked past a plaque on the platform that recorded that the distance from Moscow to Vladivostok was precisely 9288 kilometres (5771 miles). I had travelled some 10,000 miles through seven of Russia's ten time zones and I felt a momentary flush of triumph. Perhaps for this reason I was already disposed to like this city on the Pacific. Although Vladivostok was only established – as a naval outpost – in 1859, it had, for me, an aura of romance that had been singularly lacking from every other city on my way here. I liked the thought that the direct route by sea to San Francisco was marginally shorter than the rail link to Moscow. And though I knew that it had been a closed city (to Soviet citizens as well as foreigners) from the mid-fifties until the collapse of the Soviet Union, I suspected that no international port, not even this one, could have been entirely immune from outside influences. I rather hoped those influences might have bequeathed to Vladivostok an identity that would distinguish it from its dourer counterparts elsewhere in the great Russian Federation.

To test my hypothesis, I headed for the heart of the city – through and past an attractive maze of turn-of-the-twentieth-century streets and apartments – to take the funicular railway up to a vantage point called the Eagle's Nest. There, like Keats's 'stout Cortès', I looked down on the port and felt some of the 'wild surmise' that, in the poet's imagination, the conquistador's men had experienced as they saw the Pacific for the first time. From where I stood the main channel out to the ocean was not frozen, though in the distance I could see an archipelago of small islands to the south and, in between, three large patches of ice, as though the whitecaps had frozen in mid-leap. In the weeks ahead, these ice-islands would spread in size until they joined up and only an ice-breaker would be able to forge a passage through them to keep the shipping lanes open. In the late afternoon, the sun's refracted light transformed the ripples of water in the bay into an abstract dance of sparkling rivulets, the magic of which would surely have seduced Matisse or Hockney into a spasm of creative genius.

I can think of hardly any major port around the world that has not stirred my timorous nautical spirit. Whether their purpose is international trade or national security or both, seaports are always restless. There are cranes and derricks, lighters and tugs, ferries and rowboats, ugly containers and graceful merchantmen of the traditional type; there are fishing fleets and warships, and usually a smatter of cruise liners and pleasure boats as well. On the one hand ports beckon and protect, on the other they hold out the promise of exploration and adventure. Even a grubby, tattered ensign drooping from a flagstaff on a ship's stern suggests an exotic destination, a distant land, the promise of spices and mystery. Even those floating armadillos – the bulk-carriers and container ships that now rule the waves – contain a hint of the unknown and the unexpected. And in a world trapped by the intricacies of GATT rounds, import levies and trade tariffs they provide the unequivocal evidence that, in this millennium, like all that have gone before, we trade with one another or we perish. Of course, ports are also very often dirty, seamy and violent, but that is part of their romance and their humanity. I relish ports, and Vladivostok did not disappoint.

The city is built on a range of steep hills separated by fingers of deep water that form a natural harbour that is protected from almost any weather. From the Eagle's Nest I looked down over the remnants of Russia's Pacific fleet, a handful of elderly destroyers and corvettes that were not in mothballs but looked as though they were unaccustomed to leaving port. (Given the deteriorating relations between Russia and the USA, it was vaguely reassuring to read that, a couple of months before my arrival, the two former superpowers had conducted a joint naval exercise off Vladivostok – though it lasted a mere two days and between them they mustered only five vessels. More significantly – and unthinkable until a few years ago – a much larger and longer Sino-Soviet air, sea and land joint exercise was due to begin a few weeks later. This was a military manifestation of an even more important strategic and diplomatic rapprochement that – especially through the UN Security Council – has an increasing capacity to frustrate America's global aspirations, for example in Iraq, Iran, Burma, Darfur and Kosovo.

Seawards to my right I had a grandstand view of the container terminal, not the largest I had seen (it is dwarfed by that of Hong Kong, for example) but busily off-loading containers from China, Korea and Japan. On the dock itself, alongside an extended high-rise block of containers, a long line of bright yellow buses (imported from China) coiled past a row of new excavators, diggers and fork-lift trucks. Strewn around the dockside were piles of girders, tubes and hawsers. Working its way along a crazed jigsaw of railway lines, a diesel engine towing a squeaking convoy of goods wagons laden with Japanese cars caused the scurry of vans and trucks, yellow lights winking, to pause impatiently. On the other side of the harbour, no more than half a mile away, a clutch of fishing boats was moored together at the quayside; they swayed in gentle harmony as a tug passed by, washing them in its wake. A clatter of groans, screeches and clunks wafted up from a repair yard, where sanders and grinders scattered showers of yellow sparks, and oxyacetylene torches, welding steel plates to the battered hull of a cargo ship, spurted blue-white tongues of 3000-degree heat into the dusk.

Vladivostok feels both isolated and insulated. Its location so close to China, Japan and Korea makes it geographically an Asian city, but psychologically it feels more Western than many parts of European Russia. And its distinctive physical identity, which must have constrained the Soviet planners from imposing their baleful vision, has allowed it to preserve a distinctive psychological identity too, so that, unlike so many Russian cities, it feels like a human habitat that has grown organically – spasmodically, haphazardly, even accidentally. Historically, Vladivostok expressed the spirit of empire; now it expresses – or rather could express – the spirit of individual and communal enterprise.

With characteristic bombast, Khrushchev once declared that Vladivostok would one day become Russia's answer to San Francisco. As the lights of the port and the surrounding city began to twinkle in the clear night air, I could almost imagine that he might be right. Cities on steep slopes have a unique advantage over their rivals on flat land – and this is especially so when they are built at the water's edge. They have a scale, shape and perspective that are defined by the contours of nature and are not nearly as susceptible to the depredations of urban sprawl. Tier upon tier, retreating from the water's edge, hotels, office blocks, shopping centres, schools, cinemas and private apartments rise as in a theatre from the stage (the waterfront) through the stalls to the circle, the balcony and finally the gods (though, unlike the theatre, it is generally more expensive at the top than at the bottom). If they are well designed by socially sensitive planners and imaginative architects, they can be both grand and intimate, beautiful and utilitarian. The problems of traffic congestion can be countered by funicular railways that provide public transport from top to bottom like the aisles that run up and down in an auditorium.

In Vladivostok by night I let my imagination run away with me in this way. For the first time I felt myself to be in a Russian city that was not yet beyond recall. Lacking the twentieth-century brutalism that has irretrievably disfigured so many of them, it has not yet attracted the investment needed to build too many of the reach-me-down substitutes for imaginative design that now pass for post-modern originality. Imagine, I thought, if Vladivostok's city fathers could blend the old and the new, bringing in a Foster or a Gehry to construct a 'landmark' public building that would give the city the national and international status that the Kremlin craves for it. Putin has invested much diplomatic capital in securing Vladivostok as the venue for the 2012 meeting of APEC (the Asia-Pacific Economic Cooperation forum for those twenty-one 'Pacific rim' member states that between them generate almost 50 per cent of world trade and 56 per cent of its GDP). But, starry-eyed as I found myself in Vladivostok by night, by day I soon realized that the city would have to transform itself rapidly if it were not simply going to reinforce the widespread impression that Russia is still a clapped-out, quasi-Third World nation that, like Angola, happens to be blessed with a superabundance of oil.

Yes, there are one or two very expensive hotels, a casino and a scatter of restaurants, but there is no sign at all – despite the cranes on a score or more of building sites – that the city fathers have a coherent masterplan to turn this backwater city into an international beacon for the twenty-first century. As elsewhere in Russia, it looked as though Vladivostok offered developers with deep pockets and not too many scruples a licence to print easy money. As it is, the nineteenth-century buildings are so dilapidated that they will probably be pulled down without thought for the heritage they represent and, judging by the new buildings that have already replaced some of them, neither Foster nor Gehry nor any of their peers will have a look in.

I walked through a potentially handsome square near the rail terminus, where a group of homeless down-and-outs, perhaps twenty men and women, were gathered around a van from which a team of volunteers was handing out soup and bread. They stood quietly waiting their turn, then retreated to a bench where they huddled together, eating and drinking with that precision that is characteristic of those for whom every mouthful matters. Their clothes were tattered and grubby, their hair unkempt, and – as in the West – they were ignored except by the Samaritans who tended them. Not far away another queue of citizens, by no means so woebegone but nevertheless shabbily dressed in lustreless clothes and wearing scuffed, worn-out shoes, waited at a fishmonger's stand; when the time came to pay for the morsels they had chosen with elaborate care they delved deep into their shopping bags to count out the kopeks, one by one.

A few metres away another trader, a diminutive figure with Asiatic features, was selling apples and oranges from the back of a beaten-up car, unaware that he was being watched by two uniformed police officers who had parked near by. After a while, they strolled up to him and took an orange each from one of the four boxes on display. As they ate they cross-examined the trader, who looked increasingly ill at ease. Then they must have asked for his papers, because he scuttled into his car and returned with a sheaf of crumpled documents. While one of the officers walked slowly around the vehicle, the other scrutinized the papers. They were clearly not in order. The two men instructed him to pack up his oranges and put them back in his car – but not before he had been required to carry three full boxes to their Lada. Then he locked his own car and obediently got into the back of the police vehicle, where he sat disconsolately until the police officers, who went over to have a cheery word with the fishmonger, were ready to depart. Eventually they drove him away, presumably for further interrogation.

Was he an unlicensed trader? An illegal immigrant? Would he be fined? Or deported? Or might he have enough money to buy his way out of trouble? No one else was remotely interested: not the passersby, nor the shoppers, nor the down-and-outs. Such tiny incidents are, of course, commonplace in any large city. But for me, in Vladivostok, they were a vivid reminder that to live on the edge of the money economy is a very fragile existence indeed. Only then did I glance up and notice that I was overshadowed by a large and familiar figure: Lenin, his arm as ever outstretched, looking into the middle distance towards the ocean over the heads of the mortals beneath him. 'So this is what it has come to!' I imagined him thinking.

Inevitably, Vladivostok has invested the APEC summit with the same promise that Birobidzhan reserves for the bridge. Down in the docks I met Vladimir, who is in charge of the port operations for FESCO, an international shipping company that owns not only the container port but the entire commercial harbour. A former ship's captain, he was a large, genial figure who appeared to be gifted with boundless enthusiasm. He was convinced that the APEC meeting would put his Vladivostok on the world map as never before. And he was similarly convinced that his home city would soon emerge as one of the great ports of the world. He was a company man, anxious to tell me the FESCO story: that it was founded in the days of the empire, that it flourished in the Soviet era and that it had recovered since the fall, that it was the biggest container company in Russia, that it offered an 'integrated' – door-to-door – service, that its shipping fleet was modern, that it was a rapidly growing transnational corporation with an annual turnover of $1 billion, that it was growing at more than 20 per cent a year, that it had just acquired the container port at St Petersburg, that it was now one of the top fifty shipping companies in the world, and that it owned sixty-eight vessels (including four ice-breakers), and that within a decade Vladivostok would rival Seattle. He said all that, though at somewhat greater length, but without any salesman's patter and with genuine pride.

'Why Seattle?' I asked, thinking of Khrushchev's alternative vision. 'Seattle is very similar to Vladivostok. Similar hills, similar buildings, similar population and room for an expanding container terminal. We can expand this container port to be two or three times its present size.' But Seattle, I noted, was also a very modern city, a very open city, a very free city. Vladimir did not demur but said, 'If you compare

Vladivostok with any other city in Siberia, it really is an international city. There is the smell of freedom here. We have a lot of different cultures living here – Russians, Europeans, Japanese, Koreans, Chinese. And we have old buildings, old streets, and the sea around us – it is very beautiful. The weather is very special too. In the summer we may have rain and fog, but in winter the sun shines every day.'

I said, redundantly, 'You are obviously very proud of your city.' He replied, 'Actually, yes, I am. It has the soul of a city. There is nowhere else to compare with it. For the young people, there are only two choices. To stay here or go to Moscow. No other city in Russia offers them a better choice.' The falling population (now around seven hundred thousand) suggests that many of them opted in favour of the capital. What was it about Moscow? 'I have nothing to say about Moscow because I don't like it. It is just a place for business – it doesn't look like a city. It has no soul,' Vladmir replied with finality. But had Vladivostok always had a 'soul'? 'Well, in the Soviet era, of course, this city was closed, a military base. And like any other military base, it was orderly and obedient. Everything was clear. You knew what you had to do and you did not have to think about the future. Everything was done for you. You did not have to worry.'

For a moment I feared that Vladimir, who was in his mid-fifties, was about to revert to the nostalgia for the Soviet past that I had heard from so many of his generation. So I was relieved when he went on to say, 'But there were a lot of rules and obstacles. You could not travel. You were not free. Even so, a port city is different. In those days, at one time or another, ten thousand Russian sailors worked at sea for FESCO. These people went around the world. They saw other cultures and they could compare them. And they brought back a lot of things that were unobtainable anywhere inland.' 'Such as?' 'Well, jeans, for example. In the eighties you could only buy jeans brought back from other countries by individual seamen. And it was the same with rock music – the Beatles, Deep Purple, Pink Floyd. So from the very beginning Vladivostok was rather different. When I was at school my friends had parents who worked at sea. And we used to listen to the music and it created a good atmosphere, a sort of freedom. At least we felt more free.' And today? 'Today we may not be as free as you are in the West, but we are at least eighty per cent free. This is very important for young people: that you are eighty per cent free and you have a hundred per cent of your life in your own hands. Yes, I prefer it today. I prefer life today. Any individual can pursue any career without obstacles so long as you are willing to work.'

Given Vladimir's enthusiasm, FESCO hardly needed a PR man to instil its merits into me, but that job fell to Igor, who was just out of university and a few months into his first job. Igor was fresh-faced, pin-striped, buttoned-up and touchingly earnest: FESCO, according to his account, was flawless in every conceivable respect. Once I had teased him out of this indiscriminate genuflection to his employer, he became an engaging companion and only too happy to show me around the city on his day off. For Igor, Vladivostok really was the best city in all Russia, although, naturally, it could be much better. 'There is no planning, no common idea. The developers just build where they want – once they have paid the officials, of course. We need a strong governor and some independence so that we could make our city as we would like it to be. At the moment, I have no expectation that this will happen. But even so, I shall stay here. I have lived in America and I have seen some of the world. I could have stayed away. But like my friends, who have all studied in America, I have come home. Why? Because this is our city and we love it. But none of us, of course, believes that it will ever rival San Francisco.'

Then, apropos of nothing I had said, he went on to tell me that he had called his dog Yukos. 'Why?' I asked. 'I wanted to name him after Khodorkovsky. I admired him. I don't like the big gap between the rich and poor that you can see here. We have just had these elections, and unfortunately people voted for United Russia – they want a strong leader. I am in a minority – I want a strong democracy. But you know, the people here are different from the rest of Russia. Putin only got fifty-four per cent of the vote here.' I felt a leap of hope: here at last was a young man with a mind of his own, a Russian for whom democracy was not a dirty word.

Igor was tentative confirmation that Vladivostok was as different as it felt: more open, more genial, more cosmopolitan. To an extent, of course, this is in the nature of a port – the ceaseless arrivals and departures, the constant movement of goods and people, the churning of cultures – but the city did seem to breathe a different air from any other place I had visited in Russia. Perhaps that is because it lies so far from the nation's capital, at the far end of another continent. Perhaps it is because it is a sentinel city on the edge of the world's largest ocean that gives it an illusion of limitless opportunity. Whatever the reason, for the first time in Russia I felt I had found a city in which I would have happily spent more time than I had allotted myself. When I mentioned this to Igor, he was visibly touched. 'Do you really mean that? Do you like our city?' He looked as proud as he sounded.

Igor took me to a downtown café to meet a group of his friends. We could almost have been 7000 miles away in Brussels or Paris, or even a similar distance across the Pacific in Berkeley, California. The coffee was excellent, the service fast and friendly, and the atmosphere casual and unhurried. There was a whisper of jazz from an invisible speaker, a hotchpotch of posters on the walls, and a bustle of conversation that, at least in my imagination, seemed to be more about arts and culture than clothes or celebrities. I was reminded of my own student days, when a corduroy jacket and an infrequently opened copy of *Das Kapital* were de rigueur for those of us who posed as serious intellectuals. Igor's three friends, however, lacked all such pretension and, in fluent English, spoke from young hearts with guileless and refreshing enthusiasm. Kirill had qualified as an architect, while Victoria and Oxana were both postgraduate students of 'global economics'. Like Igor, they had all studied in America, but the experience had been underwhelming. Vladivostok was their home, and they were quite certain that it offered them a better future than anywhere else in the world.

By the standards of contemporary Britain they were remarkably old-fashioned, their conversation peppered with terms like 'duty' and 'service' and 'doing something for my country'. Nor did they talk about money or fame, but of 'helping their city'. Yes, they liked pop music and modern clothes, but it was soon evident that they had a sense of moral and civic purpose, and that they did not define themselves in those terms, which was both endearing and admirable. They were all members of a discussion group that met every weekend to discuss ways of making the world about them a better place. Their earnest idealism might have been easy to mock, but they were so devoid of self-righteousness that they could hardly fail to impress. Kirill, the young architect, said that he thought Vladivostok would become a 'a great city' within the decade. There were, he avowed, two hundred construction sites, and before long – in time for the APEC summit – new skyscrapers would appear on the horizon. Oxana enthused about Russian culture and the Russian people, saying, 'In America they care about money far more than we do here. And I don't want to be like them. Here I have friends, I understand people. And maybe I can do something for my city.' Igor added, 'We have a strong social network here, with our friends and the friends of our friends. There is always someone to support you,' which prompted Victoria to chip in to say, 'Yes, we like the atmosphere of this city, the architecture and the spirit.'

They wanted Vladivostok to become more open and welcoming to foreigners. 'We have to do this,' Igor explained. 'We have to change this city so that anyone from anywhere can come here and spend their money and give us the chance to develop. I think the future of the world is a world without borders in which all nations live together without committing crimes against each other.' It was said with such touching sincerity that I almost wanted to end the conversation at that point. In retrospect, I rather wish I had.

We started to talk about freedom. 'So you don't need "a strong man" at the centre?' I asked, remembering what Igor had said about his dog Yukos, and hoping that at last I had fallen in with a group of people who really understood the value of transparency, the rule of law and democracy. I could not have been more wrong. One after the other, in the most sincere and serious way, they not only disabused me, but demonstrated the hold that Putinism now has on so many thoroughly decent Russians. As the other three nodded in agreement, Victoria said, 'Putin has really done something for Russia. I would like our government to do more for the people – to be more Soviet, if you like…but we don't need too much democracy because people are lazy and they need someone to tell them what to do.' Oxana added, 'I like the fact that Putin is strong at home and the way he represents Russia in the world.' I suddenly found myself psychologically back with the disdainful glitterati in St Petersburg, asking the same questions and now fearful of hearing the same depressing answers 'So do you think this is a free country?' I asked. 'Yes,' Oxana replied. 'You think the media is free, totally free?' I asked incredulously. 'Yeah, I think they are totally free. In fact I think they need to be controlled more.' 'More controlled?' I repeated, aghast. 'Yeah.' 'By whom?' 'I don't know – maybe by the government.'

They were so direct and so good-natured that I pressed on, hoping that their young minds might still be impressionable enough for me to have some countervailing influence. 'How can Russia succeed in the world, in the global market to which you belong, without being open, transparent and accountable?' I asked. Kirill shrugged and, as though my question was not particularly relevant, said simply, 'I just don't know. I really don't know. I have nothing to say about it.' But so far from this opening up a Platonic dialogue about freedom and democracy, the confusion became worse. Oxana, who had studied 'global economics' in the United States, said, 'When you start being open, or changing in ways that other countries might want, I think you become weak…. You lose the power to control. I think the government is afraid of making our country weaker.' Echoing her sentiments, Victoria added, 'I think our government is not yet confident in its powers. Russia has been at the bottom and is now working its way up again. I think maybe when our position is really strong then we will be able to be open.'

These young people could not have been less venal. They weren't sharks wanting to get rich quick in the kleptocracy of Putin's Russia, they had a social conscience and they wanted the best for their country, but, intelligent and articulate as they were, they lacked any political compass. Disorientated by Putin's autocratic 'sovereign' democracy, they had heard quite enough about 'hanging chads' in Florida, the atrocities in Abu Ghraib and the scandal of Guantanamo Bay to reject – almost out of hand – any instruction from outside about the values of Western democracy. 'I don't think democracy is always the best way,' Igor said (shattering in an instant my earlier faith in his apparently progressive views). 'I have a lot of examples of how democracy really became an awful thing. Think of Germany before the war. It all started with democracy. And in the United States, even when most people disagree with the official course taken by the government, they can do nothing about it.'

I wanted to argue from first principles, but I now knew I would be wasting my time, so I simply said, 'Well, the Americans can get rid of their President. If you don't have democracy, if you don't have a real vote, if it is a sham, you can end up with a regime that you can't get rid of. I'm not saying you get another Stalin, but you can go backwards.' It was to no avail. 'I think that is an extreme case,' Igor replied. 'I think there is a middle way. Something more like the Chinese parliament. Something like that would probably be accepted here. You can have an open economy – transparency, if you like – but politically the central authority, the centre of power, would not be so open, not so democratic.' I wanted to bang their nice young heads together, saying, 'Do you realize what you are saying? Do you really think China has the answer? The National People's Congress? Do you know about their record on human rights? Do you know what democracy means there? Do you know what freedom means?' Instead I asked them, one by one, 'Have you got enough democracy in Russia?' And one by one they answered, 'Yes', 'Yes', 'Yes' and 'Yes' again before Victoria said decisively, 'I think we want our country to be strong and we want to be proud of it. So this means we need a really strong leader who can make our country strong in the world again.' I concluded ruefully that although I had travelled 10,000 miles in one direction, in this respect – if only in this respect – I had succeeded only in going round in circles.

## A SUMMING UP

I had set out on this journey with Sir Winston Churchill's aphorism – 'a riddle wrapped in a mystery inside an enigma' – as my lodestar. But along the way I had gradually discovered that in Putin's Russia there is no great riddle, not much mystery and very little that is enigmatic. To invest Russia with riddles and mysteries is both to indulge a romance and to excuse too much. On my final evening in Vladivostok I made a note, off the top of my head, of the most memorable moments and encounters that I had experienced on my journey and I applied to them the 'enigma' test: were there hidden meanings that I had missed, obscurities that I had failed to penetrate?

I thought first of the wild places. The storm in the White Sea on my way to Solovki, where our overloaded ferry almost drowned us all. Solovki itself, its mythical past with monks and miracles, its sinister Gulag role, and its present, uneasy reincarnation as a place of pilgrimage. Then there was the bare grandeur of the tundra gradually giving way to the taiga: the mosses, lichens, stubby shrubs, bleached rocks and sparkling streams yielding to the deep, dark, unending, absorbing forest of spruce, pine and silver birch on a scale that is almost intimidating. The lakes, rivers and forests of Karelia, filled with mythological sprites and hobgoblins and pre-Christian symbolism, were gloomily entrancing and alien. Further south, also on a scale that no little Englander can really comprehend, lay the steppe and the Black Earth belt, where millions of hectares of rich soil could, properly stewarded, feed all Russia and leave grain to spare. And after that the Caucasus – 'and the mountains', in Tolstoy's lost-in-wonder and almost lost-for-words phrase. For me, though, it was not the high peaks in the distance that stole my heart, but the uplands, the hanging valleys half lost in mist, an eagle wafting and swooping on currents of thin air; and further east, at the other end of the Caucasus, the mountains of Dagestan, the sheer black cliffs, the forbidding *Götterdämmerung* heights that most nearly beckoned my unwary imagination towards the mystery of the heavens.

Beyond the Urals – not much to recall about them, except the triumph of reaching that psychological border between West and East, Europe and Asia – there was more forest, the great boreal forest of the Siberian taiga, thin soil and poor land, for thousands of miles in every direction. Little there to excite the spirit until we pressed southeast from Tomsk towards the Altai mountains, out of the taiga and back into the southern steppe, where the land seemed almost lush with the green fields and ripened corn that reassure the peasant in all of us. And then the Altai itself, more obscure and mysterious and filled with partially resolved riddles of history and culture than anywhere else on my journey. There the snow fell out of an autumn sky, dusting the high chaparral and muffling the moaning roar of the maral deer, and the long silence of the past seemed to hold the present in suspended animation. And then I had come to the wild lands, the mountains of the Buryat people and their Lake Baikal, where in the dead of winter I felt myself drawn towards the metaphysics of shamanism, touched by a sense of the numinous inspired by a small lone tree sprouting from a rock in the snow beneath a heavenly vault of blue sky.

Of course the imagination likes to soar and drift, and in Russia, where the landscape is so immense, this is more tempting and easier to indulge than in most parts of our hurried and hassled world. You do gasp, sometimes physically, at the scale of the experience – not only the forests and mountains, but the lakes and rivers that lace through even the most barren land, linking almost every place of human habitation throughout the country. It is overwhelming and, in retrospect, has left me both exhilarated and drained. How is it possible, I ask myself, really to comprehend the immensity of the challenge that faces the inhabitants of this vastness? But that is not a riddle or a mystery or an enigma: it is a basic question about survival and endurance and character.

And that is where my journey has been most deeply rewarding. I started with a latent suspicion, almost a fear, of the Russian people. From my side of the language and culture barrier they seemed – collectively – abrupt, rough and uncouth. The young seemed already pockmarked by poverty. By middle age people looked old, worn and tired. And the old themselves? Well, the old were few and far between in a country where male life expectancy is now still only fifty-nine years. I saw few smiles and heard little laughter. I sensed too a suspiciousness on their part, a distrust, almost a resentment of the foreigner, who seemed by his very presence to rebuke their national catastrophe. I still feel some of that, but I hope I have now been disabused of a general prejudice that may be dangerously closer to racism than I would like to admit.

Again, it is the moments, the individual encounters, that matter, that help you to get closer to the truth. I must have spoken to hundreds of people in the course of my journey, and in scores of these conversations we explored at least some way below the surface of our lives. For the most part I was a guest, offered food and drink in abundance, with a simple warmth and generosity that looked for nothing in return. In Murmansk there was the war veteran Yevgraf, whose eyes filled with tears as he played his accordion and recalled the camaraderie with the British sailors who helped him save his country in the Great Patriotic War. And later, in Volgograd, the old woman weeping at the desecration of her husband's grave but praying that the sun would always shine on friendship between the Russian and British peoples. I had been a little intimidated by the Karelian babushka, the white witch who took a healing knife to my back, but later she looked at me with compassion when she detected a psychological ailment as the cause of my trouble. There was more sun than shade, in so many places: in the outdoor sulphur bath at Pyatigorsk, where a huge woman from the Arctic rocked with laughter as she placed my crabby little hand beside her great welder's paw, but who could not hold back a tear when she recalled her love of the north to which she would now never return; on the fishing boat with the one-armed leprechaun Valentin, who had once electrocuted himself and nearly did the same for us, but for whom life was a lottery, a 'casino'; with the potato-diggers in the ruined collective farm near Voronezh, where a peasant raised herself from her toil to say that if I really wanted to help, I should send her a combine harvester and then chortled at the sheer absurdity of the proposition, and where, in a cottage garden, a pensioner called Lena said that the only thing that mattered in life was 'health and peace'; with Igor, the former ship's purser, now an aide to the British Honorary Consul in Novorossiysk, sitting at a Black Sea resort as he chortled with the sheer joy of being alive in the country he loved; and at the Caucasian wedding, where the young danced with ferocious joy and the old watched them, benignly content that their traditions were still being passed down through the generations.

But, in retrospect, I do not think primarily of those moments of shared delight. Inevitably, since I was trying to understand better the Russian psyche, my focus, perhaps obsessively, was on the past as much as the present, excavating for memories of yesterday to help explain the perspectives of today, trying to discover whether the past really was 'another country' or whether the Russians are deeply in denial, unable to contemplate – because it is so unbearable and unforgivable – their own brutal, cruel and bloody history. But in all this exploration, much of which was profoundly saddening and frustrating, I discovered again and again a humanity that rebuked my irritation at the blank faces and the 'inscrutable' stares that look rudely through you as you pass in the street or along the corridor of a train.

And that humanity, often against the odds, inspired in me a growing respect and admiration. In St Petersburg, Ilya, the social scientist, took me to the communal flat that had once been his home, opening my eyes not only to the physical squalor of that life, but to the anti-materialism and idealism that had allowed Russians to endure extreme privation for generations. Diana, the newspaper editor, taught me about the tenacity that, even in the brash, self-seeking capitalist pigsty of post-Soviet Russia, still allows the human spirit to soar in search of freedom. On the collective farm outside Voronezh the sad bear of a boss, Alexander, contemplating the financial wreckage of his agricultural cooperative, showed that staunch attitude towards triumph and disaster that Kipling revered. I had been touched by Anatoly, the initially crusty archaeologist at Staraya Ladoga, who later fed me bread and cheese and drowned me in vodka as he spoke of his 'trepidation' when he touches a twelfth-century icon and almost broke my heart when he said despairingly, 'After 1917, Russia lost the twentieth century.' In Dagestan, Khan's intellectual zest and his tribal instincts laid bare the troubled soul of the Caucasus more memorably than any detached history could emulate; his idiosyncratic affection for his mountain people, and even for their atavism, was a reminder that Russia is far more diverse and individual than I had realized before making this journey. Similarly in the Altai the maral herders, who reproached me for kicking the embers of the fire and who could hardly understand what I meant when I asked dumbly if they had to work hard in order to survive, clearly believed that they lived at the centre of the universe; they were indomitable.

In Samara, Sergey, the regional editor of *Novaya Gazeta*, was, in his quite different way, indomitable as well, battling obstinately, single-handedly, in potentially mortal combat against a repressive state. Maria, the Soviet émigrée on the train, now an alien in her own land, saddened and perplexed but determined to see it through, was one of the voices – like the car dealer in the plane to Ekaterinburg, whose name I never discovered, who believed that the middle classes would one day reclaim their rights to democracy – who offered me some scintilla of hope that the Russians were not doomed to the eternal twilight zone of Putin's 'sovereign' democracy. Marina, the director of the Red Cross in Irkutsk, did not flinch from blaming the authorities for the city's HIV epidemic, even though she knew that whistle-blowing made more enemies than friends in the stifling pyramid of power with which she had to do business. Olga, the devotee of the Decembrists and Khodorkovsky's champion, had no illusions but she did not despair, confident that her young students would imbibe the Volkonsky values. Her wise humanity, like that of so many other individuals in so many more chance encounters, reminded me – as I did often need to be reminded – that the sulphurous blanket of bad faith that has now half-suffocated Russia cannot entirely poison what is honourable and good and kind in the long-suffering soul of its people. She – they – give hope that Sergey Kovalev's lament for the death of democracy in Russia may be premature or that, at some point in the not too distant future, a resurrection may occur.

The auguries are poor, though. The Kremlin's grip is tightening all the time. The judiciary, parliament and the media have all been suborned to the crypto-fascist state that Putin's bloodless *coup d'état* has so cleverly constructed. As a child of the Cold War, for whom the fall of the Berlin Wall was the most exhilarating public moment of my adult life, I kept having to ward off the gloom induced by the triumph of Putinism. Of course, in the global bubble where we now all jostle for survival there is little option for Western governments but to conduct business more or less 'as usual' with the Kremlin. But this should not stop anyone from exercising a modicum of intellectual and ethical discrimination about the nature of the Russian state. It is dismaying that so many otherwise discerning individuals – not so much inside as outside Russia – have allowed themselves to be seduced into a form of moral relativism that allows them to excuse Putin's 'sovereign' democracy on the grounds that Russia's tormented past obliges us to suspend judgement about the present. So they concede that the Duma may indeed be a sham parliament, but counter that the Russians say the same things about the Palace of Westminster. And, yes, Russian television may be controlled by the Kremlin but – did I not know? – the Russians believe the BBC is run by the government. You say the judiciary is in thrall to the Kremlin? Well, don't British ministers bully the judges? You say they trample on human rights in Russia? Well, tell the Russians about the British record since 9/11! 'So that's all right, then?' I want to retort. 'It's their life and their land and it's no business of ours?'

Of course, for many of those who have a genuine love of Russia, as much as for those who want to exploit its potential for commercial advantage, the answer to my rhetorical question is, 'Precisely so. The Russians will be the authors of their own salvation. Leave it to them.' In a sense they are right; we have very little choice in the matter. Outsiders are not going to shape Russia's destiny. For the foreseeable future that power is vested in the hands of the powerful cliques that circle each other in and around the Kremlin – the competing oligarchs and their allies and agents in the security services and the armed forces – that have worked intimately with the outgoing president and his clan to create Putinism. We may find that Dmitry Medvedev favours a rhetoric that is less crude than that adopted by his predecessor, but to suppose that the new president will deviate from the course set by Putin is to indulge a flight of fancy. The Kremlin power-brokers may have their internecine rivalries, but they are united in their objectives at home and abroad. There can be precious little doubt, to quote the last few words of Ted Hughes's chilling poem 'Hawk Roosting', that it is their intention 'to keep things like this'.

But in the future, whenever I feel that surge of impotent resentment at the excesses of the Kremlin I shall have, as a wonderful counterweight, my greater understanding of the Russian people, those many individuals who have welcomed me into their lives and for whom I now feel lasting affection and respect. I have been blessed by the experience.

My journey to the airport took a little over an hour. But I had already left Russia. I knew that I would be asked, 'Would you do it all again?' My answer would have to be an unequivocal 'No.' It had been an endurance test that I would not wish to repeat. But to the other question: 'Are you glad that you did it?' I could now – rather to my surprise – answer, with an equal absence of equivocation, 'Yes.' This was in large measure, as I have already suggested, because the journey gave me a matchless opportunity to discover a land and its people that would otherwise have been quite out of reach. My horizons have been – quite literally – broadened and my understanding of Russia and its place in the world has been immeasurably enhanced. This opportunity – if it is not too portentous an observation – is the privilege to which the reporter is given unique access. And reporting has always been at the heart of my working life.

As I got closer to the airport, my spirits soared. Looking out of the mini-bus window, I registered nothing except the elation of knowing that I had not only accomplished my professional journey but I had completed a personal odyssey as well. I had started out, 10,000 miles earlier, in a state of emotional turbulence, homesick, uncertain, fearful and confused. I had left behind a life in which there had been great joy and much pain. I was hoping to chart a new course, but not at all certain that I could do it. Knowing that I was more fragile than I hope I appeared, all those whom I love had given unstintingly of their compassion. But in the end, recovery is a solitary process. We are the sole inhabitants of our identity. We create ourselves and we re-create ourselves, the same but always changing. I felt that the test of character demanded by the professional journey paled beside the challenge of holding my fragmented psyche together on my long internal journey. And my sense that I had now achieved the latter, for which the exterior journey had been the accidental reagent, gave me sudden boundless hope. In that horrible phrase, I had not been 'fit for purpose' when I embarked on my Russian adventure. Now I knew that I was – or as much as I was likely to become. For what precise purpose I did not know and it did not much matter. I still had professional ambition, or rather the urge to work, but I had a far more important aspiration. I had my family, my children, and I had Jessica. They were the future. I felt blessed beyond measure by that knowledge and profoundly grateful for the voyage of self-realization that the journey from Murmansk to Vladivostok had given me.

By the time I was in the airport lounge, insulating myself with a Bloody Mary for the fifteen-hour journey ahead, I was already psychologically back home. To confirm the impression, Jeremy Clarkson and his fellow boy-racers were on the flat-screen TV above my head driving a trio of beaten-up jalopies across an African desert. 'Africa,' I thought. 'Africa, a Journey to the Heart of a Continent and Its People.' Sounds like a good title. It might be a good idea. I had another Bloody Mary and fairly vaulted up the steps of the plane without even a goodbye.

# HISTORICAL TIMELINE

859        Vikings under Rurik capture Novgorod and found Rus.

980        Vladimir the Great becomes ruler of breakaway portion of Rus
           centred on Kiev. Attempting to Westernize and raise Kievan
           Rus's international status, he chooses Greek Orthodoxy as
           state religion.

1223–40 Mongol invasions of Russia by Golden Horde (1237 fall of
           Moscow, 1240 fall of Kiev).

1462       Ivan the Great (Ivan III) becomes prince of Muscovy (until
           death in 1505). He ousts Mongols from his territory and
           expands it.

1533       Ivan the Terrible (Ivan IV) becomes prince of Muscovy
           (until death in 1584). He continues expulsion of Mongols
           and eventually proclaims himself first tsar.

1582       First successful Russian incursions into Siberia.

1682       Peter the Great (Peter I) becomes tsar (until death in 1725).
           He embarks on reforms, Westernization and territorial and
           military expansion.

1762       Catherine the Great (Catherine II) becomes empress (until
           death in 1796). She introduces reforms based on Enlighten-
           ment principles and expands boundaries of Russian Empire
           as far as Caspian Sea.

| 1812 | Napoleon invades Russia and reaches Moscow, but winter weather forces his armies to retreat. |
|------|------|
| 1825 | Abortive Decembrist coup against autocratic and repressive Tsar Nicholas I. |
| 1839 | Publication of *A Hero of Our Time* by Lermontov. |
| 1842 | Publication of *The Overcoat* by Gogol. |
| 1853–6 | Crimean War. |
| 1866 | Publication of *Crime and Punishment* by Dostoevksy. |
| 1869 | Publication of *War and Peace* by Tolstoy. |
| 1877 | Publication of *Anna Karenina* by Tolstoy. |
| 1891 | Construction of Trans-Siberian Railway starts. |
| 1902 | First performance of *From the Lower Depths* by Gorky. |
| 1904–5 | Russo-Japanese War, in which Russian Empire defeated by a new power on world stage. |
| 1905 | First Russian revolution. |
| 1910 | Death of Tolstoy. |
| 1912 | Posthumous publication of *Hadji Murat* by Tolstoy |
| 1914 | Start of World War I. |
| 1917 | October/Bolshevik revolution and overthrow of last tsar, Nicholas II (murdered with wife and children a year later). St Petersburg, briefly renamed Petrograd, now becomes Leningrad and capital is moved to Moscow. |
| 1918 | End of World War I, followed by Civil War ending in 1922 with defeat of Whites (supporters of old tsarist regime) by Reds (Bolsheviks). The blueprint for Stalin's Gulag system (officially instituted in 1930) introduced by Lenin. |
| 1922 | Establishment of Soviet Union. |
| 1924 | Death of Lenin. |
| 1928 | Stalin assumes supreme power in Soviet Union and initiates first Five-Year Plan, involving collectivization of agriculture and systematic destruction of kulak class. Widespread famine results. |
| 1937 | Start of Stalin's purges, with millions sent to Gulag or executed. |

1939  Hitler and Stalin sign Non-Aggression Pact. Start of World
       War II.

1941  Hitler invades Soviet Union and so brings it into World War
       II (Great Patriotic War).

1942  German forces reach Stalingrad in August and besiege city.

1943  In February, remaining German forces begin retreat from
       Stalingrad and, effectively, from Soviet Union.

1945  End of World War II and start of Cold War between West
       and its former ally. Soviet forces occupy most of eastern
       Europe, with Berlin and Vienna divided cities.

1953  Death of Stalin.

1956  Soviet leader Khrushchev repudiates Stalin, his policies and
       'personality cult'.

1964  Brezhnev becomes leader of Soviet Union.

1965  First oil produced in Siberia.

1985  Gorbachev becomes Soviet leader following brief periods in
       office by Andropov and Chernenko. He initiates reformist
       policies of *glasnost* (openness) and *perestroika* (reconstruc-
       tion) and supports moves for independence among Soviet
       satellite states.

1989  Fall of Berlin Wall and collapse of Communist regimes
       in eastern Europe (Poland, Hungary, East Germany,
       Czechoslovakia, Romania, Bulgaria).

1991  Yeltsin becomes Russian president. At end of year, Soviet
       Union dissolved to be replaced by Russian Federation and
       independent states e.g. Ukraine, Belarus, Georgia. Gorbachev
       resigns from a role that no longer exists.

1999  Yeltsin appoints Putin as prime minister of Russian Federation.
       Yeltsin resigns as president of Russian Federation.

2000  Putin becomes president.

2004  Putin re-elected for second term. Beslan massacre.

2008  Putin steps down as president. Medvedev elected as his
       successor, inviting Putin to become prime minister.

# SELECT BIBLIOGRAPHY

Rather than compile an exhaustive list of the books and documents that I dipped into to help me better understand Russia, I thought it more useful to list the books that gave me special delight or rare illumination. Of course, Leo Tolstoy's *Anna Karenina* and *War and Peace* are essential reading if you want to understand the 'soul' of Russia in the nineteenth century and today. But his last, very short novel, *Hadji Murat* (Hesperus) is a masterpiece. His better known *The Cossacks* is also indispensable; likewise many, if not all, of his short stories in *The Death of Ivan Ilych and Other Stories* (Signet Classics) and *How Much Land Does a Man Need and Other Stories* (Penguin Classics), many of which are animated by a moral intensity of purpose in the form of parables. Gogol's *Dead Souls* and the *Collected Tales of Nicolai Gogol* are merciless and lacerating satires that could have been written yesterday. *Sketches from a Hunter's Album* by Ivan Turgenev provides the mesmerising insights of a literary pointillist into the serf-stricken society of his times. Dostoevsky's masterpiece *Crime and Punishment* chisels into the psyche of an amoral society with a pitiless integrity that gives it eternal relevance; *The Best Short Stories of Fyodor Dostoevsky* (Modern Library Classics) and *A Gentle Creature and Other Stories* (OUP) are mordant but often touching as well. Mikhail Lermontov's *A Hero of Our Time*, his only novel (and short at that), captures the essence of ennui and bad faith with a brilliance that rivals all his nineteenth-century peers. Two little-known novels from a familiar twentieth-century canon stand out: *The Foundation Pit* (Harvill Press) by Andrey Platonov is a chilling satire on the cruelties of collectivization, and Alexander Zinoviev's penetrating *Homo Sovieticus* (Atlantic Monthly Press) is a bitter but witty study of the extent to which the Soviet Union imprisoned the psyche of even the most apparently liberated exile.

Among a cornucopia of reports, diaries, memoirs, sketches, biographies and autobiographies I have been particularly stimulated by *St Petersburg – A Traveller's Companion* (Interlink Books) edited by Laurence Kelly, and the same author's biography of Lermontov, *A Tragedy in the Caucasus* (Tauris Parke Paperbacks); Colin Thubron's elegant and incisive *In Siberia* (Chatto & Windus); Anna Politkovskaya's *A Small Corner of Hell – Dispatches from Chechnya* (University of Chicago Press); *Russia Under the Old Regime* (Penguin) by Richard Pipes, which provides a scholarly but riveting account of the baleful impact of tsarism on succeeding generations; *Natasha's Dance* (Penguin) by Orlando Figes, which combines scholarship with readability; Antony Beevor's brilliant and horrifying *Stalingrad* (Penguin); *Tolstoy* by A.N. Wilson (W.W. Norton) and Alexander Werth's 1928 translation of *The Diary of Tolstoy's Wife 1860–1901* (Victor Gollancz), a tragic self-portrait that gives a raw account of Sofya's tempestuous marriage to Leo, both of which throw great light on life at Yasnaya Polyana; and, in a very different vein, two penetrating academic studies – *How Russia Really Works* (Cornell University Press) by Alena V. Ledeneva, and *The Siberian Curse* (Brookings Institution Press) by Fiona Hill and Clifford Gaddy.

# INDEX

babushkas 147, 148, 149, 153, 284, 537;
  singers 49–51
Bader, Douglas 143
*Baikal* (ferry) 452, 453
Baikal Lake 321, 439, 449, 450, 452–3,
  454–5, 535
Baikal mountains 450
Baikal Port 450–1
bakers 299
Bakewell, Joan 339
Balkaria 168
Baltic 29, 95, 222, 285–6
Baltic Sea 54
bandits 169, 171
Basargin, Nikolay 461
Basayev, Shamil 200
Bath Blues Festival 1970 383–4
bath-houses (*banya*) 103–5
Batu 232
Bay of Ecstasy 455
BBC2 3
BBC Radio 4 458
BBC World Service 353
BBDO 117–21
Beethoven, Ludwig Van 79, 465
Beevor, Anthony 236–7
Begelman, David 510
Beijing 471, 494
Beijing Airport 494
Beijing University 471
Beijing–Moscow relations 490, 494, 516
Beirut 306–7; Green Line 21, 170
Belarus 508
Belorussky station, Moscow 36
Belsen 315
Beluga caviar 223–9, 236
Berlin 243
Berlin Wall 5, 539
beryllium 339
Besak, Nicholas 53
Beslan 66, 189–93, 199
Betjeman, John 76
'big business' 262–71
Birobidzhan 506–14, 516, 519, 527
Black Death 232; *see also* Great Plague
Black Earth Country 138, 143–4, 152, 155,
  535
Black Sea 4, 29, 54, 87, 138, 173
Black Sea resorts 161, 164–8, 184, 537
Blackman, Honor 473
Blagoveshchensk 481, 489–93, 495–7,
  500–3, 505–6
Blair, Tony 256, 263, 361, 487
blood feuds 205–6
Bloomsbury Group 158, 159, 466

boat trips: in Karelia 47–8; on Lake Ladoga
  85–8; on Onego Lake 39–41; on the River
  Ob 376–7, 379–82; *see also* ferries
bogs 394–6
Bohemia 232
Bolshevik Revolution 1917 4, 30, 76–7, 91,
  182, 197, 223, 328; and the Cossacks 213;
  and the Jewry 508; seeds of the 454
Bolsheviks 14, 75, 136; and the Cossacks
  213; and the execution of Nicholas II 345,
  346; and the Gulags 31, 34, 36; and St
  Petersburg 71
Bolshevism 113, 154, 157, 297
Bolshoi theatre 115, 116
'Boreal Boris' 391–3
Boris Godunov 383
Boris (PHM worker) 484–5, 486
Borisovska 156
Bosnia 169
Bosporus 165
Boxer Rebellion 493
boyars 56–7, 59
Boyle, Andrew 384
BP (British Petroleum) 350, 361, 369, 370,
  371–5; health and safety 374–5; *see also*
  TNK-BP
'brain drain' 409
Brando, Marlon 365
Brezhnev, Leonid 108, 312–13
Brezitsky, Sergey 364
bribery 120, 184, 270, 392, 401
Bridge, The 515–19
Britain 14, 17, 29, 157, 361; *see also* England;
  Northern Ireland
British Broadcasting Corporation (BBC) 7,
  44, 91, 111–12, 138, 383, 540; War
  Correspondents 21; *see also* BBC2; BBC
  Radio 4; BBC World Service
Bronze Age nomads 417
*Bronze Horseman, The* (Falconet) 52, 53–4,
  137, 461
Browne, Lord 361, 374
Bruce (BBDO employee) 119
bubonic plague 385; *see also* Black Death;
  Great Plague
Buchenwald 315
Buckley, Bill 316–17
Buddhism 436
Bukharin, Nikolai 301
Bukovsky, Vladimir 309
Bulgaria 91, 492
Burma 523
Buryat people 434–6, 440, 455, 535
Buryat Republic 433, 436
Bush, George W. 121, 256, 263, 354
butchers 209

European Union (EU) 153, 266, 369;
  Samara Summit 280
'evil empire', Soviet Union as 109

factories 262, 272, 327–8
Famagusta 169
famine 154–9
Far East (Russian) 478, 496, 509, 514, 515
farms, collective 147, 149–53, 158–9, 198–9,
  263, 293, 303, 389, 420, 537, 538
fascism 315–17, 355; see also crypto-fascism
Federer, Roger 49
ferry journeys, Kem-Solovetskie Ostrava 25–8
FESCO 527, 528, 529
Figes, Orlando 58, 130, 145, 234, 305, 318,
  345, 346, 458, 464
Financial Times (newspaper) 468
Finland 31
Finland Station, St Petersburg 76–7
Finnish tourists 11
fire rituals 427, 438–9
First World War 20–1, 344
fishing 86–7
Fleming, Renée 82, 83–4
Fleshler, Olga 465, 466, 469–70, 471, 539
flying 142–3, 256, 259–60, 322–4
Flynn, Errol 399
Fontanka 58, 60
Fontanka Canal 51
food 18, 260, 329, 498–9, 513, 516
Foreign Office 168, 185, 196, 210
forests 386–94, 396–7, 439, 535; see also
  timber
Foster, Norman 525
Fountain House 58
Fowles, John 145
France 29
Frederick II, Holy Roman Emperor 232
free market 113
freedom 99–101, 142, 528–9, 532–4; media
  66–7, 99–100, 116, 142, 255, 267–8, 276,
  279–80, 291, 532, 540
FSB (Federal Security Service) 16, 193, 200,
  256–7, 267, 277, 278–9, 329, 361
fur 326, 327, 492

G8 summits 121, 255–6
Galich, Alexander 405
Galina (teacher) 485–6
Galsworthy, John 399
gas 2, 4, 113, 148, 167, 256, 258, 265, 295,
  322, 369, 373, 478, 494
Gazelle bus company 265
Gazprom 369–70
Gehry, Frank 525

Genghis Khan 231, 232, 434
Georgia 285–6
Georgian restaurants 260–1
Gergiev, Valery 82–3, 84
German air raids: on Leningrad 77, 80, 86; on
  Murmansk 14, 15, 16, 19; on Stalingrad
  239–40, 242, 243
German army 238–43; Panzer divisions 79,
  98, 238–9; and the siege of Leningrad 81;
  Sixth Army 241
German (monk) 28, 29
German navy 17
German submarines 19
German troops 82, 238, 435
Germany 14, 55, 63, 76, 92, 98, 151, 314,
  315, 421, 454, 533
glasnost 2, 91, 110, 255, 308, 331–2, 512
global warming 395–6
Gogol, Nikolai 4, 68–70, 75, 98, 280; Dead
  Souls 69–70; 'Diary of a Madman' 12, 13,
  21, 68; The Overcoat 68–9, 70
gold 113, 256, 317, 328, 478–87, 491–2
Gold Standard 478
Golden Horde 222, 232, 234, 295, 418
Gorbachev, Mikhail 2, 4, 91, 108, 110, 254,
  255, 307, 312–13, 488, 512; interview
  with the author 110–13, 115
Gordeyev, Alexander 153
Gorky, Maxim 35–7, 76–7, 297–301, 305,
  306, 331
Gorno-Altaisk 421, 422
grain 293, 303
Grand Café, Volgograd 237, 249
graphite 515
Great Famine 154–9
Great Northern War 1700–21 54
Great Patriotic War 14, 17–20, 90–1, 98,
  213, 281, 284, 307, 511, 536; see also
  Second World War
Great Plague 385; see also Black Death
Great Siberian Highway 328
Great Siberian Route 456
Greek Orthodox Church 92, 93
Greene, Graham 168
Greenpeace 392
Grigoriev, Alexey 388
Grigory (herdsman) 423, 426–9
gross domestic product (GDP) 258
Grozny 194
Guardian (newspaper) 157
Guatemala 169
Gulags 307, 309, 314–15, 378–9, 415, 435,
  534; common criminals (shpana) 31–2;
  deaths 31, 34, 247; disease 32; female
  prisoners 32; pecking order 31–2; political

Tartarstan 293–9
Tashkent 362–3
Tatars 295–7, 326–7
Tatiana, Grand Duchess 345
Tatiana (film-maker) 99–100
tax inspectors 270
taxes 234
Tchaikovsky, Pyotr Ilyich 79
tea 22
teachers 192, 410–11, 412–13, 462–3, 484–6
Technopark 409
television 100, 116
Terek delta 214
Terek River 217
Teresa (translator) 43, 46
Terror 30, 79, 160
terrorism 166, 168–9, 171, 181–3, 184, 195, 210–11; Beslan 190, 192; of Lenin 30, 31, 33, 378; of Stalin 30, 31, 34, 79, 153–61, 247, 299, 307, 318, 362, 378, 511, 517
Texas oil plant explosion 2005 374
Thailand 421
Thatcher, Denis 110–11
Thatcher, Margaret 110, 111
Thubron, Colin 322, 406, 408, 441, 461
timber 308, 322, 386–94, 397, 439, 492, 494
*Time* magazine 79, 505
Time to Live initiative 447–8
Timofeevich, Ermak 325–7, 343
*Tirpitz* (battleship) 17
Tiumen 384–5
TNK-BP 361–6, 368–71, 372–5
Tobolsk 345
*Today* (TV programme) 383–4
Tolstoy, Andrey 132
Tolstoy, Ekaterina 301
Tolstoy, Ivan 132
Tolstoy, Leo 4, 124–38, 145, 146, 152, 172, 297, 300, 306, 460, 467, 535; *Anna Karenina* 123, 124, 127–8, 130–1, 274; and the Caucasus 177, 179, 358; and the Cossacks 211, 214; death 135, 136–7; gambling 125–6; grave 133; *Hadji Murat* 190, 201–3, 205; 'On Anarchy' 135–6; school of 133; *The Cossacks* 214; *The Raid* 179; *War and Peace* 123, 458
Tolstoy, Marya 134
Tolstoy, Sofya 131, 133–4, 135
Tolstoy, Vladimir 132–3
tombs 88–9, 114, 159–61, 417–18
Tomsk 382–404, 439, 535
Tony (Caucasus guide) 168–9, 170, 171
tourism 11, 164, 416–17

train journeys: Circumbaikal Line 451, 452, 453, 454; Ekaterinburg–Nizhnevartovsk 350–1, 354–9; Moscow–Tula 123–4; Murmask–Kem 22–5; Volgograd–Moscow 251–3; Voronezh–Novorossiysk 161–3; *see also* Trans-Siberian Railway
Trans-Siberian Railway 356, 382, 401, 404, 451–2, 454, 455–8, 470–1, 505–6, 515–16, 519–21
Triads 393
tribalism 173
Trotsky, Leon 35, 345, 346
Tsar Emerald Corporation 339, 341–2
Tsarskoe Selo 356
TU-114 262–3
tuberculosis 32, 35, 446
Tuchman, Barbara 21
Tula 123, 126
Tupolev aircraft 259, 262–3, 264, 266
Tupper, Harmon 452–3
Turgenev, Nicholas 145–6, 175, 459
Turkey 29, 164, 204
Turkish forces 21
Turkmenistan 167
Tverdushev brothers 328
Twin Towers attacks 2001 195
Tygda 478, 479, 483–8

U2 spy plane incident 450
Uganda 169, 445
Ukraine 124, 158, 264, 285–6, 293, 508; Orange Revolution 332
unemployment 51
Union of Orthodox Flag Bearers 107
United Nations 263
United Nations Security Council 523
United Russia 402, 403, 503, 504, 505, 529
United Russia Aluminium 265
United States 63, 109, 272, 345, 377, 405, 450, 529–30, 533; Great Lakes 455; politics 402–3; relations with Russia 257–8, 354, 523; and the Second World War 14; *see also* American imperialism; Americanization; anti-Americanism
United States navy 16
United States troops 359
university 23–4, 485–6
Urals 4, 95, 302, 306, 315, 317–19, 321–3, 325–7, 338, 384, 452, 456, 510, 535
uranium 362, 383
Ustinov, Peter 163
Utekin, Ilya 71–4, 538
utilities 148
Uzbekistan 362, 391
Valentin (fisherman) 85–8, 537

# PICTURE CREDITS

BBC Books would like to thank the following individuals and organizations for providing photographs and for permission to reproduce copyright material. While every effort has been made to trace and acknowledge copyright holders, we would like to apologize should there be any errors or omissions. Abbreviations: *t* top, *b* bottom, *c* centre, *l* left, *r* right, *tl* top left, *tr* top right, *i* inset.

## Plate Section 1
Page 1 (both) James Pursey; 2–3 RIA Novosti; 4 (both) Mentorn Media Ltd; 5*t* James Pursey; 5*b* Corbis/Ludovic Maisant; 6*tl* RIA Novosti; 6*tr* Corbis; 6*b* Alamy/Michael Klinec; 7*t* James Pursey; 7*b* Alamy/Authors Image; 8*t* Corbis; 8*b* Corbis/Free Agents Limited.

## Plate Section 2
Page 2*t* Mentorn Media Ltd; 1*c* Corbis/Michael Nicholson; 1*b* RIA Novosti; 2*t* James Pursey; 2*b* David Niblock; 3*t* Mentorn Media Ltd; 3*c* James Pursey; 3*b* and 4–5 David Niblock; 6*t* James Pursey; 6*b* Corbis/Peter Turnley; 7*t* Corbis/EPIX; 7*b* AP/PA Photos; 8*t* James Pursey; 6*c* and *b* Mentorn Media Ltd.

## Plate Section 3
Page 1*t* Mentorn Media Ltd; 1*c* David Niblock; 1*b* and 2*tl* Jamie Muir; 2*tr* and *b* David Niblock; 3*t* and *b* Mentorn Media Ltd; 3*c* David Niblock; 4*t* Mentorn Media Ltd; 4*b* David Niblock; 5*t* Corbis/Bettmann; 5*c* and *b* David Wallace; 6–7 RIA Novosti; 7*i* and 8 (all) David Wallace.

## Plate Section 4
Page 1*t* David Wallace; 1*b* David Niblock; 2*t* Mentorn Media Ltd; 2*b* David Wallace; 3*t* Mentorn Media Ltd; 3*c* George Carey; 3*b* Corbis/Brian A. Vikander; 4–5 George Carey; 6*t* AP/PA Photos; 6*b* Ilya Naymushin/AFP/Getty Images; 7*t* Mentorn Media Ltd; 7*b* Alamy/Iain Masterton; 8 James Pursey.